T0192128

Lecture Notes in Computer Science 13893

Founding Editors

Gerhard Goos
Juris Hartmanis

Editorial Board Members

The series Lecture Notes in Computer Science (LNCS), including its subseries Lecture Notes in Artificial Intelligence (LNAI) and Lecture Notes in Bioinformatics (LNBI), has established itself as a medium for the publication of new developments in computer science and information technology research, teaching, and education.

LNCS enjoys close cooperation with the computer science R & D community, the series counts many renowned academics among its volume editors and paper authors, and collaborates with prestigious societies. Its mission is to serve this international community by providing an invaluable service, mainly focused on the publication of conference and workshop proceedings and postproceedings. LNCS commenced publication in 1973.

Irene Garrigós · Juan Manuel Murillo Rodríguez ·
Manuel Wimmer

Editors

Web Engineering

23rd International Conference, ICWE 2023
Alicante, Spain, June 6–9, 2023
Proceedings

 Springer

Editors
Irene Garrigós (iD)
University of Alicante
Alicante, Spain

Juan Manuel Murillo Rodríguez (iD)
University of Extremadura
Cáceres, Spain

Manuel Wimmer (iD)
Johannes Kepler University Linz
Linz, Austria

ISSN 0302-9743   ISSN 1611-3349 (electronic)
Lecture Notes in Computer Science
ISBN 978-3-031-34443-5   ISBN 978-3-031-34444-2 (eBook)
https://doi.org/10.1007/978-3-031-34444-2

This Springer imprint is published by the registered company Springer Nature Switzerland AG
The registered company address is: Gewerbestrasse 11, 6330 Cham, Switzerland

Preface

The International Conference on Web Engineering (ICWE) aims to promote research and scientific exchange related to Web Engineering and associated technologies. Thus, the conference covers the many different aspects of Web Engineering including the design, creation, maintenance, operation, and usage of Web applications. ICWE aims to bring together researchers and practitioners from various disciplines in academia and industry to tackle the emerging challenges in the engineering of Web applications, study the problems and opportunities of its associated technologies, and reflect the impact of those technologies on society and culture.

The International Society of Web Engineering (ISWE) has been promoting ICWE since its inception and has contributed greatly to making it the flagship conference for web engineering.

Previous editions of ICWE took place in Bari, Italy (2022), Biarritz, France (2021) [virtually], Helsinki, Finland (2020) [virtually], Daejeon, South Korea (2019), Cáceres, Spain (2018), Rome, Italy (2017), Lugano, Switzerland (2016), Rotterdam, The Netherlands (2015), Toulouse, France (2014), Aalborg, Denmark (2013), Berlin, Germany (2012), Paphos, Cyprus (2011), Vienna, Austria (2010), San Sebastian, Spain (2009), Yorktown Heights, USA (2008), Como, Italy (2007), Palo Alto, USA (2006), Sydney, Australia (2005), Munich, Germany (2004), Oviedo, Spain (2003), Santa Fe, Argentina (2002), and Cáceres, Spain (2001).

This volume contains the full research papers, short research papers, posters, demonstrations, PhD symposium papers, and tutorials of the 23rd International Conference on Web Engineering (ICWE 2023), held during June 6–9, 2023, in Alicante, Spain.

The ICWE 2023 edition received 77 submissions, out of which, after a single-anonymous reviewing process in which each submission received three reviews, the Program Committee selected 18 full research papers (23% acceptance rate) and seven short research papers (41% acceptance rate). Additionally, the Program Committee accepted seven demonstrations and posters, and three contributions to the PhD symposium. Four tutorials were also accepted: *(i)* Developing Distributed WoT Applications for the Cloud-to-Thing Continuum; *(ii)* Quantum Web Services: Development and Deployment; *(iii)* Automated Web GUI Generation from High-Level Interaction Design with Discourse Models; and *(iv)* A Practical Introduction for Developing and Operating Hybrid Quantum Applications, along with three workshops: 3nd International Workshop on Big data driven Edge Cloud Services (BEC 2023); 2nd International Workshop on the Semantic WEb of EveryThing (SWEET 2023); 2nd International Workshop on Web Applications for Life Sciences (WALS 2023).

The comprehensive program would not have been possible without the support of the many people that contributed to the successful organization of this event. We would like to thank all the chairs for their dedication and hard work. Our thanks goes also to Omar Benjelloun (Google, France), Schahram Dustdar (Vienna University of Technology, Austria), and Nuria Oliver (ELLIS Unit Alicante Foundation, Spain) who agreed to be our keynote speakers. We are grateful to Springer for making possible the publication of this volume. Furthermore, we are grateful to the Program Committee members and reviewers for their thorough reviews and constructive discussions. Last but not least, we would like to thank the authors for their excellent work and all the participants who contributed to the success of this conference.

June 2023   Irene Garrigós
                                                    Juan Manuel Murillo Rodriguez
                                                                      Manuel Wimmer

Organization

General Chair

Irene Garrigós   University of Alicante, Spain

Program Committee Chairs

Juan Manuel Murillo Rodriguez   University of Extremadura, Spain
Manuel Wimmer   Johannes Kepler University Linz, Austria

Tutorial Chairs

Antonio Garmendia   Universidad Autónoma de Madrid, Spain
William Van Woensel   University of Ottawa, Canada

Workshop Chairs

Tommi Mikkonen   University of Jyväskylä, Finland
Sven Casteleyn   Universitat Jaume I, Spain

Demonstrations and Posters Chairs

Cinzia Cappiello   Politecnico di Milano, Italy
Sebastian Heil   Chemnitz University of Technology, Germany

PhD Symposium Chairs

Alessandro Bozzon   Delft University of Technology, NL
Sergio Firmenich   Universidad Nacional de La Plata and CONICET,
     Argentina

Proceedings Chair

César González-Mora   University of Alicante, Spain

Publicity Chairs

In-Young Ko   Korea Advanced Institute of Science and
                               Technology, South Korea
Nathalie Moreno   University of Málaga, Spain

Sponsor Chair

Rafael Lafont   FUNDEUN, Spain

Local Chairs

Jose Norberto Mazón   University of Alicante, Spain
Jose Jacobo Zubcoff   University of Alicante, Spain

Web Chair

Alberto Berenguer   University of Alicante, Spain

Program Committee

Myriam Arrue   University of the Basque Country, Spain
Mohamed-Amine Baazizi   Sorbonne Université, France
Marcos Baez   Bielefeld University of Applied Sciences,
                               Germany
Maxim Bakaev   Novosibirsk State Technical University, Russia
Luciano Baresi   Politecnico di Milano, Italy
Devis Bianchini   University of Brescia, Italy
Gabriela Bosetti   VeryConnect, UK
Andreas Both   Leipzig University of Applied Sciences / DATEV,
                               Germany
Alessandro Bozzon   Delft University of Technology, The Netherlands
Marco Brambilla   Politecnico di Milano, Italy

Antonio Brogi	Università di Pisa, Italy
Lola Burgueño	University of Málaga, Spain
Maxime Buron	Inria, France
Christoph Bussler	Oracle Corporation, USA
Jordi Cabot	Luxembourg Institute of Science and Technology, Luxembourg
Carlos Canal	University of Málaga, Spain
Javier Luis Canovas Izquierdo	Universitat Oberta de Catalunya, Spain
Cinzia Cappiello	Politecnico di Milano, Italy
Sven Casteleyn	Universitat Jaume I, Spain
Richard Chbeir	Univ. Pau & Pays Adour, France
Dickson K.W. Chiu	University of Hong Kong, China
Pieter Colpaert	Ghent University, Belgium
Shridhar Devamane	APS College of Engineering, India
Tommaso Di Noia	Politecnico di Bari, Italy
Oscar Diaz	University of the Basque Country, Spain
Schahram Dustdar	Vienna University of Technology, Austria
Jutta Eckstein	Independent, Germany
Alejandro Fernandez	Universidad Nacional de La Plata and CONICET, Argentina
Pablo Fernandez	University of Seville, Spain
Sergio Firmenich	Universidad Nacional de La Plata and CONICET, Argentina
Luca Foschini	University of Bologna, Italy
Flavius Frasincar	Erasmus University Rotterdam, The Netherlands
Piero Fraternali	Politecnico di Milano, Italy
Martin Gaedke	Chemnitz University of Technology, Germany
Jose García-Alonso	University of Extremadura, Spain
Alejandra Garrido	Universidad Nacional de La Plata and CONICET, Argentina
Hüseyin Uğur Genç	TU Delft, The Netherlands
Julián Grigera	Universidad Nacional de La Plata and CONICET, Spain
Hao Han	Konica Minolta, Japan
Radu Tudor Ionescu	University of Bucharest, Romania
Epaminondas Kapetanios	University of Hertfordshire, UK
Tomi Kauppinen	Aalto University, Finland
Alexander Knapp	Universität Augsburg, Germany
In-Young Ko	Korea Advanced Institute of Science and Technology, South Korea
Nora Koch	University of Seville, Spain
István Koren	RWTH Aachen, Germany

Anelia Kurteva	TU Delft, The Netherlands
Maurizio Leotta	Università di Genova, Switzerland
Faiza Loukil	Univ. Savoie Mont Blanc, France
Maristella Matera	Politecnico di Milano, Italy
Jose-Norberto Mazon	Universidad de Alicante, Spain
Santiago Melia	Universidad de Alicante, Spain
Tommi Mikkonen	University of Helsinki, Finland
Madhulika Mohanty	INRIA Saclay, France
Nathalie Moreno	Universidad de Málaga, Spain
Michael Mrissa	InnoRenew CoE, University of Primorska, Slovenia
Martin Musicante	UFRN, Brazil
Tobias Münch	Münch Ges. für IT- Solutions mbH, Germany
Elena Navarro	University of Castilla-La Mancha, Spain
Guadalupe Ortiz	UCASE Software Engineering Group, Spain
Frank Pallas	Technische Universität Berlin, Germany
Oscar Pastor	Universidad Politécnica de Valencia, Spain
Cesare Pautasso	University of Lugano, Switzerland
Alfonso Pierantonio	University of L'Aquila, Italy
Nicoleta Preda	University of Versailles, France
I.V. Ramakrishnan	SUNY Stony Brook, USA
Werner Retschitzegger	Johannes Kepler University Linz, Austria
Filippo Ricca	Università di Genova, Italy
Thomas Richter	Rhein-Waal University of Applied Sciences, Germany
Tarmo Robal	Tallinn University of Technology, Estonia
Gustavo Rossi	Universidad Nacional de La Plata and CONICET, Argentina
Abhishek Srivastava	Indian Institute of Technology Indore, India
Zhu Sun	Macquarie University, Australia
Kari Systä	Tampere University of Technology, Finland
William Van Woensel	University of Ottawa, Canada
Markel Vigo	University of Manchester, UK
Erik Wilde	CA Technologies, Switzerland
Marco Winckler	Université Côte d'Azur, France
Yeliz Yesilada	Middle East Technical University NCC, Turkey
Nicola Zannone	Eindhoven University of Technology, The Netherlands
Gefei Zhang	HTW Berlin, Germany

Additional Reviewers

Alfonso Diaz, Iván David
Allani, Sabri
Berardinelli, Luca
Berrocal, Javier
Cornacchia, Giandomenico
Fernsel, Linda
Hammoud, Ibrahim
Lei, Yu
Li, Chen
Liu, Hongyang
Matey, Miguel
Morichatta, Andrea
Sassi, Salma
Tocchetti, Andrea
Weinreich, Rainer

ICWE 2023 Partners

Universitat d'Alacant
Universidad de Alicante

Contents

User Privacy Engineering

User Behaviour Characterization

User-Centered Technologies

Ph.D Symposium

Tutorials

Architecting the Web in the Cloud Continuum

DCM: Dynamic Client-Server Code Migration

Sebastian Heil[✉][iD] and Martin Gaedke[iD]

Technische Universität Chemnitz, Chemnitz, Germany
{sebastian.heil,martin.gaedke}@informatik.tu-chemnitz.de

Abstract. The underlying Client/Server architecture of the Web inherently raises the question of the distribution of application logic between client and server. Currently, this distribution is static and fixed at design time, inhibiting dynamic and individual load distribution between clients and server at runtime. The benefits of dynamic migration allow balancing the needs of users, through increased responsiveness, and software providers, through better resource usage and cost reductions. Recent additions to the Web environment like WebAssembly provide a technological basis to move units of code at runtime. However, making use of them to extend a web application with dynamic code migration capabilities is challenging for web engineers. To that end, we devise a novel distributed Client/Server software architecture for web applications that supports dynamic migration of code at runtime, addressing the technical challenges of dependency management, distribution of control and data flow, and the required communication and interfaces. Our novel software architecture aims at providing a point of reference to web engineers seeking to extend their web applications with dynamic code migration capabilities and to contribute to the current re-consideration of the Web environment in the light of the standardization and wide-spread support of WebAssembly in all major browsers. Our experiments with 3 scenarios show that implementing such architecture is not only feasible but also that the impact on performance is negligible.

Keywords: Web Infrastructure · Software Architecture · Code Mobility · WebAssembly · WebSockets

1 Introduction

Current Web applications are developed and executed on top of an established stack of technologies. The underlying Client/Server architecture of the Web inherently raises the question of the distribution of application logic between client and server. The design space for software architects is wide, ranging from relatively thin clients where most of the application logic is executed on the server side – e.g. making use of server-side MVC frameworks such as Django, ExpressJS, Laravel or Rails – to architectures in which more computations are run client-side in the browser and the server provides a minimal interface to

I. Garrigós et al. (Eds.): ICWE 2023, LNCS 13893, pp. 3–18, 2023.
https://doi.org/10.1007/978-3-031-34444-2_1

the underlying data layer – e.g. with client-side frameworks such as React, Vue, Angular, or Svelte combined with high usage of AJAX.

While deciding the right distribution for a given web application depends on various factors and individual requirements, the distribution is static and fixed at design time. The mapping of units of code to either the client or server side is decided a priori and cannot be changed later dynamically at runtime, allowing to react to situational events and conditions. Especially in light of the ever-increasing heterogeneity of user devices on the client side, this static design time decision does not support balancing responsiveness/usability requirements by users, resource usage, and economic considerations by the software providers.

The availability of JavaScript on the server side via NodeJS and the support for executing server-side languages on the client side via WebAssembly [15], however, establishes more uniform client- and server-side platforms on top of which the vision of code mobility [1] at runtime becomes relevant and achievable for the Web. The benefits are a dynamic and individual distribution of load between clients and server as well as potential cost reductions for software providers.

The objective of this paper is to devise a novel distributed Client/Server software architecture for web applications that supports dynamically changing the location of execution of units of code at runtime. We address the technical challenges of dependency management and compilation, distribution of control and data flow, and the required communication and interfaces and propose solutions for each of the challenges. The resulting architecture as well as a supporting infrastructure was implemented and put to test in several scenarios.

The remainder of this paper is structured as follows: in Sect. 2 we outline our proposed solution architecture and the supporting infrastructure, Sect. 3 positions our work against existing code mobility paradigms and approaches, in Sect. 4 we evaluate the feasibility of the architecture in 3 scenarios and show that the performance overhead is negligible, and Sect. 5 concludes the paper with an outlook on directions for future work.

2   The DCM Architecture

In this section, we present our solution to enable dynamic code migration between client and server at runtime based on standardized Web technologies. We propose a novel software architecture – the DCM Architecture – that empowers Web Engineers to add dynamic code migration capabilities to the web applications they build with a dedicated focus on minimizing the impact/requirements on the development activities. Figure 1 provides an overview of the main components of the DCM Architecture and their interactions with each other. The DCM Architecture specifies a supporting dynamic migration infrastructure (in blue) that can be embedded into a web application (in black), on top of which Web Engineers can control the migration through simple configuration. Our approach comprises solutions to three main challenges:

1. the specification and compilation of migratable code fragments for client and server,

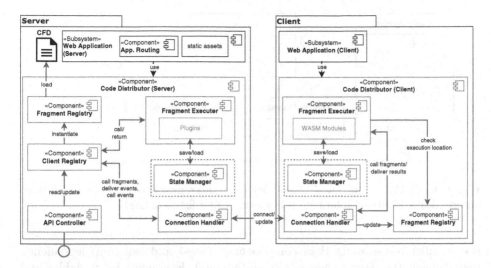

Fig. 1. Main Components and Interactions of the DCM Architecture enabling Dynamic Code Migration between Client and Server at Runtime. Supporting Infrastructure is Highlighted in Blue, Automatically Generated Artifacts are Highlighted in Green. (Color figure online)

2. the orchestration of execution/control flow of these fragments between client and server, and the
3. synchronization of fragment distribution information and redirection of data flow at runtime.

The following subsections detail our solutions to these three challenges.

2.1 Generation and Compilation of Code Fragments

In this subsection, we outline our concept of migratable code fragments, how Web Engineers can specify these parts of the codebase to be executable on server and client side, the required metadata and its semi-automatic extraction, as well as the validation, compilation and deployment of executable modules from the specified code fragments.

Specification of Code Fragments. To allow the Web Engineer to specify migratable subsets of the web application's codebase that can be dynamically moved between client and server at runtime, we define these as *Code Fragments*. A code fragment $CF = (D_i, L, T, M)$ consists of the specification of its source document $D_i \in \mathfrak{C}$ within the codebase $\mathfrak{C}$ and limits $L = (\alpha, \omega)$ (line numbers $\alpha, \omega \in \mathbb{N}$) within D_i, its type $T \in \{function, variable, typedefinition\}$ and the migration-relevant metadata M. Limits can be expressed either via code annotations in the source code itself or externally by numerical specification. In DCM, the level of granularity for specifying executable code fragments is on the level of individual functions to provide a balance between fine-grained control

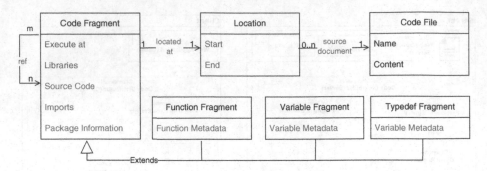

Fig. 2. Code Fragments Data Model. Web Engineer provided information in blue, automatically identified information in green. (Color figure online)

(i.e. smaller re-use units than components/classes) and isolation/dependency management (i.e. larger than sets of statements). Fragments for variables and type definitions are required to handle imports of the functions but are not executable on their own.

As shown in Fig. 2 a fragment aggregates Web Engineer-provided information and information automatically identified through static code analysis of the codebase. In addition to location and fragment type information D_i, L, T, Web Engineers specify the intended initial execution location (server or client), libraries used, and referenced other fragments. The automatically identified information comprises the actual source code as specified by the location information, imports from other sources, package information, and structural information of functions/variables/type definitions such as function parameters. Information about all code fragments is aggregated in the artifact denoted as CFD (code fragment description) in Fig. 1. A sample excerpt of the manually specified parts of a CFD can be seen in listing 1.1.

Syntax Analysis allows to automatically derive information from the codebase necessary for the compilation of code fragments without requiring manual specification by the Web Engineer and thus significantly reducing the required effort. Our approach operates on the *abstract syntax tree (AST)* resulting from parsing the source code and identifying tokens and their relations according to the grammar of the programming language in use. Generating the AST from the source code requires language-dependent tooling. To extract the data about imports from other sources, package information, and structure of functions/variables/type definitions, the AST is traversed, and the collected data merged with the specifications manually made by the Web Engineer.

```
1  fragments:
2  ...
3    - id: 6
4      name: GetHash
5      runOn: client
6      location: { filepath: shared/shared.go }
7      libs: [crypto/sha256, encoding/hex]
8      ...
9    - id: 21
10     name: CreateEmployee
11     runOn: client
12     dependsOn: [6]
13     location: { filepath: shared/employee.go }
14 ...
```

Listing 1.1. Sample excerpt of a Code Fragment Description

Compilation of Code Fragments. To support execution of code fragments specified by the Web Engineer in the CFD on server and client, they need to be compiled for both target platforms. The compilation target on the server side depends on the specific language and platform (typically shared objects, dynamic-link libraries etc.), the compilation target on the client side is WebAssembly. Server-side compiled artifacts are managed as plugins, client-side compiled artifacts as WebAssembly modules, both of which can be dynamically loaded at runtime.

The compiler input for building the language-specific plugins and WebAssembly modules is automatically created based on the codebase and the metadata of each code fragment. As parts of this information are user-provided, a CFD Validator checks the structural validity and completeness of the CFD. Errors such as duplicate fragments or missing required information are reported with additional debug information so that the Web Engineer is supported in fixing them. If validation is passed, automatic code generation and transformation is performed. The generated code for plugin and WebAssembly fragments handles imports and dependencies to turn them into separately compilable units of code. This requires consideration of all fragments' metadata together as duplicate imports resulting from dependency chains need to be resolved. The existing codebase is modified so that invocations of code declared as migratable fragment are redirected to the Fragment Executer. This allows executing either the server-side plugin or forwarding the control and data flow to the client-side DCM infrastructure to be handled by the corresponding WebAssembly module. DCM infrastructure components (c.f. Code Distributor in Fig. 1) are injected. The resulting modified codebase is then compiled for server and client and plugins and WebAssembly modules (including JS glue code) are moved to the correct directories for availability for the server and client side code distributor. In particular, WebAssembly modules need to be deployed to the directory serving static assets (JavaScript, CSS) so they can be loaded via HTTP(S) on the client side.

2.2 Dynamic Migration of Code Fragment Execution

To enable the execution location of code fragments to dynamically change at runtime, the DCM architecture specifies infrastructure that handles their life cycle, and the distribution of control and data flow. These are the `Code Distributor` components on the server and client side (cf. Fig. 1). They manage the loading, execution, and termination of plugins/WebAssembly modules respectively, and synchronize the required incoming/outgoing data flows and events.

Code Distributor (Server). Architecturally, the `Code Distributor` component can be either embedded with the web application itself or an external stand-alone proxy-like server process, potentially on a different host. Unlike approaches like HTML5 Agents [14], we propose a direct embedding due to lower required resources/operations and maintenance efforts and lower communication complexity. Embedding requires adding the DCM library to the web application's imports and registering routes for the `Code Distributor` in the application-internal routing. These steps can be automated in the codebase modifications of the compilation step described in Sect. 2.1. The `Code Distributor` checks incoming client requests and signals connection errors. For valid requests, it performs session management using a `Client Registry`. Together with the `Fragment Registry`, it keeps track of all code fragments and enables different individual fragment distribution patterns per client. Both registries are initialized from the Web Engineer's specifications of available code fragments and their initial execution location in the CFD. The fragment distribution status is synchronized with each client's `Code Distributor`, updates in the fragments' execution location trigger the required steps for control and data flow migration via the `Fragment Executer`. To execute a fragment on the server side, the `Fragment Executer` loads and executes the compiled plugin fragment. The fragment's state is monitored by the `State Manager` to be able to restore it after migration. In particular, this comprises changed/initialized variables, loops, and time functions. Changes in resources shared with other fragments are synchronized. The `API Controller` provides a RESTful interface to monitor and control the dynamic code migration. It interfaces the fragment distributions per client and allows to change them in order to trigger a migration at runtime. This enables scenarios in which an automated decision system can determine optimal distributions based on runtime measurements of load, network bandwidth, etc.

Code Distributor (Client). The client-side DCM infrastructure mirrors the `Fragment Executer` and `State Manager` components described above for execution and state management. While the server-side `Code Distributor` is implemented in the web application's backend language, its client-side equivalent is implemented in JavaScript and served via the application's static web resources. The `Fragment Executer` handles loading, initialization, and invocation of fragments previously compiled to WebAssembly modules and the data conversions between JavaScript and backend language's type system within the WebAssembly modules. Information about the execution is retrieved from the Fragment Registry before each invocation, which is synchronized with the server side. Similar to offloading approaches like MAUI [4] and ThinkAir [9], fragments are initially executed locally until updates are received to enable execution during connection establishment and initialization. Likewise, connection losses lead to local client-side execution as fallback. Fragments are executed as tasks via a pool of WebWorkers.

2.3   Client/Server Synchronization and Data Flow Redirection

The DCM code distributor components need to constantly exchange information bidirectionally in order to synchronize fragments and distribution state and to maintain the data flow from and to fragments when they change their execution location. This subsection outlines the corresponding communication channels and protocol. We propose to employ WebSockets for communication, offering a bidirectional connection between client and server-side DCM infrastructure, as it currently is supported by more browsers than the new WebTransport W3C standard. Messages within the WebSocket connections are represented in JSON. The Connection Handler components establish client-server WebSocket connections on initialization. Clients identify themselves via JSON Web Tokens (JWT) which are included in all communications to allow the server to handle fragment distributions for each client individually. Client and server communicate by exchanging events represented as JSON via the WebSocket connection.

Table 1 shows the main events of the DCM communication protocol. There are events for two different purposes: a) to exchange information required for the management of fragments and distribution state, and b) to enable the redirection of data flow for fragments where caller and callee are not on the same side.

Through the codebase modifications described in Sect. 2.1, both client and server Fragment Executer serve as proxies between the caller of a fragment and the fragment code itself. Data flows in and out of the fragments via function parameters, return values, and global variables. The information about these is gathered and contained in the CFD as described above. At runtime, each Fragment Executer checks the current execution location of the called fragment and redirects the data flow if the location is not local. The callFunction event allows specifying an optional defer property that tells the Fragment Executer to execute the invoked fragment in the background, enabling other fragments to be executed during a long-running computation in the initially called fragment.

Table 1. DCM Communication Protocol Events.

Name	Payload	Description
updateFragments	[object] fragmentStatusList	triggered whenever there is a change in the fragments' distribution to synchronize Client and Server Distributor
callFunction	string funcName, [object] params, boolean defer?	triggered when a fragment is called remotely, to pass incoming data to the called fragment
functionResult	string funcName, object result	triggered when a fragment invokation yields a result to return it to the caller

3   Related Work

Code mobility has long been a topic of research interest for distributed systems [1]. While, *Code on Demand* is the pre-dominant code mobility paradigm on the Web, the availability of NodeJS and the *WebAssembly* standard [15] has opened opportunities for other paradigms such as *Remote Evaluation* and *Mobile Agents* in the recent Web environment.

Code on Demand. [1] is the most widely used code mobility paradigm in Web applications. The ability of the client to request and execute code from the server at runtime is supported via HTML script tags allowing to load JavaScript files and execute them in the browser. Popular client-side frameworks like React, Vue, Angular, or Svelte imply an architecture in which JavaScript code is loaded at runtime and dedicated infrastructure – Content Delivery Networks (CDNs)– to support faster provision of the most commonly loaded framework code artifacts are used. Most prominently, the Code on Demand mobility paradigm was included as the sixth architectural constraint of REST [6] which forms the architectural blueprint for many current Web applications. Beyond common Code on Demand practice, Sparkle [13] additionally supports capturing, migrating, and restoration of application state. Unlike the DCM architecture, Code on Demand mobility is unidirectional, from server to client, and, while the actual code artifacts are migrated at runtime, the decision to execute them on the client side is fixed at design time for common Web applications using JavaScript, or, for recent platform-dependent approaches like Blazor[1], Web Assembly.

Remote Evaluation. [1] approaches allow a unidirectional change of the execution location of a unit of code from client to server. Offloading approaches like MAUI [4], CloneCloud [3], or ThinkAir [9] focus on supporting computationally weaker mobile devices by running computations on the server. Like DCM, MOJA [2] and PIOS [12] make use of a uniform platform of client and server side and MOJA also uses WebSockets for communication. Unlike the DCM architecture, however, the direction is only from client to server, and due to building on

---

[1] https://dotnet.microsoft.com/en-us/apps/aspnet/web-apps/blazor.

NodeJS, they are bound to JavaScript, while the use of WebAssembly modules in DCM potentially enables using and migrating arbitrary languages. Both Code on Demand and Remote Evaluation approaches do not consider redirections of data flow or transfer of state as they focus on unidirectional code mobility.

Mobile Agents. [1] approaches are focused on moving entire software components at runtime across the network. Telescript [5] was an early approach that enabled mobile agents by providing a dedicated object-oriented language supporting the migration of objects as software agents to other *places* at runtime, including the ability to interrupt the execution of an agent and continue it in the new place. Instead of requiring a dedicated language, many mobile agents approaches like Java Aglets [10] employ the threading and networking capabilities of the Java platform [1]. Aglets combine Java Aplets and Servlets, specifying lifecycle methods for Java objects that support their creation, cloning, dispatching, retraction, activation/deactivation and messaging to move them between client and server. Execution of Aglets can be paused and resumed with the previous state in a new location. HTML5 Agents [14] implement the mobile agents paradigm on top of standardized Web technologies: HTML5, CSS, JavaScript. It makes use of the platform uniformity on client and server through NodeJS. Liquid.js [7] is another contemporary mobile agents framework making use of Web standards such as WebRTC and WebWorkers. It focuses on a seamless user experience for moving Web Components, via polymer.js, across multiple heterogenous devices to allow them to "follow" the user. Disclosure [8] addresses the JavaScript-runtime-specific challenge in cross-device liquid computing to handle closures. To enable execution state of the migrated component, it proposes an instrumentation-based technique that has a limited runtime penalty of 0–15%. In comparison to DCM, mobile agents approaches have a lower level of granularity, moving components as a whole, including its code. The moved component therefore no longer exists at its origin and moves freely between peer hosts. The implied design-level security challenges of mobile agents [1] are less severe in DCM, as code migrates only between client/server of the same application and its redundancy means that "new code" cannot be easily introduced. The lack of an established platform particularly in browsers is considered an important reason for the limited success of mobile agents [1]. DCM leverages the changed situation of wide browser support for WebAssembly similar to containers in [11].

4   Evaluation

To evaluate the proposed DCM architecture and infrastructure, we instantiated these using the language platform and compiler toolchain of Go. Our experiments are based on three scenarios that put different aspects of the architecture and infrastructure under test to investigate the performance impact of the proposed solution. In the following, we describe the material and evaluation procedure, report the obtained results, and discuss them.

4.1   Material and Procedure

The Go-based evaluation implementation of DCM is available online for review. To facilitate and homogenize repeated evaluation runs and measurements under equal conditions, the evaluation setup was container-virtualized using Docker. Our experimental evaluation comprises three scenarios with different configurations each. Scenario I covers the analysis and compilation steps necessary to create executable modules described in Sect. 2.1. Scenario II tests the required network communication between the client and server side `Code Distributor` components with regard to stability and delays. Scenario III evaluates the behavior of migration and fragment execution at runtime. All evaluation materials and test scripts are provided online[2]. The test runs of the scenarios used the following hardware: Server: AMD EPYC Processor (2 CPUs @ 3.7 Ghz), 4 GB RAM, Debian Linux 10 64-bit. Client: Intel Core i5-4690K (4 CPUs @3.5 GHz), 16 GB RAM, Windows 10 Pro 64-bit (Build 19044). Network delay between server and client measured via ping ranges between 16.5 ms and 44.6 ms.

Scenario I. This scenario investigates the analysis and compilation of code fragments and the impact of different codebase sizes on each involved component. Two popular open source projects in Go language were selected as material from Github: wire[3] at about 200 and terraform[4] at about 1200 Go source files. For terraform, a docker configuration was created to simulate the settings for integration into a project by a web engineer. Additionally, a custom test suite in Go with 7 Go files and a high number of fragments dedicatedly testing different computations, errors, and data type handling was created. For all three sample projects, CFDs were manually created (wire: 5, terraform: 6, custom: 37 fragments). For each of the three samples, the test script would perform the three automatic steps of *code analysis*, *fragment generation*, and *compilation*. Each step was repeated five times and execution time was captured.

Scenario II. This evaluation scenario tests the network connections and communication timings between server and client side of the DCM architecture. To that end, the timings for different cases are measured: the round-trip time for an echo signal between client and server, the time until the initial WebSocket connection to the client is established and it has received the first fragment list update and the time between receiving a migration command via the server-side interface and the client receiving the new information. The measurements are implemented in a custom test application using a modified version of the DCM infrastructure with extended access to the WebSocket connection and inbuilt time measurements. *Echo time* is measured by the client sending an echo event to the server until receiving the response. *Initialization time* measurement is triggered by a page reload on the client, requesting the list of fragments and execution locations until it receives it. *Command time* is measured from the server side receiving a location update command via the API, forwarding the information to the client until it is received.

---

[2] https://github.com/heseba/dcm.
[3] https://github.com/google/wire.
[4] https://github.com/hashicorp/terraform.

Scenario III. This scenario showcases the migration and fragment execution at runtime. It tests the execution results before and after execution of fragments on server and client. To simulate long-running, side-effect-free computations, two algorithms were implemented in Go and JavaScript: Fibonacci and nth prime. These are run as server-side fragment plugin and as client-side WebAssembly module, as well as in plain JavaScript as baseline. The scenario comprises three test cases: *Single* tests the computation of the Fibonacci to $n = 100$. *Iterated* tests the computation of the Fibonacci to $n = 93$ (the limit of Go's `int64`) repeated in a loop for 1000 times. *Prime* tests the behavior for optimized vs. non-optimized execution conditions by computing the 500.000th prime number. The optimized conditions run 50 iterations within the fragment itself, whereas non-optimized execution invokes the fragment 50 times. During the longer executions, the system behavior by incoming migration commands was observed.

4.2   Results

Scenario I. Table 2 shows the time measurements for scenario I for the three samples per each step collected in 5 test runs $r_{I,1}$ to $r_{I,5}$. The test runner script was executed in a running docker container. All test runs were completed successfully. The DCM infrastructure assisted the CFD specification by showing hints, e.g. for missing dependencies or attributes. All fragments could be successfully compiled and were automatically deployed to the correct directories.

Table 2. Scenario I Measurements: test runs $r_{I,1}$ to $r_{I,5}$.

Sample	Step	$r_{I,1}$	$r_{I,2}$	$r_{I,3}$	$r_{I,4}$	$r_{I,5}$
Wire	code analysis	41 ms	42 ms	39 ms	39 ms	37 ms
	frag. generation	48 ms	48 ms	53 ms	49 ms	55 ms
	compilation	18 ms	18 ms	19 ms	19 ms	21 ms
Terraform	code analysis	1,841 ms	1,589 ms	1,559 ms	1,577 ms	1,542 ms
	frag. generation	192 ms	178 ms	179 ms	176 ms	174 ms
	compilation	457 ms	436 ms	421 ms	410 ms	386 ms
Custom	code analysis	3 ms	3 ms	3 ms	3 ms	3 ms
	frag. generation	63 ms	59 ms	59 ms	61 ms	61 ms
	compilation	13,734 ms	7,198 ms	7,131 ms	7,413 ms	7,141 ms

Scenario II. Table 3 shows the time measurements for the network communications of scenario II for each test case collected in 5 test runs $r_{II,1}$ to $r_{II,5}$. Additionally, we tested connection recovery behavior. The mean recovery time from a connection loss was 15 s. After a client-side page reload, the system could successfully reconnect the `Code Distributor` components of client and server in presence of several other connected clients. The mean roundtrip time was 21 ms ($\sigma = 1$ ms). Initialization took 42.8 ms on average ($\sigma = .45$ ms). A fragment update command was distributed in 43.8 ms ($\sigma = .45$ ms).

Table 3. Scenario II Measurements: test runs $r_{II,1}$ to $r_{II,5}$.

Time Measurement	$r_{II,1}$	$r_{II,2}$	$r_{II,3}$	$r_{II,4}$	$r_{II,5}$
Echo time	22 ms	20 ms	22 ms	20 ms	21 ms
Initialization time	43 ms	43 ms	43 ms	42 ms	43 ms
Command time	44 ms	43 ms	44 ms	44 ms	44 ms

Scenario III. Table 4 shows the time measurements of the three test cases in different configurations. All measurements are with browser-side caching enabled and excluding the initial loading times of WebAssembly modules. These were measured at a mean of 44 ms ($\sigma = 12$ ms). Fragments could be successfully migrated between server and client. Computed fragment execution results of WebAssembly modules and server plugins were always identical.

Table 4. Scenario III Measurements: number of elements and iterations and overall execution times for JavaScript, WebAssembly and Server plugins.

Case	Elem.	Iter.	JS	WASM	Plugin
Single	100	1	0.1 ms	60.6 ms	28.1 ms
Iterated	93	10	0.3 ms	638 ms	246 ms
	93	1,000	30 ms	69,326 ms	24,179 ms
Prime	100,000	10	2.21 s	3.8 s	0.74 s
	500,000	50	132.56 s	185.04 s/159.45 s*	21.03 s

* optimized

4.3 Discussion

Scenario I. The measurements show that analysis and compilation times depend on the complexity of the codebase. Expectedly, the more files in the codebase, the longer the AST-based analysis time and the time to generate the fragment code due to the higher number of comparisons between CFD and the fragment code. However, even for larger projects like Terraform with about 1200 code files analysis times remain well under 2 s and generation times well below 1 s. The compilation time directly depends on the number of fragments from the generation step. The impact of the overall times through our infrastructure on the regular compilation and deployment activities for Web applications can be considered negligible, especially as the added time does not occur at runtime but at design time and thus less frequent. In our experiments, we further observed some difficulties to manage the fragment IDs manually. This could be improved through a UI with automatic ID assignment or non-integer expressive fragment names as identifiers. No further difficulties were encountered in the three test cases and the DCM infrastructure's hints with automatic correction proposals facilitated executing scenario I.

Scenario II. Our experiments show that the underlying WebSocket connections could be reliably established and managed for different clients. Automatic re-connects improve the user experience in presence of network errors. The relatively low and constant times for all three test cases, placed well within the range of the test setup's raw network delay (16.5–44.6 ms), exhibit a very low impact on the runtime performance of a Web application implementing the DCM architecture and are barely noticeable by end users.

Scenario III. WebAssembly plugins on the client side exhibit higher execution times compared to native JavaScript and server plugins for all three test cases. This is particularly due to the additional loading time of WebAssembly modules, even with caching enabled. Considering the WebAssembly execution time without the mean loading time of 44 ms, results are much closer to the server plugin times. Apart from not requiring comparable initial loading times, the advantage of native JavaScript over both fragment types for lower numbers of elements and iterations stems from the speculative optimizations of V8 runtime's JIT compiler Turbofan, creating shapes for monomorphic functions. With higher numbers of elements and iterations, this advantage reduces relative to the advantage of compiled language execution compared to interpretation, leading to better times for server plugins and similar times with WebAssembly (excluding module loading times as mentioned above).

Threats to Validity. Our experiments aim at providing a proof of concept for the feasibility of the DCM architecture and some first insights on its implementation supported by the DCM infrastructure. *Internal validity* can be threatened by the execution of the experiments' manual activities by one single student assistant familiar with the architecture and toolchain. However, we are not making particular claims about Web Engineers' experience, effort, or difficulty, which would require a user study involving developer test subjects with diverse demographics. The specific choice of public real-world projects in scenario I can have influenced the results, but we selected two popular Go projects from Github at different sizes and from different domains. All reported time measurements were automatically measured based on integration in the scenarios' code without the potential for subjective biases. Furthermore, all evaluation materials are available on GitHub for replication. *External validity* of our experiments is limited specifically by the choice of the Go ecosystem. While valid for demonstrating feasibility, the measurement results cannot be generalized to other WebAssembly-compilable languages, as the code analysis, fragment generation, and compilation are dependent on the available AST parsers, compilers, and language features. For that reason, further experimentation with other languages is required for a more general understanding of the DCM architecture. Generalization of our results beyond feasibility, e.g. concerning the applicability of DCM in different application domains, is not intended and would require dedicated experimentation with qualitative empirical approaches. *Construct validity* is threatened for the command time measurements of scenario II. Unlike measurements of scenario I, III, and for echo time and initialization time, the command time is based on start and end time stamps from two different host systems. While a dedicated study of performance would require more sophisticated instrumentation to synchronize the system clocks, we argue that the command time measurements are still valid to show the general dimension of the impact of DCM. We do not make specific numerical claims for these measurements beyond. Both hosts' clocks were synchronized via NTP with an expected prevision in the 5–100 ms[5] range, so that even for large synchronization differences command times would reach a maximum of 250 ms, not violating our claims to low impact on performance perceived by end users.

5 Conclusion and Future Work

In this paper, we proposed a novel software architecture for Web applications enabling dynamic migration of code fragments at runtime. It enables differing fragment distributions individually per each client-server pair to better adapt to situational availability of client/server resources. Unlike previous code mobility approaches, it is platform-agnostic, leveraging W3C standardized and established technologies such as WebAssembly and Web Sockets. Based on extensive experimentation with the DCM architecture, we provided insights on how to address the main challenges of specification and compilation of migratable code fragments, orchestration of fragment execution control flow, and distribution management and redirection of data flow at runtime. To that end, we devise a supporting infrastructure that supports Web Engineers to make use of DCM. To evaluate the proposed architecture and infrastructure, we reported and discussed the results of experimentation with three different scenarios addressing different architectural aspects and performance impact of the solution. All implementation and experimental materials are provided to allow the Web Engineering community to replicate our experiments and extend the approach. Our experiments provided a proof of concept for the feasibility of the DCM architecture, some first insights on its implementation supported by the proposed infrastructure, and indicate that the impact on performance from the required fragment management and communication can be limited to negligible levels.

While these results are promising and showcase the potential of the WebAssembly standard for extending the capabilities of the current Web application infrastructure in the context of code mobility, we also identified some limitations and directions for future work. Running well for migrating atomic, side-effect free functions at runtime, state management, a code mobility challenge for a long time [1], is hard the more stateful these functions are. Suitable mechanisms for interruptions of long-running functions with restoring of internal states are an open challenge the achievability of which depends also on the specific language platforms. Also, due to the current limitations of exchanging data between JavaScript and WebAssembly as numerical data via the Heap,

---

[5] cf. http://www.ntp.org/ntpfaq/NTP-s-algo.htm.

fragments with data flows comprising complex structured data that cannot be easily transformed, require the development of more sophisticated serialization techniques or potential future extensions of the WebAssembly standard for supporting object transformations. Conceptually our work establishes a basis for the dynamic migration of code fragments at runtime. To fully leverage the benefits of situationally balancing responsiveness/usability requirements by users with resource usage and economic considerations by software providers for each individual client, an automatic decision system is required. It could optimize the fragment distribution at runtime based on information on the individual hardware capabilities and, particularly, through measurements of current load on client and server side, interacting with DCM via the provided API. The creation of such a decision system and the integration with dynamic code migration like in DCM are promising directions for future research to which we plan to contribute first insights from currently ongoing experiments.

Acknowledgements. The authors would like to thank Alexander Senger for his valuable contributions to the proof-of-concept implementation of the DCM architecture and the evaluation experiments.

References

1. Carzaniga, A., Picco, G.P., Vigna, G.: Is code still moving around? Looking back at a decade of code mobility. In: Proceedings of the of ICSE 2007 Companion, pp. 9–20. IEEE (2007)
2. Xu, C., Murray, N., Qiao, Y., Lee, B.: MOJA - mobile offloading for JavaScript applications. In: Proceedings of the ISSC/CIICT 2014, pp. 59–63. Institution of Engineering and Technology (2014)
3. Chun, B.G., Ihm, S., Maniatis, P., Naik, M., Patti, A.: CloneCloud: elastic execution between mobile device and cloud. In: Proceedings of the 6th EuroSys, p. 301. ACM Press, New York, New York, USA (2011)
4. Cuervo, E., et al.: MAUI: making smartphones last longer with code offload. In: Proceedigs of the 8th MobiSys, p. 49. ACM Press, New York, New York, USA (2010)
5. Domel, P.: Mobile telescript agents and the web. In: COMPCON 1996. Technologies for the Information Superhighway Digest of Papers, pp. 52–57. IEEE Comput. SocComputer Society Press (1996)
6. Fielding, R.T.: Architectural Styles and the Design of Network-based Software Architectures. University of California, Irvine (2000). Doctoral dissertation
7. Gallidabino, A., Pautasso, C.: The liquid web worker API for horizontal offloading of stateless computations. J. Web Eng. **17**(6), 405–448 (2019)
8. Kim, J.Y., Moon, S.M.: Disclosure: efficient instrumentation-based web app migration for liquid computing. In: Di Noia, T., Ko, I.Y., Schedl, M., Ardito, C. (eds.) ICWE 2022. Lecture Notes in Computer Science, vol. 13362, pp. 132–147. Springer, Cham (2022)
9. Kosta, S., Aucinas, A., Hui, P., Mortier, R., Zhang, X.: Thinkair: Dynamic resource allocation and parallel execution in the cloud for mobile code offloading. In: Proceedings of the IEEE INFOCOM, pp. 945–953. IEEE (2012)

10. Lange, D., Oshima, M.: Mobile agents with Java: the Aglet API. World Wide Web **1**, 1–18 (1998)
11. Mäkitalo, N., et al.: WebAssembly modules as lightweight containers for liquid IoT applications. In: Brambilla, M., Chbeir, R., Frasincar, F., Manolescu, I. (eds.) ICWE 2021. LNCS, vol. 12706, pp. 328–336. Springer, Cham (2021). https://doi.org/10.1007/978-3-030-74296-6_25
12. Park, S., Chen, Q., Yeom, H.Y.: PIOS: a platform-independent offloading system for a mobile web environment. In: 2013 IEEE 10th CCNC, pp. 137–142 (2013)
13. Siu, P.P.L., Belaramani, N., Wang, C.L., Lau, F.C.M.: Context-aware state management for ubiquitous applications. In: Yang, L.T., Guo, M., Gao, G.R., Jha, N.K. (eds.) EUC 2004. LNCS, vol. 3207, pp. 776–785. Springer, Heidelberg (2004). https://doi.org/10.1007/978-3-540-30121-9_74
14. Voutilainen, J.P., Mattila, A.L., Systä, K., Mikkonen, T.: HTML5-based mobile agents for Web-of-Things. Informatica **40**(1), 43–51 (2016)
15. WebAssembly Community Group: WebAssembly Specification - WebAssembly 2.0 Draft 15 December 2022 (2022). https://webassembly.github.io/spec/core/

Code Vectorization and Sequence of Accesses Strategies for Monolith Microservices Identification

Vasco Faria and António Rito Silva[✉][iD]

INESC-ID, Instituto Superior Técnico, University of Lisbon, Lisbon, Portugal
{vasco.faria,rito.silva}@tecnico.ulisboa.pt

Abstract. Migrating a monolithic application to a microservice architecture can benefit from automated methods that accelerate migration and improve the results of decomposition. One of the current approaches that guide software architects on the migration is to group monolith domain entities into microservices, using the sequences of accesses of the monolith functionalities to the domain entities. In this paper, we enrich the sequence of accesses solution by applying code vectorization to the monolith, using the *Code2Vec* neural network model. We apply *Code2Vec* to vectorize the monolith functionalities. We propose two strategies to represent a functionality, one by aggregating its call graph method vectors and the other by extending the sequence of accesses approach with vectorization of the accessed entities. To evaluate these strategies, we compare the proposed strategies with the sequence of accesses strategy and an existing approach that uses class vectorization. We run all these strategies over a large set of codebases and then compare the results of their decompositions in terms of cohesion, coupling, and complexity.

Keywords: Monolith · Microservices · Microservices Identification · Static Analysis · Machine Learning · Architecture Migration

1 Introduction

As microservice architectures prove their value over monoliths, an increasing number of monoliths are being migrated to the microservices architecture, which provides significant benefits in terms of scalability, agile development, and maintainability. Despite these advantages and depending on the size and complexity of a monolith codebase, this migration process can become very complex and expensive, which makes it worth the use of tools to automate some steps of the migration.

Abdellatif et al. [1] present, in a survey on the modernization approaches of legacy systems, several migration approaches for the automatic identification

This work was partially supported by Fundação para a Ciência e Tecnologia (FCT) through projects UIDB/50021/2020 (INESC-ID) and PTDC/CCI-COM/2156/2021 (DACOMICO).

I. Garrigós et al. (Eds.): ICWE 2023, LNCS 13893, pp. 19–33, 2023.
https://doi.org/10.1007/978-3-031-34444-2_2

of microservices in monolith systems. These approaches are classified by their inputs, processes, and outputs. These approaches work on a codebase's representation obtained by applying collection tools, which can be static if they rely only on the monolith source code, or dynamic if they require the monolith execution to collect data. However, according to this study, it can be observed that most approaches for monolith migration perform a static analysis of the source code, followed by a clustering algorithm in conjunction with similarity measures, that define the distances between the elements of the monolith that will constitute the microservices.

In what concerns the collection part, the static analysis, though the mainly used technique, becomes difficult to scale because it depends on the particular programming languages and frameworks used in the monolith implementation, which requires continuous effort in the implementation of static analyzers. On the other hand, there is a report that the use of dynamic collection techniques presents some problems with the completeness of the collection and the management of a large amount of collected data [4].

The goal of this paper is to study whether an approach that does not require a complex data collection using static analysis can generate good decompositions. This would remove some bottlenecks of previous work, since the collector would not be restricted to a particular programming language, web development stack, and object-relational mapper.

This approach is inspired by the work of Al-Debagy and Martinek [2], who analyze monolith code as a natural language processing problem (*NLP*). They use a neural network model called *Code2Vec* for microservices identification. This model uses abstract syntax trees (*AST*) of the monolith methods and the lexical interpretation of its tokens to calculate a numerical vector, representing as much information about the methods as possible. With this tool, they generate vectors associated with monolith classes and measure the quality of the decomposition in terms of cohesion and coupling metrics. However, they do not analyze the monolith from the perspective of the monolith functionality sequences of accesses, which is one of the most common approaches, e.g. [7,16].

In particular, in [16], a large number of monolith codebases are used for an extensive analysis of the identification of microservices in a monolith, which uses the monolith functionality sequences of accesses. The study analyzes the results by applying coupling, cohesion, and complexity metrics to the generated decompositions.

In this paper, we leverage on [2,16], by integrating their perspective to verify the following research questions, using a larger number of codebases:

1. Does the use of *Code2Vec* with the functionality perspective provide better results than sequences of accesses in [16]?
2. Does the application of the functionality perspective provide better results than Al-Debagy and Martinek [2]?
3. Does the input parameters of the proposed strategies impact the results of the evaluation metrics?

The proposed solution starts with a data collection phase, where a new collector is used to extract all the methods of a monolith codebase, along with all their information (package, class, type, source code, and method calls). During this phase, the *Code2Vec* model is used to generate the respective vector for each method. Then we test two different strategies to generate the functionalities vectors.

For evaluation, we apply the different strategies to a large set of codebases, and then compare the results using cohesion, coupling, and complexity metrics.

After this section, Sect. 2 discusses work related to the application of machine learning techniques in software migration. Section 3 presents new strategies for the identification of microservices in monolith systems. Section 4 evaluates and compares the new strategies with previous work, and finally Sect. 5 presents the conclusions of this work.

2   Related Work

Since the emergence of microservice architectures, migrating monoliths to these architectures has been an increasingly active topic [1].

There are approaches [7,14,16] that use the monolith functionalities sequences of accesses to the monolith domain entities to feed an aggregation algorithm that proposes candidate decompositions for microservices. These approaches can use static analysis of the monolith code, e.g. [16], or dynamic execution of the monolith to collect the sequences of accesses. Andrade et al. [4] compare the use of static and dynamic collection for microservice identification. They conclude that while in static analysis the data collection needs to be adapted to each programming language or framework, which requires tool adaption effort for each new programming language of full-stack technology, the dynamic collection of data has a worse coverage, though generating a huge amount of data. Based on these results, our research intends to explore the use of lexical analysis, a form of static analysis that requires less effort because it is more language and technology independent.

On the other hand, several approaches for the identification of microservices, or grouping classes into packages, apply lexical analysis.

Hammad and Banat [6] propose a technique that uses the K-Means clustering algorithm [8] to group a set of classes into packages, where the similarity measure presented consists of how many relevant tokens two classes have in common. This approach did not achieve good results in terms of modularity, because the tokens must be identical in order to find a similarity between two parts of the code, which ignores all words that belong to the same semantic or lexical field.

Mazlami et al. [12] present three formal coupling strategies to generate a weighted graph from the meta-information of a monolithic codebase. They decompose the generated graph using a graph-based clustering algorithm. One of the strategies follows the same logic as the previously mentioned approach [6], based on coupling two classes that contain the same tokens, but considering their frequency. Although this strategy presents a worse execution time compared to their other approaches, it shows better results in reducing team size and average domain redundancy.

Brito et al. [5] use topic modeling to identify services according to domain terms, where words with higher probabilities indicate a possible good topic. They also mention that the extraction of relevant tokens could be easier with a pure Natural Language Processor (NLP), but the results would be worse. This topic modeling approach is also agnostic of the development stack, but the results depend on an optimal extraction of lexical tokens, using specific parsers for each language to extract and process ASTs as input to the model, which means increasing its complexity. As a result of their work, the model shows good cohesion values of the identified microservices, with the trade-off of generating a high number of clusters to achieve good values in a metric that evaluates whether microservices follow the principle of single responsibility [11].

There are not many approaches besides clustering when it comes to machine learning techniques to decompose monolith applications into microservices. However, the use of NLPs has been increasing due to their significant progress in performing lexical analyzes, making the data collection phase easier and more generic. Ma et al. [10] propose a solution based on Word2Vec [13], a widely used machine learning method in NLP, to match existing microservices with new requirements. Their approach only works for applications where scenarios are written in a common language describing the features of the target system and that already follow a microservices architecture since their goal is to discover where to place new requirements. They use the vectors generated by the Word2Vec model as the similarity measure between scenarios. Leveraging on the Word2Vec [13] work, Alon et al. [3] created Code2Vec, a neural network model trained to represent methods as fixed-length numerical vectors, also called code embeddings. Al-Debagy and Martinek [2] propose an approach to decompose a monolith application into microservices using Code2Vec [3], by extracting the code embeddings of the methods. Using these vectors, they define a class embedding as the aggregation of its methods' embeddings. After testing, they found that the mean is the most suitable aggregation function to define a class embedding. The results of this novel approach show high cohesion values since all the semantically similar classes are grouped in a microservice, making this solution achieve even better results than the other approaches they consider in the evaluation.

Overall, although there is some work on the use of Code2Vec for the identification of microservices in a monolith, it does not follow an approach in which the data collected from the monolith are based on the functionalities accesses to domain entities. Additionally, there is a lack of studies that compare approaches for a large number of codebases using different quality metrics.

3   Solution

The solution uses Code2Vec [3], which is a neural network model trained to represent methods as fixed-length numerical vectors, also called code embeddings.

In machine learning, an embedding is a low-dimensional vector that represents high-dimensional data, preserving the most information possible. Although the model is designed for method naming, the learned code embeddings can be used for several other applications.

3.1 Data Collection

The first step of our approach consists of extracting all the necessary information from the monolith codebase and preparing it. This is done using the JavaParser library[1], which is a popular static analysis tool used to parse and modify Java code by generating an interactive abstract syntax tree and providing a symbol resolution module. JavaParser also provides a type resolution module (symbol-solver) that can combine different type solvers to increase the capability of solving complex references like superclass methods.

For the data collection, we explore all the codebase files, recurring to the type solvers of the JavaParser. For each java file, our parser starts by identifying the package, the class/interface name, the annotations, and all the present methods as well as checking if the class extends another.

Each time the parser finds a new method, its respective body is converted into a code embedding by the *Code2Vec* model, which we save along with the method signature. Also, inside each method body, the parser looks for all methods' invocations and tries to solve their signature using the type solvers. If the invoked method belongs to external libraries of the codebase, those invocations are discarded.

Since the evaluation is applied to monoliths implemented using Spring-Boot and an Object-Relational Mapper (*ORM*), each code embedding is characterized in terms of Spring-Boot architectural elements: Controller, Entity, Service, Repository, and Configuration classes. This categorization is used to verify whether some parts of the monolith code can provide more accurate results and to identify the starting point of each functionality (Controller) and the monolith persistent domain entities (Entity).

3.2 Functionality Vectorization Strategies

We propose two functionality vectorization strategies to represent a functionality as an embedding by using the functionality call graph, or the functionality sequence of accesses to domain entities. The purpose of these strategies is to represent each microservice as a set of functionalities, and thus to understand which functionalities should be implemented in the same microservice.

Figure 1 presents the **Functionality Vectorization by Call Graph** (*FVCG*) strategy, which represents each functionality as the call graph of its methods' invocations, where the first method is the controller where the functionality starts executing. By traversing a method call graph it is possible to

---

[1] https://javaparser.org/.

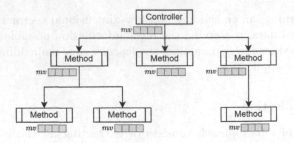

Fig. 1. Extraction of a functionality call graph vector.

reach loops, so to overcome this problem, a maximum depth parameter on the call graph is considered to compute the vector.

After discovering all the methods and the respective code embeddings, represented in Fig. 1 by the mv vectors, that belong to the call graph of a functionality for a given depth, we apply the mean weighted function to those embeddings to obtain the embedding representing the functionality. The method annotations are used to infer each method type. The following weights for method types are considered:

- w_c: The controllers weight;
- w_s: The services weight;
- w_e: The entities weight;
- w_i: The remaining methods (e.g., auxiliary or unclassified methods) weight, which will be referred to as intermediate.

The weights are positive values that should sum exactly 100 ($w_c + w_s + w_e + w_i = 100$).

In addition to the weight parameters, the d parameter in the depth of the call graph determines the number of method vectors to consider. The study will help to understand the level of computational effort required in the construction of the vectors. For instance, if vectors computed using low depth provide good results, it will significantly reduce computational effort. On the other hand, if the weights are irrelevant, the data collector will not need to recognize the type of each method, which is a positive aspect to make the collector framework and architecture agnostic.

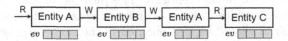

Fig. 2. Extraction of a functionality sequence of accesses vector, where R stands for read and W stands for write.

Figure 2 presents the **Functionality Vectorization by Sequences of Accesses** (*FVSA*) strategy, which represents each functionality as the sequence of its accesses to domain entities, where read accesses are distinguished from write accesses. It uses the sequences of accesses performed by a functionality and associates with each access the embedded vector of the accessed entity, ev. The entity embedded vector is computed by first identifying the entity methods, and then calculating the mean of that method's embeddings.

Having functionality sequences of accesses and the entities' embeddings, the functionality embedding is the weighted average of the entities' embeddings of all the entities possibly accessed during the functionality execution. Two weights, read and write, are considered. The weight values are positive and should sum exactly 100. Note that, as in the previous vectorization, the parameters will be used to assess the impact of distinguishing reads from write accesses in the quality of the generated decompositions.

4   Evaluation

To answer the research questions, we compare the *Code2Vec* decompositions generated using the *Code2Vec* similarity measures built on the monolith functionalities with the decompositions generated using sequences of access, as in [15], the decompositions generated using vectors for classes built with *Code2Vec*, as in [2], and the decompositions that only consider vectors for entities, which is a subcategory of the previous strategy [2].

4.1   Strategy Comparison

The strategy by Al-Debagy and Martinek [2] represents a microservice as a set of classes. They use **Class Vectorization** (*CV*), where each class has an embedding calculated as the mean of its methods embeddings, a technique already applied in the *FVSA* strategy.

Nevertheless, there are approaches where microservices are represented by monolith domain entities, instead of their classes, to highlight that the main aspect of a microservice is the independence of its database from other microservices databases. Therefore, we use another strategy adapted from the *CV* strategy, in which, rather than representing a microservice as a set of classes, it is represented as a set of entities. The **Entity Vectorization** (*EV*) strategy only considers the classes in the *CV* strategy that are entities.

The third strategy we are going to compare is **Sequence of Accesses** (*SA*). We consider four similarity measures based on access sequences [15]. They aggregate the entities in the monolith domain that are accessed by the same functionalities. The main idea behind these measures is that in a microservices architecture it is necessary to minimize the number of distributed transactions. Therefore, by having all domain entities that are accessed by a functionality in the same cluster, the functionality can execute as a single transaction. The four similarity measures distinguish the type of access, read and write, and whether the accesses are consecutive in the sequence. The *SA* strategy uses the four similarity measures by assigning weights to each one of them, so their sum should be 100.

To compare the different strategies, they must produce the same type of decomposition clusters. However, the strategies produce three different types of decompositions. *SA* and *EV* strategies generate clusters of entities, *FVCG* and *FVSA* strategies generate clusters of functionalities, and the *CV* strategy generates clusters of classes. Therefore, to compare the results, it is necessary to convert a decomposition type into the other. Since the metrics to be used in the evaluation are calculated on clusters of domain entities, the decompositions are converted into clusters of entities' decompositions.

To convert a cluster of classes into an entity's clusters, it is only necessary to remove all the non-entity classes from the clusters, which can lead to empty clusters and so we discard those clusters.

The functionalities clusters are converted into clusters of entities by counting the functionalities entity accesses present in each cluster. This is, each domain entity's access by a functionality of a given cluster increases the probability that the entity will be part of the cluster. Then, for each domain entity, we look for the cluster where it has more accesses and assign it to that cluster. Subsequently, since this conversion may also result in empty clusters, these are discarded.

4.2 Decomposition Generation

To evaluate the strategies, it is necessary to generate a significant number of decompositions, varying the number of clusters and the weights of the strategies. In terms of the number of clusters, for codebases up to 10 entities, a maximum of 3 microservices are generated, between 10 and 20 a maximum of 5 microservices, and for more than 20 the maximum number of microservices is 10.

We start at a minimum of 3 microservices and generate all possible decompositions by varying the strategy's parameters. Then we repeat the process by increasing by one the number of microservices to generate, until we reach the maximum number of microservices. The strategies that don't represent a microservice by a set of entities may result in empty clusters. Therefore, the real number of clusters of the generated decompositions is smaller than the requested one. To overcome this issue, we continue to increase the requested number of microservices and generate the respective decompositions until we achieve one that results in a number of clusters larger than the maximum value.

The number of decompositions generated for each strategy depends on the number of its parameters, since we explore all the possible combinations. For the weight parameters, we need to create all combinations where the sum of the weights equals 100, using intervals of 10. In the *FVCG* strategy, we decided to vary the depth parameter from 1 to 6.

A hierarchical clustering algorithm is applied to the strategies vectors and distances, using the Euclidean distance. A dendrogram is generated, which is cut to generate decompositions with different numbers of clusters.

4.3   Evaluation Metrics

Three metrics are used to evaluate the quality of a generated decomposition: coupling, cohesion, and complexity. Cohesion measures the principle of single responsibility, coupling reflects the interdependence between microservices, and complexity measures the effort required to migrate a functionality from a monolith to a microservice architecture [15].

An additional metric is built that combines the three metrics, to evaluate which decompositions have a better balance between them, as presented in the Eq. 1. Note that the complexity is divided by the maximum complexity of all decompositions, to obtain a value between 0 and 1, this is called uniform complexity. The cohesion has a negative value because a higher cohesion is better than a lower cohesion, whereas a lower coupling (complexity) is better than a higher coupling (complexity).

$$combined(d) = \frac{1 + \frac{complexity(d)}{max\_complexity(D)} + coupling(d) - cohesion(d)}{3} \tag{1}$$

4.4   Codebase Sample

To collect the sample codebases for this experiment, a list of GitHub repositories that depend on the Spring Data JPA library[2] was filtered to exclude codebases with less than five domain entities and controller classes. After that, the remaining codebases were sorted by the number of GitHub stars and manually selected from the top to keep the sample quite diverse in terms of codebase sizes. From these codebases we still had to exclude a few because of the dependence on libraries that generate methods from annotations on compile time, making these methods not available for a static analysis.

The selection process led to a relatively large number of monolith codebases (85)[3], with an average number of code lines of around 25 thousand and a standard deviation of 33 thousand lines of code, which indicates a high variation of the codebases size.

To validate the research questions, we compare the strategies for the cohesion, coupling, complexity and combined metrics, using decompositions for the 85 codebases chosen for different numbers of clusters. To measure whether differences in the results of the strategies are statistically significant, we apply the Welch's t-test [17].

4.5   Results

To answer the research questions, we went through all generated decompositions to calculate the respective values for cohesion, coupling, complexity, and combined metrics. With these values, it is possible to compare the strategies and

---

[2] https://github.com/spring-projects/spring-data-jpa/network/dependents.
[3] List available in *0. The Data* of https://github.com/socialsoftware/mono2micro/ blob/feature/code2vec/README.md.

look for any correlation between the parameters of the proposed strategies and the metrics values.

Each strategy generated a different number of decompositions derived from the number of parameters and from the conversion of functionalities' clusters to entities' clusters. Note that *FVCG* has the largest number of parameters. Therefore, it was decided to perform an analysis on the best decompositions of each codebase for each strategy and number of clusters. In this way, the same number of decompositions is considered for each strategy. Furthermore, since the number of decompositions associated with strategy *FVCG* is significantly higher, 131.168 while *FVSA* only has 503, it is also relevant to understand which parameters can be discarded, if any, to minimize the number of decompositions that must be generated.

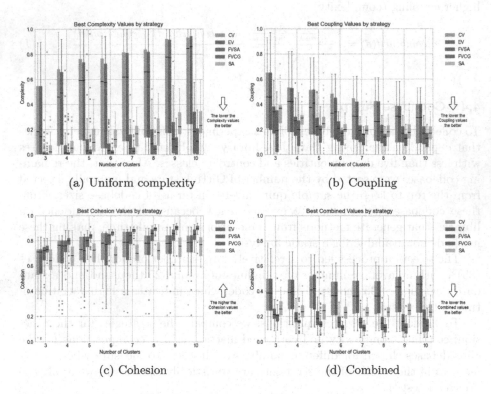

(a) Uniform complexity   (b) Coupling

(c) Cohesion   (d) Combined

Fig. 3. Evaluation metrics applied to the best decompositions of the 85 codebases for each metric.

When looking at Fig. 3 it can be observed that the new strategies perform well when compared with the other strategies. Additionally, the *FVCG* strategy distinguishes itself from *FVSA* by having better results for all metrics. Also, the *FVCG* strategy proves to be more interesting because it does not require such an in-depth analysis of the code as the *FVSA* strategy and is more independent of the technology stack.

A detailed analysis is performed in the context of the three research questions.

Does the Use of *Code2Vec* with the Functionality Perspective Provide Better Results than Sequences of Accesses? To answer the first research question, the proposed strategies that rely on feature vectorization and the *Code2Vec* model (*FVSA, FVCG*) are compared with the *SA* strategy, which clusters entities by their access sequences. When comparing the *FVSA* strategy with *SA*, it will be possible to conclude the impact of the *Code2Vec* model on the sequence of entity accesses. And the comparison of *FVCG* and *SA* strategies will indicate if only the use of *Code2Vec* can achieve better results than the very detailed static code analysis used in the *SA* strategy.

In terms of complexity, Welch's t-test only accepts the hypothesis that 2 strategies have the same mean values when comparing the *FVSA* and *SA* strategies, and the number of clusters is 4 or 5. In all other cases, including the *FVCG* strategy, as shown in Fig. 3a, most of the values of the proposed strategies are lower than those of the *SA* strategy, leading to the conclusion that the use of the *Code2Vec* model with a functionality perspective generates less complex decompositions.

Regarding coupling, in Fig. 3b the *FVSA* and *SA* strategies have very similar results, which can be validated with the results of Welch's t-test, which accepts the hypothesis that the strategies have the same average coupling values for every number of clusters except for 3 and 5. The *FVCG* strategy obtains better results than the *SA* strategy, since Welch's t-test rejects that both strategies have the same mean for every number of clusters, and the *FVCG* coupling results are lower than those of the *SA* strategy.

When it comes to the cohesiveness of the proposed strategies 3c, the values are better compared to the *SA* strategy. Welch's t-test rejects all the hypotheses that the *FVCG* and *FVSA* strategies have the same mean cohesion values when compared to the *SA* strategy. This implies that the decompositions generated by the *Code2Vec* proposed strategies have more cohesive microservices than by using the *SA* strategy.

In general, when applying the combined metric (Fig. 3d) to these strategies, the results of Welch's t-test also reject the hypothesis that the strategies have the same mean values for every comparison between the proposed strategies (*FVCG* and *FVSA*) and the *SA* strategy. With these results, it is possible to conclude that the use of the *Code2Vec* model with a functionality perspective on the sequence of accesses improves the results, but when only the functionalities vectorization without the sequence of accesses is used, it is possible to achieve even better results.

Does the Application of the Functionality Perspective Provide Better Results Than Al-Debagy and Martinek's Class Perspective? To answer the second research question, the proposed strategies (*FVSA, FVCG*) are compared with the *CV* strategy, proposed by Al-Debagy and Martinek, and the *EV* strategy, which is an adaptation of *CV*.

Calculating Welch's t-test between the proposed strategies and the CV strategy, it is possible to reject the hypothesis of having the same complexity, cohesion, coupling, and combined means for every number of clusters. These results show that these strategies are quite different as can be seen in Fig. 3 and that the results of the CV strategy are worse for every metric than the ones of the $FVCG$ and $FVSA$ strategies.

The EV strategy was implemented, which only considers classes that represent domain entities, because candidate decompositions are clusters of entities. But this strategy ended up getting the same results as the CV strategy, since Welch's t-test accepts that it has the same average across all strategies and for all numbers of clusters, which led to Welch's t-test also rejecting the hypothesis that this strategy has the same means as the proposed strategies across all metrics and for all numbers of clusters.

This evaluation shows that the use of $Code2Vec$ with a class perspective generates worse decompositions, since the class vectors are heavily influenced by each class type due to its respective lexical tokens, but may be a good approach to cluster classes into packages to organize the code by class types as in [6].

Does the Input Parameters of the Proposed Strategies Impact the Results of the Evaluation Metrics? To answer the third research question, we analyze the parameters of each of the proposed strategies.

Starting with the $FVCG$ strategy, there are five parameters to analyze, the maximum depth (d) in which the call graph is explored, and the four weights to control which method types are more relevant.

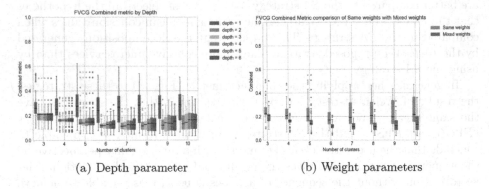

(a) Depth parameter   (b) Weight parameters

Fig. 4. Input parameter analysis for $FVCG$: (a) depth parameter for the combined metric; (b) equal weights vs best weights for the combined metric.

Figure 4a shows the results of the depth variation. Welch's t-test between a depth of 1 and a depth of 2 shows that there is a significant difference between the results, and so depth 1 provides worse results than higher depths. But, when calculating an OLS regression for depths greater than 1, it allows us to reject the hypothesis that by increasing the depth more than 2 better results are obtained, because *p-value* is smaller than the significance level.

Therefore, it is impossible to conclude, for depths greater than 1, that any given depth is better than another. Since smaller depths require less computation, it is possible to rely just on depth 2, in which only the functionality controller method and the methods it invokes there are used.

This leads us to conclude that when using a lexical approach with functionalities call graph, only the first methods of each functionality are needed since they present most of the lexical tokens present in the entire functionality call graph.

On the other hand, the regression between the method type weights for the combined metric rejects the hypothesis that a different combination of the method type weights affects the evaluation metric results because *p-value* is less than the significance level.

As it is not possible to find a perfect combination of method type weights, we did an additional analysis of the best decompositions for each codebase and number of clusters. This allows us to understand whether the use of the same weights for all types of method can achieve good results compared to all possible weight combinations (Fig. 4b). But Welch's t-test results reject the hypothesis that the combined metric mean values using the same value for each weight produce better results than a particular weight combination when looking for the best decomposition.

For the *FVSA* strategy, there are only two parameters to analyze, the two types of access weights, write and read.

The regression between the weights of the access types for the combined metric allows us to reject the hypothesis that a different combination of the weights of the access types affects the results, because *p-value* is less than the significance level.

4.6   Threats to Validity

The *FVCG* strategy was only implemented to support Java codebases, but since it is possible to change *Code2Vec* to accept more languages, it can easily be generalizable, just by creating a new parser for each language. The parser only needs to generate the methods ASTs.

Due to the codebases selection process, we believe that the 85 selected codebases are representative of monolith systems. Although all codebases use the Spring framework, it does not bias the results because the frameworks used to develop web monoliths implement the same architectural patterns.

There may be some correlation between coupling and complexity metrics, so the results of the proposed new combined metric may be biased. Nevertheless, the results are still promising when analyzing each metric separately.

The conversion of functionality clusters to entity clusters may bias the results. However, the strategies that applied this conversion have shown better results.

4.7 Lessons Learned

– It is possible to perform a lexical analysis of the AST with a neural network model and obtain better results than a complex static analysis that captures the functionality sequences of access to domain entities.
– Adding a neural network model to the static analysis of entity accesses ($FVSA$ strategy) improves its results.
– The $FVCG$ strategy is shown to provide the best results, when compared with the sequence of accesses strategy, and it is only necessary to apply a depth of 2 in the call graph generation, which dramatically improves performance.

5 Conclusion

As the majority of monolith decomposition approaches perform a static analysis of the source code followed by a clustering algorithm, this work aimed to simplify and generalize this process by recurring to a lexical analysis independent of the technology stack.

The *Code2Vec* model was used to understand that a simple lexical analysis strategy can overcome, in terms of complexity, coupling, and cohesion, a more complex analysis that has to extract the functionalities domain entities accesses sequences.

Analyzing monoliths as a set of functionalities was shown to provide better results than the monolith class vectorization strategy.

We conclude that the $FVCG$ strategy, which only relies on the call graph for functionality vectorization, provides the best results. Additionally, it is possible to reduce the number of parameter combinations to choose the best decomposition by only using depth 2 for the call graph generation.

The approach code and the experimental results are publicly available[4] and they are integrated in a monolith microservices identification pipeline [9].

References

1. Abdellatif, M., et al.: A taxonomy of service identification approaches for legacy software systems modernization. J. Syst. Softw. **173**, 110868 (2021). https://doi.org/10.1016/j.jss.2020.110868
2. Al-Debagy, O., Martinek, P.: A microservice decomposition method through using distributed representation of source code. Scalable Comput. Pract. Exp. **22**(1), 39–52 (2021). https://doi.org/10.12694/scpe.v22i1.1836
3. Alon, U., Zilberstein, M., Levy, O., Yahav, E.: code2vec: learning distributed representations of code. Proc. ACM Program. Lang. **3**(POPL), 1–29 (2019). https://doi.org/10.1145/3290353
4. Andrade, B., Santos, S., Silva, A.R.: From monolith to microservices: static and dynamic analysis comparison (2022). https://doi.org/10.48550/ARXIV.2204.11844

---

[4] https://github.com/socialsoftware/mono2micro/tree/feature/code2vec.

5. Brito, M., Cunha, J., Saraiva, J.: Identification of microservices from monolithic applications through topic modelling. In: Proceedings of the ACM Symposium on Applied Computing, pp. 1409–1418 (2021). https://doi.org/10.1145/3412841. 3442016
6. Hammad, M., Banat, R.H.: Automatic class decomposition using clustering. In: Proceedings - 2021 IEEE 18th International Conference on Software Architecture Companion, ICSA-C 2021, pp. 78–81 (2021). https://doi.org/10.1109/ICSA-C52384.2021.00019
7. Jin, W., Liu, T., Cai, Y., Kazman, R., Mo, R., Zheng, Q.: Service candidate identification from monolithic systems based on execution traces. IEEE Trans. Softw. Eng. **47**(5), 987–1007 (2021). https://doi.org/10.1109/TSE.2019.2910531
8. Lloyd, S.P.: Least squares quantization in PCM. IEEE Trans. Inf. Theory **28**, 129–136 (1982). https://doi.org/10.1109/TIT.1982.1056489
9. Lopes, T., Silva, A.R.: Monolith microservices identification: Towards an extensible multiple strategy tool. In: 2023 IEEE 20th International Conference on Software Architecture Companion (ICSA-C), pp. 127–131 (2023). https://doi.org/10.1109/ICSA-C57050.2023.00034
10. Ma, S.P., Chuang, Y., Lan, C.W., Chen, H.M., Huang, C.Y., Li, C.Y.: Scenario-based microservice retrieval using Word2Vec. In: Proceedings - 2018 IEEE 15th International Conference on e-Business Engineering, ICEBE 2018, pp. 239–244 (2018). https://doi.org/10.1109/ICEBE.2018.00046
11. Martin, R.C.: Agile Software Development: Principles, Patterns, and Practices. Pearson, USA (2002)
12. Mazlami, G., Cito, J., Leitner, P.: Extraction of microservices from monolithic software architectures. Proceedings - 2017 IEEE 24th International Conference on Web Services, ICWS 2017, pp. 524–531 (2017). https://doi.org/10.1109/ICWS.2017.61
13. Mikolov, T., Chen, K., Corrado, G., Dean, J.: Efficient estimation of word representations in vector space (2013). https://doi.org/10.48550/ARXIV.1301.3781
14. Nunes, L., Santos, N., Rito Silva, A.: From a monolith to a microservices architecture: an approach based on transactional contexts. In: Bures, T., Duchien, L., Inverardi, P. (eds.) ECSA 2019. LNCS, vol. 11681, pp. 37–52. Springer, Cham (2019). https://doi.org/10.1007/978-3-030-29983-5_3
15. Santos, N., Silva, A.R.: A complexity metric for microservices architecture migration. In: 2020 IEEE International Conference on Software Architecture (ICSA), pp. 169–178 (2020). https://doi.org/10.1109/ICSA47634.2020.00024
16. Santos, S., Silva, A.R.: Microservices identification in monolith systems: functionality redesign complexity and evaluation of similarity measures. J. Web Eng. **21**, 1543–1582 (2022). https://doi.org/10.13052/jwe1540-9589.2158
17. Welch, B.L.: The generalization of 'Student's' problem when several different population variances are involved. Biometrika **34**(1–2), 28–35 (1947). https://doi.org/10.1093/biomet/34.1-2.28

HYAS: Hybrid Autoscaler Agent for Apache Flink

Alexandros Nikolaos Zafeirakopoulos and Euripides G. M. Petrakis[✉]

School of Electrical and Computer Engineering, Technical University of Crete (TUC),
Chania, Crete, Greece
azafeirakopoulos@tuc.gr, petrakis@intelligence.tuc.gr

Abstract. Apache Flink is a distributed processing engine for stateful computations over unbounded and bounded data streams. Despite its versatility, Apache Flink cannot automatically and optimally adjust its computing resources to match the requirements of the incoming workload. HYAS agent monitors and models Flink's responsiveness based on changes in operator idleness, backpressure and input record lag. The decision process instructs Flink to adjust its parallelism to keep up with the workload. The performance of HYAS has been assessed experimentally on an Apache Flink deployment on Kubernetes on the Google Cloud Platform using synthetic and real-life workloads. HYAS successfully maintains application performance and provides a better performance-to-cost ratio than existing methods.

Keywords: Stream Processing · Autoscaling · Kubernetes · Apache Flink

1 Introduction

Apache Flink [1] is a state-of-the-art platform for large-scale low-latency, fault-tolerant batch, and stateful stream processing. Applications are defined as sequences of operations that run in parallel on different workers (i.e. servers). The parallelism of an application translates to the number of workers allocated to that application. Streaming tasks are often long-running and workload fluctuations may occur during the lifetime of an application. Operations in Apache Flink can be stateful (i.e. past events can influence the way current events are processed). Being distributed and stateful, Apache Flink complicates the scaling (i.e. changing the parallelism) of the application because different workers have to share the same state.

Static provisioning of computing resources can prove inefficient and costly. If few resources are allocated (under-provisioning), the application will not keep up with the increasing workload leading to performance reduction (i.e. increased latency or non-responsiveness). If too many resources are allocated (over-provisioning) some workers will be idle. Flink's parallelism can be changed by stopping the job, taking a save point of the current state of the stream, and then restarting the job with different parallelism from this snapshot. Flink's state

I. Garrigós et al. (Eds.): ICWE 2023, LNCS 13893, pp. 34–48, 2023.
https://doi.org/10.1007/978-3-031-34444-2_3

must be written on permanent storage. This is an asynchronous action in order not to disturb pipeline flow. However, restoring from a save point can take a significant amount of time during which incoming records are not being processed (i.e. downtime). Once the application is restarted, it should try to catch up on any accumulated records.

HYAS combines features of both proactive and reactive methods and is categorized as a *hybrid* method. It constantly monitors and maintains the performance of Apache Flink based on predictions of the workload and takes scaling decisions proactively based on rule and threshold policies. Workload predictions are expressed by the rate of change of unprocessed records (i.e. lag). HYAS prevents Flink from unnecessary scaling by incorporating idle time and backpressure metrics of task operators. Compared to existing approaches [10,13] this is a distinctive and also desirable feature of HYAS.

Apache Flink and HYAS are deployed on Kubernetes[1] and Google Kubernetes Engine (GKE) on the Google Cloud Platform (GCP). HYAS is evaluated on a click fraud detection application that ran for many hours using synthetic (i.e. Gaussian and spike) workloads and also, a real-life workload producing up to many (i.e. more than 20) thousand records per second. HYAS is compared with Smilax [5] and Horizontal Pod Autoscaler (HPA) of Kubernetes taking decisions reactively based on CPU utilization metrics. The experimental results demonstrate that HYAS always makes accurate predictions of the real workload and stress of Flink operators, and allows for accurate and cost-efficient scaling. It results in reduced application latency and better utilization of computing resources. This leads to less infrastructure cost for the clients (i.e. in GCP clients are charged based on the utilization of worker machines).

Related work on FLINK autoscaling is discussed in Sect. 2. HYAS and Apache Flink deployment on Kubernetes is discussed in Sect. 3. HYAS autoscaler solution is presented in Sect. 4 followed by evaluation and experimental results in Sect. 5. Conclusions, system extensions and issues for future research are discussed in Sect. 6.

2 Related Work

Existing resource allocation policies for Apache Flink are mostly *reactive* (e.g. [7,14]). They respond to non-anticipated changes of the workload and adjust the parallelism of the system. They are easy to implement but, leave room for both over or under-utilization of resources [12]. DS2 [7] enables automatic scaling of Apache Flink applications. A controller assesses the running application at the operator level in order to detect possible bottlenecks in the data flow (i.e. operators that slow down the whole application). Contrast to existing methods (e.g. [5,14]) that scale Flink at the Job level (i.e. multiple operators or tasks may execute in a job), DS2 is designed to adjust the parallelism of each operator separately in order to maintain high throughput. Autopilot [14] is a proprietary solution for the Ververica platform which is designed to drive multiple high throughputs, low latency stream processing applications on Apache Flink.

---

[1] https://github.com/apache/flink-kubernetes-operator.

There are also solutions that have been incorporated into the real-time analytics platforms of commercial cloud providers: Apache Heron[2] is the stream processing engine of Twitter; Dataflow[3] is a serverless autoscaling solution that supports automatic partitioning and re-balancing of input data streams to servers in the Google Cloud Platform.

Proactive methods (e.g. [5]) attempt to anticipate future changes in the system performance and take the necessary scaling actions before such changes occur. Compared to reactive methods they are characterized by improved performance and reduced utilization of resources. They resort to machine learning for the characterization of the workload during a training phase. The solution is tailored to the local characteristics of the workload and might be unstable. As a result, the training phase must run periodically (or when the workload prediction is not in range). This is inefficient and costly. Proactive scaling methods are not quite mature yet and have not been incorporated into commercial real-time analytics platforms.

Initial ideas for a statistical machine learning model for the scaling of resources are discussed in [2]. Smilax [5] exploits these ideas to auto-scaling Flink. During a training phase, a reactive scaler collects workload and performance information and adjusts the number of worker machines whenever the performance limit (i.e. the SLA) is violated. Smilax builds a statistical machine learning model which registers the optimal mapping between workload, performance, and number of servers. Model fitting takes place at run time from production data. As soon as the model is deemed stable, the agent switches to optimal mode. The model is then used for predicting the performance of the application and for making scaling decisions proactively (i.e. before SLA violations occur). The stability of the model is constantly monitored and as soon as a model change is detected (e.g. the workload becomes unpredictable), the agent switches back to reactive mode to start collecting new data in order to build a new performance model.

Varga et al. [13] is a hybrid auto-scaling model for Apache Flink jobs on Kubernetes based on *consumer lag* (i.e. number of records waiting to be processed) and *idle time* (i.e. time that a worker machine is idle) metrics. The authors analyze the relationship between the size of the state that is stored on the disk, the downtime, and the time to load the state (before the task is restarted) after a scale operation. They established a linear relationship between state size and the duration of saving Flink's state on the disk.

3   HYAS and Flink Deployment on Kubernetes

The Flink cluster consists of a Job Manager and a number of Task Managers (workers). The Job Manager controls the operation of the entire cluster: it schedules the workers, reacts to finished or failed tasks, load balances the workload among Task Managers, and coordinates checkpoints and recovery from failures.

---

[2] https://incubator.apache.org/clutch/heron.html.
[3] https://cloud.google.com/dataflow.

The Task Managers are the machines (servers) that execute the tasks of a work-flow. A task represents a data flow (i.e. a chain of one or more operators) that can be executed in a single thread or server. The data flows or Jobs or pipelines (i.e. operations chained together) form directed graphs (job graphs), that start with one or more sources and end at one or more sinks. A task can be executed in parallel (on separate Task Managers). Each parallel instance of a task is a subtask. The number of subtasks running in parallel is the parallelism of that particular task.

Apache Flink provides an extensive toolbox of operators for implementing transformations on data streams (e.g. filtering, updating state, aggregating). A job graph comprises multiple operators combined together. An operator is the lowest granularity unit that can be assigned to a thread (or machine) and scaled independently (a task slot). Operators can be grouped into tasks to be executed and scaled together in task slots. A third alternative is to map the entire job to a task slot. Accordingly, the options for scaling FLINK are by operator, task, or Job. Pipeline scaling is the only option to achieve an evenly-balanced load across tasks and operators that minimizes their interdependencies and communication [10].

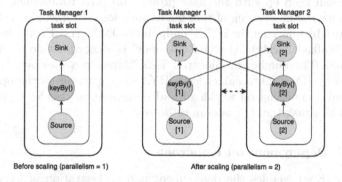

Fig. 1. An Apache Flink data flow before and after scaling.

HYAS opted for Pipeline scaling (the third option). Each Task Manager executes the entire data flow and this is the lowest granularity unit that is scaled. Rescaling actions (e.g. adding or removing workers) will modify the parallelism of all operators of a subtask at the same time. Figure 1 illustrates a data flow with parallelism 1 (on the left) and the same data flow with parallelism 2 (after scaling).

Reactive Mode [8] (in Flink v1.13) automates much of the work for scaling a Flink Job based on resource consumption metrics provided by a third-party service (e.g. Prometheus). The amount of resources to be added (or removed) is determined by an autoscaler mechanism such as the Horizontal Pod Autoscaler[4]

---

[4] https://kubernetes.io/docs/tasks/run-application/horizontal-pod-autoscale/.

(HPA) of Kubernetes or HYAS (in this work). Flink Job Manager handles the rest of the work for stopping, saving and restarting our job with the new parallelism. For the time being, Reactive Mode is only possible with Application Mode[5] (i.e. each Job is controlled by a dedicated Job Manager offering resource isolation between application deployments).

An application receives data records from streaming sources (e.g. databases, the Web, etc.) via Apache Kafka [9]. This is a broker service where applications send information. To handle large message loads, a streaming application collects the data into multiple queues (Kafka partitions). The queues may span different topics. The queues can cover different topics and each topic can be assigned a number of queues. The number of topics and the number of queues per topic is user-defined. Each Task Manager subscribes to a topic to read data from one or more queues of that topic. The records are evenly distributed among the queues to balance the load among the Task Managers.

The incoming workload is monitored by inspecting Apache Kafka queues. The workload represents the number of records per second the system receives. Kafka queues are empty if the system consumes (processes) the received data at a rate higher than the production rate; otherwise, the data remains in the queue (slow records). The average length of Kafka queues is an indicator of whether the system can keep up with the data production rate. Prometheus service[6] is responsible for the monitoring of running applications. Prometheus retrieves the Kafka metrics by querying the HTTP endpoint of JMX[7] (i.e. Prometheus cannot connect to Kafka directly). Apache Zookeeper[8] is a coordination service for the Kafka queues. The number of allocated Task Managers varies over time and it is regulated by HYAS autoscaler agent. HYAS agent monitors the operation of all tasks and, depending on workload and performance, decides to change the parallelism of a task (i.e. to scale-up or down).

3.1   Flink Deployment on Kubernetes

Kubernetes (K8s) enables the deployment and orchestration of Containerized applications across server infrastructures (e.g. the cloud). Applications services are grouped in Pods that span different Nodes (VMs) within the same or different server infrastructures. Each Node runs a container-optimized Operating System (OS) and hosts several Pods depending on Node resources and resource demands of Pods. Applications run in clusters of Nodes (the Node pool). A Node Pool is configured with the CPU, RAM, storage space, and OS requirements so that each Node is initialized to meet the resource needs of the application. The Cluster can host a finite number of Nodes, sharing hardware, software, and network. A Kubernetes Cluster includes at least one Worker Node and a Master Node (or Control Plane) which hosts all Kubernetes components. The Kubernetes cluster

---

[5] https://nightlies.apache.org/flink/flink-docs-master/docs/deployment/overview/.
[6] https://prometheus.io.
[7] https://docs.oracle.com/en/java/javase/15/jmx/.
[8] https://zookeeper.apache.org.

is deployed in the Google Cloud Platform (GCP). The Google Kubernetes Engine (GKE) is responsible for controlling the Cluster. The Google Compute Engine (GCE) controls the Node Cluster. A valuable component of the Control Plane is the Kubernetes Scheduler [4]. It monitors the cluster and binds each Pod to a Node based on several criteria such as Pod, Node resources, and user preferences.

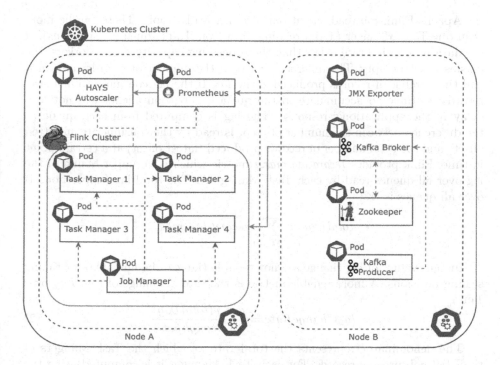

Fig. 2. Apache Flink deployment on Kubernetes.

The Flink Kubernetes Operator [6] allows to host (i.e. operate and control) Flink deployments on Kubernetes. Figure 2 illustrates a Flink deployment (i.e. an application) with HYAS autoscaler and supporting services on two Nodes (the Control Plane is not shown). Node A comprises an Apache Flink Cluster with one Job Manager and 4 Task Managers as Pods. The number of allocated Task Managers is controlled by HYAS which also runs in a Pod. HYAS can also run on a separate machine outside the Kubernetes cluster (so that it does not consume cluster resources). It receives metrics from Apache Kafka (i.e. average queue size) and Flink (e.g. CPU, RAM utilization) through Prometheus (also a Pod on node A). HYAS takes scaling decisions and instructs the Job Manager and the Control Plane (CP) to scale up (or down) Task Managers. New Pods (i.e. Task Managers) can be added or defalcated. If Node A has not sufficient resources to host new Pods, a new Node is added to the Cluster to host the new Pods. Conversely, it can deallocate empty Nodes. Node B contains the

Apache Kafka Cluster, Zookeeper, and the data producer application as Pods. The Kafka producer is a custom load-testing application that can also run outside Kubernetes on a separate server.

4   HYAS Autoscaler Agent

An Apache Flink job reads input data from a Kafka topic. There can be more than one Task Manager (TMs) reading data from Kafka queues (partitions). If the data production rate is less than the processing capacity of the workers, the queues will be empty. The difference between the number of records consumed and the number of records produced is the *lag*. If the lag continues to increase, records continue to accumulate in the queues, and soon clients will notice a delay in the application's response. The lag is computed from each queue as the difference between the number of records read by the consumer (committed offset) and the total number of records produced (latest offset) at a certain point in time. Flink provides *record_lag_max_i* metric which is an upper bound of the lag over all queues read by each Task Manager i. The total lag (upper bound) over all queues is [13]

$$total Lag = \sum_{i \in TMs} record\_lag\_max_i \tag{1}$$

Instant values of lag change are not reliable (i.e. can be unstable) for taking scaling decisions. A more reliable metric is the rate of change of *totalLag* over 1 min

$$lagChangeRate = \frac{deriv(totalLag)}{Throughput} \tag{2}$$

The denominator represents the total rate at which the Task Mangers of the Flink job process records. For each Task Manager it is computed using the *records_consumed_rate* metric of Flink

$$Throughput = \sum_{i \in TMs} records\_consumed\_rate_i \tag{3}$$

If *LagChangeRate* > 0 over 1 min, the parallelism must increase. The reverse is not always true: even if *lagChangeRate* $\leq$ 0 the application might still need all its Task Managers until all records are processed. If the decision is to scale-up, the new parallelism (*Parallelism'*) is computed by a multiplier of the current parallelism (*Parallelism*)

$$Parallelism' = \lceil Parallelism \times (lagChangeRate + 1) \rceil \tag{4}$$

Equation 4 is also intuitively correct. On constant lag change rate (i.e. *lagChangeRate = 0*) the addition of 1 in Eq. 4 results in the same value of parallelism. If the rate of change of lag equals 1, adding 1 in Eq. 4 will suggest doubling the number of Task Managers, which is also correct. However, scaling actions require that the Flink Job is stopped and then restarted with the new parallelism from a snapshot. In the meantime, records keep accumulating in the queues and Eq. 4 alone might result in a high parallelism value. This can be corrected for a short time interval and until the accumulated records are processed.

Although increasing the parallelism will speed up processing, in rare cases (e.g. *lagChangeRate* can be high after restarting a Flink Job), this might result in over-provisioning and excess charges for the client (i.e. in the cloud, the client is charged by the number of machines). There are cases where not all operators of a FLIK pipeline are equally stressed and the slowest operators limit the performance of the pipeline. Backpressure [11] is a measure of the stress of individual operators. It is commonly used to express the situation where a system is receiving data at a higher rate than it can process during a temporary load change (i.e. a spike). A possible action is to "backpressure" the entire pipeline from sink to the source, and throttle the source in order to adjust the speed to that of the slowest part of the pipeline, arriving at a steady state. This is how most stream processing engines react to backpressure.

Flink handles backpressure [3] using local buffers pools for each operator and guarantees that no records are lost even if the operator is stressed. In HYAS, backpressure is used to prevent unnecessary scaling. For example, on student load changes, *lagChangeRate* can be greater than 0 although the operators can still handle the load. If the operators are not stressed yet, HYAS should better wait before taking a decision to scale. If the operators are also stressed and *lagChangeRate > 0* then HYAS instructs Flink to scale up. The *backPressureMsPerSecond* metric of Flink takes values between 0 and 1000 and indicates how much back-pressured an operator is. Equation 5 returns a boolean value if the pipeline is back pressured or not. The overall backpressure condition of a Task Manager is computed as the maximum backpressure over all operators.

$$isBackPressured = if(max_{taskOperators} backPressureMsPerSecond == 1000) \tag{5}$$

Lag and backpressure are metrics for taking reliable decisions to scale up but not to scale down. HYAS takes decisions to scale down based on *idleTimeMsPerSecond* metric of Flink. It represents the amount of time (in milliseconds) an operator is idle (i.e. it has no records to process). It takes values between 0 (for operators processing records at the maximum capacity) and 1000 (when an operator is idle). In HYAS, the minimum idle time over all operators is used to describe the idle condition of the Task Manager as a whole. Equation 6 computes idle time over all operators. A value above a (user-defined) threshold, causes Flink to scale down.

$$idleTime = min_{taskOperators}(idleTimeMsPerSecond) \tag{6}$$

For scaling up, the number of Task Managers can be increased by more than one at a time (according to Eq. 4) to quickly catch up with the workload and avoid application latency. For scaling down, the parallelism is gradually adjusted to avoid unnecessary scaling if the workload increases soon after. Algorithm 1 summarizes how HYAS works. The cool-down period between scaling actions is 90 s (i.e. no scaling decisions will be made for this period of time) to cover the required downtime of Flink when restarting with the new parallelism. Also the conditions in lines 8 and 10 must hold for a period of 1 min to avoid unnecessary scaling due to small variations in *LagChangeRate*.

Algorithm 1. HYAS scaling policy.

1: **while** True **do**

2:     $totalLag = \sum\limits_{i \in TaskManager} record\_lag\_max_i$

3:     $Throughput = \sum\limits_{i \in TaskManager} records\_consumed\_rate_i$

4:     $lagChangeRate = \frac{deriv(totalLag)}{Throughput}$

5:     $Parallelism' = \lceil Parallelism \times (lagChangeRate + 1) \rceil$

6:     $idleTime = min_{taskOperators}(idleTimeMsPerSecond)$ ▷ over 1 minute

7:     $isBackPressured = max_{taskOperators}backPressureMsPerSecond == 1000$ ▷ over 1 minute

8:     **if** $lagChangeRate > 0$ and $isBackPressured$ **then**

9:         scaleUp(Parallelism')

10:    **else if** $idleTime \geq threshold$ **then**

11:        scaleDown(Parallelism - 1)

The threshold value in line 10 allows control of how quickly the algorithm will change parallelism. A threshold value close to 0 (e.g. 100) means that Task Managers will be removed if they are still processing records at full capacity. A threshold value closer to 1000 (e.g. 900) will keep Task Managers running longer than they need to, as they are processing records at a low capacity and the load could be shared across fewer machines. The optimal calculation of the threshold value is important to avoid situations where a Task Manager is removed but immediately afterward the latency increases again and a scaling decision must be made. If no information is available about how smooth the workload is, a threshold value of 500 represents a good balance between having idle Task Managers and releasing Task Managers too early when there are still records to process.

5   Evaluation

HYAS is assessed using a click fraud detection application. This type of fraud occurs on the Internet in pay-per-click (PPC) online advertising applications. Website owners post advertisements and receive re-numeration based on how many Web users click on the advertisements. Fraud occurs when a person or software imitates a legitimate user by clicking on an advertisement without having actual interest in it. The application receives records from a Kafka topic with elements User-IP, User-ID, time-stamp, and event type (e.f. "click"). The application attempts to detect fraud by searching for the following patterns every 60 s: (a) Counts of User IDs per unique IP address, (b) Counts of IP addresses per unique User ID, and, (c) Click-Through Rate (CTR) per User ID. The application receives records from a Kafka topic which has the following JSON format:

"ip": "205.0.44.187",
"userID": "e61b8f7a-5029-433a-9e44-79d5f514d309",
"timestamp": 1595431611,
"eventType": "display/click"

The production rate of these records is represented using the FIFA Worldcup 98 dataset[9]. Figure 3 is the workload distribution of the requests made to the Website (per second) between April 30, 1998, and July 26, 1998 (GMT+2 time zone). During this time period, the Website received 1,352,804,107 requests. The entry to Apache Kafka is the 9.5-hour slice of most request activity between 1998-06-30 14:00 and 1998-06-30 22:30. Additional results are obtained from artificial workloads simulating a Gaussian and Spike workload.

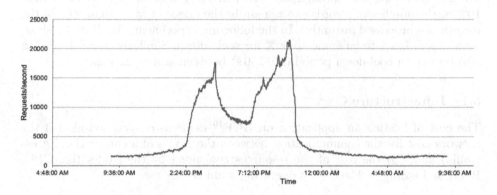

Fig. 3. FIFA 98 World Cup workload.

Apache Flink is deployed on a Kubernetes Cluster with e2-standard-8 machines in the Europe-west1-d region of the Google Cloud Platform (GCP). A Node Pool is configured with 8 virtual CPUs, 32 GB Ram, and 40 GB SSD space for each Node (VM). Apache Flink is deployed as a Flink Application Cluster with Reactive Mode enabled. The application is submitted as a single running job running (initially) in a Node. Each Pod represents a Task Manager. A scale-up operation will create new Pods in the same or in a new Node (i.e. if the current Node has no sufficient resources to host the new Pod). A scale-down

---

[9] https://github.com/nimamahmoudi/worldcup98-dataset.

operation might cause the deletion of unnecessary Pods and the de-allocation of empty Nodes. The Kafka producer is a python script that simulates a "click" action (i.e. a record) each with a randomly generated IP, user ID, and timestamp. The production rate follows the FIFA 98 Workload. The records are evenly distributed (in round-robin) to 60 Kafka partitions of a single topic. The Flink Job runs up to 6 Task Managers that consume records from 10 partitions each.

The performance of HYAS is compared against the Horizontal Pod Autoscaler (HPA) the state-of-the-art autoscaler solution of Kubernetes. The CPU target utilization for scale-up is 90% for scale-up and 60% for scale-down. Each time the current utilization (over all Pods) surpasses these values, HPA instructs the Job Manager to adjust the Parallelism accordingly by adding or removing Pods. HPA imposes a "stabilization" period (i.e. 300 s) after scaling down in order to reduce the fluctuation of the Parallelism. During stabilization, no scaling action can take place.

HYAS's performance is also compared against Smilax [5]. Smilax is a proactive autoscaler that encompasses a training phase for building the model of the workload. The model is sensitive to workload fluctuations. Training repeats periodically whenever the workload is not consistent with the model. Once a model has been computed, Smilax switches to optimal phase and takes scaling decisions reactively based on an SLA metric. The SLA is defined as the ratio between the average queue lag and throughput. The SLA threshold is 90% (i.e. less than 10% of the number of records can remain in the queue or more than 90% of the records are processed instantly). In the following experiment, the SLA threshold for scale-up is set to 90% and to 60% for scale-down. Similarly to HPA, Smilax also imposes a cool-down period (i.e. 240 s) between scaling actions.

5.1   Infrastructure Cost

The cost of hosting an application on GCP[10] depends on two factors, (a) the network cost for the communication between the Nodes of a cluster (i.e. Egress traffic) and, (b) the cost of the resources consumed by the Nodes (i.e. CPU, RAM and storage). The cost of operating a cluster is

$$TotalCost = Cost_{CPU} + Cost_{RAM} + Cost_{Traffic} + Cost_{Storage}. \qquad (7)$$

Intra-cluster (Ingress) communication of Pods within each Node is not charged. In the following experiments, each Node is allocated 8vCPU and 32GB RAM. Egress traffic is charged according to the size of data exchanged between the Nodes of a cluster. GCP charges each VM per hour of usage. Equation 8 expresses the cost of hosting an application on GCP. Egress cost is computed as a function of the total number and size of the messages exchanged between the micro-services. The Egress cost from Node i to Node j is expressed $t_e(i \rightarrow j)$. The double summation in the formula takes also into account the cost from Node j to Node i. The hourly cost of a cluster is computed as the summation of the

---

[10] https://cloud.google.com/compute/all-pricing.

following terms (i.e. n is the number of Nodes):

$$Cost_{cpu} = n \cdot 8vCPU \cdot CPU_{cost} \cdot hours; \; CPU_{cost} = \$0.023993/vCPU/hour$$
$$Cost_{ram} = n \cdot 32GB(RAM) \cdot RAM_{cost} \cdot hours; \; RAM_{cost} = \$0.003216/GB/hour$$
$$Cost_{egress} = Egress_{cost} \cdot \sum_{i=1}^{n} \sum_{j=1, j \neq i}^{n} t_e(i \to j); \quad\quad Egress_{cost} = \$0.01/GB$$
$$Cost_{storage} \simeq 0. \tag{8}$$

5.2   Experimental Results

The purpose of the following experiments is to demonstrate the effectiveness of the HYAS autoscaler method. As will be shown in the results, HYAS takes scaling decisions ahead of time (i.e. before the decline is observed), exhibits faster application latency (i.e. response time) under stress, and yields lower total infrastructure costs on the Google Cloud Platform for a given period (e.g. one hour).

Table 1 summarizes the performance of all methods. HYAS achieves lower application latency, lower resource utilization (i.e. average usage of Pods in the duration of the experiment), and, lower infrastructure costs compared to both HPA and Smilax. Infrastructure cost accounts mainly for the number of Pods (i.e. VMs) utilized. Egress traffic is below 100GB for all methods and accounts for less than $1 for all methods. Table 1 depicts also the relationship between latency (in minutes) and the maximum lag under stress. Obviously, Flink is stressed during workload spikes. This is the point in time where latency occurs (i.e. all methods perform the same under a smooth workload). The latency reported in the experiments accounts for the time each method takes to empty its queue when the second (steeper) spike occurred (Fig. 3).

Table 1. Performance of autoscaler methods on the FIFA WorldCup workload.

Method/Measurement	HYAS	HPA	Smilax
Average usage of machines (VMs)	1.6	1.8	1.8
Maximum lag (number of records)	16,663	32,184	25,206
Application latency (minutes)	11	25	14
Infrastructure cost (USD/hour)	0,24	0,27	0,27

Figure 4 illustrates the resource allocation during the experiment by all methods. Notice that, all methods handled the first spike, between 14:00 – 19:00 time, gracefully. This is not true for the second (steeper) spike between 19:00 – 23:00 time. HPA and Smilax tend to adjust Flink's parallelism faster than HYAS. This results in greater resource utilization and infrastructure cost for the client. However, this does not translate to improved application latency, and HYAS is faster than its competitors. This is attributed to HYAS policy to defer scaling based on three metrics (i.e. lag change, idle time, and backpressure) which better represent the stress of the Flink Job, than CPU or queue length alone. This prevented Flink from unnecessary scaling. HYAS reacted to the bigger (second) spike with only 1 scaling action. HPA made it with no scaling action at all but this is the source of the low application latency (i.e. 25 min) reported in Table 1. All response times do not include the downtime for Flink to restart the Job.

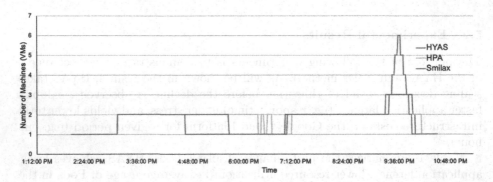

Fig. 4. Allocation of machines during the experiment for the FIFA FIFA WorldCup workload.

Similar results are obtained from testing on simulated (but realistic) workloads. Table 2 illustrates results from testing on a Gaussian workload that generated up to 18,000 records (i.e. peak load) for a period of 1 h. Table 3 illustrates results from testing on a spike workload that generated up to 20,000 records (i.e. peak load) for a period of 5 min. The results for infrastructure cost are projected to the hour.

Table 2. Performance of autoscaler methods on the Gaussian workload.

Method/Measurement	HYAS	HPA	Smilax
Average usage of machines (VMs)	1.7	1.9	3
Maximum lag (number of records)	17,316	19,325	43,783
Application latency (minutes)	5	6	14
Infrastructure cost (USD/hour)	0.25	0.29	0.44

Figure 5 illustrates the resource allocation for the Gaussian and the Spike workload during the life time of the experiment.

Table 3. Performance of autoscaler methods on the Spike workload.

Method/Measurement	HYAS	HPA	Smilax
Average usage of machines (VMs)	1.6	1.9	3.2
Maximum lag (number of records)	24,117	34,162	53,896
Application latency (minutes)	3	7	10
Infrastructure cost (USD/hour)	0.25	0.28	0.50

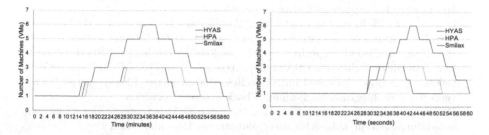

Fig. 5. Allocation of machines during the experiment for the Gaussian (left) and the Spike workload (right).

6   Conclusions and Future Work

HYAS monitors Flink's resources and adjusts its parallelism based on changes in the input's record lag, operator idleness, and backpressure. Restarting the Flink Job with a new parallelism (from a save point) can take a significant amount of time during which no records are processed. Once restarted, Flink must try to catch up to any records accumulated in the queues. HYAS handles this issue more effectively than other methods tested in this work yielding faster responses (i.e. improved latency) and less infrastructure (monetary) cost. Finding the correlation between the state size to be stored and idle time (downtime) before restarting a Flink Job would lead to a more accurate estimation computation of the idle period. The less downtime, the fewer records are accumulated in the queue. This is an important issue for future research.

Scaling Flink at the operator level is still controversial [10] but requires further investigation. HYAS takes full advantage of the Reactive Mode feature in Flink v1.13. This automates much of the work for scaling but it is only available with Application Mode. A future version might work also with Session Mode. That would enable HYAS to scale multiple Flink Jobs (i.e. more than one application) simultaneously sharing the same cluster of Task Managers. Finally, the HYAS decision-making agent is threshold-based. Threshold-based rules are simple to implement but their performance depends on the quality of user-defined thresholds. More elaborate methods based on machine learning can be applied to tailor threshold values to the characteristics of the workload.

Acknowledgment. We are grateful to Google for the Google Cloud Platform Education Grants program. The work has received funding from the European Union's Horizon 2020 - Research and Innovation Framework Programme H2020-SU-SEC-2019, under Grant Agreement No 883272- BorderUAS.

References

1. Apache Flink - Stateful Computations over Data Streams (2022). https://flink. apache.org, The Apache Software Foundation
2. Bodik, P., Griffith, R., Sutton, C., Fox, A., Jordan, M., Patterson, D.: Statistical machine learning makes automatic control practical for internet datacenters. In: Hot Topics in Cloud Computing (HoTCloud 2009), pp. 195–203. USENIX Association, San Diego, California, USA (2009). https://doi.org/10.5555/1855533.1855545
3. Celebi, U.: How Apache Flink Handles Backpressure (2015). https://www. ververica.com/blog/how-flink-handles-backpressure, ververica
4. GCP: Kubernetes Scheduler (2022). https://kubernetes.io/docs/concepts/ scheduling-eviction/kube-scheduler/, kubernetes Documentation
5. Giannakopoulos, P., Petrakis, E.G.M.: Smilax: statistical machine learning autoscaler agent for Apache Flink. In: International Conference on Advanced Information Networking and Applications (AINA-2021), pp. 433–444. Toronto, ON, Canada (2021). https://doi.org/10.1007/978-3-030-75075-6_35
6. Flink Kubernetes Operator (2023). https://github.com/apache/flink-kubernetes-operator, Version: v1beta1
7. Kalavri, V., Liagouris, J., Hoffmann, M., Dimitrova, D., Forshaw, M., Roscoe, T.: Three steps is all you need: Fast, accurate, automatic scaling decisions for distributed streaming dataflows. In: 13th USENIX Symposium on Operating Systems Design and Implementation (OSDI 2018), pp. 783–798. Carlsbad, CA (2018). https://www.usenix.org/conference/osdi18/presentation/kalavri
8. Metzger, R.: Scaling Flink automatically with Reactive Mode (2021). https://flink. apache.org/2021/05/06/reactive-mode.html
9. Narkhede, N., Shapira, G., Palino, T.: Kafka the Definitive Guide, Real Time Data and Stream Processing at Scale. O'Reilly Media (2017). https://kafka.apache.org/
10. Paul, F.: Autoscaling Apache Flink with Ververica Platform Autopilot (2021). https://www.ververica.com/blog/autoscaling-apache-flink-with-ververica-platform-autopilot, Ververica Platform
11. Phelps, J.: Backpressure Explained - The Resisted Flow of Data Through Software (2019). https://medium.com/@jayphelps/backpressure-explained-the-flow-of-data-through-software-2350b3e77ce7
12. Rampérez, V., Soriano, J., Lizcano, D., Lara, J.A.: FLAS: a combination of proactive and reactive auto-scaling architecture for distributed services. Futur. Gener. Comput. Syst. **118**, 56–72 (2021). https://doi.org/10.1016/j.future.2020.12.025
13. Varga, B., Balassi, M., Kiss, A.: Towards autoscaling of Apache Flink jobs. Acta Univ. Sapientiae Inform. **13**(1), 39–59 (2021). https://doi.org/10.2478/ausi-2021-0003
14. Autopilot (2022). https://docs.ververica.com/user_guide/application_operations/ autopilot.html, Ververica Platform

Machine Learning for Web Engineering

Optimizing ML Inference Queries Under Constraints

Ziyu Li[1]([envelope]), Mariette Schönfeld[1], Wenbo Sun[1], Marios Fragkoulis[2], Rihan Hai[1], Alessandro Bozzon[1], and Asterios Katsifodimos[1]

[1] TU Delft, Delft, The Netherlands
{z.li-14,m.a.e.schonfeld,w.sun-2,r.hai,
a.bozzon,a.katsifodimos}@tudelft.nl
[2] Delivery Hero SE, Berlin, Germany
marios.fragkoulis@deliveryhero.com

Abstract. The proliferation of pre-trained ML models in public Web-based model zoos facilitates the engineering of ML pipelines to address complex inference queries over datasets and streams of unstructured content. Constructing optimal plan for a query is hard, especially when constraints (e.g. accuracy or execution time) must be taken into consideration, and the complexity of the inference query increases. To address this issue, we propose a method for optimizing ML inference queries that selects the most suitable ML models to use, as well as the order in which those models are executed. We formally define the *constraint-based ML inference query optimization problem*, formulate it as a Mixed Integer Programming (MIP) problem, and develop an optimizer that maximizes accuracy given constraints. This optimizer is capable of navigating a large search space to identify optimal query plans on various model zoos.

Keywords: Machine learning inference query · Constrained-based query optimization · Predicate ordering

1 Introduction

Machine learning (ML) is increasingly used to process unstructured documents (i.e. text, images, videos), or data streams [6,9,21,24]. Take, for instance, the scenario of a self-driving car: when it detects (at certain proximity) that a person is crossing the road, or that another car has turned its emergency lights on, the car has to trigger an emergency action (e.g., breaking hard). This can be modeled as a complex *ML inference query*, and represented as a Boolean expression [5,12]: (road ∧ person) ∨ (car ∧ light). The literals in the expression are combined using operations such as *and* (conjunction) and *or* (disjunction).

While ML models can be (and often are) tailored to specific inference tasks, there is a growing interest in the reuse and re-purposing of pre-trained ML models [8]. This shift, mostly motivated by computational, economic, and environmental considerations, is evident from the proliferation of public, pre-trained ML

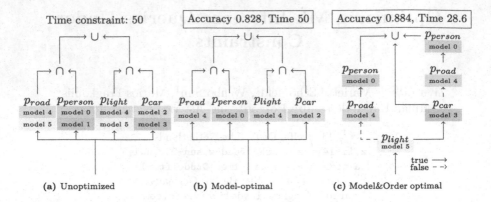

Fig. 1. Alternative ML query plans for the running example query.

model zoos on the Web, such as HuggingFace and PyTorch Hub[1]. These hubs contain thousands of pre-trained models for diverse ML inference needs such as object recognition, sentiment analysis or audio classification. These models are described by metadata detailing their inference capabilities (e.g. identified object classes), and performance (e.g. accuracy and execution time). With the help of the model zoos, ML inference query plans – i.e. complex workflows of ML models as the one shown in Fig. 1 – can be executed by leveraging existing ML models through easily accessible APIs, providing greater flexibility in defining ad-hoc queries.

ML inference queries are often subject to specific performance constraints (e.g. inference execution time, accuracy) [11,18]. In such cases, the selection of a set of models becomes quite complicated: an analyst may manually define a query plan that is excessively expensive and/or inaccurate if they lack considerable systems skills or time. Instead, an *optimizer* could automate the selection of (a set of) ML model(s) from the model zoo, so that the query could be answered under specific execution constraints. That way, data analysts/engineers can focus on the analytical task at hand, while ML researchers and engineers can independently focus on ML model development and enhancement.

Contributions. We propose a method (depicted in Fig. 2) to select the best ML models as well as their execution order, given a complex ML inference query and execution constraints. We formulate the problem of inference query optimization with constraints as a mixed integer program (MIP) and jointly optimize model assignment and predicate ordering (indicated as *model- & order-optimal* optimizer). The model assignment deals with the mapping of models to predicates, while predicate ordering decides the order in which to evaluate them. The contributions of this paper can be summarized as follows:

– We formulate the problem of ML inference query optimization as a (MIP) and propose a MIP-based optimizer that exploits model zoos.

---

[1] https://huggingface.co/, https://pytorch.org/hub/.

- Our approach is the first that jointly optimizes model assignment and predicate ordering, leveraging the selectivity (i.e., the probability of a predicate to evaluate `true`) of model-based predicates to decide their order of execution.
- We evaluate our `Bypass: Model- & Order-optimal` optimizer against baselines (Sect. 5), showing that our proposed optimizer can generate plans that significantly outperform the baselines in diverse model zoos on different constraint settings.

2   Related Work

ML Inference Query Optimization. The development of specialized models for fast inference of object detection queries has received considerable attention [7,8,17,20]. More recently, related research is targeting the processing efficiency of larger ML inference query [1,3,4,10,18]. NoScope [10] and PP [18] filtered irrelevant frames by training and deploying special lightweight binary classifiers, and Tahoma [1] trained model cascades to process video frames. The cheaper models are trained to achieve very low false negative rates, so that they did not filter out valid tuples/images/frames, since these can be validated by more accurate and expensive models downstream.

The most related work to ours is PP [18]. Our work is complementary to PPs, as it aims at reusing the plethora of existing models available in public and enterprise model zoos without retraining, and at optimally navigating the performance to accuracy trade-off of existing models. PP generates query plans for ML inference queries by first pre-selecting the predicates with a heuristic solution before optimizing the query plan, thus the query plan is suboptimal.

Multiple-objective Query Optimization. We model the ML inference query optimization problem presented in this paper as a multiple-objective query optimization problem with a bounded objective method. Notably, the problem at hand can also be modeled with other methods for multiple-objective optimization [15,19,22,23], which seek to find the set of query plans that dominate all others in terms of the trade-off between two conflicting objectives. However, the problem we tackle in this paper is different from the classic single- and multi-objective query optimization problems in existing literature due to the special treatment that accuracy requires as well as the consideration of predicate ordering in our specific problem setting.

3   Problem Definition

In this section, we define the notions of a *model zoo* and its metadata, and *ML inference query*. We also formalize the *ML inference query optimization problem*. Note that in this work, we consider the case of ML models that perform *classification* tasks.

Table 1. Execution time C of models in a model zoo.

	p_{road}	p_{person}	p_{light}	p_{car}
model 0	∞	25	∞	∞
model 1	∞	35	∞	∞
model 2	∞	∞	∞	20
model 3	∞	∞	∞	40
model 4	5	∞	5	∞
model 5	10	∞	10	∞

Table 2. Example accuracy A of models in a model zoo.

	p_{road}	p_{person}	p_{light}	p_{car}
model 0	0	0.90	0	0
model 1	0	0.95	0	0
model 2	0	0	0	0.91
model 3	0	0	0	0.93
model 4	0.94	0	0.91	0
model 5	0.96	0	0.95	0

3.1   Metadata of a Model Zoo

We formalize the metadata representation of a model zoo [14] as $\mathcal{R}(M, I, P, A, C)$, where M denotes the set of pre-trained ML models; I denotes the set of classes that M can infer; P denotes the corresponding set of a Boolean predicates over the inference classes I; A and C represent the matrices with the dimensions of $|M| \times |P|$, which store the values of model accuracy and execution time, respectively. C is depicted in Table 1 while A is depicted in Table 2. In the following, we explain how we utilize the metadata of a model zoo as prior information in ML inference query optimization in Sect. 4.

3.2   ML Inference Queries

Given a model zoo $\mathcal{R}(M, I, P, A, C)$, we write an ML inference query in the form of $(p_1 \wedge ... \wedge p_i) \vee ... \vee (p_j \wedge ... \wedge p_k)$, where each p_l is a Boolean predicate representing the inference class inferred by the ML model m_l ($1 \leq l \leq k$). According to the closed-world assumption, we assume that an input ML inference query Q can be answered by a given model zoo $\mathcal{R}$. Note that it is possible that one model is selected for multiple predicates.

CNF and DNF Queries. In above definition, Q is in the *disjunctive normal form (DNF)*, where the clauses $Q_1 \vee \cdots \vee Q_l$ are connected by disjunctions. An ML inference query Q and its subqueries Q_i are Boolean queries. In the rest of the paper, for brevity, we will refer to *ML inference queries in CNF* simply as *CNF queries* (similarly for the DNF ones).

3.3   ML Inference Query Plan

We define a ML inference query plan as the orchestration of ML models supporting the execution of a ML inference query. Note that each predicate can be associated with several models before optimization (Fig. 1(a)). Figure 1(b) presents the query plan with an optimized model assignment, where each predicate is covered by a model. All the models process all the data and results are generated with union. We call this type of query plan a *sequential* plan. Figure 1(c) depicts a plan with optimized model assignment and execution order as a bypass plan [13], where we refer to this type of query plan as *bypass* plan.

3.4 Problem Definition

Given a ML inference query Q, we aim for an optimization target that maximizes the accuracy with constraint on the execution time. The *Accuracy-maximizing Model Assignment (AMA) problem* is defined as follows: given a model zoo $\mathcal{R}$, an ML inference query Q, and an upper bound C_{bound} on execution time, the goal is to assign a model $m \in M$ for each predicate $p \in P$, which maximizes the accuracy a_Q with the constraint of execution time c_Q. Formally, the objective function to optimize is:

$$\text{Maximize: } a_Q = f_{acc}(Q)$$
$$\text{Subject to: } c_Q \leqslant C_{bound}$$

In the above definition, we denote the function to compute a_Q as $f_{acc}(Q)$, which is detailed in Sect. 4.2. The cost of the query plan c_Q is measured by the average inference time on one data instance. C_{bound} represents the given execution time bound that the computation cost of the query should respect.

In a similar way, we can define the *Execution-time-minimizing Model Assignment (EMA) Problem*, where the goal is to assign a model $m \in M$ for each predicate $p \in P$, which minimizes the average execution time on each tuple, i.e., c_Q, with the constraint that the minimum accuracy of the query a_Q stays above a lower bound A_{bound}. We do not detail this version of the problem, for the lack of space, but the interested reader can refer to an extended version of our paper[2].

4 Optimizing ML Inference Queries

Given an ML inference query, the goal is to generate query plan which maximizes the accuracy and satisfies the constraint on execution time. In this section, we outline our optimization and execution workflow for ML inference query in Sect. 4.1. We then present a mixed-integer programming formulation (Sect. 4.2–4.6) for the ML inference query optimization problem as defined previously, including accuracy model, execution time model, objective function, and other relevant components. Due to space limit, we refrain from including the implementation details such as formulation equations and linearization of quadratic terms. Instead, we provide descriptions of the key components and refer the reader to our extended paper version.

4.1 Approach Overview

As depicted in Fig. 2, users can define an ML inference query with ML model-based predicates. To optimize the query, our MIP-based optimizer leverages the metadata of a model zoo containing information about the available models and their performance in terms of accuracy and execution time. The input of our query optimizer also includes the metadata about *selectivity*, i.e., statistics

---

[2] Extended version: https://www.wis.ewi.tudelft.nl/assets/files/opt-ml-query.pdf.

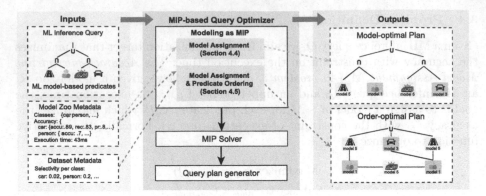

Fig. 2. Approach overview.

regarding the portion of data that a predicate returns as true. Both types of metadata are retrieved from a metadata management tool (e.g. [14]). The query optimizer then parses and optimizes the query. Given different input information, the MIP-based optimizer applies different optimization approaches to generate plans that satisfy the constraints.

Modeling as Mixed Integer Programming. The first step in the optimization phase is mathematical modeling, where the optimizer takes in different types of metadata and formulate their relationships. To tackle the *Accuracy-maximizing Model Assignment* (AMA) problem in Sect. 3.4, we resolve *model assignment*, i.e., mapping between ML models and predicates, and *predicate ordering*, i.e., deciding the execution order of predicates.

- *Model assignment.* With the model zoo metadata alone (yellow dashed arrows), the optimization only assign models to predicates adhering to an execution time constraint.
- *Predicate ordering.* To exploit the execution time budget and aim for higher effectiveness, we adopt *bypass* [13] plans and predicate ordering. The bypass plan consists of branches that execute only a defined subset of data, filtered based on prior outcomes. Bypass plans can greatly reduce execution cost by preventing the execution of models on unnecessary data. Together with predicate ordering, we manage to further increase efficiency and take full advantage of the budget by assigning better models for higher effectiveness with the available resource. The optimizer makes use of the selectivity metadata (red dashed arrows). We assume that selectivity is a property of an existing labeled dataset, and is known in advance.

In this work, we jointly optimize model assignment and predicate ordering given time constraints, and have shown significant performance for the objective goal (see Sect. 5 for details).

MIP Solver and Plan Generation. After modeling, we take the constraints and variables, and feed them to a MIP solver. We use *Gurobi* as the optimization

---

Algorithm 1: BypassPlanGen

Input : query *query*, model-predicate mapping *mapping*,
execution order of predicates (random or optimized) *order*,
indication of the current branch *flag*

Output: bypass plan *plan*

1 *plan* = NULL
2 predicate $p \leftarrow$ the first predicate in the *order*
3 **if** *p is not empty* **then**
4   current node $m = mapping[p]$
5   *suborder* $\leftarrow$ the remaining order after removing *p*
    // Positive branch
6   *subquery* $\leftarrow$ subquery of *query* where *p* is substituted with **true**
7   *pos_branch* = BypassPlanGen(*subquery, mapping, suborder*, **true**)
    // Negative branch
8   *subquery* $\leftarrow$ subquery of *query* where *p* is substituted with **false**
9   *neg_branch* = BypassPlanGen(*subquery, mapping, suborder*, **false**)
    // Generate the plan as a binary tree ([root node, left child, right child])
10   *plan* = [*m, pos_branch, neg_branch*]
11 **end**
12 **return** *plan*

---

solver. The outcomes of the solver is optimized model assignment, i.e., mapping between models and predicates, as well as the execution order of the predicates.

Given the model assignment and predicate execution order, the plan generator produces plans in different mechanisms, e.g., sequential plan with `Model-optimal` plan and bypass plan with `Model- & Order-optimal` plan. Sequential plan is a set of ML models executing on all the data. The execution order does not have an impact on the results. Conversely, in bypass plans, models process the data with filtering conditions, allowing the data flow to be divided based on the **true** or **false** results of the predicates. Algorithm 1 presents the pseudo code for generating the bypass plan. The algorithm generates a binary tree as a bypass plan, with the ML models represented as nodes and the predicate filtering conditions indicated by the edges. The root node processes full set of data while the child nodes processes data filtered with different conditions.

4.2 Modeling Accuracy

We now explain the procedure of estimating query accuracy a_Q, i.e., $f_{acc}(Q)$ in the problem definition. The intuition is that the query performance is dependent on the performance of models assigned to the predicates. We assume that predicates are independent to each other (the same assumption made in [18]), i.e., the outcome of one predicate does not impact the performance of others. The accuracy of a conjunctive query, e.g., `road` $\wedge$ `person`, can be estimated by multiplying the accuracy of each model, $a_{road} * a_{person}$. The accuracy of a disjunctive query, e.g., `car` $\vee$ `bus`, can be computed using the inclusion-exclusion principle, as $a_{car} + a_{bus} - a_{car} * a_{bus}$. In the same way, we can calculate the accuracy of more complex Boolean expressions. It is worth noting that the accuracy model is contingent upon the independence assumption, and serves as an indicator of query performance. The actual, real-world query results may be impacted by predicate correlation: when two predicates have high correlation, the performance of one model can influence the output of another. In future work we can leverage the correlated performance of a model (given the output of another) to align the estimation of query accuracy with its actual value.

4.3   Modeling the Execution Time

The measurement of execution time is determined by the form of the outcome plan, i.e., *sequential* (a set of models processing all the data) and *bypass* (models processing different subset of data based on the outcomes of the previous executed ones). Execution time is denoted by $f_{time}(Q)$.

Sequential Plan. In this case, the optimization does not take into account selectivity. The execution plan is a set of selected models executing on complete data. When computing the execution time, we only need to consider whether a model is selected, and we sum the cost of all the selected models. The models' execution time should be measured only once: the model can be executed once on the input and can output predictions for multiple classes.

Bypass Plan. In this case, not every model needs to process all the data: models in the subsequent steps only have to process a subset of the origin data filtered on the outputs of the previously executed models. The plan's execution time for this mechanism is measured with the sum of all the selected model cost proportioned to the data it need to process. For example in Fig. 1c, p_{car} processes images from two different data flows: images with light but without person (light $\wedge$ ¬person), and images with light and person but without road (light $\wedge$ person $\wedge$ ¬road). The execution cost of answering p_{car} is the execution cost of running the model proportioned to the amount of data it need to process, which is determined by the input data flows. The key challenge is to determine the portion of data processed by each predicate, which we will tackle in Sect. 4.5.

4.4   Modeling Model Assignment

Model assignment is the mapping between models and predicates. It determines the models used to answer predicates. To perform model assignment, we set a few constraints: *i*) we need to allocate exactly one model to each predicate; *ii*) only models with non-zero accuracy on a predicate can be assigned. Note that a model can be assigned to answer multiple predicates. Figure 1(b) presents the plan that only takes into account of model assignment that maximizes the accuracy given the time constraint.

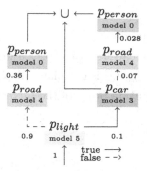

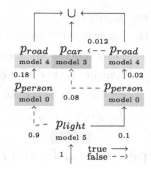

(a) Model & Order-optimal bypass plan
(cost: 28.55)

(b) Bypass plan with random predicate order
(cost: 38.4)

Fig. 3. Bypass plans with different predicate execution order (numbers near by the arrows indicating the selectivity of the predicates in that path).

4.5 Modeling Predicate Ordering

Predicate ordering has a significant impact when we generate a bypass plan. If the plan is a sequential execution of models without filtering any data, the results are the union of the predictions of all the models and the execution order will not make an effect on the results. On the other hand, a predicate in a bypass plan can filter insignificant data, which results in different execution cost when adopting a different execution order of the predicates.

The emphasis of predicate ordering is to measure the selectivity of predicates, clauses and subqueries, given a certain order, i.e., the portion of data that retained by the previous answered predicates. For example, consider a query $p_{road} \wedge p_{person}$. If the execution order is $p_{road} \rightarrow p_{person}$, the portion of data processed by p_{road} is 100%, while p_{person} the portion of data where p_{road} returns true. If p_{road} returns false, the whole query returns false, which ends the evaluation. The portion of data processed by p_{person} is thus the selectivity of p_{road}. When the execution order changes and p_{road} is answered before p_{person}, the amount of data being processed in general is different from the previous plan. Thus, when considering bypass plan, predicate ordering matters, and selectivity of predicates are taken into account.

Take the previous query as example. In Fig. 3, we present two bypass plans based on different predicate execution order. Though the model assignment is the same, the execution cost of these plans are different. Figure 3(b) shows the plan when we jointly optimize model assignment and predicate ordering. The predicate execution order follows $p_{light} \rightarrow p_{car} \rightarrow p_{road} \rightarrow p_{person}$, which achieves lower cost than random predicate order in Fig. 3(a).

4.6 Objective Function and Constraints

Our proposed `Model-` & `Order-optimal` approach has transformed the objective functions into the following forms. Given an execution time constraint (solving the AMS problem):

Maximize: $f_{acc}(Q)$

Subject to: Exactly one model is assigned to a predicate;

Only models with non-zero accuracy can be assigned to a predicate;

Execution time of the query plan $f_{time}(Q)$ is calculated depending on the type of output plan and execution order of the predicates;

$f_{time}(Q) \leqslant C_{bound}$

5   Experimental Evaluation

In this section, we empirically evaluate our method on both real and synthetic datasets, covering different modalities, i.e., texts and images. We first evaluate the efficacy of the optimizer with other competing methods on different datasets, and observe significant performance of our advanced optimizer. We then evaluate the optimizers' optimization time on a synthetic setting with different query sizes, which verifies the complexity of the problem.

5.1   Experimental Settings

Datasets and Evaluation Metrics. We used public datasets covering object detection in images with COCO [16] as well as sentiment analysis in text with TweetEval [2]. *COCO* contains 123K images and 80 distinct classes of objects, lending themselves to complex queries with multiple predicates. *TweetEval* is a corpus of tweets collected from Twitter. We focus on 18 inference classes, belonging to different categories, such as text sentiments, entity types, etc. We finetune some NLP models to fit Tweeteval to perform the tasks. We use F1-score to measure the quality of the models, and milliseconds per instance for execution time. Each dataset is divided into a validation set (60%) and a test set (40%). We use the validation set to measure selectivity on each dataset, as well as execution time. The query execution time shown in the following is obtained by executing the queries on the test set.

Model Zoos. We collected all of our pre-trained from HuggingFace (NLP tasks) and PytorchHub (object detection). To navigate the space of different model zoos that may be encountered in the real world, we manually curated different types of model zoos – each with different characteristics in terms of included models, the inference classes they support, as well as accuracy and performance characteristics. Those are summarized in Table 3:

– *Real-World:* Model Zoo ❶ contains 48 real-world models that can tackle NLP tasks. Each model in this model zoo, covers all inference classes of the NLP tasks. Model Zoo ❷ includes 33 models that can be used in object detection tasks in images; each model in this model zoo covers all object classes in COCO.

– *Synthetic: Model Zoo* ❸ , *Model Zoo* ❹ are derived from Model Zoo ❷. Each of the 33 models has 5 variants; to that end, we have introduced a 0–30% accuracy penalty to all models uniformly, while we have also added an execution time

Table 3. Summary of model zoos.

Repo. Name	Modality	Class Coverage	Performance Variation	Number of Models
Model Zoo ❶	Text	All	None	48
Model Zoo ❷	Image	All	None	33
Model Zoo ❸	Image	1	Accuracy, Cost	165
Model Zoo ❹	Image	13 (avg)	Accuracy, Cost	165

penalty of 0–50%. By applying these variations we obtain 165 models in total. These three model zoos differ in terms of the inference classes that the models can answer (see Table 3).

Optimization Methods. We compare four strategies for optimizing ML inference query given a certain constraint. Note that there are two ways to execute the query plans: in *sequential*, i.e., not applying bypass and executing the plans in sequence; and in *bypass*, i.e., executing the plan using the bypass mechanism, given a predicate execution order.

Baseline 1 - `Sequential: Greedy`. This optimizer applies greedy heuristic and loops over predicates and selects the model with the highest rank greedily, i.e., $\frac{accuracy}{cost}$ (similar to predicate ordering based on rank). The optimizer stops when every predicate is assigned to a model and the constraint is met.

Baseline 2 - `Sequential: Model-optimal`. The model selection optimizer relies on MIP to optimize the model assignment under constraints, as compared to the greedy optimizer that approximates model assignment.

Baseline 3 - `Bypass: Model-optimal`. This baseline extends Baseline 2. Given the model assignment optimized with `model-optimal` approach, this baseline generates bypass plan.

Proposed method - `Bypass: Model- & Order-optimal`. This approach jointly optimizes for both model assignment and predicate ordering and create a bypass plan. It takes into account of the *selectivity* of predicates in a dataset and creates bypass plans.

Queries. Since there are no benchmark queries that we could use from other works for our datasets, we adopted a similar approach as [18] to curate queries. We generate queries for two scenarios: comparing optimizer quality (Sect. 5.2, 5.3) and measuring optimization time (Sect. 5.4).

Optimizer Performance. We manually curated 10 queries (exemplified in Table 4) for image analysis (classes adopted from COCO), and 6 queries for text processing (tasks including name entity recognition, topic classification and sentiment analysis), in CNF and DNF forms. The queries range from 2 to 6 predicates with varying constraints on execution cost.

Query Optimization Time. We generate a set of queries in different complexity levels (the number of predicates ranging from 2 to 64), in total, 60 queries in CNF and DNF. The classes are adopted from COCO. For each predicate, we sample the classes with a uniform distribution.

Table 4. Examples of different ML inference queries (accuracy measured by F1-score, and cost measured by average inference time per instance).

Modality	Example Query	Constraint
text	e.g., ner=`person` ∧ sentiment=`negative` ∧ (topic=`news` ∨ topic=`sport`)	e.g., accuracy > 80%
image	e.g., `person` ∧ (`car` ∨ `bike`) ∧ `emergency_light`	e.g., cost < 100 ms

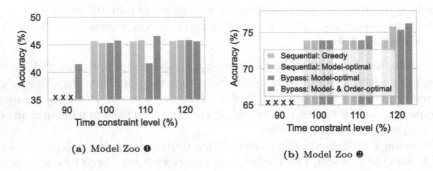

(a) Model Zoo ❶   (b) Model Zoo ❷

Fig. 4. Average speedups of query execution time compared to the *Greedy* approach on the query workload with different accuracy constraints.

Exec. Time Constraints. We create a number of experiment settings by enumerating different execution time bounds to verify optimizers' performance on different levels of constraints. We regard *Baseline 1* as the reference and record the minimum time constraint on which it can generate a query plan. The time constraints are set to be proportional to the minimum time constraint with scales of {80%, 90%, 100%, 110%, 120%} (we have observed that the performance converges from 120% onwards).

Hardware. We perform our experiments on a Ubuntu server with a single GPU (Nvidia A40, 8 GB RAM).

5.2 Using Uniform Model Zoos

We analyse the behavior of our optimizer using the model zoos Model Zoo ❶ and Model Zoo ❷. In this experiment we consider the constraint of 100% to be the execution time that allowed the `Sequential:Greedy` optimizer to find a solution to all the queries. We constrain the execution time to gradually increase from 90% - 120% to observe how the optimizers behave with different constraints. We present those results in bar plots (e.g., Fig. 4). The first observation is that when we put a low constraint on the execution time, our solution, `Bypass: Model- & Order-optimal`, succeeds to find proper solutions. Since the models used in both model zoos ❶ and ❷ have very similar accuracy, we do not observe large differences. It is worth noting that generating a bypass plan for the `Model-optimal`

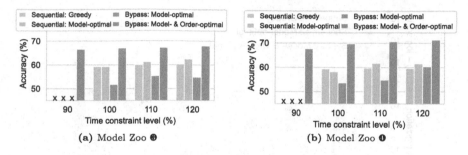

Fig. 5. The average accuracy on the query workload with different time (objective) constraint levels.

query plan can lead to a reduction in accuracy. This is because the random ordering of predicates can sometimes result in poor performance when a low-performing model is executed early in the process. Applying bypass plan can increase efficiency when executing the plan, however, with early filtering, this approach may wrongly filter data in an early stage, leading to decrease in accuracy.

5.3 Using Model Zoos with Diverse Model Distributions

We study the effect of diverse accuracy and execution time distributions, and class coverage in model zoos. More specifically, we run experiments using Model Zoo ❸ where each model answers exactly one inference class and Model Zoo ❹ average of 13 inference classes per model. We want to see if in such constrained environment the order optimizer can bring benefits.

Figure 5 shows the accuracy of all queries, for different values of execution time constraint. We observe that Bypass: Model- & Order-optimal consistently obtains higher query accuracy than the baselines. As in earlier experiment, bypass plans do not gain benefits when execution time is constrained. While Bypass: Model- & Order-optimal jointly optimizes for both model selection and predicate ordering can make use of predicate ordering and perform early filtering, making better use of execution time budget.

Results show that using bypass plans can lead to higher efficiency, while not necessarily increasing accuracy. The Bypass: Model- & Order-optimal optimizer outperforms the other baselines and can achieve higher query accuracy, especially given very diverse model zoos with different execution time and accuracy tradeoffs.

5.4 Query Optimization Time

We now evaluate the scalability of different approaches. We are interested in finding the limit of the Bypass: Model- & Order-optimal optimizer, with respect to the number of predicates that can be included in a query. Note that for brevity we exclude Baseline 3 (Bypass: Model-optimal): converting a given plan to its

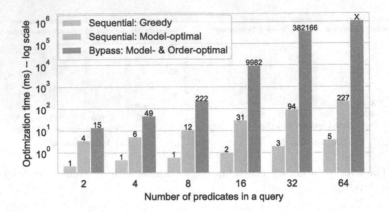

Fig. 6. Optimization time on queries with varying number of predicates.

bypass version requires a very small fraction of the optimization time. Thus, `Bypass: Model-optimal` in this case does not differ from `Bypass: Model- & Order-optimal`. We evaluate the efficiency of our optimizers in generating a query plan by varying the number of predicates in a query as shown in Fig. 6. The experiments were performed on Model Zoo ❹.

All the optimizers show exponential increase in execution time with the increase of predicate number in a query (Fig. 6 is plotted in log scale), except the `Sequential:Greedy` approach. The exponential increase also hints that the problem we are tackling has a very high complexity (Sect. 3). We observe that the advanced optimizers require much longer time to generate a plan as the number of predicates increases. In fact, when accuracy is constrained, the optimization time for 64 predicates did not finish (X). Future work can focus on applying approximation schemes to increase efficiency.

6 Conclusions and Future Work

In this paper we address the problem of ML inference query optimization, which aims for high accuracy given constraints on execution time. We formulate the problem as an MIP to perform optimal model selection and predicate ordering. Our optimizer that considers both model selection and predicate ordering achieves high performance, especially when the constraints are tight. In future work, we will consider additional objectives, such as model power consumption and memory footprint. Further research can focus on *i*) exploring multi-objective optimization problems, *ii*) applying approximation schemes in the MIP formulation of the problem and *iii*) lifting the assumptions made in this paper, considering especially the correlation of inference predicates and concept drift.

References

1. Anderson, M.R., et al.: Physical representation-based predicate optimization for a visual analytics database. In: 2019 IEEE 35th ICDE, pp. 1466–1477. IEEE (2019)
2. Barbieri, F., et al.: TweetEval: unified benchmark and comparative evaluation for tweet classification. arXiv preprint arXiv:2010.12421 (2020)
3. Cai, Z., et al.: Learning complexity-aware cascades for pedestrian detection. IEEE PAMI **42**(9), 2195–2211 (2019)
4. Cao, J., et al.: Thia: accelerating video analytics using early inference and fine-grained query planning. arXiv preprint arXiv:2102.08481 (2021)
5. Chang, J.Y., Lee, S.: An optimization of disjunctive queries: union-pushdown. In: Proceedings of COMPSAC, pp. 356–361. IEEE (1997)
6. Chowdhary, K., et al.: Natural language processing. In: Chowdhary, K.R. (ed.) Fundamentals of Artificial Intelligence, pp. 603–649. Springer, New Delhi (2020). https://doi.org/10.1007/978-81-322-3972-7_19
7. Howard, A.G., et al.: MobileNets: efficient convolutional neural networks for mobile vision applications. arXiv preprint arXiv:1704.04861 (2017)
8. Huang, J., et al.: Speed/accuracy trade-offs for modern convolutional object detectors. In: Proceedings of the IEEE CVPR, pp. 7310–7311 (2017)
9. Jiang, J., et al.: Chameleon: scalable adaptation of video analytics. In: Proceedings of SIGCOMM, pp. 253–266 (2018)
10. Kang, D., et al.: NoScope: optimizing neural network queries over video at scale. arXiv preprint arXiv:1703.02529 (2017)
11. Karanasos, K., et al.: Extending relational query processing with ml inference. CIDR (2020)
12. Kastrati, F., Moerkotte, G.: Generating optimal plans for Boolean expressions. In: IEEE ICDE, pp. 1013–1024. IEEE (2018)
13. Kemper, A., et al.: Optimizing disjunctive queries with expensive predicates. ACM SIGMOD Rec. **23**(2), 336–347 (1994)
14. Li, Z., Hai, R., Bozzon, A., Katsifodimos, A.: Metadata representations for Queryable ML model zoos. arXiv preprint arXiv:2207.09315 (2022)
15. Li, Z., et al.: Optimizing machine learning inference queries for multiple objectives. In: 39th ICDE Workshop on DBML. IEEE (2023)
16. Lin, T.-Y., et al.: Microsoft COCO: common objects in context. In: Fleet, D., Pajdla, T., Schiele, B., Tuytelaars, T. (eds.) ECCV 2014. LNCS, vol. 8693, pp. 740–755. Springer, Cham (2014). https://doi.org/10.1007/978-3-319-10602-1_48
17. Liu, W., et al.: SSD: single shot multibox detector. In: Leibe, B., Matas, J., Sebe, N., Welling, M. (eds.) ECCV 2016. LNCS, vol. 9905, pp. 21–37. Springer, Cham (2016). https://doi.org/10.1007/978-3-319-46448-0_2
18. Lu, Y., et al.: Accelerating machine learning inference with probabilistic predicates. In: Proceedings of the SIGMOD, pp. 1493–1508 (2018)
19. Papadimitriou, C.H., et al.: Multiobjective query optimization. In: Proceedings of the Twentieth ACM SIGMOD-SIGACT-SIGART Symposium on Principles of Database Systems, PODS 2001, pp. 52–59. Association for Computing Machinery, New York (2001)
20. Redmon, J., et al.: YOLO9000: better, faster, stronger. In: Proceedings of the IEEE CVPR, pp. 7263–7271 (2017)
21. Shen, H., et al.: Fast video classification via adaptive cascading of deep models. In: Proceedings of the IEEE CVPR, pp. 3646–3654 (2017)

22. Trummer, I., Koch, C.: Approximation schemes for many-objective query optimization. In: Proceedings of the 2014 ACM SIGMOD International Conference on Management of Data, pp. 1299–1310 (2014)
23. Trummer, I., Koch, C.: Multi-objective parametric query optimization. SIGMOD Rec. 45(1), 24–31 (2016)
24. Zhang, H., et al.: Live video analytics at scale with approximation and delay-tolerance. In: 14th USENIX (NSDI), pp. 377–392 (2017)

LiquidAI: Towards an Isomorphic AI/ML System Architecture for the Cloud-Edge Continuum

Kari Systä[1][✉], Cesare Pautasso[2], Antero Taivalsaari[1,3], and Tommi Mikkonen[4]

[1] Tampere University, Tampere, Finland
kari.systa@tuni.fi
[2] USI, Lugano, Switzerland
cesare.pautasso@usi.ch
[3] Nokia Bell Labs, Tampere, Finland
antero.taivalsaari@nokia-bell-labs.com
[4] University of Jyväskylä, Jyväskylä, Finland
tommi.j.mikkonen@jyu.fi

Abstract. A typical Internet of Things (IoT) system consists of a large number of different subsystems and devices, including sensors and actuators, gateways that connect them to the Internet, cloud services, end-user applications and analytics. Today, these subsystems are implemented with a broad variety of programming technologies and tools, making it difficult to migrate functionality from one subsystem to another. In our earlier papers, we have predicted the rise of *isomorphic* IoT system architectures in which all the subsystems can be developed with a consistent set of technologies. In this paper we expand the same research theme to machine learning technologies, highlighting the need to use ML in a consistent and uniform fashion across the entire Cloud-Edge continuum.

Keywords: Isomorphic Software · Software Architecture · Internet of Things · IoT · Web of Things · WoT · Artificial Intelligence · AI · Machine Learning · ML · Software Deployment · Deployment in the Large · Programmable World

1 Introduction

A typical Internet of Things (IoT) system consist of a large number of computational elements. These elements include sensors and actuators, gateways that connect them to the Internet, cloud services, end-user applications running on mobile devices, and different kinds of analytics capabilities. Today, these computational elements are implemented with a broad variety of programming technologies and tools; for instance, IoT device development is still carried out primarily with traditionally embedded systems languages and tools, while web application and cloud backend development use an entirely different set of tools

I. Garrigós et al. (Eds.): ICWE 2023, LNCS 13893, pp. 67–74, 2023.
https://doi.org/10.1007/978-3-031-34444-2_5

and technologies. This diversity makes it difficult to migrate functionality across the end-to-end system from one computational element to another. Instead, the functionality must be implemented using toolchains that are only applicable to certain types of components in the overall system. Any deployment changes typically imply a tedious re-implementation of the corresponding functionality.

Modern IoT systems and applications associated with them can generate and handle huge amounts of data. This has enabled Machine Learning (ML) and Artificial Intelligence (AI) in various use cases, ranging from smart home and smart city applications to healthcare, retail and industrial systems. Although IoT devices are generally assumed to be connected, not all the data from them can be moved to the cloud for processing because of privacy, latency or limited connectivity reasons. Thus, it is necessary to keep some computations close to the source of data, while other computations can run in the cloud. In many use cases there is a need to transfer data and computations seamlessly between different parts of the system, though. We have discussed this *cloud-edge continuum* in our earlier papers [22]. A recent literature study defined cloud continuum as *"an extension of the traditional cloud towards multiple entities (e.g., edge, fog, IoT) that provide analysis, processing, storage, and data generation capabilities"* [13]. Given the rapidly increasing use of ML technologies, we expect that the same technical challenges that apply to conventional computations shall emerge also in the context of ML technologies across the cloud-edge continuum.

The LiquidAI vision presented in this paper promises savings in the development effort by allowing flexible, dynamic, decentralized deployment of intelligent functions across the cloud-edge continuum. This is achieved by using a compatible set of technologies in all the subsystems, thus allowing different parts of the system to run the same code in an isomorphic fashion [12,20]. The LiquidAI concept builds upon liquid software – a paradigm in which software applications can flow from one computing node to another in a seamless fashion [8,23]. As a follow-up to our earlier work, we expand the liquid software concept to ML models that have an important role in today's IoT development and summarize the research challenges associated with it.

2 Background and Motivation

2.1 Artificial Intelligence in the Context of IoT

In recent years, processing and storage capabilities have grown dramatically, cloud computing has become commodity, data science has blossomed due to increasing amounts of data, and ML has emerged as everyday technologies even in devices with limited processing capabilities and resources such as mobile phones. These changes are leading us to a *Programmable World* [21], in which everyday things around us are becoming connected and programmable.

More broadly, the emergence of the IoT is acting as a catalyst for major changes in the development mindset. IoT developers must consider factors that are unfamiliar to many application developers today. Such factors include:

- multidevice programming of heterogeneous, diverse types of devices;
- the reactive, always-on nature of the overall system;
- intermittent, potentially unreliable nature of connectivity;
- the distributed, dynamic, and potentially migratory nature of software; and
- the general need to write software in a fault-tolerant and defensive manner.

In general, a typical IoT application is *continuous* and *reactive*. On the basis of observed sensor readings, computations get triggered (and retriggered) and may eventually result in various actionable events. In the context of the overall end-to-end system, programs are essentially *asynchronous, parallel* and *distributed*. In addition, the computational elements in the overall end-to-end system are typically heterogeneous and may possess very different processing capabilities and storage capacities.

In the context of this paper, we wish to highlight two areas especially:

- *Intelligence in the Edge.* In "classic" IoT systems, the majority of computation and analytics are performed in the cloud in a centralized fashion. However, in recent years there has been a noticeable trend in IoT system development to move intelligence closer to the edge (see, e.g., [9,10]).
- *Rise of Swarm Intelligence.* In IoT systems that consist of a massive number of devices overall, device topologies can be expected to be highly dynamic and ephemeral (e.g. [16,18]). This dynamism calls for technologies that can cope with dynamically changing *swarms* of devices and their dynamically evolving responsibilities at the holistic system level.

2.2 Liquid Software

Liquid software makes it possible for data and applications to move seamlessly between multiple devices and screens [23]. The concept of liquid software emerged originally in the context of multiple device ownership [8], referring especially to those use cases in which an individual user needs to use software applications in an uninterrupted fashion on different types of computing devices such as mobile phones, tablets, desktop computers and TVs – without having to explicitly install and/or launch applications anew or manually transfer data between those devices [23]. In recent years, liquid software technologies have expanded into IoT and other systems that do not necessarily have user interfaces [12]. In those contexts, liquid software typically refers to seamless transfer or migration of computations from one part of the system to another in order to best utilize the available computational resources. Moreover, liquid stream processing has been proposed, wherein data from Web-enabled sensors are gathered and sent for processing across a peer-to-peer cloud of computing peers [1].

The prerequisites of liquid software in the context of the IoT are (i) uniform API for accessing features of different subsystems, and (ii) a common runtime that is fast but small enough for embedded devices yet powerful enough to implement lightweight containers in order to deploy applications everywhere. In addition, (iii) an orchestrator is needed that will guide the deployment and potential migration of the different subsystems based on device proximity, connectivity and battery levels.

3 LiquidAI: Premises and Design Goals

3.1 The LiquidAI Vision

The requirement to run – and optionally also train – ML models and analytics algorithms in the edge increases the demand for consistent programming technologies in the overall end-to-end system. Our vision is that the required algorithms can be decomposed so that their components can be flexibly located and migrated in the cloud-edge continuum. Then, when requirements and network topology later evolve, the components can be relocated at different nodes in the IoT network. Moreover, security and privacy related issues must be reconsidered. Then, one can flexibly allocate and migrate functions across the cloud-edge continuum, considering available network bandwidth, latency, and computational resources.

To manifest an infrastructure capable of running such algorithms, the characteristics of liquid software need some revision. As stated above, the basic features include a uniform API, a common runtime, components that can be deployed and re-deployed at the cloud-edge continuum, and an orchestrator that can allocate and reallocate components. In addition, the creation of ML models requires reconsideration. Instead of creating individual ML models to process the given data, processing shall take place in a piecemeal fashion following the flow of data from the edge to the cloud, typically using techniques such as federated learning [11] and streaming data pipelines. To enable such piecemeal processing, monolithic ML models must be avoided and replaced with models that perform simple tasks and then forward the results to the next node for further processing.

Next, we present the design and research goals to reach the vision above.

3.2 Design Goals for LiquidAI

Uniform API. One of the key challenges in realizing the LiquidAI vision is the heterogeneous nature of the development languages, environments and tools, and the APIs and data formats that are associated with those technologies. There is a need for APIs to access resources on heterogeneous sets of devices, as well as for operations to manage data streams and various infrastructure features.

In the area of machine learning, application code needs to control the machine learning components (AI functions). API features shall be coherent and accessible from all relevant programming languages. Candidate base solutions in this area include the Web Thing API [3] and various service discovery protocols, which lack support for liquidity.

The research questions for a uniform liquid API include the following:

- What kind of an API allows liquid components to communicate with each other regardless of their current location?
- How can the API support access to streaming data in a unified fashion when the functions for processing the data streams may migrate as well?
- How wide a selection of programming languages can be supported and catered to with consistent APIs?

Common Runtime. By *runtime* we refer to technologies such as virtualization or virtual machines (VMs) that allow applications to run on top of the computing hardware – preferably independently of its physical architecture. In our context it is not enough to support built-in system applications only but also those that can be deployed and uninstalled dynamically.

The runtime shall support *strong* migration of software, where both the code and its current execution state can be transferred across different devices [4]. Such runtimes for liquid software have several and partially conflicting requirements: performance, hardware independence, support for various development paradigms, programming languages, and security. As concrete examples, WebAssembly and Node.js are both candidate runtimes for liquid applications. Due to virtualization, the runtime solutions that are used in the context of liquid software may not meet the performance requirements of machine learning applications. Moreover, runtimes used for ML applications may not support liquidity. Pathway to a compelling solution includes the following research challenges:

- What are the functional requirements of ML models towards the runtime?
- What are the performance and scalability requirements of ML models?
- How much can resource consumption be reduced if the runtimes for model training, validation, testing and inference in production are separated?

Decomposition and Deployment. Decomposition of software is essential for software maintainability, task allocation, and effective utilization of distributed computational elements. In addition to providing maintainability to software and its development, decomposition should split the software so that its components, optionally including ML features, can roam across the cloud-edge continuum. This places new requirements on decomposition. These observations have inspired a lot of research (e.g. [5,15]). Today's state of the art approaches advocate the use of containers and orchestration to dynamically manage VM images and select specific node(s) according to algorithmic requirements (e.g. [2]). Unfortunately, this approach is rather heavyweight because of the use of containers, and thus lighter alternatives would be preferred (e.g. [17]).

Since ML models are key elements of LiquidAI systems, decomposing and deploying them across the cloud-edge continuum has received a lot of attention on a broad variety of use cases (e.g. [15]). However, isomorphic use of such functions is a new research direction that will be fundamental to achieving flexible composition of future IoT systems. Furthermore, when an application or component is deployed onto a target device, the software and required metadata have to be encapsulated in a proper way. The deployment, initialization and monitoring of the software may also require a specialized protocol, which should support both traditional and ML components. Based on the observations above, research questions related to decomposition include the following:

- What kind of decompositions are technically feasible for ML components, in relation to working practices in this field?
- Which solutions are compatible with the requirements of liquid deployment?

– What is the lifecycle of liquid functions, including both traditional and ML software?
– How to update liquid ML components with minimal disruption to system behavior?

Orchestration. Decomposition of LiquidAI systems into separate components introduces an orchestration challenge: how can multiple components ensure reliable end-to-end execution, provide scalability with large datasets and potentially massive amount of devices, as well as react to changing situations? Because IoT is largely about data, it is assumed that many of the target applications involve data streams. The foundation for orchestrating data streams across an IoT network has already been laid out in the Web Liquid Streams framework [1]. That framework helps developers create stream processing topologies and run them across a peer-to-peer network of connected devices and Web browsers. ML models are often also used for processing data via a series of pipes and filters (e.g. [14,19]). In our vision, pipes are represented by connections in the stream processing topology, and filters are then dynamically deployed on the common runtime and communicate via the uniform API. We have identified the following research questions:

– How can the orchestrator control the migration of ML models?
– How to manage and monitor ML models in liquid context?
– How to ensure reliability and trustworthiness a distributed system where stateful components may roam between locations?
– How can performance, memory and bandwidth be optimized if ML models are partitioned across a pipeline operating on a common data stream?
– What is state for processing streaming data with AI functions?

Liquid Features. In our earlier work [6] we have investigated the architecture and design issues of liquid software. Much of the earlier research has focused on user interfaces and especially user interface adaption to a *set of* devices with different usage modalities (phones, tablets, laptops, TVs, etc.) In LiquidAI, most system components are headless (have no user interface), and therefore many aspects need to be revisited and extended. First, the handling of state – seamless data transfer and state synchronization is a key characteristic of liquid software. In LiquidAI, the viewpoint might be different given that the presence of data streams and learning – especially incremental learning – can be regarded as a form of state. Second, while the LiquidAI concept has no user sessions roaming across devices, applications still need to take full advantage of all devices that they run across. There is a need to optimize performance, including both computing and network traffic, with tradeoff factors such as power consumption and latency. The research questions related liquid functionality include:

– Do machine-learning components have a state?
– How can liquid components adapt to different hardware characteristics?

Security and Privacy. Because many of the LiquidAI systems will deal with sensitive data, they should be decomposed in such a fashion that privacy and access rules are enforced. So far, relatively small amount of research has been directed into security features needed by liquid software at large given that the prime use case has been personal computing experience in which all the devices have the same owner. Furthermore, security related concerns in IoT are common in general (e.g. [7,24]), which underlines research needs on this topic. Important research questions include the following:

- How to provide security for liquid software across the cloud-edge continuum?
- How to ensure privacy guarantees with a set of ML components learning from or processing data streaming pipelines?
- How containers for liquid software can prevent leaks of sensitive data?

4   Conclusions

In this paper, we presented a vision and a tentative research agenda for LiquidAI – a framework in which machine learning and data streaming can coexist and be flexibly orchestrated in IoT networks. The vision extends our earlier work on liquid software applications, refocusing the technology to end-to-end IoT systems. As part of this work, we have formulated the concept and identified a set of research questions that must be answered in order to realize the vision. We hope that this paper, for its part, encourages the Web engineering research community to collaborate with us on finding answers to these research questions.

Acknowledgments. This work has been supported by Business Finland (project LiquidAI, 8542/31/2022).

References

1. Babazadeh, M., Gallidabino, A., Pautasso, C.: Decentralized stream processing over web-enabled devices. In: Dustdar, S., Leymann, F., Villari, M. (eds.) ESOCC 2015. LNCS, vol. 9306, pp. 3–18. Springer, Cham (2015). https://doi.org/10.1007/978-3-319-24072-5_1
2. Debauche, O., Mahmoudi, S., Mahmoudi, S.A., Manneback, P., Lebeau, F.: A new edge architecture for AI-IoT services deployment. Procedia Comput. Sci. **175**, 10–19 (2020)
3. Francis, B.: Web Thing API. https://webthings.io/api/. Accessed 25 Jan 2023
4. Fuggetta, A., Picco, G.P., Vigna, G.: Understanding code mobility. IEEE Trans. Software Eng. **24**(5), 342–361 (1998)
5. Gallidabino, A., Pautasso, C.: The LiquidWebWorker API for horizontal offloading of stateless computations. J. Web Eng. **17**, 405–448 (2019). https://doi.org/10.13052/jwe1540-9589.17672
6. Gallidabino, A., Pautasso, C., Mikkonen, T., Systä, K., Voutilainen, J.P., Taivalsaari, A.: Architecting liquid software. J. Web Eng. **16**(5–6), 433–470 (2017). https://doi.org/10.26421/JWE16.5-6, https://www.rintonpress.com/journals/jweonline.html#v16n56

7. Gurunath, R., Agarwal, M., Nandi, A., Samanta, D.: An overview: security issue in IoT network. In: 2018 2nd International Conference on I-SMAC (IoT in Social, Mobile, Analytics and Cloud), pp. 104–107. IEEE (2018)
8. Hartman, J.J., et al.: Joust: a platform for liquid software. Computer **32**(4), 50–56 (1999)
9. Keshavarzi, A., van den Hoek, W.: Edge intelligence-on the challenging road to a trillion smart connected IoT devices. IEEE Design Test **36**(2), 41–64 (2019)
10. Liu, Y., Peng, M., Shou, G., Chen, Y., Chen, S.: Toward edge intelligence: multiaccess edge computing for 5G and internet of things. IEEE Internet Things J. **7**(8), 6722–6747 (2020)
11. Ludwig, H., Baracaldo, N.: Federated Learning: A Comprehensive Overview of Methods and Applications. Springer, Cham (2022)
12. Mikkonen, T., Pautasso, C., Taivalsaari, A.: Isomorphic internet of things architectures with web technologies. Computer **54**(7), 69–78 (2021)
13. Moreschini, S., Pecorelli, F., Li, X., Naz, S., Hästbacka, D., Taibi, D.: Cloud continuum: the definition. IEEE Access **10**, 131876–131886 (2022)
14. Pääkkönen, P., Pakkala, D.: Reference architecture and classification of technologies, products and services for big data systems. Big Data Res. **2**(4), 166–186 (2015)
15. Peltonen, E., et al.: The many faces of edge intelligence. IEEE Access **10**, 104769–104782 (2022)
16. Puschmann, D., Barnaghi, P., Tafazolli, R.: Adaptive clustering for dynamic IoT data streams. IEEE Internet Things J. **4**(1), 64–74 (2016)
17. Raghavendra, M.S., Chawla, P.: A review on container-based lightweight virtualization for fog computing. In: 2018 7th International Conference on Reliability, Infocom Technologies and Optimization (Trends and Future Directions)(ICRITO), pp. 378–384. IEEE (2018)
18. Seeger, J., Deshmukh, R.A., Sarafov, V., Bröring, A.: Dynamic IoT choreographies. IEEE Pervasive Comput. **18**(1), 19–27 (2019)
19. Sena, B., Garcés, L., Allian, A.P., Nakagawa, E.Y.: Investigating the applicability of architectural patterns in big data systems. In: Proceedings of the 25th Conference on Pattern Languages of Programs, pp. 1–15 (2018)
20. Strimpel, J., Najim, M.: Building Isomorphic JavaScript Apps: From Concept to Implementation to Real-World Solutions. O'Reilly Media, Sebastopol (2016)
21. Taivalsaari, A., Mikkonen, T.: A roadmap to the programmable world: software challenges in the IoT era. IEEE Softw. **34**(1), 72–80 (2017)
22. Taivalsaari, A., Mikkonen, T., Pautasso, C.: Towards seamless IoT device-edge-cloud continuum: In: Bakaev, M., Ko, I.-Y., Mrissa, M., Pautasso, C., Srivastava, A. (eds.) ICWE 2021. CCIS, vol. 1508, pp. 82–98. Springer, Cham (2022). https://doi.org/10.1007/978-3-030-92231-3_8
23. Taivalsaari, A., Mikkonen, T., Systä, K.: Liquid software manifesto: the era of multiple device ownership and its implications for software architecture. In: 2014 IEEE 38th Annual Computer Software and Applications Conference, pp. 338–343. IEEE (2014)
24. Zhang, Z.K., Cho, M.C.Y., Wang, C.W., Hsu, C.W., Chen, C.K., Shieh, S.: IoT security: ongoing challenges and research opportunities. In: 2014 IEEE 7th International Conference on Service-oriented Computing and Applications, pp. 230–234. IEEE (2014)

Predicting Crowd Workers Performance: An Information Quality Case

Davide Ceolin[1](✉)(iD), Kevin Roitero[2](iD), and Furong Guo[3](iD)

[1] Centrum Wiskunde & Informatica, Amsterdam, The Netherlands
davide.ceolin@cwi.nl
[2] University of Udine, Udine, Italy
kevin.roitero@uniud.it
[3] Vrije Universiteit Amsterdam, Amsterdam, The Netherlands

Abstract. Supervised machine learning tasks require human-labeled data. Crowdsourcing allows scaling up the labeling process, but the quality of the labels obtained can vary. To address this limitation, we propose methods for predicting label quality based on worker trajectories, i.e., on the sequence of documents workers explore during their crowdsourcing tasks. Trajectories represent a lightweight and non-intrusive form of worker behavior signal. We base our analysis on previously collected datasets composed of thousands of assessment data records including information such as workers' trajectories, workers' assessments, and experts' assessments. We model such behavior sequences as embeddings, to facilitate their management. Then, we: (1) use supervised methods to predict worker performance using a given ground truth; (2) perform an unsupervised analysis to provide insight into crowdsourcing quality when no gold standard is available. We test several supervised approaches which all beat the baseline we propose. Also, we identify significant differences between trajectory clusters in terms of assessments and worker performance. The trajectory-based analysis is a promising direction for non-intrusive worker performance evaluation.

Keywords: Crowdsourcing · Behavioral Analysis · Worker performance

1 Introduction

Crowdsourcing platforms changed the way researchers define and disseminate human computation tasks, and find workers willing to participate in such tasks. These platforms allow millions of human-labeled data to be collected in a short period at a far cheaper cost than that of experts [5]. However, without any supervision, the quality of crowdsourced data might vary greatly, for instance, when the skill level of workers and the difficulty of the task do not match [33,42]. Data about the crowd worker interactions with such platforms are useful to understand how workers behave in such tasks and, possibly, assist information management

© The Author(s), under exclusive license to Springer Nature Switzerland AG 2023
I. Garrigós et al. (Eds.): ICWE 2023, LNCS 13893, pp. 75–90, 2023.
https://doi.org/10.1007/978-3-031-34444-2_6

through worker performance prediction [2]. Compared to other crowdsourcing quality control methods such as taking the average or the majority over the repeated labels of each example [11], behavioral traces are easy to obtain and allow estimating worker performance on an individual basis. At the same time, behavior data might be sparse because they are composed of combinations of a possibly high number of different actions. So, we model behaviors as embeddings, which have been demonstrated to allow reducing dimensionality while preserving behavior similarity [20]. We focus on one specific class of behavior data, worker trajectories, i.e., sequences of documents that workers inspect during their tasks. These are easy to obtain, privacy-preserving, and non-intrusive. Specifically, we address these research questions:

RQ1: Can specific crowdsourcing trajectories be used to predict worker performance?

RQ2: Do the distributions of trajectories correlate with worker performance?

To address our research questions, we instruct an experiment using two datasets of crowdsourced information quality assessments for which we also have a ground truth at our disposal. First, we employ supervised machine learning to analyze correlations between worker trajectories, worker errors, and ground truth. Second, we use unsupervised clustering to group worker trajectories, check the correlation between worker scores and trajectories clusters, and assess the worker performance in each of the clusters. This second approach aims at inspecting whether trajectories-based clusters are capable of grouping together items of information with the same quality levels, measured according to different quality dimensions. Our results show that supervised learning based on trajectories outperforms a random baseline. Clusters based on trajectories differ in terms of workers' scores, confidence values, and worker performance. This paper extends and improves the original work carried out by the third author, under the first and second authors' supervision [19].

This paper continues as follows. Section 2 discusses related work. Section 3 describes the datasets used and the models employed to address the research questions. Section 4 presents the experimental evaluation. Section 5 concludes.

2   Related Work

Assessing the quality and truthfulness of items of information is gaining attention and importance [12]. A line of research investigated such issues with (semi-)automatic methods for fact-checking. [27] proposed a deep neural network architecture to detect and stop the spread of misinformation; [26] proposed to gather crowdsourcing labels to detect and analyze assessor bias; [25] proposed to leverage topic models on Twitter to identify misinformation. [24,34] collected thousands of labels for the truthfulness of political and COVID19-related statements using crowdsourcing, studying the effect of using different scales to gather the assessments. Related work also investigated the credibility of sources. [15] conducted a survey to understand the perceived level of trust in news sources, while [4] investigated the credibility of statements related to climate change. Other work addressed information quality focusing on peculiar phenomena that occur when dealing with misinformation. [30] investigated echo chambers and epistemic bubbles, [14] considered ideological echo chambers, and [18] focused on the effect of search engines and social networks. [7] investigated the usage of argument mining to identify low-quality information (though, in the context of product reviews). [38] dealt with multidimensional scales for gathering relevance assessments. [43] and [41] considered a framework for multidimensional relevance. [6,29] investigated the usage of a multidimensional scale on debated topics addressing facts about vaccines. Our work is complementary to [3], although they focus on keystrokes, which are more invasive than worker trajectories. Concerning worker behavior analysis, [20,37] both focus on the use of embeddings, and [21] studied crowd worker behavior focusing on abandonment.

3   Methods

3.1   Datasets

Original Data. We focus on the dataset collected by [34][1], which sampled statements from two popular sources of information used to perform fact-checking: Politifact [39] and ABC [1]. Politifact contains more than 12,000 statements from U.S. politics which are assessed by experts on a 6-level truthfulness scale (quoted from [32]): *true*: "The statement is accurate and there's nothing significant missing"; *mostly-true*: "The statement is accurate but needs clarification [...]"; *half-true*: "The statement is partially accurate [...]"; *mostly-false*: "The statement contains an element of truth [...]"; *false*: "The statement is not accurate"; *pants-on-fire*: "The statement is not accurate and makes a ridiculous claim". ABC contains more than 500 statements about Australian politics and is labeled by the Australian Broadcasting Corporation using a 3-level truthfulness scale: *positive* if the statement is true, *negative* if the statement is false, and *in-between* otherwise. They sampled a balanced dataset, 10 statements for each of the two main political parties (i.e., Republican and Democratic for Politifact, and Labor and Liberal for ABC) for each truthfulness level, for a total of 180 statements (120 for Politifact and 60 for ABC). Then, they evaluated the truthfulness of such statements using a crowdsourcing setting. Their results show that, after appropriate data processing, a high level of agreement between the crowd workers and the expert judges can be reached. We employ the dataset obtained by asking workers to re-assess the same statements detailed in [34].

Crowdsourced Data. This dataset was collected using Amazon Mechanical Turk. Access to the task was restricted to US workers only, who were asked to evaluate the truthfulness of statements using a multidimensional scale composed of the following dimensions, selected relying on previous work [6,29]: *Correctness*, to indicate how much the item is accurate (vs. wrong); *Neutrality*, to

---

[1] Available at https://github.com/KevinRoitero/crowdsourcingTruthfulness.

indicate that how neutral is the item (vs. biased); **Comprehensibility**, to indicate how much the information is understandable; **Precision**, to indicate how much the information is precise and not vague; **Completeness**, to indicate how much the item is complete; **Speaker's Trustworthiness**, to indicate how reliable is the item's source; **Informativeness**, to assess how useful the item is to derive information. Assessors were also asked to report the **Overall Truthfulness** of the piece of information under consideration and their **Confidence** in the score assessed, and also to provide a URL of the source of information accessed to evaluate the piece of information. Each Human Intelligence Task (HIT) was designed as follows. When the assessor starts the task, s/he fills a profiling questionnaire (e.g., income range, age, education level, political views, opinion on climate change, and the U.S. southern border). Given that the statements assessed are political, these questions were meant to identify factors that could affect the worker's bias, if any. Then, s/he is asked 3 Cognitive Reflection Test questions, to measure his/her tendency to answer using non-correct "intuitive" responses. Then, the worker is presented with 11 statements, 6 from Politifact, 3 from ABC, and '2 gold questions' for quality check. For each statement, the assessor expressed a judgment for each dimension using the following Likert Scale: *Completely Disagree* (-2), *Disagree* (-1), *Neither Agree Nor Disagree* (0), *Agree* ($+1$), *Completely Agree* ($+2$). The quality of the collected data is ensured through the assessment of two 'gold questions'. Also, workers should spend at least 2 cumulative seconds on each statement. To ensure fair treatment, multiple tests were performed and the average time spent was commensurated with the U.S. Minimum Salary Wage of 7.25 USD per hour, resulting in a reward of 2 USD for each HIT. The study has been approved by the University of Queensland Ethics Committee. Workers were informed about their rights, and the data collection was compliant with the law. See [36] for additional details.

3.2   Behavioral Logging and Embeddings

In the crowdsourcing experiment above, a behavioral logger was employed to collect information about worker trajectories recording the following actions: **finish** (the worker finished the task); **next** (the worker clicked the next button); **back** (the worker clicked the back button); **document** $d_i, i \in \{1, 9\}$ (document inspected by the worker at a given time). These actions define the trajectory of workers when performing the task. E.g., $[Next, d7, d9, d8, d6, d5, d4, d3, d2, d3, d1]$ means that the worker clicked the *Next* button in the task interface, finished the surveys; then, he inspected the documents with the order of 7, 9, 8, 6, 5, 4, 3, 2, 3 and 1. Note that here d_i represents the document ids relative to the task. Different workers evaluated different document sequences (e.g., $d1$ for *worker*$_1$ will differ from $d1$ for *worker*$_2$). To take the trajectories as input for the considered machine learning models, we transform the sequences of actions into 25-dimensional embeddings by assigning every action with an identifier. For this purpose, we use the tokenizer from the Official TensorFlow implementation of the BERT Model [9] with our custom vocabulary (i.e., the actions). Inspired by [37], we apply BERT [13] to embed the trajectories. Trajectories' size varies, and their average length is about 25. To foster data manageability, we pop the tails of long trajectories, and we pad short trajectories into 25 dimensions with 0s. Further analyses confirmed that the effects of such approximation on the model performance are negligible. The trajectory example we mentioned before after embedding becomes $[17, 15, 12, 14, 13, 11, 10, 9, 8, 7, 6, 0, 0, \ldots, 0]$.

3.3 Models

Supervised Machine Learning. We apply supervised algorithms to predict the difference between workers' scores and experts' scores based on workers' trajectories. These algorithms belong to three classes, i.e., algorithms that treat trajectories embeddings as unordered and ordered one- and bi-directionally. In the first class of algorithms, the trajectories embeddings are considered as a set of features. Considering the example above, the embedding is split into 25 distinct unordered features with values $17, 15, 12, 14, 13, 11, 10, 9, 8, 7, 6, 0, 0, \ldots, 0$. We apply Random Forest (RF) in this case. RF is an ensemble learning method for classification that does not require dimensionality reduction, shows a fast training time, and is easily deployable. In the second class of algorithms, trajectory embeddings are treated as temporally ordered sequences. We employ neural network algorithms like Gated Recurrent Unit (GRU) [10] and Long short-term memory (LSTM) [22], which have proven to be effective at modeling sequential information [17]. We also consider convolutional neural networks (CNN) [23], which can be employed to model sequences using "n-grams" and have a lower training time than other neural networks. In the third class of algorithms, trajectories are processed bidirectionally by bi-LSTM and bi-GRU [35].

Unsupervised Machine Learning. We use clustering to understand if similar worker trajectories imply significantly similar worker performance. Also, we evaluate whether similar trajectories imply that the quality level of the items assessed is similar. We try different combinations of methods to cluster the trajectories: K-means [28] with and without dimensionality reduction; Density-based spatial clustering of applications with noise (DBSCAN) [16] with and without dimensionality reduction. We use these two popular methods as representative of two different philosophies of clustering: K-means is centroid-based, while DBSCAN is density-based. We use Principal Component Analysis (PCA) to reduce dimensionality, and the Elbow method to identify the parameter k.

4 Experimental Evaluation

4.1 Dimension Importance and Scale Alignment

After collecting the data through crowdsourcing, it is worth investigating if all the considered dimensions are useful and provide a signal. Given that we have the ground truth labels only for the dimension named *Overall Truthfulness*, and also considering that the expert and crowd assessors used two different sets of truthfulness scales (i.e., a 6-level categorical scale for Politifact, a 3-level categorical

Table 1. Strategies to align the scales of workers' and Politifact experts' scores.

	Politifact scores						Workers scores				
	0	1	2	3	4	5	-2	-1	0	+1	+2
M3	-1	0	0	0	0	1	-1	0	0	0	1
M00	-2	-2	-1	0	1	2	-2	-1	0	1	2
M11	-2	-1	-1	0	1	2	-2	-1	0	1	2
M22	-2	-1	0	0	1	2	-2	-1	0	1	2
M33	-2	-1	0	1	1	2	-2	-1	0	1	2
M44	-2	-1	0	1	2	2	-2	-1	0	1	2

Table 2. Aggregation strategies employed to align of workers' and ABC experts' scores.

	ABC scores			Workers scores				
	0	1	2	-2	-1	0	+1	+2
N0	-1	0	1	-1	0	0	0	1
N1	-1	0	1	-1	-1	0	0	1
N2	-1	0	1	-1	0	0	1	1
N3	-1	0	1	-1	-1	0	1	1

scale for ABC, and a 5-level Likert scale for the crowdsourcing setting), we can not directly compare the expert and crowd judgments to test our hypothesis. Thus, we fitted an ANOVA model and we computed the ω^2 effect size index [31] to measure the effect of the dimensions to *Overall Truthfulness*. (ω^2 is used to analyze the impact of components in information systems, see, e.g., [40].) *Correctness* has a large effect on *Overall Truthfulness* ($\omega^2 = 0.251$). *Comprehensibility*, *Trustworthiness*, and *Neutrality* have a small effect ($0.01 < \omega^2 < 0.02$). *Neutrality*, *Precision*, and *Completeness* have no effect ($\omega^2 < 0.005$). *Overall Truthfulness* cannot be obtained by a combination of other dimensions.

The expert scores of the Politifact dataset are on a 6-level scale, while the workers' scores are on a 5-level scale. To estimate the differences between workers' scores and experts' scores, we need to align them. We identify two types of strategies (6 strategies in total, *M3, M00, M11, M22, M33, M44*) for the Politifact dataset. First, we align the 5- and 6-level scales with a 3-valued scale (*3*). Then, we identify five other alignments based on aggregations of the 6-level scale of experts' scores to a 5-level scale. The details are reported in Table 1, where we assigned numeric labels to textual categories: *pants-on-fire* is assigned with 0, *false* with 1, etc. Similarly, we devise several strategies to align the 3-level scale of the ABC dataset with the crowdsourced scale (*N0, N1, N2, N3*; see Table 2).

4.2 Supervised Machine Learning

Experimental Setting. The 25-dimensional embeddings are taken as inputs for the supervised machine learning model, while the target is the difference between

Table 3. Macro average F1 scores of algorithms for Politifact dataset. *M3* is the strategy that leads to higher scores, and RF is on average the most effective algorithm.

Algorithm	M3	M00	M11	M22	M33	M44	(Macro Average)
baseline	.25	.21	.19	.18	.15	.18	.19
RF	.63	**.45**	**.48**	**.50**	**.47**	**.47**	**.50**
GRU	.49	.24	.28	.27	.36	.25	.32
LSTM	.49	.31	.31	.34	.28	.29	.34
CNN	.51	.28	.38	.32	.39	.42	.38
CNN+ GRU	**.64**	.37	.36	.40	.41	.41	.43
CNN+ LSTM	.54	.38	.35	.43	.35	.33	.40
Bi-LSTM	.53	.27	.26	.36	.34	.21	.33
Bi-GRU	.53	.28	.29	.31	.34	.26	.34
	.51	.31	.32	.35	.34	.31	

experts' scores and workers' scores. Given that the dataset is imbalanced in terms of the difference between worker scores and ground truth, (e.g., with aggregation strategy *M00* in Politifact dataset, the number of worker scores that are the same as ground truth is 290, while the rest is 1006) we use Synthetic Minority Over-sampling Technique (SMOTE) [8] to balance the dataset and reduce the risk of overfitting. Additional inspection shows that SMOTE significantly improves the model performance when predicting the minority category. We employ the macro-average F1 score as an effectiveness metric, computed by considering the metric for each class, and then averaging the results together. We focus on F1 because our ideal system would have a balanced trade-off between precision and recall. We split the dataset into training (80%), validation (10%), and test set (10%). We use a randomly chosen target class as a baseline. We also apply the set of supervised classification algorithms introduced above. The architecture complexity of all supervised algorithms is shown in Table 5, which indicates that RF has the shortest training time and the least parameters, LSTM has the longest training time, and Bi-LSTM has the most parameters. Tables 3 and 4 report macro average F1 scores obtained when predicting the difference between workers' scores and ground truth using the different aggregation strategies.

Results and Discussion. The effectiveness scores of the supervised classification algorithms are higher than the ones obtained by the baseline (see Tables 3 and 4). This suggests that we can use worker trajectories as a basis to identify high- and low-quality worker contributions. Among the algorithms tested, we find that RF has the lowest architecture complexity as we mentioned before, and is the best performing algorithm on average. Instead, bidirectional models which have complex architectures and long training time as shown in Table 5, obtain relatively low F1 scores for almost any aggregation strategy. This result

Table 4. Macro average F1 scores of algorithms for ABC dataset. *N1* and *N3* lead to higher scores, and RF is on average the most effective algorithm.

Algorithm	N0	N1	N2	N3	
baseline	.35	.39	.34	.34	.36
RF	**.63**	**.61**	**.51**	.51	**.57**
GRU	.45	.45	.43	.48	.45
LSTM	.48	.43	.47	.54	.48
CNN	.45	.55	**.51**	**.58**	.52
CNN + GRU	.43	.54	.50	.57	.51
CNN + LSTM	.53	.50	.44	.49	.49
Bi-LSTM	.44	.47	.44	.42	.44
Bi-GRU	.47	.51	.48	.45	.48
	.47	**.49**	.46	**.49**	

Table 5. Algorithm statistics. RF has the shortest training time and the least parameters, LSTM has the longest training time, and Bi-LSTM has the most parameters.

Algorithm	Layers	Params	Training time (s)
RF	-	**3**	**0.15**
GRU	5	33,867	52.26
LSTM	5	86,667	102.09
CNN	8	29,771	16.46
CNN + GRU	13	197,323	83.80
CNN + LSTM	13	105,163	57.42
Bi-LSTM	5	237,067	83.89
Bi-GRU	6	65,931	91.18

suggests that the trajectories order, and especially the bidirectional order of the trajectories in the computed embedding space is not very useful for predicting the worker performance. Another possible explanation for the relatively poor performance of the neural network algorithms is that these models with complex architectures require a large amount of training data, and our datasets might not be big enough. Thus, we find that in this setting, traditional machine learning algorithms and simpler neural networks like CNN (combined or not with GRU layer) achieve higher effectiveness scores. As we can see from Table 3, the performance achieved on *M3* is higher than the other Politifact aggregation strategies. *M3* has a 3-level scale Politifact experts' scores, while other strategies have a 5-level scale. The higher performance might be explained by the coarser granularity. *N1* and *N3* are, on average, the best-performing mappings (Table 4).

4.3 Unsupervised Machine Learning

Experimental Setting. We test the K-means and DBSCAN, with and without dimensionality reduction. Only K-means with dimensionality reduction identifies clusters that correspond to significantly different distributions of worker performance. Dimensionality reduction plays an important role because of the high dimensionality of the embeddings. On both datasets, we get 9 principal components and 6 clusters (Elbow method). We use the Kruskal-Wallis H-test to check the significance of differences among worker scores.

Table 6. P-values obtained by testing the differences across trajectories-based clusters in terms of workers' scores or experts' scores or workers' confidence levels (Politifact on the left, ABC right). All workers' scores and workers' confidence levels are significant.

Target	M3	M00	M11	M22	M33	M44	N0	N1	N2	N3
workers	.01	.01	.01	.01	.01	.01	.51	.62	.78	.87
experts	.40	.29	.16	.39	.17	.17	.62	.62	.62	.62
confidence	.00	.00	.00	.00	.00	.00	.13	.03	.02	.01

Table 7. Shapiro-Wilk test on worker performance. Only α with *N0* are not normal.

	M3	*M00*	*M11*	*M22*	*M33*	*M44*	*N0*	*N1*	*N2*	*N3*
Acc	0.80	0.99	0.46	0.54	0.42	0.42	0.11	0.43	0.70	0.23
α	0.51	0.88	0.33	0.51	0.64	0.64	**0.04**	0.28	0.38	0.1

Results and Discussion – Worker Scores and Trajectories. There are significant differences between workers' scores across different trajectories clusters for the Politifact dataset (c.l. 0.05), independent of the aggregation strategies adopted (see Table 6). However, there is no statistically significant difference between experts' scores across trajectories-based clusters. This means that workers' trajectories are correlated to their assessments, but not to the actual quality of the documents. Table 6 shows that there is no statistically significant difference between experts' scores and workers' scores across trajectories-based clusters for ABC dataset. There are differences in workers' confidence across trajectories-based clusters for the ABC dataset (see Fig. 1). A Kruskal-Wallis H-test did not show any significant difference in the distribution of documents across clusters: trajectories are not significantly affected by the documents evaluated.

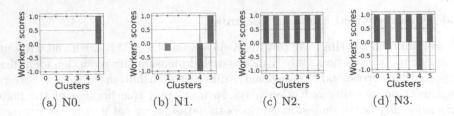

(a) N0.   (b) N1.   (c) N2.   (d) N3.

Fig. 1. Workers' scores across clusters with different aggregation strategies (ABC).

Results and Discussion – Worker Performance and Trajectories. To measure worker performance, we select the accuracy metric and a metric of agreement, namely Krippendorff's α. Accuracy measures the degree to which the worker scores match the real truthfulness; Krippendorff's α is an inter-annotator agreement measure, indicating the agreement between worker and expert. For completeness, we also tested the use of Cohen's κ inter-annotator agreement measure. Since it shows results that closely resemble α, we focus on α. As we can see from Table 10 and Table 11, Krippendorff's α coefficients for Politifact and ABC dataset are all below 0.2, indicating that the overall agreements of workers' and experts' assessments are low. To check if trajectories clusters

Table 8. P-values of t-tests for worker performance values (only for normally distributed ones) (Politifact). Correlation is independent of the specific strategy and performance significantly varies across clusters. Accuracy, α coefficient. Cluster id $\in [0, 5]$

	Acc						α					
	0	1	2	3	4	5	0	1	2	3	4	5
M3	0.31	0.10	0.10	0.53	**0.03**	**0.02**	0.30	0.06	0.37	0.68	0.11	**0.01**
M00	**0.02**	0.89	**0.01**	0.17	0.78	0.20	**0.03**	0.53	**0.01**	0.12	0.47	0.35
M11	0.17	0.26	**0.01**	0.05	0.76	0.17	0.45	0.06	0.21	0.21	**0.45**	**0.45**
M22	**0.04**	**0.04**	0.50	0.89	0.17	**0.02**	**0.02**	0.09	0.52	0.52	0.52	**0.02**
M33	0.74	0.22	**0.02**	**0.04**	**0.04**	0.74	0.60	0.40	**0.01**	0.06	**0.04**	0.86
M44	0.74	**0.04**	**0.02**	**0.04**	0.74	0.22	0.60	0.06	**0.01**	0.04	0.86	0.40

Table 9. P-values of t-test for worker performance across clusters. Cluster id $\in [0, 5]$.

	Acc						α					
	0	1	2	3	4	5	0	1	2	3	4	5
N0	0.08	0.08	0.73	**0.04**	0.12	**0.02**	-	-	-	-	-	-
N1	0.77	0.08	0.06	**0.02**	0.47	**0.04**	0.31	0.08	**0.04**	**0.02**	0.97	0.05
N2	0.58	0.51	0.58	**0.03**	0.16	**0.01**	0.68	0.76	0.68	**0.04**	0.08	**0.01**
N3	0.55	0.25	0.25	0.90	**0.01**	0.06	0.62	0.22	0.29	0.68	**0.01**	0.09

identify significantly different worker performance distributions, we run pairwise t-tests on the performance distribution of each pair of clusters, both for accuracy and α. Since the t-test assumes the normality of data, we check normality using the Shapiro-Wilk test. The results shown in Table 7 indicate that only the Krippendorff's α coefficients with $N0$ across clusters are not from normal distributions, while other worker performance values across clusters are from normal distributions. We apply a one-sample t-test on the performance score of each cluster as follows: we obtain a 6-valued vector of performance indicators (accuracy or $alpha$, one per cluster), and then we iteratively compute the t-test, comparing the resulting vector against each of its elements. We use this method to test whether any of the elements would represent the mean of a Normal distribution of which the vector represents a plausible sample. In other words, this tells us whether the indicators obtained are similar to each other or not. We obtain similar results both when the compared value is kept and removed from the vector. Results (when the compared value is kept in the vector) are shown in Tables 8 (Politifact) and 9 (ABC). Both tables show that there are significant differences in accuracy scores and α coefficients across trajectories-based clusters with all aggregation strategies for the worker performance values that are normally distributed with all aggregation strategies. Regarding the not-normally distributed α coefficients with $N0$, we performed a qualitative analysis. We can note from Table 11 that two of these values imply low agreement ($\sim$0.2) and four imply no agreement ($<$0). Again, this suggests that the coefficients are not

Table 10. Distributions of worker scores and performance in clusters (Politifact). Mean (μ), variance (σ^2), accuracy (Acc), and Krippendorff's α. Cluster id $\in [0, 5]$.

	0				1				2			
	μ	σ^2	Acc	α	μ	σ^2	Acc	α	μ	σ^2	Acc	α
M3	.16	.28	.52	.02	.28	.25	.49	.00	.11	.30	.56	.08
M00	.30	1.60	.27	.07	.56	1.38	.23	.00	.81	1.06	.31	.10
M11	.41	1.59	.21	−.00	.56	1.38	.22	−.00	.81	1.06	.27	.05
M22	.56	1.38	.22	−.01	.52	1.54	.18	−.05	.24	1.49	.20	−.01
M33	.41	1.59	.28	.09	.56	1.38	.22	−.00	.81	1.06	.16	−.09
M44	.31	1.60	.22	.02	.52	1.54	.28	.08	.81	1.06	.16	−.09
	3				4				5			
	μ	σ^2	Acc	α	μ	σ^2	Acc	α	μ	σ^2	Acc	α
M3	.17	.31	.46	−.12	.06	.30	.58	.13	.01	.25	.56	.11
M00	.41	1.59	.24	.04	.52	1.54	.15	−.09	.24	1.49	.20	− 01
M11	.52	1.54	.20	−.03	.30	1.60	.25	.05	.24	1.49	.21	.00
M22	.41	1.59	.21	−.01	.81	1.06	.25	.03	.30	1.60	.25	.05
M33	.52	1.54	.28	.08	.24	1.49	.20	−.01	.30	1.60	.22	.02
M44	.24	1.49	.20	−.01	.41	1.59	.28	.09	.57	1.38	.22	−.00

uniformly distributed among clusters. Different trajectories imply different levels of agreement. Since we identify a significant difference in workers' performance across clusters, we leverage the multidimensional assessment in the crowdsourced dataset to get additional insights. We saw in Sect. 4.1 that Correctness, Trustworthiness, Informativeness, and Comprehensibility have an effect on the overall quality assessment. When restricting our attention to clusters, such effects might differ. Thus, we check if (1) the distribution of information quality dimension scores significantly differs among clusters and if (2) information quality dimension scores correlate with worker performance. Information quality dimensions scores correlate with trajectories clusters but not with worker performance. We conclude that trajectories signal aspects of quality other than truthfulness.

Results and Discussion – Confidence Level and Trajectory. Crowd workers are asked to rate their confidence in the assessments provided. After hypothesis testing to check if there is a correlation between workers' *confidence level* and worker trajectories, the results are shown in Table 6 and we find there are statistically significant differences of *confidence level* across trajectories-based clusters for all aggregation strategies in the Politifact dataset and most aggregation strategies in the ABC dataset. We suppose that *confidence level* correlates with worker performance. So, we compute the Pearson's correlation coefficients between means of *confidence level* and worker performance (accuracy and Krippendorff's α coefficient). The results show a linear correlation between confidence values and accuracy scores for Politifact dataset with aggregation strategy *M11*, *M33* and *M44*, and a linear correlation between confidence values and α coefficients for Politifact dataset with aggregation strategy *M33* and *M44* (c.l. 0.05). Hence, also the *confidence level* can be used for predicting worker performance.

Table 11. Distributions of worker scores and performance (accuracy, and α coefficient) in clusters (ABC). Mean (μ), variance (σ^2), accuracy (Acc), and α coefficient (α).

	0				1				2			
	μ	σ^2	Acc	α	μ	σ^2	Acc	α	μ	σ^2	Acc	α
N0	.11	.32	.34	−.04	.10	.24	.35	−.07	.18	.15	.42	−.03
N1	.02	.45	.34	−.03	−.03	.47	.38	.06	.03	.34	.39	.02
N2	.43	.47	.38	.04	.45	.40	.38	.04	.58	.24	.42	.08
N3	.36	.66	.27	−.13	.29	.71	.42	.11	.31	.64	.37	.04
	3				4				5			
	μ	σ^2	Acc	α	μ	σ^2	Acc	α	μ	σ^2	Acc	α
N0	.00	.30	.51	.20	.14	.31	.34	−.09	.18	.35	.49	.19
N1	−.04	.39	.35	−.02	−.13	.42	.47	.18	.08	.48	.45	.16
N2	.48	.44	.27	−.16	.34	.53	.45	.18	.41	.45	.49	.20
N3	.42	.56	.39	.08	.21	.73	.42	.12	.31	.62	.45	.15

Results and Discussion – Profile Features and Trajectory. The datasets used provide also a set of profile features about the workers: *worker age, education level, income level, political views, consideration level, southern border views, environment views* and answers to three simple calculation problems. Besides worker scores and worker performance, we also check if there is a correlation between trajectories and worker static features, i.e., we check if using trajectory data provides different information from worker profile data. For both the Politifact and the ABC datasets, workers' *political views* and *southern border views*, which are two political-related questions, show a correlation with trajectory. So, while the worker profile as a whole does not directly correlate with worker trajectory, a specific and subjective portion of it does. In the future, we will extend these analyses of the links between subjective features and worker trajectories.

4.4   Discussion Highlights

Overall, we learned the following lessons. **(1) Limited Intrusion behavior detection.** Worker behavior can be an indicator of their performance. We adopt a coarse and high-level behavior representation that balances the trade-off between the worker's right to privacy, and the need to evaluate worker performance. **(2) Trajectory analysis can quantify subjective confidence.** Worker trajectory is an objective measure of the worker's actions. Worker confidence is a subjective measure. The correlation we identified between the two indicates that the former is a predictor of the latter. We also identify limitations in our work, i.e., the fact that the datasets analyzed are specific to a given use case, that they are limited in size, and that the trajectories do not consider timestamps.

5   Conclusion and Future Work

We study the correlation between workers' trajectories and the performance of quality assessments. We use two datasets (ABC and Politifact) that contain multidimensional information quality assessments and fact-checked ground truths. First, we align ground truth with the crowdsourcing assessment scale; second, we model worker trajectories as embeddings; third, we perform a set of supervised analyses to test the possibility of using trajectories as a basis for performance evaluation; and, fourth, we perform a set of unsupervised analyses to evaluate in-depth the usefulness and significance of trajectory-based clustering. We find that worker trajectories can be used to predict worker performance for information quality assessment when ground truth is available (RQ1). With the 3-level scale aggregation *M3* of Politifact algorithms achieve the best average performance. This is likely due to the coarser granularity. We also found that our predictions did not sensibly benefit from taking into account trajectory orders. To investigate this aspect further, we will extend the size of the datasets evaluated and consider timestamps. Concerning RQ2, we employ unsupervised clustering methods on workers' trajectories and we look for significant differences among clusters in terms of scores and worker performance. There are significant differences in worker scores across different trajectory clusters for the Politifact dataset. For the ABC dataset, the differences in worker scores across clusters are not significant, although Fig. 4.3 hints at the possible differences in the distributions. We evaluate information quality through accuracy and inter-rater reliability. We find that trajectory clusters correlate with worker performance and worker scores. Multidimensional scores do not correlate with overall truthfulness within clusters except in the case of strategy N2 (ABC dataset). We find significant differences between trajectories-based clusters and worker-relevant features: workers' political views and workers' confidence values. The two politics-related questions do not correlate to workers' performance while there is a linear correlation between confidence values and workers' performance only for the Politifact dataset. Worker trajectories provide a lightweight, non-intrusive, yet promising means for a performance assessment that we will explore further in the future.

Acknowledgments. This research has been partly supported by the Netherlands eScience Center project "The Eye of the Beholder" (project nr. 027.020.G15).

References

1. ABC and RMIT University: RMIT ABC Fact Check (2021). https://apo.org.au/collection/302996/rmit-abc-fact-check. Accessed 10 June 2021
2. Agichtein, E., Brill, E., Dumais, S., Ragno, R.: Learning user interaction models for predicting web search result preferences. In: SIGIR, p. 3–10. ACM (2006)
3. Benham, R., Mackenzie, J., Culpepper, J.S., Moffat, A.: Different keystrokes for different folks: visualizing crowdworker querying behavior. In: CHIIR, pp. 331–335. ACM (2021)
4. Bhuiyan, M.M., Zhang, A.X., Sehat, C.M., Mitra, T.: Investigating differences in crowdsourced news credibility assessment: raters, tasks, and expert criteria. PACMHCI **4**, 1–26 (2020)
5. Callison-Burch, C.: Fast, cheap, and creative: Evaluating translation quality using amazon's mechanical turk. In: EMNLP 2009, pp. 286–295. ACM (2009)
6. Ceolin, D., Noordegraaf, J., Aroyo, L.: Capturing the ineffable: collecting, analysing, and automating web document quality assessments. In: Blomqvist, E., Ciancarini, P., Poggi, F., Vitali, F. (eds.) EKAW 2016. LNCS (LNAI), vol. 10024, pp. 83–97. Springer, Cham (2016). https://doi.org/10.1007/978-3-319-49004-5_6
7. Ceolin, D., Primiero, G., Wielemaker, J., Soprano, M.: Assessing the quality of online reviews using formal argumentation theory. In: Brambilla, M., Chbeir, R., Frasincar, F., Manolescu, I. (eds.) ICWE 2021. LNCS, vol. 12706, pp. 71–87. Springer, Cham (2021). https://doi.org/10.1007/978-3-030-74296-6_6
8. Chawla, N.V., Bowyer, K.W., Hall, L.O., Kegelmeyer, W.P.: Smote: synthetic minority over-sampling technique. JAIR **16**, 321–357 (2002)
9. Chen, C., et al.: Tensorflow official model garden (2020). https://github.com/tensorflow/models
10. Cho, K., van Merriënboer, B., Gulcehre, C., Bahdanau, D., Bougares, F., Schwenk, H., Bengio, Y.: Learning phrase representations using RNN encoder-decoder for statistical machine translation. In: EMNLP, pp. 1724–1734. ACL (2014)

11. Dekel, O., Shamir, O.: Vox Populi: collecting high-quality labels from a crowd. In: COLT (2009)
12. Demartini, G., Mizzaro, S., Spina, D.: Human-in-the-loop artificial intelligence for fighting online misinformation: challenges and opportunities. IEEE Bull. **43**(3), 65–74 (2020)
13. Devlin, J., Chang, M.W., Lee, K., Toutanova, K.: Bert: Pre-training of deep bidirectional transformers for language understanding (2019)
14. Eady, G., Nagler, J., Guess, A., Zilinsky, J., Tucker, J.A.: How many people live in political bubbles on social media? evidence from linked survey and Twitter data. SAGE Open 9(1), 2158244019832705 (2019)
15. Epstein, Z., Pennycook, G., Rand, D.: Will the crowd game the algorithm?: using layperson judgments to combat misinformation on social media by downranking distrusted sources. In: CHI, pp. 1–11. ACM (2020)
16. Ester, M., Kriegel, H.P., Sander, J., Xu, X.: A density-based algorithm for discovering clusters in large spatial databases with noise. In: KDD, pp. 226–231. AAAI Press (1996)
17. Fang, H., Zhang, D., Shu, Y., Guo, G.: Deep learning for sequential recommendation: Algorithms, influential factors, and evaluations (2020)
18. Flaxman, S., Goel, S., Rao, J.M.: Filter bubbles, echo chambers, and online news consumption. Public Opin. Q. **80**(S1), 298–320 (2016)
19. Guo, F.: Analyzing Workers Trajectories for Performance Evaluation - An Information Quality Assessment case (2021). Master's Thesis
20. Han, L., Checco, A., Difallah, D., Demartini, G., Sadiq, S.: Modelling user behavior dynamics with embeddings. In: CIKM 2020, pp. 445–454 (2020)
21. Han, L., et al.: All Those Wasted Hours: On Task Abandonment in Crowdsourcing. In: WSDM, pp. 321–329. ACM (2019)
22. Hochreiter, S., Schmidhuber, J.: Long short-term memory. Neur. Comp. **9**(8), 1735–1780 (1997)
23. Kalchbrenner, N., Grefenstette, E., Blunsom, P.: A convolutional neural network for modelling sentences. arXiv preprint arXiv:1404.2188 (2014)
24. La Barbera, D., Roitero, K., Demartini, G., Mizzaro, S., Spina, D.: Crowdsourcing truthfulness: the impact of judgment scale and assessor bias. In: Jose, J.M., et al. (eds.) ECIR 2020. LNCS, vol. 12036, pp. 207–214. Springer, Cham (2020). https://doi.org/10.1007/978-3-030-45442-5_26
25. Li, G., et al.: Misinformation-oriented expert finding in social networks. WWW **23**(2), 693–714 (2020)
26. Lim, S., Jatowt, A., Färber, M., Yoshikawa, M.: Annotating and analyzing biased sentences in news articles using crowdsourcing. In: LREC, pp. 1478–1484. ELRA (2020)
27. Liu, Y., Wu, Y.F.B.: FNED: a deep network for fake news early detection on social media. TIST **38**(3), 1–33 (2020)
28. Macqueen, J.: Some methods for classification and analysis of multivariate observations. In: Berkeley Symposium on Mathematical Statistics and Probability, pp. 281–297 (1967)
29. Maddalena, E., Ceolin, D., Mizzaro, S.: Multidimensional news quality: a comparison of crowdsourcing and nichesourcing. In: INRA, vol. 2482. CEUR-WS.org (2018)
30. Nguyen, C.T.: Echo chambers and epistemic bubbles. Episteme **17**(2), 141–161 (2020)
31. Olejnik, S.F., Algina, J.: Generalized eta and omega squared statistics: measures of effect size for some common research designs. Psych. Methods **8**, 434–47 (2004)

32. PolitiFact: The Principles of the Truth-O-Meter: PolitiFact's methodology for independent fact-checking (2020). https://www.politifact.com/article/2018/feb/12/principles-truth-o-meter-politifacts-methodology-i/

33. Redi, J.A., Hoßfeld, T., Korshunov, P., Mazza, F., Povoa, I., Keimel, C.: Crowdsourcing-based multimedia subjective evaluations: A case study on image recognizability and aesthetic appeal. In: CrowdMM, pp. 29–34. ACM (2013)

34. Roitero, K., et al.: The COVID-19 infodemic: can the crowd judge recent misinformation objectively? In: CIKM, pp. 1305–1314. ACM (2020)

35. Schuster, M., Paliwal, K.: Bidirectional recurrent neural networks. TSP **45**(11), 2673–2681 (1997)

36. Soprano, M., et al.: The many dimensions of truthfulness: crowdsourcing misinformation assessments on a multidimensional scale. IP&M **58**(6), 102710 (2021)

37. Sun, F., et al.: Bert4rec: Sequential recommendation with bidirectional encoder representations from transformer. In: CIKM, pp. 1441–1450. Springer (2019)

38. Uprety, S., et al.: Quantum-like structure in multidimensional relevance judgements. In: Jose, M., et al. (eds.) ECIR 2020. LNCS, vol. 12035, pp. 728–742. Springer, Cham (2020). https://doi.org/10.1007/978-3-030-45439-5_48

39. Wang, W.Y.: "Liar, Liar Pants on Fire": a new benchmark dataset for fake news detection. In: ACL 2017, pp. 422–426. ACL (2017)

40. Zampieri, F., Roitero, K., Culpepper, J.S., Kurland, O., Mizzaro, S.: On topic difficulty in IR evaluation: the effect of systems, corpora, and system components. In: SIGIR, pp. 909–912. ACM (2019)

41. Zhang, Y., Zhang, J., Lease, M., Gwizdka, J.: Multidimensional relevance modeling via psychometrics and crowdsourcing. In: SIGIR, pp. 435–444 (2014)

42. Zheng, H., Li, D., Hou, W.: Task design, motivation, and participation in crowdsourcing contests. Int. J. Electron. Commer. **15**, 57–88 (2011)

43. Zuccon, G., Leelanupab, T., Whiting, S., Yilmaz, E., Jose, J.M., Azzopardi, L.: Crowdsourcing interactions: using crowdsourcing for evaluating interactive information retrieval systems. Inf. Retr. **16**(2), 267–305 (2013)

IoT and WoT Engineering

WebAssembly in IoT: Beyond Toy Examples

Pyry Kotilainen[✉], Viljami Järvinen, Juho Tarkkanen, Teemu Autto,
Teerath Das, Muhammad Waseem, and Tommi Mikkonen

University of Jyväskylä, Jyväskylä, Finland
{pyry.kotilainen,viljami.a.e.jarvinen,juho.a.tarkkanen,
teemu.a.autto,teerath.t.das,muhammad.m.waseem,tommi.j.mikkonen}@jyu.fi

Abstract. WebAssembly enables running the same application code in
a range of devices in headless mode outside the browser. Furthermore,
it has been proposed that WebAssembly applications can be made isomorphic so that they can be liberally allocated to a set of computers
that comprise the runtime environment. In this paper, we explore if
WebAssembly truly enables the development of comprehensive IoT applications with the same ease as more traditional techniques would enable.

Keywords: WebAssembly · Web of Things · Internet of Things · IoT

1 Introduction

There has been a lot of interest in using WebAssembly (Wasm) outside the
browser [2]. It has been proposed as a small-memory portable operating system
(OS) [34], as well as a solution to improve modularity [17] or performance [16].
In particular, the cloud-edge continuum has been used as a target, either as an
OS [13] or by evaluating applicability in serverless computing [19], to support
services at the edge. However, many demonstrators have been small-scale implementations, focusing on demonstrating a single claim or feasibility of a proposed
approach with WebAssembly.

In industry, WebAssembly has been proposed as a tool for addressing performance [5], size [17], and to some extent security issues [9] that more traditional
web technologies – in particular JavaScript – introduce. Numerous enterprises,
such as Google, eBay, and Norton have already started using WebAssembly
instead of JavaScript in many of the projects with the aim to enhance the performance of services, such as Tenserflow.js applications [4], a barcode reader [26],
and pattern matching [27].

Furthermore, WebAssembly could tackle some major challenges of the Internet of Things (IoT), which has become a key technology enabler for several
diverse and critical daily life applications such as healthcare, transportation, and
industrial automation, among others. The fragmented nature of IoT applications
requires a more profound understanding of various programming languages and

I. Garrigós et al. (Eds.): ICWE 2023, LNCS 13893, pp. 93–100, 2023.
https://doi.org/10.1007/978-3-031-34444-2_7

prior knowledge of technologies, which makes it more complex for developers to implement and manage a typical end-to-end IoT system without impediments.

One of the prominent solutions for addressing these challenges is to adopt an isomorphic IoT system architecture, which provides feasibility in developing the whole system with the same set of technologies [20]. With this in mind, WebAssembly is the way-forward approach that supports the development of isomorphic IoT architecture. The possible benefits of having such an architecture include reducing the complexity of the IoT system, improving the overall performance, and decreasing the overhead of developers from implementing fragmented IoT applications [20].

In this paper, we discuss WebAssembly in the IoT application context. Furthermore, we analyse the feasibility of an isomorphic IoT architecture using WebAssembly based on our experiences gained with a prototype implementation. Finally, we analyze WebAssembly's suitability as a platform for full-stack IoT applications and propose its potential use in IoT in the short term.

2   Background and Motivation

2.1   Isomorphic IoT Systems

While isomorphism is a well-established concept in mathematics, in software development the concept has emerged relatively recently. In the context of web applications, isomorphism refers to the ability to run the same code both on the backend (cloud), and in the frontend (web browser) [29]. More broadly, isomorphic software architectures feature software components that do not have to be modified ('change their shape') when running across the different hardware or software components of the system. Examples of isomorphic systems include Java and its 'write once, run everywhere' promise [1], Unity 3D engine, Universal Windows platform, which enables running the same code in Windows 10, Xbox One gaming machines and HoloLens devices, and liquid web applications [21].

Several different levels of isomorphism can be identified [20]. At the first level, isomorphism refers to the consistent use of the same development technologies across the different computational elements in the entire system. In contrast with such *static*, development-level isomorphism, in *dynamic* isomorphism, a common runtime engine or virtualization solution is used so that the same code can run in different computational elements without recompilation. In an even more advanced system, dynamic migration of code from one computational element to another is enabled.

In the IoT context, the same, isomorphic software can ideally be deployed throughout the end-to-end system to run on edge devices, gateways, mobile clients and cloud services. With its characteristics, WebAssembly is a natural candidate for such use, as discussed below.

2.2   WebAssembly in a Nutshell

WebAssembly is a low level code format designed for efficiency together with hardware- and platform-independence among other things [28]. WebAssembly offers dynamic isomorphism, as a standard runtime interpreter is used to execute the code. Therefore, WebAssembly can be used as a runtime environment for applications developed using different languages, but compiled for the WebAssembly interpreter.

While the origins of WebAssembly are inside the browser, the developer community has started to realise its significance outside the browser, in particular as a unifying environment for heterogeneous devices [2,15,31,33]. Indeed, WebAssembly's conservative memory usage and somewhat near-native performance make it suitable for constrained environments like IoT devices [6]. Moreover, facilities such as *WebAssembly System Interface* (WASI) [3] have been introduced, to access system resources when running WebAssembly outside the browser.

3 Design and Implementation

3.1 Development Goals and Initial Architecture

The goal of our development approach was straightforward – go all the way to build isomorphic IoT applications with WebAssembly. In more technical sense, the target was to

G1: Demonstrate that isomorphic web applications can be freely located to form a functioning IoT network;
G2: Demonstrate that various WebAssembly modules from different repositories can be used to implement the applications;
G3: Demonstrate that applications can configure themselves upon deployment to liberate developers from rigid, development-time configurations.

The technical framing for the demonstrations was to use a microservice architecture consisting of various IoT devices [10]. Within this architecture, heterogeneous devices could easily be discovered and used in accordance to their characteristics, such as varying processing power and peripheral features, because application code could move inside the system. Computations would then be executed when and where best suited, taking into account the state of the system and the capacity of the different subsystems.

Device discovery would be performed with mDNS for advertising available IoT-devices to the orchestrator. For querying the capabilities of discovered devices, a ReSTful endpoint providing the answers would be placed on each IoT device. For machine-to-machine (M2M) communication between the IoT-devices using CoAP was planned, to demonstrate that IoT specific protocols are feasible. Finally, all functionality running on the different IoT-devices – in particular executing WebAssembly binaries – would be controlled by the host process, which we call *supervisor*.

3.2 Development and the Reality Check

From the beginning, we realized that relying on external components would be necessary, building on earlier experience with IoT systems [22]. Hence, in

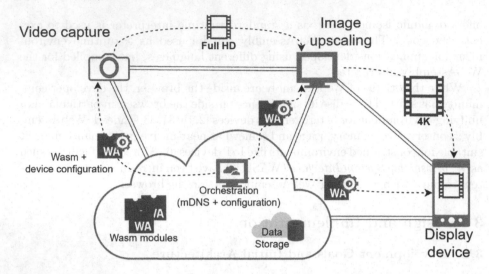

Fig. 1. Overview of the function of the proposed system. In this case, a low quality video is sent from a source to an intermediary device with resources for upscaling the video and then sent to a device with a screen to display the upscaled video.

parallel to composing our first application specific WebAssembly routines, we started with an inventory of suitable 3rd party WebAssembly components we could use. Unfortunately, it turned out that if we wanted to rely on widely used, reliable technologies, we would have to look beyond WebAssembly. For instance, as the ReSTful endpoint we decided to use a Python framework *Flask*, not a WebAssembly derivative. As the development went on, the same thing kept repeating – with almost every feature, some new open source component, not implemented with WebAssembly, crept in because it simply was not technically feasible for the team to implement everything in WebAssembly with a reasonable development time. The most essential learnings are listed below.

During the development, a repeating problem was the features of different WebAssembly runtime implementations. Some of the WASI implementations lacked key functions for our use cases. For instance, networking – or even access to the underlying OS's file system – meant that we had to implement our supervisor function without directly using WebAssembly. Obviously a layer of unnecessary abstraction is a burden when running on constrained IoT-devices, but this was considered the simplest way forward, and we would know where the superfluous function is. In the end, we used Python3 and the WebAssembly runtime *Wasm3* [18], because the selection of libraries they provide fit our planned use cases, e.g. cameras and sensors controlled with laptop and Raspberry PIs, respectively.

Application programming with WebAssembly raised some concerns with respect to data objects and secure and refined interfaces to access the data. Because multiple programming languages can be used to compose WebAssembly code, it seems that a common and accepted way of using non-primitive datatypes in WebAssembly is based on pointers, as described in [12]. This impression is reinforced by examples of using WebAssembly's memory like an integer-indexable array [23], which is adopted also in practice and business (e.g. [15]). Hence, while WebAssembly might help in dealing with problems such as buffer overflow and running code from untrusted sources in a sandbox [14,31], dangers still seem to exist [11]. Such security concerns are especially unfavorable considering the potential of code reuse with existing C/C++ libraries compiled to WebAssembly.

The application development stage also introduced challenges related to combinining IoT device architecture and general microservice architecture. A way to comprehensively, extensively and even automatically describe the interfaces between different WebAssembly modules was needed. In our work, we took the Web of Things Thing description [7] and OpenAPI [25] as the baseline. Actual descriptions could be made with different interface description languages, such as Smithy, which is used by the WasmCloud [33] project. Even parsing the WebAssembly binaries (i.e., the *modules*) for their exports using Kaitai [8] was considered, but abandoned as we wanted to enforce fundamentally API-like descriptions. Finally, for generating APIs, Swagger [30] was selected, because it supports OpenAPI by its design. However creating a comprehensive, all-purpose implementation was considered an overkill, and we turned to existing research prototypes for inspiration. Unfortunately, earlier work and existing implementations where WebAssembly is used in a way that is aligned with our goals do not support any WebAssembly targeting language in application development, but only one language. The WiProg system as proposed by Li, Dong and Gao [12] uses language-specific constructs tied to C/C++. With WasmCloud [33], in contrast, the currently available languages are Rust and TinyGo.

When considering existing implementations, the closest match with our needs was provided by the Losant [15] project. However we did not wish to commit to using their service to construct our applications. In the end, we wrote our own prototype version of the required functions, targeted to exact use cases we had in mind. The available device server entries and deployment instructions are defined in JSON, and the actual package management and deployment was implemented in JavaScript.

3.3   Results and Observations

At the present phase of the development, there is a running demonstrator, where isomorphic code can be run in WebAssembly environment. However, while WebAssembly is at the core and applications are written in WebAssembly, everything that surround the apps is something else, most often JavaScript, Node.js, or Python, simply because a dominant design already existed. Moreover, building the corresponding function from scratch would have been a major engineering effort, not simple experimentation. Hence, the grand goal to use WebAssembly to implement every part of the architecture was deemed to fail. In hindsight, this could have been overcome by using a monolithic architecture instead of microservices, which by definition embrace technology integration.

4   Discussion

To summarize the experiences from our development, there are numerous aspects that truly fulfilled the WebAssembly promise. For instance, running old code, implementing fast algorithms, was considered feasible, and the new tools and techniques, in particular Rust, form pieces for a really developer-friendly IoT technology stack. Hence, potential for future development truly exists.

However, forming full technology stacks – or even forming one's own – was deemed difficult with WebAsssembly. There was little support for accessing resources or to support integration between different microservices or subsystems, implemented with different technologies. We attribute the above to WASI implementations, which are still immature, and to calling WebAssembly modules from other languages, which is made cumbersome, in particular when dealing with complex data structures. One needs to use generated glue code even with single WebAssembly modules, if these form meaningful business entities, which by definition often is the case with microservices. Moreover, implementation-specific differences in essence imply that it is easy to be bound to a particular virtual machine in a project, instead of being able to use different ones in different devices, based on characteristics of the device. These issues have been overcome by others (e.g. [12,33]) by simply avoiding excessive interfacing, and enforcing a monolithic architecture.

With the above observations in mind, WebAssembly is well suited for small, independent, yet security and/or performance dependent routines that are called when needed, instead of aiming at a full WebAssembly IoT stack. Such use of WebAssembly resembles its role inside the browser where it can have a limited, supporting role in some performance-heavy places, not as a fundamental piece in the tech stack to build on in large scale. This approach has been proposed by [24]. However, even performance advantages have been partially challenged [32].

5   Conclusions

Using WebAssembly outside the browser has gained a lot of interest recently. In this paper, we have studied using it as a comprehensive technology for IoT applications. In conclusion, we were able to use WebAssembly for key functions, but the technology was complemented by readily available subsystems and extensions using some other technology. Therefore, we believe that WebAssembly is presently applicable in the IoT domain, but to speed up executions and to produce security gains, instead of being a comprehensive development stack. This resembles the role of WebAssembly inside the browser, where particular tasks can be run independently inside the WebAssembly virtual machine. However, even in this role several complications exist in the IoT domain, such as lack of comprehensive standards, lack of OS implementation, and the dominance of de-facto implementations composed with dynamic languages and other less rigid techniques than WebAssembly. To this end, in our future work, candidate subjects to study include the use of artificial intelligence and machine learning (AI/ML) related features, encryption and decryption in general, and domain specific algorithms.

Acknowledgments. This work has been supported by Business Finland (project LiquidAI, 8542/31/2022).

References

1. Arnold, K., Gosling, J., Holmes, D.: The Java Programming Language. Addison Wesley Professional, Boston (2005)
2. Bryant, D.: WebAssembly outside the browser: a new foundation for pervasive computing. Keynote at ICWE'20, 9–12 June, Helsinki, Finland (2020)
3. Bytecode Alliance: Welcome to WASI. https://github.com/bytecodealliance/wasmtime/blob/main/docs/WASI-intro.md. Accessed 05 Dec 2022
4. Smilkov, D., Thorat, N., Yuan, A.: Introducing the WebAssembly backend for TensorFlow.js. https://blog.tensorflow.org/2020/03/introducing-webassembly-backend-for-tensorflow-js.html. Accessed 11 Mar 2020
5. De Macedo, J., Abreu, R., Pereira, R., Saraiva, J.: On the runtime and energy performance of webassembly: is WebAssembly superior to JavaScript yet? In: 2021 36th IEEE/ACM International Conference on Automated Software Engineering Workshops (ASEW), pp. 255–262. IEEE (2021)
6. Hall, A., Ramachandran, U.: An execution model for serverless functions at the edge. In: Proceedings of the International Conference on Internet of Things Design and Implementation, pp. 225–236. IoTDI 2019, Association for Computing Machinery, New York, NY, USA, April 2019. https://doi.org/10.1145/3302505.3310084
7. Kaebisch, S., Kamiya, T., McCool, M., Charpenay, V., Kovatsch, M.: Web of Things (WoT) Thing Description. https://www.w3.org/TR/wot-thing-description/. Accessed 09 Dec 2022
8. Kaitai project: Kaitai home page. https://kaitai.io/. Accessed 24 Jan 2023
9. Kim, M., Jang, H., Shin, Y.: Avengers, assemble! Survey of WebAssembly security solutions. In: 2022 IEEE 15th International Conference on Cloud Computing (CLOUD), pp. 543–553. IEEE (2022)
10. Kotilainen, P., Autto, T., Järvinen, V., Das, T., Tarkkanen, J.: Proposing isomorphic microservices based architecture for heterogeneous IoT environments. In: Taibi, D., Kuhrmann, M., Mikkonen, T., Klünder, J., Abrahamsson, P. (eds.) Product-Focused Software Process Improvement. PROFES 2022. LNCS, vol. 13709, pp. 621–627. Springer, Cham (2022). https://doi.org/10.1007/978-3-031-21388-5_47
11. Lehmann, D., Kinder, J., Pradel, M.: Everything old is new again: binary security of {WebAssembly}. In: 29th USENIX Security Symposium (USENIX Security 20), pp. 217–234 (2020)
12. Li, B., Dong, W., Gao, Y.: Wiprog: a webassembly-based approach to integrated IoT programming. In: IEEE INFOCOM 2021-IEEE Conference on Computer Communications, pp. 1–10. IEEE (2021)
13. Li, B., Fan, H., Gao, Y., Dong, W.: ThingSpire OS: a WebAssembly-based IoT operating system for cloud-edge integration. In: Proceedings of the 19th Annual International Conference on Mobile Systems, Applications, and Services, pp. 487–488 (2021)
14. Long, J., Tai, H.Y., Hsieh, S.T., Yuan, M.J.: A lightweight design for serverless function as a service. IEEE Softw. **38**(1), 75–80 (2020)
15. Losant IoT Inc: Embedded Edge Agent. https://docs.losant.com/edge-compute/embedded-edge-agent/overview/. Accessed 09 Nov 2022

16. Mäkitalo, N., Bankowski, V., Daubaris, P., Mikkola, R., Beletski, O., Mikkonen, T.: Bringing WebAssembly up to speed with dynamic linking. In: Proceedings of the 36th Annual ACM Symposium on Applied Computing, pp. 1727–1735 (2021)
17. Mäkitalo, N., et al.: WebAssembly modules as lightweight containers for liquid IoT applications. In: Brambilla, M., Chbeir, R., Frasincar, F., Manolescu, I. (eds.) ICWE 2021. LNCS, vol. 12706, pp. 328–336. Springer, Cham (2021). https://doi.org/10.1007/978-3-030-74296-6_25
18. Massey, S., Shymanskyy, V.: wasm3: The fastest WebAssembly interpreter, and the most universal runtime. https://github.com/wasm3/wasm3. Accessed 09 Dec 2022
19. Mendki, P.: Evaluating WebAssembly enabled serverless approach for edge computing. In: 2020 IEEE Cloud Summit, pp. 161–166. IEEE (2020)
20. Mikkonen, T., Pautasso, C., Taivalsaari, A.: Isomorphic Internet of Things architectures with web technologies. Computer **54**(7), 69–78 (2021)
21. Mikkonen, T., Systä, K., Pautasso, C.: Towards liquid web applications. In: Cimiano, P., Frasincar, F., Houben, G.-J., Schwabe, D. (eds.) ICWE 2015. LNCS, vol. 9114, pp. 134–143. Springer, Cham (2015). https://doi.org/10.1007/978-3-319-19890-3_10
22. Mikkonen, T., Taivalsaari, A.: Software reuse in the era of opportunistic design. IEEE Softw. **36**(3), 105–111 (2019)
23. Mozilla: WebAssembly. https://developer.mozilla.org/en-US/docs/WebAssembly/JavaScript_interface/Memory. Accessed 05 Jan 2023
24. Oliveira, F., Mattos, J.: Analysis of WebAssembly as a strategy to improve JavaScript performance on IoT environments. In: Anais Estendidos do X Simpósio Brasileiro de Engenharia de Sistemas Computacionais, pp. 133–138. SBC (2020)
25. OpenAPI Initiative: OpenAPI Specification. https://github.com/OAI/OpenAPI-Specification. Accessed 09 Dec 2022
26. Padmanabhan, S., Jha, P.: WebAssembly at eBay: A Real-World Use Case. https://tech.ebayinc.com/engineering/webassembly-at-ebay-a-real-world-use-case/. Accessed 22 May 2019
27. Raymond Hill. 2019.: gorhill/uBlock. https://github.com/gorhill/uBlock. Accessed 09 Dec 2022
28. Rossberg, A.: Introduction - WebAssembly 1.1 (Draft 2022–04-05). https://www.w3.org/TR/wasm-core-2/intro/introduction.html. Accessed 12 Jan 2022
29. Strimpel, J., Najim, M.: Building Isomorphic JavaScript Apps: From Concept to Implementation to Real-World Solutions. O'Reilly Media, Sebastopol (2016)
30. Swagger project: Swagger home page. https://swagger.io/. Accessed 24 Jan 2023
31. Vetere, P.: Why wasm is the future of cloud computing. https://www.infoworld.com/article/3678208/why-wasm-is-the-future-of-cloud-computing.html. Accessed 09 Dec 2022
32. Wang, W.: Empowering web applications with WebAssembly: are we there yet? In: 2021 36th IEEE/ACM International Conference on Automated Software Engineering (ASE), pp. 1301–1305. IEEE (2021)
33. wasmCloud Project: wasmCloud home page. https://wasmcloud.com/. Accessed 30 Jan 2022
34. Wen, E., Weber, G.: Wasmachine: bring IoT up to speed with a WebAssembly OS. In: 2020 IEEE International Conference on Pervasive Computing and Communications Workshops (PerCom Workshops), pp. 1–4. IEEE (2020)

Applying Discrete Event Simulation on Patient Flow Scenarios with Health Monitoring Systems

Anastasiia Gorelova[1]([⊠]), Santiago Meliá[1], Diana Gadzhimusieva[1], and Alexandra Parichenko[2]

[1] Universidad de Alicante, Carretera de San Vicente S/N, 03690 San Vicente del Raspeig, Alicante, Spain
{anastasiia.gorelova,santi}@ua.es, dg67@alu.ua.es
[2] Institute for Materials Science and Max Bergmann Center of Biomaterials, Dresden University of Technology, Budapester Str. 27, 01069 Dresden, Germany
alexandra.parichenko@tu-dresden.de

Abstract. Despite technological advances, today there are still many treatments that have not been addressed by remote monitoring due to the absence of reliable monitoring devices and/or Health Monitoring Systems (HMS). In addition, there are situations where the deficiency of data due to the lack of a real scenario or device makes it impossible to use artificial intelligence (AI) techniques. However, this problem could be solved with simulation, being a fundamental mechanism for predicting and forecasting not-existing scenarios. In this paper, we proposed the use of Discrete-Event Simulation (DES) to model complex HMS scenarios. We have integrated a simulation module based on Matlab Simulink, into the MoSTHealth framework, so that the digital twins (DTs) modelled by the framework are elements of the DES scenario that the medical expert can easily parameterize through a mobile interface. A case study has been defined on the use of a wearable device (under development) that collects relevant hormone levels in real time, during infertility treatment. The DES simulation demonstrates an increase in the number of patients seen by one physician by 88,8%. In addition, the average waiting time for consultation decreased by 36.5%.

Keywords: Web of things (WoT) · MATLAB · Simulink · SimEvents · infertility treatment · simulation · biosensor · Model Driven Engineering (MDE) · Digital Twin · Discrete-Event Simulation (DES)

1 Introduction

Despite of continuous medical and technological advances, today there are still treatments, that have not been addressed by remote monitoring due to the absence of reliable devices and Health Monitoring Systems (HMSs) that accurately provide real-time information to a patient and a physician. HMSs help clinicians to improve their effectiveness and efficiency in the treatments, helping them to make better decisions based on real data from previous cases, and even allowing them to simulate new scenarios for forecasting the future.

I. Garrigós et al. (Eds.): ICWE 2023, LNCS 13893, pp. 101–108, 2023.
https://doi.org/10.1007/978-3-031-34444-2_8

Infertility treatment is one of these treatments, where real-time monitoring of certain hormone levels can not only increase the effectiveness of therapy, but also prevent a range of side-effects of different gravity [1–3].

In order to understand the advantages that the implementation of an HMS can bring to the hospital system, it is necessary to make a forecast to find out whether it helps doctors to reduce consultation times, improve the efficiency of treatments, etc. However, when researchers face with a new HMS scenario, it doesn't have enough information, which makes impossible the implementation of AI techniques, since it requires a certain amount of data for appropriate analysis, training and performance. At this point, it is necessary to reproduce the conditions using techniques that help experts to make decisions. One of the solutions to handle the lack of data is to carry out a software simulation [4]. Simulation is a fundamental method [5] for forecasting, anticipating and generating data and requirements needed during both the development and adoption of complex scenarios, for cost reasons or simply because it is currently not possible to reproduce them.

One of the complex scenarios are patient flow scenarios, which is the movement of patients through a healthcare facility. It involves the medical care, physical resources, and internal systems needed to get patients from the point of admission to the point of discharge while maintaining quality and patient/provider satisfaction. In simulations of patient flow is widely used the queuing theory, which is a methodology based on mathematical models to study the movement of people, objects or information [6]. However, the queuing theory has a set of limitations, which are the basic assumptions for application of queuing models [7]. In fact, queuing models still not close enough to the operational process in a healthcare environment. However, there are more complete methods such as Discrete Event Simulation (DES), which describes the chronological sequence of events [8] that occur in a deterministic or non-deterministic (stochastic) manner. Thus, DES techniques are considered more flexible and naturalistic than Markov models in queuing theory [9]. DES is a modelling and analysis methodology that allows final users, (e.g. hospitals, clinical staff, and healthcare delivery organizations, etc.) to ask "what if?" questions, to develop new healthcare systems and treatment strategies, to evaluate the impact of existing systems, to predict the implications of changes on patient flow, and to investigate the complex interactions between system variables [10].

One of the aspects that needs to be addressed in today's health systems - is an increase of the HMS adoption to achieve an appropriate integration with the clinical workflow [11, 12]. One way of doing so, is to involve health experts to take part in the definition and maintenance of the monitoring system. To do that, our project is based on Model-Driven Engineering (MDE) paradigm [13] that raises the level of abstraction at which this HMS configuration takes place, and by providing a simplified scenario model. In addition, MDE allows to reduce the development time and maintenance of the HMS through the definition of an automated development process, which starts with the definition of the domain and scenario models, from which the simulation is animated. Once the simulation has been validated, the final implementation of the HMS is generated using a MDE approach such as OOH4RIA [14]. This approach reduces significantly the development costs of a new HMS and allows the medical expert to modify the solution at any time.

2   Related Work

The most common application of simulation in patient flow is related to the emergency and radiology departments. In [15], authors performed a simulation, using DES software, to simulate queues in emergency department, proposing scenarios to reduce parameters such as: waiting time, utilization of each server, etc. Authors of [16], analyzed a workflow process in a radiology department, with implementation of DES to explore a complex interaction. Arrival, service and waiting times for each patient have been estimated and a software program has been proposed, in order to improve operations planning and control process by managers, using forecasting system. Suthihono et al. [17], identified a set of scenarios to prevent accumulation of patients, following social distancing protocol. DES was used to select the most effective scenario. The most approximate work to our project is an article [8], where the authors propose a DES model for receiving patients who suffer from heart disease. A patient has an IoT device that provides continuous communication between the patient and the healthcare team. Through simulation, authors demonstrate the correlation between the number of patients arriving and the resources needed to provide quality services.

As a result of the review, no papers on simulated fertility treatment were found.

3   MoSTHealth: A Framework for Modeling and Simulating HMS Based on Digital Twins

The MoSTHealth framework [18], based on a set of disciplines such as DT, WoTs, DES, Machine Learning and MDE, that allows to the modelling, simulating and providing a rapid deployment of different remote healthcare monitoring scenarios with IoT medical devices. Figure 1 shows an overview of a HMS scenario for a fertility treatment using the MoSTHealth framework. The doctor proposes a remote treatment to the patient in which the most important telemetries are collected using a hormone biosensor (female hormones) and a smart band (e.g. heart rate, temperature, oxygen saturation, physical activity, etc.). Both wearables send the information to the patient's smartphone app via Bluetooth, which sends it to the MoSTHealth system using an internet connection. However, as mentioned above, the biosensor is still under development, and the system needs to provide a prediction of the data, when real data is not yet available. Therefore, the MoSTHealth system applies modelling and simulation techniques based on real-time simulation to reproduce the behaviour of complex devices using Digital Twins. On the other hand, MoSTHealth applies DES scenarios that represents the real world, through simulation on an asynchronous event-by-event basis and the generation of a detailed performance report [19]. The simulation itself will be conducted in Matlab, which will be called from the MoStHealth backend, using the MATLAB Engine API for.NET.

In the next section, DES will be used to simulate how patient flow would change if we make use of technology such as a Health Monitoring System and an under-development hormone wearable. The biosensor is currently at the development stage at the chair of "Material science and nanotechnology" of the Technical University of Dresden. In this case, DES helps us to understand the impact of such a hormone biosensor in the hospital system, prior to its implementation.

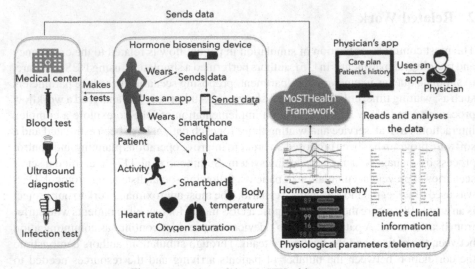

Fig. 1. Overview of the MoSTHealth process

4 A DES Case Study: A Patient Flow in a Fertility Clinic with or Without HMS with Hormone Biosensor

The purpose of simulating patients' flow in a fertility clinic, is to determine the number of served patients and the average waiting time for a consultation [10], and further comparison with simulation of proposing treatment. For the specific scenario of the fertility clinic, we include an integration with the DES simulation, based on, MATLAB Simulink tool, specifically with the SimEvents toolbox, that provides a DES engine based on a graphical notation. Initially, a model of traditional infertility treatment is created, taking as example a flowchart depicting the patient process in the fertility center, which follows ISO 9001 standard [20]. Since a patient arrival and serves rates are not predictable, the simulation model should be stochastic [21]. To approximate the random process: a generator of entities or "patients" (Fig. 2 and Fig. 3) follows a Poisson arrival process and a service time has a negative exponential distribution. In fact, the Poisson and negative exponential distributions have the same random dynamic [22]. To introduce the data of a real clinic in the simulator, a health expert provided it via the MoSTHealth mobile interface. In this experiment the data has been provided by Dr. Manuel Lillo Crespo, deputy director of the HLA Vistahermosa Hospital in Alicante.

As can be seen in Fig. 2, in case of traditional infertility treatment, a patient comes to a medical center and gets in first queue, waiting for registration. Once registered, the patient gets in another queue, depending on a propose of visit. So, in this simulation there are 3 patient queues: (i) directly to a consultation with a physician; (ii) to an examination, e.g., an ultrasound; (iii) to carry out an analysis. Once obtained results of examination or analysis, the patient comes to consultation with physician.

In the case of an infertility treatment with an HMS and a hormone biosensor (Fig. 3), the number of queues on site is reduced and an alternate type of patient appears (online patients). Patient Twin, is a digital representation of real patient. In addition to the patient

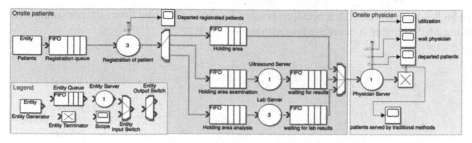

Fig. 2. Simulation model of patients' flow in a fertility center, with one attending physician.

twin, there are a device and a careplan twins in the model. The careplan is a set of activities suggested by the physician (consultations, daily goals, diet, injections, etc.). Some activities require a physician and others not. Thus, a certain part of patients receives a care without an intervention of medical staff. Another part of patients has a pre-scheduled appointment, so they queue up for an online consultation with a physician, which takes less time than an onsite consultation. The third digital twin in the simulation model is the Device twin, which represents digitally the hormone biosensor. If the biosensor detects hormone levels that are considered as alarming, the patient gets priority in the queue for an online consultation with the physician. Importantly, the digital twins are resources within the DES modelling. These resources have behavior and data defined from MoSTHealth framework.

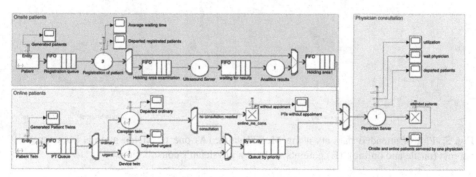

Fig. 3. Simulation model of patients' flow in a fertility center with one attending physician, using the HMS with hormone biosensor.

5   Results

Graphs Fig. 4 and Fig. 5 illustrate the correlation between the number of patients (y-axis) and time in seconds (x-axis). Simulation time has been equated to 12 h of visiting times in health centers. As a result of simulations, in case of traditional treatment, one physician can only attend to 36 patients per day (Fig. 4). However, the physician can attend up to 68 patients per day (Fig. 5AB), applying MoSTHealth with hormone biosensor, which is an 88,8% more efficient that previous results. Regarding waiting times for consultations, using MoSTHealth, it decreased on average by 36.5%.

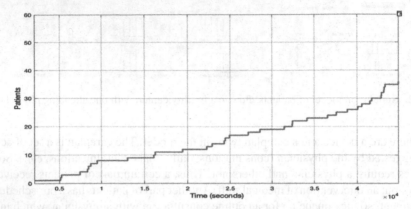

Fig. 4. Plot of attended patients in case of traditional infertility treatment.

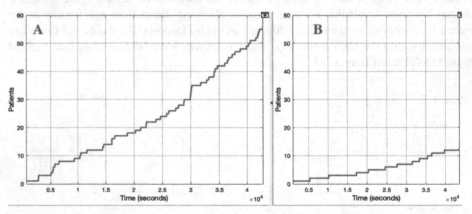

Fig. 5. Plot of attended patients using MoSTHealth, (A) one physician attends both types of patents (onsite and online); (B) patients without a physician's consultation.

After experimenting with the change of resources, we have detected, that better results can be achieved by separating the roles of the doctors, i.e., instead of one physician attending to both types of patients (online and onsite), splitting the tasks and assigning one physician to attend only the online patients and another to attend only the onsite patients.

6   Conclusions and Future Works

In the current paper, we presented a resource optimization through results of DES applied on traditional and the HMS infertility treatment with a novel hormone biosensor. This simulation is part of the MoSTHealth framework, which by modelling and simulating

HMS scenarios, forecasts the effect of the implementation of devices, patients and care plans through its digital twins. The result of this simulation shows that the establishment of an HMS with the biosensor improves the number of patients attended per day by 88,8%, and patient waiting time by 36.5%. The implementation of this device is considered appropriate, showing an optimization in the daily work of doctors, and a shorter waiting time for patients. These aspects focus mainly on optimizing patient flow, thus affecting the organization of work and the fertility center itself.

In future works, we will perform a real-time simulation of the treatment and the hormone biosensor itself. Thanks to the use of the framework, patients and doctors will be able to interact with the mobile interfaces with the digital twins, with the purpose of assessing aspects such as satisfaction, intention of adoption, and validation of a device even before is implemented.

Acknowledgments. We are grateful to Dr. Manuel Lillo Crespo, for providing information about patients' flow in Vistahermosa Hospital in Alicante.

Funding. This work has been funded by SkoPS project EU (Ref 2020-1-DE01-KA226HE-005772), co-funded by the Spanish Ministry of Science and Innovation under contract PID2019-111196RB-I00 (Access@IoT).

References

1. Nivin Todd, Irregular Periods and Getting Pregnant. Medical review (2020). https://www.webmd.com/infertility-and-reproduction/guide/in-vitro-fertilization
2. Fauser, B.C.J.M.: Patient education: Infertility treatment with gonadotropins (Beyond the Basics) (2021)
3. Ovulation Induction. University of California San Francisco. https://www.ucsfhealth.org/education/ovulation-induction
4. Broutonlab. How to Deal With the Lack of Data in Machine Learning. https://broutonlab.com/blog/how-to-deal-with-lack-of-data-in-machine-learning
5. Malpas, J.: Donald Davidson, The Stanford Encyclopedia of Philosophy (Winter 2012 Edition), Edward N. Zalta (ed.). https://plato.stanford.edu/entries/simulations-science/#Wha ComSim
6. Queuing Theory Definition, Elements, and Example. Investopedia (2022). https://www.investopedia.com/terms/q/queuing-theory.asp
7. Mehandiratta, R.: Applications of queuing theory in health care (2011). Chitkara University, Punjab. ISSN (Online): 2229–6166
8. Karboub, K., Mohamed, T., Moutaouakkil, F., Sofiene, D., Dandache, A.: Emergency patient's arrivals management based on IoT and discrete simulation using ARENA. In: Habachi, O., Meghdadi, V., Sabir, E., Cances, J.-P. (eds.) UNet 2019. LNCS, vol. 12293, pp. 234–244. Springer, Cham (2020). https://doi.org/10.1007/978-3-030-58008-7_19
9. Discrete Event Simulation (DES). In: Kirch, W. (eds.) Encyclopedia of Public Health. Springer, Dordrecht (2008). https://doi.org/10.1007/978-1-4020-5614-7_818
10. Jacobson, S.H., Hall, S.N., Swisher, J.R.: Discrete-event simulation of health care systems. In: Hall, R. (eds.) Patient Flow. International Series in Operations Research & Management Science, vol. 206, pp. 273–309. Springer, Boston, MA (2013). https://doi.org/10.1007/978-1-4614-9512-3_12

11. Marzkin, A.: How COVID-19 Could impact Digital Health. Health Advances Blog. Reflections on Healthcare & Life Sciences Innovation. Publication date: April 2020. https://health advancesblog.com/2020/04/01/how-covid-19-could-impact-digital-health/
12. Cicibas, H., Özkan, S.: Adoption factors of health monitoring systems for smart healthcare: a systematic review, pp. 43–50 (2019)
13. Bézivin, J.: In search of a basic principle for model driven engineering. Novatica J. Spec. Issue 5(2), 21–24 (2004)
14. Meliá, S., Gómez, J., Pérez, S., Díaz, O.: Architectural and technological variability in rich internet applications. IEEE Internet Comput. 14(3), 24–32 (2010)
15. Haghighinejad, H.A., et al.: Using queuing theory and simulation modelling to reduce waiting times in an Iranian emergency department. Int. J. Community Based Nurs. Midwifery 4(1), 11–26 (2016). PMID: 26793727; PMCID: PMC4709818
16. Idigo, F., et al.: Workflow estimation of a radiology department using modelling and simulation. Int. J. Adv. Oper. Manag. 12, 122 (2020). https://doi.org/10.1504/IJAOM.2020.108261
17. Suthihono, Y.A., Kusumastuti, R.D.: A simulation of patient queuing system on MRI system at tertiary referral hospital in Indonesia. In: 2021 6th International Conference on Management in Emerging Markets (ICMEM), Bandung, Indonesia, 2021, pp. 1–6 (2021). https://doi.org/10.1109/ICMEM53145.2021.9869416
18. Gorelova, A., Meliá, S.: Applying a healthcare web of things framework for infertility treatments. In: Di Noia, T., Ko, I.Y., Schedl, M., Ardito, C. (eds.) Web Engineering. ICWE 2022. LNCS, vol. 13362, pp. 426–431. Springer, Cham (2022). https://doi.org/10.1007/978-3-031-09917-5_30
19. Babulak, E., Wang, M.: Discrete event simulation. Aitor Goti (Hg.): Discrete Event Simulations. Rijeka, Kroatien: Sciyo, p. 1 (2010)
20. Bento, F., Esteves, S.: Establishing a quality management system in a fertility center: experience with ISO 9001. (2016). https://doi.org/10.5935/MedicalExpress.2016.03.02
21. Leonelli, M.: Simulation and Modelling to Understand Change. School of Human Sciences and Technology at IE University, Madrid, Spain (2021). https://bookdown.org/manuele_leon elli/SimBook/
22. Palvannan, R.K., Teow, K.L.: Queueing for healthcare. J. Med. Syst. 36, 541–547 (2012). https://doi.org/10.1007/s10916-010-9499-7

User Privacy Engineering

Streamlining Personal Data Access Requests: From Obstructive Procedures to Automated Web Workflows

Nicola Leschke[✉] , Florian Kirsten , Frank Pallas , and Elias Grünewald

TU Berlin, Information Systems Engineering, Berlin, Germany
{nl,f.kirsten,fp,eg}@ise.tu-berlin.de

Abstract. Transparency and data portability are two core principles of modern privacy legislations such as the GDPR. From the regulatory perspective, providing individuals (data subjects) with access to their data is a main building block for implementing these. Different from other privacy principles and respective regulatory provisions, however, this right to data access has so far only seen marginal technical reflection. Processes related to performing *data subject access requests (DSARs)* are thus still to be executed manually, hindering the concept of data access from unfolding its full potential.

To tackle this problem, we present an automated approach to the execution of DSARs, employing modern techniques of web automation. In particular, we propose a generic DSAR workflow model, a corresponding formal language for representing the particular workflows of different service providers (controllers), a publicly accessible and extendable workflow repository, and a browser-based execution engine, altogether providing "one-click" DSARs. To validate our approach and technical concepts, we examine, formalize and make publicly available the DSAR workflows of 15 widely used service providers and implement the execution engine in a publicly available browser extension. Altogether, we thereby pave the way for automated data subject access requests and lay the groundwork for a broad variety of subsequent technical means helping web users to better understand their privacy-related exposure to different service providers.

Keywords: Data Subject Access Request · Process Automation · Web Automation · Privacy · Privacy Engineering · Data Access · Data Portability · GDPR

1 Introduction

Modern privacy regulations such as the GDPR or the CCPA comprise a broad variety of obligations to be fulfilled by service providers (*controllers*) processing personal data of individuals (*data subjects*). Besides concepts broadly recognized in the technical domain – such as security, data minimization/anonymization,

I. Garrigós et al. (Eds.): ICWE 2023, LNCS 13893, pp. 111–125, 2023.
https://doi.org/10.1007/978-3-031-34444-2_9

etc. – this also includes provisions and rights regarding *transparency* and *data portability*. Taking the GDPR as a blueprint example for other privacy regulations herein, users have a right to access (RtA), obligating service providers to provide them with "a copy of the personal data undergoing processing" (Art. 15 (3)) upon request.

This right is considered essential in empowering data subjects to make well-informed and self-sovereign decisions regarding, e.g., which services (not) to use (anymore), which data to share with them, etc. [17]. In addition, the RtA is also an indispensable prerequisite for exercising other privacy rights [32], such as the right to rectification or deletion (Art. 16/17) and also facilitates novel practices of data reuse for individual as well as collective purposes [33,34,40].

The manifold possible benefits notwithstanding, the RtA is rarely used in practice. Some even say it is "ignored, inefficient, underused and/or obsolete" [5, p. 4]. This lack of use can largely be attributed to the fact that request processes as implemented in practice are tedious and error-prone from the perspective of data subjects who, in turn, all too often abstain from pursuing data access or from successfully completing a respective request [9].

To address these shortcomings, we propose to render DSARs more accessible and less obstructive for data subjects by means of web automation and a higher order process automation language explicitly tailored to the specifics of DSARs. In particular, we contribute:

- a generalized data access process model covering manual, web-based and API-driven DSAR implementations found in practice
- a formalized data access request process automation language (DARPAL) facilitating the automation of data access requests for said three cases across a broad variety of service providers
- a fully functional prototype of a browser-based runtime and a corresponding process repository allowing for "one-click" data access request, and
- an initial corpus of 15 provider-specific, automatically executable DARPAL documents particularly including the most important large-scale service providers and thereby demonstrating the practical viability of our approach.

These contributions unfold as follows: In Sect. 2, we introduce relevant background and related work from the legal and process perspective to DSARs as well as on web automation in general. On this basis, we delineate our general approach in Sect. 3, develop our generalized process model in Sect. 4, and subsequently transfer it into our DARPAL language (Sect. 5). Prototypical implementations for the runtime and the process repository as well as the initial corpus are presented in Sect. 6, followed by a discussion and conclusion (Sect. 7).

2   Background and Related Work

Relevant background and related work regards the legal givens for DSARs and respective challenges and shortcomings, real-world implementations of data access processes, and web automation in general. These foundations shall be briefly introduced before delineating our approach.

2.1   Right to Data Access

At the core of any modern privacy regulation is the right of data subjects to know whether and, if so, what data about them is being processed and by what means. This includes transparency information that can be obtained before the data is processed (*ex-ante transparency*) [20,21], for example through privacy statements, as well as after the data has been processed (*ex-post transparency*) [23]. One important part of ex-post transparency is the RtA, which includes the right to obtain a copy of the personal data undergoing processing.

Under the GDPR, for instance, the RtA is defined in Art. 15. Besides general obligations addressing ex-ante transparency as defined in Art. 15(1), Art. 15(3) declares that data subjects have the right to receive, upon request, a copy of all personal data relating to them and processed by a controller. In the following, we will refer to a respective request as *"data subject access request (DSAR)"*. Closely related to the RtA is the right to data portability, as codified in Art. 20 GDPR. It grants data subjects the right to receive a copy of personal data *they provided* in a *"structured, commonly used and machine-readable format"*. Despite this difference of scope, service providers often do not differentiate between data access and data portability [10, p. 79f] and handle both with the same functionality and interfaces like "checkout" dashboards or "archive downloads". To avoid overly legalese elaborations, we will thus not further distinguish between RtA and RtDP herein but rather refer to them conjointly as RtA and to said interfaces as *"RtA endpoints"*.

As for the practical implementation of such data access, various challenges have been identified, ranging from controllers not fulfilling their obligations in matters of data completeness [3,9,30] or response time[1] [9,25,39] over a lack of authentication processes, enabling the unauthorized access to personal data [10, 11,15], to incomprehensible responses [9,30,40]. Last but not least, data subjects often have difficulties locating the RtA endpoint [35]. Altogether, this severely hinders the execution of the RtA, raising the question of how the process of executing data requests can be streamlined and made more accessible.

2.2   Data Access Process

From a data subjects perspective, the execution of a DSAR is composed of two sub-processes: the actual data access process (which we will refer to as DAP), and the privacy enactment, which covers all subsequent activities building upon the data retrieved through the DAP, such as data mapping, visualization, exploration, or (collective) decisionmaking [3,30,40]. However, these enactment activities are rather subject to socio-technical and human-computer-interface research and shall therefore be considered out of scope herein. Real-world implementations of DAPs, in turn, can be categorized into one of the following three distinct approaches:

---

[1] The controller has to fulfill the request without delay, but no later than within 30 days that might even be extended up to 60 days, if the data subject is informed about the delay in the first 30 days (Art. 12 (3) GDPR).

Manual DAPs require data subjects to identify the responsible data protection officer and make a written (mail, e-mail) or oral (e.g., phone call) request to get a copy of the data, which may either be received via e-mail or as a printed copy [9,35,39]. From the perspective of a data subject, these manual processes cannot be automated, except from using text generation tools that assist in formulating proper request texts.[2]

Web-based DAPs, in turn, use a web form as RtA endpoint. In this process, the data subject needs to identify the URL of the form, fill in the form fields and submit the request form.[3] The subsequent communication is usually handled via e-mail, allowing for a download of the retrieved data [39]. Such a web-based process is somewhat more automated than a manual process, nonetheless, it offers even more automation potential.

Finally, **API-based DAPs** are characterized by enabling third-party tools to handle authentication, configuration, and request through, e.g., a (standardized) API as proposed in [22], privacy dashboards [37], or personal information management systems (PIMS) [24]. Basically, this approach can facilitate tools that fully automate the RtA on the data subject side.[4] However, such processes are, in practice, rarely implemented [10,35,39].

2.3   Web Automation

As there are many repetitive tasks to handle in the daily interaction with websites, approaches to automate those tasks have been widely discussed [8,13,29], culminating in the research area of web automation. Web automation tools can be applied for different purposes and audiences: from allowing developers to automatically test web pages [31,38], over business use-cases involving abstractions of manual work [4,29], to improved accessibility, e.g. for visually-impaired users [7,36]. The to-be-automated tasks and corresponding actions are wrapped in a so-called macro [13]. In general, two approaches for generating macros can be distinguished: declaring a sequence of actions (sometimes referred to as handcrafting [36]), like, e.g., used in Chickenfoot [8], and programming by demonstration (PBD) [6,13,29]. The latter approach is more attractive for end-users, like the data subjects in the RtA process, because it requires less [28] or even no programming knowledge at all [6]. Therefore, we concentrate on PBD, which can be executed in two steps: first, a list of tasks needs to be identified, and then these tasks are automated by using record and replay techniques [12]. Those tasks can either be reconstructed by observing user actions [12,28] or application states [13,26].

Above-mentioned traditional PBD mainly addresses single page applications, however, in modern web applications, the to-be-automated tasks might be distributed across web pages. For that specific case, an intersection with AI-enabled

---

[2] Examples of such DAP specific text generators are datenanfragen.de or mydatadoneright.eu.

[3] Instructions for such processes can for example be found at justgetmydata.com.

[4] An API-based DAP is followed, e.g., by the aeon prototype (aeon.technology) that integrates a few big service providers.

robotic process automation (RPA) [1,27] can be identified, resulting in the research field of web RPA [2,16].

3 Proposed Approach

As identified in Sect. 2.1, current real-world implementations of the RtA broadly lead to data subjects not being able to or abstaining from actually exerting it. There is thus a significant need for improving the prevailing status quo of data access. Given their broad use in practice (especially by large-scale service providers) and their already semi-automated nature, we here see particular potential in the automation of web-based DAPs. More specifically, the primary goal behind the work presented herein is to automate the request-parts of DAPs, which are the necessary basis for subsequent data checkouts (for a more detailed analysis of the DAP, see Sect. 4 below) and to thereby make them more accessible and less obstructive for data subjects. In addition, albeit less focused on herein, we also want to pave the way for technically supported DAPs for manual and API-driven approaches across highly variable and provider-specific interfaces.

In a first step, we propose a generalized process model for DAPs that covers manual, web-based, and API-driven DAPs and a broad variety of respective real-world implementations. In particular, this model distinguishes between the sub-processes for submitting a request (data request process, *DRP*) and for checking out the personal data after provision (data checkout process, *DCP*). Of these, we thenceforth primarily focus on the DRP (see above).

Building upon that process model, we introduce a formal language called DARPAL allowing to represent provider-specific, heterogeneous DRPs – which we refer to as provider-specific *DRP specifications* herein – in a unified, formalized, and to-be-executed form. To fulfill the primary goal, such a representation must comprise all automation-relevant parameters, such as the specific RtA endpoint or the to-be-automated workflow itself, as well as the parameters available for customizing the data to be retrieved. In addition, the language shall be defined in such a way that it also covers manual and API-driven approaches to facilitate later extensions in line with the secondary goal.

Based on this language, we aim to make respective provider-specific DRP specifications automatically executable on the data subject side without any intermediary party being involved in the actual DRP execution. In addition, actually executing such DRPs should be as accessible and easy-to-use as possible for data subjects. Employing modern techniques of web automation, we thus strive to provide a browser-based execution engine particularly tailored to the specific givens of DRPs that automates respective requests as far as possible using the parameters provided in a DRP specification. Last but not least, we also aim to make DRP specifications codified in our formal language publicly available and accessible in an extensible process repository and to pre-fill this repository with a base corpus of formalized DRP specifications for broadly used service providers, especially including GAFA[5].

---

[5] GAFA represents the four tech-companies Google, Apple, Facebook, and Amazon.

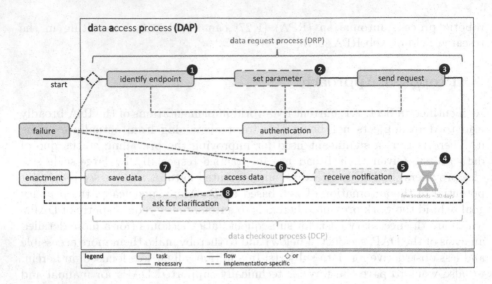

Fig. 1. Generic data access process.

Together, these components – language, browser-based execution engine, process repository, and base corpus – shall then provide the necessary basis for "one-click" DRPs. At the same time, successfully automating DRPs for a substantial number of service providers also validates the suitability of our generalized process model and our formal language. All these components shall thus be elaborated on in more detail below.

4   Modeling Data Access Processes

Data subjects wishing to exercise their RtA are following a *data access process (DAP)*, a generalized depiction of which is given in Fig. 1. In general, the DAP can be simplified as a sequential process that can be divided into two sub-processes [35], which we denote *data request process (DRP)* and *data checkout process (DCP)*, and that can be delineated as follows:

Data Request Process (DRP): To initiate a DRP, a data subject first has to identify and navigate to the controller-specific RtA endpoint. Secondly, some providers require providing further request parameters, e.g., a specific time frame that should be contained in the retrieved data, while others are satisfied by the statement that data access is requested. Afterwards, the request can be sent. Of particular interest to reach our primary goal are web-based DRPs, which can be refined as depicted in Fig. 2. Within this approach, the RtA endpoint is represented as a web-page or -form, and also the customization is made via a web-form. In most cases, the web form is only available for authenticated users, so sometimes further authentication processes are dismissed, but in other cases, there are (multiple) authentication steps in place [14].

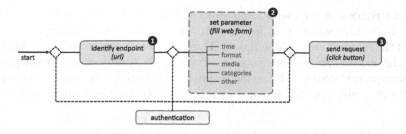

Fig. 2. Model of a web-based DRP.

Even though these steps seem to be quite easy to handle, in reality, the DRP is quite complicated. For instance, it has been empirically shown that even the very first step is far from straightforward for data subjects, who already struggled in identifying the correct RtA endpoint [3]. This is due to the fact that RtA endpoint addresses are either wrapped in lengthy privacy policies or are decoupled from the main service experience, e.g., a web form is only accessible via privacy settings hidden in some menu [35]. Additionally, the request parameters to be provided can be complex and hard to understand. For example, a non-technical data subject can hardly judge which data format should be used for the download [35].

Data Checkout Process (DCP): After the request was successfully made (and, thus, the DRP completed), the DCP starts with a waiting period, the duration of which can range from a few seconds (e.g., Google Takeout) up to the legally specified maximum of 30 days. During this period, the service provider processes the request and creates the response.[6] Then, some service providers send the compiled data directly to the data subject, while others send a notification that it is available for download [9]. Finally, the data subject can access and save a copy of the data. Within the DCP, clarification can be required [35] at various stages, arising from both the service provider (see, e.g., [5]) and the data subject side, especially when above-mentioned challenges with the RtA emerge.

Authentication: Throughout the whole DAP, multiple authentication steps might be required, which can vary from weak evidence like giving the full name of the data subject [14], logging into a user account or a verified mail account [25], to proving the identity with an ID-card [9]. Again, data subjects often fail in the authentication steps (or are at least demotivated from proceeding), especially since some authentication processes require multiple clarification messages between the data subject and the service provider, ultimately leading to a DAP not being completed successfully [35]. However, Joris et al. [25] found that only a fraction of service providers included in their study had implemented at least one identification measure. This can lead to an abuse of the RtA, as already mentioned above.

---

[6] Respective provider-side processes are considered out of scope herein.

End of Process: After the DCP has successfully finished, the enactment phase can be started. In some cases, feedback to the service provider is required, especially if the received data is incomplete. This may lead to a renewed DCP. Furthermore, the process can also end with an error [35]. Data subjects abort the process at various points because they no longer know what to do [9] or because the service provider does not respond (in time) or refuses to process the request [39].

5   DARPAL: Process Automation Language

Based on the general process depicted above, we now define a formal automation language specifically tailored to the domain of DRPs. Our *data access request process automation language (DARPAL)* is provided as JSON Schema specification and pays regard to the particularities of DRPs as follows:

First, DARPAL allows specifying the **requestInterface**, reflecting the RtA endpoint from Sect. 2.1 above, in a way that covers as many real-world DRP-implementations as possible. In the light of the different DAP categories to be found in practice and their specifics (see Sect. 2.2), DARPAL thus allows to specify different request interface attributes for manual, web-based, and api-based DRPs. For each of these cases, it must be specified whether it is available and the respective means of authentication (e.g. "password" or "id-card") can be specified. Besides this, the definition of the request interface attributes varies between said three cases: In case of a manual process, the interface is an *address*, *email*, or *phone* number, while for web-based DRPs it is the *startUrl* of the request form and for APIs it is the *endpointUrl* and possibly an additional set of *apiParameters*.

For web-based request interfaces – which we consider the primary target for automating DRPs herein – a generic second-level field *workflowContainer* is introduced. It is of type object and has the sub-fields *automationEngine*, *workflow*, *version*, and *verified*. We decided to provide a generic solution allowing for different automation engines to be used for executing the ultimate workflow. Therefore we need to reference the automation engine. The workflow itself is also an array of objects specific to the respective automation engine. These objects are not subject to further constraints (except for being a JSON object), because they are of an engine-specific format. The fields *version* and *verified*, in turn, serve secondary purposes that shall not be discussed in more detail here.

Besides the so-structured requestInterface definition, the second concept that needs to be reflected by DARPAL are request parameters, which refine the content of the copy that is to be requested. For example, Facebook has a "download your information" page for logged-in users with a request form that has many options regarding the file format and content of the DSAR, while LinkedIn has a web form where authenticated users have the choice between requesting a full copy or selected general information blocks. Given that these parameters become relevant independently from the automation level of the interface (e.g., the file format can be of relevance for manual DRPs as well), they are specified in a separate **requestParameter** section.

Table 1. First and second-level building blocks of DARPAL. Mandatory elements are denoted by a *.

meta			requestInterface		
name*			manual		
version*					available*
_hash*					address
					email
requestParameter					phone
timeRange*					authentication
	allTime*		webinterface		
	customRange*				available*
mediaQuality					startUrl
dataFormat*					authentication
additionalProperties					workflowContainer
			api		
					available*
					endpoint
					authentication
					apiParameters

Following our model depicted in Fig. 2, we allow for the fields *timeRange*, describing the period for which the copy is created, *dataFormat*, describing the file type of the copy, *mediaQuality*, describing the preferred quality of media files within the copy, and *categories* if only specific types of personal data shall be included in the copy. Service-specific other fields can be provided via the *additionalProperties* field. For example, Linkedin allows to select special *categories* of personal data that shall be requested.

For identifying provider-specific DARPAL documents, we additionally need to provide **meta** information in a third DARPAL section. These meta-information especially include the name of the service provider the document refers to, as well as information about the version and a hash of the document. Together, these three sections make up the DARPAL document structure depicted in Table 1. Additionally, there are some fields that are required for document identification, however, they have no further semantic meaning and are therefore not elaborated here. The respective JSON-Schema definition also providing more details on field formats/data types etc. is available online.[7]

6   Prototypical Implementation

To make DRPs as accessible as possible, we implemented the *"data access request assistant (DARA)"* system, consisting of a process repository component pre-filled with 15 real-world DARPAL specifications[8], an automation engine in the

---

[7] github.com/DaSKITA/darpal.
[8] github.com/DaSKITA/darpal-documents.

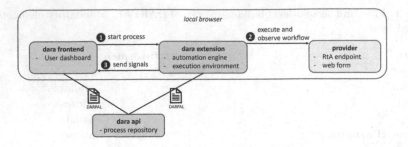

Fig. 3. Architecture of the DARA system.

form of a publicly available browser extension and a user interface, altogether providing fully functional "one-click" DRPs. A general overview can be found in Fig. 3. Each of these components shall be elaborated on in more detail below.

Process Repository: The storage and processing of the available DRP specifications is done in a separate process repository, which we refer to as DARA API[9]. In addition to providing automation engines with the necessary DRP specifications, the process repository is also conceptualized (but not yet implemented) to handle quality assurance and lifecycle management of the stored DARPAL documents[10]. It was realized as Python-based REST-API via FastAPI. For each covered service provider, it offers a separate endpoint with GET, POST and DELETE routes.

Currently, the DARA API includes a base corpus of 15 DARPAL specifications, describing the DRPs of broadly used service providers. These are retrieved and employed by both, the DARA extension and the DARA frontend. The workflows within the specifications are enriched with signals reporting the status of the DAP to the frontend. For example, we send a "started execution" event to the execution environment for proper handling as soon as the provider's DRP page was loaded successfully and no redirection to a login portal occurred. Statistics collection and crowdsourcing functionalities were not yet implemented in the current prototype, however, they are planned for future versions.

Browser Extension: For our prototype, we chose an approach based on a browser extension because of the accessible and cross-platform installation procedure through the browsers' extension stores. To execute the DRP in the user's browser, we built the DARA extension[11] based on the Automa[12] project. The Automa automation engine uses a simple block-based user interface to build browser workflows. We configured Automa to include a content-script in our frontend, which listens for user commands like the execution of a particular DRP or, respectively, the workflow it includes.

---

[9] github.com/DaSKITA/dara-api.

[10] For instance, statistics on successful and failed local workflow executions shall in future versions be reported back to the repository. With this data, likely outdated and dysfunctional workflows could be marked respectively.

[11] github.com/DaSKITA/dara-extension.

[12] www.automa.site.

When an automated DRP is triggered, either directly via the extension or via the frontend, the DARA extension executes it in a new browser tab, which is automatically opened in the background. After successful execution, this tab is closed and a "success" signal is sent to the frontend. However, if the execution fails or takes longer than expected, an "interaction required" signal is sent, and the user can switch to the background tab. To additionally enable non-technical users to add or update (individual, local) DRP specifications, we build upon the workflow recording functionality of Automa. We modified the recording functionality so that per default, XPath is used to select HTML elements, as in our experience XPath provided a more stable selector than using CSS classes.

Frontend: Via a dashboard[13], the user is first asked to install the DARA extension. Afterwards, the user assesses the DRP specifications available via the DARA API and selects the service provider for which a DRP shall be executed. While executing a DRP in a non-active tab through the web extension, the user is informed about the execution state and in case manual interaction is required, the option to switch to the browser-tab in question is displayed. Currently, the frontend is available in German, with further languages to be added soon.

Preliminary User Study: In a preliminary pre-study, we asked 14 users (not familiar with our implementation before) to request their data from two of the fifteen service providers we provide DARPAL specifications for. For the first chosen service, the users had to follow the DRP without the use of our prototype or any other instructions. It took them on average 4.3 min to finish the DRP. 29% of the users were not able to successfully send a request at all. Overall, only half of the user group considered executing their RtA again. The second service was requested using our prototype. The users chose to send a request to Amazon, Apple, Google, Instagram, LinkedIn, and Vinted. In all cases, it took them less than two minutes to complete the request (with an average of one minute), and 86% of the users stated they are willing to repeat the process on a regular basis, with the same and other service providers.

Even though being of highly preliminary nature and hardly generalizable so far, these results are definitely encouraging and at least support the basic viability of our approach. Following up on the more technical groundwork presented herein, a more in-depth user study is planned in the near future.

7   Discussion and Conclusion

With our contributions as a whole, we provide significant improvements for data subjects exercising their RtA. Formerly tedious web-based data requests are condensed into automated "one-click" DRPs. Still, the approach pursued herein carries inherent needs for creating a multitude of provider-specific DARPAL documents separately. Our prototype partially tackles this problem with a dedicated recording function. Still, service providers immensely obfuscate their page sources, perform random changes to the document object model, or follow other

---

[13] github.com/DaSKITA/dara-frontend

strategies preventing effective web automation. Future versions of our prototype aim to counteract this problem with crowdsourcing features. Nonetheless, such options also include abuse potentials (spamming, security and trust issues etc.). Thwarting these remains a nontrivial challenge. Perspectively, DRP automation could substantially profit from documented APIs, which unfortunately exist far too rarely so far. We, thus, emphasize the regulatory need for documented APIs [18], optimally with queryable metadata according to Art. 15(1) GDPR.

Further developments in DARPAL could include a generic process representation, which could then be consumed by different automation engines and translated into their specific representation before execution. For the moment, however, we used Automa as the mere engine and workflow format and did not run into relevant limitations. For greater interoperability, however, others should be supported as well.

We encourage data subjects to request their data from as many services as possible. However, we solely addressed the DRP herein, while the DCP and enactment processes are not yet included. Still, they are very important to make access requests useful. In particular, the received data packages need to be prepared for actual interpretation, summary, risk identification, or visualization. Only with such data post-processing, data subjects can actually make sovereign evaluations and decisions regarding their usage and the processing activities of a service offering [40]. Respective functionalities are natural candidates for extending our solution further in the future. This would also be in line with requests from two of our study participants explicitly asking for data retrieval and analysis support to also be provided. Still, our approach shall serve as stable ground for respective upcoming work dealing with the actual data presentation tasks needed for a meaningful enactment stage.

Another promising next step for fostering the RtA across platforms is to extend the scope from webpage-based services to, e.g., native mobile apps (for instance through deep-linking). Similarly, our system could also be integrated with Personal Information Management Systems (PIMS) or Personal Data Stores (PDS) [24]. These aim to manage granular data access based on, among others, purpose-specific consent provisions for selected categories of personal data. Our contributions can be used to import such data, possibly also to perform data transfers in the vein of the RtDP.

Altogether, the contributions presented herein thus provide a solid ground for much more structured, automated, and sovereign DRPs, illustrating that and how web automation can fill a gap left open by existing regulations. This can not only have an instant effect on the actual exercise of the RtA, but also pave the way for a broad variety of future research endeavors in the context of the RtA, the RtDP, and technically mediated ex-post transparency in general.

Acknowledgements. We thank our students Majed Idilbi, Christopher Liebig, Ann-Sophie Messerschmid, Moriel Pevzner, Dominic Strempel, and Kjell Lillie-Stolze, who contributed to the initial proof-of-concept within the scope of a study project [19]. Special thanks go to Johanna Washington, who kindly supported us to conduct the user experiment.

The work behind this paper was partially conducted within the project DaSKITA, supported under grant no. 28V2307A19 by funds of the Federal Ministry for the Environment, Nature Conservation, Nuclear Safety and Consumer Protection (BMUV) based on a decision of the Parliament of the Federal Republic of Germany via the Federal Office for Agriculture and Food (BLE) under the innovation support program.

References

1. van der Aalst, W.M.P., Bichler, M., Heinzl, A.: Robotic process automation. Bus. Inf. Syst. Eng. **60**(4), 269–272 (2018). https://doi.org/10.1007/s12599-018-0542-4
2. Agostinelli, S., Lupia, M., Marrella, A., Mecella, M.: Automated generation of executable RPA scripts from user interface logs. In: Asatiani, A., et al. (eds.) BPM 2020. LNBIP, vol. 393, pp. 116–131. Springer, Cham (2020). https://doi.org/10.1007/978-3-030-58779-6_8
3. Alizadeh, F., Jakobi, T., Boden, A., Stevens, G., Boldt, J.: GDPR reality check - claiming and investigating personally identifiable data from companies. In: 2020 IEEE European Symposium on Security and Privacy Workshops (EuroS&PW), pp. 120–129 (2020). https://doi.org/10.1109/EuroSPW51379.2020.00025
4. Amershi, S., Mahmud, J., Nichols, J., Lau, T., Ruiz, G.A.: LiveAction: automating web task model generation. ACM Trans. Interact. Intell. Syst. **3**(3), 1–23 (2013). https://doi.org/10.1145/2533670.2533672
5. Ausloos, J., Dewitte, P.: Shattering one-way mirrors - data subject access rights in practice. Int. Data Priv. Law **8**(1), 4–28 (2018). https://doi.org/10.1093/idpl/ipy001
6. Barman, S., Chasins, S., Bodik, R., Gulwani, S.: Ringer: web automation by demonstration. In: Proceedings of the 2016 ACM SIGPLAN International Conference on Object-Oriented Programming, Systems, Languages, and Applications, pp. 748–764. OOPSLA 2016, Association for Computing Machinery (2016). https://doi.org/10.1145/2983990.2984020
7. Bigham, J.P., Lau, T., Nichols, J.: Trailblazer: enabling blind users to blaze trails through the web. In: Proceedings of the 14th International Conference on Intelligent User Interfaces, pp. 177–186 (2009)
8. Bolin, M., Webber, M., Rha, P., Wilson, T., Miller, R.C.: Automation and customization of rendered web pages. In: Proceedings of the 18th Annual ACM Symposium on User Interface Software and Technology, UIST 2005, pp. 163–172. Association for Computing Machinery, New York (2005). https://doi.org/10.1145/1095034.1095062
9. Bowyer, A., Holt, J., Go Jefferies, J., Wilson, R., Kirk, D., David Smeddinck, J.: Human-GDPR interaction: practical experiences of accessing personal data. In: Proceedings of the 2022 CHI Conference on Human Factors in Computing Systems, CHI 2022, pp. 1–19. Association for Computing Machinery (2022). https://doi.org/10.1145/3491102.3501947
10. Bufalieri, L., Morgia, M.L., Mei, A., Stefa, J.: GDPR: when the right to access personal data becomes a threat. In: 2020 IEEE International Conference on Web Services (ICWS), pp. 75–83 (2020). https://doi.org/10.1109/ICWS49710.2020.00017
11. Cagnazzo, M., Holz, T., Pohlmann, N.: GDPiRated – stealing personal information on- and offline. In: Sako, K., Schneider, S., Ryan, P.Y.A. (eds.) ESORICS 2019. LNCS, vol. 11736, pp. 367–386. Springer, Cham (2019). https://doi.org/10.1007/978-3-030-29962-0_18

12. Chasins, S., Barman, S., Bodik, R., Gulwani, S.: Browser record and replay as a building block for end-user web automation tools. In: Proceedings of the 24th International Conference on World Wide Web, WWW 2015 Companion, pp. 179–182. Association for Computing Machinery, New York (2015). https://doi.org/10.1145/2740908.2742849
13. Cypher, A., Halbert, D.C.: Watch What I Do: Programming by Demonstration. MIT Press, Cambridge (1993)
14. Di Martino, M., Meers, I., Quax, P., Andries, K., Lamotte, W.: Revisiting identification issues in GDPR 'right of access' policies: a technical and longitudinal analysis. Proc. Priv. Enhanc. Technol. **2022**(2), 95–113 (2022)
15. Di Martino, M., Robyns, P., Weyts, W., Quax, P., Lamotte, W., Andries, K.: Personal information leakage by abusing the GDPR 'right of access'. In: Fifteenth Symposium on Usable Privacy and Security (SOUPS 2019), pp. 371–385. USENIX (2019)
16. Dong, R., Huang, Z., Lam, I.I., Chen, Y., Wang, X.: WebRobot: web robotic process automation using interactive programming-by-demonstration. In: Proceedings of the 43rd ACM SIGPLAN International Conference on Programming Language Design and Implementation, PLDI 2022, pp. 152–167. Association for Computing Machinery (2022). https://doi.org/10.1145/3519939.3523711
17. Fialová, E.: Data portability and informational self-determination. Masaryk Univ. J. Law Technol. **8**(1), 45–55 (2014)
18. Gill, D., Metzger, J.: Data access through data portability. Eur. Data Prot. Law Rev. **8**(2), 221–237 (2022)
19. Grünewald, E., Pallas, F.: Datensouveränität für Verbraucher:innen: Technische Ansätze durch KI-basierte Transparenz und Auskunft im Kontext der DSGVO, pp. 1–17. Alexander Boden, Timo Jakobi, Gunnar Stevens, Christian Bala (Hgg.): Verbraucherdatenschutz - Technik und Regulation zur Unterstützung des Individuums (2021). https://doi.org/10.18418/978-3-96043-095-7_02
20. Grünewald, E., Pallas, F.: TILT: A GDPR-aligned transparency information language and toolkit for practical privacy engineering. In: Proceedings of the 2021 Conference on Fairness, Accountability, and Transparency. FAccT 2021, Association for Computing Machinery, New York (2021). https://doi.org/10.1145/3442188.3445925
21. Grünewald, E., Wille, P., Pallas, F., Borges, M.C., Ulbricht, M.R.: TIRA: an OpenAPI extension and toolbox for GDPR transparency in RESTful architectures. In: 2021 IEEE European Symposium on Security and Privacy Workshops (EuroS&PW). IEEE Computer Society (2021)
22. Hansen, M., Jensen, M.: A generic data model for implementing right of access requests. In: Gryszczyńska, A., Polański, P., Gruschka, N., Rannenberg, K., Adamczyk, M. (eds.) Privacy Technologies and Policy. APF 2022. Lecture Notes in Computer Science, pp. 3–22. Springer, Cham (2022). https://doi.org/10.1007/978-3-031-07315-1_1
23. Hildebrandt, M.: Behavioural biometric profiling and transparancy enhancing tools. Fidis Deliverable 7.12 (2009). https://doi.org/10.13140/RG.2.2.21363.32808
24. Janssen, H., Cobbe, J., Singh, J.: Personal information management systems: a user-centric privacy utopia? Internet Policy Rev. **9**(4), 1–25 (2020)
25. Joris, G., Mechant, P., De Marez, L.: Exercising the right of access: a benchmark for future GDPR evaluations. In: 70th Annual ICA Conference : Open Communication, Proceedings (2020)
26. Lau, T., Wolfman, S.A., Domingos, P., Weld, D.S.: Programming by demonstration using version space algebra. Mach. Learn. **53**, 111–156 (2003)

27. Leno, V., Dumas, M., Maggi, F.M., La Rosa, M.: Multi-perspective process model discovery for robotic process automation. In: Proceedings of the Doctoral Consortium Papers Presented at the 30th International Conference on Advanced Information Systems Engineering (CAiSE), vol. 2114, pp. 37–45. CEUR-WS (2018)
28. Leshed, G., Haber, E.M., Matthews, T., Lau, T.: CoScripter: automating & sharing how-to knowledge in the enterprise. In: Proceedings of the SIGCHI Conference on Human Factors in Computing Systems, CHI 2008, pp. 1719–1728. Association for Computing Machinery, New York (2008). https://doi.org/10.1145/1357054.1357323
29. Little, G., Lau, T.A., Cypher, A., Lin, J., Haber, E.M., Kandogan, E.: Koala: capture, share, automate, personalize business processes on the web. In: Proceedings of the SIGCHI Conference on Human Factors in Computing Systems, CHI 2007, pp. 943–946. Association for Computing Machinery, New York (2007). https://doi.org/10.1145/1240624.1240767
30. Mahieu, R., Asghari, H., van Eeten, M.: Collectively exercising the right of access: individual effort, societal effect. Internet Policy Rev. **7**(3) (2018)
31. Mickens, J., Elson, J., Howell, J.: Mugshot: deterministic capture and replay for javascript applications. In: Proceedings of the 7th USENIX Conference on Networked Systems Design and Implementation, p. 11. USENIX Association (2010)
32. Murmann, P., Fischer-Hübner, S.: Tools for achieving usable ex post transparency: a survey. IEEE Access **5**, 22965–22991 (2017)
33. Pallas, F., Hartmann, D., Heinrich, P., Kipke, J., Grünewald, E.: Configurable per-query data minimization for privacy-compliant web APIs. In: Proceedings of the 2022 ICWE International Conference on Web Engineering, Bari (2022). https://doi.org/10.1007/978-3-031-09917-5_22
34. Pallas, F., et al.: Towards application-layer purpose-based access control. In: Proceedings of the 35th Annual ACM Symposium on Applied Computing, pp. 1288–1296 (2020)
35. Petelka, J., Oreglia, E., Finn, M., Srinivasan, J.: Generating practices: investigations into the double embedding of GDPR and data access policies. Proc. ACM Hum. Comput. Interact. **6**(CSCW2), 1–26 (2022)
36. Puzis, Y., Borodin, Y., Puzis, R., Ramakrishnan, I.: Predictive web automation assistant for people with vision impairments. In: Proceedings of the 22nd International Conference on World Wide Web, pp. 1031–1040 (2013)
37. Schufrin, M., Reynolds, S.L., Kuijper, A., Kohlhammer, J.: A visualization interface to improve the transparency of collected personal data on the internet. IEEE Trans. Visual Comput. Graph. **27**(2), 1840–1849 (2021). https://doi.org/10.1109/TVCG.2020.3028946
38. Sharma, M., Angmo, R.: Web based automation testing and tools. Int. J. Comput. Sci. Inf. Technol. **5**(1), 908–912 (2014)
39. Urban, T., Tatang, D., Degeling, M., Holz, T., Pohlmann, N.: A study on subject data access in online advertising after the GDPR. In: Pérez-Solà, C., Navarro-Arribas, G., Biryukov, A., Garcia-Alfaro, J. (eds.) DPM CBT-2019. LNCS, vol. 11737, pp. 61–79. Springer, Cham (2019). https://doi.org/10.1007/978-3-030-31500-9_5
40. Veys, S., Serrano, D., Stamos, M., Herman, M., Reitinger, N., Mazurek, M.L., Ur, B.: Pursuing usable and useful data downloads under GDPR/CCPA access rights via co-design. In: SOUPS @ USENIX Security Symposium (2021)

In2P-Med: Toward the Individual Privacy Preferences Identity in the Medical Web Apps

Ha Xuan Son[1], Khoi N. H. Tuan[2], Loc C. P. Van[2], Phuc T. Nguyen[3], Khanh H. Vo[3], Huong H. Huong[3], Khiem G. Huynh[3], Khoa D. Tran[3], Anh T. Nguyen[3], Nghia H. Huynh[3], Ngan T. K. Nguyen[4], Duy T. Q. Nguyen[3], Bang K. Nguyen[3], and Nghia Duong-Trung[5(✉)]

[1] RMIT University (SGS), 702 Nguyen Van Linh, 7th District, Ho Chi Minh City, Vietnam
ha.son@rmit.edu.vn
[2] VinCSS Internet Security Services JSC, Long Bien, Ha Noi, Vietnam
khoinht@ieee.org
[3] FPT University, Nguyen Van Cu street, Ninh Kieu District, Can Tho City, Vietnam
[4] FPT Polytechnic, 22nd street, Cai Rang District, Can Tho City, Vietnam
[5] German Research Center for Artificial Intelligence (DFKI), Alt-Moabit 91C, 10559 Berlin, Germany
nghia_trung.duong@dfki.de

Abstract. With the advancement of technology, people are now able to monitor their health more efficiently. Mobile phones and smartwatches are equipped with sensors that can measure real-time changes in blood pressure, SPO2, and other attributes and public them to service providers via web applications (called web apps) for health improvement suggestions. Moreover, users can share the collected health data with other people, such as doctors, relatives, or friends. However, using technology-based approaches has raised the issue of privacy. Some health web apps, by default, intrusively gather and share data. Additionally, smartwatches may monitor people's health status 24/7. This can be cumbersome as they would have to configure each device manually. To this end, we have developed a privacy-preference prediction mechanism in the web apps called In2P-Med: the individual privacy preferences identity for the medical data. To capture individual privacy preferences in the web apps, our model learns users' privacy behavior based on their responses in different medical scenarios. In practice, we exploited several machine learning algorithms: SVM, Gradient Boosting Classifier, Ada Boost Classifier, and Gradient Boosting Regressor. To prove its effectiveness, we set up several scenarios to measure the accuracy and the satisfaction level in the two participant groups (i.e., expert and normal users). One key point in this research's selection of participants is its focus on those living in developing countries, where privacy violation issues are not a common topic.

Keywords: Privacy preferences · Medical data · Medical web applications · Semi-supervised Learning

© The Author(s), under exclusive license to Springer Nature Switzerland AG 2023
I. Garrigós et al. (Eds.): ICWE 2023, LNCS 13893, pp. 126–140, 2023.
https://doi.org/10.1007/978-3-031-34444-2_10

1   Introduction

Monitoring health with technological devices and web apps has gained great popularity in this day and age. In fact, the market value of health monitoring devices in 2019 was $25,78.56 million and is predicted to soar to $44,861.56 million in 2027[1]. The devices can track multiple values like blood pressure, heart rate, and sleep quality and send them to a web app for visualization. Based on the collected data (called Evidence-based disease management [16,18]) from these sensors, several approaches could detect the corresponding diseases. Furthermore, these devices can monitor users' metrics everywhere due to their portability. Thanks to these gadgets, hospitals can better support their patients, and people can take care of their health more efficiently. However, due to the vast amount of data that can be collected, the use of health-monitoring devices and web apps faces doubt from those value data privacy [14]. Thus, there is a demand for a solution that manages how personal data is collected by health devices and web apps.

Conventionally, users can manually adjust their privacy preferences via web apps' or devices' settings. However, this can be cumbersome and may not be effective. On the other hand, an automated solution that can suggest security settings for a user based on his/her personality or privacy preference can bring better results [28]. In this paper, we introduce our privacy preference prediction solution. Our system learns a user's security perspective and makes suitable suggestions for changing privacy settings.

Due to some economic barriers in developing countries, their citizens lack healthcare services and institutions. Thus, the privacy issues of the medical data are ignored. Currently, there are no medical data protection standards like the developed countries (e.g., European countries - GDPR[2]) to protect the user privacy issues. To address this drawback, our model focuses on individual privacy preferences w.r.t medical data - especially, in developing countries. Our dataset explores the feedback from the developing countries' citizens, e.g., Asia, Africa, and Latin America.

Moreover, most current health systems are focused on protecting users' medical data [23,26]. For example, Son et al. [24] emphasizes the importance of user privacy preferences that are placed alongside the system's privacy policy. This means that the requestor must satisfy both privacy policy and privacy preferences in order to be able to access the patient's medical data. Besides, Hoang et al. [8] provide a mechanism to handle conflicts between the privacy policy and privacy preferences where it depends on prioritizing patient treatment or reducing the risk of personal information leakage. In addition to the above studies, the systems that build smart contract models for medical facilities using Blockchain technology also take care of users' privacy preferences, for example, Nghia et al. [5–7]. In these studies, the patient role was given full discretion in

---

[1] https://www.alliedmarketresearch.com/patient-monitoring-devices-market.

[2] The GDPR document is available at https://edps.europa.eu/data-protection/data-protection/glossary/d_en#data_minimization.

sharing their data with stakeholders. Moreover, the priority of treatment is also exploited in the approach of [13, 25], where patients allow access to their personal data in case of an emergency. Also, in the medical-related system, several studies deployed the individual privacy preference based on blockchain technology (e.g., blood donate [12, 20] or IoT medical sensors [30] via the transmission messages protocol [19]).

To make this suggestion function works, we introduce In2P-Med: an individual privacy preferences w.r.t medical data based on a Machine Learning system, i.e., built based on Semi-Supervised Learning. The reason for choosing the Semi-Supervised Learning method is to be able to reduce the amount of data required while preserving the prediction accuracy. The data for this system was gathered via a questionnaire. This questionnaire aims to learn respondents' perspectives or attitudes toward privacy. We distribute the questions to two types of people. The former type was people who had a background in IT and privacy, such as IT students (i.e., expert participants), while the latter group included various types of people called average users (i.e., normal participants) - see Sect. 5.2. who responded to the questionnaire on the Internet.

The key contributions of this paper are three-fold, including i) designing the individual privacy preferences architecture w.r.t medical data (i.e., In2P-Med - Sect. 3); ii) balancing the user burden and accuracy based on the semi-supervised learning approach (i.e., Implementation - Sect. 4); and iii) proving the effectiveness of the In2P-Med based on the two participant dataset.

2   Related Work

Privacy problems have always been captivating researchers. To discover potential privacy infringement from browsing the Internet with a mobile phone, Collin Mulliner [17] tracked all HTTP headers sent to web services providers. From this activity, he could estimate the amount of covertly leaked personal information. Threats that come from unsecured applications have also been meticulously summarized by Jain et al. in their paper [9].

There have been multiple papers introducing various approaches to adjust privacy preferences dynamically. These proposed approaches do not only apply to applications but also to a wide range of other cases.

By introducing a Context-aware Privacy Policy Language (CPPL), Behrooz et al. [3] aimed to minimize the number of privacy policies that need analysis. In their work, the language filters policies that are relevant to the current scenario using context. The expectation of this research is to enhance the user experience of mobile users in general.

To cope with the issue of ever-changing contexts, Alom et al. [1] proposed a context-based privacy management system that utilizes machine learning algorithms. In their system, privacy preferences for a new context are automatically determined based on existing ones. To be specific, the authors build a classifier that can detect which users' preferences may be changed as well as the extent of that change. Therefore, given a new scenario, the classifier can predict users' choices. In their work, Lin et al. [15] also use machine learning to determine the most appropriate privacy preferences for the users. This is done after the system has created a collection of candidate configurations for a particular user.

Bahirat et al. [2] proposed a data-driven approach to designing privacy-setting profiles for IoT devices. Using scenario-based input, the system generates a collection of default privacy settings for the devices, and it is the responsibility of the users to pick one manually.

Knijnenburg et al. [10] introduced a system that supports privacy decisions by modeling privacy concerns. This approach is also known as user-tailor privacy, in which users are provided with private information and non-invasive controls. However, given the variance in people's perspectives on privacy, creating a general privacy model can be complicated.

There are also methods of adjusting privacy preferences specifically for smartphones. For instance, by taking contextual information into account, Yuan et al. [32] developed a machine learning-based privacy model for sharing photos. In their work, Sanchez et al. [22] developed a privacy preference recommendation system for personalized fitness apps. In their approach, the first profile users' traits and data permission preferences with machine learning clustering algorithms before designing privacy setting recommendation strategies. In their attempts to preserve users' privacy when using health applications, V. Koufi et al. [11] proposed an access control framework used in PHRManager. PHRManager is an Android app that gives authorized users access to Personal Health Records.

3 In2P-Med Architecture

Figure 1 shows the interaction process among the parties in the proposed model, including i) Users; ii) Personal data; iii) People; iv) service providers, and v) In2P-Med. The main roles and responsibilities of these parties in the system are presented as follows:

User (also known as the data owner): they have the right to make a decision whether to share their personal data by responding with consent (Yes) or disagree (No). The data in their possession includes normal data (i.e., easy to share) and personal data (i.e., medical data). **Personal data**: the data that needs to be protected because they are highly identifiable. As a result, a malicious user can obtain other types of user data based on the exploitation of this data pool. This study focused on grouping personal data in the medical environment. Which can be exploited by sensors or smartphones (e.g., heart rate, SPO2, calories burned). **People**: Can act as a user (in some specific cases). **People** represent other users (in the same or not the same system) who have a relationship (e.g., relative, friend,) with the owner of the data. This party can have more than one relationship with the data owner. **Service providers**: the party provides the necessary medical services to users (e.g., health monitoring, disease diagnosis, online doctor)[3]. This target group provides a specific type of health care service; in return, the user must provide the data requested by the service provider. In a traditional environment, users have to provide virtually any type of data to service providers, ignoring privacy risks [29]. Previous studies have shown that applications collect more data than what they need for the supported services [27]. In this paper, any data manipulation request must be accompanied by a corresponding purpose to eliminate this drawback. **In2P-Med**: this party automatically identifies privacy preferences for each individual. Specifically, this model identifies users' privacy behaviors based on their responses to service providers' access requests. Besides, Fig. 1 also depicts five main components of In2P-Med including: data types; relationship(s); context; access request(s); and purpose(s). The relationship between In2P-Med and the remaining parties is presented as follows:

– **Data types**: the types of data (e.g., location, heart rate, etc). In fact, the identification of personal data also depends on the user's sense of privacy. Each individual will make a different decision depending on many factors. It is not possible to define all possible possibilities in this study. So we're targeting the kind of medical data that are being exploited by the user's sensors, wearable devices, and smartphones. To ensure that our survey achieves its stated objectives (i.e., risks of personal information disclosure), we also emphasized in our survey that these medical data can easily be exploited through their device without any notification to the user.
– **Relationship(s)**: This group of attributes also greatly affects the issue of sharing personal data. A user can easily share their walking record (e.g., steps, distance traveled, start and end locations) for a day with his/her friends or personal training etc. Users will share or not share their data depending on each specific relationship.
– **Context**: depending on the specific context, users can (not) share their data regardless of same data type and relationship. For example, in healthcare scenarios (hospitals, clinics), heart rate data can be shared with **People** as healthcare workers (e.g., doctors, nurses); however, same data types and relationships but different contexts (e.g., sports participation) - users can opt-out of sharing. To be able to capture each user's data sharing behavior, we exploit sub-attributes (i.e., data types; relationship(s); access request(s); purpose(s)) on the context-specific (see Sect. 4.3 for more details).
– **Access request(s)**: This component is closely associated with the service provider. In contrast to **People**, where users voluntarily share their data with a specific purpose (i.e., decided by themselves), the data retrieval process for service providers is the opposite. Specifically, the structure must include the party of the request for access (e.g., medical or fitness apps) and the corresponding purpose (discussed in the next section). Users judge between the benefits and risks of privacy to make a decision.

---

[3] The service provider can reserve several services, but we target the medical environment.

– **Purpose(s)**: One of the important pieces of information to decide whether
  users share their data or not is the purpose of access. In particular, a series of
  analyses have shown that requests for supporting the application's service will
  be accepted more than advertising purposes. To clarify this, we also emphasize
  the importance of access intent in our survey scenarios (see Sect. 4.3 for more
  details).

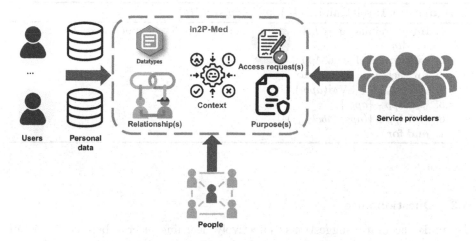

Fig. 1. In2P-Med architecture.

4 Implementation

4.1 Self-training

Self-training or "Self-learning" is the most basic of pseudo-labelling approaches
[31]. They consist of a single supervised classifier that is iteratively trained on
both labeled data and unlabeled data that has been pseudo-labeled in previous
iterations of the algorithm. At the initial procedure, a supervised classifier is
trained on only the labeled data. The outcome of the classifier is used to obtain
predictions for the unlabeled data. Then, the most confident of these predictions
is added to the labeled data set, and the supervised classifier is re-trained on
both the original labeled data and the newly obtained pseudo-labeled data. This
procedure is typically iterated until no more unlabeled data remain.

Several applications and variations of self-training have been put forward.
For instance, Rosenberg et al. [21] applied self-training to object detection problems, and showed improved performance over a state-of-the-art (at that time)
object detection model. Dopido et al. [4] developed a self-training approach for
hyperspectral image classification. They used domain knowledge to select a set of
candidate unlabeled samples, and pseudo-labeled the most informative of these
samples with the predictions made by the trained classifier.

4.2   Algorithm

Algorithm 1 applies self-training model to label the *apps* in *UApp* dataset. Specifically, it applies the SVM algorithm (several supervised methods) to pseudo-label the apps in the unlabeled data set (*UApp*) (see line 4). For the other supervised learning algorithm, we do the same idea.

Algorithm 1: selfTraining(*LApp*,*UApp*,*supAlg*)

1: **input**:training apps *LApp*, target apps *UApp*, list of supervised algorithms *supAlg*.
2: **output**: label for *UApp*.
3: **for** each $app_i \in Uapp$ **do**
4:     $label_{app_i} = \text{SVM}(app_i)$;
5:     $UApp$ - $\{app_i\}$;
6:     $LApp \cup \{(app_i, label_{app_i})\}$;
7: **end for**

4.3   Questionnaire

To make accurate suggestions, effectively learning users' behaviours is of paramount importance. We have meticulously designed a questionnaire for the learning purpose. Our questionnaire focuses on observing how users will adjust their privacy preferences in multiple contexts. To be specific, from our questions, we expect to answer three queries:

1. Given a specific context, how will participants share different types (e.g., heart rate, SPO2, burned calories) of data with other people (e.g., friends, relatives, doctors)?
2. Given a specific context, how will participants share the data for a certain purpose (e.g., analysis, education, ads)?
3. Given a specific context, how will participants share data with service providers (e.g., medical apps, fitness apps)?

For each query, we develop an appropriate type of question. In each question, there are a number of parameters whose values can be activities, individuals, permissions, etc. Participants have three options, they may completely agree, completely disagree or partly agree with the statement.

5   Experiments

5.1   Experiment Setting

In our tests, each participant had to take part in two phases i) they make their choice about whether to share medical data in each context different in the training period ii) they participate in the evaluation of the prediction results from our algorithms and give the satisfaction level of the corresponding algorithms. To achieve this goal, we have developed a web application to satisfy requires interaction with participants through the two phases mentioned above. Specifically, participants label questions that share data during the learning phase (i.e. data set training data), then give their feedback on the labels generated by the models predict in the testing phase (i.e. test data set), and finally rate their satisfaction level on our predictive models.

More precisely, in the first phase, participants were asked to label each sentence ask (i.e. Yes (Y), No (N), or Maybe (M)) about sharing data in each term-specific scene as described in Sect. 4.3. During the training phase, participants have to give answers to all 20 questions over a while. The minimum time is 10 min (an average of 30 s for an answer). After the labelling, the collected training dataset is built using algorithms learning is covered in Subsect. 4.2, specifically the -based approach to supervised learning and semi-supervised learning. To evaluate learning strategies, during the beta phase, the web app displays 20 new questions for those who participate. We randomly select prediction strategies instead of trying to define strategies according to the expected degree of accuracy. The main purpose is to remove all user prejudices about the algorithms in the back, which will be better than the previous algorithms. Specifically, four predictive models (five assessment questions/per model) are applied in this paper, including SVM, Gradient Boosting Classifier, Ada Boost Classifier, and Gradient Boosting Regressor.

For each new question in the experimental phase, the participants gave feedback on the labels, i.e. agree (Y) or disagree (N) - and in the case of disagreement, they must provide the correct label. For example, our forecast label is "Y", but their expected result is "M". They will give feedback on the label as no agree (N) and reselect the outcome they expected. In addition, in the 20 questions at a stage of the test phase, we reused four questions that appeared in the test phase corresponding to four predictive models. Specifically, each prediction model will have four sentences of new questions, and 1 question is randomly selected out of 20 questions during the experimental stage. The main purpose of this work is to divide into two groups of people based on their choices for that question for both periods, specifically, the selection group, the same selection, and the different selection group. The details of this comparison will be presented in Sect. 5.4.1. Finally, we collected the satisfaction level of the participants with the project guesses generated by each model. Participants can answer Yes (100%), No (0%), or Maybe (50%). The average time for answering each question at the test stage was 30 s. So each person participating in the survey must spend at least 20 min completing both learning and testing. To remove unsatisfactory answers, we have set the timer to track participants' time answering questions. If they spent less than the desired time (i.e. less than 30 s for a question), participants could not move on to the next question.

5.2 Participants

The primary purpose of this paper is to build an automatic medical data-sharing model that meets the privacy requirements of the users. We also want to explore the issue of sharing private data in developing countries where privacy is not widely aware of, especially in terms of sensitive data like medical. To achieve the above purposes, we conducted surveys. Our models are in countries in Asia, Africa, and Latin America. Besides that, there is a difference between the survey respondents on security and privacy, we categorized the differences between these two groups of users. Specifically, in the expert user group, we collected feedback from students as well as teachers who are studying and working at FPT University (Vietnam) majoring in Information Security at two campuses in Ho Chi Minh City. Ho Chi Minh City and Can Tho. For the normal user group, we used the tool Microworkers[4] to collect user feedback participants from developing countries.

Expert Users: For expert users (students and teachers of information security), we sent an email to the students who participated in the survey for four weeks (September 2021). There were a total of 20 qualified participants out of 32. The majority of participants were disqualified for not answering enough required questions. The average age of participants is 21.5, with the oldest and youngest being 29 and 18, respectively. Besides, about 15% of the participants were female (3/20).

Normal Users: The main purpose of this user group is to satisfy the requirement of diversity in terms of age, education, gender, and culture. We choose developing countries in two regional groups, including Latin America and Asia-Africa. We got 209 valid responses out of 296 participants. Each participant was paid $3. The number of participants belonging to the above two regional groups is 85 and 124, respectively. The mean age is 31.06 (minimum is 18 and oldest is 70) and 28.29 (the smallest age is 18 and the largest is 59). Out of a total of 85 responses, 42 were female (49.41%). The number for Asia-Africa is 25.6% (32 out of 125 participants).

5.3 Confusion Matrix

We used conventional measures to evaluate the accuracy of the proposed learning methods. Specifically, we exploited the 3X3 confusion matrix corresponding to the three labels (Y, N and M) (Table 1), where the columns represent the predicted labels (generated from approaches) and possible rows of values actual (participant opinion) and cells represent Error (E) or True Positive (TP). From the confusion matrix, we determined the evaluable metrics given in Table 2.

---

[4] https://www.microworkers.com/.

Table 1. Confusion matrix

	Predicted value: Y	Predicted value: N	Predicted value: M
Actual value: Y	TP_Y	$E_{Y,N}$	$E_{Y,M}$
Actual value: N	$E_{N,Y}$	TP_N	$E_{N,M}$
Actual value: M	$E_{M,Y}$	$E_{M,N}$	TP_M

Table 2. Metrics definition

$Accuracy$	$(TP_Y + TP_N + TP_M)/\#samples$
Pre_Y	$TP_Y/(TP_Y + E_{N,Y} + E_{M,Y})$
Pre_N	$TP_N/(TP_N + E_{Y,N} + E_{M,N})$
Pre_M	$TP_M/(TP_M + E_{Y,M} + E_{N,M})$
Re_Y	$TP_Y/(TP_Y + E_Y, N + E_{Y,M})$
Re_N	$TP_N/(TP_N + E_{N,Y} + E_{N,M})$
Re_M	$TP_M/(TP_M + E_{M,Y} + E_{M,N})$
$F1_X$	$2* (Pre_X * Re_X)/(Pre_X + Re_X)$, where $X \in \{Y, N, M\}$

5.4   Evaluation

In the evaluation, we performed a series of measurements to find the most appropriate algorithm in detecting the sharing behavior of personal medical data, given a specific context. Specifically, in the first test, we compared the accuracy obtained by different learning approaches (specifically between supervised learning and semi-supervised learning). We first compared the semi-supervised soft clustering method and the hard clustering techniques. This comparison aims to evaluate whether a semi-supervised system has good accuracy even with a reduced training set.

In the second test, we compared the accuracy of the proposed prediction models, namely SVM, Gradient Boosting Classifier, Ada Boost Classifier, and Gradient Boosting Regressor. As the results displayed in Sect. 5.4.1, the semi-supervised-based approach gave better results than the supervised approach. Therefore, we apply the semi-supervised model to all four proposed algorithms.

Supervised Learning and Semi-supervised Learning Comparison. In this section, in addition to demonstrating which approaches (in particular supervised learning and semi-supervised learning) provide better prediction results with small data sets, we also wanted to test the difference between homogeneous and heterogeneous user groups in terms of data sharing decisions.

To achieve the above goals, we first compare the accuracy between supervised learning and semi-supervised learning approaches by building a training set that is a subset of the original training set (with 10, instead of 20 questions). Specifically, in the new dataset, the number of questions in the shuttered train is ten and in the test set is 30 (including ten questions transferred from the

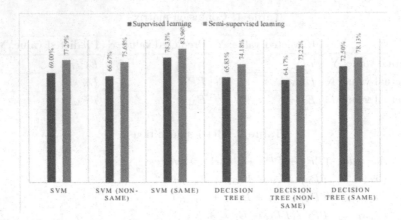

Fig. 2. The accuracy of SVM and Decision tree in supervised and semisupervised learning approaches.

train set). The main purpose for this reallocation of questions is that we wanted to aim for an approach that can balance the effort spent by the user to build the training set and the accuracy of the applied algorithm. A good approach that can satisfy the above criteria is the one that only has a small number of questions in the training set and ensures an acceptable accuracy. To meet the above requirements, we used a semi-supervised learning approach for the SVM algorithm, decision tree, and supervised learning for both SVM and Decision tree. We compared the accuracy of the SVM algorithm for both approaches as well as two different algorithms (SVM and decision tree) to get the most general view when choosing strategies to build predictive models.

Figure 2 shows the accuracy between SVM and Decision tree on both approaches: semi- and supervised learning. It shows that the semi-supervised-based approach is always better than supervised learning for both SVM and Decision tree algorithms as well as groups of participants (same and non-same). SVM algorithm has higher accuracy than the Decision tree for all cases. Besides, the Same answer group has the highest accuracy in each algorithm. This proves that the approach based on semi-supervised learning gives high accuracy even when trained on a small data set. In the following section, we apply a semi-supervised learning approach to delve into the analysis of accuracy, F1 score as well as the satisfaction of survey participants.

Answer Prediction Model Accuracy. Figure 3 depicts the accuracy of four predictive models for all three datasets (expert, Asia-Africa, and Latin America). The group with the lowest accuracy was experts from 60–71%, while the highest accuracy group was the group of participants from Asia-Africa and Latin America from 76.20% to 83.81%. This proves that the behavior of the user group is often easier to capture than the expert user group. Indeed, based on a manual analysis of users' comments on the reasons for their choice, we found that the difference between the two groups of users lies in the context of sharing personal data in the medical environment. In the case of ordinary users, they only care about the object to be shared or the type of data requested. Meanwhile, the experts evaluated all 3 groups of data, the shared audience, and especially their context. In particular, they are very careful when sharing high-risk data (motion data, location) with any individual (including relatives and friends). On the other hand, user groups are often more comfortable sharing personal data. They are willing to trade personal information to choose the services or utilities that the services or applications bring. Moreover, they trust the personal data protection mechanism of the service or application as well as the group of people who share it closely (relatives, friends).

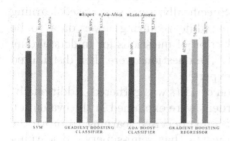

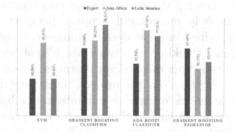

Fig. 3. Accuracy level of four classification models.

Fig. 4. Satisfaction level of four classification models.

Satisfaction Level. This section evaluates the satisfaction level of four prediction algorithms for all three datasets. Specifically, all approaches have high satisfaction for all three datasets (from 90% to 98.81%). The algorithm with the highest satisfaction is the Gradient Boosting classifier (95%–98.81%). Meanwhile, the algorithm with the lowest satisfaction level is SVM (95%–98.81%). This experiment proves that the semi-supervised learning-based approach brings about a high level of satisfaction for all three groups of participants.

Table 3. Comparison of the four prediction models for the test dataset.

		Approach 1			Approach 2			Approach 3			Approach 4		
		Y (%)	N (%)	M (%)	Y (%)	N (%)	M (%)	Y (%)	N (%)	M (%)	Y (%)	N (%)	M (%)
Expert-based	Precision	75.86%	55.10%	72.73%	88.46%	63.64%	66.67%	90.91%	41.18%	70.37%	NaN	62.99%	NaN
participants	Recall	62.86%	77.14%	53.33%	67.65%	75.68%	68.97%	60.61%	72.41%	50.00%	0.00%	100.00%	0.00%
(N=20)	F1	68.75%	64.29%	61.54%	76.67%	69.14%	67.80%	72.73%	52.50%	58.16%	NaN	76.54%	NaN
Crowd-based in Latin	Precision	85.00%	75.63%	87.65%	90.75%	73.17%	80.00%	86.29%	78.00%	75.00%	NaN	78.57%	NaN
American participants	Recall	92.12%	83.33%	65.14%	92.37%	83.33%	62.92%	95.54%	75.73%	58.06%	0.00%	100.00%	0.00%
(N=85)	F1	88.42%	79.30%	74.74%	91.56%	77.92%	70.44%	90.68%	76.85%	65.46%	NaN	88.00%	NaN
Crowd-based in Asia	Precision	89.07%	57.48%	84.47%	87.79%	62.81%	87.63%	90.15%	61.29%	83.53%	NaN	76.20%	NaN
-Africa participants	Recall	93.30%	71.57%	60.00%	93.50%	78.63%	56.29%	96.75%	72.38%	54.20%	0.00%	100.00%	0.00%
(N=124)	F1	91.13%	63.76%	70.16%	90.56%	69.83%	68.55%	93.33%	66.38%	65.74%	NaN	86.49%	NaN

F1 Score. Finally, we measured the score F_1 for each label (Y, N, M) in all three datasets (Expert, Asia-Africa, America Latin). The F_1 score considers both the precision and the recall aspect (see Table 1). There is a difference in approach four compared to the other approaches: this algorithm does not correctly predict any Yes or No answer options, but only predicts all possible answer options. This can be seen as a minus when applied to these models to identify user behavior in complex contexts.

6   Conclusion

This paper has introduced In2P-Med, a solution on how to learn users' privacy preferences and suggest appropriate settings for medical data (i.e., health-monitoring devices and apps scenarios). Specifically, semi-supervised learning can help understand people's perspectives while requiring fewer data to be explained in great detail. Moreover, a collection of questions for understanding users' thinking on privacy was also shown. The questions were then distributed to two types of participants (normal and expert).

At the end of the project, the satisfaction of users was gathered. Additionally, four models on how to minimize users' burdens were explained in the evaluation section. In this section, we also compare semi-supervised learning to prove the effectiveness of our model. The result indicates that semi-supervised learning can potentially conserve users' privacy.

The paper is the first attempt toward a user-centric model for healthcare systems, so it is extremely urgent to identify future development directions. Specifically, we plan to analyze user behavior to build a set of privacy settings recommendations for new users to apply to the medical system. A blockchain-based solution is a potential option to validate service providers' claims about how much data mining is required. On the other hand, an extensive and in-depth study (e.g., increasing the number of participants, compared with users in developing countries) will also be launched soon.

Acknowledgement. This work would not have been possible without the support of Mr. Le Thanh Tuan in implementation and evaluation process. We also express our sincere gratitude to the students and crowd-workers who joined our survey.

References

1. Alom, M.Z., et al.: Helping users managing context-based privacy preferences. In: 2019 IEEE International Conference on Services Computing (SCC), pp. 100–107. IEEE (2019)
2. Bahirat, P., He, Y., Menon, A., Knijnenburg, B.: A data-driven approach to developing IoT privacy-setting interfaces. In: 23rd International Conference on Intelligent User Interfaces, pp. 165–176 (2018)

3. Behrooz, A., Devlic, A.: A context-aware privacy policy language for controlling access to context information of mobile users. In: Prasad, R., Farkas, K., Schmidt, A.U., Lioy, A., Russello, G., Luccio, F.L. (eds.) MobiSec 2011. LNICST, vol. 94, pp. 25–39. Springer, Heidelberg (2012). https://doi.org/10.1007/978-3-642-30244-2_3

4. Dópido, I., Li, J., Marpu, P.R., Plaza, A., Dias, J.M.B., Benediktsson, J.A.: Semisupervised self-learning for hyperspectral image classification. IEEE Trans. Geosci. Remote Sens. **51**(7), 4032–4044 (2013)

5. Duong-Trung, N., Quynh, N., Tang, T., Ha, X.: Interpretation of machine learning models for medical diagnosis. Adv. Sci. Technol. Eng. Syst. J. **5**(5), 469–477 (2020)

6. Duong-Trung, N., Son, H.X., Le, H.T., Phan, T.T.: On components of a patient-centered healthcare system using smart contract. In: Proceedings of International Conference on Cryptography, Security and Privacy, pp. 31–35 (2020)

7. Duong-Trung, N., Son, H.X., Le, H.T., Phan, T.T.: Smart care: integrating blockchain technology into the design of patient-centered healthcare systems. In: Proceedings of the 4th International Conference on Cryptography, Security and Privacy, pp. 105–109. ICCSP 2020 (2020)

8. Hoang, N.M., Son, H.X.: A dynamic solution for fine-grained policy conflict resolution. In: Proceedings of the 3rd International Conference on Cryptography, Security and Privacy, pp. 116–120 (2019)

9. Jain, A.K.: Addressing security and privacy risks in mobile applications. IT Prof. **14**(5), 28–33 (2012). othes

10. Knijnenburg, B.P.: Privacy? I can't even! making a case for user-tailored privacy. IEEE Secur. Priv. **15**(4), 62–67 (2017)

11. Koufi, V., et al.: Privacy-preserving mobile access to personal health records through Google's android. In: 2014 MOBIHEALTH, pp. 347–347. IEEE (2014)

12. Le, H.T., Nguyen, T.T.L., Nguyen, T.A., Ha, X.S., Duong-Trung, N.: Bloodchain: a blood donation network managed by blockchain technologies. Network **2**(1), 21–35 (2022)

13. Le, H.T., et al.: Patient-Chain: patient-centered healthcare system a blockchain-based technology in dealing with emergencies. In: Shen, H., et al. (eds.) PDCAT 2021. LNCS, vol. 13148, pp. 576–583. Springer, Cham (2022). https://doi.org/10.1007/978-3-030-96772-7_54

14. Lim, S., Oh, T.H., Choi, Y.B., Lakshman, T.: Security issues on wireless body area network for remote healthcare monitoring. In: International Conference on Sensor Networks, Ubiquitous, and Trustworthy Computing, pp. 327–332. IEEE (2010)

15. Lin, J., Liu, B., Sadeh, N., Hong, J.I.: Modeling users' mobile app privacy preferences: restoring usability in a sea of permission settings. In: 10th Symposium On Usable Privacy and Security ({SOUPS} 2014), pp. 199–212 (2014)

16. Luong, H.H., et al.: Feature Selection Using Correlation Matrix on Metagenomic Data with Pearson Enhancing Inflammatory Bowel Disease Prediction. In: Ibrahim, R., Porkumaran, K., Kannan, R., Mohd Nor, N., Prabakar, S. (eds.) International Conference on Artificial Intelligence for Smart Community. LNEE, vol. 758, pp. 1073–1084. Springer, Singapore (2022). https://doi.org/10.1007/978-981-16-2183-3_102

17. Mulliner, C.: Privacy leaks in mobile phone internet access. In: 2010 14th International Conference on Intelligence in Next Generation Networks, pp. 1–6. IEEE (2010)

18. Nguyen, H.T., et al.: Enhancing inflammatory bowel disease diagnosis performance using chi-squared algorithm on metagenomic data. In: Anh, N.L., Koh,

SJ., Nguyen, T.D.L., Lloret, J., Nguyen, T.T. (eds.) Intelligent Systems and Networks. LNNS, vol. 471, pp. 669–678. Springer, Singapore (2022). https://doi.org/10.1007/978-981-19-3394-3_77

19. Nguyen, L.T.T., et al.: BMDD: a novel approach for IoT platform (broker-less and microservice architecture, decentralized identity, and dynamic transmission messages). PeerJ Comput. Sci. **8**, e950 (2022)

20. Quynh, N.T.T., et al.: Toward a design of blood donation management by blockchain technologies. In: Gervasi, O., et al. (eds.) ICCSA 2021. LNCS, vol. 12956, pp. 78–90. Springer, Cham (2021). https://doi.org/10.1007/978-3-030-87010-2_6

21. Rosenberg, C., et al.: Semi-supervised self-training of object detection models (2005)

22. Sanchez, O.R., Torre, I., He, Y., Knijnenburg, B.P.: A recommendation approach for user privacy preferences in the fitness domain. User Model. User-Adapted Interact. 1–53 (2019)

23. Son, H.X., Chen, E.: Towards a fine-grained access control mechanism for privacy protection and policy conflict resolution. Int. J. Adv. Comput. Sci. Appl. **10**(2) (2019)

24. Son, H.X., Hoang, N.M.: A novel attribute-based access control system for fine-grained privacy protection. In: Proceedings of the 3rd International Conference on Cryptography, Security and Privacy, pp. 76–80 (2019)

25. Son, H.X., Le, T.H., Quynh, N.T.T., Huy, H.N.D., Duong-Trung, N., Luong, H.H.: Toward a blockchain-based technology in dealing with emergencies in patient-centered healthcare systems. In: Bouzefrane, S., Laurent, M., Boumerdassi, S., Renault, E. (eds.) MSPN 2020. LNCS, vol. 12605, pp. 44–56. Springer, Cham (2021). https://doi.org/10.1007/978-3-030-67550-9_4

26. Son, H.X., Nguyen, M.H., Vo, H.K., Nguyen, T.P.: Toward an privacy protection based on access control model in hybrid cloud for healthcare systems. In: Martínez Álvarez, F., Troncoso Lora, A., Sáez Muñoz, J.A., Quintián, H., Corchado, E. (eds.) CISIS/ICEUTE -2019. AISC, vol. 951, pp. 77–86. Springer, Cham (2020). https://doi.org/10.1007/978-3-030-20005-3_8

27. Son, H.X., et al.: A risk assessment mechanism for android apps. In: International Conference on Smart Internet of Things, pp. 237–244. IEEE (2021)

28. Son, H.X., et al.: PriApp-Install: learning user privacy preferences on mobile apps' installation. In: Su, C., Gritzalis, D., Piuri, V. (eds.) Information Security Practice and Experience. ISPEC 2022. LNCS, vol. 13620, pp. 306–323. Springer, Cham (2022). https://doi.org/10.1007/978-3-031-21280-2_17

29. Son, H.X., et al.: A risk estimation mechanism for android apps based on hybrid analysis. Data Sci. Eng. **7**(3), 242–252 (2022)

30. Thanh, L.N.T., et al.: IoHT-MBA: an internet of healthcare things (IoHT) platform based on microservice and brokerless architecture. Int. J. Adv. Comput. Sci. Appl. **12**(7) (2021)

31. Triguero, I., et al.: Self-labeled techniques for semi-supervised learning: taxonomy, software and empirical study. Knowl. Inf. Syst. **42**(2), 245–284 (2015)

32. Yuan, L., Theytaz, J., Ebrahimi, T.: Context-dependent privacy-aware photo sharing based on machine learning. In: De Capitani di Vimercati, S., Martinelli, F. (eds.) SEC 2017. IAICT, vol. 502, pp. 93–107. Springer, Cham (2017). https://doi.org/10.1007/978-3-319-58469-0_7

User Behaviour Characterization

Hierarchical Transformers for User Semantic Similarity

Marco Di Giovanni(iD) and Marco Brambilla(✉)(iD)

Politecnico di Milano, Milan, Italy
{marco.digiovanni,marco.brambilla}@polimi.it

Abstract. The investigation of users' behaviour on Web and Social Media platforms usually requires to analyze many heterogeneous features, such as shared textual content, social connections, demographic traits, and temporal attributes. This work aims to compute accurate user similarities on Twitter just using the textual content shared by users, a feature known to be easy and quick to collect. We design and train a 2-stages hierarchical Transformer-based model, whose first stage independently elaborates single tweets, and its second stage combines the embeddings of the tweets to obtain user-level representations. To evaluate our model we design a ranking task involving many accounts, automatically collected and labeled without the need for human annotators. We extensively investigate hyper-parameters to obtain the best model configuration. Finally, we check whether the obtained embeddings reflect our idea of similarity by testing them on further tasks, including community visualization, outlier detection, and polarization quantification.

1 Introduction

Nowadays social media take significant parts of the lives of a large number of people, as the increasing number of active users and shared content testifies.

The analysis of users' behaviours on social media platforms became an important branch of research since it allows customization of the overall personal experience [7]. User profiling helps in recommendations [9,10] as well as detection of profile duplicates [24] and social threats [18].

Computing user similarity often requires heterogeneous information about users. Examples of selected features are the *textual-content* shared by users [16], the *social graphs* involving users (e.g., the follower/friend graph, the mention graph, or more advanced alternatives) [10], *shared links* and their source [22], and so on.

However, the definition of similarity between users is not straightforward and becomes even more challenging when multiple kinds of features are involved. In this work we investigate how using only the textual content shared by users can lead to accurate similarity measures.

The main advantage of working on textual data, independently of the underlying social graph that is commonly used in previous works, is that the former

I. Garrigós et al. (Eds.): ICWE 2023, LNCS 13893, pp. 143–157, 2023.
https://doi.org/10.1007/978-3-031-34444-2_11

approach can detect similarities even between users that are far apart from each other or even belonging to different connected components of the graph. Moreover, the complete social graph is usually expensive to build due both to the magnitude of active users in the main social networks, and also because this information is usually slow and expensive to extract. Finally, our approach can easily adapt to many text-based social networks, such as Twitter, Facebook, and Reddit, while the graph structure is more dependent on the platform.

We select *Twitter* as the Social Networking to investigate since it is worldwide used to communicate and stay informed, and it mainly relies on textual data. Our goal is to compute user embeddings that accurately reflect their semantic similarities. We train hierarchical models to map the textual content of tweets shared by users into high-dimensional dense vectors. We expect our map to transform similar users into vectors close to each other.

In this work, we exploit the recent successes of NLP to generate high-dimensional semantic embeddings such as Transformer-based models [26] like BERT [6] or GPT-3 [5], applied to users to encode similarities. We use Transformer-based models, previously pre-trained on Twitter texts, in a hierarchical approach [19]. We train our models with a triplet-like loss [13], where we minimize the distance between positive pairs of users and maximize the distance between negative ones. One of the main differences compared to previous works [16,21,22,24], where a careful manual selection of small collections of users is likely to bias the results, is that we evaluate the models on a large set of users automatically obtained from Twitter. We can accomplish this due to a carefully designed evaluation process that does not require manually annotated labels. We compare our models with baselines, and we extensively investigate the hyper-parameters to obtain the best configuration overall.

We formulate and answer the following research questions: **(RQ1)**: How can we evaluate the best model to compute semantic user similarity in a fully reproducible approach without influencing the results with biased selections of small sets of users? **(RQ2)**: How can we apply to tens of posts a Transformer-based model, widely known to be effective on single texts or pairs of texts with limited length? **(RQ3)**: Do the obtained embeddings reflect our idea of similarity? Can we use them for further tasks?

Our contribution can be summarized as follows: *(i)* We collect a large dataset of Twitter users, we design an automatic labelling approach, and we share the code and the parameters to reproduce it; *(ii)* We train and release a Hierarchical Language Model to compute accurate user similarity; *(iii)* We extensively investigate hyper-parameters to obtain the best configuration of the model; and *(iv)* We test whether the obtained embeddings are accurate when applied to other tasks.

The structure of the paper is the following: we summarize related works in Sect. 2, we describe how we collected and cleaned our dataset in Sect. 3, we show our approach and the selected baselines in Sect. 4, we report and discuss results in Sect. 5 and we inspect the obtained embeddings in Sect. 6. We conclude in Sect. 7.

2   Related Work

In this section, we summarize the related works about user similarity and state-of-the-art language models. To the best of our knowledge, no previous studies applied Transformer-based Language Models to user profiling and similarity.

User Profiling and Similarity. User profiling is a research field whose purpose is to profile users of a platform to personalize their experience. We distinguish between approaches relying on multiple heterogeneous features (Comprehensive) and approaches based solely on content.

Comprehensive approaches require multiple features to compute similarities. These approaches are often slower and their performance is not guaranteed to be higher since similarity is usually poorly defined in this context. Twitter research team first proposed *Who-To-Follow* [10] approach, whose goal is to recommend potential users to follow. It is based on common connections and shared interests. The core of the architecture is Cassovary, a graph-processing engine that implements the main graph recommendation algorithms, applied to the Twitter "follow" graph. They also proposed a *similar-to* framework [9] where similar users are detected by comparing four signals: cosine follow score, number of suggestions' followers, page rank score, and historic follow-through rate. An alternative approach [27] is designed to include Affinity Propagation to obtain communities. Similar users are defined with several metrics based on many different features. TSIM is another system for discovering similar users on Twitter [1], that quickly detects users similar to a specific user by computing seven different signals.

Content-based approaches are preferred since usually content of tweets is quickly available and the definition of textual similarity has been recently largely investigated. Our proposed approach is content-based and we define similar users as users that share semantically similar tweets. Twitter-based User Modeling Service (**TUMS**) [25] is a service that generates semantic user profiles by exploiting tweets and producing a list of topics or entities a user was interested in at a specific point in time. The approach [16] works by building a network representing semantic relationships between words occurring in the same tweet. The graph is exploited to compute network centrality measures and finally, user similarity is computed with cosine similarity. Finally, an interesting approach defines content-based similarities to detect Twitter communities with syntactic and semantic feature vectors [21]. The authors apply TF-iDF vectorizations on different kinds of words and also vectorized users through topic analysis (LDA) incorporating the semantics of tweets. We compared our approach to theirs in the Evaluation Section.

One of the most important differences between our study and previous works is the magnitude of the number of users involved in the experiments, without the need of human annotators, thanks to the carefully designed evaluation strategy.

Language Models. Language models became popular after the surprisingly accurate performances of *BERT* [6], a deep Transformer-based [26] model pre-trained in an unsupervised way on large corpora of text using two self-supervised techniques: Masked Language Models (MLM) task and Next Sentence Prediction (NSP) task. *RoBERTa* [15] is an improved pre-training of BERT-base architecture, including dynamic masking, Next Sentence Prediction formats, larger batch size, and a BPE vocabulary of $50K$ subwords units. *BERTweet base* [17] is a BERT-base model pre-trained using the same approach as RoBERTa on $850M$ English Tweets, outperforming previous SOTA on Tweet NLP tasks. *Sentence BERT* [23] are BERT-base models trained with siamese or triplet approaches on Natural Language Inference (NLI) and Semantic Textual Similarity (STS) data. We select a suggested base model from the full list of trained models: stsb-roberta-base-v2 (S-RoBERTa). **Twitter4SSE** exploits Twitter's intrinsic powerful signals of relatedness (quotes and replies) to generate semantically similar embeddings training a Transformer model with a triplet approach [8].

Many alternatives have been proposed to process **long texts** with variations of BERT [2,28]. An alternative is performed by using a hierarchical approach to process long texts through **Hierarchical Transformers** [19] that combine chunks of long texts into a single embedding.

3   Data Collection and Preprocessing

In this section we briefly describe how we collected and cleaned raw data, and the selection of users to include in the training and evaluation datasets. We focus on the first research question **(RQ1)** while designing an approach to build large datasets in a fully reproducible way.

Data Collection. We select Twitter as the social media platform on which we perform our analyses, but the whole approach and experiments can be easily transferred to other platforms with a few small changes. Retweets typically indicate endorsement [3]: when a user retweets another user, it typically agrees with the content of the retweeted post. We use this feature to build our groundtruth for similar users: two users are similar if at least one of them retweeted at least once a tweet shared by the other. We remove clear exceptions of extreme behaviours, such as users that retweeted by too many users, in the cleaning phase. This similarity assumption is not always true when *quotes* are involved instead of retweets, since the original comment attached to the tweet could include criticisms and objections to the original tweet.

We build our dataset from *Archive Team Twitter*[1]. We do not download tweets from Twitter official API since it does not guarantee reproducible results: the same request made at different times and by different accounts could result in different collected data. We remark that we do not include sensitive information in our analysis. The full approach involves only the textual content shared by users, cleaned as described later by removing the screen names of users. We use

---

[1] https://archive.org/details/twitterstream.

the ids of users only to group tweets shared by the same user. We select English tweets, filtered accordingly to the "lang" field provided by Twitter, posted in November and December 2020. They amount to about 27 GB of compressed data. We collect texts of tweets, including replies and quotes but excluding retweets, and ids of users that posted them, and, in parallel, we collected pairs of ids of users if one of them retweeted the other. This second collection is performed to obtain a groundtruth of similar users, since we assumed that users that retweet each other are similar. We collected a total amount of $38M$ tweets and $95M$ pairs of users from retweets.

Data Cleaning. Before performing any analysis, we clean the obtained texts, since tweets are known to be extremely noisy. We remove mentions (appearing as the symbol @ followed by a screen name) and URLs, frequently attached to tweets. We standardize spaces replacing tabs, newlines, and multiple consecutive spaces with a single whitespace and we lowercase the full texts. Finally, we remove texts shorter than 20 characters, since they are too short and do not contain enough information to be processed. After the cleaning procedure about $29M$ texts tweeted by $10M$ unique users remain. Since we collected data tweeted during a 2-months window, we remove users that posted too many tweets, since they may be bots. We set the maximum number of tweets to 60 (about 1 per day). We also remove users with less than 5 tweets collected, as we do not have enough information to perform the following analysis on them. We obtain $1.4M$ different users that we define *Good Users*. We also clean the connections between users, removing from pairs of ids of users retweeting each other, and the auto-retweets (when a user retweets one of its own tweets), duplicate pairs (when a user retweets more than once another user or when two users both retweet each other) and pairs where at least one of the users in not what we have previously defined as Good User. Finally, we remove users with more than 50 connections, since those accounts contradict our assumption of user similarity given from retweet connections because they retweet or are retweeted too much to be considered similar to all of the other users. We finally obtain about $1.9M$ connections between $950k$ unique users.

Training and Evaluation. We split the dataset for *training and evaluating* the approach. We first generate our evaluation dataset by randomly selecting 5k users (out of the about 50k users with at least 5 connections), each one paired with 5 randomly selected users from the connected ones. Our final evaluation benchmark consists of comparing a user with 30 other candidate users, 5 of them considered similar to it since they share at least one retweet connection, and 25 of them considered not similar, randomly selected among the other users. We remove connections involving the previously selected users and we create the training set with the remaining pairs of connected users. From each user, we collect the first n tweets posted. This number is analyzed in detail in the Evaluation Section and defines the final size of the training dataset.

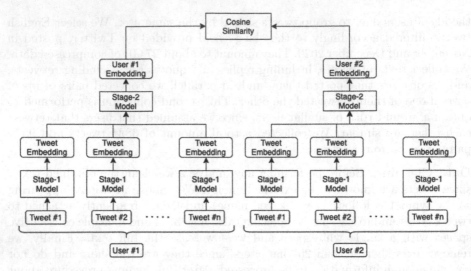

Fig. 1. Schema of the Hierarchical approaches.

4 Methodology

In this section, we describe our hierarchical approaches and some baselines. We also include brief technical details to support complete reproducibility of the results. Our approach is inspired by [19], where the authors build a hierarchical model to process long documents. They exploit a hierarchical approach to process a long single document that cannot fit into a standard BERT architecture due to length limitations. Instead, our data are multiple short documents (i.e., texts of tweets) from the same user, which naturally fits the hierarchical structure. Thus we answer the second research question (**RQ2**) by building a hierarchical Transformer-based approach. Our hierarchical approaches are composed of two stages: a *tweet embedding* stage and a *user embedding* stage. The complete pipeline is shown in Fig. 1.

Stage-1: Tweet Embedding. We obtain embedding of tweets using one of the following four Transformer-based models that share the same architecture but are pretrained with different approaches and datasets: *RoBERTa*[2], *BERTweet*[3], *Sentence BERT*[4], and *Twitter4SSE*[5].

We test them by freezing and unfreezing their weights during the training step. BERTweet and Twitter4SSE models, being pretrained on texts from Twitter, are able to successfully deal with the intrinsic noise of data from social media, thus no further special cleaning is required (such as dealing with hashtags, abbreviations, and typos).

---

[2] https://huggingface.co/roberta-base.
[3] https://huggingface.co/vinai/bertweet-base.
[4] https://huggingface.co/sentence-transformers/stsb-roberta-base-v2.
[5] https://huggingface.co/digio/Twitter4SSE.

Stage-2: User Embedding. We test three techniques to process Twitter embeddings to generate accurate user embeddings:

- **MEAN:** the simplest approach to merge tweet embeddings into a fixed size vector representing user embeddings is to compute their MEAN. This approach can be performed without limits on the number of tweets n per user when the weights of the Stage-1 model are frozen (no training is performed when we select this variant). However we test this approach also unfreezing the weights of the Stage-1 model, thus we limit the number of tweets per user, also for a fair comparison with other variants;
- **Recurrence over BERT (RoBERT):** the embeddings of tweets are used as input of a Recurrent Model. We select a 2-layer LSTM model with hidden size of 768.[6] We use the last output as the user embedding. We test this approach both freezing and unfreezing the weights of the Stage-1 model;
- **Transformer over BERT (ToBERT):** the embeddings of tweets are used as input of a Transformer Model with 2 encoding layers (EL) and 2 decoding layers (DL), 16 heads, and 0.1 dropout. We also experimented with a model with 1 encoding and 1 decoding layer and without dropout (more details are reported below). Transformers output one embedding for each input, so we select the MEAN of all output embeddings as the user embedding. We test this approach both freezing and unfreezing the weights of the Stage-1 model.

To evaluate our proposal, we compare our approaches with two simple non-hierarchical alternatives:

- **TF-iDF:** Term Frequency-inverse Document Frequency is a classical vectorizer of documents belonging to a corpus. It can be applied to documents of any length. We consider the concatenation of the tweets of a single user as a single document. We use the TfidfVectorizer implemented in scikit-learn [20], testing with or without bigrams, with or without English stopwords and different values of minimum document frequency. We report results of the best set of hyperparameters.
- **Naive Transformers:** similar to TF-iDF, we consider a single document the concatenation of the tweets of a single user. We tokenize the documents and use them as inputs to a Transformer model, which truncates them at 128 tokens. We test four Transformer models previously described.

We select **Multiple Negative Loss (MNLoss)** [12] as our loss funcion for every trainable model: given a batch of positive pairs of users $(a_1, p_1), ..., (a_n, p_n)$, we assume that (a_i, p_j) is a negative pair for $i \neq j$ (i.e., we assume that a user did not retweet posts from any of the other $n - 1$ users). This assumption is valid for small batches due to the big total number of users and the approach selected to collect data. We use AdamW optimizer, learning rate 2×10^{-5}, linear scheduler with 10% warmup steps on a single NVIDIA Tesla P100.

---

[6] Preliminary experiments with different number of layers show evident advantages with respect to a single layer architecture, but not clear improvements when using deeper architectures.

5   Evaluation

In this section we report and discuss results of our models compared to variants and baselines to find the best approach overall. When not stated differently, we use 20 tweets per user, thus $124k$ pairs of users in the training set. More details about dataset sizes are reported in Fig. 2.

We evaluate the models by comparing three metrics, commonly used for similar tasks. These metrics evaluate different aspects of the rankings and we generally obtain compatible scores.

- **Mean Average Precision (MAP)** between the binary labels (connected or not connected by retweets) and the similarities. It summarizes a precision-recall curve. In this setting, it ranges from 0.17 when the 5 connected candidates receive similarity score of 0 and the 25 not connected candidates receive similarity score of 1, to 1, when the similarities are the opposite;
- **Mean Reciprocal Rank (MRR) @k** is a ranking quality measure defined as the reciprocal of the rank of the first relevant element, if not greater than k. We set $k = 10$. MRR@10 ranges from 0, if none of the 5 connected users are ranked in one of the first 10 positions, to 1 if the most similar user is connected;
- **normalized Discounted Cumulative Gain (nDCG)** [14] is a ranking-quality metric obtained normalizing Discounted Cumulative Gain (DCG). In this setting the scores range from 0.35 to 1, the higher the better. Thus, 1 represents a perfect ranking: the first ranked document is the most relevant one, the second-ranked document is the second most relevant one, and so on.

Stage-1 Model Comparison. Firstly we investigate the best initialization model. For each experiment, we keep the same hyper-parameters and the same Stage-2 model is trained on top of it: ToBERT with 2 encoding layers (EL) and 2 decoding layers (DL), 0.1 dropout, and MEAN pooling. We test RoBERTa, BERTweet, S-RoBERTa, and Twitter4SSE. Table 1 shows that Twitter4SSE is the best initialization. As expected, this model, trained to generate accurate tweet embeddings, outperforms both the model trained on Tweets using only MLM (BERTweet) and the model trained to generate accurate sentence embeddings on formal data (S-RoBERTa).

MEAN Stage-2 Models Comparison. We test the MEAN Stage-2 approach on the four Stage-1 models with and without freezing their weights. Table 2 shows that unfreezing the weights leads to better results, even if the batch size has to be reduced to 10 and the number of tokens per tweet is reduced to 32 to fit in memory. We confirm that the best Stage-1 model is Twitter4SSE for these configurations too.

ToBERT Hyperparameter Comparison. We investigate the best hyperparameter configuration of the Stage-2 Transformer model (ToBERT). We investigate with 1 and 2 encoding and decoding layers (EL-DL), with and without

Table 1. Comparison of Stage-1 models.

Model	MAP	MRRO10	nDCG
RoBERTa	81.1	94.2	90.8
BERTweet	83.7	95.3	92.2
S-RoBERTa	81.3	94.4	91.0
Twitter4SSE	**84.2**	**95.6**	**92.4**

Table 3. Comparison of ToBERT Stage-2 models.

Model	EL-DL D	MAP	MRR@10	nDCG
ToBERT 1-1	0.1	84.3	95.8	92.6
ToBERT 2-2	0	**84.5**	**96.0**	**92.7**
ToBERT 2-2	0.1	84.2	95.6	92.4

Table 2. Comparison of MEAN Stage-2 models.

Stage-1	Frozen	MAP	MRR@10	nDCG
RoBERTa	yes	33.3	64.0	60.1
S-RoBERTa	yes	33.2	63.8	60.1
BERTweet	yes	33.3	63.7	60.7
Twitter4SSE	yes	33.3	64.0	60.1
RoBERTa	no	80.8	94.3	90.7
S-RoBERTa	no	81.2	94.7	91.0
BERTweet	no	83.1	95.3	91.9
Twitter4SSE	no	**83.6**	**95.8**	**92.3**

Table 4. Full Comparison of Models and Baselines.

Model	MAP	MRR@10	nDCG
Random	25.3	36.0	51.8
TF-iDF	59.6	79.3	77.9
PROPN [21]	59.5	79.3	77.8
LDA [21]	30.4	45.7	57.1
Naive RoBERTa	55.5	85.1	76.9
Naive S-RoBERTa	42.4	73.6	60.7
Naive BERTweet	53.0	82.3	75.1
Naive Twitter4SSE	70.1	90.1	85.1
Twitter4SSE MEAN	83.6	95.8	92.3
RoBERT_fr	79.8	94.0	90.2
RoBERT	83.0	95.1	91.8
ToBERT_fr	82.3	94.9	91.5
ToBERT	**84.5**	**96.0**	**92.7**

dropout. We fix Twitter4SSE as initial model. Table 3 shows that 2 EL and 2 DL without dropout is the best overall configuration (Table 4).

Full Comparison. We compare the performance of the models with a Random baseline and with the two best approaches from [21].

Naive approaches underperform Hierarchical approaches confirming an advantage to encode single tweets independently. The hierarchical approach with a Stage-1 Twitter4SSE model and a Stage-2 Transformer model outperforms the other alternatives. We notice a gap in performance with respect to the same model with a Stage-2 LSTM model, empirically proving the goodness of transformer layers with respect to recurrent layers in this setting while confirming that the sequential nature of tweets is not critical. TF-iDF best approach (including bigrams, excluding English stopwords and words that appeared less than 5 times in the whole dataset) is comparable to Naive Transformers, whose alternative initialized from Twitter4SSE is the only model that clearly outperforms the not-trained baseline. However, its performance is far from the Hierarchical alternatives. PROPN [21] does not improve classical TF-iDF approaches while LDA [21] reaches performances marginally higher than a random baseline in our setting. Finally, as expected, when unfreezing the weights of Stage-1 models, the performance increases even if we had to reduce the batch size (models denoted with _fr are the frozen variants).

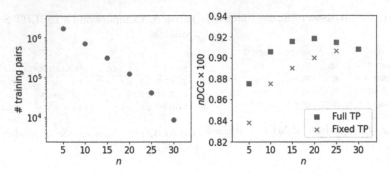

Fig. 2. *Left*: Distribution of the total number of pairs of users in our collection with respect to the minimum number of tweets posted n. *Right*: $nDCG \times 100$ of models (red crosses) when the training set is fixed and (green squares) when we include the full set of pairs of users. (Color figure online)

Selection of Number of Tweets per User. Now we inspect the number of tweets to process per user n. To perform a fair comparison, we build the test set as described in the Data Section with users that have tweeted at least 30 tweets, and we keep it fixed for every experiment. First we check if a greater number of tweets per user implies a better accuracy by selecting all the remaining users with at least 30 tweets as training set. We train models by changing n and we report the results in Fig. 2 (right, red crosses). As expected, a greater number of tweets per users results in a better model, when the number of pairs of training users is fixed.

However, in the Fig. 2 (left) we show how a greater n implies a lower number of users since we have a limited collection of tweets. Thus we investigate what is the best trade-off between the number of users and the number of tweets per user. Figure 2 (right, green squares) shows the performance of models trained changing the number of tweets per user, including every user available. A peak around 20 tweets suggests our best trade-off. However, we remark that this number is highly dependent on our collection since the number of downloaded tweets is high but finite (2 complete months). Expanding the collection time window will result in a different trade-off, since we could be able to collect a greater number of users. We remark that Fig. 2 (right, red crosses) shows that the performances plateau at about $n = 25$, thus expanding the collection window will influence the results but not the best values of the number of tweets per user to process.

Selection of Number of Training Epochs. One could argue that a lower number of users could be compensated increasing the number of epochs. We investigate how this hyper-parameter influences the results in Fig. 3. The left plot shows how simply increasing the number of training epochs scarcely improves the performance of the model, while the computational time linearly increases. Moreover, the performance immediately reaches a plateau and the model risks overfitting due to the lack of an evaluation dataset. The right plot shows the

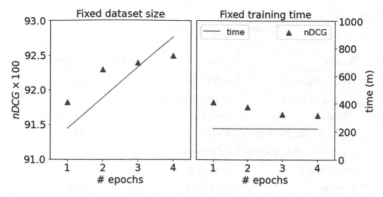

Fig. 3. $nDCG \times 100$ score (purple triangles) and training time in minutes (blue lines) of models trained for different epochs. (left): Fixed training dataset; (right): Reduced training dataset to keep the training time constant. (Color figure online)

performance when the dataset is reduced to keep the training time constant, e.g., when the number of training epochs is set to 2, we reduce the training set by half, when the number of training epochs is set to 3, we remove two-thirds of the training data and so on. As expected, increasing the number of epochs does not compensate for the removed data.

6   Further Analyses

In this section, we answer the third research question **(RQ3)** by checking whether the obtained embeddings and the similarity scores actually reflect our idea similarity between users, and how to use these embeddings for other tasks, such as community visualization, outlier detection and polarization direction detection. The results of this section prove that our main assumption is valid.

In this section, we exploit **Twitter lists** to generate sets of similar users. Twitter lists are collections of users' handles, called members, and they can be followed by other users to get activities related to the members of the list in their feeds. We select a set of public lists reported in Table 5. For each user in the list, we collect the last 20 tweets, including retweets.

The whole analysis is performed using a hierarchical model with a frozen Stage-1 Twitter4SSE model and a Stage-2 ToBERT model with 2 layers, 0.1 dropout rate, MEAN pooling, trained using 20 tweets for each user for one epoch.

6.1   Community Visualization

We visualize reduced embeddings performing PCA with two principal components. Figure 4(a) shows an example of PCA applied to embeddings of the five communities of Table 5 about sports (first five lines: NBA collects Basketball

Table 5. Selected lists of users.

Name	Owner	Members	Followers
NBA teams	@chicagobulls	31	360
NFL (Teams)	@Sportsguy786	32	443
Clubs	@MLB	43	3759
NHL Team Accounts	@NHL	37	9190
Chess Grandmasters	@chesscom	36	18
technology	@verified	20	1437
foodies	@verified	11	500
charity-ngo	@verified	23	631
Democrats	@tweetcongress	51	262
Republican	@tweetcongress	108	1118

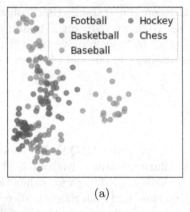
(a)

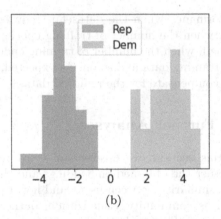
(b)

Fig. 4. (a) 1st and 2nd Principal Components of members of five sport-related lists. (b) Histogram of one-dimensional LDA projections of members of Republicans and Democrats lists.

Clubs, NFL Football Clubs, MBL Baseball Clubs, NHL Hockey Clubs, and Chess players). We observe that members of the same lists are clustered, even if the topics of the selected communities are similar since they are all related to sports. As expected, the community of Chess players is more separated from members of other lists, since chess is a much different sport.

6.2   Outlier Detection

Members of a list do not always share on Twitter content about the same topic. This happens because not everybody uses Twitter to tweet about the topic that they are known for. We can use our model and the obtained user embeddings to detect outliers, i.e., users that are not similar to users in the community for the content shared, even if they are members of the same list. We tested this approach by applying Local Outlier Factor (LOF) [4] algorithm on three lists of users and we manually inspected the results. When applied to embeddings of *technology* list, it outputs one outlier (@majornelson). After manually inspecting the 20 processed tweets, we discover that this account mainly tweets about videogames, while the rest of the members share technology news in general. When applied to the *foodies* list, LOF outputs only @BryanVoltaggio as outlier, a chef that mainly retweets about topics different from food. When applied to *charity-ngo* list, we obtain the official account of Charlize Theron (@CharlizeAfrica), an actress that founded Charlize Theron Africa Outreach Project (CTAOP). We clearly notice that even if some of the tweets from the personal account are actually related to CTAOP, her feed is much different from other NGO members of the list.

6.3 Polarization Direction Detection

Given two communities that are polarized by definition, we use the embeddings to define a one-dimensional subspace of the 768-dimensional space of embeddings, that represents the polarization direction. In this example, we pick the list of Democrats and the list of Republicans as the two polarized communities. We perform Linear Discriminant Analysis (LDA) [11] to obtain the one dimensional projection of the user embeddings. Figure 4(b) shows how the users of the two political parties are projected in the new subspace. However, we can potentially project every user and obtain their expected inclination. As expected, the distributions are clearly separated and generate a linear subspace quantifying the polarization.

This approach can be extended using every pair of communities that defines a polarizing topic, similar to the American structure of politics, but not when the sides are more than two. We can also use this approach when we have only two users, instead of two lists of users, to generate the polarization direction, for example selecting only the most representative accounts for each side of a debate.

7   Conclusion

In this work, we aimed to identify the best approach to embed users so that the obtained vectors reflect our idea of similarity. We restrict the analysis on Twitter and, in particular, to the textual content of tweets. We design a scalable approach to obtain large pairs of similar users exploiting the "retweet" feature of Twitter without human annotators. We verify that a Hierarchical Transformer model outperforms classical and straightforward approaches, and we perform ablation to check the best initialization model and hyper-parameters. The whole approach, including the dataset generation, is language-independent so we plan to evaluate it on other languages spoken on Twitter. We evaluate our work on a large validation set to obtain more general results than previous works.

Finally, we apply the obtained embeddings to other tasks, e.g., visualization of communities and outlier detection, confirming that they reflect our concept of similarity.

Future works include the evaluation of the influence of the selected time window on the user embeddings since topics discussed on Twitter are highly related to contemporary events.

References

1. Almahmoud, H., AlKhalifa, S.: TSim: a system for discovering similar users on twitter. J. Big Data **5**, 1–20 (2018). https://doi.org/10.1186/s40537-018-0147-2
2. Beltagy, I., Peters, M.E., Cohan, A.: Longformer: the long-document transformer (2020)
3. Boyd, D., Golder, S., Lotan, G.: Tweet, tweet, retweet: conversational aspects of retweeting on twitter. In: 2010 43rd Hawaii International Conference on System Sciences, pp. 1–10 (2010). https://doi.org/10.1109/HICSS.2010.412
4. Breunig, M., Kriegel, H.P., Ng, R., Sander, J.: LOF: identifying density-based local outliers, vol. 29, pp. 93–104 (2000). https://doi.org/10.1145/342009.335388
5. Brown et al., T.: Language models are few-shot learners, vol. 33, pp. 1877–1901. Curran Associates, Inc. (2020)
6. Devlin, J., Chang, M.W., Lee, K., Toutanova, K.: BERT: pre-training of deep bidirectional transformers for language understanding. In: Proceedings of the 2019 Conference of the North American Chapter of the Association for Computational Linguistics, pp. 4171–4186. Association for Computational Linguistics (2019). https://doi.org/10.18653/v1/N19-1423
7. Eke, C.I., Norman, A.A., Shuib, L., Nweke, H.F.: A survey of user profiling: state-of-the-art, challenges, and solutions. IEEE Access **7**, 144907–144924 (2019). https://doi.org/10.1109/ACCESS.2019.2944243
8. Giovanni, M.D., Brambilla, M.: Exploiting twitter as source of large corpora of weakly similar pairs for semantic sentence embeddings (2021)
9. Goel, A., Sharma, A., Wang, D., Yin, Z.: Discovering similar users on twitter. In: Workshop on mining and learning with graphs (2013)
10. Gupta, P., Goel, A., Lin, J., Sharma, A., Wang, D., Zadeh, R.: WTF: the who to follow service at twitter. In: Proceedings of the 22nd International Conference on World Wide Web, WWW 2013, pp. 505–514. ACM, New York (2013). https://doi.org/10.1145/2488388.2488433
11. Hastie, T., Tibshirani, R., Friedman, J.: The Elements of Statistical Learning. Springer Series in Statistics. Springer, New York (2001)
12. Henderson, M., et al.: Efficient natural language response suggestion for smart reply. ArXiv (2017)
13. Hoffer, E., Ailon, N.: Deep metric learning using triplet network. In: Feragen, A., Pelillo, M., Loog, M. (eds.) SIMBAD 2015. LNCS, vol. 9370, pp. 84–92. Springer, Cham (2015). https://doi.org/10.1007/978-3-319-24261-3_7
14. Järvelin, K., Kekäläinen, J.: Cumulated gain-based evaluation of IR techniques. ACM Trans. Inf. Syst. **20**(4), 422–446 (2002). https://doi.org/10.1145/582415.582418
15. Liu, Y., et al.: RoBERTa: a robustly optimized BERT pretraining approach. arXiv e-prints arXiv:1907.11692 (2019)

16. Mizzaro, S., Pavan, M., Scagnetto, I.: Content-based similarity of twitter users. In: Hanbury, A., Kazai, G., Rauber, A., Fuhr, N. (eds.) ECIR 2015. LNCS, vol. 9022, pp. 507–512. Springer, Cham (2015). https://doi.org/10.1007/978-3-319-16354-3_56

17. Nguyen, D.Q., Vu, T., Tuan Nguyen, A.: BERTweet: a pre-trained language model for English tweets. In: Proceedings of the 2020 Conference on Empirical Methods in Natural Language Processing, pp. 9–14. ACL (2020). https://doi.org/10.18653/v1/2020.emnlp-demos.2

18. P, S., Chatterjee, M.: Detection of fake and cloned profiles in online social networks (2019). https://doi.org/10.2139/ssrn.3349673

19. Pappagari, R.R., Żelasko, P., Villalba, J., Carmiel, Y., Dehak, N.: Hierarchical transformers for long document classification. In: 2019 IEEE Automatic Speech Recognition and Understanding Workshop (ASRU), pp. 838–844 (2019)

20. Pedregosa, F., et al.: Scikit-learn: machine learning in Python. J. Mach. Learn. Res. **12**, 2825–2830 (2011)

21. Ramponi, G., Brambilla, M., Ceri, S., Daniel, F., Di Giovanni, M.: Content-based characterization of online social communities. Inf. Process. Manage. **57**(6), 102133 (2020). https://doi.org/10.1016/j.ipm.2019.102133

22. Razis, G., Anagnostopoulos, I.: Discovering similar twitter accounts using semantics. Eng. Appl. Artif. Intell. **51**(C), 37–49 (2016). https://doi.org/10.1016/j.engappai.2016.01.015

23. Reimers, N., Gurevych, I.: Sentence-BERT: sentence embeddings using Siamese BERT-networks. In: Proceedings of the 2019 Conference on Empirical Methods in Natural Language Processing. Association for Computational Linguistics (2019)

24. Shoeibi, N., Shoeibi, N., Chamoso, P., Alizadehsani, Z., Corchado Rodríguez, J.: Similarity approximation of twitter profiles (2021). https://doi.org/10.20944/preprints202106.0196.v1

25. Tao, K., Abel, F., Gao, Q., Houben, G.-J.: TUMS: twitter-based user modeling service. In: García-Castro, R., Fensel, D., Antoniou, G. (eds.) ESWC 2011. LNCS, vol. 7117, pp. 269–283. Springer, Heidelberg (2012). https://doi.org/10.1007/978-3-642-25953-1_22

26. Vaswani, A., et al.: Attention is all you need (2017)

27. Vathi, E., Siolas, G., Stafylopatis, A.: Mining interesting topics in twitter communities. In: Núñez, M., Nguyen, N.T., Camacho, D., Trawiński, B. (eds.) ICCCI 2015. LNCS (LNAI), vol. 9329, pp. 123–132. Springer, Cham (2015). https://doi.org/10.1007/978-3-319-24069-5_12

28. Zaheer, M., et al.: Big bird: transformers for longer sequences (2020)

User Identity Linkage via Graph Convolutional Network Across Location-Based Social Networks

Qian Li, Qian Zhou, Wei Chen$^{(\boxtimes)}$, and Lei Zhao

School of Computer Science and Technology, Soochow University, Suzhou, China
20204227004@stu.suda.edu.cn, {qzhou0,robertchen,zhaol}@suda.edu.cn

Abstract. In the past few decades, we have witnessed the flourishing of location-based social networks (LBSNs), where many users tend to create different accounts on multiple platforms to enjoy various services. Benefiting from the large-scale check-in data generated on LBSNs, the task of location-based user identity linkage (UIL) has attracted increasing attention recently. Despite the great contributions made by existing work on location-based UIL, they usually investigate the task with data mining methods, which are hard to extract and utilize the latent features contained by check-in records for more precise user identity linkage. In view of the deficiencies of existing studies, we propose a graph convolutional network (GCN) based model namely GCNUL that consists of a GCN-based encoder, an interaction layer, and a classifier, to fully exploit the spatial features hidden in check-in records. Specifically, the GCN-based encoder aims to exploit the spatial proximity of check-in records and mine user mobility patterns. The interaction layer is developed to capture deep correlations between users' behaviors explicitly. The extensive experiments conducted on two real-world datasets demonstrate that our proposed model GCNUL outperforms the state-of-the-art methods.

Keywords: User identity linkage · Graph convolutional network · Location data · Spatial features

1 Introduction

Recently, location-based social networks (LBSNs) such as Twitter, Instagram, and Foursquare, have grown in popularity. Many users tend to register different accounts on multiple platforms to enjoy diverse services. At the same time, the check-in information associated with the status shared by users provides a significant opportunity for understanding user behaviors. Inspired by this, the task of location-based **U**ser **I**dentity **L**inkage (UIL), which aims to identify the same user across location-based social networks, has attracted increasing attention recently, due to the wide range applications of it, such as friend recommendation [4] and link prediction [23].

The mainstream work on UIL can be collectively referred to as attribute-based methods [6,15,16,18,21,24], where the user profiles, friend network, and

© The Author(s), under exclusive license to Springer Nature Switzerland AG 2023
I. Garrigós et al. (Eds.): ICWE 2023, LNCS 13893, pp. 158–173, 2023.
https://doi.org/10.1007/978-3-031-34444-2_12

user-generated contents (e.g., tweets and posts) are exploited to solve the task. Different from them, the recent wrorks [3,5,13,20] try to link user accounts across multiple platforms based on location information. Generally, they mainly focus on solving the following two challenges: 1) Data sparsity. Unlike the trajectory data that are automatically recorded by GPS equipments with fixed and short time intervals, the check-in records are user-driven, i.e., the user decides when and where to post. This results in large time and space intervals between check-ins. 2) Data heterogeneity. Due to the different usage behaviors of users, the properties of mobility data (e.g., time interval) are drastically different across services. For example, Foursquare enthusiasts may share more statuses than their WhatsApp comments. To address these challenges, traditional studies have proposed many statistical techniques by extracting features and calculating the similarity between user accounts. To name a few, the studies [3,13] introduce kernel density estimation (KDE) based methods, which can alleviate data sparsity but is inevitably time-consuming. Additionally, Feng et al. [5] try to solve the UIL task with a deep learning model DPLink. Specifically, they introduce a pre-training mechanism to mitigate data heterogeneity, and then utilize a recurrent network (RNN) as an encoder to extract trajectory features.

Despite the achievements of above-mentioned studies, they still suffer from some critical limitations. 1) They have not fully considered users' geographic preferences from the spatial perspective. In general, a user's active range is usually centered on some individual areas, such as home areas and work regions. Furthermore, a user usually prefers to visit geographically close locations, so his/her footprints on different location-based social networks may also be geographically adjacent. That is to say, a user's check-ins present a certain spatial distribution, which reflects the mobility pattern of the user. Therefore, we try to model the discrete check-in records via local spatial graphs in this work and achieve more precise UIL by fully utilizing the latent spatial features learned from the local spatial graphs. 2) The deep sequence model DPLink [5] has advantages in modeling trajectory data that are composed of continuously sampled points but performs poorly in modeling discrete check-in records [14].

Having observed the drawbacks of existing work, we propose a graph convolutional network (GCN) based model GCNUL to improve the performance of UIL by mining the latent spatial features in check-ins and explicitly capturing the correlations between users' behaviors. In detail, GCNUL consists of a GCN-based encoder, an interaction layer, and a classifier. First, we divide the space into cells and convert each user's check-ins into a set of cells. Note that the cells here have coordinates, which contain more information and are different from the previous grid-based division strategy [2,3]. Particularly, we only utilize the location information of check-ins without considering the temporal information, since the experimental results in [2] have demonstrated that the temporal information negatively affects modeling user behaviors on sparse check-in data. Next, we construct a local spatial graph based on the spatial proximity of cells for a given account pair. Notably, there are two types of edges in the graph, one exists between cells of each account, and the other exists between cells of two accounts.

Then, the GCN-based encoder is designed to incorporate the spatial features and generate cell representations, and obtain the user representations by feeding the cell embeddings into the max-pooling layer. Subsequently, we introduce an interaction layer composed of the basic interaction (i.e. subtraction and product) and a co-attention mechanism to explicitly capture the deep correlation between two user accounts. Finally, we employ a multi-layer perception (MLP) as a classifier to perform the UIL task.

The main contributions of our work are summarized as follows:

- To the best of our knowledge, this is the first deep learning method that tries to exploit the latent spatial features in check-ins to address the location-based UIL task.
- We propose a GCN-based model namely GCNUL, where an encoder is developed to exploit the spatial features, and an interaction layer is devised to explicitly capture the deep correlation between users' behaviors.
- We conduct extensive experiments on two real-world datasets and the results demonstrate that GCNUL outperforms the state-of-the-art methods.

2   Related Work

Generally, the related work can be roughly divided into two categories, i.e., attribute-based methods, and location-based methods.

Attribute-Based Methods. Early methods employ multiple user attributes to implement the UIL task, including user profiles (e.g., user name, gender), users' social networks, and user-generated content (e.g., tweets, and posts). Zafarani et al. [21] investigate the possibility of linking identities across various communities on the web by usernames and first formally define the user identity linkage problem. Mu et al. [15] propose a unified framework based on latent user space modeling by utilizing the basic user profiles. Vosecky et al. [18] introduce a method to match web profiles from different domains and further extend its effectiveness by incorporating the user's social network. Since then, information in social networks is widely used to perform the UIL. Zhou et al. [24] propose the friendship-based user identification algorithm, which calculates a matching degree for all candidate user matched pairs. Gao et al. [6] propose a knowledge distillation framework that models user-generated content to link user identities. Although so many attributes can be utilized, they all have limitations, such as the possibility of falsification of user information and the difficulty of obtaining a complete social network.

Location-Based Methods. Recent work has investigated the possibility of linking user identities based on location data. Han et al. [8] utilize the location data generated by users in social networks to solve the UIL task and propose a co-clustering-based framework, where account clusterings in temporal and spatial dimensions are carried out synchronously. Riederer et al. [17] propose a generic and self-tunable algorithm. Specifically, location and time are first divided into bins of corresponding geographic regions or time intervals, and the similarity between two accounts is measured based on their co-occurrence in the bins. Chen et al. [3] propose a grid-based KDE method to alleviate the data sparsity problem when computing user similarity and improve computation efficiency by dividing the space into cells. Xue et al. [20] introduce a k-means clustering based approach to link user identities with spatio-temporal data. Li et al. [13] consider the inherent correlation between spatial and temporal information in user check-in records and present a KDE-based solution. Besides, they utilize the inconsistency among check-in records to compute penalties for trajectory similarity. Feng et al. [5] propose a deep learning method named DPLink, which pre-trains the model by a simple task to alleviate the data heterogeneity problem.

Although the above studies have been proven effective on UIL, none of them consider the latent spatial features in check-ins. In view of this, we propose a novel framework GCNUL to make up for the shortcoming of existing work. The key intuition is that GCN [10] can be used to learn complex topologies to capture spatial dependencies. In the recent past, there has been a surge in exploiting spatio-temporal data for tackling relevant tasks, such as taxi demand prediction [19] and pedestrian trajectory prediction [1].

3   Problem Definition

In this section, we define the notations used throughout this paper and describe the location-based UIL problem.

Definition 1. *Check-in record.* *Let $r = (u, l, t)$ be a check-in record generated by a user u, where l is defined as (lat, lng) with lat denotes latitude and lng denotes longitude, and t is the timestamp of this check-in. The set of check-in records is defined as $R = \{r_1, r_2, \cdots, r_n\}$.*

Definition 2. *Location-based User Identity Linkage (Location-based UIL).* *Given a user account pair (u_1^i, u_2^j) where $u_1^i \in U_1$ and $u_2^j \in U_2$, i and j means the index of user, U_1 and U_2 denote the set of user accounts on two platforms. Each user account is associated with a set of check-in records, i.e., R_1^i and R_2^j. Our goal is to learn a binary classifier f that infers whether u_1^i and u_2^j refer to the same natural person or not, i.e.,*

$$f(u_1^i, u_2^j) = \begin{cases} 1, & u_1^i, u_2^j \text{ belong to the same user.} \\ 0, & \text{otherwise.} \end{cases} \tag{1}$$

4   Proposed Model

As presented in Fig. 1, our proposed model GCNUL consists of four components: the construction of cells, a GCN-based encoder, an interaction layer, and a classifier. The details of these components are introduced as follows.

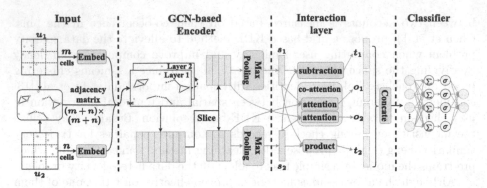

Fig. 1. Overview of the proposed model GCNUL

4.1 Construction of Cells

Due to the sparsity of check-in records, it is necessary to compress the data space. Some studies use landmarks or road intersections [9] in city maps to delineate areas to compress data. However, complete road network data is not publicly available for every city. Considering this, a simple strategy commonly used for spatio-temporal data analysis is to divide the overall space into grids [12], and then treat each grid as a token. Similarly, we divide the space into equal-sized cells. The difference is that we set the granularity of cells by controlling the coordinates' precision and represent each cell's position with the coordinates of its center, which is the basis of building graphs in Sect. 4.2. Compared with grids, each cell is naturally bound to a spatial location (i.e., longitude and latitude) to preserve user mobility patterns while compressing the data space.

Specifically, we set the size of cells by controlling the number of decimal digits n_d in the coordinates, which can refer to Sect. 5.5. For instance, given two coordinates (20.37075, 112.13872) and (20.36673, 112.14277), they will fall into the same cell with the coordinate (20.37, 112.14) when n_d is set to 2. We can defer the cell size is $1\,\text{km} \times 1.1\,\text{km}$ according to the conversion between coordinates and distance that the distance differs by about $10\,\text{km}$ for every $0.1°$ of longitude and the distance difference is about $11\,\text{km}$ for every $0.1°$ of latitude. The demonstration can refer to Fig. 2 and the formulas are as follows:

$$c_i.lat = round(r_j.lat, n_d) \, , \; c_i.lng = round(r_j.lng, n_d) \qquad (2)$$

where r_j is the j-th check-in of a user, c_i represents the i-th cell of the user, and $round(\cdot)$ means round a number to a given precision in decimal digits.

4.2 GCN-Based Encoder

Based on the construction of cells, all check-in records of each user are converted into a set of non-repetitive cells. Afterward, considering the inherent sparsity of discrete check-ins, we first employ all cells of two users to exploit the spatial

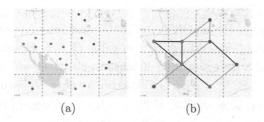

(a)   (b)

Fig. 2. An example of converting check-ins into cells and building graphs. The red and blue dots in (a) and (b) represent the check-ins and cell centers of the two accounts respectively. The black lines and green lines in (b) indicate the edges between cell centers of the same account and the edges between cells of two accounts respectively. (Color figure online)

features via constructing the local spatial graph. Then, we employ a GCN-based approach on this graph and mine users' mobility patterns according to the spatial features. The motivation for this is that personal preferences are hidden in the user's check-ins. The key intuition is that people prefer to visit locations [7] that are geographically closer. Furthermore, the footprints of the same user on different location-based social networks are spatially similar. These regularities reflect the user mobility pattern.

Local Spatial Graph Construction. Specifically, for any account pair u_1 and u_2 on two platforms, and their respective cell sets $C_1 = \{c_1^1, \cdots, c_1^m\}$ and $C_2 = \{c_2^1, \cdots, c_2^n\}$, we first construct a local spatial graph $G = (V, E)$ by building edges between Geographically close cells. Each $v_i \in V$ represents a cell and E is the set of edges. In particular, there are two types of edges, i.e., *inner-account edges* and *cross-account edges*. The former edges exist between cells of the same account and focus on mining the mobility pattern of one user. The latter edges exist between cells of two accounts and help capture the spatial proximity between the two accounts' mobility patterns. The detailed process of building two types of edges is as follows.

$$e_{ij} = \begin{cases} 1, & dist\,(c_i, c_j) \leq \delta \ \& \ c_i \text{ and } c_j \text{ belong to two users} \\ 1, & dist\,(c_i, c_j) \leq \delta \ \& \ c_i \text{ and } c_j \text{ belong to the same user} \\ 0, & otherwise. \end{cases} \quad (3)$$

where $dist(\cdot)$ is the spherical distance and δ is a predefined threshold which is discussed in Sect. 5.5. c_i and c_j represent the i-and the j-th cell respectively.

Based on the graph above, we construct an adjacency matrix $A \in \mathbb{R}^{(m+n)\times(m+n)}$, where each element A_{ij} satisfies: $A_{ij} = e_{ij}$. Besides, the self-adjacency matrix $\tilde{A}$ is obtained by adding the adjacency matrix A and the identity matrix I.

GCN-Based Encoding. Given two user accounts u_1 and u_2 from different platforms, we can readily employ GCN on the constructed graph to obtain each cell representation by aggregating the neighboring nodes' information.

Specifically, for a user account u_1, we stack m one-hot vector representations of grids to form the matrix $X_1 \in \mathbb{R}^{m*m}$ and feed X_1 into an embedding layer to obtain initial embeddings $H_1^{(0)}$ of cells: $H_1^{(0)} = Embedding(X_1)$ where $H_1^{(0)} \in \mathbb{R}^{m*d}$ and d is the embedding dimension. Likewise, we can obtain cell representations $H_2^{(0)} \in \mathbb{R}^{n*d}$ of u_2. Then, we concatenate $H_1^{(0)}$ and $H_2^{(0)}$ to obtain the syncretic node representations $H^{(0)}$, i.e., $H^{(0)} = Concat\left(H_1^{(0)}, H_2^{(0)}\right)$ where $H^{(0)} \in \mathbb{R}^{(m+n)*d}$. Finally, we feed $H^{(0)}$ into the GCN-based encoder along with the self-adjacency matrix $\tilde{A}$. The hidden state of the nodes in each GCN layer is:

$$H^{(l+1)} = LeakReLU\left(\tilde{A}H^{(l)}W^{(l)}\right) \tag{4}$$

where $H^{(l)}$ is the node representations of the l-th layer, and $W^{(l)} \in \mathbb{R}^{d*d}$ is the linear transformation matrix at the l-th layer.

After obtaining the final node representations $H^{(l)}$ by GCN, we first slice $H^{(l)}$ to obtain the cell representations of u_1 and u_2, i.e., $H_1 = \left\{h_1^1, \cdots, h_1^m\right\}$ and $H_2 = \left\{h_2^1, \cdots, h_2^n\right\}$. Note that, $h_1^i \in \mathbb{R}^d$ is a cell representation of u_1. Then, we feed H_1 into a max-pooling layer to obtain the fix-length vector representation $s_1 \in \mathbb{R}^d$ of u_1, i.e., $s_1 = MaxPooling(H_1)$. The final vector representation s_2 of u_2 is obtained in the same manner.

4.3 Interaction Layer

After extracting the information of mobility patterns through the above encoder, we have the user representations (i.e., s_1 and s_2) and cell representations (i.e., H_1 and H_2) of u_1 and u_2 respectively. Based on these representations, we design an interaction layer including the basic interaction module and the co-attention module to explicitly capture the deep correlation between users' behaviors. Notably, the basic interaction module based on subtraction and product is used to capture the coarse-grained correlation between users' behaviors. The co-attention module is devised to capture the fine-grained correlation between users' behaviors by considering the interaction between one user's representation and the cell representations of another user. The details are as follows.

In the base interaction module, we capture the correlation between users' behaviors from different perspectives by performing subtraction and multiplication on s_1 and s_2, where the subtraction reflects their differences and the multiplication reflects their similarities. The specific formulas are as follows:

$$t_1 = s_1 - s_2, \quad t_2 = s_1 \odot s_2 \tag{5}$$

where t_1 and t_2 are coarse-grained correlations obtained based on two user representations, and $\odot$ represents the elementwise (Hadamard) product.

In the co-attention module, we design a co-attention mechanism for pair inputs to capture the fine-grained correlation between two users' behaviors. This is achieved by the interaction between one user's representation and another user's cell representations. We first calculate the attention score vector based on

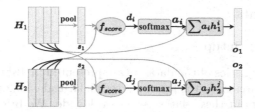

Fig. 3. Co-attention mechanism.

one user's representation and the cell representations of another user. Then, a weighted sum vector is generated based on this attention score vector and the cell representations of another user. Particularly, we apply this attention mechanism to assign larger weights to discriminative places that are most relevant to users. The details of the co-attention mechanism are shown in Fig. 3.

Formally, given the u_1's vector representation s_1 and u_2's cell embedding matrix H_2 respectively, we utilize the Hadamard product to obtain the attention score d_j of each cell of u_2. Then, we normalize the attention scores to generate the weights a. Finally, we use the weights a and H_2 to get a weighted sum vector o_2. Likewise, another weighted sum vector o_1 can also be obtained based on the representations of u_2 and all cells' representations of u_1.

$$d_j = dot(s_1, h_2^j), \tag{6}$$

$$a_j = \frac{exp(d_j)}{\sum\limits_{k}^{n} exp(d_k)} \ , \ o_2 = \sum\limits_{j}^{n} a_j h_2^j. \tag{7}$$

4.4 Classifier

The MLP-based classifier is designed to transform the UIL task into a binary classification task between arbitrary account pairs.

To be specific, we first concatenate the outputs of the above modules to obtain the input z of the classifier. Then, we feed z into MLP to obtain the representation of hidden layer $\tilde{z}$. Finally, the probability p indicating that two accounts belong to the same user is obtained through the sigmoid function:

$$z = concat\,(s_1, \ s_2, \ t_1, \ t_2, \ o_1, \ o_2) \tag{8}$$

$$\tilde{z} = tanh\,(W_1 z + b_1)\,, \ \ p = sigmoid\,(W_2 \tilde{z} + b_2) \tag{9}$$

where W_1, W_2, b_1 and b_2 denote the learnable parameters of the classifier.

Eventually, in the training stage, we use Adam for optimization. The model is trained by minimizing the binary cross-entropy loss function. Given a user account pair (u_1, u_2), the loss function of our model is defined as:

$$Loss = -\sum\limits_{i=1}^{n} [\, y_i\, log\, p_i + (1 - y_i)\, log\,(1 - p_i)\,] \tag{10}$$

where y_i is the ground-truth label.

5   Experiments

5.1   Experiment Setup

Datasets. The statistics of the datasets are presented in Table 1. Each check-in record in both datasets is in the form of (user id, latitude, longitude, timestamp). Note that the users in these datasets are worldwide. We briefly describe these datasets as follows. **1) Foursquare-Twitter (FS-TW).** Foursquare is a popular location-based social network, Twitter is a microblog social network, and both applications provide users with basic location-based services, such as sharing status with location information. The FS-TW dataset is provided by [17,22] and only retains users with more than one check-in record on both platforms. **2) Instagram-Twitter (IG-TW).** Instagram is a popular photo-sharing application. Users often share pictures and videos with location information via cell phones, desktops, laptops, etc. The IG-TW dataset is provided by [17] and filtered in the same way as the FS-TW dataset.

Table 1. Statistics of datasets.

Dataset	Domain	Users	Records Count	Time Span
FS-TW	FourSquare	862	13177	2006.10–2012.11
	Twitter	862	174618	2008.10–2012.11
IG-TW	Instagram	1717	337934	2010.10–2013.09
	Twitter	1717	447366	2010.09–2015.04

Data Preprocessing. Here we explain in detail how to divide the training/validation/testing set. The proportion of training, validation, and testing data is 6:1:3. For two user account sets U_1 and U_2 on two platforms, the number of samples will be very large if we adopt the cartesian product approach, i.e., $U_1 \times U_2 = \{(u_1^i, u_2^j) \mid u_1^i \in U_1, u_2^j \in U_2)\}$, where any two accounts form a pair. Similar to the studies [5,6,13], we construct positive and negative samples based on the ratio of 1:2.

Baselines. We compare the performance of our approach with that of the state-of-the-art location-based UIL methods. Particularly, DPLink is a deep learning-based method, and the rest are based on traditional machine learning methods.

GKR-KDE [3]: This is a grid-based KDE method to alleviate the data sparsity problem when calculating user similarity, and tackle the data missing problem by dividing the space into cells.

KMUL [20]: KMUL introduces a k-means clustering based approach to obtain the cluster center representations of users, and then link user accounts according to the distance between the cluster center representations.

UIDwST [13]: This model is a KDE-based method to exploit the correlation between spatial and temporal information in user check-in records and impose penalties on conflicting check-in records when calculating the similarity.

DPLink [5]: DPLink proposes a deep learning method that pre-trains the model by a simple task to address the heterogeneity of data and introduces a co-attention mechanism to capture potential correlations between trajectories.

Parameter Settings and Metrics. After tuning parameters on the validation set, we find the best parameters for our proposed model GCNUL. Specifically, the number of GCN layers n_g is 2. The output dimension of GCN is set to 500. The distance threshold δ is initialized as 20 km, and the number of decimal digits n_d is 1. Note that use the parameter setting recommended in the original paper, and fine-tune them on each dataset to be optimal. We evaluate the performance of the above methods by metrics commonly used in classification tasks, including precision, recall, and F1 score. Precision represents the proportion of all samples predicted to be positive that are actually positive. Recall means the percentage of correctly identified positive samples. F1 is used to reconcile the balance, meaning the summed mean of the two indicators. Our main code is publicly available.[1]

5.2   Performance Comparison

We compare the performance of our method with that of four baselines through the above metrics. Due to differences in datasets and data processing details, we adjust the hyperparameters of all baselines instead of using the hyperparameters of original papers to ensure the best results on the F1 score. The results are shown in Table 2, where the best results are highlighted in bold.

Table 2. Performance comparison of GCNUL with baselines on two datasets.

Method	FS-TW			IG-TW		
	Precision	Recall	F1	Precision	Recall	F1
GKR-KDE	0.7565	0.7915	0.7736	0.9331	0.9186	0.9258
KMUL	0.6707	0.6448	0.6575	0.8476	0.7868	0.8161
UIDwST	0.7455	0.7915	0.7678	0.9504	0.8915	0.9200
DpLink	0.6737	0.7413	0.7059	0.7763	0.8004	0.7882
GCNUL	**0.8699**	**0.8263**	**0.8475**	**0.9519**	**0.9593**	**0.9556**

Observed from the experimental results in Table 2, GCNUL outperforms all baselines in terms of precision, recall and F1 score. This can be attributed to two aspects: 1) The GCN-based encoder models user mobility patterns based on the

---

[1] https://github.com/liqian0126/GCNUL.

spatial features hidden in check-ins. 2) The interaction layer explicitly captures the correlation between users' behaviors. GKR-KDE and UIDwST demonstrate comparable performance on the two datasets and achieve better performance than all methods except for our proposed GCNUL. This is because they all adopt a KDE-based method to measure the proximity of two user check-in records, which is feasible and effective on UIL. The performance of KMUL is inferior to the above two methods. This is because the user representation that KMUL generates for UIL tasks via the k-means algorithm is less efficient. Meanwhile, the strategy for measuring similarity in KMUL is too simple. Note that, GKR-KDE, KMUL and UIDwST are all methods based on statistical techniques, which cannot mine the latent spatial features in check-ins effectively. Apart from these statistical technique-based methods, the deep learning-based method DPLink is also inferior to our proposed model GCNUL, observed from Table 2. This is due to that DPLink utilizes RNNs as encoders and sequential models cannot efficiently handle discrete check-in records. In addition, we find that all methods perform better on the IG-TW dataset than on the FS-TW dataset. The reason is that the FS-TW dataset is small-scale and sparse, which can refer to Table 1.

5.3   Ablation Study

To verify the effect of each module in our model, we design four variants (i.e., GCNUL-NoG, GCNUL-NoI, GCNUL-NoSD, and GCNUL-NoC) for ablation study and conduct experiments on the FS-TW dataset. In detail, GCNUL-NoG is the model without the GCN-based encoder, and we directly implement the max-pooling operation on the output of the embedding layer to obtain the user's representation. GCNUL-NoI is the model with the interaction layer stripped, i.e. the vector encoded by GCN is directly fed to the classifier. To further validate the effect of the components in the interaction layer, we remove the basic interaction and the co-attention separately and name them GCNUL-NoSD and GCNUL-NoC, respectively.

Table 3. Results of ablation study on FS-TW.

Variants	Precision	Recall	F1
GCNUL-NoG	0.5144	0.5521	0.5326
GCNUL-NoI	0.8125	0.8533	0.8324
GCNUL-NoSD	0.8397	0.8494	0.8445
GCNUL-NoC	0.8066	0.8533	0.8293
GCNUL	**0.8699**	**0.8263**	**0.8475**

According to the experimental results in Table 3, GCNUL-NoG has the most serious performance decline of about 37% in F1. This demonstrates the necessity of using GCN-based encoders to model user mobility patterns by mining the spatial features in check-ins. In addition, we can observe that GCNUL-NoI also has a performance drop, which verifies the effectiveness of applying the interaction layer to capture the correlation between users' behaviors. Furthermore, we have further analysis on the interaction layer: 1) The performance of GCNUL-NoSD has a slight decrease compared to GCNUL. It indicates that the basic interaction module contributes to mining the correlation between user mobility patterns. 2) In contrast, GCNUL-NoC performs worse than GCNUL-NoSD. This illustrates that the co-attention module can capture the finer-grained correlation between users' behaviors compared to the basic interaction module, which effectively improves the performance of the UIL task.

5.4   Effect of Two Types of Edges in the Graph

As mentioned in Sect. 4.2, the constructed local spatial graph has two types of edges. In order to verify the effect of the two types of edges, we conduct experiments. The experiment results are shown in Table 4, where *w/o inner-edges* represents the variant with inner-account edges removed, and *w/o cross-edges* denotes the variant with cross-account edges removed. From Table 4, we observe that either of the two types of edges has a crucial impact on the results of the UIL task. In particular, the performance of GCNUL drops more significantly after removing the cross-account edges. This is because the inner-account edges focus on mining users' visit preferences and mobility patterns while ignoring the spatial proximity of two users' mobility patterns, which is effective for linking user identities across platforms.

Table 4. Experiment results about the effects of two types of edges on FS-TW.

Variant	Precision	Recall	F1
w/o inner-edges	0.7938	0.7876	0.7907
w/o cross-edges	0.5519	0.5135	0.5320
GCNUL	**0.8699**	**0.8263**	**0.8475**

5.5   Effect of Hyperparameters

Due to limited space, we follow the practice of other work and only show the impact of a few key hyperparameters on the testing set. The results are shown in Fig. 4, Fig. 5, and Fig. 6. One can see that the values of the three metrics on IG-TW are always higher than those on FS-TW because the IG-TW dataset is denser and more spatially distributed.

Varying Number of GCN Layer n_g. We can observe that the changing trend of F1 score in Fig. 4(a) is similar to that in Fig. 4(b), but the curve in Fig. 4(a) is slightly more obvious. In fact, this phenomenon is related to the inherent over-smoothing property of GCN [11] which causes the nodes to be indistinguishable.

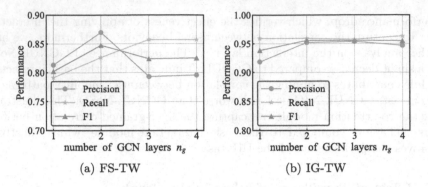

Fig. 4. Performance of GCNUL w.r.t. varied number of GCN layers n_g.

That is to say, during the training of GCN, the node representations tend to converge to the same value as the number of layers and iterations of the network increase. Besides, our proposed model GCNUL on two datasets achieves the best result when the number of GCN layers is 2.

Varying Number of Decimal Digits n_d. This is an important parameter that controls the granularity of cells. One can see from Fig. 5 that the F1 score first increases significantly and then decreases gradually with the increase of n_d. Obviously, a too-large cell granularity may cause more records of two user accounts to be divided into the same cell, which makes it difficult for our model to distinguish correctly. Conversely, a too-small cell granularity will reduce the ability of cells to compress the data space and thus fail to alleviate the data sparsity problem. GCNUL achieves the best results when the n_d is 1. This indicates that moderate granularity enables GCNUL to better extract latent information hidden in user mobility patterns.

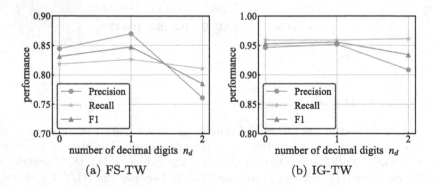

Fig. 5. Performance of GCNUL w.r.t. varied number of decimal digits n_d.

Varying Distance Threshold δ. This parameter determines the density of the local spatial graph. Observed from Fig. 6, we find that the F1 score first increases significantly and then decreases gradually with the increase of δ. This is because the δ is directly related to the number of edges in the graph. When δ is set to a large value, the dense graph causes each node may aggregate repeated and redundant information as the network deepens, resulting in difficulty in extracting distinguishable features. On the contrary, when δ is set to a small value, node representations will contain less useful information, resulting in difficulty in processing the UIL task.

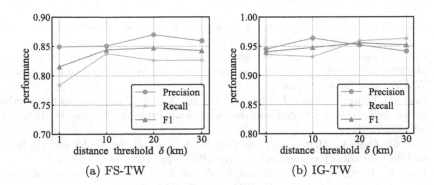

Fig. 6. Performance of GCNUL w.r.t. varied distance threshold δ.

6 Conclusion

In this paper, we propose the first deep learning-based model named GCNUL for UIL on discrete check-in records. Compared with existing approaches, Our model fully exploits the latent spatial features in check-in records and explicitly captures correlations between users' behaviors. Specifically, we apply a GCN-based encoder on the constructed local spatial graphs to mine user mobility patterns by modeling the spatial features. Then an interaction layer is introduced to explicitly capture the correlation between users' behaviors. We conduct extensive experiments on two LBSNs datasets, and the results demonstrate that GCNUL outperforms the state-of-art methods. In the future, we intend to implement UIL on continuous GPS data and design an efficient and general solution.

Acknowledgments. This work is supported by the National Natural Science Foundation of China No. 62272332, the Major Program of the Natural Science Foundation of Jiangsu Higher Education Institutions of China No. 22KJA520006.

References

1. Bae, I., Jeon, H.G.: Disentangled multi-relational graph convolutional network for pedestrian trajectory prediction. In: AAAI, pp. 911–919 (2021)
2. Chen, W., Wang, W., Yin, H., Zhao, L., Zhou, X.: HFUL: a hybrid framework for user account linkage across location-aware social networks. VLDB J. **2022**(1), 1–22 (2022)
3. Chen, W., Yin, H., Wang, W., Zhao, L., Zhou, X.: Effective and efficient user account linkage across location based social networks. In: ICDE, pp. 1085–1096 (2018)
4. Dong, Y., et al.: Link prediction and recommendation across heterogeneous social networks. In: ICDM, pp. 181–190 (2012)
5. Feng, J., Zhang, M., Wang, H., Yang, Z., Zhang, C., Li, Y., Jin, D.: DPLink: user identity linkage via deep neural network from heterogeneous mobility data. In: WWW, pp. 459–469 (2019)
6. Gao, H., Wang, Y., Shao, J., Shen, H., Cheng, X.: UGCLink: user identity linkage by modeling user generated contents with knowledge distillation. In: IEEE, pp. 607–613 (2021)
7. Gao, Q., Zhou, F., Zhang, K., Trajcevski, G., Luo, X., Zhang, F.: Identifying human mobility via trajectory embeddings. In: IJCAI, pp. 1689–1695 (2017)
8. Han, X., Wang, L., Xu, L., Zhang, S.: Social media account linkage using user-generated geo-location data. In: ISI, pp. 157–162 (2016)
9. Jin, F., Hua, W., Xu, J., Zhou, X.: Moving object linking based on historical trace. In: ICDE, pp. 1058–1069 (2019)
10. Kipf, T.N., Welling, M.: Semi-supervised classification with graph convolutional networks. In: ICLR, pp. 1–14 (2017)
11. Li, Q., Han, Z., Wu, X.: Deeper insights into graph convolutional networks for semi-supervised learning. In: AAAI, pp. 3538–3545 (2018)
12. Li, X., Zhao, K., Cong, G., Jensen, C.S., Wei, W.: Deep representation learning for trajectory similarity computation. In: ICDE, pp. 617–628 (2018)
13. Li, Y., Ji, W., Gao, X., Deng, Y., Dong, W., Li, D.: Matching user accounts with spatio-temporal awareness across social networks. Inf. Sci. **570**(2021), 1–15 (2021)
14. Li, Y., Sang, Y., Chen, W., Zhao, L.: Linking check-in data to users on location-aware social networks. In: Khanna, S., Cao, J., Bai, Q., Xu, G. (eds.) PRICAI 2022. LNCS, vol. 13629, pp. 489–503. Springer, Cham (2022). https://doi.org/10.1007/978-3-031-20862-1_36
15. Mu, X., Zhu, F., Lim, E.P., Xiao, J., Wang, J., Zhou, Z.H.: User identity linkage by latent user space modelling. In: SIGKDD, pp. 1775–1784 (2016)
16. Nie, Y., Jia, Y., Li, S., Zhu, X., Li, A., Zhou, B.: Identifying users across social networks based on dynamic core interests. Neurocomputing **210**(2016), 107–115 (2016)
17. Riederer, C.J., Kim, Y., Chaintreau, A., Korula, N., Lattanzi, S.: Linking users across domains with location data: theory and validation. In: WWW, pp. 707–719 (2016)
18. Vosecky, J., Hong, D., Shen, V.Y.: User identification across social networks using the web profile and friend network. Int. J. Web Appl. **2**(1), 23–34 (2010)
19. Wang, Y., Yin, H., Chen, H., Wo, T., Xu, J., Zheng, K.: Origin-destination matrix prediction via graph convolution: a new perspective of passenger demand modeling. In: SIGKDD, pp. 1227–1235 (2019)

20. Xue, H., Sun, B., Si, C., Zhang, W., Fang, J.: KMUL: a user identity linkage method across social networks based on spatiotemporal data. In: IEEE, pp. 111–117 (2021)
21. Zafarani, R., Liu, H.: Connecting corresponding identities across communities. In: ICWSM, pp. 354–357 (2009)
22. Zhang, J., Kong, X., Yu, P.S.: Transferring heterogeneous links across location-based social networks. In: WSDM, pp. 303–312 (2014)
23. Zhang, J., Yu, P.S.: Integrated anchor and social link predictions across social networks. In: IJCAI, pp. 2125–2132 (2015)
24. Zhou, X., Liang, X., Zhang, H., Ma, Y.: Cross-platform identification of anonymous identical users in multiple social media networks. IEEE Trans. Knowl. Data Eng. **28**(2), 411–424 (2016)

Emotions Intensity Prediction in Online Discussions Using Time Series Forecasting

Maksymilian Marcinowski[✉] [iD]

Poznan Supercomputing and Networking Center, Poznań, Poland
ksymilian@man.poznan.pl

Abstract. Toxic behaviors such as aggression, harassment, and insults are the scourge of social media and online discussion sites. Conflictual interactions of this type finally lead dialogues off the rails and as a result the dialogue loses its essence. Preventing a discussion from such incidents requires the ability to predict such situation. This, in turn, presents the challenge of modeling and understanding the dynamics of dialogues and thus predefining the factors that may change throughout their course.

In this work we propose to take an emotional intensity of discussion posts as such factor and to model an emotional trajectory of the dialogue. Therefore we also present an approach for modeling the dynamics using time series representation of dialogue. Finally we perform an experiment of time series forecasting on collection of such conversational time series with state-of-the-art deep learning model in order to make a prediction about emotional intensity value of upcoming post.

Keywords: online discussion · emotions intensity · dialogue modeling

1 Introduction

Incidents of antisocial, offensive interactions constantly obstruct social network communication. Bullying, insults and personal attacks in posts and comments often deprive users of the chance to have a substantive online discussion. Analysis of the conversational dynamics may help in predicting potential appearance of such derailment and breakdown - this however needs definition of the conversational aspects that change in time. While there are prior works that take up the matter of breakdown prediction focusing on rhetorical aspects of conversations [23] and its structure [20], we can hypothesize that it is possible to extract, analyze, and forecast conversational dynamics using an emotional factor - emotions intensity - and widespread representation of such trajectory with its ups and downs.

Therefore in this paper we aim to answer the following research questions:

RQ1 is it possible to recognize emotional aspects of the post in the online dialogue such as emotional intensity level,

RQ2 is it possible to estimate the emotional intensity level of the upcoming post in the online conversation,

© The Author(s), under exclusive license to Springer Nature Switzerland AG 2023
I. Garrigós et al. (Eds.): ICWE 2023, LNCS 13893, pp. 174–188, 2023.
https://doi.org/10.1007/978-3-031-34444-2_13

RQ3 how accurately we can predict the facts of increase or decrease of emotional intensity between posts in the course of online conversation.

For this purpose we propose a new approach for recognition of emotional intensity in online conversation posts. Then we also introduce a new approach for modeling online conversation and forecasting its trajectory of emotional intensity as a time series.

My main contributions are as follows:

i) introduction for evaluation of emotional intensity of posts in online conversations and representing them as a time series of emotion-intensity-based values

ii) conducting a reproducible experiment to forecast intensity of emotions using deep neural networks trained on prepared time series with the goal of verifying the performance of the time series forecasting with respect to state-of-the-art model's baseline configurations in predicting emotional escalation in conversation.

I hope that our approach to modeling online conversations in form of time series may provide new aspects for online discussions analysis and facilitate steps necessary for predicting their potential breakdown, like recognizing common features in dialogues and overcoming the problem of conversations' unknown finishing line (the moment of closure or breakdown).

2   Related Works

2.1   Emotion Recognition and Intensity Prediction

The analysis of emotions in text has been a topic of gaining interest among researchers for several years. This is related to the opportunities arising from the development of automated text analysis and the increasing public availability of text data. Potential applications such as social opinion mining, emotion-aware dialogue systems or advanced moderation of social media communication, as well as relevant datasets like MELD [18], EmoryNLP [21], DailyDialog [13] and Convokit [23] are guiding this topic to even more specific area of ERC - Emotion Recognition in Conversations, where the task is to identify the emotions occurring during the discussion. ERC focuses then on the conversational factors like the topic, intentions and impact of the emotions in online dialogues. [19] BERT, language representation model created in 2018 [4], gave new possibilities in contextual text analysis, including area of contextual emotion recognition. Huang et al. [8] adapted BERT-based model into emotion prediction task with one sentence context. Chatterjee et al. [3] presenting SemEval-2019 Task 3 also included BERT-based models in the *Top systems* section. Although other approaches, e.g. with use of transfer learning from hierarchical generative dialogue model [5] or Contextual Reasoning Networks that are to help in understanding context of conversations from a cognitive perspective [7], have been studied, BERT is still the most common model to develop and leverage with advanced features [22].

ERC mainly focuses on recognizing particular emotion as a category from the chosen model of emotions but in recent years there has been a development in such emotion analysis in text that handles estimating emotion intensity, emotion as a number. In 2017 Mohammad and Bravo-Marquez [16] created a dataset of tweets annotated with four scores (corresponding to the intensity of anger, joy, fear and sadness) and trained SVM regression models based on several combinations of NLP features and lexicons as well as investigated which aspects of such utterances impact emotion intensity the most. With use of this and other provided datasets they also held WASSA-2017 Shared Task on Emotion Intensity and SemEval-2018 Task 1. Basing on them Kulshreshtha et al. [12] examined efficiency of deep neural networks combined with transfer learning and lexicon-based features in emotions intensity prediction. One of the latest works from Kajiwara et al. [10] that distinguishes emotions between the writer's and readers' ones, provides evaluating posts from social media with eight values from 0 to 3 that correspond to the intensity of eight main Plutchik's emotions and shows results of training three classification models (one of which is BERT) with such dataset. Nonetheless these papers concern emotions intensity in single separate utterance and there was no research about change of emotions intensity through the whole dialogue.

2.2   Conversation Modelling for Breakdown Prediction

The topic of aggressive, unacceptable behaviors that lead conversations off the rails has been recently taken up by many researchers but early papers approach this task in post-hoc way, so they analyze harmfulness of already posted content. The first study about forecasting such situation was introduced by Zhang et al. [23] who investigated an impact of initial utterances on whole conversation derailment. An approach still considered as state-of-the-art in conversation modelling was proposed by Chang et al. [2]. They introduced a new architecture tailored to the problem of forecasting conversational dynamics - Conversational Recurrent Architecture for ForecasTing. CRAFT bases on hierarchical recurrent encoder-decoder and consists of two components: a generative one that learns in unsupervised way to represent this dynamics and a supervised one that tunes the representation in order to forecast online its further trajectory. Kementchedjhieva and Søgaard [11] carried out the same experiment as Chang et al. did, however they used BERT model instead of CRAFT and managed to obtain better results on some data. Also Janiszewski et al. [9] were inspired by this approach and enhanced the HRED architecture which as well allowed to obtain premising results. Their model also returns new type of information about dialogue - time-to-breakdown. More explainable conversational model was presented by Saveski et al. [20] who studied relationship between structure and toxicity in conversations on Twitter. They collected numerical features related to derived structures of dialogues like reply trees (size, depth, Wiener index) and follow graphs (size, density, modularity) to use them in predicting next reply's and whole conversation's toxicities.

3 Datasets

To define intensity of emotions quantitatively we used two different models of emotions, both of which indirectly allow to represent emotional aspect as a numerical value.

EmoWordNet [1] is a lexicon, describing 67 000 words and terms from English WordNet with 8 emotion scores for each one. The values, spanned between 0 and 1 and adding up to 1 for each term, represent the intensity of 8 emotions: **afraid, amused, angry, annoyed, don't care, happy, inspired** and **sad**. Sample from EmoWordNet lexicon is presented in Table 1.

Table 1. Example of an EmoWordnet record

term	afraid	amused	angry	annoyed	don't care	happy	inspired	sad
activated	0.0	0.0	0.099	0.0	0.0	0.713	0	0.188

Plutchik's model is a theory of emotions which assumes the existence of eight basic emotions (**anger, anticipation, disgust, fear, joy, sadness, surprise** and **trust**) as well as their more and less intense derivations (like **annoyance** and **rage** as levels of **anger** or **contempt** composed of **anger** and **disgust**) and illustrates relations between them on a wheel. Intensity of the emotions is meant by the level of the wheel.

After picking proper models of emotions we nominated datasets of dialogues that are or can easily be described with the chosen models. Thereafter we chose datasets containing conversations that are substantive but sometimes derail.

EmoWikipediaTalkPages is a dataset of posts that also come from the first round of "Conversations-Gone-Awry" corpus collection provided by Zhang et al. [23] but it also contains annotations of these posts with emotions from Plutchik's model. The annotations were made with the help of 63 respondents - volunteers, students aged 20–25 years whose task was to choose on Plutchik's wheel one dominating emotion for each of the comments/posts presented to them. Each post was annotated by 3 respondents to check the reliability of annotation. The number of conversations in the dataset is 586 of which 237 are the derailed ones which lose their substantial point and end with insults and harassment. The dataset was introduced by Marcinowski and Ławrynowicz in 2020. [15] The **Conversations Gone Awry** corpus [23] consists of posts in online discussions from Wikipedia Talk Pages that according to crowdsourced annotations derail into personal insults. It contains 4.188 conversations with nearly 30.000 posts.

3.1 Datasets Preprocessing and Evaluation

Dialogues from the aforementioned datasets required adapting so that they could be modelled as time series first. By that we mean preprocessing them and evaluating their intensity level according to the preselected methods.

I convert the emotions in the EmoWikipediaTalkPages dataset into numbers, according to their intensity in Plutchik's model: emotions in the first level of the model are assigned a value of 1, emotions in the second level of the model and primary dyads are assigned a value of 2, the most intense emotions are assigned a value of 3 and the *none* annotation is assigned a value of 0. The final emotional intensity of a post is the exact mean level of three emotions the post was annotated with.

The Conversations-Gone-Awry corpus (hereinafter called CGA corpus) is preprocessed with NLTK suite – each post from the dataset is lemmatised and cleared of "stop words" – and evaluated in two experimental ways shown in Fig. 1

1. where the scores of particular emotions in each term are summed up for each post and divided by the number of terms in the post to provide 8 mean emotion scores of each post then the maximum of these values for each post was selected, so the final value of post (X_n) is defined as the average maximal mean emotion score, hereinafter called *average score*
2. where the final value of post (X_n) is defined as highest value among the intensity of any emotion present in any term of the post, hereinafter called *maximal score*

Statistics for each method of emotions intensity evaluation are presented in Table 2.

Table 2. Statistics for emotions' intensity evaluations

evaluation	min value	max value	mean	median
CGA corpus - max score	0.0000	1.0000	0.4486	0.3868
CGA corpus - avg score	0.0004	0.7257	0.0294	0.0133
Plutchik's model annotations	0.0000	3.0000	1.3734	1.3333

3.2 Time Series Representation of a Conversation

A time series is a sequence of time-ordered observations whose measurements are made with a precise time step, which can be constant or non-constant (then we are dealing with a so-called unevenly spaced time series). The problem of time series forecasting concerns fitting a model that can predict values of upcoming observations referring to previous observations. If S $= <s_1, s_2, \ldots, s_i>$ is a sequence of past observations in time series, then the task is to predict the value $s_i + 1$ and following ones with the lowest possible error.

Let us define online conversation as a sequence of events - posts - that appear in non-regular intervals in time. Hence, if we evaluate every post with numerical feature, we can create time series that illustrates the change of this feature throughout the conversation. Such representation enables us to overcome a problem of unknown horizons of conversations and to make forecasts dynamically. We propose to create time series with emotional intensity of the posts aimed at presenting the dialogue's emotional trajectory. Furthermore, considering the

Sentence: I need time.

Evaluation based on Plutchik's model annotation:

	Annotation 1	Annotation 2	Annotation 3	mean level of intensity
I need time.	apprehension (intensity level: 1)	pensiveness (intensity level: 1)	sadness (intensity level: 2)	(1+1+2)/3 = 1,33

Emotional intensity of the sentence by 'Plutchik's model annotations': **1,33**

Evaluation based on EmoWordNet:

	I	need	time.	mean
afraid	0.052089349	0.115980463	0.106601594	0.0915571353
amused	0.156761645	0.116377358	0.138042555	0.1370605193
angry	0.087090734	0.102394325	0.101707483	0.0970641806
annoyed	0.143208913	0.130030549	0.121004963	0.1314148083
don't care	0.168120457	0.121926461	0.127749571	0.1392654963
inspired	0.119559521	0.126993069	0.129452179	0.1253349233
happy	0.214331870	0.166309632	0.159480696	**0.1800407326**
sad	0.058837512	0.119988143	0.115960960	0.0982622050

Emotional intensity of the sentence by 'maximal score': **0.214331870**

Emotional intensity of the sentence by 'average score': **0.1800407326**

Fig. 1. Example post's emotional intensity evaluation

fact that except of the first post in the conversation each of the following posts is a reply to an earlier one, we propose that such conversation emotional trajectory can be represented as a time series in two manners, in accordance with two established orders of posts in a conversation:

- whole conversation as one time series with posts ordered according to the time of appearance - hereinafter called "chronological order"
- conversation as a collection of branches arranged in post-reply context, each of which is one time series - hereinafter called "contextual order".

So the chronological order will give one, long time series covering whole conversation while the contextual order will give more but shorter time series. The examples of both orders are shown in Fig. 2.

Here we make an assumption that the exact time interval between appearance of two following posts does not impact on their emotional intensity, the following posts arc for sure the adjacent observations in time series as well, so we omit the non-regularity factor and cast the time dimension such as we can forecast the time series as the evenly spaced ones.

After the evaluation process, each of three collections of evaluated posts is arranged into univariate time series (with emotional intensity as a variable) adequately to their appearance in the dialogues in datasets. Metadata collected in

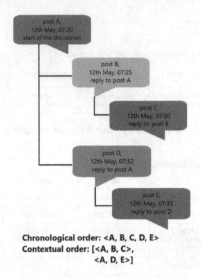

Chronological order: <A, B, C, D, E>
Contextual order: [<A, B, C>,
                          <A, D, E>]

Fig. 2. Example conversation's chronological and contextual orders

EmoWikipediaTalkPages allows to arrange posts only in the chronological order. Conversations-Gone-Awry contains metadata so that posts can be arranged in both orders.

After completing all time series collections, time series containing any zero value are removed from each of the collections of posts evaluated with use of the EmoWordNet lexicon (both maximal and average scores) - such a value of the emotional intensity of the post meant that the post does not contain any term listed in the lexicon.

The summary of created time series collections included in the process of learning are presented in the Table 3.

Table 3. List of the time series collections used in the experiment

id	dataset/evaluation	order	ts count	avg ts length
CGAmaxCh	CGA corpus - max score	chrono	3821	6.175
CGAmaxCo	CGA corpus - max score	context	8378	3.159
CGAavgCh	CGA corpus - avg score	chrono	4188	6.253
CGAavgCo	CGA corpus - avg score	context	8624	3.160
Plutchik	mean Plutchik's level	chrono	137	4.117

4   Experiment

The aim of the experiment is to examine what accuracy can be achieved in estimating upcoming post's emotional intensity level and predicting direction of the

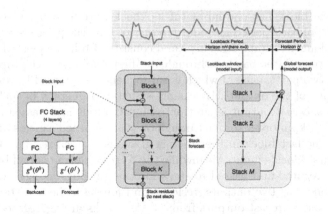

Fig. 3. N-Beats model architecture [17]

change in emotional intensity of the posts throughout the online conversations which verifies usefulness of time series representation of conversations.[1]

In order to answer the questions we use an implementation of the state-of-the-art time series forecasting architecture based on deep neural networks - N-Beats [17] - that can be trained on multiple time series, which is a crucial feature in developing a common model for a whole collection of online conversations.

I also investigate what impact have the emotional intensity evaluation method and the length of the training sequence given to the model on the learning effects.

4.1   N-Beats

N-Beats (Neural Basis Expansion Analysis Time Series Forecasting) model [17] is a type of artificial neural network focused on forecasting univariate time series forecasting. The model is built of chain of subsequent stacks each of which consists of several blocks shown in the Fig. 3 The blocks are responsible for generating partial forecast basing on the local features of the time series. Then the stack combines partial forecasts made by the blocks inside and pass on results to the next stack.

The implementation of the model, available in *darts* library [6], takes two main input arguments:

- length of the **lookback period** on which the model learns the characteristics of the time series (*input_chunk_length*)
  length of the **forecast period** to predict by the model (*output_chunk_length*)

---

[1] notebooks and preprocessed collections are publicly available: https://github.com/mmarcinowski/Emotions-Intensity-Prediction.

Each basic block has one input (of lookback period size) and two outputs (*backcast* of lookback period size and *forecast* of forecast period size) - with the principle of doubly residual stacking - and consists of fully connected layers with ReLU activation. After passing through the first four layers the input is being divided into two parts, each of which is subsequently processed by another layer and put to one of the outputs. Blocks are structured in stack in such a manner that block's *backcast* output is subtracted by its input and passed as an input to the next block, in order to put through only not learned aspects of the batch. *Backcast* of the last block in the stack is given as a stack residual to the next stack as its first block's input. Meanwhile the *forecast* outputs of all blocks in the stack are aggregated and passed to stack forecast output. So each stack, except for the last one, has two outputs: residual and forecast, the last stack has only the forecast one. Forecast outputs from all the stacks are aggregated and given as a model output, the global forecast.

4.2   Experiment Setup

Having time series collections ready, we perform the experiment using N-Beats model with the following parameters (which are default for this implementation):

- number of stacks: 30
- number of blocks in every stack: 1
- number of fully-connected layers preceding the final layers in each block: 4
- number of neurons in each fully-connected layer in every block: 256
- loss function: mean squared error
- optimizer: Adam
- learning rate: 0.001
- number of epochs:
- output chunk length: 1

In order to investigate impact of the emotional intensity evaluation method and the size of training sequence on the results, it is now needed to train separate instance of the model for every time series collection with different *input_chunk_length* argument values (from 1 to 4 for CGA and 1 to 2 for Plutchik). The task of the models is to predict the emotional intensity value of the last item (*output_chunk_length* $= 1$) of all time series in the collection, hence at the end every collection is trimmed of time series whose number of observations was lower than *input_chunk_length* $+$ *output_chunk_length*. Then, each final collection is randomly split into training, validation and test sets at a ratio 3:1:1. All final training configurations are given in Table 4.

Table 4. List of final training configurations

id	collection id	N-Beats input chunk length	training samples
1	CGAmaxCh	1	2292
2	CGAmaxCh	2	2292
3	CGAmaxCh	3	2056
4	CGAmaxCh	4	1857
5	CGAmaxCo	1	5026
6	CGAmaxCo	2	2725
7	CGAmaxCo	3	1532
8	CGAmaxCo	4	1400
9	CGAavgCh	1	2512
10	CGAavgCh	2	2512
11	CGAavgCh	3	2270
12	CGAavgCh	4	2064
13	CGAavgCo	1	5174
14	CGAavgCo	2	2800
15	CGAavgCo	3	1579
16	CGAavgCo	4	1443
17	Plutchik	1	95
18	Plutchik	2	95

The model returns the value of the emotional intensity of the last item in each time series ("upcoming post"). To compare exact forecasts performances of the model we compute mean absolute percentage error (MAPE) between real and predicted values of the "upcoming posts" in all time series. We compare models used for forecasting data of different scales due to different methods of evaluation, MAPE in such a case provides reliable results [14]. Moreover we examine how effectively the model is able to predict the fact of increase or decrease of the next emotion's intensity in relation to the preceding one, as we see such ability important for predicting emotional escalation and as a result a potential outbreak of intense emotions that may result in conversation breakdown. Therefore we also use mean directional accuracy (MDA) metric which compares actual and predicted forecast directions - upward or downward.

4.3   Results

To answer research questions RQ2 and RQ3, an experiment of forecasting emotional intensity of the next post in conversation was made. The performance was measured with MAPE to verify model's power for forecasting exact value and with MDA to check whether this exact value is correctly predicted as greater or lower than the previous observation. In Table 5 configuration results (averaged over 10 runs) are presented.

Table 5. Results of time series forecasting

configuration id	MAPE value	MDA value
1	325.084	0.753
2	41.867	0.739
3	46.363	0.695
4	47.857	0.684
5	47.270	0.722
6	**41.827**	0.734
7	45.957	0.728
8	54.761	0.664
9	325.085	0.654
10	354.108	0.640
11	199.640	0.682
12	227.583	0.685
13	183.222	0.693
14	253.336	0.631
15	251.734	0.643
16	239.802	0.612
17	63.747	**0.762**
18	48.412	0.619

Mean Absolute Percentage Error. In most cases the error exceeds the value of observation. Networks trained on contextually-arranged time series basing on posts from Conversations-Gone-Awry corpus evaluated with *maximal score* have achieved best mean errors with minimum of 41.827% for *input_chunk_length* parameter equal to 2. Nonetheless this metrics illustrates exact precision of models, while the actual ability to predict emotional escalation in conversation is measured with MDA (Figs. 4 and 5).

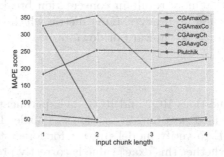

Fig. 4. MAPE scores depending on input chunk length

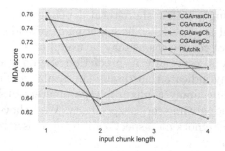

Fig. 5. MDA scores depending on input chunk length

Mean Directional Accuracy. The highest MDA value - 0.762 - was scored by a network trained on posts annotated with emotions from Plutchik's model with *input_chunk_length* parameter equal to 1. It means that with such configuration model was able to predict over three-fourths situation of emotional escalations and deescalations in conversations. It is premising result considering that CRAFT model in Chang et al. [2] had 66.5% accuracy of derailment prediction on the same set of conversations.

5   Conclusions

In this work we introduced emotions intensity as a factor of online discussion dynamics with time series as its representation and presented results of an experiment of predicting upcoming post's emotions intensity value in online conversation using state-of-the-art deep neural network for time series forecasting.

I proposed three methods of evaluation of discussion posts' emotional intensity which are based on two models: EmoWordNet lexicon and Plutchik's model of emotions, and with these methods we evaluated posts from two conversational datasets: Conversations-Gone-Awry and EmoWikipediaTalkPages. Thereafter we presented two possible orders in which evaluated posts can be arranged when creating time series representation of dialogue.

In order to examine possible baseline accuracy of estimating upcoming post's emotional intensity value and prediction of such value change direction, we performed the forecasting experiment using default configuration of state-of-the-art deep neural network for forecasting time series - N-Beats, that we trained with prepared data and evaluated with all evaluation methods conversations-based time series. Through the experiment we investigated the impact of different lengths of input sequence (*input chunk length*) on the forecasting performance.

The experiment shows that forecasting exact emotional intensity value of upcoming post is a demanding task. Mean error of prediction rarely has been falling below 50% of forecast observation. However one of the evaluation methods allowed to reach some prediction stability on the lower level. Meanwhile the accuracy of predicting emotional escalations and deescalations in some cases exceeded 75%. Lower length of input sequence allowed to achieve higher accuracy scores which would suggest that short-term dependencies are the most important in conversational time series. The experiment provides premises that time series representation of conversations may be useful and may help in forecasting their emotional aspects, especially in prediction the emotional intensity direction change which may indicate that discussion escalates. The subject of further research may be tuning many configurable parameters of N-Beats in order to adapt it to conversational time-series' specificity. We believe that accurate forecast of such dialogues' emotional aspects will bring closer to possibility of their breakdowns prediction.

References

1. Badaro, G., Jundi, H., Hajj, H., El-Hajj, W.: EmoWordNet: automatic expansion of emotion lexicon using English WordNet. In: Proceedings of the Seventh Joint Conference on Lexical and Computational Semantics, pp. 86–93. Association for Computational Linguistics (2018). https://doi.org/10.18653/v1/S18-2009

2. Chang, J.P., Danescu-Niculescu-Mizil, C.: Trouble on the horizon: forecasting the derailment of online conversations as they develop. In: Proceedings of the 2019 Conference on Empirical Methods in Natural Language Processing and the 9th International Joint Conference on Natural Language Processing, EMNLP-IJCNLP 2019, Hong Kong, China, 3–7 November 2019, vol. 1865, no. 10, pp. 4742–4753 (2019). https://doi.org/10.18653/v1/D19-1481

3. Chatterjee, A., Narahari, K.N., Joshi, M., Agrawal, P.: SemEval-2019 task 3: EmoContext contextual emotion detection in text. In: Proceedings of the 13th International Workshop on Semantic Evaluation, pp. 39–48. Association for Computational Linguistics, Minneapolis (2019). https://doi.org/10.18653/v1/S19-2005, https://aclanthology.org/S19-2005

4. Devlin, J., Chang, M.W., Lee, K., Toutanova, K.: BERT: pre-training of deep bidirectional transformers for language understanding. In: Proceedings of the 2019 Conference of the North American Chapter of the Association for Computational Linguistics: Human Language Technologies, Volume 1 (Long and Short Papers), pp. 4171–4186. Association for Computational Linguistics, Minneapolis (2019). https://doi.org/10.18653/v1/N19-1423, https://aclanthology.org/N19-1423

5. Hazarika, D., Poria, S., Zimmermann, R., Mihalcea, R.: Conversational transfer learning for emotion recognition. Inf. Fusion **65**, 1–12 (2021). https://doi.org/10.1016/j.inffus.2020.06.005, https://www.sciencedirect.com/science/article/pii/S1566253520303018

6. Herzen, J., et al.: Darts: user-friendly modern machine learning for time series. J. Mach. Learn. Res. **23**(124), 1–6 (2022). http://jmlr.org/papers/v23/21-1177.html

7. Hu, D., Wei, L., Huai, X.: DialogueCRN: contextual reasoning networks for emotion recognition in conversations. In: Proceedings of the 59th Annual Meeting of the Association for Computational Linguistics and the 11th International Joint Conference on Natural Language Processing (Volume 1: Long Papers), pp. 7042–7052. Association for Computational Linguistics, Online (2021). https://doi.org/10.18653/v1/2021.acl-long.547, https://aclanthology.org/2021.acl-long.547

8. Huang, Y.H., Lee, S.R., Ma, M.Y., Chen, Y.H., Yu, Y.W., Chen, Y.S.: EmotionX-IDEA: emotion BERT - an affectional model for conversation (2019)

9. Janiszewski, P., Lango, M., Stefanowski, J.: Time aspect in making an actionable prediction of a conversation breakdown. In: Dong, Y., Kourtellis, N., Hammer, B., Lozano, J.A. (eds.) ECML PKDD 2021. LNCS (LNAI), vol. 12979, pp. 351–364. Springer, Cham (2021). https://doi.org/10.1007/978-3-030-86517-7_22

10. Kajiwara, T., Chu, C., Takemura, N., Nakashima, Y., Nagahara, H.: WRIME: a new dataset for emotional intensity estimation with subjective and objective annotations. In: Proceedings of the 2021 Conference of the North American Chapter of the Association for Computational Linguistics: Human Language Technologies, pp. 2095–2104. Association for Computational Linguistics, Online (2021). https://doi.org/10.18653/v1/2021.naacl-main.169, https://aclanthology.org/2021.naacl-main.169

11. Kementchedjhieva, Y., Søgaard, A.: Dynamic forecasting of conversation derailment. In: Moens, M., Huang, X., Specia, L., Yih, S.W. (eds.) Proceedings of the 2021 Conference on Empirical Methods in Natural Language Processing, EMNLP 2021, Virtual Event/Punta Cana, Dominican Republic, 7–11 November 2021, pp. 7915–7919. Association for Computational Linguistics (2021). https://doi.org/10.18653/v1/2021.emnlp-main.624

12. Kulshreshtha, D., Goel, P., Kumar Singh, A.: How emotional are you? Neural architectures for emotion intensity prediction in microblogs. In: Proceedings of the 27th International Conference on Computational Linguistics, pp. 2914–2926. Association for Computational Linguistics, Santa Fe (2018). https://aclanthology.org/C18-1247

13. Li, Y., Su, H., Shen, X., Li, W., Cao, Z., Niu, S.: DailyDialog: a manually labelled multi-turn dialogue dataset. In: Proceedings of the Eighth International Joint Conference on Natural Language Processing (Volume 1: Long Papers), pp. 986–995. Asian Federation of Natural Language Processing, Taipei (2017). https://aclanthology.org/I17-1099

14. Makridakis, S.: Accuracy measures: theoretical and practical concerns. Int. J. Forecast. 9(4), 527–529 (1993). https://EconPapers.repec.org/RePEc:eee:intfor:v:9:y:1993:i:4:p:527-529

15. Marcinowski, M., Ławrynowicz, A.: On emotions in conflict Wikipedia talk pages discussions. In: Bielikova, M., Mikkonen, T., Pautasso, C. (eds.) ICWE 2020. LNCS, vol. 12128, pp. 293–301. Springer, Cham (2020). https://doi.org/10.1007/978-3-030-50578-3_20

16. Mohammad, S., Bravo-Marquez, F.: Emotion intensities in tweets. In: Proceedings of the 6th Joint Conference on Lexical and Computational Semantics (*SEM 2017), pp. 65–77. Association for Computational Linguistics, Vancouver (2017). https://doi.org/10.18653/v1/S17-1007, https://aclanthology.org/S17-1007

17. Oreshkin, B.N., Carpov, D., Chapados, N., Bengio, Y.: N-beats: neural basis expansion analysis for interpretable time series forecasting (2020)

18. Poria, S., Hazarika, D., Majumder, N., Naik, G., Cambria, E., Mihalcea, R.: MELD: a multimodal multi-party dataset for emotion recognition in conversations. In: Proceedings of the 57th Annual Meeting of the Association for Computational Linguistics, pp. 527–536. Association for Computational Linguistics, Florence (2019). https://doi.org/10.18653/v1/P19-1050, https://aclanthology.org/P19-1050

19. Poria, S., Majumder, N., Mihalcea, R., Hovy, E.H.: Emotion recognition in conversation: Research challenges, datasets, and recent advances. IEEE Access 7, 100943–100953 (2019)

20. Saveski, M., Roy, B., Roy, D.: The structure of toxic conversations on Twitter. In: Proceedings of the Web Conference 2021, WWW 2021, pp. 1086–1097.

Association for Computing Machinery, New York (2021). https://doi.org/10.1145/3442381.3449861, https://doi.org/10.1145/3442381.3449861

21. Zahiri, S.M., Choi, J.D.: Emotion detection on tv show transcripts with sequence-based convolutional neural networks. In: Workshops at the Thirty-Second AAAI Conference on Artificial Intelligence (2018)

22. Zanwar, S., Wiechmann, D., Qiao, Y., Kerz, E.: Improving the generalizability of text-based emotion detection by leveraging transformers with psycholinguistic features. In: Proceedings of the Fifth Workshop on Natural Language Processing and Computational Social Science (NLP+CSS), pp. 1–13. Association for Computational Linguistics, Abu Dhabi (2022). https://aclanthology.org/2022.nlpcss-1.1

23. Zhang, J., Chang, J.P., Danescu-Niculescu-Mizil, C., Dixon, L., Thain, N., Taraborelli, D.: Conversations gone awry: detecting warning signs of conversational failure. In: Proceedings of ACL (2018)

User-Centered Technologies

Speed Up the Web with Universal CSS Rendering

Lucas Vogel$^{(\boxtimes)}$ and Thomas Springer

Technical University Dresden, 01069 Dresden, Germany
lucas.vogel2@tu-dresden.de

Abstract. Achieving fast page load and upholding conversion rates requires continuous effort for web applications ever-growing in size and complexity. Consequently, developing new methods for optimizing and speeding up page load is a constant effort of the web community. Existing methods aim to reduce the amount of render-blocking code in the render pipeline to improve the time until render. However, a recent study revealed a tremendous optimization potential remaining, especially for CSS, since only ≈ 15% of render-blocking CSS code is used until render [12]. In this paper, we present `Essential`, an improved server-side CSS renderer. It is based on the popular `Critical` package [10], which increases the code efficiency and prepares websites by extracting render-critical elements "Above-the-Fold" and delaying the remaining code asynchronously. `Essential` renders the CSS of the whole page, as well as eliminates code duplicates to optimize the rendered result. Our evaluation results show that `Essential` more than triples code efficiency and decreases the transferred render-critical CSS by 65.9% compared to the original while maintaining a high visual similarity and matching or surpassing the performance of `Critical`.

Keywords: universal rendering · CSS rendering · render-critical · Above-the-Fold · improved loading times · render pipeline · web page optimization

1 Introduction

In recent years, the size of web pages has continued to increase, according to the HTTP archive [5]. In general, however, larger websites that are not optimized result in longer load times due to the amount of data being downloaded. As can be seen in Fig. 1, both JavaScript and CSS are responsible for the majority of the code transferred but are only partially used for rendering the page. In particular, CSS is only used by ≈ 15.9% and has the most significant optimization potential [12]. Slower websites, in turn, significantly negatively impact the conversion rate of a given page and, thus, financial consequences [13]. This is still an ongoing issue. The "Milliseconds make Millions" study from 2020, commissioned by Google, showed that decreasing loading times by only 0.1 s increases

© The Author(s), under exclusive license to Springer Nature Switzerland AG 2023
I. Garrigós et al. (Eds.): ICWE 2023, LNCS 13893, pp. 191–205, 2023.
https://doi.org/10.1007/978-3-031-34444-2_14

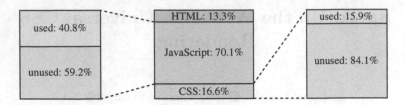

Fig. 1. Proportion of HTML, JavaScript, and CSS in an average web page (top) and the ratio of used/unused JavaScript and CSS for page render (bottom). Source: [12]

the conversion rates of retail pages by 8.4% [3]. Therefore, the motivation for optimizing websites originates not only from a user experience perspective but also from an economic background. Currently, optimizing the CSS of a page requires high development effort, which in turn results in increased costs, as existing tools do not produce entirely satisfactory results. This paper focuses on optimizing CSS, more specifically, by optimizing existing rendering techniques with minimal effort for the developer. By creating an automatic and easily integrable approach, development costs can be kept low and simultaneously allow for creating complex and dynamic web pages while reaching loading speed goals. Furthermore, by reducing the amount of data transferred to a client, the energy required to load a web page will also decrease. We argue that existing solutions for optimizing CSS, like `Critical`, can result in a worse user experience than without the optimization. `Critical` is a popular "Above-the-Fold" CSS rendering framework that splits CSS into "critical" and "uncritical" parts needed for rendering. One reason for its limitation is that delaying styling information which is render-critical for HTML sections "Below-The-Fold" might result in a user seeing unstyled HTML, as well as possibly experiencing large amounts of layout shift, as this "uncritical" CSS does not block the rendering process. A significantly worse user experience can overshadow the increased loading performance created by splitting the CSS in this way. Additionally, the CSS produced by `Critical` can be optimized further, mainly by removing code duplicates. The contributions of this paper will be twofold: First, we present an improved version of a universal CSS renderer that we call `Essential`, built on top of the `Critical` package. It eliminates the limitations of `Critical` by rendering the whole page at once and optimizing the produced CSS further to increase code usage until rendering. Secondly, an extensive evaluation compares the techniques and discusses the differences between the original pages and their modified counterparts.

The paper is organized as follows: in Sect. 2, important fundamentals and techniques are summarized, followed by the related work in Sect. 3. Next, the concept is described in Sect. 4 and evaluated in Sect. 5. The evaluation also contains a discussion about limitations and future work. The conclusion then follows in Sect. 6.

2   Background

In this section, the most important fundamentals used in this paper are explained.

Render-Blocking CSS: CSS can be inserted into a web page in three different ways: as a linked external file, a `<style></style>`-block or inline with the `style=""`-attribute. By default, all three methods will prevent showing the website until their included CSS is fully loaded and parsed. As a result, this behavior is called render-blocking. With CSS, only external files can be made non-render-blocking by either utilizing the `media` attribute or by using JavaScript. However, only using the `media` attribute without JavaScript can be limiting. For example, it results in CSS only applying for one specific screen size, which might result in a development overhead due to extra files needed. Therefore, to improve the loading time of a web page, the amount of render-blocking CSS has to be reduced as much as possible.

First Contentful Paint: The performance of a web page can be measured with various markers which are reached while a web page is loading. Regarding CSS, one of the most crucial performance markers is the First Contentful Paint (FCP). FCP describes the point in time when the first user-visible content is shown. Improving the efficiency of CSS code on a page by reducing unused code will impact the FCP, as less data has to be loaded, and parsing will be quicker, which is why it is used as one of the performance markers in the evaluation.

DOM Content Loaded: While FCP represents the beginning of rendering user-visible content, the *DomContentLoaded* event end marks the point in time when the DOM is constructed entirely, and no style-sheet document is blocking the execution of JavaScript [4]. This marker is chosen, as it shows improvements in executing render-blocking resources, like CSS linked without delay in the `HEAD` of an HTML document. Improving CSS execution times, in general, will be visible in the *DomContentLoaded* event end marker due to reduced render-blocking content, depending on browser implementation. For that reason, it will be included in the evaluation.

Critical CSS: The goal of CSS is to separate the presentation and content of a given web page [2]. Generally, no strict binding of HTML elements and CSS selectors is present. This entails that one CSS block or CSS file included in a page might have code that does not match any HTML elements of the current page. If this code is loaded in a render-blocking way, the FCP will be later than necessary as unused CSS code was loaded and parsed. Critical CSS, in turn, describes all CSS code that is render-*critical*, i.e., used while rendering the part of the page presented at and after the FCP. Ideally, the developed technique will separate and load only the actual critical CSS in a render-blocking way.

Above-the-Fold: When rendering a page on a screen, the content visible without scrolling is called "Above-the-Fold". This area describes a height of 100vh from the top of the page in CSS measurement units. This term often describes techniques that optimize web page loading speed by splitting resources at the described point. For example, by post-loading the content "Below-the-Fold" and directly serving the content from "Above-the-Fold", performance improvements to the FCP can be made, as the initial page size is reduced.

CSS Rendering: Rendering CSS can be done by utilizing a remote-controlled browser on a server. More specifically, popular frameworks like Penthouse or Criticalare using this technique [9,10]. In simple terms, the browser opens the final web page and waits until it is fully loaded. Then, JavaScript is used to split CSS into an AST representation (Abstract Syntax Tree) to extract the CSS selectors. Next, a selection method like the popular "css-mediaquery"[1]-library can be applied to match selectors. As a result, the delivered CSS can be split into two parts: CSS, which is necessary for the page to be displayed correctly, and CSS, which does not match the visible elements. For libraries like Critical, this rendering is only done for the visible part of the page "Above-the-Fold".

Differences Between SSR and CSS Rendering: Server-side rendering (SSR) is often associated with rendering the web page, focusing on the page content. This might not include CSS optimizations, like reducing the CSS code to only the necessary sections. One example is Angular Universal, where the content is rendered, but CSS is not optimized as of the time of writing[2]. Furthermore, SSR is often associated with breaking dynamic JavaScript, as the frontend code often has to be adapted to preliminary changes in the DOM. The term "CSS rendering", as used in this paper, only describes the optimizations on the CSS code itself, not the HTML DOM content. Therefore, CSS rendering can only cause a problem under one specific circumstance: when the JavaScript code depends on checks for element properties described by CSS, like the width or color of an element, if this CSS code is not loaded yet due to being flagged as "uncritical". As it is possible to program web pages without said checks and with the goal of CSS rendering of styling all visible elements correctly, the described error is unlikely to cause real-world issues.

Shortcomings of Critical and Above-the-Fold Rendering: As described in Sect. 2, the critical CSS is only rendered for a section of the whole page by Critical. Figure 2 shows a simplified loading behavior for an unoptimized website and a web page with critical CSS rendering. It is visible that splitting CSS can theoretically be beneficial for the overall loading time. Excluding speculative parsing in this example, removing uncritical CSS from the critical rendering path shortens the time until a web page can be displayed, as shown by the yellow triangles in Fig. 2. However, suppose, for example, user input changes the page in a way that requires CSS from the uncritical CSS file. In that case, the rendering might be delayed to a point in time even after the corresponding original loading behavior has finished rendering the page. A blue triangle displays the worst-case loading time. One such behavior is scrolling too soon after loading on the page, which moves the viewport away from the rendered section. However,

---

[1] npmjs.com/package/css-mediaquery.

[2] angular.io/guide/universal.

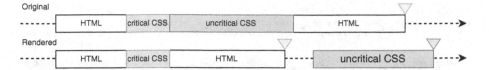

Fig. 2. Simplified visualization of loading a Web page with and without Critical, describing the best-case and worst-case render times, marked with a yellow and blue triangle, respectively (Color figure online)

this is worsened by the technology itself, as improving the loading time also reduces the time to interactive (TTI), which describes the time until the user can interact with the page. As a result, classical "Above-the-Fold" critical CSS rendering can lead to faster loading times and a worse user experience.

3 Related Work

In this section, approaches that optimize the loading of CSS are discussed.

3.1 "Critical CSS Rules — Decreasing Time to First Render by Inlining CSS Rules for Over-the-fold Elements"

In paper [7], the authors describe a method of rendering CSS "Above-the-Fold" by utilizing PhantomJS to match all CSS declarations of the HTML elements [7]. If the match is inside the viewport that describes the part "Above-the-Fold", the CSS class is marked as "critical". Afterward, all critical CSS declarations are combined and inserted into a `style` element in the web page's header. All other "non-critical" CSS declarations are loaded asynchronously and will, therefore, not block the rendering of the page. However, by only marking the elements "Above-the-Fold" as critical, the rest of the page might take significantly longer to load, depending on the network speed or amount of resources. This could not sufficiently be proven otherwise, as the exact setup used for testing is missing in the paper.

3.2 Critical CSS Tools

Various techniques exist to render CSS, like `Critical`, Critical-CSS, and Penthouse [1,9]. However, Critical-CSS is now archived and not maintained, and `Critical` is based on Penthouse with automatic style-sheet extraction. Therefore, the technique with the most advanced high-level interface is `Critical`. All three techniques render CSS. However, the current popular frameworks (`Critical` and Penthouse) only utilize a viewport to render CSS. If the whole page were rendered, improvements might still be possible, with results that more closely match the real-world use-case of users that start scrolling as soon as possible after the FCP. Furthermore, `Critical` provides an option to insert critical CSS internally into the HTML of the page. However, no data on this modification or inlining performance exists and will be analyzed as part of this paper.

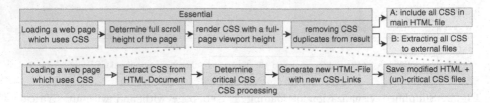

Fig. 3. Workflows of `Essential` (top) and CSS processing like `Critical` (bottom).

3.3 "On the Impact of the Critical CSS Technique on the Performance and Energy Consumption of Mobile Browsers"

As described by Janssen et al. in their experiment, using Critical CSS can reduce loading times and improve the time until FCP [6]. The test was run using a remote-controlled Smartphone connected to a Raspberry Pi, which also hosted the tested websites. They converted 40 randomly selected Websites from the Tranco list [11], and compared them to their original counterpart. This selection might impact the validity of the results, as the data set might be too small for comparable results. Furthermore, the version of the Tranco list was not given, and a table of used web pages is missing.

3.4 "Eliminating Code Duplication in Cascading Style Sheets"

As described in the thesis of Davood Mazinanian, a significant problem of CSS is code duplication [8]. While Mazinanian proposes a solution for reducing CSS, the core target of the work is different from the goal of this paper, as it does not explicitly focus on render-critical CSS. However, this removal of duplicated code can also be applied after extracting critical CSS code and will therefore be included in the concept of this work.

As shown by the described techniques and articles, all existing approaches have limitations. This mainly includes papers that evaluated only a small selection of web pages or missing information on the parameters used, like the version of the page list. Furthermore, existing techniques show the potential that has yet to be researched. In detail, this means extending the strict limitation to identify render-critical CSS only "Above-the-Fold" to the complete page to support immediate user interaction after FCP.

4   General Concept

Our approach, which we call `Essential`, aims to extract the minimal amount of CSS that needs to be loaded in a render-blocking way to render a full page for FCP. The key idea is that by extracting the render-critical CSS for the whole page and not just for the part *Above-the-Fold* and removing duplicated CSS, the efficiency of CSS and the time to First Contentful Paint will be improved.

As a result, the user can start scrolling without waiting for the uncritical CSS to be loaded to see a correctly styled page, assuming that "uncritical" CSS existed on the original page. This stands in contrast to techniques like Critical, where all CSS (necessary for the page elements) Below-the-Fold is marked as uncritical. Secondly, we further hypothesize that browsers are not optimized for large amounts of internal code, which is why we will evaluate two versions: including all CSS in the HTML file (path A in Fig. 3) and moving all CSS to external files (path B in Fig. 3). This will be evaluated as packages like Critical allow for including all critical CSS in the main HTML file. CSS rendering like Penthouse or Critical use, among other things, puppeteer[3] as a base framework, which is a remote-controlled browser tool. With a page loaded, queries of CSS selectors can be executed to find all matches of CSS selectors on a given page. By testing the location of the found elements, the selectors can be grouped into critical and non-critical. Special effort has to be made to keep the correct order of selectors due to the cascading property of CSS, as well as consider nested selectors in special rules like @media. The renderer proposed in this paper is based on the Critical pipeline since its extraction behavior can be reused. As shown in Fig. 3, the Essential pipeline significantly extends the Critical approach to prevent the "Above-the-Fold"-Split and to further increase the code efficiency for CSS files by the following steps:

First, the whole page is processed instead of the "Above-the-Fold"-Split only. This is achieved by a puppeteer-controlled Chromium browser that opens up the target web page to extract the entire scrollable page height via JavaScript. The given page height is used to execute Critical, which will render the whole page's critical CSS. This step increases the amount of render-critical CSS, as the whole page is now used while checking. Critical is configured so that <style>-elements are also considered, and the results will be saved in external CSS files. Second, the resulting page is cleaned to increase its code efficiency. In this step, all found CSS code duplicates are removed (exact matches, including sections of preexisting CSS, which is not removed by Critical), which includes excess <style>-elements. This results in the following setup: one HTML file, with one file for render-critical CSS and one file for non-render-critical CSS. At this stage, the HTML file only contains links to both files and, at most, internal styles. A second reason for using Critical to extract CSS is to utilize the given CSS generator. This results in clean and valid CSS code, making this proposed method, especially the next stage, more robust against different validity stages of CSS code. Still, Critical is not perfect and still throws errors at invalid web pages. However, utilizing the implemented extraction feature and the described generator validates the usage of Critical at this point.

In the next stage, the extracted render-critical files of Criticalwill be inserted Into the main HTML document, as shown in Fig. 3, marker "A". This will increase the HTML file size, as described above, but removes one render-critical external CSS file call. When rendering a page optimized with the regular version of Critical without modifications, it is possible to scroll on the page,

---

[3] npmjs.com/package/puppeteer.

even though the non-critical CSS is still loading. At this point, the user might experience a broken page "Below-the-Fold" with the pure `Critical` optimized page or see a section with misaligned content. In order to see and use this section of the page correctly, the user would have to wait for all the non-critical CSS to load, which can take as long or longer as loading the same page without optimizations by `Critical`. Furthermore, the HTML of a `Critical`-optimized page usually already contains all necessary HTML content when delivered, but not all of the CSS. Rendering the entire page height will prevent this behavior, as all transmitted HTML elements visible on a given page will be styled, not just "Above-the-Fold". As a result, the setup with option "A", shown in Fig. 3, now contains only a single HTML file containing all render-critical CSS and an asynchronously loaded CSS file with the non-render-critical parts. Comparing sizes, the expected size of the now-generated HTML file is larger than the sum of the HTML and render-critical CSS when using `Critical` in its default setting but smaller than the sum of the HTML and CSS of the original. However, displaying the now-generated file at this stage directly matches the loading behavior of the original closer than using the same file optimized by `Critical` alone. For version "B", shown in Fig. 3, the critical CSS is saved as an external ".css"-file. Additionally, all internal style elements are removed, and the external file is linked in the `HEAD` of the document. `Essential` was implemented using Node.js and the software packages described in Sect. 4. `Critical` was used in version `4.0.1`, with `extract` and `inline` set to `true`, as necessary by the following optimization and recommended by `Critical` for best performance[4]. Puppeteer was used in version `13.5.2`, running `HeadlessChrome/101.0.4950.0`, and the `css`-package in version `3.0.0`.

5   Evaluation

For evaluation, we compare `Essential` with the unmodified render pipeline of Chrome and the closest competitor, `Critical`. We consider the CSS code efficiency and the resulting loading performance, particularly the time to FCP, as key metrics that motivated the development of `Essential`. We further evaluate how much impact `Essential` and `Critical` have on the visual appearance of pages by comparing the pages produced by these two frameworks with the unmodified version. This is also necessary, as the visual impact of removing code duplicates is not researched until now. Conversion times are evaluated to quantify and compare the overhead introduced using `Essential`.

General Setup: For this evaluation, the top 1000 web pages of the Tranco list were downloaded (ID: 5Y67N) [11]. In order to fetch the websites, the pages were downloaded with an automated script, including all resources, using Chrome version 103. In total, 869 web pages out of the top 1000 could be downloaded successfully. The remaining pages could not be reached, for example, due to unavailability from Germany, where the test was carried out.

---

[4] As stated at the time of writing (June 2022) at npmjs.com/package/critical in section "Why should critical-path CSS be inlined?".

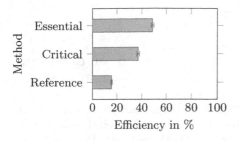
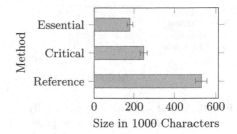

Fig. 4. Measured average CSS code efficiency (CSS used until render)

Fig. 5. Measured average code size of all transferred (render-critical) CSS in characters

5.1 Code Efficiency

The *puppeteer* framework was used to test code efficiency to control a headless Chromium browser. Using the code coverage provided by Chromium, the used CSS efficiency is calculated by the used sections of code, e.g., if all CSS code is used until render, it will result in a code efficiency of 100%.

As shown in Fig. 4, `Essential` outperforms both `Critical` and the reference version in terms of code efficiency. On average, the reference uses 15.6% of the delivered CSS code. `Critical` improves this value to 37.1%, while `Essential` further increases code efficiency to 48.8%. This might be driven mainly by a smaller amount of delivered CSS, as shown in Fig. 5. When assuming an ASCII encoding with one character represented by one Byte, the delivered measured CSS of the reference pages would, on average, result in 529.9 KB. `Critical` reduces the delivered code to 246.4 KB, while `Essential` transfers 180.1 KB of CSS. This is equivalent to a 65.9% decrease in delivered code in relation to the original CSS. As a frame of reference, a recent study showed, when analyzing the top 10.000 web pages, that on average, CSS made up 437.4 KB of the downloaded data from a total page size of 3.3 MB when combining the transmitted HTML, CSS, and JavaScript [12].

5.2 Visual Similarity

In order to verify that the rendering resulted in a visually similar page, `puppeteer` was used to open all variations of every page and create a screenshot of the loaded state. These screenshots were then converted to the same size with the `sharp`-library[5] to be compared by `pixelmatch`[6], which requires same-sized images, by filling in the empty space with a contrasting color. As a result, all screenshots have the same maximum size in both dimensions. Then, `pixelmatch` is used to create a similarity score with a threshold of 0.0 and the same-sized screenshots. This setup magnifies even minor visual errors, for example, if the

---

[5] npmjs.com/package/sharp.
[6] npmjs.com/package/pixelmatch.

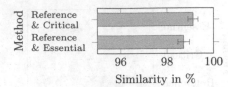

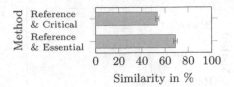

Fig. 6. Visual similarity between fully rendered versions, based on a pixel-by-pixel comparison. Note: The x-axis starts at 95% to highlight differences.

Fig. 7. Visual similarity between versions, based on a pixel-by-pixel comparison. Both `Critical` and `Essential` were loaded without the "uncritical" CSS.

page is marginally larger or smaller. However, we argue that visual similarity is one of the most important aspects of CSS rendering and is, therefore, explicitly used.

As shown in Fig. 6, both versions have a visual similarity of over 98.5%. It must be noted that this test only tests fully rendered pages, including uncritical files, to check the final results. Differences can include even minimal shade changes as this compares on a pixel-by-pixel basis. In general, both versions show a high level of similarity.

In contrast to the fully rendered pages, a second test was performed, removing all CSS marked "uncritical" by both `Critical` and `Essential`. Figure 7 shows that `Essential` has a significantly higher similarity to the original page than `Critical`. The remaining similarity is explained by the "Above-the-Fold"-part of a web page being rendered correctly. Identically to the previous visual similarity test, a worst-case scenario is chosen to compare based on a pixel-by-pixel comparison. It is, therefore, visible that the improvements made by `Essential` have a positive impact on web page similarity compared to `Critical`. This is also shown in the example Fig. 8, where the screenshots of wordpress.org are displayed, optimized with `Critical` and `Essential`, without the CSS marked as "uncritical" in both versions. This page was chosen as the differences between both techniques are clearly visible: with `Critical`, all elements "Below-The-Fold" are not rendered correctly, which is what the user would see if the "uncritical" CSS loads too slowly.

5.3   Conversion Times

For using a rendering framework in a real-world scenario, the conversion times matter as they determine the area of application, e.g., a subsecond rendering might be applicable for real-time use, or a slower conversion might be utilized on a CDN. In this section, the times before and after rendering with the `Critical`- and `Essential`-package were measured. The results showed that out of the 869 downloaded pages, 650 converted correctly using `Critical`. One of the limiting factors of non-convertible web pages is the inclusion of invalid CSS code, as browsers fail as silently as possible when encountering a CSS error. The convertible pages with `Essential` took an average of 7.62 s to convert per page on a

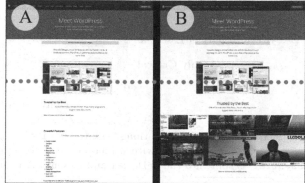

Fig. 8. Screenshots of wordpress.org optimized using (A): `Critical` and (B): `Essential`, both without loading the "uncritical" CSS. The green dotted line marks the "Above-The-Fold" line for a standard 1920×1080 display. The image on the left shows an overview of the entire page, and the image on the right highlights the top section of the same web page above and below the "fold". There, the differences in layout and lack of elements of version "A" compared to version "B" are visible. (Color figure online)

2020 MacBook Pro with a 2.3 GHz Intel i7. This measurement results from the combined times of `Critical` for `Essential`, with an average of 3.224 s, and the `Essential`-exclusive improvements that run on top of `Critical`, with an average of 4.397 s. In Fig. 9, these measured speeds are also compared to converting the webpages with a non-modified configuration of `Critical`. Improved hardware might also improve the conversion times when, e.g., running the framework on a server with improved hardware. In this case, both software versions might be less suitable for real-time conversion. However, with an average conversion time in the single-digit second range, application areas like CDNs or as part of a CI chain are achievable. For example, `Essential` could be called to create *critical* and *uncritical* files every time the developer modifies the page as part of the deployment process.

5.4 Loading Times

To test the differences before and after rendering, the different versions are loaded by a `puppeteer`-controlled Chromium version 105.0 and Firefox Nightly version 105.0a1 browser, with a network speed limitation of the Apple "Network Link Conditioner"[7] DSL-preset with a download link speed of 10 Mbps. To test the impact of different versions, multiple configurations were chosen:

– the original web page as the reference page
– a pure `Critical` version without modifications

---

[7] developer.apple.com/download/more/?q=Additional%20Tools.

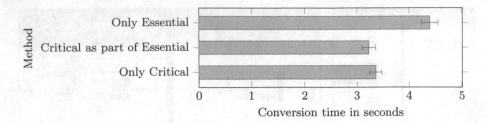

Fig. 9. Compared conversion times. "Only `Critical`" is a conversion of a web page using the `Critical`-package with a non-modified configuration. The conversion with `Essential` is split into the `Critical` and `Essential`-exclusive parts.

- a modified `Critical` version necessary for `Essential` as described in Sect. 4
- an `Essential` version with exclusively internal render-blocking CSS (version "A" from Fig. 3)
- and one `Essential` version with exclusively external CSS (version "B" from Fig. 3)

As shown in Fig. 10, all CSS rendering modifications show a significant improvement over the unmodified page speed. However, keeping all resources external has a negative impact on performance in this test configuration, both for Firefox and Chrome. In contrast, on average, `Essential` performed similarly to `Critical`, and increasing the viewport did not increase the time until FCP. Likewise, the additional CSS from `Essential` has similar results. Therefore, CSS rendering positively impacts loading time until FCP, and the differences between techniques that include CSS in the HTML file are minor.

In contrast to the FCP, the timing differences until "DomContentLoad" are more prominent, particularly between the two browsers. Primarily Firefox benefits largely from any form of CSS rendering, as shown in Fig. 11. Most notably, `Essential` did not only match the loading speed of `Critical` but surpassed the performance of all other techniques when used with external CSS, even though more CSS affecting a larger section of the page is transmitted. This can be explained by the improved code efficiency, as shown in Subsect. 5.1. In contrast to Firefox, the exclusively internal version of Chrome was also faster than `Critical`. As they are the same files at the same loading speed, this difference can be explained by varying implementations and optimizations of internal and external CSS and how it is rendered in the browser. Still, both versions show a significant improvement, as Firefox is generally faster at reaching the performance event in all cases.

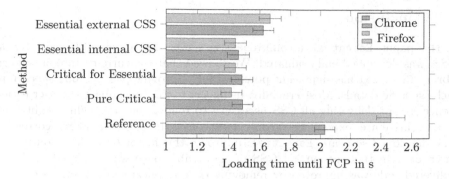

Fig. 10. Average time measurements until the First Contentful Paint at 10 Mbps for different versions. The x-axis starts at 1s to highlight differences.

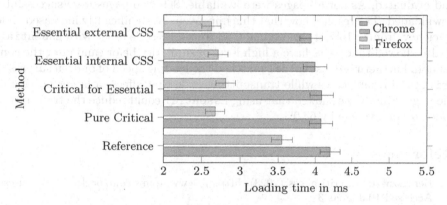

Fig. 11. Average time measurements until the "DomContentLoaded"-event end at 10 Mbps for different versions. The x-axis starts at 2s to highlight differences.

5.5 Limitations and Future Work

As with all web crawlers, the analysis of web pages will be limited to the start page of a website, for example, a login screen. This page might be optimized differently than the web application, which is reachable with user interaction. Even though the efficiency of Essential is higher than both the original web page and Critical, it is still below 50%. We speculate this is partially due to media queries, which allow for a responsive design. The CSS declarations inside such a query might purposefully not be activated due to screen size. This CSS code is, therefore, not used for page rendering. However, it is still necessary for the page to work as intended. Furthermore, not all web pages can be loaded and parsed. Critical was used to increase the AST-render capabilities to reduce the impact of the parsing limitation. However, there are still web pages that could not be rendered, for example, by including non-valid CSS code. Future work will include researching more flexible CSS to AST converters.

6   Conclusion

In this paper, `Essential`, a comprehensive server-side rendering framework for CSS, was developed and evaluated. We showed that the current state-of-the-art library `Critical` has significant potential for improving page loading speed but lacks specific details. Most crucially, using `Critical` can impact the user experience by not delivering all CSS necessary to render the page. This might lead to a negative user experience, as only a section of the page is rendered correctly. The developed software, `Essential`, improves this factor by building on top of `Critical`. In this version, all CSS of the visible page was rendered, and the delivered code was improved by removing code duplicates. Both improvements together resolve the described issues of `Critical`. For the evaluation, the top 1000 most popular web pages, according to the Tranco list, were downloaded and evaluated. As not all pages were available, 869 web pages were successfully downloaded. The results show that this improvement significantly increased code efficiency, from $\approx 16\%$ of the original CSS to $\approx 49\%$ code usage with `Essential`. It also showed that pages have a high level of similarity before and after the conversion. Furthermore, `Essential` matched the loading speed of or even surpassed `Critical` in some cases while transmitting code that affects a larger portion of the page. Finally, we showed that using `Essential` could reduce the transmitted code size on average by 65.9%.

References

1. Beregszaszi, A.: critical-css (2023). https://www.npmjs.com/package/critical-css. Accessed 10 Jan 2023
2. Bos, B., Çelik, T., Hickson, I., Lie, H.W.: Cascading style sheets level 2 revision 2 (CSS 2.2) specification (2016). https://www.w3.org/TR/CSS22. Accessed 10 Jan 2023
3. Google, Deloitte Digital and 55 the data company: Milliseconds make millions - a study on how improvements in mobile site speed positively affect a brand's bottom line (2020). https://www2.deloitte.com/content/dam/Deloitte/ie/Documents/Consulting/Milliseconds_Make_Millions_report.pdf. Accessed 10 Jan 2023
4. Grigorik, I.: Measuring the critical rendering path (2023). https://web.dev/critical-rendering-path-measure-crp. Accessed 8 Jan 2023
5. HTTP Archive: HTTP Archive: State of the Web (2023). https://httparchive.org/reports/state-of-the-web. Accessed 10 Jan 2023
6. Janssen, K., Pelle, T., de Geus, L., van der Gronden, R., Islam, T., Malavolta, I.: On the impact of the critical css technique on the performance and energy consumption of mobile browsers. In: Proceedings of the International Conference on Evaluation and Assessment on Software Engineering (EASE) (2022)
7. Jovanovski, G., Zaytsev, V.: Critical css rules-decreasing time to first render by inlining css rules for over-the-fold elements. In: Postproceedings of 2016 Seminar on Advanced Techniques and Tools for Software Evolution (SATToSE), pp. 353–356 (2016)
8. Mazinanian, D.: Eliminating code duplication in cascading style sheets. Ph.D. thesis, Concordia University (2017)

9. Ohlsson Aden, J.: penthouse (2023). https://www.npmjs.com/package/penthouse. Accessed 10 Jan 2023
10. Osmani, A.: critical (2023). https://www.npmjs.com/package/critical. Accessed 10 Jan 2023
11. Pochat, V.L., Van Goethem, T., Tajalizadehkhoob, S., Korczyński, M., Joosen, W.: Tranco: a research-oriented top sites ranking hardened against manipulation. arXiv preprint arXiv:1806.01156 (2018)
12. Vogel, L., Springer, T.: An in-depth analysis of web page structure and efficiency with focus on optimization potential for initial page load. In: Di Noia, T., Ko, IY., Schedl, M., Ardito, C. (eds)International Conference on Web Engineering, pp. 101–116. Springer, Cham (2022). https://doi.org/10.1007/978-3-031-09917-5_7
13. Wiegand, M.: Portent (2023). https://www.portent.com/blog/analytics/research-site-speed-hurting-everyones-revenue.htm. Accessed 10 Jan 2023

Collaborative Web Accessibility Evaluation: An EARL-Based Workflow Approach

Juan-Miguel López-Gil[(✉)] [iD], Oscar Díaz[iD], and Mikel Iturria

ONEKIN Research Group, University of the Basque Country (UPV/EHU),
20018 Donostia-San Sebastián, Spain
{juanmiguel.lopez,oscar.diaz}@ehu.eus, miturria003@ikasle.ehu.eus
http://www.ehu.eus

Abstract. The Web Accessibility Guidelines are designed to help developers ensure that web content is accessible to all users. These guidelines provide the foundation for evaluation tools that automate inspection processes. However, due to the heterogeneity of these guidelines and the subjectivity involved in their evaluation, humans are still necessary for the process. As a result, evaluating accessibility becomes a collaborative endeavor wherein different human experts and tools interact. Despite quickly being noticed by the W3C, it has largely been overlooked in the existing literature. Tool vendors often focus on providing a thorough evaluation rather than importing, integrating, and combining results from diverse sources. This paper examines an EARL-based document-centric workflow. It introduces a dedicated editor for EARL documents that accounts for the life-cycle of EARL documents where evaluation episodes feedback on each other. Expert evaluations were conducted (n = 5 experts), not so much about the tool itself but its ability to facilitate a collaborative approach.

Keywords: Web engineering · Web accessibility · Web accessibility evaluation · Browser extension · Aggregation

1 Introduction

Web accessibility evaluation (WAE) is the process of determining how accessible a website is for individuals with disabilities [18]. The evaluation process typically involves manual testing, automated testing tools, and user testing with people with disabilities. This places WAE as a computer-assisted collaborative endeavor. Indeed, W3C describes this scenario as one where *"a group of evaluators may want to arrange for shared access to certain evaluation tools or to ensure that they have access to a broad range of evaluation tools across the group as a whole. Using an agreed-upon template for reporting the results of evaluations can greatly facilitate coordination between different evaluators."* [7]. This quote warns against using a single WAE tool by a single WAE expert [20], and rather promotes an evaluation process involving two or more people with evaluation episodes feedbacking to each other, potentially using different WAE tools [16].

© The Author(s), under exclusive license to Springer Nature Switzerland AG 2023
I. Garrigós et al. (Eds.): ICWE 2023, LNCS 13893, pp. 206–220, 2023.
https://doi.org/10.1007/978-3-031-34444-2_15

This vision is supported by the W3C's Evaluation and Report Language (EARL) [21], a vendor-neutral and platform-independent format for expressing the results of Web accessibility evaluations. Regrettably, EARL has not received much support from tool vendors, who are more interested in providing one-size-fits-all solutions than in complementing each other. As a result, evaluators are left on their own when it comes to combining different EARL reports. This can be a significant stumbling block in the way toward collaborative WAE. The question arises about

RQ: How could evaluators be assisted in gradually and collaboratively elaborating EARL documents?

The vision is for a single EARL document to be gradually enriched as distinct evaluators provide their feedback manually or assisted through WAE tools. This calls for dedicated editors that handle EARL reports throughout their life cycle (hereafter referred to as 'handlers'). Accordingly, we can then refine our research question as follows:

RQ: How would a dedicated handler for EARL documents look like?

In addressing this question, we contribute to the existing body of literature by:

- a life-cycle for EARL documents (Sect. 4),
- a handler utility for supporting this life-cycle (Sect. 5),
- an evaluation of the use of this handler by five experts (Sect. 6).

We start by outlining the current state of affairs.

2   Accessibility Evaluation: A Crowded Tool Panorama

The more the services and content move to the Web, the more significant the impact of accessibility evaluation. As WAI gained importance, WAE tools started to crop up. As of October 2022, the W3C WAE Tools list contains 167 tools. Manca et al. provide a view of the design criteria for evaluation tools and surveys of most existing tools [17]. Broadly, tools are usually grouped along with three primary purposes, namely, [1]:

- *Automated Testing* where guidelines can be translated to code pieces is verified. Its prompt and effortless feedback makes automated testing normally used as a first accessibility test. These tools can be generic as accounting for most of the W3C guidelines (e.g., TAW 3.0, WAVE, SiteImprove, or AChecker), or rather focus on a specific accessibility aspect (e.g., Contrast Checker that focuses on the color contrast),
- *Manual Inspection Accessibility* where expert human evaluators inspect guidelines of a subjectivity matter. Brajnik et al. [6] demonstrate the ability of expert users to detect accessibility violations with more reliability than tools, specifically when it involves using a website in such a way that certain sensory, motor, or cognitive capabilities are artificially reduced. It is convenient to use manual inspection techniques throughout the design process as they can early identify potential design problems [1].

– *User Testing* where participants with disabilities are asked to perform several tasks to collect empirical data individually. Support software for user testing is being produced to make these evaluations more agile.

The main premise of this work is that existing tools complement each other, providing different focuses. This was noticed in different studies, especially [20], where the very same website was evaluated with different tools and resulted in distinct insights. Since this study goes back to 2013, we were interested in assessing the extent to which this point still holds. To this end, we replicated the study by using two popular tools *AccessMonitor* and *AChecker* on six websites selected because they are public organizations of different types, which can give an idea of the state of accessibility in public organizations[1], and check to see whether major evaluation differences still hold. Table 1 depicts the results. Cells kept the number of occurrences detected by *AccessMonitor* vs those of *AChecker* (e.g., "4/0" in the 'Passed' row stands for 4 success criteria passed as determined by *AccessMonitor* vs 0 success as determined by *AChecker*). We can see divergences in all possible outcomes for the analyzed web pages. It can be concluded that *AccessMonitor* is more strict in detecting failures in the success criteria. In contrast, *AChecker* has a higher standard for determining success in the criteria it evaluates.

Table 1. Diversity of results between *AccessMonitor* vs *AChecker*

Result Type	EU	Brussels	WHO	UN	UNESCO	MIT
Passed	4/0	3/0	4/0	3/0	1/0	0/2
Failure	4/0	6/4	3/2	3/1	9/4	2/2
Can't tell	4/18	3/15	2/17	1/8	6/15	16/4
Not Present	0/0	0/0	0/0	0/0	0/0	0/0
Not Checked	38/32	38/31	41/31	43/41	34/31	32/42

The bottom line is that both tools complement each other. This diversity in the methods and tools at play favors a wealth of insights contributing to a more thorough evolution. The downside rests on the effort of combining a heterogeneous set of terms and insights into a single report. If manually conducted, this effort might put off evaluators from teaming up. This moves us to the next section.

---

[1] European Union main web page: https://european-union.europa.eu/index_en; Brussels City Hall main web page: https://www.brussels.be/; World Health Organization main web page: https://www.who.int/home; United Nations main web page: https://www.un.org/en/; UNESCO main web page: https://www.unesco.org/en; MIT main web page: https://www.mit.edu/.

3   Accessibility Evaluation: A Collaborative Effort

W3C early notices the collaborative nature of accessibility evaluation by introducing the following scenarios [7]:

- a group of colleagues distributed within a larger organization; for instance, Web developers from different units of a large corporation working together
- a Web development or quality assurance team within a larger organization, which brings in outside experts to help them conduct evaluations in the short term and helps them build improved capability for in-house evaluation over the long term
- a small business whose mission is to provide accessibility evaluation services and which does so with a multi-disciplinary team
- disability advocates from different organizations collaborate online to monitor the accessibility of Web sites
- a group of individuals distributed across related organizations such as government agencies, each with the obligation to monitor the accessibility of their Web site, who combine their diverse expertise & perspectives for higher quality evaluations

Despite W3C's explicit recommendation, collaboration in WAE has been largely overlooked. We are unaware of guidelines for carrying out accessibility evaluations when conducted collaboratively. Without the aim of being exhaustive, we conducted some literature readings where complex evaluation scenarios are introduced (Kumar and Owsto [12], Abdul Latif and Masrek [13], Faouzi [3]). Some general guidelines could be derived:

- hybrid evaluation outperforms tool-only evaluation. Intermingling human-based evaluation (accounting for subjectivity) and tool-based evaluation (accounting for scalability) nicely feedback each other,
- delaying human intervention. Human participation, no matter whether evaluation experts or disabled users, tend to be costly and cumbersome. Avoid involving humans from the onset. Rather than conducting some general assessment using automatic tools, pinpointing weak areas, and focusing human attention on these areas,
- evaluation is a process rather than a one-shot effort. If websites are thought to evolve frequently, then accessibility evaluation becomes a continuous practice. This seems to suggest that results from an evaluation cycle might serve as the basis for the next cycle.

Unfortunately, the lack of traces prevents guidelines from being sustained in empirical evidence.

Along with the above W3C scenario, we introduce our running example (see Fig. 1):

1. *Expert1* selects a generic-purpose tool such as *AChecker* to get an overview of the accessibility status for the page at hand. The report casts some limitations on the accessibility of the web page. *Expert1* takes the *AChecker* output to

the W3C's Evaluation Report tool to add whatever comment she considers appropriate.

2. *Expert2* is invited for an interview on this web page. A manual report is produced and uploaded into *EARLER*. Notice that the report may not cover all guidelines and can be focused on specific issues detected.

3. *Expert3*, informed by insights after *Expert2* participation, runs *AccessMonitor*, which is appreciated by its performance in detecting this sort of issue. As anecdotally proved by Table 1, *AccessMonitor* complements *AChecker*.

4. *Expert4* takes the aggregated result so far and uses an automatically aggregated report using both *AccessMonitor* and *AChecker* as a template to analyze how to detect possible issues.

For our purposes, we would like to note that: (1) different people might participate; (2) different tools might be involved; and (3) the evaluation process may unfold throughout distinct evaluation episodes. The question is how to harmonize the freedom of evaluators to choose their tools with the need to team up in producing a single report.

A step forward is the W3C's Evaluation and Report Language (EARL), a vendor-neutral and platform-independent format for expressing the results of Web accessibility evaluations in the pursuit of portability [21]. Regrettably, EARL has not received much support from tool vendors, who are more interested in providing one-size-fits-all solutions than in complementing each other. Alternatively, we advocate for a document-centric model where EARL documents sit at the center while moving among WAE tools. Next, we introduce a life cycle for EARL documents.

4   A Life-Cycle for EARL Documents

This section elaborates on requirements for EARL-document handlers as utilities to support the life-cycle of an EARL document (see Fig. 2). Precisely, the following events are reckoned to be supported by EARL-document handlers:

- **New/Import**. Evaluators can provide a brand-new subjective evaluation right away without resorting to any WAE tool. Alternatively, EARL reports from previous evaluations can also be imported so that evaluators can have a head-start by tapping into someone else's EARL report. An *EARLER* session's output can be the next *EARLER* session's input.

- **Upgrade**. Upon loading, documents can be enriched with supplementary information. Upgrades can be either manual or assisted. The former permits evaluators to provide their subjective evaluation. By contrast, assisted upgrades are those conducted with the help of a WAE tool.

- **Export**. The exportation of a document incorporates metadata concerning the origin of the document. Provenance metadata encompasses information regarding the individuals and activities involved in the document's creation and can be employed to evaluate its quality, dependability, or credibility. The usage of the W3C's PROV ontology is suggested as a standard [22]. Although

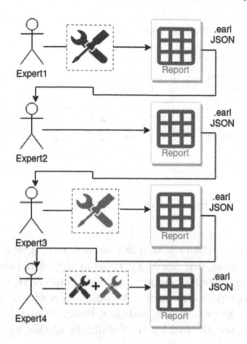

Fig. 1. Running example: 4 experts & 2 tools team up to deliver a single report

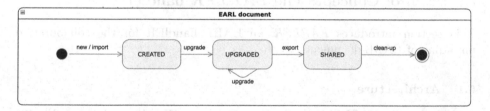

Fig. 2. The life-cycle of an EARL document

our scenario is not as open as those for which this standard was designed, the capability to monitor the sequence of changes would allow us to consider alternative trust metrics, such as the involvement of specific individuals, the implementation of proper testing procedures, or the verification that the evaluation procedures were executed in the correct sequence.

– **Clean-up**. Evaluators may opt to eliminate the current document and commence anew. This process may involve the import of a new document or the selection of a different WAE tool.
– **Render**. EARL documents are structured according to the JSON-LD format, with a focus on machine processing rather than human readability. An EARL handler should provide a user-friendly visual representation of the document, regardless of its current state.

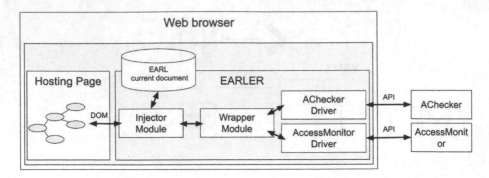

Fig. 3. EARLER architecture

WAE collaboration is then realized as a sequence of these events conducted by *different* evaluators using *distinct* WAE tools at *different* points in time. EARL handlers assist in this interplay among evaluators and WAE tools in their double role of hubs and provenance auditors. As hubs, they enable drivers to tap into existing WAE tools. As provenance auditors, handlers may record who did what and when. The next section tackles the feasibility of this vision.

5 Proof of Concept: The *EARLER* handler

This section introduces *EARLER*, an EARL handlER for the collaborative unfolding of EARL documents.

5.1 Architecture

Architecturally, *EARLER* is realized as Chrome's Web Extension (see Fig. 3). This decision was made to facilitate the smooth and risk-free implementation of the approach proposed in this work, which we believe is crucial for the widespread adoption of this nascent approach.

5.2 Graphical-User Interface Gestures

Once installed and activated, *EARLER* overlays the current web page with a lateral toolbar (see Fig. 5). This toolbar is the handler for *the current document*, i.e., the EARL document that is locally kept in the web extension. This toolbar holds two regions. Although web accessibility analysis tools can evaluate a whole website, EARLER currently works a page at a time.

The upper region . It accounts for the events of the life-cycle of EARL documents, namely:

- *New/Import*, which provides the means to initialize *the current document*,

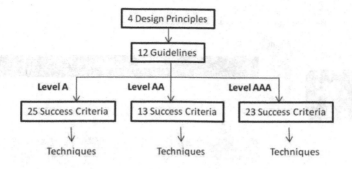

Fig. 4. WCAG 2.0 data model

- *Assisted Upgrade*, where WAE tools are invoked, their results are scraped from the tool's page, and finally, these results are combined with those of the current EARL document (see later). So far, *EARLER* support *AccessMonitor* [2] and *AChecker* [11]. More WAE tools can be added by providing their corresponding drivers,
- *Manual Upgrade*, which permits evaluators to directly edit *the current EARL document* through combo boxes and text boxes,
- *Export*. Once the evaluation ends, *the current document* can be exported, ready to be consumed by an EARL-compliant tool. In addition, the PROV data model is used to enrich the EARL document with provenance data obtained automatically from local variables (e.g., current user, current time, current IP).
- *Clean-up*, which resets the EARL document to its initial state.

The lower region. It renders *the current EARL document*. EARLER supports three renderings (see Fig. 5):

- in terms of *Passed (P), Failure (F), Can't tell (CT), Not Present (NP)* and *Not Checked (NC)*
- in terms of the EARL model (see Fig. 4: guidelines are first listed, where drop-down menus are arranged along with the W3C criteria, which are hierarchically arranged according to the structure of the WCAG 2 guidelines (i.e., principle, guideline, and success criterion). Mimicking the WAVE tool, click on a criterion for the affected HTML elements on the host page to be highlighted. Click again on the criterion for the host page to scroll down to the next affected HTML element.

5.3   Merge Algorithm

A critical issue is combining EARL documents. Consider that the current EARL document contains the results from a previous evaluation episode with *AccessMonitor*. To upgrade this document, the evaluator launches the 'Assisted Upgrade' by selecting the *AChecker* driver. Internally, this causes an HTTP

Fig. 5. *EARLER* at work: After a web accessibility report is generated or uploaded, found issues are displayed in the table in the lateral bar. In the example in the Figure, a possible error in the success criterion 2.4.1 (bypass blocks) is spotted during *Assisted Upgrade* using *AccessMonitor* and *AChecker* (table in the lateral bar). When the possible error is clicked on the HTML snippet in the lateral bar, its web page counterpart is framed by a red rectangle (upper part of the web page).

request whose HMTL result is scraped to produce an EARL transient document. The merge algorithm governs how EARL documents are combined. Figure 1 outlines the process.

Table 2 presents the results of the algorithm applied to the sample websites described in Sect. 2. The cells of the table contain a triplet in the form of $n1/n2/n3$, where $n1$, $n2$, and $n3$ represent the number of occurrences identified by a previous evaluation with *AccessMonitor* (held in the current document), the current evaluation with *AChecker* (kept in a transient document), and the merged result, respectively. For example, the cell *('European Union', 'Passed')* has the value of *"4/0/2"*, which means that 4 success criteria were passed without any issues by the *AccessMonitor* evaluation, and 0 success criteria were passed without any issues as determined by the *AChecker* evaluation. The merged result is **2**. This result represents the number of success criteria passed without any issues based on the combined evaluations of both tools[2]. This is a strict merging approach. If there is one failure, the merging would consider that as a failure. A more lenient approach may be necessary to avoid minor errors halting the merging process. This calls for configuration options to tune EARLER to website specifics, an alternative that is left for further research.

EARLER provides proof-of-concept for a workflow-based approach to WAE evaluation. EARLER is open source and available for download at[3]. We would be thrilled for the community to check it out with their scenarios.

6   Proof-of-Value: Evaluation

Collaborative WAE evaluation is still not widely studied in the academic community. Hence, the first evaluation is about the need for such collaboration, using EALER or not. This is conducted through an Expert Interview (n = 5) [5]. Next, we tackle how such collaborative evaluation can be conducted through EARLER. Here, the aim is to assess the perceived usefulness and ease of use of EARLER, we resort to the Technology Acceptance Model (TAM) questionnaire.

6.1   Capturing the Insights About Collaborative Evaluation: An Expert Interview

Goal. *Capturing* the insights about collaborative evaluation *with respect to* web accessibility *from the point of view of* evaluation experts *in the context of* disseminating UX evaluators from the Universities of the Basque Country and Lleida. Notice that the goal is not evaluating EARLER but the need to support collaborative practices, using EARLER or not.

Instrument. We resort to Expert Interviews [5]. We consider an individual 'an expert' based on her skill in software quality and web accessibility evaluation.

---

[2] It's worth noting that if even a single error is detected, the corresponding success criterion is labeled as *Failed*.

[3] https://github.com/Itusil/TFG.

Algorithm 1. Merging of EARL documents

Input: the current document & the transient document
Output: Adequately scored success criteria
    issueList $\longleftarrow$ List of success criteria with accessibility-related issues in any of the report documents
    for Each success criterion in the *issueList* **do**
        listOccurrences $\longleftarrow$ Occurrences related with the success criteria in any of the reports
        if any occurrence labeled as *"Failure"* in *listOccurrences* **then**
            Outcome := *"Failure"*
        else if any occurrence labeled as *"Can't tell"* in *listOccurrences* **then**
            Outcome := *"Can't tell"*
        else if any occurrence labeled as *"Passed"* in *listOccurrences* **then**
            Outcome := *"Passed"*
        else if any occurrence labeled as *"Non checked"* in *listOccurrences* **then**
            Outcome := *"Non checked"*
        else if any occurrence labeled as *"Non present"* in *listOccurrences* **then**
            Outcome := *"Non present"*
        end if
    end for
    return Outcome

At least two years of experience in web accessibility evaluation were required to participate. We could not obtain all the experts locally but also at the University of Lleida. Five experts qualified, three males and two females, three from the University of the Basque Country and two from the University of Lleida.

Table 2. EARL document merging: sample cases

Result Type	EU	Brussels	WHO	UN	UNESCO	MIT
Passed	4/0/2	3/0/1	4/0/1	3/0/2	1/0/0	0/2/0
Failure	4/0/4	6/4/8	3/2/5	3/1/4	9/4/11	2/2/4
Can't tell	4/18/18	3/15/15	2/17/17	1/8/8	6/15/16	16/4/18
Not Present	0/0/0	0/0/0	0/0/0	0/0/0	0/0/0	0/0/0
Not Checked	38/32/26	38/31/26	41/31/27	43/41/36	34/31/23	32/42/28

Process. We mimicked the W3C scenario where *"a group of evaluators may want to arrange for shared access to certain evaluation tools"*. Specifically, we wanted to convey the need for combining results for distinct evaluations. To this end, we consider seven cases, one for each of the websites that serve to illustrate the diversity of results between *AccessMonitor* vs *AChecker* (see Table 1). To this end, EARLER was used to evaluate these sites first with *AccessMonitor*, and next *AChecker*, and most importantly, the results were combined. The results were delivered to the experts (see Table 2) for discussion. We stress that the aim

Table 3. TAM questionnaire results. The TAM questions are described in [9]

TAM question	U1	U2	U3	U4	U5	Mean	Dev
1) Using this product at work would help me complete	6	7	7	6	7	6.6	0.55
2) Using this product would improve my job performance	6	7	7	7	7	6.8	0.45
3) Using this product would increase my productivity	6	7	7	6	7	6.6	0.55
4) Using would increase my effectiveness at work	6	7	6	5	7	6.2	0.84
5) Using this product would make it easier to do my job	7	7	7	6	7	6.8	0.45
6) I would find this product useful at work	7	6	7	7	7	6.8	0.45
7) Learning how to handle the product would be easy	7	6	5	7	7	6.4	0.89
8) I would find it easy to let the product do what	6	6	6	6	7	6.2	0.45
9) My interaction with this product would be clear	6	6	6	6	7	6.2	0.45
10) I would find this product flexible to work with	6	5	5	7	7	6	1.00
11) It would be easy for me to become agile	7	6	6	6	7	6.4	0.45
12) I would find it easy to use	7	7	6	7	7	6.8	0.45
Mean	6.4	6.4	6.2	6.3	7.0	6.5	0.3
Dev	0.5	0.7	0.7	0.6	0.0	0.5	0.3

Table 4. UMUX-Lite results

UMUX-Lite question	U1	U2	U3	U4	U5	Mean	Dev
This system's capabilities meet my requirements	1	2	1	2	1	1.4	0.55
This system is easy to use	1	2	2	1	1	1.4	0.55
Mean	1	2	1.5	1.5	1	1.4	0.42
Dev	0.00	0.00	0.71	0.71	0.00	0	0.39
UMUX-Lite score (percentage)	100	83.33	91.67	91.67	100	93.33	6.97

of this evaluation is not EARLER itself but the need for tools like EARLER, i.e., the need for supporting collaborative evaluation. The interviews were conducted individually, both in person and via *Skype*, and lasted an average of 30 to 45 min. For the sake of common terminology, the interviews started with a comprehensive introduction to accessibility principles and methods, followed by an EARLER demo.

Results. Experts agreed on the importance of combining different perspectives and skills during the evaluation. In addition, some collaborative practices emerged during the interview, specifically:

- evaluation does not need to start from scratch but may tap into a previous report. This seems to back the 'import' facility,
- evaluation might combine both subjective and assisted evaluation. This seems to back the interplay of the manual upgrade and the assisted upgrade

Threats to validity. We regard the main threats as interpretive validity and generalizability. *Interpretive Validity* is how well researchers capture participants' meaning of events or behaviors without imposing their perspective. To improve interpretative validity, we began the session with a brief presentation on the study's objectives and the proposed intervention. This presentation was aimed at establishing common terminology and avoiding misunderstandings. Apart from that, we confirmed the expert evaluation's conclusions by soliciting participant feedback. As for *Generalizability*, it concerns the applicability of conclusions to similar settings and groups. In this respect, we tap into five experts with at least two-year experience in conducting accessibility studies. The main risk comes from their procedures being biased toward the academic world. It is honest to recognize we do not yet have strong empirical evidence about the need for accessibility evaluation to be collaborative, except the one from the W3C.

6.2   Assessing EARLER Acceptance: A TAM Evaluation

Goal. *Assess* the ease of use and usefulness of EARLER *with respect to* Web accessibility evaluation *from the point of view of* evaluation experts *in the context of* collaborative evaluation.

Instrument. The Technology Acceptance Model (TAM) questionnaire [9] and the UMUX-Lite questionnaire [14], both based on a seven Likert scale. Multiple acceptance questionnaires were used to test EARLER as they can provide insights, improve the accuracy of predictions and provide a more nuanced and complete picture of the technology in question [19].

Results. Table 3 shows the results of the TAM questionnaire. The scores range from 1 to 7, with 7 being the best possible score. As specified in TAM [9], the first six questions describe perceived usefulness, which achieved a mean of 6.63. As for the last six questions, they describe the perceived ease of use, reaching a mean of 6.33. According to TAM, good ratings of usefulness and ease of use (perceived usability) influence the intention to use, influencing the actual likelihood of use.

The results for the UMUX-Lite questionnaire are displayed in Table 4. The table shows the marks each expert answered for each question and the mean and standard deviation values for each question and each expert. Scores range from 1 to 7, with 1 representing the highest attainable score. The mean result for UMUX-Lite responses for all experts was 1.4 out of 7. It also shows each expert's UMUX-Lite score [14], which achieved a mean of 93,33 in a ranking from 0 to 100, where 100 is the maximum achievable value. On the other hand, the System Usability Scale (SUS) [8], one of the most commonly used questionnaires to evaluate the perceived usability of a given system, consists of ten questions on a five-point Likert scale that provides a score from 0 to 100 range [4]. There is a correspondence between SUS and UMUX-Lite scores, as [15] demonstrated.

Threats to Validity. We should indicate a risk of Selection bias since participants were recruited locally from academia. This is unfortunate as the need for the thoroughness that collaborative evaluation can bring about might be argumentatively better appreciated by practitioners. Furthermore, the successful adoption of collaborative evaluation depends on the collaborative culture within the hosting organization, thus potentially influencing the validity of the results.

7   Conclusions

The W3C soon recognized the collaborative nature of WAE, which involves multiple experts and tools working together to produce an EARL document gradually. This raised the research question of how to assist users in the process of gradually creating EARL-based documents. To address this challenge, we propose a document-centric approach where EARL documents are incrementally constructed with the help of dedicated editors. The feasibility of this approach is demonstrated through EARLER, a Chrome web extension designed to manage EARL documents. In this approach, experts interact by exchanging EARL documents, and a preliminary evaluation has shown that subjects appreciate the complementarity of EARLER compared to existing evaluation tools. Based on these positive results, we believe that EARL editors have the potential to become a valuable tool in the accessibility evaluator's toolkit. We hope to further validate this hypothesis through additional evidence gathered from the ease of installing EARLER.

EARLER, similar to early online document collaboration, relies on email with an attached document for sharing purposes [10]. This places the management of stakeholders outside of EARLER's scope, resulting in a lack of control over the participants and the fate of the EARL document during the transition. In contrast, advanced systems for document collaboration, such as wikis, provide complete version history and store all comments and activities associated with a document. EARLER has the potential to move in this direction, but this would require a centralized architecture where a server maintains copies of the documents for remote access. In this scenario, sections of an EARL document would be considered wiki pages, raising questions about the topology of the organization conducting the evaluation. The W3C scenarios for collaborative evaluation suggest various topologies, ranging from peer-to-peer to more centralized ones, might be possible.

Acknowledgement. This work is co-supported by MCIN/AEI/10.13039/501100011033 and the "European Union NextGeneration EU/PRTR" under contract PID2021-125438OB-I00.

References

1. Abascal, J., Arrue, M., Valencia, X.: Tools for web accessibility evaluation. In: Yesilada, Y., Harper, S. (eds.) Web Accessibility. HIS, pp. 479–503. Springer, London (2019). https://doi.org/10.1007/978-1-4471-7440-0_26
2. acessibilidade.gov.pt: Accessmonitor (2023). https://accessmonitor.acessibilidade.gov.pt/. Accessed 03 April 2023
3. Al Mourad, M., Kamoun, F.: Accessibility evaluation of Dubai e-government websites: findings and implications. J. E-Gov. Stud. Best Practices (2013)
4. Bangor, A., Kortum, P.T., Miller, J.T.: An empirical evaluation of the system usability scale. Intl. J. Human-Comput. Inter. **24**(6), 574–594 (2008)
5. Bogner, A., Littig, B., Menz, W.: Introduction: expert interviews-an introduction to a new methodological debate. In: ogner, A., Littig, B., Menz, W. (eds.) Interviewing Experts, pp. 1–13. Springer (2009)

6. Brajnik, G., Yesilada, Y., Harper, S.: The expertise effect on web accessibility evaluation methods. Human-Comput. Interact. **26**(3), 246–283 (2011)
7. Brewer, J.: Using combined expertise to evaluate web accessibility (2022). https://www.w3.org/WAI/test-evaluate/combined-expertise/
8. Brooke, J., et al.: SUS-A quick and dirty usability scale. Usability Eval. Ind. **189**(194), 4–7 (1996)
9. Davis, F.D.: A technology acceptance model for empirically testing new end-user information systems: theory and results. Ph.D. thesis, Massachusetts Institute of Technology (1985)
10. Gazzè, D., La Polla, M.N., Marchetti, A., Tesconi, M., Vivaldi, A.: WorkMail: collaborative document workflow management by Email. In: Luo, Y. (ed.) CDVE 2012. LNCS, vol. 7467, pp. 14–23. Springer, Heidelberg (2012). https://doi.org/10.1007/978-3-642-32609-7_2
11. Greg Gay, C.L.: Achecker (2023). https://achecker.achecks.ca/checker/index.php. Accessed 03 April 2023
12. Kumar, K.L., Owston, R.: Evaluating e-learning accessibility by automated and student-centered methods. Educ. Tech. Res. Dev. **64**(2), 263–283 (2016)
13. Latif, M.H.A., Masrek, M.N.: Accessibility evaluation on Malaysian e-government websites. J. E-Government stud. Best Practices **2010**, 11 (2010)
14. Lewis, J.R., Utesch, B.S., Maher, D.E.: UMUX-LITE: when there's no time for the SUS. In: Proceedings of the SIGCHI Conference on Human Factors in Computing Systems, pp. 2099–2102. CHI '13, Association for Computing Machinery, New York (2013). https://doi.org/10.1145/2470654.2481287
15. Lewis, J.R., Utesch, B.S., Maher, D.E.: Investigating the correspondence between UMUX-LITE and SUS scores. In: Marcus, A. (ed.) DUXU 2015. LNCS, vol. 9186, pp. 204–211. Springer, Cham (2015). https://doi.org/10.1007/978-3-319-20886-2_20
16. MACAKOĞLU, Ş.S., Peker, S.: Web accessibility performance analysis using web content accessibility guidelines and automated tools: a systematic literature review. In: 2022 International Congress on Human-Computer Interaction, Optimization and Robotic Applications (HORA), pp. 1–8 (2022). https://doi.org/10.1109/HORA55278.2022.9799981
17. Manca, M., Palumbo, V., Paternò, F., Santoro, C.: The transparency of automatic web accessibility evaluation tools: design criteria, state of the art, and user perception. ACM Transactions on Accessible Computing (2022)
18. Thatcher, J., et al.: Constructing accessible web sites. Apress, Berkeley, CA (2002). https://doi.org/10.1007/978-1-4302-1116-7, http://link.springer.com/10.1007/978-1-4302-1116-7
19. Venkatesh, V., Davis, F.D.: A theoretical extension of the technology acceptance model: four longitudinal field studies. Manage. Sci. **46**(2), 186–204 (2000)
20. Vigo, M., Brown, J., Conway, V.: Benchmarking web accessibility evaluation tools: measuring the harm of sole reliance on automated tests. In: Proceedings of the 10th International Cross-Disciplinary Conference on Web Accessibility, pp. 1–10. W4A '13, Association for Computing Machinery, New York (2013). https://doi.org/10.1145/2461121.2461124
21. W3C: Evaluation and report language (earl) overview (2023). https://www.w3.org/WAI/standards-guidelines/earl/. Accessed 03 April 2023
22. W3C: Prov model primer (2023). https://www.w3.org/TR/2013/NOTE-prov-primer-20130430/. Accessed 03 April 2023

In a Hurry: How Time Constraints and the Presentation of Web Search Results Affect User Behaviour and Experience

Garrett Allen[✉][iD], Mike Beijen[iD], David Maxwell[iD], and Ujwal Gadiraju[iD]

TU Delft, Delft, The Netherlands
{g.m.allen,u.k.gadiraju}@tudelft.nl, m.f.beijen@student.tudelft.nl,
maxwelld90@acm.org

Abstract. Time constraints are commonplace in our daily lives. While literature in recent years from the *Information Retrieval (IR)* community has increased our understanding of the effects of time constraints on search, practical effects on search outcomes have rarely been evaluated. Little is known about how different search interfaces influence search outcomes and experiences in time-constrained search. This constitutes a knowledge gap that we aim to address in our work. Through a pre-registered 4 × 4 between-subjects crowdsourced user study, we investigate the influence of four different interfaces (*list view, grid-based view, absence of result snippets*, and *linear scanning pattern view*) on search outcomes and experiences under imposed time constraints (*no constraint* and constraints at *two, five*, and *eight* minutes). Results from our study indicate that user task performance is considerably affected by time constraints. In addition, as time constraints are tightened, a trade-off between querying rates and click depths arises. While no interaction effects between SERP interfaces and time constraints were ultimately found, findings from this study form an essential foundation for future work on how search result presentation may assist those searchers under strict time constraints.

Keywords: web search · time constraints · user interfaces · search behaviour analysis · task performance · user experience

1 Introduction

Time constraints are commonplace in our lives, and can arise from various causes—such as a report deadline, or public transport disruption. Such constraints likely influence how we interact with the world around us, and can affect our judgement and decision-making abilities. Of course, the activity of searching for information is also subject to time constraints, which in turn can introduce pressure. Amongst other effects, experiencing these constraints and/or pressures has resulted in observations where individuals change their search strategies [23]. Differences in online search behaviour measures—such as

© The Author(s), under exclusive license to Springer Nature Switzerland AG 2023
I. Garrigós et al. (Eds.): ICWE 2023, LNCS 13893, pp. 221–235, 2023.
https://doi.org/10.1007/978-3-031-34444-2_16

query rates, dwell times, and the time spent examining documents—have also been observed [7,8]. Such behavioural changes come with consequences. This could lead to a decrease in effectiveness, as demonstrated in a clinical decision-making study where the gained accuracy from using a web-based medical search system decreased from 32% to 6% as time pressure increased [38]. The literature on the effects of time constraints on web search task performance however provides limited insights. Therefore, directing research efforts into how a search engine may assist searchers under time pressure is justified. While search engines cannot mitigate the time pressure that (some) of their users may be experiencing, search engines *can* change the presentation of results on the *Search Engine Results Page (SERP)*—with designs to support time-constrained users. Various adaptations of SERPs (e.g., [18,19,28]) have been explored, yet the extent to which elements of the SERP may cater to individuals under time constraints in terms of task performance is a knowledge gap worthy of additional examination.

This work aims to investigate how different time constraints influence *task performance, user behaviour*, and *user experience*. We conducted a pre-registered, crowdsourced 4×4 between-subjects factorial design user study and examined the effects of four different SERP interfaces on user experience: *(i)* a standard *list-based view*; *(ii)* a *grid-based view*; *(iii)* a *list-based view without result snippets*; and *(iv)* a *linear scanning pattern view*. We explored whether an affinity for technology moderates the relationship between time constraints and task performance, over scenarios with no constraints present—and with time constraints of two, five, and eight minutes. We address the following research questions.

RQ1 *How do different time constraints influence task performance?*
RQ2 *How do different time constraints affect search behaviour?*
RQ3 *In what way are different UI designs susceptible to the effect of time constraints?*
RQ4 *What impact do different SERP interfaces have on user experience?*
RQ5 *To what extent does Affinity for Technology Interaction serve as a moderating variable for task performance?*

Our results show that stricter time constraints decrease task performance considerably—and as a result, some search behaviour measures are influenced. Exploratory results suggest that as time constraints tighten, a trade-off between query rate and click depth arises. While no significant interaction between SERP interfaces and time constraints emerged, this work lays an important foundation for future work on how search result presentation may assist time-constrained searchers. In line with open science principles, we publish all the materials, including questionnaires and data collected in this study on the *Open Science Framework*.[1]

---

[1] https://osf.io/3wx42/—last accessed 10th October, 2022.

2   Related Work

2.1   SERP Interfaces

Early work in the *noughties* by Dumais et al. [10] explored SERP layouts by grouping seven experimental interfaces into traditional list interfaces, such as those used by Google or Bing, and category interfaces[2]. The authors found that category-based interfaces were more effective than list interfaces in terms of search time. Additionally, inline summaries displayed underneath a search result's title, as are commonplace on contemporary SERPs, were found to be more useful than their hover summary counterparts. A hover summary was only provided when the user hovered over the related document's title. Through the addition of contextual information (including the *PageRank* score [32], overall and export popularity, and awards won), Schwarz and Morris [37] identified a significant improvement in credibility assessment of search results—increasing the accuracy to equal a user assessing the web page in its entirety.

Regarding user evaluation, Kammerer and Gerjets [19] investigated how the user interface may facilitate search result evaluations using a traditional list interface, and a tabular interface with results sorted into three categories: subjective, objective, and commercial. The findings showed that in the tabular interface, participants paid less attention to commercial results and more to objective results. While using tabular or "grid" interfaces [20], participants are motivated to select more trustworthy search results and to divide attention more equally between the results [18]. In a similar interface *without* categories, Joachims et al. [17] found that a greater number of results were inspected before the first result was clicked—thereby decreasing the role of the search result's ranking. This interface was provided as a means of mitigating the effects of position bias.

Investigating search result snippets, Clarke et al. [4] reported short or absent snippets have a negative effect on click-through rates. Maxwell et al. [28] found that longer snippets do not improve task performance, while Cutrell and Guan [9] found the opposite, adding information to search snippets improved task performance. In the same work, Cutrell and Guan [9] suggest designing SERP to focus the user's attention on the result metadata, i.e., the URL and title, to address the problem of long snippets being problematic for navigational search tasks. Therefore, in this work we explore whether using a SERP sans snippets within a time constrained environment and a SERP with snippets re-positioned to the right side of the other result data has an effect on user behaviour.

Various SERP have been designed with a specific goal in mind. Salmerón [36] for example compared a conventional, list-based design with a SERP consisting of a graphical overview presenting the relationship between web pages. Participants of this study were asked to examine the text of the result pages in both interfaces as if preparing for a test, after which they would be assessed on their comprehension. By signalling the relationships between web pages, an increased inter-text comprehension was provoked. Focusing on learning, Roy et al. [35]

---

[2] The category interface is akin to a search *directory*, much like how early commercial web search engines presented documents (like *Yahoo!*).

investigated the inclusion of active learning tools in the SERP interface, and found that note-taking increased the number of facts covered in post-task written essays by 34%—and highlighting resulted in 34% more subtopics covered. The SERP may also be used to reduce the *Search Engine Manipulation Effect (SEME)* [11] through low and high bias alerts [12]. In the same work, Epstein et al. [12] found that the SEME caused users to focus more on lower-ranked results. In contrast, Wu et al. [41] found adding an answer module to the SERP makes users focus more on the top results, but also improved user engagement and user satisfaction. User engagement also played an important role in the work by Foulds et al. [14], who concluded that users retrieved relevant documents faster—and with less frustration—when using a SERP without advertisements present. In response to users lacking familiarity with how search engines retrieve results and the findings of an investigation into user trust in search engines, Pan et al. [33] suggested the need for providing short explanations on SERP. Following this suggestion, Ramos and Eickhoff [34] experimented with search results explanations in terms of query term contribution bars per search result. Novin and Meyers [30] called for greater transparency in SERPs—establishing that search result explanations lead to increased transparency and search efficiency. There is a rich and varied body of work around SERP interfaces, yet little work addresses the *interplay between these interfaces and time pressured searchers*.

2.2 Time Pressure and Web Search

The effects of time on search is a well-researched topic. As previously mentioned, van der Vegt et al. [38] investigated the effects of time-constrained searching within the medical domain. They found that the accuracy of using an online medical search system decreased as time pressure increased. Crescenzi et al. [6] investigated the effects of time pressure through a crowdsourced user study, and found that participants who perceived to be under time pressure experienced lower search satisfaction and higher task difficulty. This work was later extended by Crescenzi et al. [8] with a comparable experimental setup, finding numerous significant effects of the time constraints on, amongst others, time pressure, task difficulty, and search performance satisfaction. In an earlier user study, Liu et al. [24] varied the presence of a time constraint. Participants subjected to no time constraints self-rated significantly higher pre-search confidence, better post-search performance, higher post-search familiarity with the topic, and greater knowledge acquisition. As for search strategy, Weenig and Maarleveld [39] found that participants adapt to time constraints via a more selective search strategy— and are not likely to accelerate their examination of items (i.e., spend less time on items). Liu and Wei [23] showed that when presented with time constraints, searchers move from a more *"economic"* search strategy to a more *"cautious"* approach. This was reflected by the fact that fewer results per query were viewed.

Delays in web search are also a topic of conversation. Crescenzi et al. [8] looked at the influence of system delays which caused participants to think the system was slower *only* when the delays were present in the second task performed. Of particular note, Arapakis et al. [1] found that the addition of query submission delays are noticed sooner by users of a fast search engine. The user's belief that the search engine would help them complete their search task decreased as this induced latency increased. In addition, Maxwell and Azzopardi [26] also experimented with delays to search. They found delays to both query submission and document download affected the behaviour of participants of their laboratory study regarding the time spent examining documents.

3   Study Design

In this study, we seek to understand the relationship between SERP interfaces and task performance, user behaviour, and user engagement while under time constraints. To this end, we conducted a 4 × 4 between-subject study, where the independent variables are the SERP interface and the time constraint. To identify proper time constraints, we turned to recent works involving search tasks with no time constraints to find insights on the search duration. We find that the average time spent on a search task ranges from a minimum of seven minutes to a maximum of ten minutes [16, 25, 42]. To ensure the constraints act as a source of time pressure, we use values of two, five, and eight minutes. We also include a no time constraint condition—acting as a baseline.

3.1   Search Task and SERP Interfaces

In a scenario-based search task, participants are instructed to imagine themselves as a journalist who has been assigned at the last minute to replace a colleague at an international forum discussion on a controversial topic, DNA cloning. Their job is to collect arguments connected to this topic in order to prepare for this role. Participants are allotted a training period with a practice topic and no time constraints to familiarize themselves with the SERP interface.

The participants perform their searches using a mock search engine, *BBT*. BBT displays the search frame on the left and the experiment frame on the right. The search results are presented according to which experimental condition the participant is randomly assigned. In the *list-view*, users are presented with the standard SERP interface that you see on mainstream search engines like Google or Bing. The *grid-view* presents the results in a 3 × 3 grid. In the *sa-view* participants are shown a SERP with no snippets included. The *ilsp-view* places the snippets to the right of the results in a traditional list view. No auto-completion is used during the search process to prevent inducing any biases. Screenshots of these interfaces can be seen on the companion page.[3]

For the duration of the task, participants can add additional arguments using an "Add argument" button below the text boxes in the experiment frame, or remove them by using the trash can icon at the top right of each argument text box. A "Review instructions" button above the text boxes allows participants to review task instructions at any time. Additionally, participants are provided

---

[3] https://sites.google.com/view/icwe2023.

with a "Finalize" button to exit early if they feel they have collected enough information or if further search does not yield additional arguments.

A timer at the top of the experiment frame shows the remaining time if any. An alert in the form of a pop-up will be given when there is one minute remaining. It is made technically impossible to copy and paste arguments into the text boxes to encourage active involvement and prevent misbehaviour. The actual search is performed using the Bing web search API.[4] Participants are free to issue any queries and (re)visit any search result as they normally would. While making use of the search engine, search behaviour is recorded using LogUI [29]. To simulate a scenario as realistic as possible, there will be no 'review' part where participants can add, alter or remove arguments in the last-minute.

3.2 Metrics and Analysis

Once time is up, participants are taken automatically to the post-task questionnaire. The questionnaire is configured to assess participants for Affinity for Technology Interaction (ATI) [15], user engagement [31], and experienced time pressure. Both the pre-task and the post-task questionnaire contained an attention check. Due to the cognitive load of the task and to prevent distraction, no attention checks are shown during the search task itself.

Table 1. Scale description for the Interpretation of Data into Arguments (D-Intrp) and the Quality of Arguments (D-Qual) metrics.

Rating	Description
0	Facts contained within one argument with no association.
1	Association of two useful or detailed facts: $A \rightarrow B$.
2	Association of multiple useful or detailed facts: $A + B \rightarrow C$; $A \rightarrow B \rightarrow C$; $A \rightarrow B \therefore C$.

(a) D-Intrp metric.

Rating	Description
0	Facts within the argument are irrelevant to the subject; facts hold no useful information or advice.
1	Facts are generalized to the overall subject matter; facts hold little useful information or advice.
2	Facts fulfill the required information need and are useful.
3	A level of technical detail is given via at least one key term associated with the technology of the subject; statistics are given.

(b) D-Qual metric.

We utilized metrics for task performance, search behaviour, and user experience in our evaluation. With the aim of assessing the quality of arguments identified by the participants, we apply techniques introduced by Wilson and Wilson [40] based on Bloom's Taxonomy [3]. We measure the number of arguments submitted by each participant (*F-Argument*), a measure analogous to *F-Fact* in [40]. At the argument level, we measure how well the participants interpret data into arguments (*D-Intrp*) and the quality of the arguments (*D-Qual*). Details

---

[4] https://www.microsoft.com/en-us/bing/apis/bing-web-search-api.

on the scales for each can be seen in Table 1a and Table 1b, respectively. D-Qual and D-Intrp are averaged across arguments into one final value per participant. At the participant level we measure the level of topic focus (*T-Depth*) by rating the coverage of subtopics on a scale of 0–3. The subtopics are: (*i*) benefits of cloning, (*ii*) safety considerations, (*iii*) ethical considerations, and (*iv*) drawbacks of cloning that are separate from safety or ethical considerations. When necessary, these metrics are adapted to fit the context of extracted arguments. Finally, we apply the ATI scale from [15] to understand to what extent ATI moderates the relationship between time constraints and task performance.

To measure search behaviour under time constraints, we capture result clicks in the form of the ranking position of the result, participant dwell time on the SERP, and perception of time pressure. We also capture whether or not participants opt to stop entering arguments early and determine the reliance on a single result for argument selection. User experience is measured using the User Experience Scale - Short Form by O'Brien et al. [31].

3.3 Participants

Participants for the user study were recruited using the online participant recruitment tool Prolific[5] and were rewarded at a rate of GBP 7.50/h for successfully completing the task, regardless of experimental condition. The required sample size of 431 participants was determined by conducting a power analysis for an ANCOVA using *G*Power* [13] with an effect size $f = 0.25$ (indicating a moderate effect), significance threshold $\alpha = 0.05/21 = 0.00238$ (due to the anticipated number of statistical tests), and a statistical power of $(1 - \beta) = 0.8$. In total, we recruited 523 participants via Prolific, with 37 submissions being excluded for failed attention checks or low-effort responses.[6] The remaining 486 submissions were marked as valid.

Table 2. Analyses performed per research question.

Research Question	Independent Variables	Dependent Variables	Covariates
RQ1	Time contraint	Task performance	SERP interface, ATI, prior knowledge, topical interest, web search experience, perception of time pressure
RQ2	Time constraint	Search behaviour	SERP interface, prior knowledge, topical interest, web search experience, perception of time pressure
RQ3	Time constraint & SERP interface	Task performance & Search behaviour	Prior knowledge, topical interest, web search experience, perception of time pressure
RQ4	SERP interface	User experience	Time constraint, prior knowledge, topical interest, web search experience, perception of time pressure
RQ5	Time constraint	Task performance	SERP interface, ATI

---

[5] https://www.prolific.co—last accessed 10th October, 2022.
[6] Participants are considered *low-effort* if they did not complete the study or were inactive for 2+ min. We also exclude application and browser tab switches.

To determine answers for each research question, we analyze the main effects via an Analyses of Covariances (ANCOVAs). The covariates, independent, and dependent variables are described in Table 2. In the event of significant main effects, interaction effects are investigated in a post-hoc analysis using Tukey's honest significant difference test. We correct for Type-I error inflation with the Holm-Bonferroni correction (adjusted $\alpha = 0.05$). All statistical analysis was performed using SPSS 26.

4   Results

4.1   Descriptive Statistics

All participants recruited were native English speakers with a mean age of 25.65 years old (SD = 9.05). The youngest participant was 18 and the oldest 72 years old. The gender distribution is skewed toward males (male: 59.9%, female: 39.3%, other: 0.8%). The participants were balanced across the experimental conditions. The highest levels of education completed most prevalent in the participant sample are high school (37.7%), graduate degree (26.7%), and technical/community college (24.5%). Our participant pool consisted of practised searchers, with 92.2% indicating using a search engine to search the web at least once per day. Prior knowledge regarding the topic of DNA cloning varied but was at a moderately low level (mean = -0.55, SD = 1.20, scale: $[-2, 2]$). Prior interest in the topic was also moderate (mean = 0.42, SD = 1.15, scale: $[-2, 2]$). Participants possessed an adequate understanding of the search task, according to self-reported scores for the task definition (mean = 1.61, SD = 0.65, scale: $[-2, 2]$). Based on the reported levels of prior knowledge and prior interest, we argue that the search task adheres to the desired characteristics of exploratory search tasks and that participants understood what was asked of them [22].

A total of 21,763 arguments were submitted, with an average of 5.69 arguments per participant. Looking at topic focus (T-Depth), the best-covered subtopic was the benefits of cloning (45.9%) followed by ethical considerations (23.0%), safety considerations (11.3%), and drawbacks of cloning (8.1%). It is worth noting that a bias for arguments in favour of the topic is present among our participants. The D-Qual, D-Intrp, and T-Depth ratings were completed by the authors. Examples of how arguments were assessed can be found in Table 3. Participants rated the traditional list-view the highest in terms of user experience (mean = 3.61, SD = 0.51). Yet, only 27.6% of participants opted to look at a second SERP. Participants did not have a preference for the interface.

4.2   Statistical Analysis

To evaluate task performance, we conducted a set of one-way ANCOVA tests. Investigating the effect of the time constraints on the level of topic focus (T-Depth) revealed a significant effect ($F(3, 476) = 9.853$, $p < 0.001$, partial $\eta^2 = 0.058$). Post-hoc analysis revealed statistically significant differences at the $p <$

Table 3. Example assessments of D-Qual, D-Intrp, and subtopic.

Argument	D-Qual	D-Intrp	Subtopic
It can save animals from possibly extinction, or even species who were already extinct.	2	0	1
The negative of DNA cloning is that is can lead to in-breeding. This is because the same genotypes are reproducing.	3	1	4
One of the best advantages of DNA cloning is, it helps infertile couples to reproduce	1	0	1
Cons: DNA cloning present a lot of ethical and religious dilemmas	2	0	3
Reproductive cloning is controversial and may cause a lot of problems, since it creates two identical organism.	2	2	3

0.001 level between the 2 min time constraint (mean = 0.77) and 8 min time constraint (mean = 1.26). No significant effect of time constraint on quality of arguments (D-Qual) was found, ($F(3, 476) = 2.159$, $p = 0.092$, partial $\eta^2 = 0.013$). The effect of time constraints on interpretation of data into arguments (D-Intrp) was found to be statistically significant ($F(3, 476) = 10.46$, $p < 0.001$, partial $\eta^2 = 0.062$). A significant difference ($p < 0.001$) between the 2 min time constraint (mean = 0.037) in relation to the 8 min time constraint (mean = 0.301) and the no time constraint conditions (mean = 0.374) was also identified. The effect of time constraints on number of arguments (F-argument) was also found to be statistically significant ($F(3, 476) = 11.82$, $p < 0.001$, partial $\eta^2 = 0.069$) with the 2 min time constraint (mean = 3.924) being significantly different to the 8 min time constraint (mean = 6.974) and no time constraint conditions (mean = 6.337) with $p < 0.001$. This indicates that a general pattern where as time constraints tighten, task performance decreases.

A one-way ANCOVA revealed a statistically significant effect of time constraints on query rate ($F(3, 477) = 34.62$, $p < 0.001$, partial $\eta^2 = 0.179$). Significant differences at the $p < 0.001$ level existed between the 2 min time constraint (mean = 0.829) in relation to the 5 min time constraint (mean = 0.437), 8 min time constraint (mean = 0.360), and no time constraint (mean = 0.267) condition. Thus, as time constraints tightened, the query rate increased. No statistically significant effects of time constraints on average length of queries was found ($F(3, 477) = 0.71$, $p = 0.545$, partial $\eta^2 = 0.004$).

Using two-way ANCOVA, no statistically significant interaction effect was found between time constraint and user interface with respect to topic focus (T-Depth; $F(9, 466) = 0.648$, $p = 0.756$, partial $\eta^2 = 0.012$), quality of arguments (D-Qual; $F(9, 466) = 1.608$, $p = 0.110$, partial $\eta^2 = 0.030$), interpretation of data into arguments (D-Intrp; $F(9, 466) = 1.653$, $p = 0.098$, partial $\eta^2 = 0.031$), number of arguments (F-Argument; $F(9, 466) = 0.627$, $p = 0.775$, partial $\eta^2 = 0.012$), query rate ($F(9, 466) = 1.268$, $p = 0.252$, partial $\eta^2 = 0.024$), and average length of queries ($F(9, 466) = 0.942$, $p = 0.488$, partial $\eta^2 = 0.018$).

A one-way ANCOVA revealed no significant effect of SERP interface on user experience ($F(3, 477) = 1.925$, $p = 0.125$, partial $\eta^2 = 0.012$).

The covariate ATI was also statistically insignificant with respect to topic focus (T-Depth; $F(1, 480) = 0.359$, $p = 0.549$, partial $\eta^2 = 0.001$), quality of arguments (D-Qual; $F(1, 480) = 0.682$, $p = 0.409$, partial $\eta^2 = 0.001$), interpretation of data into arguments (D-Intrp; $F(1, 480) = 2.185$, $p = 0.140$, partial $\eta^2 = 0.005$), and number of arguments (F-Argument; $F(3, 480) = 0.095$, $p = 0.758$, partial $\eta^2 = 0.000$).

5   Discussion

How do Different Time Constraints Influence Task Performance? With RQ1, we expected to find that stricter time constraints reduced task performance, and in fact found that 3 of the 4 task performance metrics (T-Depth, D-Intrp, F-Arguments) decreased significantly as time constraints tightened. These findings are in line with similar works reporting reduced task performance related to the presence of a time constraint [7]. Moreover, in line with [38], we find significant differences in task performance between different lengths of time constraints.

How do Different Time Constraints Affect Search Behaviour? For RQ2, we anticipated seeing various effects from time constraints on search behaviours. However, our results indicate only an increased query rate for participants in stricter time constraints. Our exploratory investigation suggests the increase in queries comes at the cost of click depth. This means that as time constraints tighten, participants rely more on fresh or reformulated queries rather than explore deeper in the results sets. Although the increased query rate corroborates prior research [5,7,23], other influences in behavioural metrics could not be established.

In What Way are Different UI Designs Susceptible to the Effect of Time Constraints? Considering the susceptibility of SERP interfaces to the effects of time constraints (RQ3), the expected outcome was that of a noticeable interaction effect between the SERP interface and the task performance metrics. However, no such interaction effects were discerned in our study.

What Impact do Different SERP Interfaces have on User Experience? Past findings have demonstrated that various elements and their presentation on the SERP have been found to impact measures related to user experience, such as informativeness [27], satisfaction [2], and difficulty [21]. As such, we expected to find that the SERP interfaces affect user experience when time constraints are present (RQ4). Counter to this expectation, our analysis showed no significant impact of the interface on perceived user experience.

To What Extent does Affinity for Technology Interaction Serve as a Moderating Variable for Task Performance? Lastly, we questioned to what extent ATI moderates the relationship between time constraints and task performance (RQ5). ATI correlates with characteristics such as technology usage and learning success [15]. Motivated by such correlations, we sought to explore the relationship between ATI and task performance, as defined in Sect. 3.2. Our exploration uncovered no clear correlations.

5.1 Caveats and Limitations

This pre-registered study has some limitations despite the careful preparations and attention devoted to its design. The generalizability of this study is limited by the fact that only one topic was used in the search task. The decision to design the study in the presented form was based on the identified knowledge gaps in related literature, maximizing the potentially contribution. As a more technical limitation, using a proxy to serve search results such that all participants would see exactly the same page would be ideal. Presumably, the absence of a proxy mainly manifested itself in personalization differences in terms of ads and some web pages not being available in certain regions. Using a proxy, however, would increase response times, possibly affecting user experience. Also, no existing solutions were satisfactory in terms of cost or ease of use. Hence, the presence of a proxy did not outweigh its drawbacks.

6 Conclusions and Future Work

We presented a user study aiming to increase an understanding of the relationships between time constraints and SERP interfaces and task performance, user behaviour, and user experience. Participants were tasked with finding arguments in favor or against a controversial topic under a time constraint while using a mock search system. Task performance was evaluated using qualitative measures to examine whether participants understood the topic more deeply.

The results of the user study show that stricter time constraints reduce task performance. Additionally, tighter time constraints affect web search behaviour in terms of increased query rate. An exploratory finding suggests this comes at the cost of click depth, which increases as time constraints loosen. Using various SERP interfaces, the susceptibility to the effects of time constraints was investigated with no sensitivity found. Also, the various SERP interfaces used did not influence the user experience, implying that user experience was neither improved nor worsened. We did not find ATI to serve as a moderating variable in the relationship between time constraints and task performance. Exploratory findings have shown that participants who stopped the task early because they believed they had collected enough arguments had comparable task performance scores to those who used all the time available. Our results have strengthened the existing literature revolving around time constraints and SERP interfaces and made contributions to the knowledge gap on the interplay between time constraints and SERP interfaces.

Turning to future work, we propose that further research is needed to establish the generalizability of this work. The limiting factor of one topic used in this study leaves an open pathway for further studies, where more than one topic is considered. The experimental setup used in this work may serve as a foundation for such future studies. Additionally, the absence of effects on user experience due to SERP interfaces used in this work warrants further investigation. Further focused investigation is required to determine whether time constraints have a clear effect on users' perceived experience with a particular interface. Findings from such a study may inform ways to design SERP interfaces which can be used in support of searchers in other directions of the information retrieval field. Finally, this study was among one of the first to study various lengths of time constraints. Further research efforts devoted to closer examination of the sensitivity between these time constraints and task performance is required.

Acknowledgments. This work was partially supported by the SURF Cooperative, the Design@Scale Lab, and the TU Delft AI initiative.

References

1. Arapakis, I., Bai, X., Cambazoglu, B.B.: Impact of response latency on user behavior in web search. In: Geva, S., Trotman, A., Bruza, P., Clarke, C.L.A., Järvelin, K. (eds.) The 37th International ACM SIGIR Conference on Research and Development in Information Retrieval, SIGIR '14, Gold Coast, QLD, Australia - 06–11 July 2014, pp. 103–112. ACM, New York, NY, USA (2014)
2. Arapakis, I., Leiva, L.A., Cambazoglu, B.B.: Know your onions: understanding the user experience with the knowledge module in web search. In: Bailey, J., et al. (eds.) Proceedings of the 24th ACM International Conference on Information and Knowledge Management, CIKM 2015, Melbourne, VIC, Australia, 19–23 October 2015, pp. 1695–1698. ACM, New York, NY, USA (2015)
3. Bloom, B.S., Engelhart, M.B., Furst, E.J., Hill, W.H., Krathwohl, D.R.: Taxonomy of educational objectives. The classification of educational goals. In: Handbook 1: Cognitive domain. Longmans Green, New York (1956)
4. Clarke, C.L.A., Agichtein, E., Dumais, S., White, R.W.: The influence of caption features on clickthrough patterns in web search. In: Proceedings of the 30th Annual International ACM SIGIR Conference on Research and Development in Information Retrieval, pp. 135–142. SIGIR 2007, Association for Computing Machinery, New York, NY, USA (2007)
5. Crescenzi, A., Capra, R., Choi, B., Li, Y.: Adaptation in information search and decision-making under time constraints. In: Proceedings of the 2021 Conference on Human Information Interaction and Retrieval, pp. 95–105. CHIIR 2021, Association for Computing Machinery, New York, NY, USA (2021)
6. Crescenzi, A., Capra, R., Arguello, J.: Time pressure, user satisfaction and task difficulty. Proc. Am. Soc. Inf. Sci. Technol. **50**(1), 1–4 (2013)
7. Crescenzi, A., Kelly, D., Azzopardi, L.: Time pressure and system delays in information search. In: Baeza-Yates, R., Lalmas, M., Moffat, A., Ribeiro-Neto, B.A. (eds.) Proceedings of the 38th International ACM SIGIR Conference on Research and Development in Information Retrieval, Santiago, Chile, 9–13 August 2015, pp. 767–770. ACM, New York, NY, USA (2015)
8. Crescenzi, A., Kelly, D., Azzopardi, L.: Impacts of time constraints and system delays on user experience. In: Kelly, D., Capra, R., Belkin, N.J., Teevan, J., Vakkari, P. (eds.) Proceedings of the 2016 ACM Conference on Human Information Interaction and Retrieval, CHIIR 2016, Carrboro, North Carolina, USA, 13–17 March 2016, pp. 141–150. ACM, New York, NY, USA (2016)
9. Cutrell, E., Guan, Z.: What are you looking for? An eye-tracking study of information usage in web search. In: Proceedings of the SIGCHI Conference on Human

Factors in Computing Systems, pp. 407–416. CHI 2007, Association for Computing Machinery, New York, NY, USA (2007)

10. Dumais, S.T., Cutrell, E., Chen, H.: Optimizing search by showing results in context. In: Jacko, J.A., Sears, A. (eds.) Proceedings of the CHI 2001 Conference on Human Factors in Computing Systems, Seattle, WA, USA, March 31–5 April 2001, pp. 277–284. ACM, New York, NY, USA (2001)

11. Epstein, R., Robertson, R.E.: The search engine manipulation effect (SEME) and its possible impact on the outcomes of elections. Proc. Natl. Acad. Sci. **112**(33), E4512–E4521 (2015)

12. Epstein, R., Robertson, R.E., Lazer, D., Wilson, C.: Suppressing the search engine manipulation effect (SEME). Proc. ACM Hum. Comput. Interact. **1**(CSCW), 42:1–42:22 (2017)

13. Faul, F., Erdfelder, E., Lang, A.G., AG, B.: G*power 3: a flexible statistical power analysis program for the social, behavioral, and biomedical sciences. Behav. Res. Methods Instrum. Comput. **39**, 175–191 (2007)

14. Foulds, O., Azzopardi, L., Halvey, M.: Investigating the influence of ads on user search performance, behaviour, and experience during information seeking. In: Scholer, F., Thomas, P., Elsweiler, D., Joho, H., Kando, N., Smith, C. (eds.) CHIIR '21: ACM SIGIR Conference on Human Information Interaction and Retrieval, Canberra, ACT, Australia, 14–19 March 2021, pp. 107–117. ACM, New York, NY, USA (2021)

15. Franke, T., Attig, C., Wessel, D.: A personal resource for technology interaction: development and validation of the affinity for technology interaction (ATI) scale. Int. J. Hum. Comput. Interact. **35**(6), 456–467 (2019)

16. Gadiraju, U., Yu, R., Dietze, S., Holtz, P.: Analyzing knowledge gain of users in informational search sessions on the web. In: Proceedings of the 2018 Conference on Human Information Interaction & Retrieval, pp. 2–11. CHIIR 2018, Association for Computing Machinery, New York, NY, USA (2018)

17. Joachims, T., Granka, L.A., Pan, B., Hembrooke, H., Gay, G.: Accurately interpreting clickthrough data as implicit feedback. SIGIR Forum **51**(1), 4–11 (2017)

18. Kammerer, Y., Gerjets, P.: How the interface design influences users' spontaneous trustworthiness evaluations of web search results: comparing a list and a grid interface. In: Proceedings of the 2010 Symposium on Eye-Tracking Research & Applications, pp. 299–306. ETRA 2010, Association for Computing Machinery, New York, NY, USA (2010)

19. Kammerer, Y., Gerjets, P.: Effects of search interface and internet-specific epistemic beliefs on source evaluations during web search for medical information: an eye-tracking study. Behav. Inf. Technol. **31**(1), 83–97 (2012)

20. Kammerer, Y., Gerjets, P.: The role of search result position and source trustworthiness in the selection of web search results when using a list or a grid interface. Int. J. Hum. Comput. Interact. **30**(3), 177–191 (2014)

21. Kelly, D., Azzopardi, L.: How many results per page?: A study of SERP size, search behavior and user experience. In: Baeza-Yates, R., Lalmas, M., Moffat, A., Ribeiro-Neto, B.A. (eds.) Proceedings of the 38th International ACM SIGIR Conference on Research and Development in Information Retrieval, Santiago, Chile, 9–13 August 2015, pp. 183–192. ACM, New York, NY, USA (2015)

22. Kules, B., Capra, R.: Constructing exploratory tasks for a faceted search interface. In: The Workshop on Computer Interaction and Information Retrieval, pp. 18–21. HCIR 2008, Microsoft Research, Redmond, WA, USA (2008)

23. Liu, C., Wei, Y.: The impacts of time constraint on users' search strategy during search process. In: Proceedings of the 79th ASIS&T Annual Meeting: Creating Knowledge, Enhancing Lives through Information & Technology. ASIST 2016, American Society for Information Science, USA (2016)

24. Liu, C., Yang, F., Zhao, Y., Jiang, Q., Zhang, L.: What does time constraint mean to information searchers? In: Elsweiler, D., Ludwig, B., Azzopardi, L., Wilson, M.L. (eds.) Fifth Information Interaction in Context Symposium, IIiX '14, Regensburg, Germany, 26–29 August 2014, pp. 227–230. ACM, New York, NY, USA (2014)

25. Liu, J., Mitsui, M., Belkin, N.J., Shah, C.: Task, information seeking intentions, and user behavior: toward a multi-level understanding of web search. In: Proceedings of the 2019 Conference on Human Information Interaction and Retrieval, pp. 123–132. CHIIR 2019, Association for Computing Machinery, New York, NY, USA (2019)

26. Maxwell, D., Azzopardi, L.: Stuck in traffic: how temporal delays affect search behaviour. In: Elsweiler, D., Ludwig, B., Azzopardi, L., Wilson, M.L. (eds.) Fifth Information Interaction in Context Symposium, IIiX '14, Regensburg, Germany, 26–29 August 2014, pp. 155–164. ACM, New York, NY, USA (2014)

27. Maxwell, D., Azzopardi, L., Järvelin, K., Keskustalo, H.: Searching and stopping: an analysis of stopping rules and strategies. In: Bailey, J., Moffat, A., et al. (eds.) Proceedings of the 24th ACM International Conference on Information and Knowledge Management, CIKM 2015, Melbourne, VIC, Australia, 19–23 October 2015, pp. 313–322. ACM, New York, NY, USA (2015)

28. Maxwell, D., Azzopardi, L., Moshfeghi, Y.: A study of snippet length and informativeness: behaviour, performance and user experience. In: Proceedings of the 40th International ACM SIGIR Conference on Research and Development in Information Retrieval, pp. 135–144. SIGIR '17, Association for Computing Machinery, New York, NY, USA (2017)

29. Maxwell, D., Hauff, C.: *LogUI*: contemporary logging infrastructure for web-based experiments. In: Hiemstra, D., Moens, M.-F., Mothe, J., Perego, R., Potthast, M., Sebastiani, F. (eds.) ECIR 2021. LNCS, vol. 12657, pp. 525–530. Springer, Cham (2021). https://doi.org/10.1007/978-3-030-72240-1_59

30. Novin, A., Meyers, E.M.: Making sense of conflicting science information: exploring bias in the search engine result page. In: Nordlie, R., Pharo, N., Freund, L., Larsen, B., Russel, D. (eds.) Proceedings of the 2017 Conference on Conference Human Information Interaction and Retrieval, CHIIR 2017, Oslo, Norway, 7–11 March 2017, pp. 175–184. ACM, New York, NY, USA (2017)

31. O'Brien, H.L., Cairns, P.A., Hall, M.: A practical approach to measuring user engagement with the refined user engagement scale (UES) and new UES short form. Int. J. Hum. Comput. Stud. **112**, 28–39 (2018)

32. Page, L., Brin, S., Motwani, R., Winograd, T.: The pagerank citation ranking: Bringing order to the web. Technical report, Stanford InfoLab (1999)

33. Pan, B., Hembrooke, H., Joachims, T., Lorigo, L., Gay, G., Granka, L.A.: In google we trust: users' decisions on rank, position, and relevance. J. Comput. Mediat. Commun. **12**(3), 801–823 (2007)

34. Ramos, J., Eickhoff, C.: Search result explanations improve efficiency and trust. In: Huang, J., Chang, Y., Cheng, X., Kamps, J., Murdock, V., Wen, J., Liu, Y. (eds.) Proceedings of the 43rd International ACM SIGIR conference on research and development in Information Retrieval, SIGIR 2020, Virtual Event, China, 25–30 July 2020, pp. 1597–1600. ACM, New York, NY, USA (2020)

35. Roy, N., Torre, M.V., Gadiraju, U., Maxwell, D., Hauff, C.: Note the highlight: incorporating active reading tools in a search as learning environment. In: Scholer, F., Thomas, P., Elsweiler, D., Joho, H., Kando, N., Smith, C. (eds.) CHIIR '21: ACM SIGIR Conference on Human Information Interaction and Retrieval, Canberra, ACT, Australia, 14–19 March 2021, pp. 229–238. ACM, New York, NY, USA (2021)

36. Salmerón, L., Gil, L., Bråten, I., Strømsø, H.I.: Comprehension effects of signalling relationships between documents in search engines. Comput. Hum. Behav. **26**(3), 419–426 (2010)

37. Schwarz, J., Morris, M.R.: Augmenting web pages and search results to support credibility assessment. In: Tan, D.S., Amershi, S., Begole, B., Kellogg, W.A., Tungare, M. (eds.) Proceedings of the International Conference on Human Factors in Computing Systems, CHI 2011, Vancouver, BC, Canada, 7–12 May 2011, pp. 1245–1254. ACM, New York, NY, USA (2011)

38. van der Vegt, A., Zuccon, G., Koopman, B., Deacon, A.: How searching under time pressure impacts clinical decision making. J. Med. Librar. Assoc. JMLA **108**(4), 564–573 (2020)

39. Weenig, M.W., Maarleveld, M.: The impact of time constraint on information search strategies in complex choice tasks. J. Econ. Psychol. **23**(6), 689–702 (2002)

40. Wilson, M.J., Wilson, M.L.: A comparison of techniques for measuring sensemaking and learning within participant-generated summaries. J. Assoc. Inf. Sci. Technol. **64**(2), 291–306 (2013)

41. Wu, Z., Sanderson, M., Cambazoglu, B.B., Croft, W.B., Scholer, F.: Providing direct answers in search results: a study of user behavior. In: d'Aquin, M., Dietze, S., Hauff, C., Curry, E., Cudré-Mauroux, P. (eds.) CIKM '20: The 29th ACM International Conference on Information and Knowledge Management, Virtual Event, Ireland, 19–23 October 2020, pp. 1635–1644. ACM, New York, NY, USA (2020)

42. Xu, L., Zhou, X., Gadiraju, U.: Revealing the role of user moods in struggling search tasks. In: Proceedings of the 42nd International ACM SIGIR Conference on Research and Development in Information Retrieval, pp. 1249–1252. SIGIR'19, Association for Computing Machinery, New York, NY, USA (2019)

A Taxonomy of User Behavior Model (UBM) Tools for UI Design and User Research

Maxim Bakaev[1]([⊠]) [iD], Sebastian Heil[2] [iD], Johanna Jagow[3], Maximilian Speicher[3] [iD], Kevin Bauer[4] [iD], and Martin Gaedke[2] [iD]

[1] Independent UX Consultant, 630132 Novosibirsk, Russia
maxis81@gmail.com
[2] Technische Universität Chemnitz, 09111 Chemnitz, Germany
{sebastian.heil,martin.gaedke}@informatik.tu-chemnitz.de
[3] Jagow Speicher Consulting, 08037 Barcelona, Spain
icwe@maxspeicher.com
[4] University of Mannheim, 68161 Mannheim, Germany
kevin.bauer@uni-mannheim.de

Abstract. The engineering of user interfaces (UIs) increasingly relies on software tools that aid in ideation, design, evaluation, etc., but involve no real users. Particularly, user behavior models (UBMs) bear the potential to improve human-centered design processes, but their adoption in practice remains low. In this paper, we present a taxonomy for UBM tools that organizes and structures them along 7 dimensions – supported job, degree of automation, focus, interface data input, user data input, output of tool, and target interface platform. We also conduct an initial evaluation with 61 existing tools, providing insights into the current state of the field. Notably, none of the investigated tools work with user characteristics or reference interfaces as input, although this would appear very practical for real projects. Our results could support UI/UX researchers and digital design practitioners in searching for the tools and further enhancing them. Ultimately, our work represents a step toward understanding and overcoming the low adoption rate of ML-based UBM tools in the industry.

Keywords: Software Classification · User-Centered Design · Human-Computer Interaction · Machine Learning

1 Introduction

In their work, engineers and designers rely on an actionable mix of existing knowledge in their respective fields and the understanding of the problem and the context at hand. Engineering effective and attractive web user interfaces (UIs) necessitates finding out the website's target visitors' needs and characteristics during the user research stage. Rigorous knowledge for transforming these into a UI is drawn from the field of human-computer interaction (HCI), where it is increasingly operationalized as user behavior models (UBMs) [1].

© The Author(s), under exclusive license to Springer Nature Switzerland AG 2023
I. Garrigós et al. (Eds.): ICWE 2023, LNCS 13893, pp. 236–244, 2023.
https://doi.org/10.1007/978-3-031-34444-2_17

In the broadest sense, UBMs in HCI are formal constructs that attempt to conceptualize, explain, or predict the behavior of human users with respect to particular interface designs without involving actual users. Many modern UI/UX engineering support software tools/systems/platforms are based on UBMs, at least to a certain extent (we shall call them *UBM tools* hereinafter), and they are in the focus of this paper. UBM tools can simulate or predict users' behavioral responses to novel designs, to optimize or inspire design features [2, 3], produce novel prototypes [4], perform quantitative analyses [5], etc. They have the potential to facilitate the development of successful interfaces for digital products, but they appear to have trouble gaining traction in the industry. In a recent survey of UI design practitioners, we found that the top reasons for non-using the AI/ML-based tools included *"never heard of those"* (91%) and *"I don't see the added value"* (21%) [6]. Thus, we concluded that the designers have little awareness of how exactly such tools could support them in their job.

In the current paper, we rely on the same collection of 61 UBM tools (see in [6]) to construct a taxonomy, which we then apply to classify them. In this way, we hope to facilitate the identification and differentiation of UBM tools for practitioners and researchers and to provide a starting point for better understanding the gap between research and practice in this area. We structure the remainder of the paper as follows. Section 2 summarizes related research and outlines the taxonomy development process. In Sect. 3, we present our novel taxonomy and classify the considered UBM tools. In the final section, we discuss our findings and potential directions for future work.

2 Related Work and the Taxonomy Development Process

A wide range of disciplines apply behavior models in one way or another, including Psychology, Biology, and Economics. In HCI, behavior models typically aim to explain or predict the response of human users to specific interface designs, which is why the HCI community commonly refers to these models as "user behavior models" (UBMs) [7]. They generally output (predict) a certain interaction quality parameter, for a particular UI (or its prototype) and a certain user group [1]. Our definition of a UBM-based tool is: *software that can, based on previously learned user behavior, instantly (more or less) and automatically produce a visual design, prototype, analysis, or validation.*

In that sense, UBM tools are a specific category of design support tools, whose overarching goal is to facilitate the development of interfaces that optimize the user experience by providing designers insights into user behaviors and their interaction with an interface without involving actual human users. This shall not be contrasted with the involvement of real users – in the IT industry, with its constrained budgets and schedules that hinder the thorough implementation of the prescribed user-centered design process, the real alternative is relying on no user data whatsoever. Strictly speaking, the name *"user-less"* tools that we used previously [6], is not entirely embracing: theoretically, a UBM tool can supplement its operation with real user data, in addition to the learned behavior.

Recently, advances in the field of Machine Learning (ML) have also spilled over into the domain of UBM tools, promising to make the lives of digital design and user researcher professionals easier automating pivotal parts of their jobs. At the most automated end of the spectrum, they could take over the entire design process and output an optimized user interface [1]. For example, researchers have shown that ML-based UBM tools can define design problems from online review narratives [8], generate interface prototypes based on sketches [9], construct behavioral personas from clickstreams and social media contents [10], and derive semantic representations of digital designs that inform user behaviors [11].

Despite their versatility and great promise to revolutionize the design work of practitioners, this new generation of UBM tools has not seen much practical usage and appears to belong predominantly to the academic realm [12]. One of the reasons for the non-usage that we can speculate about concerns the extensive upfront effort required to find a suitable tool and integrate it into existing design processes [13]. We believe that developing a taxonomy can provide a better overview of the UBM tool landscape with its different capabilities and purposes, facilitating researchers' and practitioners' navigation of the field.

Taxonomies related to software are manifold: many of them target specific subject matters and are created ad-hoc for practical purposes [14]. The substantial stages in a taxonomy development process, based on [15, Table 1], are as follows:

1. **Planning:** Identify the business needs and the objectives of the taxonomy. Define the list of key users and survey the users' needs.
2. **Identification and extraction of information:** Explore sources of information, extract the terms, and identify the candidate categories.
3. **Design and construction of the taxonomy:** Define the first level of the taxonomy design (about 7 categories) and the subsequent levels.
4. **Testing and validation:** Validate the use to which the taxonomy is intended and apply the content of the taxonomy.

The two intended groups of our taxonomy users are: 1) digital design practitioners, who often have problems finding and recruiting real users, especially specialized ones [6], and would benefit from awareness of the UBM tools' and the specific support they can provide, and 2) authors of design support tools, who need to position them in the market and invent new functionality, could analyze the competitors and identify unoccupied segments.

The sources of information were by and large the official websites of the tools, at which we arrived by sending queries to global search engines (details on the queries and the tools' selection can be found in [6]). Overall, we collected 61 classification items, some of which are not individual tools, but series, e.g., *Clicks/CTR prediction* or *Browser web analytics plug-ins*. Like for lanthanides and actinides series in Mendeleev's Periodic Table, the properties of items within them are virtually indistinguishable in the context of UI/UX design. The full list of the collected items is available in the Online Appendix of [6] (https://github.com/heseba/UserlessDesignSurvey).

The technology for the actual design and construction of software taxonomies is not very well detailed, and a lot is left to the experts. The initial generation of the UBM tools taxonomy structure and the categories was done by the first authors of this paper, based on his 15 years of experience in HCI and over 20 years of experience in web UIs engineering. The process was largely top-down, but inspired by the list of tools. The validation was performed by all the other authors, whereas the application of the categories to classify the 61 items was done by the second author of this paper.

In the first level, there were 7 categories, each of which got from 3 to 11 possible values (sub-categories), so the taxonomy structure turned out to be rather shallow. The categories were largely orthogonal, and each of the UBM tools would be simultaneously classified in each category. The values were not necessarily mutually exclusive, but in most instances, only one of the values should apply to a classified item.

3 A Taxonomy of User Behavior Models-Based Tools

Most of the categories that we initially identified for the taxonomy were rather universal for software products in general: supported job, input and output, target platform, degree of automation. These were tailored for the considered domain: e.g., input was detailed into *Interface data input* and *User data input*, as per UBMs. The values in the second level of the taxonomy were also by and large made domain-dependent.

In this section, we present the taxonomy categories and values and demonstrate its application to classify the 61 tools. More complete taxonomy data can be found in the Online Appendix[1]. A reader shall not consider the classification that we propose to be strictly correct and complete. Instead, we welcome the tools' developers and the research community to make corrections to our initial classification.

Designer's/Researcher's Job. As with any software made for professionals, the tools need to fulfill or support a certain task in the user's work process. Design and evaluation (assessment/analysis/testing/validating/checking) appear to be the most frequent ones in the digital design field, followed by ideation (Table 1).

Table 1. UBM Tools' taxonomy: by *Designer's/researcher's job.*

Value	Tools
Design (generative)	MenuOptimizer, GRIDS, UIZard Design Assistant, Material Design guidelines, 10 more tools
Evaluation	Usability Smells Finder, Qualidator, USEFul, WaPPU, AIM, CogTool, Cogulator, WAVE, ViCRAM, 27 more tools
Other (ideation, reference)	Paper2Wire, Sketch2Code, WebRatio, 8 more tools

Degree of Automation. Classically, depending whether the transformation of the input to the output is done with the involvement of a human (*Semi-automatic*) or without it (*Automatic*). *Instrumental* corresponds to software that supports certain intermediate operations (technical aid, computation, code generation, etc.), while most of the work is supposed to be done by the user (Table 2).

Focus. This category is the most domain-specific one and involves both theoretical interaction aspects known in HCI and practical goals of UI engineering (Table 3).

---

[1] https://github.com/heseba/UBMToolsTaxonomy.

Table 2. UBM Tools' taxonomy: by *Degree of automation.*

Value	Tools
Automatic	Paper2Wire, WaPPU, AIM, Zyro Heatmaps, UIS Hunter, W3C Validator, VisualMind AI, 15 more tools
Semi-Automatic	MenuOptimizer, GRIDS, UIZard Design Assistant, Test.ai, Tricentis Tosca, Eggplant
Instrumental	Figma, Cogulator, Selenium, Appium, TestComplete, Ranorex Studio, IBM Rational Rhapsody, 25 more tools
None	Material Design guidelines

Table 3. UBM Tools' taxonomy: by *Focus (interaction aspect or goal).*

Value	Tools
Technical (correctness of code, URIs, etc.)	Browser web analytics plugins, Web Vitals, Test.ai, W3C Validator, SortSite
Motor behavior	CogTool, Cogulator, KLM Calculator
Visual perception	GRIDS, AIM, ViCRAM, VisualMind AI
Cognitive (e.g., readability)	MenuOptimizer, WaPPU, Zyro Heatmaps, Eye-gaze/ROI prediction, CogTool, Cogulator, KLM calculator
Subjective/emotional	AIM, VisualMind AI
Marketing	Clicks/CTR prediction
Simulation	Selenium, Katalon, iMacros, Robot Framework, Capybara, Cucumber, Twist, Ranorex Studio, 6 more tools
Accessibility	Qualidator, WAVE, AChecker, SortSite, Level Access WebAccesibility, Color/Contrast checkers
Guidelines / patterns / standards	Usability Smells Finder, Qualidator, USEFul, Material Design Guidelines, UIS Hunter
Other	Adobe XD, Figma, Sketch, JustInMind, Balsamiq, Origami Studio, Sketch2Code, UIZard Design Assistant, CaseComplete, AXIOM, Mendix Studio, 9 more tools

Interface Data Input. This category corresponds to one of the classical input components for a UBM, which can be of different types (Table 4). This input is optional, as some tools are not concerned with a particular UI or require the user to create it.

Table 4. UBM Tools' taxonomy: by *Interface data input.*

Value	Tools
Code	Usability Smells Finder, WaPPU, AIM, Test.ai, AChecker, SortSite, Selenium, Katalon, Twist, ViCRAM, 22 more tools
Image	Zyro Heatmaps, Eye-gaze/RoI prediction, UIS Hunter
Model	Cogulator, KLM Calculator, IBM Rationa Rhapsody, WebRatio, CaseComplete, Appian, AXIOM, Mendix Studio
Prototype	MenuOptimizer, GRIDS, CogTool
Sketch	UI-image-to-GUI-skeleton, Paper2Wire, Sketch2Code, UIZard Design Assistant
A reference interface	–
None	Figma, Axure, Mockplus, uizard.io, InVision, Balsamiq, JustInMind, Material Design Guidelines, 3 more tools

User Data Input. Some representation of the target user, (e.g., such *User characteristics* as age or gender obtained from user research) is another classical input for a UBM (Table 5). Some UBM tools do not explicitly ask to input user data but cover all users or contain implicit knowledge (e.g., about the significant visual factors).

Table 5. UBM Tools' taxonomy: by *User data input.*

Value	Tools
User model	–
User interaction data/logs	Usability Smells Finder, Clicks/CTR prediction
User survey data	WaPPU
User characteristics	–
Other	XCUITest, UIS Hunter, CogTool, KLM Calculator, Cogulator, Selenium, Appium, Tricentis Tosca, Twist, 11 more tools
Implicit/none	Adobe XD, Balsamiq, Sketch, GRIDS, Paper2Wire, Qualidator, AIM, Appian, AXIOM, VisualMind AI, 23 more tools

Output of the Tool. This category corresponds to the added value that the tool can provide to designers, user researchers, or even product managers (Table 6).

Target Interface Platform. The interface platforms are different in the employed technologies and interaction modes and in the maturity of related HCI techniques (Table 7). Many design support tools promote themselves as specific to a certain platform.

Table 6. UBM Tools' taxonomy: by *Output (added value).*

Value	Tools
Errors/warnings/"smells"	Usability Smells Finder, Qualidator, USEFul, UIS Hunter, W3C Validator, WAVE, AChecker, SortSite, 5 more tools
Guidelines/recommendations	–
Interface metrics	Qualidator, WaPPU, AIM, ViCRAM, VisualMind AI
Usability/interaction metrics (time, error, subjective, etc.)	WebVitals, CogTool, Cogulator, KLM Calculator
Business KPIs (e.g., CTR, sales, subscriptions, etc.)	Clicks/CTR prediction
Code	IBM Rational Rhapsody, WebRatio, Appian, AXIOM, Mendix Studio
Interface-related image (e.g., heatmaps) or visualization	Zyro Heatmaps, Eye-gaze/RoI prediction
Interface model/prototype	MenuOptimizer, GRIDS, Sketch2Code, UIZard Design Assitant, 8 more tools
Simulated interactions	Selenium, Eggplant, Linux Desktop Testing Project, Robot Framework, Behat, Twist, Ranorex Studio, 7 more tools
User classification/profiling	–
Other	CaseComplete

Table 7. UBM Tools' taxonomy: by *Target UI platform.*

Value	Tools
Web	GRIDS, Usability Smells Finder, Qualidator, WaPPU, AIM, Web Vitals, W3C Validator, WAVE, Selenium, iMacros, Behat, WebRatio, ViCRAM, VisualMind AI, 10 more tools
Mobile	XCUITest, Appium, AXIOM, Mendix Studio
Desktop	MenuOptimizer, Linux Desktop Testing Project
Embedded (vending machines, kiosks, cars, etc.)	–
Hybrid	Zyro Heatmaps, Test.ai, CogTool, Cogulator, Katalon, Eggplant, Ranorex Studio, IBM Rational Rhapsody, 18 more tools
Other (AR/VR, voice, etc.)	–
N/A	CaseComplete

4   Conclusion

UI/UX design practitioners frequently perceive jobs that involve actual users as particularly costly and time-consuming, leading them to reduce this central component of the user-centered design methodology to a minimum [3]. This reduction, however, causes them to waste valuable time and resources developing designs that users eventually reject. Meanwhile, design support tools based on UBMs can provide insights into user interactions with an interface even in the absence of actual human users.

In this paper, we have developed a 2-level taxonomy incorporating 7 categories and 48 values (sub-categories) in total, which we applied to classify the 61 items that we previously collected [6]. It provides a comprehensive overview of the existing landscape of UBM tools, allowing researchers and practitioners to navigate and identify different tools based on their capabilities and features. This can also help identify underpopulated segments and provide inspiration for developing new software features.

Our taxonomy and the associated classification yield some noteworthy insights: in particular, there are no tools that require *user characteristics* as inputs, although this data is readily available in real projects. Another input that surprisingly none of the identified tools accepts are *reference interfaces*, even though they are often of considerable use in the ideation phase of design processes, e.g., to produce slightly changed versions of a single design mockup or an existing website design. Finally, none of the existing tools focus on *embedded, AR/VR, and voice*, which reveals a clear opportunity in the market.

We would like to note several limitations of our work. First, **knowing** about a design support tool and **using** it is not the same, as we have previously learned from the negative correlation discovered in our practitioners' survey [6]. Awareness that can be facilitated by the taxonomy is necessary, but not sufficient – ultimately, the adoption of a design support tool would depend on the added value it provides. Second, our classification is far from being complete and perfect, as the collection of the tools started in 2021, so the landscape might have changed somehow. Still, we believe that the proposed taxonomy categories and values have long-term validity and utility.

References

1. Oulasvirta, A.: Can computers design interaction? In: Proceedings of the 8th ACM SIGCHI Symposium on Engineering Interactive Computing Systems, pp. 1–2. ACM, New York, USA (2016)
2. Grigera, J., Garrido, A., Rivero, J.M., Rossi, G.: Automatic detection of usability smells in web applications. Int. J. Hum. Comput. Stud. **97**, 129–148 (2017)
3. Speicher, M., Both, A., Gaedke, M.: Ensuring web interface quality through usability-based split testing. In: Casteleyn, S., Rossi, G., Winckler, M. (eds.) ICWE 2014. LNCS, vol. 8541, pp. 93–110. Springer, Cham (2014). https://doi.org/10.1007/978-3-319-08245-5_6
4. Buschek, D., Anlauff, C., Lachner, F.: Paper2wire: A case study of user-centred development of machine learning tools for UX designers. In: Proceedings of the Conference on Mensch und Computer, pp. 33–41. MuC '20. ACM, New York (2020)
5. Bakaev, M., Heil, S., Khvorostov, V., Gaedke, M.: Auto-extraction and integration of metrics for web user interfaces. J. Web Eng. **17**(6&7), 561–590 (2019)

6. Bakaev, M., Speicher, M., Jagow, J., Heil, S., Gaedke, M.. We don't need no real users?! Surveying the adoption of user-less automation tools by UI design practitioners. In: Di Noia, T., Ko, IY., Schedl, M., Ardito, C. (eds.) Proceedings of the 22nd International Conference on Web Engineering, pp. 406–414. Springer, Cham (2022). https://doi.org/10.1007/978-3-031-09917-5_28

7. Massimo, D., Ricci, F.: Harnessing a generalised user behaviour model for next-poi recommendation. In: Proceedings of the 12th ACM Conference on Recommender Systems, pp. 402–406 (2018)

8. Hedegaard, S., Simonsen, J.G.: Extracting usability and user experience information from online user reviews. In: Proceedings of the CHI 2013, pp. 2089–2098 (2013)

9. Moran, K., et al.: Machine learning-based prototyping of graphical user interfaces for mobile apps. IEEE Trans. Softw. Eng. **46**(2), 196–221 (2018)

10. Zhang, X., Brown, H.F., Shankar, A.: Data-driven personas: constructing archetypal users with clickstreams and user telemetry. In: Proceedings of the CHI 2016, pp. 5350–5359 (2016)

11. Li, T.J.J., Popowski, L., Mitchell, T., Myers, B.A.: Screen2vec: semantic embedding of GUI screens and GUI components. In: Proceedings of the CHI Conference on Human Factors in Computing Systems, pp. 1–15 (2021)

12. Lu, Y., Zhang, C., Zhang, I., Li, T.J.J.: Bridging the Gap between UX Practitioners' work practices and AI-enabled design support tools. In: CHI 2022 Extended Abstracts, pp. 1–7 (2022)

13. Bakaev, M., Speicher, M., Heil, S., Gaedke, M.: I don't have that much data! Reusing user behavior models for websites from different domains. In: Bielikova, M., Mikkonen, T., Pautasso, C. (eds.) Proceedings of the 20th International Conference on Web Engineering, pp. 146–162, Springer (2020). https://doi.org/10.1007/978-3-030-50578-3_11

14. Usman, M., Britto, R., Börstler, J., Mendes, E.: Taxonomies in software engineering: a systematic mapping study and a revised taxonomy development method. Inf. Softw. Technol. **85**, 43–59 (2017)

15. Bayona-Oré, S., Calvo-Manzano, J.A., Cuevas, G., San-Feliu, T.: Critical success factors taxonomy for software process deployment. Softw. Qual. J. **22**(1), 21–48 (2012). https://doi.org/10.1007/s11219-012-9190-y

Tools and Techniques for Advanced Web Engineering

On the Energy-Efficiency of Hybrid UI Components for Mobile Cross-Platform Development

Stefan Huber[1][(✉)] , Mario Döller[2] , and Michael Felderer[1,3,4]

[1] University of Innsbruck, 6020 Innsbruck, Austria
`mail@stefanhuber.at`
[2] University of Applied Sciences Kufstein, 6330 Kufstein, Austria
`mario.doeller@fh-kufstein.ac.at`
[3] German Aerospace Center (DLR), 51147 Cologne, Germany
`michael.felderer@dlr.de`
[4] University of Cologne, 50923 Cologne, Germany

Abstract. The increasing use of mobile apps in everyday life has led to an increased demand for efficient and cost-effective mobile development methods. One such method is mobile cross-platform development (MCPD), which enables the creation of apps from a single codebase for multiple platforms. However, previous research has shown that MCPD approaches can have higher energy consumption than native development approaches. In order to address this issue, this paper proposes the use of Hybrid UI components, which are a combination of native and web technologies, as a means to improve the energy efficiency of cross-platform UI components. Four selected Hybrid UI components were implemented and evaluated regarding their energy-efficiency against native and hybrid mobile development. Results indicate that for two UI components, a substantial increase in energy-efficiency was achieved. However, for the other two UI components, no improvement, and in one case, even a degradation in energy consumption was observed. The study concludes that Hybrid UI components are a promising approach, but further research is needed to ensure their energy-efficiency in all cases.

Keywords: Energy-efficiency · Mobile cross-platform development · Empirical Study

1 Introduction

Mobile apps are omnipresent in our daily lives, providing us with a variety of important services. The availability of these services is bound to the limited battery capacity of today's smartphones. Since the advancement of battery technology is highly challenging [24], energy-efficient mobile apps are critical for increasing user satisfaction. Improving the energy-efficiency of mobile apps is considered as a difficult task for practitioners, primarily due to a lack of knowledge and lack of appropriate tools [21].

ⓒ The Author(s), under exclusive license to Springer Nature Switzerland AG 2023
I. Garrigós et al. (Eds.): ICWE 2023, LNCS 13893, pp. 247–261, 2023.
https://doi.org/10.1007/978-3-031-34444-2_18

Developing mobile apps for multiple platforms poses another challenge for practitioners [2,17], as it typically requires creating and maintaining a separate codebase for each platform. Practitioners commonly choose mobile cross-platform development (MCPD) approaches, which allow the development of mobile apps that can run on multiple platforms, such as iOS and Android, using a single codebase [15]. This approach clearly saves resources for development, testing and maintenance compared to building separate apps for each platform.

Previous research [16] showed that MCPD approaches have a higher energy consumption than Android native when considering UI interactions. Therefore, this paper introduces Hybrid UI components, which are a combination of native UI components and web technologies. The research hypothesis of the proposed approach is that energy-intensive parts of the UI component are handled by the native implementation, such as animations and interactivity and the content is provided with web technologies (HTML, CSS, JavaScript) to keep the cross-platform availability. For the popular hybrid MCPD approach, Hybrid UI components would act as easy-to-use drop-in replacements for web-only UI components.

The goal of this paper is to evaluate the energy-efficiency of Hybrid UI components in a thorough and controlled experiment. Thus, the main contributions of this paper are: (1) an implementation of four selected Hybrid UI components; (2) an experimental comparison of Hybrid UI components against other mobile development approaches; (3) a discussion of the results and a discussion on the implications for cross-platform development; (4) a comprehensive replication package containing all research artifacts.

The remainder of this paper is organized as follows. Section 2 introduces the concept of Hybrid UI components. Section 3 gives an overview of relevant related research. Section 4 outlines the design and execution of the experiment, the experimental subjects, and the applied analysis procedure. Section 5 presents the results of this study, which is followed by the discussion thereof in Sect. 6, and a separate discussion on the threats to validity is given in Sect. 7. Finally, Sect. 8 concludes this paper.

2   Hybrid UI Components

MCPD refers to all mobile development approaches that enable developers to build apps from a single codebase or model for multiple mobile platforms. Researchers have conducted extensive studies on the various existing MCPD approaches, and have classified them accordingly [4,13]. Based on developer popularity and usage, approaches that utilize web technologies, such as the hybrid mobile development approach, have been found to be widely adopted in industry [25].

The hybrid mobile development approach allows for embedding a web app inside a mobile app. Generally, the mobile app provides a fullscreen WebView to render the web content. A WebView is a UI component, available for all mobile platforms, which allows displaying web content inside a mobile app. By using

  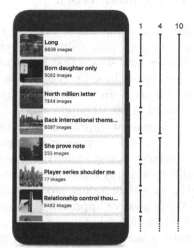

Fig. 1. Dialog Capacitor UI Component

Fig. 2. Dialog Hybrid UI Component

Fig. 3. Different divisions of list items inside separate WebViews for the Scrolling Hybrid UI component

web technologies (HTML, CSS, JavaScript), the web content can be styled and programmed to mimic the look and feel of the underlying mobile platform, e.g., Android or iOS. For the efficacy of mobile developers, open-source UI component libraries exist, which provide out-of-the-box web components with the look and feel of mobile platforms. Figure 1 shows a Dialog UI component inside a hybrid mobile app. The embedded WebView is set fullscreen inside the mobile app. The Dialog UI component, including animation and interactivity aspects, are fully built with web technologies, which mimic the look and feel of Android.

Hybrid UI components, as envisioned in this paper, are considered an extension of the hybrid MCPD approach. As existing research has shown, native development has a lower energy consumption [16], when considering UI interactions, than other mobile development approaches. Therefore the concept of Hybrid UI components is based on the assumption to provide energy-intensive parts of a UI component, such as animations and interactivity, by the native UI component and wrap a WebView inside the component to display the contents with web technologies to not compromise the cross-platform characteristic.

Figure 2 shows a Dialog UI component, implemented as a Hybrid UI component. The Dialog is using the Android native `AlertDialog` for interactive aspects, such as the open and close animations. The content is displayed inside a WebView with cross-platform web technologies. For a developer using a hybrid development approach, such as Capacitor, Phonegap or Apache Cordova, Hybrid UI components would be an easy-to-use drop-in replacement for respective UI components.

3   Related Work

There is a substantial body of research in the field of energy optimization for mobile apps, primarily focused on the Android native development approach [3]. Studies have shown that refactoring code smells [5,20] or following performance-based guidelines [9] can significantly reduce the energy footprint of Android native apps. However, these findings, although significant, cannot be directly applied to MCPD approaches.

A general approach to influence energy consumption, which is applicable to all mobile development approaches, is regarded with the coloring of user interfaces. Today's smartphones are equipped with OLED displays, which have a different energy consumption depending on the lightness of the color pixels. Thus, UIs providing a dark mode could substantially reduce energy consumption [11]. A less invasive approach is presented in [1]. The authors introduce an approach for indistinguishably changing color values, by transforming them into another color space and by that reduce energy consumption.

Besides adapting color values Valerio et al. [22] suggested usability improvements, to increase user efficiency and by that save energy. Furthermore, dimming parts of the screen, which are not important for a user's current task have been proposed. Intuitively, the area covered by the user's fingers could be completely dimmed, as proposed by the authors of FingerShadow [6]. ShiftMask [18] is another approach, which dims parts of the screen, which are not in the focus of a user.

Considering the energy-efficiency of MCPD approaches, existing studies have primarily focused on comparative analysis. Thus, studies on various aspects of MCPD approaches have been conducted, including comparisons of the energy-efficiency of sensors [7], algorithm benchmarks [19], UI interactions [16], media playback [8] and common app features [12]. To the best of our knowledge, this study is the first to focus on improving the energy-efficiency of an MCPD approach. Since the widespread use of MCPD approaches by practitioners, we hope this study fosters more research interest in optimizing the energy-efficiency of MCPD approaches.

4   Study Design

For planning, execution and analysis of this study, established guidelines for empirical research were followed, as described in the handbook of Wohlin et al. [23]. All research artifacts have been made available publicly as a comprehensive replication package[1].

4.1   UI Components and Interaction Scripts

In this study, four commonly used UI components, namely Dialog, Drawer, Scrolling, and Sheet, were examined as experimental subjects. These components are displayed in Fig. 4 and are widely used in mobile apps. To cover a broad

---

[1] https://github.com/stefanhuber/ICWE-2023.

Fig. 4. Screenshots of the UI elements considered in this study: (1) Dialog, (2) Drawer, (3) Scrolling and (4) Sheet

spectrum of UI components, we aimed to diversify the selection as much as possible. The components were implemented using three development approaches: Android native, the hybrid development approach Capacitor[2], and our proposed approach as Hybrid UI components.

The Android native UI components were included in the study as a benchmark for comparison with the Hybrid UI component counterparts. Previous research has shown that Android native has the lowest energy consumption among different mobile development approaches, when considering UI interactions [16]. On the other hand, the hybrid development approach Capacitor was included as a baseline for comparison with Hybrid UI component counterparts. Following the goal of this research, Hybrid UI components should have a lower energy consumption than the Capacitor implementations, to be regarded as an optimization.

Realistic test scenarios were created by rendering the UI components with content generated from publicly available fake data APIs. This was especially important for the Scrolling component, which required a large amount of image and textual data. To ensure reproducibility of the results, the scripts used to gather the fake data are also provided as part of the replication package.

For each of the four UI components, repeatable UI interaction scripts were created. The scripts were implemented with the UI Automator Android testing framework[3], which was selected according to the guidelines provided by Cruz et al. [10]. The interaction scripts can be started from the controlling computer and can be reused with each implementation of the UI components. A detailed description of each interaction script is provided in Table 1.

---

[2] https://capacitorjs.com/.

[3] https://developer.android.com/training/testing/ui-automator.

Table 1. Interaction scripts for UI components

UI component	Interaction description	Exp. subjects	Duration (seconds)
Dialog	The dialog is opened by clicking a button, left open for approx. 1.5 s and then closed again by clicking outside of the dialog. The interaction is repeated 5 times	3	16.7
Drawer	The drawer is opened by a left-to-right swipe gesture, left open for approx. 1.5 s and then closed again by clicking outside of the drawer. The interaction is repeated 5 times	3	16.7
Scrolling	The list is scrolled through by executing 5 consecutive bottom-to-top swipe gestures, with approx. 1 s waiting time between the swipe gestures	5	8.6
Sheet	The sheet is opened by clicking a button, left open for approx. 1.5 s and then closed again by clicking outside of the sheet. The interaction is repeated 5 times	3	16.7

Overall the study had 14 implementations of UI components (experimental subjects). For the 3 UI components Dialog, Drawer, and Sheet, a variant with each development approach was provided, resulting in 9 experimental subjects. For the Scrolling UI component, 3 different variants (discussed in Sect. 4.2) for the hybrid UI component were provided and 2 variants for the other development approaches, resulting in 5 experimental subjects.

4.2   UI Component Implementation Details

All implementations of the UI components follow the Material design guidelines[4]. This is the default design system used in Android apps. By following that practice we could make sure that for typical smartphone users the different UI component implementations are indistinguishable, as they have the same look and feel.

The Android native implementation of the UI components uses all the corresponding default UI components from the Android SDK. That is, the `AlertDialog` for the Dialog component, the `DrawerLayout` for the Drawer component and the `BottomSheetDialog` for the Sheet component. The Scrolling component was implemented with the `RecyclerView`, which makes use of the concept of virtual scrolling.

Virtual scrolling is an efficient approach to implement scrolling, especially for resource-constrained devices like smartphones. For a scrollable list, only the items which are within the displayable area of the screen are loaded and rendered.

---

[4]   https://material.io.

While scrolling, as soon as a list item is leaving the visible area, it is reused and rendered with different content on the other end of the list, which enters the visible area of the screen.

Capacitor is a hybrid mobile development approach, therefore web technologies could be used. For the UI component implementations, the JavaScript library React[5] was used together with the Ionic[6] mobile UI library. Ionic is a popular library for mobile UI components built with web technologies. The library closely follows the Material design guidelines for the Android components and by that mimics the look and feel of the native implementations. From the Ionic library the `ion-alert` component was used for implementing the Dialog, the `ion-menu` component for implementing the Drawer and the `ion-action-sheet` component for implementing the Sheet component. Similar to the Android native implementation for Scrolling a virtual scrolling approach was used. Thus, an additional React component, named `Virtuoso`[7], was used for that purpose. To style the list items, we employed corresponding CSS styles from the Ionic library.

As envisioned, the Hybrid UI components should be built upon native UI components and wrap a WebView inside, for displaying the content. Thus, for implementing the Dialog, Drawer and Sheet component, the native Android `AlertDialog`, `DrawerLayout` and `BottomSheetDialog` were used as a basis. The visible area of the respective UI component was rendered with an embedded WebView. The contents of the WebViews were created with web technologies to mimic the exact same look and feel as for the native counterpart.

For Hybrid UI components, scrolling was implemented based on the virtual scrolling approach. Similar to Android native a `RecyclerView` was used and WebViews were used as scrollable items. Inside the WebViews the actual list items with respective styling and content were rendered. Since inside a WebView, more than one list item could be rendered and a reduction of the amount of WebViews inside the RecyclerView should increase the energy-efficiency, three variants of the component were implemented. The variants divide different amounts of list items into a WebView. Thus, we implemented the default approach with one list item per WebView, an approach with four list items per WebView and an approach with ten list items per WebView. In Fig. 3 a visualization of the variants is given. Thereby the line sections on the right indicate how list items are divided into WebViews.

For Hybrid UI components, scrolling was also implemented using the virtual scrolling approach. Like in the Android native implementation, a `RecyclerView` was used, and WebViews were used as scrollable items. The actual list items with their corresponding styling and content were rendered inside the WebViews. We implemented three variants of the component, that divide different numbers of list items into a WebView. As a hypothesis, we considered that by reducing the amount of WebViews the energy-efficiency should be increased. The first variant is the default approach with one list item per WebView, the second variant is an

---

[5] https://reactjs.org/.
[6] https://ionicframework.com/.
[7] https://virtuoso.dev/.

approach with four list items per WebView, and the third variant is an approach with ten list items per WebView. Figure 3 illustrates these variants. The line sections on the right indicate how the list items are divided into WebViews.

4.3   Energy Measurement

The energy measurements were collected with a hardware-based metering approach, as this allows for exactly collecting the energy consumed by the device. The Monsoon High Voltage Power Monitor[8] was used, as it has a Python-based API, to precisely control the measurement process and is commonly used in similar study designs. The Samsung Galaxy S21 Android device was prepared to be usable with the power monitor. An overview of the device specifications is listed in Table 2.

The preparation of the device included removing the device's battery and assembling the power monitor as the only power source. Throughout the experiments, the device was supplied with a constant voltage of 4.3V in order to infer reliable and repeatable measurements.

4.4   Experimental Setup and Execution

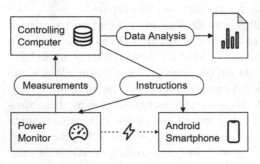

Fig. 5. Overview of experimental setup

Table 2. Samsung Galaxy S21 Android Device Specifications

Android:	Version 13
CPU:	Snapdragon 888 $1 \times 2.9\,\text{GHz}$, $3 \times 2.8\,\text{GHz}$, $4 \times 2.2\,\text{GHz}$
RAM:	8 GB
Display:	AMOLED 1080×2400 pixels

The experimental setup consists of a controlling computer and a smartphone with a power monitor as its sole power supply. The Android Debug Bride (adb) was used to connect the controlling computer with the smartphone via Wi-Fi. The controlling computer was also connected to the power monitor to read and control the energy measurements. An overview of the experimental setup is given in Fig. 5.

Before starting the experiment, the smartphone was prepared by following these steps:

---

[8] https://www.msoon.com/high-voltage-power-monitor.

– All required apps containing the UI components and the accompanying interaction scripts were installed and tested.
– All background services, such as GPS or Bluetooth were deactivated and all
other active apps were closed.
– The device was put into a do-not-disturb-mode, to prevent any kind of notifications to interfere with the experiment execution.

For the actual execution of the experiment, a Python script on the controlling
computer was prepared. The script randomly selects one of the experimental
subjects and its corresponding interaction script.

The scripts open the app under test on the smartphone. Parallel to running
the interaction script, the energy is metered with the power monitor. In addition,
before and after starting the interaction script the idle energy consumption of
the app is measured. The mean of the idle energy consumption is deducted from
the energy consumption of the interaction with the UI component. With this
procedure, the actual and isolated energy consumption of the UI component
and respective interaction could be approximated. The power monitor can only
collect the energy consumed by the whole smartphone. Therefore, the deduction
of the idle energy consumption of the app under test was used to approximate
the energy consumption of the UI component.

To minimize measurement bias, at least 30 identically and independently
repeated samples were collected for each experimental subject. Thus, the controlling script ended the experiment after enough samples were available. Overall
the experiment procedure yielded 420 samples.

4.5   Experimental Variables and Hypothesis

The stated research goal of this study, is to investigate, whether there are significant differences in energy consumption among different UI component implementations. To achieve this, statistical hypotheses were formulated. The independent variables are the UI component and the development approach, while
the dependent variable is the energy consumption in Joules for interacting with
the specific UI component.

For each experimental subject the respective mean μ_{ij} was calculated, with
$i \in \{an, c, hu\}$ for the development approaches Android native, Capacitor, and
Hybrid UI and further $j \in \{di, dr, sc, sh\}$ for the UI components Dialog, Drawer,
Scrolling and Sheet.

To investigate the differences in energy consumption of the UI component
interactions, with regard to the different development approaches, a two-tailed
null hypothesis (H_0) and corresponding alternative hypothesis (H_a) were formulated:

$$H_{0,ij} : \mu_{hu,j} = \mu_{ij}, \qquad \forall i \in \{an, c\}, j \in \{di, dr, sc, sh\}$$

$$H_{a,ij} : \mu_{hu,j} \neq \mu_{ij}, \qquad \forall i \in \{an, c\}, j \in \{di, dr, sc, sh\}$$

The $H_{0,ij}$ hypothesis states that there is no significant difference in energy consumption between Hybrid UI components with regard to the other development approaches. In contrast, the alternative hypothesis $H_{a,ij}$ states that there is a significant difference in energy consumption between Hybrid UI components and the other examined development approaches.

4.6   Data Analysis

From the experiment execution 30 samples, for each UI component, were obtained. A sample represents the energy consumption of a UI component in Joule when executing the respective interaction script.

The permutation test [14] was selected to determine statistical significance, due to the fact that the majority of the samples were failing to meet the assumptions of normality (based on Shapiro-Wilk test with $\alpha = 0.05$). The permutation test is a non-parametric test and has no assumptions on the distribution of the samples.

As the obtained samples from the Hybrid UI components were used in multiple hypothesis tests (once with Android native and once with Capacitor) the chance of Type-I errors is increased with respect to our target $\alpha = 0.05$ level. Thus, after applying a Bonferroni correction an α of 0.025 is used to determine significance.

Finally, to complement the hypothesis testing and to determine the magnitude of the differences in energy consumption, effect sizes are calculated. The non-parametric Cliff's Delta was selected as the appropriate effect size measure.

5   Results

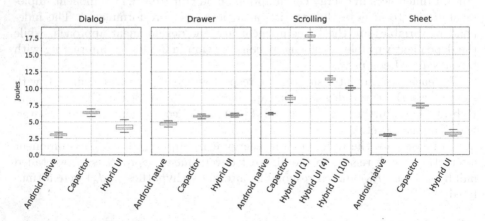

Fig. 6. Energy consumption of different UI component implementations, based on the execution of the test script

Figure 6 shows a descriptive overview of the results in the form of a box plot. The different UI components, considered in this study, are shown in separate charts. Each chart represents the energy consumption in Joules along the y-axis and the implementation approaches along the x-axis. For the Scrolling UI component, the three variants of the Hybrid UI implementation are shown. The number in parentheses accounts for the number of list items, which are rendered within a WebView.

Furthermore, Table 3 lists the results of the statistical analysis. For the Scrolling component, the results of the Hybrid UI component with ten list items per WebView are used in the statistical comparisons, as it is the most energy-efficient according to the descriptive results.

Considering the results regarding the comparison of Hybrid UI components and Android native components, clearly, all results show a statistically significant difference. Further, when interpreting the effect sizes for Android native the Dialog, Drawer, and Scrolling components are more energy-efficient, by a large extent than the Hybrid UI implementations. For the Sheet component, the Android native implementation is more energy-efficient than the Hybrid UI counterpart, but to a lesser extent.

The results regarding Capacitor show that there is a significant difference between the Dialog, Scrolling, and Sheet components. For the Drawer component, the H_0 hypothesis could not be rejected. By interpreting the effect sizes Hybrid UI components are more energy-efficient, by a large extent, than the Capacitor counterpart. For the Scrolling component, the opposite is true, Capacitor is more energy-efficient than the Hybrid UI implementation.

Table 3. Results of statistical analysis for comparing Android native and Capacitor against Hybrid UI components

UI Components	Android native		Capacitor	
	P-Value Perm. Test	Cliff's Delta	P-Value Perm. Test	Cliff's Delta
Dialog	0.00312	0.94872	0.00002	**−0.93375**
Drawer	0.00002	0.95000	0.28722	0.47051
Scrolling	0.00002	1.00000	0.00002	0.99872
Sheet	0.00576	0.57500	0.00002	**−0.95000**

6 Discussion

The proposed Hybrid UI approach for the Dialog and Sheet components has the potential to significantly reduce energy consumption by on average ~38.3% and ~54.7%, respectively, when compared to the Capacitor hybrid development method. This represents a substantial improvement, as the user experience and visual appearance remain completely unchanged.

Simultaneously, it must be noted that while the Hybrid UI implementation of the Drawer component resulted in slightly higher energy consumption compared to the Capacitor implementation (~1.4% on average), it was not a significant difference. On the other hand, a significant increase in energy consumption was observed for the Scrolling component when using the Hybrid UI component implementation. Further analysis revealed that the number of list items per WebView was a key factor in reducing energy consumption. As a result, the observed increase in energy consumption varied from over ~109.6% (one list item per WebView) to as low as ~18.6% (ten list items per WebView).

In this first implementation of Hybrid UI components, the wrapping native UI components were used as provided by the Android SDK. However, it was found that in the case of the Drawer and Scrolling UI components, this might not be the optimal approach, as these native components were not designed with our use case in mind.

A first runtime analysis of the implementation of the Drawer and Scrolling Hybrid UI components revealed that unnecessary re-renderings of the WebViews were triggered by the underlying native UI component. This seems to be mainly the case when a UI component leaves and enters the displayable area of the screen. For example, at times the Drawer UI component was re-rendered when sliding into the displayable area, although it was already rendered once. This would not have been necessary if the wrapped content inside the WebView didn't change. To improve the performance of these Hybrid UI components, a more in-depth analysis of the inner workings of the native wrapper UI component is required, and potential adaptations on how the re-rendering approach could be tweaked to fit the use case of Hybrid UI components better. This could involve making changes to the way the native wrapper component handles the triggering of re-renderings based on the state of the WebView contents.

Developing and maintaining a comprehensive UI component library using web technologies, that replicate the look and feel of native UI components, such as Ionic, is a significant undertaking. Besides the goal of being more energy-efficient, another advantage of Hybrid UI components is that the need for implementing and maintaining interactivity and animation features is eliminated, as the native UI components can be utilized. Developers solely need to focus on styling the content for Hybrid UI components. However, a disadvantage of this approach is, that it cannot be used directly within a web or progressive web app anymore.

We have shown the feasibility of using Hybrid UI components for the Android platform by implementing four selected UI components. The approach is highly extendable and other UI components, such as navigation bars, navigation rails, snackbars, time and date pickers, navigation tabs, and others, can be implemented as well. Although we have not tested the approach on the iOS platform, to the best of our knowledge, Hybrid UI components are transferable to iOS as well. However, examining energy-efficiency on iOS is challenging, as the platform is highly restricted for such kinds of experiments.

Hybrid UI components were designed as an extension to the hybrid MCPD approach to reduce energy consumption. Previous research has found that other MCPD approaches [16], such as React Native, consume more energy during UI interactions than the hybrid development approach. Therefore, Hybrid UI components could be used in conjunction with other MCPD approaches to decrease energy consumption.

7   Threats to Validity

There are potential threats to the validity of this study, which should be considered in the context of our results.

External Validity. We aimed for a hardware-based measurement approach, in order to have exact results. The preparation of the device, by removing the battery, makes it useless for other purposes. A replication with other devices was economically unfeasible. Therefore, we selected a modern and representative device (Samsung has the largest market share of all Android device manufacturers). To address this limitation, we prepared a publicly available replication package, which is compatible with other Android devices, to facilitate future replications.

Internal Validity. A smartphone is a complex system comprised of a variety of hardware and software components. In our measurement setup, the proper elicitation of the causal relationship between our treatment (development approach) and the outcome (energy consumption) could be disturbed by the presence of confounding factors. To mitigate this threat, we took several measures to eliminate known confounding factors such as background services, other active apps, and notifications. Additionally, we randomly selected subjects before starting each experimental run. These measures helped to substantially mitigate the threat of potentially disturbing factors and increase the internal validity of our study.

Construct Validity. The execution of the experiment was preceded by an extensive planning phase, in which all aspects of the experiment, including the goal, treatments, variables, and hypotheses, were clearly defined and established a priori. By adhering to this methodology, we ensured that the design of the experiment accurately reflected the construct under study.

Conclusion Validity. The analysis procedure was carefully chosen to ensure the correct conclusions could be drawn from the results. We conducted a check for normality of the samples to select an appropriate hypothesis test and corresponding effect size measure. Additionally, to account for the fact that the Hybrid UI component samples were reused in comparison with other development approaches, we applied a conservative correction of the target α level. The raw measurements and the accompanying analysis are included in the replication package for independent review.

8   Conclusion

In summary, our study demonstrates the potential of Hybrid UI components in reducing energy consumption in MCPD approaches, particularly when used together with the hybrid MCPD approach. We implemented and evaluated a diverse set of four UI components and found that two of them showed a substantial improvement in energy efficiency, while the results for the other two were inconclusive. However, we could identify first indications, which could be used to also improve the energy-efficiency of the Drawer and Scrolling UI components.

As future work, we plan to implement and evaluate more Hybrid UI components for Android as well as for iOS. Our study has demonstrated the potential of this approach in reducing energy consumption in mobile applications, but further research is needed to fully optimize all of the offered UI components. By providing clear and measurable improvements in energy-efficiency, we hope to motivate developers of MCPD frameworks and apps to participate in the continued use and development of this approach.

References

1. Agolli, T., Pollock, L., Clause, J.: Investigating decreasing energy usage in mobile apps via indistinguishable color changes. In: 2017 IEEE/ACM 4th International Conference on Mobile Software Engineering and Systems (MOBILESoft), pp. 30–34. IEEE (2017)
2. Ahmad, A., Li, K., Feng, C., Asim, S.M., Yousif, A., Ge, S.: An empirical study of investigating mobile applications development challenges. IEEE Access **6**, 17711–17728 (2018)
3. Baresi, L., Griswold, W.G., Lewis, G.A., Autili, M., Malavolta, I., Julien, C.: Trends and challenges for software engineering in the mobile domain. IEEE Softw. **38**(1), 88–96 (2020)
4. Biørn-Hansen, A., Grønli, T.M., Ghinea, G.: A survey and taxonomy of core concepts and research challenges in cross-platform mobile development. ACM Comput. Surv. (CSUR) **51**(5), 1–34 (2018)
5. Carette, A., Younes, M.A.A., Hecht, G., Moha, N., Rouvoy, R.: Investigating the energy impact of android smells. In: 2017 IEEE 24th International Conference on Software Analysis, Evolution and Reengineering (SANER), pp. 115–126. IEEE (2017)
6. Chen, X., Nixon, K.W., Zhou, H., Liu, Y., Chen, Y.: Fingershadow: an OLED power optimization based on smartphone touch interactions. In: 6th Workshop on Power-Aware Computing and Systems (HotPower 14) (2014)
7. Ciman, M., Ombretta, G.: An empirical analysis of energy consumption of cross-platform frameworks for mobile development. Pervasive Mob. Comput. **39**, 214–230 (2017)

8. Corbalan, L., et al.: Development frameworks for mobile devices: a comparative study about energy consumption. In: 2018 IEEE/ACM 5th International Conference on Mobile Software Engineering and Systems (MOBILESoft). ACM/IEEE, Gothenburg, Sweden (2018)

9. Cruz, L., Abreu, R.: Performance-based guidelines for energy efficient mobile applications. In: 2017 IEEE/ACM 4th International Conference on Mobile Software Engineering and Systems (MOBILESoft), pp. 46–57. IEEE (2017)

10. Cruz, L., Rui, A.: On the energy footprint of mobile testing frameworks. IEEE Trans. Softw. Eng. **47**(10), 2260–2271 (2019)

11. Dash, P., Hu, Y.C.: How much battery does dark mode save? An accurate oled display power profiler for modern smartphones. In: Proceedings of the 19th Annual International Conference on Mobile Systems, Applications, and Services, pp. 323–335 (2021)

12. Dorfer, T., Demetz, L., Huber, S.: Impact of mobile cross-platform development on CPU, memory and battery of mobile devices when using common mobile app features. Procedia Comput. Sci. **175**, 189–196 (2020)

13. El-Kassas, W.S., Abdullah, B.A., Yousef, A.H., Wahba, A.M.: Taxonomy of cross-platform mobile applications development approaches. Ain Shams Eng. J. (2017)

14. Good, P.: Permutation Tests: A Practical Guide to Resampling Methods for Testing Hypotheses. Springer Science & Business Media, New York (2013). https://doi.org/10.1007/978-1-4757-2346-5

15. Heitkötter, H., Hanschke, S., Majchrzak, T.A.: Evaluating cross-platform development approaches for mobile applications. In: Cordeiro, J., Krempels, K.-H. (eds.) WEBIST 2012. LNBIP, vol. 140, pp. 120–138. Springer, Heidelberg (2013). https://doi.org/10.1007/978-3-642-36608-6_8

16. Huber, S., Demetz, L., Felderer, M.: A comparative study on the energy consumption of progressive web apps. Inf. Syst. **108**, 102017 (2022)

17. Joorabchi, M.E., Mesbah, A., Kruchten, P.: Real challenges in mobile app development. In: 2013 ACM/IEEE International Symposium on Empirical Software Engineering and Measurement, pp. 15–24. IEEE (2013)

18. Lin, H.Y., Hsiu, P.C., Kuo, T.W.: Shiftmask: dynamic oled power shifting based on visual acuity for interactive mobile applications. In: 2017 IEEE/ACM International Symposium on Low Power Electronics and Design (ISLPED), pp. 1–6. IEEE (2017)

19. Oliveira, W., Oliveira, R., Castor, F.: A study on the energy consumption of android app development approaches. In: Proceedings of the 14th International Conference on Mining Software Repositories, pp. 42–52 (2017)

20. Palomba, F., Di Nucci, D., Panichella, A., Zaidman, A., De Lucia, A.: On the impact of code smells on the energy consumption of mobile applications. Inf. Softw. Technol. **105**, 43–55 (2019)

21. Pinto, G., Castor, F.: Energy efficiency: a new concern for application software developers. Commun. ACM **60**(12), 68–75 (2017)

22. Vallerio, K.S., Zhong, L., Jha, N.K.: Energy-efficient graphical user interface design. IEEE Trans. Mob. Comput. **5**(7), 846–859 (2006)

23. Wohlin, C., Runeson, P., Höst, M., Ohlsson, M.C., Regnell, B., Wesslén, A.: Experimentation in Software Engineering. Springer Science & Business Media, Berlin, Heidelberg (2012). https://doi.org/10.1007/978-3-642-29044-2

24. Wu, F., Maier, J., Yu, Y.: Guidelines and trends for next-generation rechargeable lithium and lithium-ion batteries. Chem. Soc. Rev. **49**(5), 1569–1614 (2020)

25. Zohud, T., Zein, S.: Cross-platform mobile app development in industry: a multiple case-study. Int. J. Comput. **20**(1), 46–54 (2021)

Human-Friendly RDF Graph Construction: Which One Do You Chose?

Ana Iglesias-Molina[1]([✉]), David Chaves-Fraga[1,2], Ioannis Dasoulas[2],
and Anastasia Dimou[2]

[1] Ontology Engineering Group, Universidad Politécnica de Madrid, Madrid, Spain
{ana.iglesiasm,david.chaves}@upm.es
[2] KULeuven – Flanders Make@KULeuven – Leuven.AI, Leuven, Belgium
{ioannis.dasoulas,anastasia.dimou}@kuleuven.bes

Abstract. Knowledge Graphs (KGs) are a powerful mechanism to structure and organize data on the Web. RDF KGs are usually constructed by declaring a set of mapping rules, specified according to the grammar of a mapping language (e.g., RML), that relates the input data sources to a domain vocabulary. However, the verbosity and (manual) definition of these rules affect their global adoption. Several user-friendly serializations for different mapping languages were proposed to facilitate users with the definition of such rules, e.g., YARRRML, SMS2, XRM, or ShExML. Still, most of them do not cover all features of the mapping languages for RDF graph construction (e.g., constructing RDF-star), or they lack tooling support. In this paper, (i) we present a set of updates over the YARRRML serialisation to empower it with the latest necessities for constructing RDF graphs; (ii) we implement these new features in a new open-source translator, Yatter, currently used in different real-use cases and international projects; and (iii) we qualitatively compare our proposal against similar state-of-the-art serialisations, and their associated translators over a set of conformance test cases. Our proposal advances the declarative construction of RDF graphs and supports users in choosing an appropriate serialisation and translator for their use cases.

Keywords: Knowledge Graphs · Mapping Languages · YARRRML

1 Introduction

Knowledge graphs have proven to be a powerful technology for integrating and accessing myriads of data available on the Web. Using mapping languages guarantees sustainable construction of RDF graphs based on a set of declarative mapping rules [18], specified according to a mapping language's grammar (e.g., R2RML [8] and RML [10]), which relates data sources to a domain vocabulary.

Several mapping languages were proposed to construct RDF graphs [18]. W3C recommends the Relational to RDF Mapping Language (R2RML) [8]) to construct RDF from Relational Databases. R2RML is a custom mapping language based on the RDF syntax. Multiple works extend R2RML [18] (e.g.,

© The Author(s), under exclusive license to Springer Nature Switzerland AG 2023
I. Garrigós et al. (Eds.): ICWE 2023, LNCS 13893, pp. 262–277, 2023.
https://doi.org/10.1007/978-3-031-34444-2_19

RML [10]) enabling its use for heterogeneous data sources. Despite efforts to conceptualize and describe these mapping languages, their manual creation process, verbosity, and complexity lead to the appearance of user-friendly serializations.

Human-friendly serialisations emerged to ease the definition of mapping rules. YARRRML [13] leverages YAML to offer a user-friendly representation to define mapping rules, while ShExML [11] extends the syntax of the ShEx constraint language [15]. XRM [21] provides an abstract syntax that simulates programming languages and SMS2 [17], proposed by Stardog[1], is loosely based on the SPARQL query language and extends the features of R2RML to create virtual RDF graphs. Each serialisation is accompanied by a system that translates their rules into mapping languages, such as RML or R2RML (henceforth abbreviated as [R2]RML). However, these serialisations and translators were not compared with each other in terms of serialisations' features and system's characteristics, even though it would help to decide which serialisation fits each use case.

In this paper, we propose YARRRML-star, by extending YARRRML to also support RML-star [9] to construct RDF-star graphs, and improve YARRRML to adhere with the latest RML updates (e.g., datatypes, joins, etc.). We developed a translator system that implements the new features, validated our proposal with test cases and compared it to other user-friendly serializations.

The contributions of this paper are: (i) the YARRRML-star[2], an extension of the YARRRML serialisation to fully cover RML and support for RML-star; (ii) Yatter[3], a new YARRRML system that implements the translation of the new features; (iii) a qualitative comparison of human-friendly mapping languages with respect to their expressiveness; (iv) conformance test cases[4] for YARRRML adapted from [R2]RML test-cases and translated to other serializations; and (v) a comparison of language conformance and other features (e.g., open vs. close source code) of the associated translators.

The remaining paper is structured as follows: Sect. 2 describes related work, and, Sect. 3, a set of relevant concepts to understand the rest of the paper. Section 4 describes the extension over the YARRRML serialization. Section 5 presents the implementation of these advances in a new translator, Yatter. Section 6 validates our proposals and their position compared to previous works and Sect. 7 outlines our conclusions and future work.

2   Related Work

Different serialisations were proposed so far to offer a user-friendly experience for constructing RDF graphs. Each serialisation is accompanied with a system to translate the mapping rules to RML or directly construct the RDF graph.

YARRRML [13] is a compact serialisation for RML and R2RML mapping rules based on YAML[5] and is currently used in several projects over different

---

[1] https://www.stardog.com/.
[2] https://oeg-dataintegration.github.io/yarrrml-spec/.
[3] https://github.com/oeg-upm/yatter/.
[4] https://github.com/oeg-upm/yarrrml-validation.
[5] https://yaml.org/.

domains [2,4,16]. Companies also incorporate YARRRML into their processes, e.g., the Google Enterprise Knowledge Graph where YARRRML is used to construct and reconcile an external RDF graph[6]. However, YARRRML is currently outdated with respect to latest developments of RML (e.g., RML-star [9]).

ShExML [11] is a mapping language for heterogeneous data sources based on Shape Expressions (ShEx) [15]. Its syntax combines declarations to handle data sources with a set of shapes that define how they should be mapped. The language's operators and support of Scala functions offer multiple possibilities for data transformation. ShExML mapping rules can be translated into RML or directly used to construct RDF graphs with the ShExML Java library[7].

The Expressive RDF Mapper [21] (XRM) by Zazuko[8] offers an abstract syntax for mapping rules aiming to resemble programming languages. XRM's system translates the mappings to [R2]RML, CARML[9] or CSVW[10], and provides code-assistance and syntax validation.

Another well-known human-friendly serialization is the Stardog Mapping Syntax 2 [17] (SMS2) supporting both structured and semi-structured data sources. SMS2 is loosely based on SPARQL CONSTRUCT queries. It follows a FROM - TO syntax, where the FROM part resembling the data source it refers to, and the TO part resembling the RDF syntax that defines how the output will be generated. This serialisation can be used to directly create RDF graphs.

3   Background

As we propose YARRRML-star extending YARRRML to also support RML-star, in this section we describe the basics of the YARRRML serialisation and how it translates to RML. To this end, we present an example in YARRRML (List 1) and its corresponding translation to RML (List 2). The YARRRML mapping rules (List 1) are grouped in sets unified under a mapping identifier, given below the **mappings** key (lines 1–2, 18). Each rule set describes how to access the input data sources and how the triples will be constructed from these data sources. The input data sources' description is specified below the **sources** key (lines 4–5, 19–20). Within, the name, path and format of the file are specified.

The **graphs** key assigns a named graph to the triples (line 3). The **subjects** key defines the IRI or Blank Node of the subjects to be generated (lines 6, 21), and the **predicateobjects** key is used for the predicate-object pairs (lines 7–16, 22–24). The **predicates** (line 9) and **objects** (line 10) keys define how predicate IRIs and object terms (IRIs, Blank Nodes or Literals) are generated.

---

[6] https://cloud.google.com/enterprise-knowledge-graph/docs/entity-reconciliation-console.

[7] https://github.com/herminiogg/ShExML.

[8] https://zazuko.com.

[9] https://github.com/carml/carml.

[10] https://www.w3.org/ns/csvw.

```
1   mappings:                          13        function: equal
2    personTM:                         14        parameters:
3     graphs: :pole-vaulters           15          - [str1, $(ID)]
4     sources:                         16          - [str2, $(ID)]
5      - [jump.csv~csv]                 17
6     subjects: :$(ID)                  18   jumpTM:
7     predicateobjects:                 19     sources:
8      - [:name, $(PERSON), en~lang]    20      - [jump.csv~csv]
9      - predicates: :jumps             21     subjects: :$(ID)-$(MARK)
10       objects:                       22     predicateobjects:
11        - mapping: jumpTM             23      - [:date, $(DATE)]
12          condition:                  24      - [:mark, $(MARK), xsd:float]
```

Listing 1: YARRRML mapping rules.

```
1   <#personTM>                         22        rr:parent "ID" ] ] .
2    a rr:TriplesMap ;                  23   <#jumpTM>
3    rml:logicalSource [                24    a rr:TriplesMap ;
4     rml:source "jump.csv" ;           25    rml:logicalSource [
5     rml:referenceFormulation ql:CSV   26     rml:source "jump.csv" ;
6    ] ;                                27     rml:referenceFormulation ql:CSV
7    rml:subjectMap [                   28    ] ;
8     rr:template ":{ID}" ] ;           29    rml:subjectMap [
9     rr:graphMap [                     30     rr:template ":{ID}-{MARK}" ] ;
10     rr:constant :pole-vaulters ];    31    rr:predicateObjectMap [
11    rr:predicateObjectMap [           32     rr:predicate :date ;
12     rr:predicate :name ;             33     rml:objectMap [
13     rml:objectMap [                  34      rml:reference "DATE" ] ] ;
14      rml:reference "PERSON";         35    rr:predicateObjectMap [
15      rr:language "en" ] ] ;          36     rr:predicate :mark ;
16    rr:predicateObjectMap [           37     rml:objectMap [
17     rr:predicate :jumps;             38      rml:reference "MARK";
18     rr:objectMap [                   39      rr:datatype xsd:float
19      rr:parentTriplesMap <#jumpTM>;  40   ] ] ] .
20      rr:joinCondition [
21       rr:child "ID";
```

Listing 2: RML mapping rules translated from List 1.

It is usually more common to use the abbreviated syntax, that needs none of the keys abovementioned (line 8, 23–24). Following this alternative, the first element of the array corresponds to the predicate, the second to the object, and optionally, the language tag (line 8) or datatype (line 24). Lastly, join conditions may be used when the desired object is the subject of another mapping set (lines 9–16). This condition requires the name of the target mapping set (line 11), and a similarity function, (usually equal). This function evaluates when the data values of the source data specified (lines 15–16) are the same to create the triple. The input parameters for this funciton that refer to the data values are str1 for the current mapping set, and str2 for the referencing mapping set.

Subjects, predicates, objects and graphs are terms that can be generated as constant values (i.e. the same term is always generated in all triples) or dynamic values (i.e. the term changes with the data value, that is enclosed inside "$()").

The YARRRML serialisation[11] also includes description of target data output (`targets`) [19], and application of functions[12] (`function`).

The YARRRML features are translated to RML (List 2) as follows: mapping rule sets are denoted by `rr:TriplesMap` (lines 1–2); input data sources with `rml:LogicalSource` (lines 3–6); subjects with `rr:SubjectMap` (lines 7–10); named graphs with `rr:graphMap` (lines 9–10); predicate-object pairs with `rr:PredicateObjectMap` (lines 11–22, 31–40); language tags with `rr:language` (line 15); datatypes with `rr:datatype` (line 39); joins with `rr:joinCondition` (lines 16–22). Term maps can be divided in three categories: `rr:constant` for constant values, `rml:reference` for data fields and `rr:template` for terms that have a constant value and one or more data fields enclosed by "{}".

4   Extending YARRRML

We extend the YARRRML serialisation to support the RDF-star construction and two updates: the dynamic datatypes and language tags, and a shortcut for join conditions. These are recent features in RML that so far were not considered in YARRRML. To illustrate the extensions, we use a CSV file as input (List 3).

```
ID , PERSON       , COUNTRY , MARK , DATE                , DATE-TYPE
1  , Lisa Ryzih   , de      , 4.40 , 2022-03-21          , date
2  , Xu Huiqin    , zh      , 4.55 , 2022-03-19T17:23:37 , dateTime
```

Listing 3: Contents of the `jump-source` logical source.

4.1   YARRRML-Star

RDF-star introduces the notion of RDF-star triples, i.e. triples that are subjects or objects of another triple. These triples are enclosed using "<<" and ">>", and can be (1) *quoted*, if they only appear in a graph embedded by another triple (List 4 lines 2,4); or (2) *asserted*, if the quoted triple is also generated outside the triple where it is quoted (lines 1–4). We extend YARRRML to specify how we can construct RDF-star graphs, aligned with the RML-star specification [14].

```
1   :1 :jumps 4.40 .
2   << :1 :jumps 4.80 >> :date "2022-03-21" .
3   :2 :jumps 4.55 .
4   << :2 :jumps 4.85 >> :date "2022-03-19T17:23:37" .
```

Listing 4: RDF-star triples.

RDF-star triples can be created in YARRRML-star (List 5) by referencing existing Triples Maps with the tags (1) `quoted` for quoted asserted triples (line 10) and (2) `quotedNonAsserted` for quoted non-asserted triples. The triple that

---

[11] https://rml.io/yarrrml/spec/.
[12] https://rml.io/yarrrml/spec/#functions.

the rule set `jumpTM` creates is used as subject in the rule set `dateTM`, creating RDF-star triples (List 4). The equivalent mapping rules in RML are in List 6.

```
1   mappings:                         7   dateTM:
2   jumpTM:                           8     sources: jump-source
3     sources: jump-source           9     subjects:
4     subjects: :$(ID)              10       quoted: jumpTM
5     predicateobjects:             11     predicateobjects:
6     - [:jumps, $(MARK)]           12     - [:date, $(DATE)]
```

Listing 5: YARRRML-star mapping rules.

```
1   <#jumpTM>                                11     a rr:TriplesMap ;
2     a rr:TriplesMap ;                      12     rml:logicalSource :jump-source ;
3     rml:logicalSource :jump-source;        13     rml:subjectMap [
4     rml:subjectMap [                       14       rml:quotedTriplesMap <#jumpTM> ];
5       rr:template ":{ID}" ] ;              15     rr:predicateObjectMap [
6     rr:predicateObjectMap [                16       rr:predicate :date ;
7       rr:predicate :jumps ;                17       rml:objectMap [
8       rml:objectMap [                      18         rml:reference "DATE" ] ] .
9         rml:reference "MARK" ] ] .
10  <#dateTM>
```

Listing 6: RML-star mapping rules translated from List 5.

4.2   Additional Updates

We enable YARRRML-star with other new features that have been incorporated into RML in the last years. We extend YARRRML to assign datatypes and language tags dynamically to objects. They are generated with the data values, in the following examples the datatype is generated dynamically with the data field `DATA-TYPE` (List 7), and the language tag with `COUNTRY` (List 8). They translates into RML as Lists 9 and 10 show.

```
- [:date, $(DATE), xsd:$(DATE-TYPE)]       - [:name, $(PERSON), $(COUNTRY)~lang]
```

Listing 7: Dynamic datatype.   Listing 8: Dynamic language tag.

```
1   rr:predicateObjectMap [              1   rr:predicateObjectMap [
2     rr:predicate :jumpsOnDate ;        2     rr:predicate :name ;
3     rml:objectMap [                    3     rml:objectMap [
4     rml:reference "DATE";              4     rml:reference "PERSON";
5     rml:datatypeMap [                  5     rml:languageMap [
6       rr:template "xsd:{DATE-TYPE}"]]];6       rml:reference "COUNTRY"]]];
```

Listing 9: Dynamic datatype in   Listing 10: Dynamic language tag
RML translated from List 7.   in RML translated from List 8.

We also incorporate a shortcut for specifying join conditions (List 11). This shortcut follows the functions' syntax (See footnote 12). It is specified as the function `join` that takes as parameters the mapping identifier (with the `mapping=` parameter key) and the similarity function to perform the join. This function can, in turn, take as parameters data values. Quoted and non-asserted triples can also be generated within join conditions by using the parameter keys `quoted=` and `quotedNonAsserted=` respectively. In the example, the join condition is performed using the `equal` function to create as objects the subjects of the mapping set `jumpTM` if the values of the fields ID from source and ID from target mapping set are the same.

The YARRRML-star extension and all the additional updates were proposed to be incorporated in the YARRRML specification and are currently under review by the KG Construction Community Group[13].

```
1  - predicates: :jumps
2    objects:
3    - function: join(mapping=jumpTM, equal(str1=$(ID), str2=$(ID)))
```

Listing 11: Abbreviated syntax for join conditions.

5 Yatter

Yatter [5] is a new open-source bi-directional YARRRML translator that supports the aforementioned new features. Yatter receives as input a mapping document in the YARRRML serialisation and the desirable output format (R2RML or RML), or the other way around. Algorithm 1 presents the procedure implemented by the system to translate an input YARRRML mapping document into [R2]RML. First, the namespaces defined in YARRRML are added together with a set of predefined ones (e.g., `foaf`[14], `rml`[15], `rdf`[16]) that are used in by [R2]RML. Second, functions, targets, and databases are identified in the entire YARRRML document and translated into RML. Each of them generates a global identifier mapped into a hash table that can be used by any `rr:TermMap`. For external source declaration, their identifiers are also mapped into a hash table for the next steps. Regarding the RDF-star support, the mapping rules are parsed to identify if it contains `quoted` or `quotedNonAsserted` keys. This determines if the translation requires producing RML-star mapping rules. If true, a hash table is also created for the mapping instances of `rml:NonAssertedTriplesMap`.

In YARRRML, lists of sources and subjects maps can be defined within the same triples map, but [R2]RML triples maps may contain only one source and one subject. Hence, for each mapping document, a list of sources and subjects is first collected and then translated depending on the desirable output format ([R2]RML[-star]). Nevertheless, multiple predicate maps and object maps are allowed within the same triples map, and they are directly translated to RML. Finally, the cartesian product of sources and subject maps together with the predicate object maps is combined to generate the desirable triples map. Before returning the mapping rules, Yatter validates that the generated output is a valid RDF graph.

---

[13] https://github.com/kg-construct/yarrrml-spec/pull/4.
[14] http://xmlns.com/foaf/0.1/.
[15] http://semweb.mmlab.be/ns/rml#.
[16] http://www.w3.org/1999/02/22-rdf-syntax-ns#.

Algorithm 1: YARRRML-star translation algorithm

Result: [R2]RML mapping document
$input\_m \longleftarrow yarrrml\_rules$;
$format \longleftarrow output\_format$;
$output\_m \longleftarrow \emptyset$;
$output\_m.add(translate\_prefixes(input\_m))$;
if $format == RML$ **then**
   | $output\_m.add(translate\_functions(input\_m))$;
   | $output\_m.add(translate\_targets(input\_m))$;
   | $is\_star, non\_asserted\_maps \leftarrow analyze\_rml\_star(input\_m)$;
end
$output\_m.add(translate\_databases\_access(input\_m))$;
$ext\_sources \leftarrow get\_external\_sources(input\_m)$;
for $tm \in M.get\_triples\_map()$ **do**
   | $source\_list \leftarrow translate\_source(format, get\_source\_list(ext\_sources, tm))$;
   | $subject\_list \leftarrow translate\_subject(is\_star, format, get\_subject\_list(tm))$;
   | $predicates\_objects \leftarrow translate\_predicates\_objects(is\_star, format, tm)$;
   | **for** $s \in source\_list$ **do**
   | | **for** $subj \in subject\_list$ **do**
   | | | $m \leftarrow combine(s, subj, predicates\_objects, non\_asserted\_maps)$;
   | | | $output\_m.add(m)$;
   | | **end**
   | **end**
end
return $validate(output\_m)$;

Although YARRRML leaves the RDF-based syntax of the mapping rules to be processed only by the RDF graphs construction systems, we also provide a human-readable output considering previous experiences [4,6,7]. This helps knowledge engineers in complex data integration contexts to easier understand if the mapping document in YARRRML represents the desirable rules of [R2]RML and, hence, if the constructed RDF graph will be correct or not. Thus, the output mapping follows a Turtle-based syntax, using predicate object lists within blank node properties[17], as recommended by the [R2]RML specifications. We also ensure the same mapping rules' order as they are defined in YARRRML. Functions, targets, and databases appear first, while for each `rr:TriplesMap`, the sequence is: source, subject map, and the set of predicate object maps.

The source code of Yatter is openly available under Apache 2.0 license (See footnote 3). Following open science best practices, each release automatically generates a dedicated DOI to ensure reproducibility[18]. The development is under continuous integration using GitHub Actions and the YARRRML test-cases

---

[17] https://www.w3.org/TR/turtle/#unlabeled-bnodes.
[18] https://doi.org/10.5281/zenodo.7024500.

(Sect. 6) have more than 80% code coverage. Yatter is available through PyPi as a module[19] to be easily integrated in any Python development.

6   Validation

We validate the extensions to YARRRML and the developed implementation by proposing and testing a set of test cases, and comparing to other proposed user-friendly serialisations and corresponding systems.

6.1   YARRRML Test Cases

Test cases are a common method to evaluate the conformance of a system [1,12]. To the best of our knowledge, previous R2RML [20] and RML [12] test cases were not translated to any human-friendly serialisation (e.g., YARRRML). Relying on [R2]RML test cases, we propose a set of representative test cases (including also the new features presented in this work) to assess the conformance of any YARRRML translator system. The proposed test cases require to be two-fold defined: to cover the complete vocabulary of the serialisation, and also have the flexibility to declare the rules (e.g., shortcuts or location of the keys).

We follow a systematic methodology for creating the YARRRML test cases. We analyzed the [R2]RML test cases and observed that several assess correct data generation. Since YARRRML serves as user-friendly serialisation for another mapping language, the focus of its test cases is not on assessing data correctness, but on covering the language expressiveness. Hence, we select 15 R2RML test cases that cover the R2RML features and manually translate them into YARRRML. Since RML is a superset of R2RML, it introduces modifications with respect to R2RML to include the definition of heterogenous datasets (e.g., `rr:LogicalTable` is superseded by `rml:LogicalSource`). We propose 8 new test cases to cover these features.

For features not covered by the RML test cases, we follow a similar procedure. We inspected the RML-star test cases [3], and translated to YARRRML the ones that provide a complete coverage of this extension. From the 16 test cases proposed to assess the conformance of RML-star, we adapt 6. Finally, as there are still no test cases proposed for RML-Target, RML-FNML, RML dynamic language tags and datatypes, we proposed another 21 test cases to cover them.

In total, we defined 50 YARRRML test cases and their corresponding translation to RML or R2RML. They are openly available[20] to be used by any YARRRML-compliant system. Yatter passes all test cases successfully.

6.2   Serialisations Comparison

We compare a set of user-friendly serialisations and languages, namely SMS2 [17], XRM [21], ShExML [11] and YARRRML [13] incorporating the updates

---

[19] https://pypi.org/project/yatter/.
[20] https://github.com/oeg-upm/yarrrml-validation.

Table 1. Features of user-friendly serialisations. BN stands for blank node, L for literal, ST for RDF-star triple, C for constant and D for dynamic. Underlined features indicate the updates of YARRRML-star, while "*" indicates that a feature is possible with the implementation but not explicit in the serialisation.

	ShExML	SMS2	XRM	YARRRML-star
LF1	BN, IRI	BN, IRI, ST	IRI	BN, IRI, ST
LF2	C, D (1..1)	C, D, (1..1)	C, D, (1..1)	C, D (0..1)
LF3	IRI	IRI	IRI	IRI
LF4	C (1..1)	C, D (1..1)	C (1..1)	C, D (1..N)
LF5	BN, IRI, L	BN, IRI, L, ST	IRI, L	BN, IRI, L, ST
LF6	C, D (1..1)	C, D (1..N)	C, D (1..1)	C, D (1..N)
LF7	C, D (0..1)	C (0..1)	C (0..1)	C, D (0..1)
LF8	C, D (0..1)	C, D (0..1)	C (0..1)	C, D (0..1)
LF9	C (0..1)	C (0..1)	C, D (0..N)	C, D (0..N)
LF10	(1..N)	(1..N)	(1..N)	(1..N)
LF11	Input	Input	Input	Input, output
LF12	Yes	No*	No*	Yes
LF13	Yes	No	No	No
LF14	Yes	Yes	No	Yes
LF15	Yes	No	No	Yes

described in Sect. 4, regarding their expressiveness. To that end, we study 15 features that tackle usual characteristics and functionalities in mapping languages. We describe each and discuss how each serialisation addresses it (Table 1).

LF1. Subject Term Type. This feature indicates what kind of RDF[-star] term the language can generate as subject. In RDF, subjects can be IRIs or blank nodes, while in RDF-star they can also be RDF-star triples. All serialisations enable the creation of subjects at least as IRIs, SMS2 and YARRRML additionally implement RDF-star triples and, along with ShExML, blank nodes.

LF2. Subject Generation. This feature indicates if subjects can be generated as constant or dynamic values; and how many subject declarations are allowed at a time. In dynamically generated values, the subject value changes with a field in the data source. In our example, the subject uses the field "ID" to generate different subject for each row of input data (List 1 line 6) . All serialisations can generate constant and dynamic subjects. For each set of rules, exactly one subject declaration is expected, i.e. one subject for predicate-object pairs. YARRRML can also accept no subject declaration, producing a blank node.

LF3. Predicate Term Type. This feature indicates if the serialisation is able to generate an IRI for a predicate and all serialisations do so.

LF4. Predicate Generation. This feature indicates if predicates can be generated as constant or dynamic values; and how many predicate declarations are allowed at a time. In dynamically generated values, the subject value changes with a field in the data source. SMS2 and YARRRML enable dynamic predicates, and YARRRML is also able to handle more than one predicate, which avoids repeating the same object for different predicates.

LF5. Object Term Type. This feature indicates what kind of RDF[-star] term the serialisation is able to generate as object. The serialisations can generate the same kinds of terms as in subjects (LF1), with the addition of literals.

LF6. Object Generation. This feature indicates if objects can be generated as constant or dynamic values; and how many predicate declarations are allowed at a time. As for subjects, all serialisations can generate constant and dynamic objects. In addition, SMS2 and YARRRML allow more than one at a time, which avoids repeating the same predicate for different objects.

LF7. Datatype. This feature indicates if datatypes can be specified constant or dynamically. All serialisations enable the optional declaration of constant datatypes, but ShExML and YARRRML also enable dynamic datatypes.

LF8. Language Tag. This feature indicates if language tags can be constant or dynamic. Just as for datatypes, all serialisations enable the optional declaration of constant language tags, XRM is the only not allowing dynamic.

LF9. Named Graph. This feature indicates if named graphs can be assigned to the generated statements and how (constant or dynamically). All serialisations enable their optional declaration as constant IRI. XRM and YARRRML also enable more than one graph assignation, and allow dynamic values.

LF10. Data References. This features indicates how many data references a term can contain when generated dynamically (i.e. when its value changes with the input data). It applies to subjects, predicates, objects, datatypes, language tags and named graphs when the serialisation allows dynamic generation. All serialisations allow more than one data reference for dynamic generation.

LF11. Data Description. This feature indicates if the input or output data (e.g., format, iteration, name, path, etc.) can be described. All serialisations can describe input data source, and YARRRML also provides the output data source.

LF12. Data Linking. This feature indicates if explicit data linking (e.g. join, fuzzy linking, etc.) can be performed with mapping rules. ShExML and YARRRML provide specific features for this end; in XRM and SMS2, however, it is not explicit, but it is possible by using SQL queries.

LF13. Nested Hierarchies. This feature indicates if different levels of a hierarchy source can be accessed in the same data iteration. ShExML is the only language that implements this feature. It is not implemented in YARRRML since it is neither supported in RML as a language feature in the time of writing.

Table 2. Features of the systems that support the different languages.

	ShExML translator	Stardog	XRM translator	YARRRML parser	Yatter
SF1	Open Source	Closed source	Closed source	Open Source	Open Source
SF2	Java	Java	Java	Javascript	Python
SF3	RDB, CSV, JSON, XML, RDF	RDB, NoSQL, CSV, JSON, GraphQL	RDB, CSV, XML	RDB, NoSQL, CSV, JSON, XML	RDB, NoSQL, CSV, JSON, XML
SF4	ShExML	R2RML, SMS, SMS2	XRM	YARRRML, R2RML, RML	YARRRML, R2RML, RML
SF5	RML, RDF	RDF	R2RML, RML, CSVW, CARML	R2RML, RML, YARRRML	R2RML, RML, YARRRML
SF6	N/A	Yes	N/A	No	Yes
SF7	Yes	Yes	N/A	No	Yes
SF8	Yes	N/A	N/A	No	Yes

LF14. Functions. This indicates if data transformations are applicable to input data (e.g. lowercase). XRM is the only serialisation not supporting it.

LF15. Conditions. This feature indicates if a statement is generated or not depending on a condition. Only ShExML and YARRRML implement this.

Discussion. All serialisations offer a rich variety of mapping features, but ShExML and YARRRML have a richer selection. SMS2 leverages the SPARQL syntax, lowering the learning curve for SPARQL users. At the same time, data processing is limited to basic SPARQL functions and the user is unable to integrate custom ones. XRM is designed to mimic natural language and adds minimal overhead with its own syntax keywords, which also makes it easy-to-learn, but provides a more limited variety of features (Table 1).

6.3   Systems Comparison

We also compare the systems that support the aforementioned serialisations: ShExML translator (See footnote 7), Stardog (See footnote 1) (with focus on how Stardog maps data sources to RDF graphs, using R2RML or SMS2), XRM translator [21], and YARRRML-parser[21] and our system, Yatter [5]. We study 8 system features to draw conclusions about them including:

SF1. Availability. Stardog and XRM are commercial systems and their implementation is not available. ShExML Java library (See footnote 7), YARRRML-parser (See footnote 21) and Yatter[22] are all available as GitHub repositories.

SF2. Programming Language. ShExML, XRM and Stardog are built in Java, YARRRML-parser in Javascript and Yatter in Python.

---

[21] https://github.com/RMLio/yarrrml-parser.
[22] https://github.com/oeg-upm/yatter/.

SF3. Input Data Sources. This feature indicates the data source formats that the system can translate, given the corresponding mapping rules. All systems support relational databases and CSV files as input data sources. Only Stardog and Yatter support NoSQL data sources.

SF4. Input Serialisation. This feature indicates the input mapping serialisation. All systems support their corresponding mapping serialisation. Additionally, Stardog can transform R2RML mapping rules to RDF graphs, whereas both YARRRML systems can translate R2RML or RML files into YARRRML.

SF5. Output Serialisation. This indicates the output mapping serialisation. XRM and YARRRML systems translate their mapping rules to [R2]RML, while XRM also supports CARML and CSVW. Stardog directly constructs the RDF graph. ShExML generates both RML mapping rules and RDF graphs.

SF6. RDF-star Support. Only Stardog and Yatter support this feature. Stardog added RDF-star statement support in one of their latest releases using the "Edge Properties" configuration. Yatter improves upon YARRRML-parser by also enabling the construction of RDF-star graphs.

SF7. Dynamic Language Tag Support. ShExML, Yatter and Stardog provide support for this feature.

SF8. Dynamic Datatype Tag Support. Yatter and ShExML are the only systems that enable the reference of datatypes dynamically.

Additionally, based on the YARRRML test cases, we develop the corresponding test cases for the other analyzed serialisations. The results of the conformance test of the analysed systems are presented online (See footnote 20).

Discussion. All systems provide a solid user experience and are -mostly- highly conformant with their corresponding serialisation. ShExML is especially useful for integrating different data sources and formats, but lacks RDF-star support, writing functions results cumbersome and the translation to RML is incomplete. Stardog works smoothly with its proprietary Stardog databases, but managing several different sources becomes complex as a different mapping rule set is required per source. XRM is installed within a coding editor, and helps actively the writing process with suggestions and warnings. YARRRML-parser supports most of the functionalities that are also implemented in Yatter but still it does not support the latest RML features. YARRRML-parser translates functions to non-standard set of RML rules, while our implementation supports the specification proposed by the W3C CG on Knowledge Graph Construction[23].

6.4   Use Cases

Constructing RDF Graphs for Research-Performing Organizations. In a previous work [4] we used YARRRML-star and Yatter to support the creation of RDF graphs for research supporting organizations with R2RML. Thanks to

---

[23] https://w3id.org/kg-construct/rml-fnml.

this setup, we created a fluent and iterative pipeline for testing and debugging the created mapping rules in a complex environment, where almost 2000 tables were mapped into RDF. Additionally, the easy-to-read RML outcome helped knowledge engineers to easily identify and fix errors during the construction of the RDF graphs.

The EU Public Procurement Data Space (PPDS). The EU PPDS constructs a decentralized KG[24], by declaratively mapping procurement data from each EU member state into the e-Procurement Ontology (ePO)[25]. YARRRML-star is the selected serialisation to ensure the maintainability of the graph construction, and it is currently used together with Yatter to develop the initial pilots. In the latest pilots, open Spanish public procurement data extracted from their national platform was mapped, where the mapping rules[26] contain dynamic language tags and complex XPath expressions.

7   Conclusions and Future Work

In this paper, we present YARRRML-star, an extension of YARRRML serialisation to fully cover the RML specification supported by a new translator, Yatter. Additionally, we compare YARRRML-star with other human-friendly mapping serialisations in terms of language features and system support over a set of conformance test cases. We demonstrated the impact of our approach over two real use cases, situating YARRRML-star and Yatter as a promising setup for constructing knowledge graphs in complex environments.

In future work, we plan to extend YARRRML-star to support collections and containers[27] in both the serialization and in Yatter. We are also planning to include more test cases to verify correctness in the inverse translation from RML or R2RML mapping rules to YARRRML-star.

Acknowledgement. The work presented in this paper is partially funded by Knowledge Spaces project (Grant PID2020-118274RB-I00 funded by MCIN/AEI/ 10.13039/501100011033) and partially supported by Flanders Make, the strategic research centre for the manufacturing industry. David Chaves-Fraga is supported by the Madrid Government (Comunidad de Madrid-Spain) under the Multiannual Agreement with Universidad Politécnica de Madrid in the line Support for R&D projects for Beatriz Galindo researchers, in the context of the V PRICIT (Regional Programme of Research and Technological Innovation).

References

1. Arenas-Guerrero, J., Iglesias-Molina, A., Chaves-Fraga, D., Garijo, D., Corcho, O., Dimou, A.: Morph-KGC^{star}: declarative generation of RDF-star graphs from heterogeneous data. Semant. Web (Under Review) (2023)

---

[24] https://europa.eu/!qx9WxQ.
[25] https://docs.ted.europa.eu/EPO/latest/.
[26] https://github.com/oeg-upm/yatter/tree/main/test/projects/PPDSTC.
[27] https://w3id.org/kg-construct/rml-collections-containers.

2. Chatterjee, A., Nardi, C., Oberije, C., Lambin, P.: Knowledge graphs for COVID-19: an exploratory review of the current landscape. J. Pers. Med. **11**(4), 300 (2021)
3. Chaves, D., Iglesias, A., Garijo, D., Guerrero, J.A.: kg-construct/rml-star-test-cases: v1.1 (2022). https://doi.org/10.5281/zenodo.6518802
4. Chaves-Fraga, D., Corcho, O., Yedro, F., Moreno, R., Olías, J., De La Azuela, A.: Systematic construction of knowledge graphs for research-performing organizations. Information **13**(12), 562 (2022)
5. Chaves-Fraga, D., Gonzalez, M., Doña, D.: oeg-upm/yatter (2023). https://doi.org/10.5281/zenodo.7643310
6. Chaves-Fraga, D., Priyatna, F., Cimmino, A., Toledo, J., Ruckhaus, E., Corcho, O.: GTFS-Madrid-Bench: a benchmark for virtual knowledge graph access in the transport domain. J. Web Semant. **65**, 100596 (2020)
7. Corcho, O., et al.: A high-level ontology network for ICT infrastructures. In: Hotho, A., et al. (eds.) ISWC 2021. LNCS, vol. 12922, pp. 446–462. Springer, Cham (2021). https://doi.org/10.1007/978-3-030-88361-4_26
8. Das, S., Sundara, S., Cyganiak, R.: R2RML: RDB to RDF mapping language. W3C recommendation, world wide web consortium (W3C) (2012). http://www.w3.org/TR/r2rml/
9. Delva, T., Arenas-Guerrero, J., Iglesias-Molina, A., Corcho, O., Chaves-Fraga, D., Dimou, A.: RML-star: a declarative mapping language for RDF-star generation. In: International Semantic Web Conference, ISWC, P&D, vol. 2980. CEUR Workshop Proceedings (2021). http://ceur-ws.org/Vol-2980/paper374.pdf
10. Dimou, A., Vander Sande, M., Colpaert, P., Verborgh, R., Mannens, E., Van de Walle, R.: RML: a generic language for integrated RDF mappings of heterogeneous data. In: Proceedings of the 7th Workshop on Linked Data on the Web, vol. 1184. CEUR Workshop Proceedings (2014). http://ceur-ws.org/Vol-1184/ldow2014_paper_01.pdf
11. García-González, H., Boneva, I., Staworko, S., Labra-Gayo, J.E., Cueva-Lovelle, J.M.: ShExML: improving the usability of heterogeneous data mapping languages for first-time users. PeerJ Comput. Sci. **6**, e318 (2020). https://doi.org/10.7717/peerj-cs.318
12. Heyvaert, P.: Conformance test cases for the RDF mapping language (RML). In: Villazón-Terrazas, B., Hidalgo-Delgado, Y. (eds.) KGSWC 2019. CCIS, vol. 1029, pp. 162–173. Springer, Cham (2019). https://doi.org/10.1007/978-3-030-21395-4_12
13. Heyvaert, P., De Meester, B., Dimou, A., Verborgh, R.: Declarative rules for linked data generation at your fingertips! In: Gangemi, A., et al. (eds.) ESWC 2018. LNCS, vol. 11155, pp. 213–217. Springer, Cham (2018). https://doi.org/10.1007/978-3-319-98192-5_40
14. Iglesias-Molina, A., Arenas-Guerrero, J., Delva, T., Dimou, A., Chaves-Fraga, D.: RML-star. W3C draft community group report (2022). https://kg-construct.github.io/rml-star-spec/
15. Prud'hommeaux, E., Labra Gayo, J., Solbrig, H.: Shape expressions: an RDF validation and transformation language. In: Proceedings of the 10th International Conference on Semantic Systems (2014)
16. Rojas, J.A., et al.: Leveraging semantic technologies for digital interoperability in the European railway domain. In: Hotho, A., et al. (eds.) ISWC 2021. LNCS, vol. 12922, pp. 648–664. Springer, Cham (2021). https://doi.org/10.1007/978-3-030-88361-4_38
17. Stardog: Sms2 (stardog mapping syntax 2) (2022). https://docs.stardog.com/virtual-graphs/mapping-data-sources

18. Van Assche, D., Delva, T., Haesendonck, G., Heyvaert, P., De Meester, B., Dimou, A.: Declarative RDF graph generation from heterogeneous (semi-) structured data: a systematic literature review. J. Web Semant. 100753 (2022)

19. Van Assche, D., Delva, T., Heyvaert, P., De Meester, B., Dimou, A.: Towards a more human-friendly knowledge graph generation & publication. In: ISWC2021, The International Semantic Web Conference, vol. 2980. CEUR (2021)

20. Villazón-Terrazas, B., Hausenblas, M.: R2RML and direct mapping test cases. W3C Note, W3C (2012). http://www.w3.org/TR/rdb2rdf-test-cases/

21. Zazuko: Expressive RDF mapper (XRM) (2022). https://zazuko.com/products/expressive-rdf-mapper/

Waiter and AUTRATAC: Don't Throw It Away, Just Delay!

Lucas Vogel$^{(\boxtimes)}$ and Thomas Springer

Technical University Dresden, 01069 Dresden, Germany
`lucas.vogel2@tu-dresden.de`

Abstract. The modern web is built with a mixture of HTML, CSS, and an increasing amount of JavaScript. Since JavaScript determines ≈70% of the overall data of websites on average, JavaScript code efficiency significantly influences their loading performance. A recent study revealed that the average JavaScript code usage until render is ≈40%. For economical and convenience reasons, a significant amount of research already focuses on optimizing the delivered data to reduce loading times. For example, a large area of research focuses on eliminating dead code, where unused functions are deleted. Code in this context is classified as "dead" when the results of the code or the whole code itself are never executed or used. Since code elimination is based on heuristics/code classification, there is always a trade-off between code elimination and missing JavaScript code that harms the correct functioning of the website. As a result, some pages do not load correctly after elimination. Even the most advanced attempts with user input emulation do not achieve 100% accuracy. In this paper, we introduce two new open-source frameworks called `Waiter`, which waits until a resource is available, and `AUTRATAC`, an **au**tomatic **tra**nspiler **t**o **a**waitable **c**ode. Both can be used separately or in combination to robustly delay pieces of JavaScript code without breaking it. For example, it allows code to be executed without loading all called functions beforehand. Therefore, when eliminating dead code optimized with `AUTRATAC`, the loading of unused functions can be delayed in a non-render-blocking way. This also opens up multiple new opportunities, as future code-splitting techniques might be significantly stricter without breaking a page. Our results show that delaying render-blocking JavaScript reduces loading times until First Contentful Paint (FCP) significantly, especially at slower network speeds. In one instance, an 85% drop in loading time was measured. Furthermore, it was visible that deferring the code with the developed frameworks still matches the total code execution time of the original render-blocking JavaScript.

Keywords: asynchronous JavaScript · code delay · code splitting · faster loading times · JavaScript framework

1 Introduction

Measurements of the HTTP Archive show that websites are getting continuously larger and more complex over the years [1]. Furthermore, the access speed

I. Garrigós et al. (Eds.): ICWE 2023, LNCS 13893, pp. 278–292, 2023.
https://doi.org/10.1007/978-3-031-34444-2_20

of web pages was already researched by Nielsen and Nah et al., which concluded that users' tolerable waiting time is approximately 2 s and that faster pages have a higher conversion rate [11,12]. As a result, for most companies, having slow web pages will directly translate into losing money. For example, reducing the loading speed of amazon.com by only 100 ms results in a 1% loss of sales, according to Greg Linden [10]. Therefore, even minor optimizations have a significant economic impact. One of the most straightforward methods of reducing loading times is to transfer fewer data. However, eliminating unnecessary code depends on the type of resource. For HTML and CSS, techniques like server-side rendering (SSR for short) already exist to minimize the amount of data by only transferring the elements used to display the page. In contrast, although various approaches exist [4,9], approaches for SSR for Javascript still have substantial limitations. This might be due to the difficulty of correctly identifying if a function or component is used, retaining the full functionality of a page while simultaneously trying to eliminate as much code as possible to reduce loading times. We argue that all approaches can be significantly improved if the "dead" code does not have to be thrown away. Instead, we propose to delay all code identified to be eliminated to avoid insufficiently eliminated code being missing and thus would break the web page's functionality.

Our approach uses async-based JavaScript code in combination with a self-developed framework to wait until code is available before it is executed. Instead of an error, the code becomes resilient to other code not being available. Therefore parts of the code can be loaded asynchronously.

The main contributions of this paper are twofold. First, the developed Waiter-framework is introduced, which uses promises to wait for a function to be called. A targeted function or variable of a code block that is not available yet will be provided as a parameter to the framework. Waiter will then call the function or provide access to the variable once available, hence the technique's name. Waiter requires wrapper code (code enclosing other code) to work. Therefore, a second developed framework AUTRATAC is introduced, which is short for automatic transpiler to awaitable code. This is our second contribution. AUTRATAC is a transpiler that converts asynchronous JavaScript into its Waiter-wrapped equivalent. Our goal is to provide an automatic open-source technique that can be used in various existing optimization techniques to "close the gap" of maintaining the full functionality of a web page. This allows future dead code elimination algorithms to optimistically select code that will never be used with a high probability of significantly reducing the amount of JavaScript code that needs to be transferred render-blocking. Code that is incorrectly classified as dead code can be asynchronously loaded on demand. Our evaluation results show that this strategy allows significantly lower loading times until FCP (First Contentful Paint) while simultaneously keeping similar execution times.

This paper is organized as follows. In Sect. 2, key terms and concepts related to code delay are introduced. In Sect. 4, the most relevant related work is discussed, followed by the general concept in Sect. 5. There, the two techniques AUTRATAC and Waiter are described in detail. Next, both frameworks are evalu-

```
1  function a(){
2      return new Promise((resolve, reject) => {
3        setTimeout(() => {
4          resolve(true) //resolve after 2 seconds
5        }, 2000)
6      })
7  }
8  a().then((result) => {//will be executed afterward
9    console.log(result) //true
10  });
11  a().then((result) => {//will also be executed afterward
12    const x = result;
13  });
```

Fig. 1. Example of a promise with "`then()`", highlighting the problem of code readability

ated in Sect. 6, focusing on both methods' performance. Furthermore, the limitations of the created approach are discussed. A summary of the paper is described in Sect. 8.

2   Background

The fundamental idea of our concept is to allow for delaying JavaScript code classified as "dead" code based on asynchronous code with async/await and promises instead of eliminating it. Therefore, we introduce the main concepts of promises and async/await in the following section.

Promises enable deferring JavaScript code and executing it asynchronously. A promise has a constructor and can be created by calling `new Promise()`. A promise can be pending (neither fulfilled nor rejected), fulfilled (completed successfully), or rejected (failed) [5]. When a promise is settled (resolved or rejected), the `then()`-method can be used to execute code afterward. However, chaining promises can be difficult, as it is harder to track which code will be executed and when. This issue can be seen in Fig. 1, in line 8 and line 11. Both code blocks will be executed after the promise is settled, but it might be challenging to read. In the shown example, they are resolved in the order they appear. To solve the readability problem, async/await can be used, which provides a simpler syntax.

async/await, or asynchronous functions are methods declared with the `async` keyword in front of it. In async functions, the `await` keyword is allowed. Furthermore, top-level async is supported in modules so that the keyword can be used even outside of functions. `Await` waits for a promise to be settled, as shown in Fig. 2. The `await` syntax shown in line 5 can be used with promises or other `async` functions (shown in line 6). Most importantly, `await` still works even if no promise is given without crashing, as shown in line 7. As a result, the await

```
1  async function b(){
2    return 2;
3  }
4  async function c() {
5    const x = await Promise.resolve(1);
6    const y = await b();
7    const z = await 3;
8    console.log(x,y,z); // 1 2 3
9  }
10 c();
```

Fig. 2. Example of async/await with promises

syntax is not only shorter and more readable, but it is also more robust than using then().

Babel is used as part of AUTRATAC to automatically convert asynchronous code into Waiter-wrapped code. This is necessary to allow easy usage of Waiter without manual insertion. Babel is a popular JavaScript-to-JavaScript transpiler framework that provides numerous features to modify code [3]. This is done by parsing JavaScript code into an Abstract Syntax Tree (AST) representation, a modification from ESTree [6]. This hierarchical structure can then be traversed and modified. Afterward, the AST will be converted back into JavaScript code.

3 Compatibility

Creating executable code by the majority of existing browsers is a major concern in our code. Promises are used primarily due to some functions not being able to work with async/await. Those challenges are described in detail in Subsect. 5.1. By default, at least 97.45% of all currently used web browsers support promises, 95.9% support async functions, and 94.88% support the await operator, according to caniuse.com at the time of writing. The major exceptions are Internet Explorer, which is now discontinued, and Opera Mini, which uses its own optimization methods to improve the loading speed of web pages. Even though most browsers already support the necessary functions, the built-in polyfill functionality of Babel can be used to increase compatibility even further.

Render-Blocking Code: JavaScript code can be inserted into a web page in three ways: inside the HTML file itself by using the <script>//code</script>-tag, externally using the src-attribute, e.g. <script src="script.js">, or inline at a tag. By default, both versions will prevent the rendering of a web page. Therefore, all resources that share this behavior are called render-*blocking*, resulting in a long loading time until the page's content is visible to a user. Resources like images do not block the rendering process and are therefore called non-render-blocking.

FCP: First Contentful Paint (FCP) is one of the most important metrics when evaluating the performance of a web page. It describes the point in time when a user can see the first content of a web page[1]. Therefore, a faster FCP describes a faster web page and a better user experience.

4   Related Work

The related work is split into two sections. First, techniques utilizing a compiler to modify JavaScript code are discussed, which can potentially be used for the frameworks developed in this paper. Secondly, various methods are shown to classify and remove JavaScript to optimize web pages.

The *Closure Compiler* is a transpiler that "compiles from JavaScript to better JavaScript," according to Google [8]. The applied improvements to the code range from removing white space and renaming variables to dead code removal and global inlining. However, the amount of applied optimization depends on the compilation level [8]. The dead code removal, advanced renaming, and inlining are only applied in the "advanced"-mode, which makes certain assumptions about the source code. If these assumptions are not met, the compiled code will not work. Therefore, the *Closure Compiler* is no viable, universal solution for advanced code optimizations like dead code removal.

The authors of *speedy.js* argue that the performance of JavaScript execution is insufficient in numerous cases, even when including all optimizations made to the JavaScript engines in recent years [13]. Therefore a subset of JavaScript (and therefore also a subset of TypeScript) is presented, which improves the performance of targeted functions. A cross-compiler is then used to produce WebAssembly, which can be executed in a browser. Like our approach, the JavaScript code is compiled into a different format to provide the desired functionality. However, this paper targets mainly the execution time of already loaded code, not optimizing the amount of code or providing code splitting techniques.

Muzeel and *JSCleaner* take different approaches to classifying and removing unused JavaScript [4,9]. However, the described papers also evaluate how many pages retain full functionality after elimination, which is crucial for the real-world success of the proposed method. One major factor of correct dead code classification is user input, which can lead to functions being called only under certain complex web page states. Some techniques, like the method proposed by Goel et al., do not consider this factor at all [7]. As the authors state in their paper, this might have skewed their results. Even advanced methods like *Muzeel*, which try to emulate every possible user input combination, cannot ensure full functionality after elimination. All described approaches can benefit from the proposed `Waiter` and `AUTRATAC` frameworks, as they can close the gap by delaying individual functions that would otherwise be eliminated. To the best of our knowledge, no work exists that enables such conversion of JavaScript code.

---

[1] web.dev/fcp.

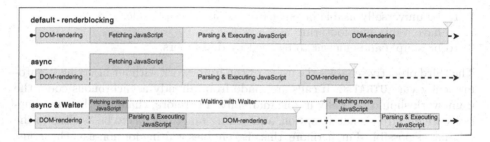

Fig. 3. Ways to load and execute external JavaScript code. The first visible render is marked with a yellow triangle. (Color figure online)

5   General Concept

The following concept generally aims to provide a developer-friendly framework to easily delay code without breaking. This allows code to be loaded in a delayed fashion, possibly providing new approaches to working with JavaScript code. One example is dead code elimination, as the code might not have to be eliminated, just loaded at a later stage. Delaying code prevents a page's rendering, as traditionally, loading JavaScript is render-blocking. However, utilizing the async-Attribute on the <script>-tag, the fetching of JavaScript can be done in parallel, which is not render-blocking. As a result, the asynchronously loaded JavaScript will improve rendering times significantly. Still, the parsing and execution use computing power while rendering the page, as shown in Fig. 3. The loaded code might contain functions that are not needed at this stage or not needed at all, for example, if they are part of a larger framework. Removing those functions is an open challenge described in Sect. 1, which can result in broken web pages. Our approach uses async/await as a concept to test if delayed code is loaded and returns the results when available. As shown in Fig. 3, adding the developed Waiter-framework allows websites to delay parts of JavaScript, with the framework handling the waiting operation. Even though using Waiter as a standalone framework is possible, implementing it in larger code bases might pose a significant challenge for developers. Additionally, Waiter only works if called in asynchronous code. Therefore, the AUTRATAC framework is created, automatically converting asynchronous code into Waiter-wrapped code. Next, both frameworks are described in detail.

5.1   Waiter Framework

The task of the Waiter framework is to wait for a requested function or resource until it becomes available and then serve it to the entity that initiated the request. For example, it enables asynchronous code to wait for the result of a function that might not have been loaded yet. The goal of constructing the described framework is threefold:

1. to be universally usable in asynchronous JavaScript code,
2. to have a minimal footprint, and
3. to be simple and efficient to be used by developers.

The third objective enables the usage of the framework without inserting it automatically via AUTRATAC. If calls are made from already asynchronous code, the framework should be easily usable manually. Therefore, changing the way functions are declared is not an option, and calling functions has to be as close to the original as possible. Furthermore, this also enables waiting for non-asynchronous, non-modified code. In other words, if a framework function is used that does not call other functions, it does not have to be asynchronous to work with Waiter. Suppose this applies to all framework functions (for example, a framework that provides a list of utility functions). In that case, the framework can be used without modifications made by AUTRATAC. In order to address both goals 1. and 3., the call syntax of Waiter is discussed next. In order to ensure a minimal footprint, goal 2. is discussed afterward.

Call Syntax: Multiple challenges have to be considered in order to define a call syntax. Most prominently, calling a function that is not defined will, by default, result in an error, even if the said function is never called. More crucially, all JavaScript execution will be stopped. One possible solution is using eval(), which evaluates text to JavaScript and executes it with the privileges of the caller. Even though it might seem like the ideal option, eval has several shortcomings. Most prominently (besides major security concerns[2]), it does not highlight errors made in the input string, making development harder. Instead, arrow functions are chosen.

Both methods work and are shown in Fig. 4, lines 2 and 4. Both will not throw an error if function b is removed and function a is not called. Line 4 is wrapped in an IIFE (Immediately Invoked Function Expression) to be executed immediately, which is only necessary in the shown example. Therefore, if the developer uses TypeScript, it is also type-safe. As a result, Waiter will be called by providing an arrow function that contains the actual function to be called. The code in Fig. 5 demonstrates how Waiter is used. The double underscore is only utilized to minimize interference with existing functions and frameworks. Renaming the framework function would not interfere with its functionality. The example also shows that the await statement is not strictly necessary inside the arrow function given as a parameter to Waiter (assuming function b is asynchronous), as the framework can work with asynchronous functions wrapped in an arrow function directly.

Availability Check Trigger: The availability of requested resources or functions has to be checked repeatedly through Waiter as it might change depending on the context. Therefore, a *MutationObserver* is ideal, as it can be configured

---

[2] developer.mozilla.org/en−US/docs/Web/JavaScript/Reference/Global_Objects/
eval.

```
1  function a(){ //is not called
2    eval('b()'); //no error
3    (
4       ()⇒b() //no error
5    )()
6  }
```

```
1  //Waiter is loaded beforehand
2
3  async function a(){
4      await __w(()⇒b())
5  }
6
```

Fig. 4. Comparison between eval and an arrow function. In this example, function b() is not defined.

Fig. 5. Example of calling a function with WaiterNo error is thrown, even if function b() is not defined.

to trigger when any part of a document changes, including adding new code via a `script` tag. According to *caniuse.com*, nearly 98.5% of all tracked browsers support this feature at the time of writing. Alternatively, checking based on a time interval is possible but might impact the code's performance or response time, which is therefore not used in the example shown. Because the test is an asynchronous function, a *MutationObserver* and a time interval could also be combined if increased backward compatibility is desired.

Implementation of the Waiter Framework: The full version of `Waiter` is available on GitHub [16]. Even in the uncompressed form, it only consists of 20 lines of code. When the code is minified, the size of the whole framework is 244 Byte in size. The framework uses the `isTesting`-Variable to prevent double execution of a requested function if the observer is triggered again while the function is running. The inner test function is called once. This prevents the code from getting stuck due to it already being loaded. In conclusion, it shows that all requirements for the framework can be met without sacrificing compatibility. Due to the single function-based framework structure, it is universally usable in asynchronous JavaScript code, with a size of 244 Byte it has a minimal footprint, and handling the availability check on its own with a short call syntax makes it to be simple and efficient to be used by developers.

5.2   AUTRATAC

As shown in Sect. 5.1, the `Waiter` framework can be integrated manually. Even though this results in the highest control for the developer, it requires all function calls to be wrapped, as shown in Fig. 5. For such a framework to be viable, an automatic converter is needed, which inserts the wrapper code automatically. This is why AUTRATAC is necessary, as it converts asynchronous JavaScript to the wrapped equivalent. Similarly to `Waiter`, the AUTRATAC framework has multiple goals to achieve:

1. It has to convert all valid asynchronous JavaScript code correctly,
2. The framework should be easy to integrate with existing software, and
3. be able to insert calls to the `Waiter` framework directly.

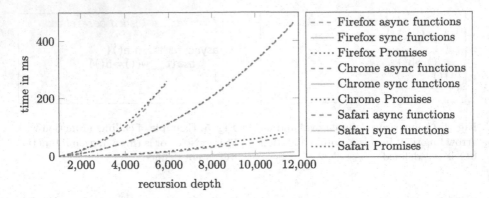

Fig. 6. The average time in milliseconds for executing recursive functions ("async," synchronous, and with promises) with different depths 100 times on Firefox, Chrome, and Safari. The recursion depth is represented on the x-axis.

5.3   Automatic Conversion of Synchronous to Asynchronous Code

As `Waiter` works in asynchronous code, the question arises if it is possible to convert all synchronous code to asynchronous code first using a Babel plugin [3]. Such a conversion might theoretically be possible. However, multiple downsides exist that prevent real-world usage. The most critical issues are discussed next.

First, the resulting overhead is the most significant downside of converting all synchronous code to the asynchronous equivalent. For example, using jQuery v3.6.0, adding an await keyword to every function and a `Waiter` wrapper to every function call would result in a 34.7% increase in file size. As this overhead might outweigh the benefits of splitting the code, a more fine-grained approach is chosen.

Secondly, chaining promises will reduce performance. Even if the file overhead is hypothetically classified as acceptable, chaining multiple asynchronous calls negatively impacts the execution time of the code, as shown in Fig. 6. There, the average execution time of a recursively called asynchronous function is shown at different recursion depths until every browser reaches its maximum call stack size. The graph shows that the performance of async-based and promise-based functions did not differ significantly in most scenarios. However, synchronous functions executed faster on every test and with every browser. Therefore, the minimization of asynchronous code is favorable.

Lastly, some additional code challenges arise. The main challenge includes the JavaScript ability to create class instances from functions, also called function-based classes. In a regular class, the constructor can be made asynchronous by wrapping the content of the constructor body in a promise, similar to what is shown in Fig. 1, with an additional resolve at the end. However, with function-based classes, every function might also be able to create a function-based class, which cannot be called when the function uses the `async` keyword, as shown in line 5 in Fig. 7. This needs a more sophisticated code analysis and wrap-

```
1  function A(){}
2  const a = new A(); //works
3
4  async function B(){}
5  const b = new B();  //will throw TypeError "B is not a constructor"
```

Fig. 7. Example of a function-based class with and without an asynchronous function

ping every function body in a promise, as it is outside the scope of this paper and part of future work. Until such a tool exists, converting only code that is already marked as asynchronous is the best option to balance code overhead and minimize additional code execution time.

5.4 Implementation

In order to make the integration of AUTRATAC as easy as possible, it was chosen to implement it as a plugin for *Babel*. The *Babel* framework is one of the most popular compilers for web applications that allows for flexible manipulation of JavaScript code by using provided functionality and plugins [3]. These plugins, by default, only need minimal setup. Babel also allows for different configurations, for example, using the plugin to convert a file or a string of code directly or as a part of a build chain. AUTRATAC is also available on GitHub [16].

6 Evaluation

In order to test both Waiter and AUTRATAC, different setups were created to evaluate their performance. In detail, the tests for Waiter include measuring the time until FCP and the JavaScript execution time for determining the total overhead and file sizes before and after inserting Waiter with AUTRATAC. Both are tested separately due to AUTRATAC being used by the developer and, in contrast, Waiter being applied on the client.

6.1 Correctness of Converted Code

The correctness of conversion with AUTRATAC is based on what Babel is classifying as a *function* or a *call*. The only additional logic consists of two tests: if a piece of code is inside an asynchronous function and if a specific *call* is already wrapped inside a call to Waiter. Even though no issues were encountered while evaluating AUTRATAC, proving that the generated code will always be valid without exceptions requires the same proof in combination with Babel, which exceeds the scope of this paper.

6.2   Loading Speed

According to the "state of JavaScript"-report by the HTTP Archive, the amount of JavaScript included in a web page differs by a significant amount [1]. As this form of code modification via `Waiter` and `AUTRATAC` requires access to the code bases of web pages, relying on a set of open-source web pages would be insufficient. The measured results would only represent the small number of converted code bases, not the results of the average web page. Therefore, an average page concerning JavaScript loading accuracy was created to solve this issue. The generated page (as well as the reference page) is also available on GitHub [2]. The structure data is based on a large-scale web page analysis. All downloadable web pages of the top 10.000 Tranco-list[3] entries were checked. The number of external, render-blocking JavaScript characters and files was counted to ensure the highest accuracy. The average JavaScript loading behavior can be replicated accurately by replicating the same number of characters spread to the exact number of external, render-blocking JavaScript files. In total, 8417 pages could be accessed and analyzed, which included an average of 94756 external and render-blocking JavaScript characters, spread to an average of 25 external files (Tranco-ID: J67Y).

Secondly, according to a Statista survey, the most popular front-end framework in 2022 is React, used by 42.62% of developers [14]. Therefore, a React project is used by utilizing the "Create React App" tool[4] and generating React code in version 18.2.0. The resulting project already includes a demo page, which will be used in this evaluation. Special care was taken to ensure that no external JavaScript file is bundled by webpack and that the React JavaScript code is deferred to keep the amount of render-blocking JavaScript consistent. The framework was also used to test if `AUTRATAC` and `Waiter` can be deployed in a real-world scenario.

As the reference page, the generated React project was modified to load all 25 files and call the containing function of each file in the main `App`. After all the calls are completed, a timestamp is saved to compare the total execution time. Comparing the total time this chained series of calls takes shows real-world applicability, as significant delays of the modified version could negatively affect user experience. More precisely, this test checks how much delay is added by delaying the external JavaScript files instead of loading them in a render-blocking way. For the web page with `Waiter`, the reference page was taken, and the JavaScript code was modified using `AUTRATAC`. Furthermore, the loaded scripts were marked as "deferred," and the `Waiter`-library was inserted into the main HTML file. It was chosen to "defer" the external files, as it ensures late execution, by waiting until the `DOMContentLoaded`-event, which allows testing the maximum code delay with the built-in options (defer, async, or none).

For the test itself, two machines were used on a local network: one hosting both versions of the web page via a node express server, the other machine (a 2020 MacBook Pro with a 2.3 GHz Quad-Core Intel i7 and 32GB 3733 MHz

---

[3] tranco-list.eu.

[4] create-react-app.dev.

RAM) loading the web pages at 2, 4, 6, 8, and 10 Mbps. In order to control the network speed, the Apple "Network Link Conditioner"[5] was used, with a Node.js wrapper to control the presets[6]. The web pages were loaded with *puppeteer*, which allows for remote-controlling a browser, using Chromium version 105.0. The presets were custom created, with 2 Mbps, 4 Mbps, 6 Mbps, 8 Mbps, and 10 Mbps, with no additional delay or package loss. The performance was measured using the Performance-API provided by Chrome and the described timestamp after calling all external functions. For both versions and every speed preset, the page was loaded 100 times, and the measurements were averaged out. The test can be replicated with the published test pages on GitHub [2].

6.3   Time Until FCP

The resulting measured times until FCP are visible in Fig. 8. The FCP was extracted using the `Performance`-API provided by *Chromium*. In all scenarios, using `Waiter` reduces the loading time significantly. This is especially visible at slower speeds, as the loading times increase exponentially. Furthermore, Fig. 8 shows that the page was visible for every measured speed in under 2 s, marked with a dotted line. This fulfills the criteria from the study of Nah et al., which state that a tolerable waiting time for information is approximately 2 s [11]. At even lower speeds, the generated web page might surpass this mark. Still, it shows that tools to reduce render-blocking JavaScript can effectively decrease the time until FCP.

6.4   Time Until JavaScript Execution

As described in Subsect. 6.2, every external JavaScript file of the test setup contains a callable function. In the main React application, all functions of all external JavaScript files are called. These calls are synchronous for the reference page, and for the modified version with `Waiter`, the calls are awaited. A timestamp is taken inside the delivered JavaScript code after the last call to the function in the last external file to compare execution times. The start timestamp is taken inside the Node application before puppeteer navigates to the page. After successfully accessing the page, the "end"-timestamp is extracted by puppeteer, and the difference is saved to a local file. Therefore, this metric includes all navigation and necessary resource loading until the page works fully. This is also why the first timestamp is taken before the page load. Suppose the difference in time until the last execution of code is significantly large. In that case, it might reduce the real-world usefulness of the framework, as it could also affect code that is executed as a result of user input and loaded by a deferred piece of JavaScript. More realistically, a significant delay of code that affects the visible elements of a page would also result in an unwanted layout shift, which

---

[5] developer.apple.com/download/more/?q=Additional%20Tools.
[6] npmjs.com/package/network-link-conditioner.

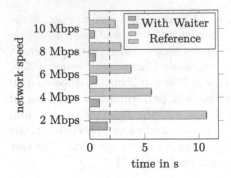

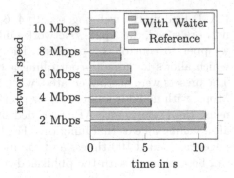

Fig. 8. Average loading time comparison until FCP between a web page optimized with and without `Waiter` at different network speeds. The dotted line highlights the 2-second mark.

Fig. 9. Average loading time comparison until all external JavaScript functions are executed between a web page optimized with and without `Waiter` at different network speeds

is not visible in the "time until FCP"-measurement. Therefore, checking this metric gives insight into the total time that initially loaded code takes.

The results are shown in Fig. 9. Both versions show near identical results, varying at maximum by only 31 ms at 6 Mpbs, and are therefore in the margin of error. Deferring code that is not needed for rendering the page can therefore be done without sacrificing significant loading time on the client device. However, it must be pointed out that specifically delaying JavaScript is the main part of the concept. Loading JavaScript code that affects visible elements on the page in a large delayed file can still decrease the user experience if done improperly. However, this scenario strongly depends on individual developer choices and the tools used to create a web page.

6.5 Transferred Data

Using the `AUTRATAC` Babel output as a reference, each function call in an asynchronous function that is converted increases by 17 characters. This matches with the code output (before webpack bundling with React); the converted 25 function calls increase the code size by 425 Characters. Additionally, the minified `Waiter` framework has an uncompressed size of 244 Byte, equivalent to 244 additional Characters, as calculated in Sect. 5.1.

6.6 Challenges and Limits

Proving that two pieces of code work identically is a significant challenge. Therefore, `AUTRATAC` only converts already asynchronous code. In the current form, `AUTRATAC` converted code correctly in all tests made in this paper. However, edge cases may exist that still need to be covered. Furthermore, the performance tests containing promises and asynchronous code show that future versions need to reduce the usage of both to prevent performance hits. In the current form, this is up to the developer to decide. By making the software open-source, we encourage collaboration on future versions capable of producing code with even higher quality and efficiency. Converting an existing synchronous JavaScript code base into an asynchronous equivalent might be theoretically possible. However, it represents a significant challenge.

7   Research Roadmap

In the future, we plan to create a dynamic code analysis, which allows for adapting the code based on the original call structure and closing currently unknown edge cases. The goal is to reduce the number of asynchronous functions as they impact performance.

8   Conclusion

This paper conceptualized and evaluated a solution for postponing asynchronous JavaScript code in a developer-friendly way. This, for example, can be used to solve the issue that, on average, over 70% of JavaScript is render-blocking, but only ≈40% of the render-blocking JavaScript is used until page render [15]. The developed method enables easy implementation of new ways to delay blocks of JavaScript, which decreases render time due to a decrease in render-blocking code. Faster web pages, in turn, result in better conversion rates and an improved user experience. As part of this paper, two frameworks were presented: `Waiter` and `AUTRATAC`. `Waiter` is a framework that enables asynchronous code to be automatically executed when it becomes available. In other words, it was shown that with the developed `Waiter` framework, loading sections of JavaScript could easily be delayed by an arbitrary amount without breaking the code. `AUTRATAC` is a support framework that converts asynchronous JavaScript code into a version that includes `Waiter` on every call. Using both frameworks together, JavaScript code can accept the absence of other code, for example, due to deferred loading. The results show that the frameworks can convert code at a large scale, even in their current prototype state, which enables new areas of code splitting. When comparing the performance of a generated average web page modified with `AUTRATAC`, a significant decrease in loading time until First Contentful Paint is visible when using `Waiter` by up to 9.1 s at 2 Mbps. Additionally, no significant difference in client code execution time was measurable. However, further research is necessary, as performance measurements showed that excessive usage of promise-based code has a negative impact on execution speed.

References

1. Archive, H.: HTTP archive: state of JavaScript (2022). https://httparchive.org/reports/state-of-javascript. Accessed 9 Jan 2022
2. waiter-and autratac: TestPages (2023). https://github.com/waiter-and-autratac/TestPages. Accessed 31 Jan 2023
3. babeljs.io: Babel - the compiler for next generation JavaScript (2022). https://babeljs.io. Accessed 10 Jan 2022
4. Chaqfeh, M., Zaki, Y., Hu, J., Subramanian, L.: JSCleaner: de-cluttering mobile webpages through JavaScript cleanup. In: Proceedings of the Web Conference 2020, pp. 763–773 (2020)
5. contributors, M.: Promise - JavaScript MDN (2022). https://developer.mozilla.org/en-US/docs/Web/JavaScript/Reference/Global_Objects/Promise Accessed 9 Jan 2022
6. estree: estree (2022). https://github.com/estree/estree. Accessed 10 Jan 2022
7. Goel, U., Steiner, M.: System to identify and elide superfluous JavaScript code for faster webpage loads. arXiv preprint arXiv:2003.07396 (2020)
8. Google: Closure Compiler - Google Developers (2020). https://developers.google.com/closure/compiler Accessed 15 Jan 2022
9. Kupoluyi, T., Chaqfeh, M., Varvello, M., Hashmi, W., Subramanian, L., Zaki, Y.: Muzeel: a dynamic javascript analyzer for dead code elimination in today's web. arXiv preprint arXiv:2106.08948 (2021)
10. Linden, G.: Slides from my talk at Stanford (2022). http://glinden.blogspot.com/2006/12/slides-from-my-talk-at-stanford.html. Accessed 9 Jan 2022
11. Nah, F.F.H.: A study on tolerable waiting time: how long are web users willing to wait? Behav. Inf. Technol. **23**(3), 153–163 (2004)
12. Nielsen, J.: Website response times. Nielsen Norman Group (2010)
13. Reiser, M., Bläser, L.: Accelerate JavaScript applications by cross-compiling to WebAssembly. In: Proceedings of the 9th ACM SIGPLAN International Workshop on Virtual Machines and Intermediate Languages, pp. 10–17 (2017)
14. statista.com: most used web frameworks among developers 2022 | Statista (2022). https://www.statista.com/statistics/1124699/worldwide-developer-survey-most-used-frameworks-web. Accessed 5 Sep 2022
15. Vogel, L., Springer, T.: An in-depth analysis of web page structure and efficiency with focus on optimization potential for initial page load. In: Di Noia, T., Ko, I.Y., Schedl, M., Ardito, C. (eds.) Web Engineering. ICWE 2022. LNCS, vol. 13362, pp. 101–116. Springer, Cham (2022). https://doi.org/10.1007/978-3-031-09917-5_7
16. waiter-and-autratac: Waiter and AUTRATAC (2023). https://github.com/waiter-and-autratac/WaiterAndAUTRATAC. Accessed 31 Jan 2023

Scraping Data from Web Pages Using SPARQL Queries

Radek Burget[✉][iD]

Faculty of Information Technology, Brno University of Technology,
Bozetechova 2, 61266 Brno, Czechia
burgetr@fit.vut.cz

Abstract. Despite the increasing use of semantic data, plain old HTML
web pages often provide a unique interface for accessing data from many
domains. To use this data in computer applications or to integrate it
with other data sources, it must be extracted from the HTML code. Currently, this is typically done by single-purpose programs called scrapers.
For each data source, specific scrapers must be created, which requires
a thorough analysis of the source page's implementation in HTML. This
makes writing and maintaining a set of scrapers a complex and time-
consuming task. In this paper, we present an alternative approach that
allows defining scrapers based on visual properties of the presented content instead of the HTML code structure. First, we render the source
page and create an RDF graph that describes the visual properties of
every piece of the displayed content. Next, we use SPARQL to query the
model and extract the data. As we demonstrate with real-world examples, this approach allows us to easily define more robust scrapers that
can be used across multiple web sites and that better cope with changes
in the source documents.

Keywords: Web scraping · Page rendering · Data extraction · RDF ·
SPARQL

1 Introduction

Web pages often provide a unique interface for accessing data from many
domains, such as e-commerce, news, movies, real estate, and a vast number
of others. Data presented in this way is easily accessible to human readers, but
due to the semi-structured nature of the HTML language used, integrating web
data sources with computer applications or other data sets is a challenging task.

In recent years, we have seen an increase in the use of structured data annotations created using JSON-LD, Microdata, or RDFa along with semantic vocabularies such as schema.org. According to Web Data Commons statistics, structured data was available in 42% of the 33.8 million domains included in the
Common Crawl corpus [3]. However, the use of structured data is growing slowly
and is limited to certain domains. A large part of the annotated documents come

I. Garrigós et al. (Eds.): ICWE 2023, LNCS 13893, pp. 293–300, 2023.
https://doi.org/10.1007/978-3-031-34444-2_21

from the major content providers such as Google, while there remains a large set of diverse "long tail" data sources whose providers are less motivated to provide the structured data.

Therefore, it is a common practice in web data integration today to use special programs called *scrapers* that extract the required data directly from the HTML code of the source pages. Currently, scrapers are typically tailored for a specific web site and identify the required data fields based on rules that have been designed by an analyst based on an examination of the HTML code. Creating scrapers requires considerable website implementation expertise, they are limited to very narrow sets of web pages, and they are very sensitive to changes in the source web pages, which can occur at any time.

In this paper, we present an alternative approach that allows defining scrapers based on visual properties of the presented content instead of the HTML code structure. Key advantages of this approach are (1) There is no need to analyze the details of the HTML code as the extraction rules are specified by the visual and textual properties of the content, and (2) the rules can be made more general, making scrapers more resistant to anomalies and changes in the source documents, and even making it possible to define scrapers that can be applied across multiple web sites.

The proposed solution is built on top of existing, widely available technologies. We use the Resource Description Framework (RDF) to represent all the details of the source page content, including its visual representation, and later SPARQL is used to query the models and extract the data. Due to the growing popularity of the semantic web, many developers are already familiar with these technologies, which we consider another advantage of the presented solution.

2   Related Work

The extraction of data from HTML documents has been the subject of research for more than 25 years. Despite this long history of research, ranging from the early string-based *wrappers* [1], through the most common DOM-oriented methods [2,6], to the sophisticated applications of machine learning methods [9,11], it is still a widely accepted practice in the industry to create procedural scrapers to perform this task. By a *scraper* we understand a single-purpose program (or procedure) that takes HTML code as its input and produces the extracted structured values as its output. Typically, scrapers are written in general-purpose languages (most often Python, JavaScript, and Ruby are mentioned in this context [4]), often combined with the use of CSS selectors or XPath to select important DOM nodes from the source page model.

The vulnerability to errors caused by changes and variations in the source documents has been a well-known feature of traditional scrapers for a long time [10]. Several approaches have been proposed that aim to provide a more robust solution. For example, in [13], the initial DOM node selection phase (based on node classification) is followed by an additional *visual validation* phase to eliminate incorrectly extracted nodes. In [7], robustness is improved by not strictly applying the XPath expressions, but by evaluating the similarity of the potential paths.

With the development of machine learning algorithms, their application to web data extraction has received increasing attention. A number of methods have been developed that use different neural network architectures for this task [8,9,11]. The results show that such approach is usable for extracting data from large sets of diverse web sites. On the other hand, such extractors are quite complex and require the preparation of large annotated data sets for training the neural networks.

Although Semantic Web technologies such as RDF and SPARQL are closely related to web development and are often used for the definition of structured data, their use for the scraping of web content has been very rare. In [5], the authors propose an RDF-based framework for mapping web content fragments to RDF resources, and the *visual selectors* can be used in addition to XPath and CSS selectors to address DOM nodes. However, the visual properties considered include only the basic font and color properties of the node itself, which does not allow, for example, taking advantage of the mutual positions of different elements on the page. In [12], we proposed an ontological model that allows to capture different aspects of web page content, and we used it to extract content from the web using a set of hard-coded procedural rules specific to the target domain. In this paper, we generalize this approach by using general SPARQL queries to define scrapers for an arbitrary application domain. This has allowed as to implement a general purpose scraping tool, which is described below.

As we will show in the next sections, the proposed approach allows to build web scrapers in a straightforward way, without the need to manually examine the source HTML code. The use of a generic query language allows to abstract from implementation details and to create robust scrapers applicable to variable source pages, while avoiding the complexity and other drawbacks of advanced machine learning methods.

3   Method Overview

Our method operates on a page rendered by a standard web browser (we use Chromium in our implementation, as we describe in Sect. 5). When rendering a page, the browser generates a tree of *boxes*, where a box represents a rectangular area in the rendered page with some content. The browsers generate the boxes from DOM elements in a manner defined by the CSS Visual Formatting Model[1].

The page processing workflow is shown in Fig. 1. It assumes a central RDF repository that stores the complete information about the page being processed and its content and on which SPARQL queries are subsequently executed. The RDF representation of this information makes use of the Box Model Ontology[2] and the Visual Area Ontology[3] that we published in [12]. The former defines

---

[1] https://www.w3.org/TR/CSS22/visuren.html.

[2] http://fitlayout.github.io/ontology/render.owl#.

[3] http://fitlayout.github.io/ontology/segmentation.owl#.

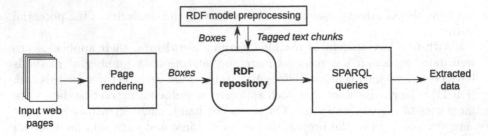

Fig. 1. Overall workflow of data extraction from source web pages using SPARQL queries.

(among other things) the concept of a *Box*, which corresponds to a box generated by a web browser during page rendering, and its properties. Similarly, the latter ontology defines the concept of a *Text Chunk*, which represents a part of a box text that has some interpretation (e.g. a product price), with the same properties as the box itself. The relevant properties of boxes and text chunks are summarized in Table 1.

Table 1. Properties of *boxes* and *text chunk* used in their RDF description. The `bounds` property assigns an object with the `positionX`, `positionY`, `width`, and `height` properties to a box or text chunk. The values of these properties are given in pixels with the origin of the coordinate system at the top left corner of the rendered page.

Property name	Description
`backgroundColor`	Background color in hex notation
`color`	Text color in hex notation
`fontFamily`	Font family name
`fontSize`	Font size in *pt* units
`fontStyle`	Average font style (0.0 for normal font, 1.0 for italic)
`fontWeight`	Average font weight (0.0 for normal font, 1.0 for bold)
`lineThrough`	Line-through text decoration
`underline`	Underline text decoration
`bounds`	Box or visual area position and size within the page
`text`	Contained text
`contentLength`	Contained text length in characters
`containsObject`	Description of a contained object such as image

After the page is rendered, we describe the generated boxes (including the values of all their properties) by RDF statements using the Box Model Ontology, and we store the statements in the RDF repository. Next, we preprocess the RDF model. This consists of the following tasks:

Tagged Text Chunk Extraction. We select all the boxes that have the text property set, create the text chunk instances with the same properties as the original boxes, and add their descriptions to the RDF repository. Optionally, we can specify a regular expression for each extracted data field that specifies its expected text format (for example, for product price). This allows us to pre-select the boxes that potentially correspond to the expected data, and possibly select a relevant substring of the box text for creating the text chunk. The created text chunks that match the regular expression are assigned a *tag* that indicates the data field to which they potentially correspond. Note that this is only a rough pre-selection of the boxes, and the regular expressions can be very general at this stage; the final extraction is done later in the query phase.

Discovery of Spatial Relationships Among Areas. We go through the list of created text chunks and we look for the pairs of text chunks that are located below each other while their x-coordinates overlap at least partially. For each such pair $(c1, c2)$ we add new statements c1 below c2 and c2 above c1 to our RDF model. Similarly, we add statements with the predicates before and after, which represent a similar relationship in the x-axis direction. For convenience, we also define the equivalent functions isAbove(), isBelow(), isBefore(), and isAfter() that can be used in SPARQL predicates.

4 Querying the RDF Model

After preprocessing, the RDF repository contains a complete RDF graph that can be queried using SPARQL. In the queries, both the visual properties of the boxes (as listed in Table 1) and their spatial relationships can be used for identifying the text chunks that contain the required data. The query may include multiple boxes whose properties can be compared arbitrarily.

We demonstrate the use of SPARQL for this task on two typical scenarios: extracting multiple records from a single input page and extracting single records from a large set of pages from different web sites.

4.1 Extraction of Multiple Records

To demonstrate the extraction of multiple repeating records from a single website, we use the cast tables on IMDb (Fig. 2). For preprocessing, we defined taggers (regular expressions) that roughly recognize the names and the episode strings and assign the tags *name* and *credit* to the corresponding text chunks. We then extract the records using the query shown in Fig. 3.

In the query, we first identify the header text chunk (hbox) that contains the "Series Cast" text. Below this header, we look for triplets of boxes that match the actor name, character name, and episodes and are arranged on one line after each other.

We chose this particular table for the demonstration because its HTML code is very complex and creating a DOM-based scraper for it is a non-trivial task. On the other hand, the visual presentation is straightforward, which makes the SPARQL code quite simple.

Series Cast

Úrsula Corberó	...	Tokio	41 episodes, 2017-2021 ₩
Álvaro Morte	...	El Profesor	41 episodes, 2017-2021 ₩
Itziar Ituño	...	Raquel Murillo	41 episodes, 2017-2021 ₩
Pedro Alonso	...	Berlín	41 episodes, 2017-2021 ₩
Miguel Herrán	...	Río	41 episodes, 2017-2021 ₩
Jaime Lorente	...	Denver	41 episodes, 2017-2021 ₩
Esther Acebo	...	Mónica Gaztambide	41 episodes, 2017-2021 ₩
Darko Peric	...	Helsinki	41 episodes, 2017-2021 ₩
Enrique Arce	...	Arturo Román	38 episodes, 2017-2021 ₩
Alba Flores	...	Nairobi	34 episodes, 2017-2021 ₩

Fig. 2. Top of the source table on IMDb

```
SELECT ?name ?character ?episodes WHERE {
  ?hbox rdf:type segm:TextChunk .
  ?hbox segm:text ?header .
  # Actor names
  ?nbox segm:hasTag r:tag-generic--name .
  ?nbox segm:text ?name .
  # Character names after the header
  ?cbox r:rel-after ?nbox .
  ?cbox segm:hasTag r:tag-generic--name .
  ?cbox segm:text ?character .
  # Episodes after the character
  ?ebox r:rel-after ?cbox .
  ?ebox segm:hasTag r:tag-generic--credit .
  ?ebox segm:text ?episodes .
  # Names are below the header
  FILTER (regex(?header, 'Series␣Cast␣')
    && flfn:isBelow(?nbox, ?hbox))
}
```

Fig. 3. SPARQL query to scrape series cast tables from IMDb

```
SELECT ?tbox ?pbox ?tfsize ?pfsize ?ty ?py WHERE {
    FILTER (?ty < ?py)
    { SELECT ?tbox ?tfsize ?ty ?tw ?th ?ttag WHERE {
        ?tbox segm:hasTag r:tag-generic--title .
        ?tbox box:fontSize ?tfsize . ?tbox box:contentLength ?tlen .
        ?tbox box:bounds ?tb . ?tb box:positionY ?ty . ?tb box:width ?tw . ?tb box:height ?th
        FILTER (?ty <= 500 && ?tlen > 10)
      } ORDER BY DESC (?tfsize) LIMIT 10 }
    { SELECT ?pbox ?pfsize ?py ?pw ?ph ?ptag WHERE {
        ?pbox segm:hasTag r:tag-generic--price .
        ?pbox box:fontSize ?pfsize . ?pbox box:bounds ?pb .
        ?pb box:positionY ?py . ?pb box:width ?pw . ?pb box:height ?ph
        FILTER (?py <= 1200)
      } ORDER BY DESC (?pfsize) LIMIT 10 }
} ORDER BY DESC (?tfsize) DESC (?pfsize) DESC(?th) DESC(?ph) DESC(?tw) DESC(?pw) ?ty ?py LIMIT 1
```

Fig. 4. SPARQL query to extract product title and price from e-commerce product pages

4.2 Extraction from Diverse Web Sites

In this scenario, the task is to extract single (*title, price*) pairs from e-commerce web pages. Again, we have prepared taggers that assign the corresponding tags to the extracted pieces of text. The corresponding query in Fig. 4 is based on the simple observation that the product title is typically placed at the top of the page (at most 500 px from the top) and the price is always lower than the title (we allow up to 1200 px from the top). Both are written in a larger font than the rest of the content. We look for instances of two different text chunks (?tbox for product title and ?pbox for price). We use a separate subquery for each of these boxes, each of which retrieves up to 10 candidate boxes that match the given condition, ordered by font size, starting with the largest font size.

In the main query, we combine the results of both subqueries, considering only the combinations where the title box is above the price box (?ty < ?py). The final order ensures that we favor the boxes with the largest font sizes, the largest width and height, and the smallest Y-positions. We use the first result in the resulting list.

5   Implementation and Experimental Results

To test the queries in a practical setting, we have implemented an experimental application[4] that allows to process any input page and execute the given query on the created RDF model. The implementation is based on our generic FitLayout framework[5], which uses the Playwright library and Chromium for rendering the pages, creates the RDF models, and stores them in an RDF4J repository. In general, the architecture allows storing multiple page models in the RDF repository and executing multiple queries on the stored page models.

We tested the Cast table extraction on 100 IMDb tables, from which we correctly extracted 43624 records. Another 2060 records were omitted because their visual appearance did not match the SPARQL query (overlapping columns in the table). This problem can be solved at the cost of making the query more complex. The product/price extraction was tested on a total of 1898 product pages from 5 different e-commerce sites that use different visual presentation of products (and very different HTML code). Both title and price were correctly extracted in all cases. The extraction results for both scenarios, including annotated screenshots of the pages, are available in a separate git repository[6].

The visual presentation-based approach using a full-featured web browser in the background implies an increased complexity of the solution. Rendering and processing a single page took from 9 s[7] for the e-commerce pages and short Cast tables up to 6 min for an extremely long page[8]. However, the time complexity can be reduced by a more precise selection of the target area of the page, as we have demonstrated for e-commerce sites, where we strictly limit the analyzed area. The browser-based solutions such as Playwright or Selenium are already being used for web scraping for a variety of other reasons, making it easy to integrate the SPARQL approach.

6   Conclusions

In this paper, we have presented an approach to define web scrapers using SPARQL queries over an RDF model of the rendered page. As we show through our experimental implementation and results, scrapers defined in this way are general enough to be applied in different scenarios including a set of different web sources with similar visual presentation. This also implies the robustness of the scrapers with respect to changes and deviations in the source documents. In addition, no knowledge of the HTML code is required to create the scrapers. We consider these features to be an advantage over traditional scrapers, which are tailored to a specific page code. The implemented solution is based on the technology already used in this area, which allows its integration into the existing infrastructure.

---

[4] https://github.com/FitLayout/sparql-web-scraping.

[5] https://github.com/FitLayout/FitLayout.

[6] https://github.com/FitLayout/sparql-web-scraping-results.

[7] On Intel(R) Core(TM) i5-9500 CPU 3.00 GHz, 16 GB RAM.

[8] The rendered page height was 183,294 pixels.

Acknowledgements. This work was supported by project Smart information technology for a resilient society, FIT-S-23-8209, funded by Brno University of Technology.

References

1. Ashish, N., Knoblock, C.A.: Wrapper generation for semi-structured internet sources. SIGMOD Rec. **26**(4), 8–15 (1997). https://doi.org/10.1145/271074.271078
2. Baumgartner, R., Flesca, S., Gottlob, G.: Visual web information extraction with Lixto. In: VLDB 2001, pp. 119–128. Morgan Kaufmann Publishers Inc., San Francisco (2001)
3. Bizer, C., Meusel, R., Primpeli, A., Brinkmann, A.: Web data commons - microdata, RDFa, JSON-LD, and microformat data sets - extraction results from the october 2022 common crawl corpus (2022). http://webdatacommons.org/structureddata/2022-12/stats/stats.html. Accessed 29 Jan 2023
4. Dilmegani, C.: Best web scraping programming languages in 2023 with stats (2023). https://research.aimultiple.com/web-scraping-programming-languages/. Accessed 05 Feb 2023
5. Fernández-Villamor, J.I., Blasco-García, J., Iglesias, C.A., Garijo, M.: A semantic scraping model for web resources - applying linked data to web page screen scraping. In: Proceedings of ICAART 2011, Roma, Italia (2011)
6. Furche, T., Gottlob, G., Grasso, G., Schallhart, C., Sellers, A.: OXPath: a language for scalable data extraction, automation, and crawling on the deep web. VLDB J. **22**(1), 47–72 (2013). https://doi.org/10.1007/s00778-012-0286-6
7. Gao, P., Han, H.: Robust web data extraction based on weighted path-layer similarity. J. Comput. Inf. Syst. **62**(3), 536–546 (2022). https://doi.org/10.1080/08874417.2020.1861571
8. Gogar, T., Hubacek, O., Sedivy, J.: Deep neural networks for web page information extraction. In: Iliadis, L., Maglogiannis, I. (eds.) AIAI 2016. IAICT, vol. 475, pp. 154–163. Springer, Cham (2016). https://doi.org/10.1007/978-3-319-44944-9_14
9. Hotti, A., Risuleo, R.S., Magureanu, S., Moradi, A., Lagergren, J.: Graph neural networks for nomination and representation learning of web elements (2021). https://doi.org/10.48550/ARXIV.2111.02168
10. Kushmerick, N.: Wrapper verification. World Wide Web **3**(2), 79–94 (2000). https://doi.org/10.1023/A:1019229612909
11. Lin, B.Y., Sheng, Y., Vo, N., Tata, S.: FreeDOM: a transferable neural architecture for structured information extraction on web documents. In: KDD 2020, pp. 1092–1102. ACM, New York (2020). https://doi.org/10.1145/3394486.3403153
12. Milicka, M., Burget, R.: Information extraction from web sources based on multi-aspect content analysis. In: Gandon, F., Cabrio, E., Stankovic, M., Zimmermann, A. (eds.) SemWebEval 2015. CCIS, vol. 548, pp. 81–92. Springer, Cham (2015). https://doi.org/10.1007/978-3-319-25518-7_7
13. Potvin, B., Villemaire, R.: Robust web data extraction based on unsupervised visual validation. In: Nguyen, N.T., Gaol, F.L., Hong, T.-P., Trawiński, B. (eds.) ACIIDS 2019. LNCS (LNAI), vol. 11431, pp. 77–89. Springer, Cham (2019). https://doi.org/10.1007/978-3-030-14799-0_7

Web Engineering Practices
and Experience

An Empirical Study of Web API
Versioning Practices

Souhaila Serbout[✉][iD] and Cesare Pautasso[iD]

Software Institute (USI), Lugano, Switzerland
{souhaila.serbout,cesare.pautasso}@usi.ch

Abstract. As Web APIs evolve, developers assign them version identifiers to reflect the amount and the nature of changes that the API clients
should expect. In this work we focus on identifying versioning practices
adopted by Web API developers by extracting and classifying version
identifiers found in a large collection of OpenAPI descriptions. In particular, we observe how frequently different versioning schemes have been
adopted for identifying both stable and preview releases (e.g., simple version counters, semantic versioning, or release timestamps). We further
study the stability of versioning schemes during APIs evolution. We also
detect APIs which offer dynamic access to versioning metadata through
dedicated endpoints as well as APIs which support clients expecting to
reach up to 14 different versions of the same API at the same time.
Overall the results offer a detailed view over current Web API versioning practices and can serve as the basis for future discussions on how to
standardize critical API versioning metadata.

Keywords: API · Web API · OpenAPI · Empirical Study · Versioning

1 Introduction

The evolution of Web APIs requires versioning practices to ease compatibility
checking and maintainability for both API providers and clients [13,19]. API
providers often use version identifiers to make changes evident to clients, allowing
them to refer to specific versions of the API on which they depend. In some cases,
providers make multiple versions of the same API available to ease the transition
for clients as they switch from retired versions to newer versions [14].

The lack of a centralized registry for Web APIs, combined with the flexibility for service providers to use their own versioning approaches [17], has led
to multiple and sometimes inconsistent practices in terms of discoverability and
notification of breaking changes [9]. Such variability in versioning practices raises
questions about the prevalence of semantic versioning [1] adoption among Web
APIs. In this study, we aim to classify the versioning schemes used for Web APIs
and to track how their adoption of changes over time and across the API release
cycle. Additionally, we aim to examine the frequency and extent of concurrent
availability of multiple API versions, as the introduction of backward incompatible changes in web APIs can have negative impacts on clients, unless both

I. Garrigós et al. (Eds.): ICWE 2023, LNCS 13893, pp. 303–318, 2023.
https://doi.org/10.1007/978-3-031-34444-2_22

old and new versions are kept in production [14]. To achieve this, we analyze a large dataset of 186,259 OpenAPI descriptions mined from GitHub, tracing the change histories of 7114 APIs, to answer the following research questions:

Q1: What is the prevalence of versioning in Web APIs? How often is version information located outside of the API metadata or discovered dynamically?
Q2: How do developers distinguish stable from preview releases?
Q3: To what extent is the practice of semantic versioning adopted in Web APIs, and are there alternative versioning schemes in use?
Q4: How often do developers switch to different versioning schemes during the lifespan of their APIs?
Q5: Has the adoption of semantic versioning changed over the past few years?
Q6: What is the prevalence of APIs with multiple versions in production? how many concurrent versions exist, and which formats are used in this case?

Answering these questions will provide valuable observations on the state of the practice regarding Web API versioning. Given the simple approach to versioning in the OpenAPI specification, there is room for different interpretations on how to encode whether an API is a stable or preview release, and different version identification strategies are possible. Our study results reveal a need for more detailed versioning metadata in the OpenAPI standard [2]. Likewise, we did not only observe the presence of a variety of formats to represent static version identifiers, but also emerging support for dynamic version discovery, as well as two or even more (up to 14) coexistent versions in production.

The remainder of this paper is organized as follows. In Sect. 2 we define basic versioning concepts and how they are expressed in OpenAPI. In Sect. 3, we describe the methodology used to collect the API artifacts. In Sect. 4, we present the results obtained from our analysis. In Sect. 5, we discuss the implications of these results and the main threats to their validity. We relate them to previous work in the field in Sect. 6. In Sect. 7, we provide a summary of our findings and offer recommendations for future research.

A replication package is available on GitHub [3].

2   Background

2.1   Semantic Versioning and Web API Versioning

The goal of semantic versioning [1] is to reflect the impact of API changes through the version identifier format MAJOR.MINOR.PATCH. The MAJOR version counter is incremented when incompatible API changes were introduced, the MINOR counter is upgraded when new functionalities were added without breaking any of the old ones, and the PATCH increases for backwards compatible bug fixes.

Several widely known package managers, such as NPM [4], Maven [21], and PyPI, adopt semantic versioning as a standard for package version identifiers. These package managers enforce the usage of semantic versioning and perform version increment checks every time the package is republished [12].

When it comes to Web APIs, in addition to informing about the version in the API metadata [13], clients may also refer to specific API version when invoking them. The version identifier can be embedded as part of HTTP request messages as a parameter or a segment in the endpoint path URL, such as: `https://<server-address>/API-URL/<version-identifier>/` as well as a part of the server URL DNS name, such as: `<server-address>` = `v1.api.com` | `v2.api.com`. Embedding version identifiers in endpoint URLs is commonly used also when multiple versions of the API coexist simultaneously.

2.2   OpenAPI Versioning Metadata

API service providers typically provide API clients with information on how to use the API through a description, which is often written in natural language [20] or based on a standard Interface Description Language (IDL), such as OpenAPI [2]. OpenAPI includes a specific required field {`"version"`: `string`} in the `info` section pertaining to the API's metadata. However, there are no constraints on the format used to represent the version identifier. Additionally, version identifiers can be embedded in the API endpoint addresses, which are stored in the `server` and `path` URLs. While the OpenAPI standard defines how developers describe their APIs, there is no centralized standard documentation manager service where developers can share API specifications. For example, SwaggerHub [5] does not impose any rules on the format of version identifiers, nor does it require developers to upgrade them when publishing a new version of the API description. We aim to study the resulting variety of version identifier formats found in a large collection of OpenAPI descriptions.

2.3   API Preview Releases

Test releases are often given specific marketing names to clearly reflect their purpose and distinguish them from stable releases. Marketing names help also to indicate the audience of the test releases, and allow users to understand that they should expect bugs [6,7,15]. In our collection, we identified the following six types of usage for preview release tags:

– *Develop:* A version under development is still in the process of being created and is not yet complete or stable. It may contain new features or bug fixes that have not yet been fully tested, and may not be suitable for use in a production environment. Developers may use dev versions to test new features and make changes before releasing a final version to the public.
– *Snapshot:* These versions are automatically built from the latest development code and are intended to be used by developers.
– *Preview:* These are unstable versions that are made available to users before the final release. Preview versions are typically released to a small group of users or testers to gather feedback and iron out any bugs or issues before the final release. They can also be used to give users a preview about new features to expect to see in the next stable version.

SWR Audio Lab - Radiohub

Version: 2.14.0
Description: This documentation is also available as [openapi.json](https://docs.radiohub.swr.digital/openapi.json) or [openapi.yaml](https://docs.radiohub.swr.digital/openapi.yaml

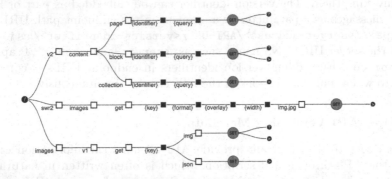

Fig. 1. Tree visualization of the endpoint structure of a subset of the SWR Audio Lab - Radiohub API (version 2.14.0) [8] (see the whole API tree) - Different version identifiers (v1, v2) are found in the path URL addresses.

- *Alpha:* These versions are considered to be very early in development and are likely to be unstable and contain many bugs. They are often released to a small group of testers for feedback.
- *Beta:* These versions are considered to be more stable than alpha versions and are often released to a wider group of testers for feedback. They may still contain bugs, but they are expected to be closer to the final release.
- *Release Candidate (RC):* These versions are considered to be very close to the final release and are often the last versions to be released before the final version. They are expected to be stable and contain only minor bugs.

Our goal is to quantify how often such types of pre-release versions are found.

3   Dataset Overview and Methodology

In this paper we analyze the versioning practices of Web APIs through an analysis of their descriptions written according to the OpenAPI specification [2]. Our dataset consists of 7,114 Web APIs, obtained from 186,259 commits pushed to 3,090 open-source GitHub repositories, belonging to 2,899 GitHub repository owners. To obtain this dataset, we filtered from 567,069 detected potential OpenAPI descriptions to include only those that: (a) belonged to APIs with more than 10 commits in their history (11,408 APIs); (b) were described in JSON/YAML files that were parsable in all commits (10,062); and (c) had at least one path specified in one of the commits (7,114), excluding descriptions of JSON schemas without any API functionality [18].

To automate the extraction, we first retrieved 5,514 distinct version identifiers from the `info.version` field in each OpenAPI description. We then searched for any of these identifiers in the URL addresses listed as part of the

Table 1. Some detectors used to classify the version identifier formats

Format	Regular Expression
integer	`/^(\d{3}|\d{2}|\d{1})+$/i`
v*	`/v\d*/i`
semver-3	`/^(v|)\d+\.\d+\.\d+$/i`
date(yyyy-mm-dd)	`/^\d{4}-\d{2}-\d{2}/`
semver-dev*	`/^(v|)\d+\.\d+(\.\d)*(\.|-)dev\d*$/i`
semver-snapshot*	`/^(v|)\d+\.\d+(\.\d)*(\.|-)SNAPSHOT\d*$/i`
date-preview*	`[date](-|\.)preview$/i`
v*alpha*	`/^v\d+alpha\d*$/i`
v*beta*	`/^v\d+beta\d*$/i`
semver-rc*.*	`/^(v|)\d+\.\d+(\.\d)*-rc\d*\.\d+$/i`

endpoints or server URL strings. For example, the Radiohub API [8] from the SWR audio lab includes the version identifier, v2, in the endpoint URLs, which reflects the major version of the API (Fig. 1).

To classify the version identifiers, we employed a set of regular expression rules (Table 1). These detectors were iteratively defined based on our observations to ensure that most of the samples could be labeled. We also distinguished between version identifiers used to describe preview releases and stable versions of the APIs. The complete list of detectors and machine-readable regular expression rules can be found in the replication package.

4 Results

4.1 Location of Version Identifiers in API Descriptions

In Table 2, we classify the dataset of APIs and commits into eight categories based on the locations of the API version identifiers. For completeness, we also include separate categories for APIs that lack version identifiers (L_{nover}) and APIs whose version identifier is discovered dynamically ($L_{dynamic}$).

We aggregate the commits of each API history as follows:

- $L_l^1 = \{api \in \textbf{APIs}, \exists c \in \mathcal{C}_{api}, L_l(c)\}$: the set of APIs where there is at least one commit where the version identifiers are located in L_l.
- $L_l^* = \{api \in \textbf{APIs}, \forall c \in \mathcal{C}_{api}, L_l(c)\}$: the set of APIs where in all the commits the version identifiers are located in L_l.

where $\mathcal{C}_{api} = \{c\}$ is the set of commits found during the history of the api, $L_l(c)$ indicates whether for commit c version identifiers are found in location $l \in \{ips, ps, ip, is, p, s, i, nover, dynamic\}$.

Static Versioning. The majority of APIs (4,445 - 62.5%) and commits (102,986 - 55%) has version identifiers located only in the `info.version` field of the API

Table 2. Number of Commits/APIs which include version identifiers in different locations of the OpenAPI description artifacts

Location info.version	path	server	#Commits Total	Identical	#APIs L_i^1	L_i^*		CV	
L_{nover}	–	–	–	2,076		168	76	(45%)	92	(54%)
$L_{dynamic}$	–	–	–	5,985		220	129	(58%)	91	(41%)
L_i	x	–	–	102,986		5022	4445	(89%)	1236	(24%)
L_p	–	x	–	915		61	12	(20%)	25	(40%)
L_s	–	–	x	70		6	1	(16%)	1	(16%)
L_{ip}	x	x	–	61,010	36,441	1512	1139	(75%)	173	(11%)
L_{is}	x	–	x	18,749	4,050	1017	741	(73%)	93	(9%)
L_{ps}	–	x	x	0	0	0	0		0	
L_{ips}	x	x	x	453	8	41	16	(39%)	5	(12%)
Total Statically Versioned				184,183	40499	7038	6354	(90%)	2390	(34%)

description metadata (L_i). The version identifiers were present in all of the server and path URLs, as well as in the info.version metadata (L_{ips}) for 453 commits belonging to 41 APIs. We did not observe any APIs that contained version identifiers in both path and server URLs but not in the info.version metadata field (L_{ps}).

When version identifiers were present in multiple locations, we checked whether the identifiers were consistent or varied across those locations. We found that the identifiers were identical in 50.49% of the commits found in the history of 406 "consistently versioned" APIs. Furthermore, we identified 168 APIs that did not include any version identifiers in any location (L_{nover}) for certain commits, with 76 of these lacking all types of versioning throughout their entire history.

Dynamic Versioning. The version information of an API can also be obtained dynamically by the client via a dedicated API endpoint. Instead of specifying the version statically in the info.version field value, clients may retrieve the API version dynamically by invoking the GET /version operation, as documented in the example {"version": "see /version below"}. This approach was detected in 220 APIs in our collection, where 129 of them were dynamically versioned during their entire history, such as the ONS Address Index API.

4.2 Evolution of Version Identifiers

Given the API history $\mathcal{C}_{api} = \{c_i\}$, we define CV as the set of APIs where we detect at least one change in the value of the version identifier between two distinct commits:

$$CV = \{api \in \textbf{APIs}, \exists c_j, c_i \in \mathcal{C}_{api}, version(c_j) \neq version(c_i)\}\}$$

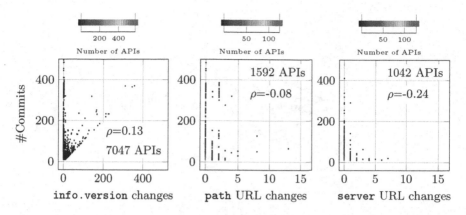

Fig. 2. Where do version identifiers change more often? Density plots of the number of commits of each API as a function of the number of version identifier changes detected in the three locations (L_i, L_p, L_s).

For each L_l, in Table 2 we report as CV the number of APIs which change their version identifiers. About one third of the APIs (2,390) undergo at least one change of version identifier throughout their history of at least 10 commits.

In Fig. 2, we present the correlation between the number of version changes in API histories and the number of commits, differentiated by the location of the version identifier. The dot color indicates the number of APIs with a given combination of version changes (x) and commits (y). As anticipated, $y > x$. A small subset of APIs (47 APIs) demonstrates frequent version changes with each commit ($y = x + 1$), while a considerable number of APIs (L_i: 5119, L_p: 1446, L_s: 973) maintain a constant version identifier ($x = 0, y \geq 10$) despite having in some cases a substantial number of commits in their history. The majority of version changes occur in the location designated as L_i, with fewer changes observed for version identifiers embedded in URLs.

By analyzing changes of the `info.version` field, we could track the API evolution through several iterations of preview releases followed by stable releases (and vice-versa). Figure 3 shows how many APIs evolved with preview and stable releases, and how many added or removed versioning information at some commit of their history. We also measured the delay between each type of release: on average, preview releases occur every 9.3 days, while stable versions are released every 18.2 days.

4.3 Classification of Version Identifier Formats

We categorize the formats employed to represent version identifiers in Table 3. The results show that the most widely utilized format for versioning API releases is Semantic Versioning (SemVer), followed by a straightforward approach using an integer to denote the major version of the API, often accompanied by a `V` prefix. All types of preview release tags are most often found in the `info.version`

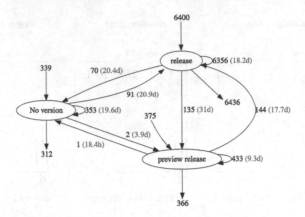

Fig. 3. Number of APIs which evolve interleaving preview and stable releases and average duration (in days) of the transitions

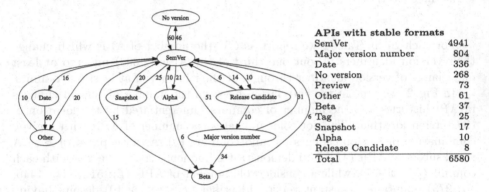

APIs with stable formats	
SemVer	4941
Major version number	804
Date	336
No version	268
Preview	73
Other	61
Beta	37
Tag	25
Snapshot	17
Alpha	10
Release Candidate	8
Total	6580

Fig. 4. Number of APIs where `info.version` identifiers formats changes were detected during their history (includes only transitions happening in ≥ 4 APIs)

metadata, while release candidate and preview tags are never found as part of path or server URLs.

The version formats for 534 out of 7114 APIs exhibited instability over time, with the most prevalent change being from the absence of a version to Semantic Versioning (SemVer). The most common format transitions are listed in Fig. 4. In contrast, 4941 APIs consistently utilized SemVer throughout their history. Table 4 provides a more detailed classification of the version identifier format used by APIs that maintained a consistent versioning scheme across all commits, including statistics on the number of commits and version identifier changes. We also include the most frequent version identifier detected in each category.

4.4   Adoption of Semantic Versioning over the Years

In our collection of 7,114 APIs, we discovered that 5,292 APIs employed semantic versioning (with 112,908 commits) at some point in their history. Additionally,

Table 3. Number of commits with version identifiers of stable (above) and preview (below) releases classified by their format and location (a more detailed classification is in the replication)

Format	Location			
	info.version	path	server	All
Major version number	29129	45310	14944	89383
SemVer	114663	788	18172	133623
Tag	845	1199	6	2050
Date	5447	299	27	5773
Other	1549	1354	0	2309
Develop	545	92	106	743
Snapshot	964	0	11	975
Preview	863	0	0	863
Alpha	3003	2339	10	5352
Beta	19410	15459	207	35076
Release Candidate	548	0	0	548

504 APIs utilized alternative formats in addition to semantic versioning (with 7,388 commits) and 4,565 APIs exclusively utilized SemVer-3 (e.g., 1.0.0) and SemVer-2 (e.g., 1.0) throughout their history.

An examination of the adoption of semantic versioning (SemVer) over time, as depicted in Fig. 5, reveals that the usage of SemVer in final release versions is consistently higher than other versioning schemes, with a relatively steady level of adoption from 2015 to 2021.

4.5   Multiple Versions in Production

Our analysis identified a total of 135 APIs that incorporate various version identifiers in their paths, as demonstrated in Fig. 6(a). Out of these, 2102 paths had two distinct version identifiers, while one API reached a maximum of 14 coexistent versions during 5 commits. In addition, 51.11% (69 APIs) demonstrated a change in the number of path versions at least once.

As an example, the RiteKit API introduced a new path with a v2 version identifier. The Agent API underwent two changes: from v1,v3,v4 to v1,v2,v3,v4 on 2017-08-02, and from v1,v2,v3,v4 to v1,v2,v3,v4,v5 on 2017-09-27. Additionally, the version declared in the metadata increased from 1.46.0 to 22.9.1 over 51 commits during a five-year period, showing an example of inconsistency between the version identifiers found in the API description metadata and the endpoints exposed to the API clients.

We categorize the version identifier formats present in APIs with multiple versions in production in Fig. 6. The predominant trend among APIs with multiple versions is to adopt a similar version format consisting of the use of a major

Table 4. How many APIs consistently use the same version identifier format in the `info.version` field during their lifespans? $min(\#\text{Commits}) = 10$, $min(\text{info.version}$ Changes$) = 0$

Format	Most Frequent Version Identifier	#APIs	#Commits				VC			
			max	avg	mdn	stdev	max	avg	mdn	stdev
semver-3	1.0.0	40.45%	3531	1031	28	17	37	496	4	0	17
semver-2	1.0	64.92%	1093	3585	30	15	116	77	1	0	4
v*	v1	80.32%	489	692	42	20	74	4	0	0	0
date(yyyy-mm-dd)	2017-03-01	4.87%	327	52	14	12	4	52	0	0	3
other	v1b3	7.23%	213	222	29	18	32	33	1	0	3
integer	1	36.30%	48	143	27	17	24	113	5	0	20
v*beta*	v1beta1	60.10%	115	360	136	35	146	3	0	0	1
date-preview*	2015-10-01-preview	11.93%	72	47	13	12	5	2	0	0	0
semver-3#	1.0.0-oas3	27.62%	33	215	32	15	41	18	2	0	4
v*beta*.*	v2beta1.1	19.44%	26	30	24	24	4	12	3	3	4
latest*	latest	52.75%	25	137	27	15	28	2	0	0	0
v*alpha*	v1alpha	51.34%	18	339	56	24	91	3	0	0	1
semver-SNAPSHOT*	1.0.0-SNAPSHOT	31.61%	18	172	32	16	38	36	5	0	9
semver-beta*	v1.0-beta	28.37%	17	113	40	29	29	9	1	0	2
v*p*beta*	v1p3beta1	23.45%	9	347	162	35	153	3	1	0	1
beta	1beta1	100.00%	7	37	15	11	9	0	0	0	0
beta*	beta	65.49%	7	47	26	26	12	0	0	0	0
semver-alpha*	1.0.0-alpha	28.04%	7	48	23	15	15	2	0	0	1
semver-2#	1.3-DUMMY	12.26%	6	24	16	15	5	3	2	2	1
semver (beta*)	1.0 (beta)	29.89%	6	58	39	46	13	46	18	26	18
date(yyyy.mm.dd)	2019.10.15	10.45%	6	24	22	24	4	24	20	24	9
#semver-3	2019.0.0	29.73%	5	37	22	17	11	3	1	2	1
semver-rc*	1.0.0-rc1	38.14%	4	190	60	20	75	8	4	5	3
semver-4	6.4.3.0	3.31%	4	23	16	17	5	9	2	0	4
semver-rc*.*	2.0.0-RC1.0	41.69%	4	85	54	63	26	0	0	0	0
v*alpha*.*	v2alpha2.6	61.76%	3	26	23	22	2	4	1	0	2
alpha*	alpha	73.85%	2	35	26	35	9	0	0	0	0
dev*	dev	98.38%	2	172	91	172	81	0	0	0	0
date(yyyy-mm)	2021-10	67.44%	2	14	13	14	1	2	1	2	1
semver-pre*.*	3.5.0-pre.0	100.00%	1	10	10	10	0	0	0	0	0
date(yyyymmdd)	20190111	29.63%	1	13	13	13	0	0	0	0	0
semver-dev*	0.7.0.dev20191230	15.52%	1	40	40	40	0	0	0	0	0
v*-date	v1-20160622	57.14%	1	18	18	18	0	2	2	2	0
semver-alpha*.*	1.1.0-alpha.1	4.94%	1	146	146	146	0	0	0	0	0

version number (MVN) often attached to the prefix V*, especially in APIs that have fewer than six concurrent versions. We observed a deviation from this trend in only 593 commits, out of which 292 commits combined different version formats, as depicted in Fig. 6(b). This deviation is more commonly seen in APIs that have more than six concurrent versions, and the most prevalent format among these is the Semantic Versioning (SemVer) format.

5   Discussion

Q1: *What is the prevalence of versioning in Web APIs? How often is version information located outside of the API metadata or discovered dynamically?*

Our study found that out of the 7114 APIs examined, only 76 were completely unversioned, and 336 started their history with no metadata version while in [15] the authors recommend using a version number from the start of the lifespan of any software artifact. Of the remaining APIs, 4445 included static version information exclusively in their metadata, while the others had version identifiers present in their Paths or Server URLs. Notably, in the case of 1896 APIs, version identifiers were present both in the `info.version` field and endpoint URLs. Conversely, none of the APIs had version identifiers both in Paths and Server URLs, without also having it in the `info.version` field. Another versioning practice was detected in the case of 220 APIs where the developers dedicated one of the endpoints to dynamically inform clients about the version of the currently deployed API.

Q2: *How do developers distinguish stable from preview releases?*

Our analysis identified specific labels indicating a different type of preview release version in 25,308 commits belonging to 535 APIs. The examination of 202 APIs revealed that they have a history covering both preview and stable releases. The absolute number and the portion of pre-releases increases during recent years (Fig. 5). The labeling accuracy appears to be confirmed also by the differences in the average delay measured for each type of release (Fig. 3).

Q3: *To what extent is the practice of semantic versioning adopted in Web APIs, and are there alternative versioning schemes in use?*

Our findings indicate that semantic versioning (SemVer) is the most widely adopted versioning scheme among API releases, specifically in the case of APIs that use the `info.version` field (60.56%). In contrast, for APIs that use alternative methods for versioning, such as embedding version identifiers in endpoints URLs or the server DNS name, the most common practice is to use shorter version identifiers that include only the major version counter. Additionally, for preview releases, SemVer is often combined with other tags to reflect the type of preview release, such as Develop, Snapshot, Alpha, Beta, or Preview. More in detail, 3-counter semantic versioning (`MAJOR.MINOR.PATCH`) is adopted more often than the 2-counter format (`BREAKING.NONBREAKING`) recommended by [13]. The fourth largest group of APIs uses "visible dates" as version identifier format (Table 4), which appears to be anti-pattern according to [15], as it would reveal how old a release has become.

Q4: *How often do developers switch to different versioning schemes during the lifespan of their APIs?*

Only 785 APIs underwent changes in their versioning scheme during their evolution. Figure 4 illustrates that, in the case of APIs that use `info.version` identifiers, the most common target format adopted by 106 APIs changing their scheme is Semantic Versioning (SemVer), which is also the most widely adopted versioning scheme among APIs that did not switch to another format.

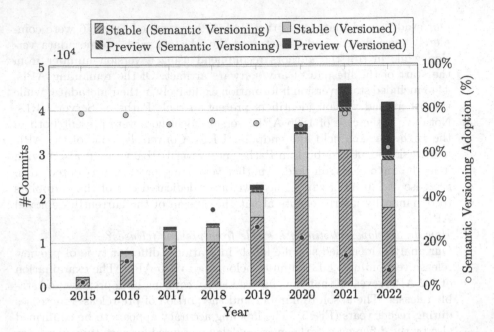

Fig. 5. Semantic versioning adoption over the years (2015–2022) in stable and preview releases considering the version identifier found in the `info.version` metadata.

Q5: *Has the adoption of semantic versioning changed over the past few years?*
    In this study, we assessed the prevalence of Semantic Versioning (SemVer) in API versioning by analyzing the utilization of the `info.version` field in stable releases of APIs that have been committed to GitHub between 2015 and 2022. Our findings showed a relatively high adoption rate of SemVer in stable releases, with a mean of 75.84% ± 4.79%. However, the adoption rate was lower for API preview releases, where the most commonly used formats did not conform to the SemVer format. Our analysis revealed a linear decline in the adoption of SemVer in preview releases from 2018 to 2022, with a significant increase in the use of simpler versioning formats, such as v*beta* or v*alpha*, which combine the major version number with a preview release tag.

Q6: *What is the prevalence of APIs with multiple versions in production? how many concurrent versions exist, and which formats are used in this case?*
    We analyzed the usage of the "two in production" evolution pattern [14,22] by examining the APIs that have paths with distinct version identifiers. Out of 7114 APIs, we found 175 with multiple version identifiers attached to their paths. The majority (119 APIs) had exactly two versions across 2,102 commits. In one case, an API supported up to 14 different versions in production across five commits.
    The commonly used format for version identifiers attached to the API path varies based on the number of coexisting versions. For APIs with fewer than

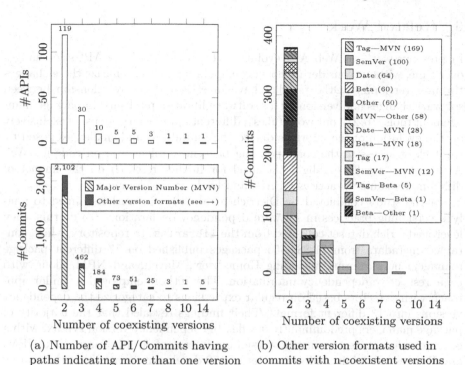

(a) Number of API/Commits having paths indicating more than one version

(b) Other version formats used in commits with n-coexistent versions

Fig. 6. Number of API having at least one commit with paths indicating more than one version

six versions, the most prevalent format is to reference only the major version. However, for APIs with more than six coexisting versions, the widely adopted format is semantic versioning. This suggests that an increased number of coexisting versions requires a more detailed identifier for proper differentiation.

5.1 Threats to Validity

– Internal validity: Our formats classification approach allowed us to accurately identify the presence of version identifiers embedded in the URL. However, this process is susceptible to errors or omissions if the version information is not already retrieved from the `info.version` or if the identifier matched in the URL is not meant to be used for versioning.

– External validity: Our study relies on API history snapshots from GitHub, potentially missing the full evolution of the APIs. Findings should be viewed with caution given the possibility of missing updates and changes. The APIs in the study come from a single platform, GitHub, and caution should be exercised in generalizing the results to APIs developed elsewhere.

6   Related Work

In previous work on Web API evolution [11] we studied the API size changes over time, without considering how developers tend to summarize these changes through versioning. Other studies have investigated the relationship between software changes and versioning for software libraries published in package management tools [16,21], our work takes a different approach by focusing exclusively on the evolution of the interface due to the limitations and challenges posed by the lack of access to the corresponding backend implementation code for Web APIs. These results highlight the need for further research on the impact of different versioning practices on API and backend development.

In the study conducted by Dietrich et al. [12], the authors aimed to analyze versioning practices in software dependency declarations. To do this, they leveraged a rich dataset collected from the libraries.io repository, which contained metadata from 71,884,555 packages published on 17 different package management platforms, including Home-brew, Maven, and NPM, along with their respective dependency information. The authors employed a similar approach with detectors based on regular expressions to categorize the dependency versions into 13 different formats. Their findings revealed that the majority of package managers predominantly use flexible dependency version syntax, with a considerable uptake of semantic versioning in case of Atom, Cargo, Hex, NPM, and Rubygems. Additionally, a survey of 170 developers showed that they rarely modified the declared dependencies' version syntax as the project evolved.

In a separate study [10], the author focused on the versioning practices adopted by developers when using continuous integration services such as GitHub Actions. The results indicated that 89.9% of the analyzed version tags followed GitHub's recommendation of only referring to the major version in the identifier, with only a small fraction (0.9%) including minor version information and 9.2% using the SemVer-3 format. This differs from our findings, where we found that SemVer-3 was the most widely adopted semantic versioning format.

7   Conclusion

Versioning in Web APIs is a fundamental practice to ensure their compatibility and ease their maintainability. In this empirical study we focused on version identifiers, observing their location, formats, and evolution. Out of 7114 APIs, the majority (5022) utilized static versioning in the API metadata, while a small fraction (220) supported dynamic discovery of the current version through a dedicated endpoint. In terms of version format, we identified 55 distinct formats used to distinguish stable and preview releases, with 535 APIs including preview versions in their Github histories. The number of preview releases pushed to Github showed an upward trend with a yearly average of 1858 commits.

With regards to metadata versions, we found that 85% of the 6580 APIs which consistently used the same format throughout their lifespan utilized Semantic Versioning. The adopted version format was unstable in 534 APIs, with 30% switching to SemVer. Our analysis indicated a steady usage rate of SemVer for 75% (on average) of API releases, while preleases adopted more often less detailed formats that only reference the major version of the API, typically with a tag (e.g., "beta" being the most frequent) to indicate their purpose.

We also observed the usage of the "two in production" evolution pattern in 175 APIs (56 with more than 2 versions). In these cases, the most prevalent format for version identifiers attached to the path was to reference only the major version, particularly among APIs with fewer than six coexisting versions.

As future work, we plan to further investigate the adherence of developers to semantic versioning guidelines and study the types of API changes that drive major or minor version changes.

Acknowledgements. The authors acknowledge Fabio Di Lauro for gathering the raw dataset, and Deepansha Chowdhary for conducting a feasibility study on it. This work was supported by the SNF with the API-ACE project number 184692.

References

1. Semantic Versioning. https://semver.org/
2. OpenAPI Initiative. https://www.openapis.org/
3. https://github.com/USI-INF-Software/API-Versioning-practices-detection
4. https://docs.npmjs.com/about-semantic-versioning
5. SwaggerHub. https://app.swaggerhub.com/
6. Release naming conventions. https://www.drupal.org/node/1015226
7. https://docs.fedoraproject.org/en-US/packaging-guidelines/Versioning/
8. SWR Audio Lab - Radiohub API. https://github.com/swrlab/swrlab/blob/main/openapi/openapi.yaml
9. Bogart, C., Kästner, C., Herbsleb, J., Thung, F.: How to break an API: cost negotiation and community values in three software ecosystems. In: Proceedings of the 24th International Symposium on Foundations of Software Engineering (FSE), pp. 109–120 (2016)
10. Decan, A., Mens, T., Mazrae, P.R., Golzadeh, M.: On the use of GitHub actions in software development repositories. In: International Conference on Software Maintenance and Evolution (ICSME), pp. 235–245 (2022)
11. Di Lauro, F., Serbout, S., Pautasso, C.: A large-scale empirical assessment of web API size evolution. J. Web Eng. **21**(6), 1937–1980 (2022)
12. Dietrich, J., Pearce, D., Stringer, J., Tahir, A., Blincoe, K.: Dependency versioning in the wild. In: Proceedings of the 16th International Conference on Mining Software Repositories (MSR), pp. 349–359 (2019)
13. Lauret, A.: The Design of web APIs. Simon and Schuster (2019)
14. Lübke, D., Zimmermann, O., Pautasso, C., Zdun, U., Stocker, M.: Interface evolution patterns: balancing compatibility and extensibility across service life cycles. In: Proceedings of the 24th EuroPLoP (2019)
15. Marquardt, K.: Patterns for software release versioning. In: Proceedings of the 15th European Conference on Pattern Languages of Programs (EuroPLoP) (2010)
16. Ochoa, L., Degueule, T., Falleri, J.R., Vinju, J.: Breaking bad? Semantic versioning and impact of breaking changes in maven central. Empir. Softw. Eng. **27**(3), 1–42 (2022)

17. Raatikainen, M., Kettunen, E., Salonen, A., Komssi, M., Mikkonen, T., Lehtonen, T.: State of the practice in application programming interfaces (APIs): a case study. In: Biffl, S., Navarro, E., Löwe, W., Sirjani, M., Mirandola, R., Weyns, D. (eds.) ECSA 2021. LNCS, vol. 12857, pp. 191–206. Springer, Cham (2021). https://doi.org/10.1007/978-3-030-86044-8_14
18. Serbout, S., Di Lauro, F., Pautasso, C.: Web APIs structures and data models analysis. In: Companion Proceedings of the 19th International Conference on Software Architecture (ICSA), pp. 84–91 (2022)
19. Varga, E.: Creating Maintainable APIs. APress (2016)
20. Yang, J., Wittern, E., Ying, A.T., Dolby, J., Tan, L.: Towards extracting web API specifications from documentation. In: Proceedings of the 15th International Conference on Mining Software Repositories (MSR), pp. 454–464 (2018)
21. Zhang, L., et al.: Has my release disobeyed semantic versioning? Static detection based on semantic differencing. In: Proceedings of the 37th International Conference on Automated Software Engineering (2023)
22. Zimmermann, O., Stocker, M., Lübke, D., Zdun, U., Pautasso, C.: Patterns for API Design - Simplifying Integration with Loosely Coupled Message Exchanges. Addison-Wesley (2022)

The Rise of Disappearing Frameworks in Web Development

Juho Vepsäläinen(✉)(iD), Arto Hellas, and Petri Vuorimaa

Aalto University, Espoo, Finland
juho.vepsalainen@aalto.fi
https://www.aalto.fi/en/department-of-computer-science

Abstract. The evolution of the web can be characterized as an emergence of frameworks paving the way from static websites to dynamic web applications. As the scope of web applications has grown, new technical challenges have emerged, leading to the need for new solutions. The latest of these developments is the rise of so-called disappearing web frameworks that question the axioms of earlier generations of web frameworks, providing benefits of the early web and simple static sites.

Keywords: web · web development · multi-page applications · JavaScript · front-end frameworks · single-page applications · islands architecture · disappearing frameworks · Astro · Marko.js · Qwik

1 Introduction

The World Wide Web (WWW) was designed to bring a global information universe into existence using the prevailing technology [2]. Over time, it grew into a whole application platform. The evolution into a platform could be characterized through the following phases: (1) the birth of the web in the early 1990s [2], (2) the introduction of AJAX in 1999 [7], and (3) rise of the Single-page applications (SPAs) starting from the early 2010s. Each of the phases was a response to the rising need for interactivity and improvements made to the browsers. For example, the introduction of AJAX let developers manipulate server data without having to refresh the whole page shown to the client. This led to more interactive experiences and, eventually, SPAs, which dominate today's dynamic web applications. As a response to SPAs, a new breed of frameworks, so-called *disappearing frameworks*, have emerged.

The purpose of this article is to examine (RQ1) why disappearing frameworks are needed, (RQ2) what disappearing frameworks are, and (RQ3) why disappearing frameworks might be the next major phase in web development. To address the first research question RQ1, we'll discuss the background leading to the current situation in Sect. 2. To understand the concept of disappearing frameworks – RQ2 – in detail, we'll delve into the concept and a couple of examples in Sect. 3. In Sect. 4 we argue why disappearing frameworks might become the next major phase in web development, addressing RQ3.

© The Author(s), under exclusive license to Springer Nature Switzerland AG 2023
I. Garrigós et al. (Eds.): ICWE 2023, LNCS 13893, pp. 319–326, 2023.
https://doi.org/10.1007/978-3-031-34444-2_23

2   Background

Originally the web was designed as a content platform. Over time, as its usage grew, so did the user requirements for interactivity. As a result, it has morphed into an application platform spanning from desktop to mobile devices and beyond. Web technologies have become a universal way to deliver software to countless users. In this section, we'll have a brief look at the major movements and their contribution as this will help us to understand the motivation behind the development of disappearing frameworks.

2.1   First Decades of the Web

Early websites of the 1990s were authored directly in key web technologies: HTML, CSS, and JavaScript. These technologies are still in use and form the building blocks of the web as we know it. Authoring websites has however changed as contents may be generated either via code or via a user interface, depending on the system. The idea of generating code is not novel, as editors such as Frontpage and Dreamweaver offered the opportunity to create websites in a graphical manner already in the 1990s.

To manage a shared state, server-side functionality implemented using technologies such as PHP [16] and cgi-bin [6] was used. These allowed the implementation of complex logic on the server side, which could be customized to fit the need of individual organizations. As the needs of organizations were often related to editing, storing, sharing, and displaying content, Content Management Systems (CMSs) such as WordPress emerged. Slowly, CMSs came to dominate the content market [24], providing benefits for both developers and users [1,3,25].

The early web applications were most often Multi-page applications (MPAs), where the application state lives on the server, and each request from the client to the server loads a new page [15]. The introduction of JavaScript in 1995 [7] and in particular Asynchronous JavaScript (AJAX) in 1999 allowed developers to move logic to the client over time, which led to the birth of JavaScript-heavy programming models such as Single Page Applications (SPAs).

2.2   The Rise of Single-Page Applications

SPAs were developed to address the constraints of MPA development, mainly the need to refresh the page when data changes [15]. AJAX was the key enabler as a technology as it allowed developers to retrieve data from the server. With the introduction of the History API in HTML5 specification in 2008, it became possible to control routing as well. To understand the differences between MPAs and SPAs, we've listed their relative merits in Table 1, summarizing [13,15,22].

SPAs set a new standard for Developer eXperience (DX) and what's expected from developer tooling. The developer-side improvements come with a cost as SPAs direct developers to rely on JavaScript and ignore native browser APIs, which have improved over time [5]. Techniques, such as progressive enhancement [8] can help, but a more significant change is required on the tooling level to address the user needs [5].

Table 1. MPA vs. SPA

Dimension	MPA	SPA
Relies on JavaScript	No	Yes [15, 22]
Initial cost of loading	Potentially low	High due to dependency on JavaScript [22]
Overall response time	Slower	Faster due to partial updates [15]
Business logic	Coupled	Decoupled [15, 22]
Refresh on navigation	Yes	No [22]
Bandwidth usage	Higher	Lower due to only transaction-related data moving between the parties [15]
Offline support	Not possible	Possible [15, 22]
Search Engine Optimization (SEO)	Excellent	Possible but difficult [13, 15, 22]
Security	Understood	Practices still being established [15]
Routing	At server	Duplicated in server and client [22], but modern frameworks, such as Next.js, mitigate the problem

2.3 The Current Front-End Development Landscape

The current front-end development landscape is dominated by React, Vue, and Angular[1]. Out of these technologies, React and Vue can be considered libraries in the sense that they have a strict focus and they omit opinions such as how routing should be implemented. Angular can be considered a framework as it comes with everything one would need to construct an application. Due to this, frameworks such as Next.js or Nuxt.js[2] have emerged as they provide structure and opinionated development practices on top of existing libraries. Regardless of the library or framework, the contemporary solutions rely on the three following key principles:

1. Component orientation – They come with component-oriented abstractions[3]
2. Templating – A solution, such as JSX, is used for modeling markup
3. Hydration – To make the components come alive, the solutions run the code at the client side. By this, we mean attaching event handlers and running component logic [12].

---

[1] Based on Stack Overflow Survey of 2022 [23], 42.6% of developers use React. For Angular, the proportion was 20.4%, and for Vue 18.8%. W3Techs [21] puts these values into perspective as there the global market share of React is around 3.7% for all websites.

[2] Based on [23], 13.5% of developers use Next.js so that means roughly one out of four React developers use Next.js. For Nuxt.js, the figure is 3.8% which means roughly one out of six.

[3] By component-oriented abstractions, we mean a way to encapsulate markup and potentially local state so that it can be reused.

Each library and framework relies on some amount of client-side JavaScript to load a web page – that is, when a website is loaded, client-side JavaScript is executed to display content. Preact and petite-vue are notable examples of implementations that try to minimize the size of the required JavaScript while keeping API compatibility with their bigger brothers.

2.4   A Need to Reconsider Technologies

Given the current solutions allow developers to build complex and dynamic web applications, what is there left to do? As pointed out in [17], analyzing the characteristics of real-world applications is difficult. It is difficult to generalize and extract best practices as they are context-specific. In a case where an MPA might be a good solution, a SPA could fare poorly. To capture and characterize specific use cases, [17] proposes a set of holotypes that can be used to make informed decisions on deciding what sorts of technical approaches one could or should make.

The key differences between the holotypes proposed in [17] relate to the following dimensions: (1) interactivity, (2) search engine optimization (SEO), (3) media type (rich or not), (4) client size (thick or not), (5) processing (server or client), (6) latency, (7) offline-capability. This list summarizes the complexity related to modern web development and associated technical choices.

The list also highlights a need to reconsider technologies used for web development. Rather than trying to fit solutions such as SPAs to various use cases, *disappearing frameworks give the option to reframe the problems and to potentially address them from an angle that could be considered a paradigm-level shift* (RQ1). This is the foundation of why we consider them as the next potential phase in mainstream web development.

3   Disappearing Frameworks

Disappearing frameworks start from close to zero cost in terms of JavaScript loaded by the client and remove it from the application as much as possible [5][4]. The shift in focus provides a strong contrast to the current mainstream JavaScript frameworks, which come with a heavy upfront cost that increases as components are added to the system [22]. Due to this shift in focus, applications are distributed into smaller sections instead of treating the whole as a single top-down system. The approach works well with MPAs as it allows developers to pull from experiences gained through building traditional systems while gaining modern DX as experienced with SPAs. As a side effect, the ideas of SPAs and

---

[4] The idea of disappearing frameworks is also in line with Transitional Web Applications (TWAs), where the key idea is to draw from both the traditional web and SPAs [5,10] to build applications with the following characteristics: (1) static site rendering is utilized for fast initial loading times (2), resiliency is achieved by allowing applications to work without JavaScript by default, and (3) consistent experience and accessibility are built-in by definition [5].

MPAs may eventually merge and become a framework-level concern allowing the developers to use what is best for the given situation. Here, we discuss the key features of disappearing frameworks: (1) islands architecture and (2) automatic islands, outlining an answer to (RQ2).

3.1   Islands Architecture

Islands architecture is the first stepping stone toward disappearing frameworks. It is an approach that can be considered further evolution of progressive enhancement. In the islands architecture, web page sections are treated as separate islands, some of which might be completely static while some might have some interactivity in them [18]. A good implementation of islands architecture should allow the developer to decide when an interactive island is loaded [9]. Controlling loading is important as it lets the developers defer secondary work or even avoid it. Deferring work is the key to improving performance and decreasing bandwidth usage, which is important e.g., in mobile contexts and search engine optimization.

Figure 1 compares the islands architecture to other contemporary architectures, namely SSR and progressive hydration. In progressive hydration, the application framework controls which portions of a page to hydrate [9]. In islands architecture, the concern is distributed so that each island can load independently from the others in an asynchronous fashion [9]. Therefore, the difference between the approaches has to do with control.

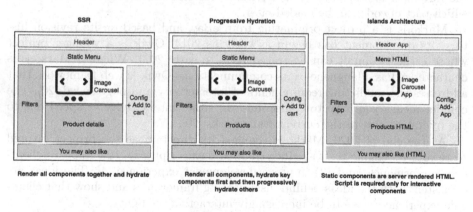

Fig. 1. Islands architecture compared [9]

The benefits of islands architecture include (1) avoidance of top-down rendering [18], (2) improved performance as there is less JavaScript to ship [9,18], (3) less problematic SEO story due to an increased amount of static content [18], (4) better accessibility and discoverability by default [9], and (5) component-orientation to encourage reuse [9]. The last point is not without problems as usage of islands can lead to composition issues since it is not trivial to compose functionality across an island boundary. Also, the SEO point comes with caveats related to SPAs and is not without complexity.

The islands architecture has been criticized since as a new approach, official support is limited [9], there's limited discussion around the idea (besides [9,14, 18]), and frameworks might claim to implement the idea while implementing it wrong [9]. In addition, the architecture might not fit a highly interactive use case such as a social media application with a high amount of interactivity [9].

Given the islands architecture has been formalized only in 2019 [18], there is no widespread usage yet. According to Hallie and Osmani [9], at least the following frameworks support it: Astro, Eleventy when combined with Preact. Out of these, only Astro was developed with the architecture in mind, whereas the other options contain the features needed for a developer to implement it. Further, Astro is not coupled to a specific library, such as React, but instead lets the developer choose and even mix solutions based on the need at hand.

3.2 Compiler-Based Approaches – Marko.js and Qwik

Both Marko.js and Qwik implement a compiler-based approach that is able to write split points for code automatically. In Qwik's case, the compiler is able to split code at the view, state, and handler level [11]. Marko.js generates split points at the sub-component level as well [4]. It is these split points that represent code that can be loaded later on demand. In earlier approaches, such as React, the developer would have to insert hints[5] for the bundler in the code to tell which part of code can be loaded later.

Marko.js is a project originating from eBay, and based on its revision history, its development has begun as early as 2014. Qwik is a younger project whose earliest commit can be traced back to early 2021. Whereas Marko.js is characterized as a language in its communications, Qwik is web framework that addresses the conflicting requirements of interactivity and page speed [20]. The conflict means you have to compromise in either interactivity or speed due to the hydration cost of the current frameworks [20].

At the end of 2020, Marko.js changed its direction as the project pivoted to rework its engine to (1) reduce shipped JavaScript size, (2), improve client-side performance, and (3) improve development experience [4]. The ideas are consistent with the ideas behind disappearing frameworks and show that client-side experiences have to be increasingly interactive yet light.

Qwik solves compromising interactivity and speed by choosing resumability over hydration, automatic code splitting, tiny runtime, and compilation over runtime cost [19]. Presently, these factors make Qwik unique when compared to options. Qwik is consistent with the idea of disappearing frameworks as it tries to make itself vanish from the application. Because of its approach, Qwik represents a paradigm-level shift in how to develop web applications. One of

---

[5] The latest ECMAScript standard supports this in the form of *import()* statement.

the ways Qwik achieves its targets is by focusing on different metrics than its predecessors, namely Time to Interactive (TTI) over Time to Load (TTL).

4   Discussion and Conclusion

To summarize, the growth of the web has been fueled by increasing requirements from both developers and users. Early web practices, including MPAs, were later complemented by developer-friendly approaches, such as SPAs. During the process, fundamental ideas of the web were put aside as applications required JavaScript to run and came with accessibility and SEO challenges. We discussed disappearing frameworks and argue that they represent the next major stage in web development as they take the best parts of SPAs and combine them with the good development practices of the early web, improving common challenges of SPAs such as search engine optimization. The existing early implementations, such as Marko.js and Qwik, show promise and the increasing popularity of Astro highlights the demand for lighter ways to develop for the web; it also demonstrates that there is room for more than one option in the ecosystem, as it provides a framework/library agnostic approach to web development. These possibilities, coupled with developer experience, lead to us believe that they might be the next major phase in web development (RQ3).

By questioning existing axioms, the emergence of disappearing frameworks leads to a group of new research questions. Given the frameworks postpone loading code, what is the optimal strategy to do it? What are the pros/cons of the solutions from a developer and a user perspective relative to the incumbent approaches? What is the cost of using the island architecture? What is the cost of using hydration based technologies in islands? Is the idea of disappearing frameworks compatible with other rising approaches, such as micro-frontends? How does the islands architecture and disappearing frameworks scale as application size grows?

Disappearing frameworks provide a refreshing take on web development as they promise benefits for both developers and users. At the same time, there are many questions related to the feasibility of the approach as no case studies exist.

References

1. Benevolo, C., Negri, S.: Evaluation of content management systems (CMS): a supply analysis. Electron. J. Inf. Syst. Eval. **10**(1), 9–22 (2007)
2. Berners-Lee, T., Cailliau, R., Groff, J.F., Pollermann, B.: World-wide web: the information universe. Internet Res. (1992)
3. Boiko, B.: Content Management Bible. Wiley, Hoboken (2005)
4. Carniato, R.: FLUURT: re-inventing Marko—dev.to (2020). https://dev.to/ryansolid/fluurt-re-inventing-marko-3o1o. Accessed 11 Jan 2023
5. Carniato, R.: Understanding transitional Javascript apps (2021). https://dev.to/this-is-learning/understanding-transitional-javascript-apps-27i2. Accessed 29 Sept 2022

6. Common Gateway Interface (2022). https://en.wikipedia.org/w/index.php?
   title=Common_Gateway_Interface&oldid=1102228140.   Page   Version   ID:
   1102228140
7. Flanagan, D., Novak, G.M.: Javascript: the definitive guide (1998)
8. Gustafson, A., Overkamp, L., Brosset, P., Prater, S.V., Wills, M., PenzeyMoog, E.:
   Understanding progressive enhancement (2008). https://alistapart.com/article/
   understandingprogressiveenhancement/. Accessed 29 Sept 2022
9. Hallie, L., Osmani, A.: Islands architecture – patterns.dev (2022). https://www.
   patterns.dev/posts/islands-architecture/. Accessed 29 Sept 2022
10. Harris, R.: Have single-page apps ruined the web? | transitional apps with rich har-
    ris, nytimes (2021), https://www.youtube.com/watch?v=860d8usGC0o. Accessed
    29 Sept 2022
11. Hevery, M.: Your bundler is doing it wrong – dev.to (2021). https://dev.to/
    builderio/your-bundler-is-doing-it-wrong-ic0. Accessed 14 Nov 2022
12. Huotala, A.: Benefits and challenges of isomorphism in single-page applications:
    a case study and review of gray literature. Master's thesis, University of Helsinki
    (2021)
13. Iskandar, T.F., Lubis, M., Kusumasari, T.F., Lubis, A.R.: Comparison between
    client-side and server-side rendering in the web development. In: IOP Conference
    Series: Materials Science and Engineering, vol. 801, p. 012136. IOP Publishing
    (2020)
14. Jones, A.: Etsy engineering: mobius: adopting JSX while prioritizing user
    experience (2021). https://www.etsy.com/codeascraft/mobius-adopting-jsx-while-
    prioritizing-user-experience/. Accessed 29 Sept 2022
15. Kaluža, M., Troskot, K., Vukelić, B.: Comparison of front-end frameworks for web
    applications development. Zbornik Veleučilišta Rijeci **6**(1), 261–282 (2018)
16. Lerdorf, R., Tatroe, K., Kaehms, B., McGredy, R.: Programming PHP. O'Reilly
    Media, Inc. (2002)
17. Miller, J.: Application Holotypes: A Guide to Architecture Decisions - JASON For-
    mat – jasonformat.com (2019). https://jasonformat.com/application-holotypes/.
    Accessed 10 Jan 2023
18. Miller, J.: Islands   architecture   (2020).   https://jasonformat.com/islands-
    architecture/. Accessed 29 Sept 2022
19. Qwik: Overview - Qwik – qwik.builder.io (2022). https://qwik.builder.io/docs/
    overview/. Accessed 14 Nov 2022
20. Qwik's magic is not in how fast it executes, but how good it is in avoiding doing
    any work – devm.io (2022). https://devm.io/javascript/qwik-javascript-hevery.
    Accessed 15 Nov 2022
21. React vs. Vue.js vs. Angular usage statistics, October 2022–w3techs.com (2022).
    https://w3techs.com/technologies/comparison/js-angularjs,js-react,js-vuejs.
    Accessed 31 Oct 2022
22. Solovei, V., Olshevska, O., Bortsova, Y.: The difference between developing sin-
    gle page application and traditional web application based on mechatronics robot
    laboratory onaft application. Autom. Technol. Bus. Process. **10**(1) (2018)
23. Stack Overflow Developer Survey 2022 – survey.stackoverflow.co. https://survey.
    stackoverflow.co/2022/. Accessed 31 Oct 2022
24. W3Techs - extensive and reliable web technology surveys (2022). https://w3techs.
    com/. Accessed 03 Oct 2022
25. Yermolenko, A., Golchevskiy, Y.: Developing web content management systems-
    from the past to the future. In: SHS Web of Conferences, vol. 110. EDP Sciences
    (2021)

On the Popularity of Classical Music Composers on Community-Driven Platforms

Ioannis Petros Samiotis[1] , Andrea Mauri[2(✉)] , Chirstoph Lofi[1] ,
and Alessandro Bozzon[1]

[1] TU Delft, Delft, The Netherlands
{i.p.samiotis,c.lofi,a.bozzon}@tudelft.nl
[2] Université Claude Bernard Lyon 1, Lyon, France
andrea.mauri@univ-lyon1.fr

Abstract. Traditionally, the popularity of classical music composers is approximated through commercial figures like album releases, record sales, or live performances. However, commercial factors only provide one piece of the overall picture. The success of community-driven platforms has profoundly changed how people consume and interact with music, and, consequently, our understanding of what popularity is. People discuss their favourite artists, archive knowledge regarding them and share their work through multimedia platforms. In this paper, we investigate how data from these platforms can provide a more comprehensive view on popularity and engagement regarding the long-tail of classical music composers. We combine album release data provided by MusicBrainz, the commitment of people in maintaining the composers' Wikipedia pages and user engagement in classical music videos on YouTube. Our analysis provides a complementary multi-faceted view on community engagement and urges future research to expand on user-generated content for a more diverse expression of popularity in the music domain.

Keywords: social media · user-generated content · music · popularity · web crawling

1 Introduction

Popularity is a desired achievement for artists, as it promotes their work, facilitates the interaction with the broader audience, and ultimately affects how people will remember them in years to come. This holds especially true in classical music, which includes centuries-long catalog of works created and reinterpreted by a long list of artists. Access to those works and their artists is essential in preserving parts of historic and cultural heritage, as classical music has fundamentally influenced western music throughout history.

Recording labels have pioneered the methods to capture audio performances, preserving a plethora of classical music pieces of the old or contemporary composers. Inevitably though, these recordings are skewed towards already established and well studied composers and their works can be found performed by various artists.

However, popularity is not only related to talent, but also former success [1] and *"the need of consumers to consume the same art as others"* [2]. When people are exposed to art, share it with others, or consume media about it, they create what is called "consumption capita" [3]. These activities have become much easier to perform with the widespread adoption of Web technologies and the availability of community-driven platforms. People from around the world with different cultural backgrounds can openly share their knowledge, experiences, and recordings with others in the ever expanding publicly-accessible knowledge bases and social media communities.

For this reason we believe that by tapping into user-generated content, we can find interesting insights on user-engagement and popularity of classical composers online. To that end, we analyze user-generated data on Wikipedia and YouTube compared to album releases retrieved from MusicBrainz[1], to investigate our hypothesis that *User-engagement on community-driven platforms develops composer popularity differently than the album release trends in classical music.* Our findings can be used to indicate to what extent those platforms potentially hold content and information about composers who have zero to low number of official album releases.

2   Related Works

Research on the multilingual online encyclopedia Wikipedia[2], has shown that it is possible to predict real-world opinions and popularity through analyzing user interaction on the platform. For example, Mestyán et al [4] presented a model using Wikipedia's user-generated content that accurately predicts movie box office success, while another study by Wei et al [5] uses user interaction on Wikipedia to predict stock market values.

YouTube[3] is a video-sharing, social media platform, which encourages a user-content-user interaction [6] and hosts a staggering amount of videos across a wide variety of categories. While research work has mostly focused on network dynamics [7–9] and opinion mining [10–12], there have been studies on popularity on the platform. Chatzopoulou et al. [13] studied the correlation between views, number of comments and ratings and popularity, while in [14] it is found that popularity on YouTube follows the conclusions of studies on "consumption capita" [15]. Related to our study, the work of Cayari [16] studies how YouTube has fundamentally affected musical art forms and has essentially changed the way people listen, share and consume music. This holds especially true for classical music, where with a quick search on the platform, it is possible to find

---

[1] https://musicbrainz.org/.

[2] https://en.wikipedia.org/wiki/Wikipedia.

[3] https://www.youtube.com/.

several results with multiple compilations of classical music works, live footage of concerts, interpretations of compositions, and educational material.

Our study is inspired by the work of Bellogin et al [17], the first comparing music artist popularity from different Web and music services. The main difference with our work is that we look into user-engagement regarding music on generic platforms that host music information among other categories. In our study, we also focus on genre-specific content on those generic platforms, rather than overall music consumption trends. Related to classical music, Schedl et al. [18] studied the online engagement of fans of classical music on Twitter and Last.fm finding that classical music is under-represented on social media, as classical music enthusiasts seem averse sharing content on both of the studied platforms. In this study we argue that we need further analysis on community-driven platforms to be able to assess the extent those platforms contain domain specific information.

3   Data Collection

We started with quantifying user engagement on Wikipedia and YouTube. We defined a list of classical music composers which we are considering for analysis in different platforms and selected a reliable source of knowledge about album releases. In this section, we outline our data collection process. The data retrieval and scripts, as well as the resulting dataset are available here[4].

DBpedia: to select the composers, we retrieved a list of their names from various classical music periods from DBpedia[5] using the Virtuoso SPARQL Query Interface[6]. We used the name contained in the URI as an unambiguous representation of a composers' name, as there could be multiple entries with the same name, but different people. We queried the composer names, using the following Yago entities available for classical music periods in DBpedia: WikicatBaroqueComposers, WikicatClassicalComposers, WikicatClassical-periodComposers, WikicatRomanticComposers, Wikicat18th-centuryClassicalComposer, Wikicat19thcenturyClassicalComposers, Wikicat20th-centuryClassicalComposers, Wikicat-21stcenturyClassicalComposers. We finally collected 5928 different composers, distributed as follows: 1126 baroque, 1025 romantic, 725 classical, 96 from eighteen century, 345 from nineteen century, 3155 from twenty century and 1383 from twenty one century. Obviously, a composer can belong to multiple periods.

Wikipedia: we used Wikipedia APIs[7] to retrieve each composer's page and related information. To ensure we retrieve the page related to the composer, we use as query the name as it appears in the "About" on DBPedia. For instance, to retrieve the page of *Alexander Müller* we use *Alexander_ Müller_ (composer)*. This also holds true for composers having the same name, like *Johann Strauss I*

---

[4] https://github.com/ipsamiotis/classical_popularity.
[5] https://wiki.dbpedia.org/.
[6] https://dbpedia.org/sparql.
[7] https://www.mediawiki.org/wiki/API:Main_page.

and his son *Johann Strauss II*. We follow the same procedure for a composer's full name on MusicBrainz and YouTube. More specifically, we retrieved: 1) the number of edits a page has received, 2) the number of users who edited the page, 3) the number of languages the page is translated to, 4) the size of the page (in KB), and 5) how many sections it contains. We use these data as a proxy to measure how many people engage on Wikipedia with a composer's entry. They show us the amount of users maintaining a page, how much are they committed in keeping the information correct and updated (number of edits), accessible to many people (languages) and complete (page length and number of sections).

MusicBrainz: Musicbrainz is a community-maintained music encyclopedia that collects metadata about music artists and their released works (albums, recordings and more). We used their up-to-date and proven reliable information on *Album Releases* per classical music composer. We retrieved this using a Python wrapper to its API[8] and in our analysis we refer to them as *Album Releases*.

YouTube: we gathered videos from YouTube using youtube-dl[9] based on the queries: ''composer name'' + ''music'' and ''composer name'' + ''live music'', resulting in a total of.184,019 video entries. The retrieved videos contained a high amount of non-relevant entries. We cleaned the dataset by discarding all videos where the composer name was not present in either the title, in one of the tags or in the description of the video. This way, we decreased the number of videos relevant to our study to 69,261. Since users also view videos and react to them by leaving a like, dislike or a comment, we also retrieved the number of: 1) likes, 2) dislikes, 3) views, 4) comments, 5) unique uploaders and 6) duration of videos. From these engagement data, we further calculated the average number of likes, dislikes, views, video duration and comments per composer.

In the final dataset we collected, we find 97% of the composers have a Wikipedia page, 87% of the composers have at least one video on Youtube, while only 70% of them have albums on MusicBrainz. Also, 63% of composers are in common to all the platforms, with Wikipedia and YouTube having the biggest overlap (99%), while MuiscBrainz lacks 31% of composers present in Wikipedia.

4   Data Analysis

We first analyse if the data we use as a proxy for user engagement on Wikipedia and YouTube is correlated. To that end, we calculated the Spearman correlation [19] of the popularity ranking of composers each data property was generating. This will give some insights into how comparable user engagement is between platforms. To investigate if user-engagement-driven popularity exhibit differences compared to the album releases, we calculate the similarity between those trends. Using the Jaccard similarity index [20], we are able to observe

---

[8] https://python-musicbrainzngs.readthedocs.io/en/v0.7.1/.

[9] https://pypi.org/project/youtube_dl/.

differences between the different popularity rankings and album releases, finding interesting results on both top-to-bottom and bottom-to-top rankings. The intuition is that by computing the Jaccard index at different level of cut-off it is possible to see how much each platform agrees on who are the top n (or bottom n) composers.

4.1   Calculating Popularity per Platform

We calculate a single popularity ranking per platform based on user activity metrics as described in Sect. 3. These metrics are related to: 1) how much the people engage with the platform in the context of classical music and 2) what kind of data they create. Their connection to popularity is based on the fact that people who are interested on a composer and are active users of those platforms, they will either create data about them, interact with data others created and/or discuss about them with other users. All these factors are an "online version" of those described on "consumption capita", which indicates the reasons why artists become famous among people, apart from their talent [3]. We first calculate the correlation of those metrics, following the methodology of [13], to find if the engagement metrics we chose are correlated with each other, to be later considered part of a platform-wide "popularity ranking". This popularity ranking, as discussed before, is being used as a proxy of real popularity of composers on those platforms.

Wikipedia: we compute the correlation of the metrics described in Sect. 3 using the Spearman coefficient. As shown in Table 1, most of the different metrics exhibit high correlation (greater than 0.5), with the least correlated being the number of languages with the page size and number of sections metadata.

Table 1. Spearman correlation the metrics of Wikipedia and Youtube

	Wikipedia				
	Sections	Languages	Revisions	Users	
Pages Size	0.82	0.38	0.72	0.69	
Sections	1	0.38	0.63	0.61	
Languages		1	0.49	0.67	
Revisions			1	0.87	
	Youtube				
	Views	Likes	Dislikes	Duration	Comments
Videos	0.86	0.85	0.81	0.89	0.05
Views	1	0.98	0.94	0.81	0.07
Likes		1	0.93	0.81	0.07
Dislikes			1	0.76	0.06
Duration				1	0.06

Youtube: we performed the same analysis on the data gathered from YouTube, finding that they are all highly correlated - as shown in Table 1 - except the number of comments. This could be explained by limitations on the number of comments which could be accessed by the APIs, so we excluded them from the final rankings. The others are consistent with the results reported in [13].

To compare the popularity of composers on Wikipedia, YouTube and album releases, we needed a single ranking per platform. To achieve this, we ranked the composers based on each metric per platform. If a composer is not present on a platform, the values of his or her platform metrics are set to 0 (e.g., for composers not present on MusicBrainz, we set their album releases number to 0). In this way we obtain list of the same length and we can compute correlation coefficients. Then, we aggregated the different rankings into a single one for each platform using the average ranking aggregation method. We then compared them using the Spearman correlation coefficient.

Table 2. Spearman correlation between the platform rankings and album releases.

	Wikipedia	MuiscBrainz
YouTube	0.42	0.34
Wikipedia	1	0.36

As Table 2 shows, all platforms are positively correlated, with YouTube and Wikpedia exhibiting a stronger correlation to each other's popularity rankings.

4.2 Popularity on Platforms and Album Releases

We then calculate the similarity between the popularity rankings derived from the community-driven platforms and the rankings obtained by looking at composers' *Album Releases*. Such comparison can inform us on the degree to which online communities engage in data creation, compared to the official recordings produced by the industry shown in the *Album Releases*. We compute similarity at different ranks, which intuitively can be encoded as "how much different rankings agree" with each other. To that end, we used the Jaccard similarity index. We observe - in Fig. 1a - that Wikipedia's and YouTube's popularity rankings are more similar to each other, than compared to the *Album Releases*. While this was expected, considering the fact that they are both community-driven platforms (see Table 2), this is still notable as both platforms have strong differences in scope and purpose. Wikipedia's ranking is closer to those of *Album Releases*, when compared to YouTube. This results actually is more in line with related work in [4,5], that shown user-engagement metrics can predict real-world popularity to a certain extent.

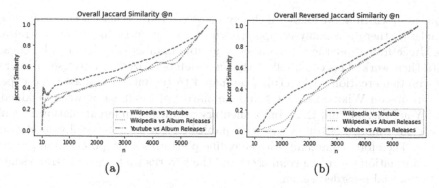

Fig. 1. Jaccard similarity at different ranking cut-offs with normal (a) and reverse ranking (b)

We compute the Jaccard similarity also looking at the bottom of the ranking, that is by looking at the long-tail of each platform. Following a reverse ordering on popularity rankings, starting from most "obscure" composers, the uniqueness of YouTube's ranking becomes more evident, as we see in Fig. 1b. The popularity of the long-tail composers on YouTube is completely dissimilar to the *Album Releases*, as it stays at 0 until we consider 1000 composers. This dissimilarity means that for composers with 0 released albums, the users still engage in data creation on YouTube. This is very encouraging for future works that need to find information regarding classical music composers, as YouTube contains video artefacts and user-engagement metadata for those composers who don't have registries with official album releases.

In the same way, Wikipedia, noticeably less severely, has low similarity with *Album Releases* as well for the first 1000 composers. This means that even composers with low-count of official album releases, there are still Wikipedia entries with stored information, generated in its entirety by the community of the platform. These findings strengthen our hypothesis that community-driven platforms behave similarly to each other and differently to *Album Releases*, potentially holding user-generated information for composers with low number of official album releases.

5 Conclusion

In this work we investigated to what extent popularity of classical music composers on generic community-driven online platforms, follows official album releases as registered in MusicBrainz. We found that Wikipedia and YouTube although they share similarities with each other regarding composers' popularity rankings, they differ on the long-tail of popularity, based on album releases. We discovered that Wikipedia's popularity ranking follows more closely the ranking found in album releases, following results from similar studies on the platform. This comes in contrast with the popularity rankings as witnessed on

YouTube, which don't follow as closely those of album releases. For example on YouTube, there are many composers who have no entry for an album release on MusicBrainz but they still garner a notable number of followers who engage with their work. This could reflect the more democratized and diverse manner of information creation on YouTube, compared to the more rule-based and expert driven one on Wikipedia. Due to the similarity of rankings between Wikipedia and YouTube, we find that complementary studies of different platforms could assist to a more holistic overview of published corpora, especially in classical music. Therefore, community-driven online platforms show potential in preserving information regarding composers and their works that are under-represented in the official recorded canon.

Acknowledgements. This work is partially supported by the European Commission under the TROMPA project (H2020 770376). We thank Cynthia C.S. Liem for her insights on popularity in music and contributions in discussions around the topic.

References

1. MacDonald, G.M.: The economics of rising stars. Am. Econ. Rev. 155–166 (1988)
2. Adler, M.: Stardom and talent. Am. Econ. Rev. **75**(1), 208–212 (1985)
3. Stigler, G.J., Becker, G.S.: De gustibus non est disputandum. Am. Econ. Rev. **67**(2), 76–90 (1977)
4. Mestyán, M., Yasseri, T., Kertész, J.: Early prediction of movie box office success based on Wikipedia activity big data. PloS One **8**(8) (2013)
5. Wei, P., Wang, N.: Wikipedia and stock return: Wikipedia usage pattern helps to predict the individual stock movement. In: Proceedings of the 25th International Conference Companion on World Wide Web, pp. 591–594 (2016)
6. Wattenhofer, M., Wattenhofer, R., Zhu, Z.: The Youtube social network. In: Sixth International AAAI Conference on Weblogs and Social Media (2012)
7. Siersdorfer, S., Chelaru, S., Pedro, J.S., Altingovde, I.S., Nejdl, W.: Analyzing and mining comments and comment ratings on the social web. ACM Trans. Web (TWEB) **8**(3), 17 (2014)
8. Paolillo, J., Ghule, S., Harper, B.: A network view of social media platform history: social structure, dynamics and content on Youtube. In: Proceedings of the 52nd Hawaii International Conference on System Sciences (2019)
9. Siersdorfer, S., Chelaru, S., Nejdl, W., Pedro, J.S.: How useful are your comments?: analyzing and predicting Youtube comments and comment ratings. In: Proceedings of the 19th International Conference on World Wide Web, pp. 891–900. ACM (2010)
10. Orellana-Rodriguez, C., Diaz-Aviles, E., Nejdl, W.: Mining emotions in short films: user comments or crowdsourcing? In: Proceedings of the 22nd International Conference on World Wide Web, pp. 69–70. ACM (2013)
11. Severyn, A., Moschitti, A., Uryupina, O., Plank, B., Filippova, K.: Multi-lingual opinion mining on Youtube. Inf. Process. Manag. **52**(1), 46–60 (2016)
12. Severyn, A., Uryupina, O., Plank, B., Moschitti, A., Filippova, K.: Opinion mining on Youtube (2014)
13. Chatzopoulou, G., Sheng, C., Faloutsos, M.: A first step towards understanding popularity in Youtube. In: 2010 INFOCOM IEEE Conference on Computer Communications Workshops, pp. 1–6. IEEE (2010)

14. Budzinski, O., Gaenssle, S.: The economics of social media stars: an empirical investigation of stardom, popularity, and success on Youtube. Ilmenau Econ. Discussion Pap. **21**(112) (2018)
15. Adler, M.: Stardom and talent. Handb. Econ. Art Cult. **1**, 895–906 (2006)
16. Cayari, C.: The Youtube effect: how Youtube has provided new ways to consume, create, and share music. Int. J. Educ. Arts **12**(6), n6 (2011)
17. Bellogín, A., de Vries, A.P., He, J.: Artist popularity: do web and social music services agree? In: Seventh International AAAI Conference on Weblogs and Social Media (2013)
18. Schedl, M., Tkalčič, M.: Genre-based analysis of social media data on music listening behavior: are fans of classical music really averse to social media? In: Proceedings of the First International Workshop on Internet-Scale Multimedia Management, pp. 9–13 (2014)
19. Myers, L., Sirois, M.J.: Spearman correlation coefficients, differences between. Encyclopedia Stat. Sci. **12** (2004)
20. Jaccard, P.: The distribution of the flora in the alpine zone. 1. New Phytol. **11**(2), 37–50 (1912)

Topio: An Open-Source Web Platform for Trading Geospatial Data

Andra Ionescu[1]([⊠]) [iD], Kostas Patroumpas[2] [iD], Kyriakos Psarakis[1] [iD],
Georgios Chatzigeorgakidis[2] [iD], Diego Collarana[3] [iD], Kai Barenscher[4],
Dimitrios Skoutas[2] [iD], Asterios Katsifodimos[1] [iD], and Spiros Athanasiou[2] [iD]

[1] Delft University of Technology, Delft, The Netherlands
{a.ionescu-3,k.psarakis,a.katsifodimos}@tudelft.nl
[2] Athena Research Center, Athens, Greece
{kpatro,gchatzi,dskoutas,spathan}@athenarc.gr
[3] Fraunhofer IAIS, Sankt Augustin, Germany
diego.collarana.vargas@iais.fraunhofer.de
[4] WIGeoGIS, Vienna, Austria
kb@wigeogis.com

Abstract. The increasing need for data trading across businesses nowadays has created a demand for data marketplaces. However, despite the intentions of both data providers and consumers, today's data marketplaces remain mere data catalogs. We believe that marketplaces of the future require a set of value-added services, such as advanced search and discovery, that have been proposed in the database research community for years, but are not yet put to practice. With this paper, we report on the effort to engineer and develop an open-source modular data market platform to enable both entrepreneurs and researchers to setup and experiment with data marketplaces. To this end, we implemented and extended existing methods for data profiling, dataset search & discovery, and data recommendation. These methods are available as open-source libraries. In this paper we report on how those tools were assembled together to build `topio.market`, a real-world web platform for trading geospatial data, that is currently in a beta phase.

Keywords: Web platform · Data trading · Data marketplace · Open-source

1 Introduction

As the economic value of data becomes more prevalent, data marketplaces (DMs) have emerged, treating data as a commodity and aiming at facilitating and streamlining data trading between data providers and data consumers. Data may be exchanged directly, by offering a dataset itself, or indirectly, by offering services on top of it [3]. DMs can be used to find and acquire specialized and high-quality data that are needed to train ML models, which are in turn crucial for many industrial or societal applications [20]. They can be general-purpose, such as AWS Data Exchange[1] or Datarade,[2] or focused to a specific industry or type of data. For instance, big geospatial data providers (e.g., Carto[3], Here[4]) have recently integrated private marketplaces into their platforms. A DM is typically expected to deal with commercial data assets; nevertheless, as pointed out in [3], there also exist some DMs that generate revenue by monetizing the effort to collect and link open data, making them more easily and readily exploitable.

In this paper, we present Topio marketplace, alongside its main design decisions and the challenges that we had to overcome when developing it. Topio is designed with **openness and reusability** in mind: all of the components are packaged as reusable libraries[5] (e.g., for data discovery, data pipelines, data profiling, etc.). We believe that these reusable libraries can provide value to both researchers and practitioners alike. We also provide descriptions of the different libraries that we have developed, alongside links to their respective repositories. These libraries can be used together to form a platform on which different data marketplaces can be built.

The goal of Topio[6] is to develop a digital single market for proprietary geospatial data, addressing the heterogeneity, disparity, and fragmentation of geospatial data products in a cross-border and inclusive manner. Our goal is inspired by, and grounded on, the real-world landscape and industry-led challenges of the fragmented geospatial data value chain. The Topio marketplace is a central hub and a one-stop shop for the streamlined and trusted discovery, remuneration, sharing, trading, and use of proprietary and commercial geospatial assets [14]. Offering high-quality value-added services, it addresses the heterogeneity, disparity, and fragmentation of geospatial data products. The platform is simple, fast, cost-effective and safe for data providers and data consumers alike. In short, we make the following contributions:

- We provide insights into the needs of users, based on conducted surveys with 122 geospatial data asset providers and consumers (Sect. 3).
- We present the underpinnings of Topio - the first marketplace for geospatial data developed for publishing and purchasing assets which integrates data management tools for profiling and discovery (Sect. 4).
- We illustrate the asset lifecycle process throughout the platform and provide a pragmatic approach towards pricing (Sect. 5).
- We outline a suite of scalable, low-cost value-added services that we built on top of industrial geospatial assets published in the platform (Sect. 6).

---

[1] https://aws.amazon.com/data-exchange/.
[2] https://datarade.ai/.
[3] https://carto.com/spatial-data-catalog/.
[4] https://www.here.com/platform/marketplace.
[5] https://github.com/opertusmundi/.
[6] https://topio.market.

2   Related Work

Data Market Platforms. Although many DMs have emerged over the last few years, they are highly diverse with respect to their characteristics, and the landscape is quite fragmented, lacking any interoperability standards [3]. Moreover, DMs have recently become an active area of research, with many works focusing on investigating pricing policies and models for data [1,7,8,10,21]. Still, DMs deal with many traditional data management challenges, such as data profiling and integration, metadata curation and enrichment, dataset search and recommendation. Such problems have also been studied in the context of data catalogs and data lakes [6,22,25]. These, however, typically deal with open datasets or data exchanged among users of the same organization, whereas data in a marketplace is an asset to be traded. This makes even more imperative the need for mechanisms to facilitate buyers to quickly and easily discover relevant datasets, and to be able to assess the suitability of a candidate dataset for a given task before proceeding to its purchase. Our assessment identified the lack of comprehensive and precise metadata as a significant deficiency of the current market landscape.

Open Data Platforms. Despite the extensive efforts of the research community towards data platforms openness, and their added benefits (e.g. developing data-driven insights and analytics modules) [24,27,28], to the best of our knowledge, there is no existing open-source platform that facilitates building and running data marketplaces. Topio is the first open-source set of tools that can be used to build a data marketplace. At the moment, Topio focuses on spatial data assets, but it can be easily extended to other data models and types.

3   User Surveys

Many data marketplaces or data sharing platforms focus on the data provider, and develop and support features tailored for the provider only [12]. Due to the difference between the viewpoints of the provider and consumer, match-making platforms have started to emerge [3,12]. With Topio, we want to develop and provide a platform which meets the requirements and preferences of both consumers and providers. Therefore, we conducted user surveys to discover and assess the qualities and features needed for a web data market platform from both perspectives: providers (27 responses) and consumers (95 responses).

3.1   Providers

The survey includes questions suitable for extracting user requirements from stakeholders with diverse backgrounds (e.g., geography, information technologies, marketing), roles (e.g., legal experts, analysts, managers, developers), and business fields (e.g., asset production, digitization, geo-marketing). The survey contains 44 questions categorized into five distinct groups: market activity, data assets, contractual life cycle, digital single market, Topio services.

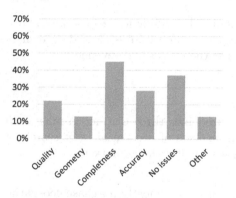 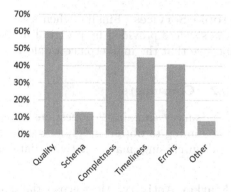

(a) Typical issues raised by the consumers to the providers.

(b) Consumers' challenges when purchasing assets.

Fig. 1. Issues raised by consumers (a) to the providers, and (b) in the survey.

Market Activity. Most data providers currently offer less than ten geospatial data assets for sale, and typically sell two to ten geospatial data assets to the same customer. Moreover, most data providers did not adopt selling the assets via a digital marketplace, and almost half do not provide their assets as a service.

Data Assets. Most of the data providers are also the producers of the assets and do not offer their assets through a catalog or other asset management system. Most geospatial data providers do not offer access to their assets via web services. However, the providers that do, mostly prefer either OGC- (e.g., WMS, WFS), or RESTful API-based services. Finally, the providers reported that most consumers raised issues regarding the completeness of the data, and quite a few reporting complaints about the quality, the accuracy and the geometry of the assets, as illustrated in Fig. 1a.

Contractual Life Cycle. More than 60% of respondents provide their terms and restrictions as part of a contract (i.e., license embedding), while signature of a contract is needed only by 57% of the participating data owners and producers, and to a high extent, a *digital* signature is also accepted. Interestingly, a high number of providers do not need a signed contract. In terms of delivery of purchased data assets, data owners and producers usually deliver the assets through their websites, followed by email and delivery via physical media.

Digital Single Market. More than 95% of the questioned data owners and producers are interested in participating in the marketplace. However, the greatest challenges of joining a digital market platform are the standardization of pricing and contracts, and payment. To participate in a digital market platform, the providers would prefer a fixed commission on the price of each asset sale with no participation fee (42%), followed by zero fees (23%).

Topio Services. Finally, when asked about the willingness to use and adopt the services provided by a digital marketplace, more than 85% of data owners believe that the marketplace would increase their sales and revenue.

3.2 Consumers

The survey contains 25 questions categorized into three distinct groups, each one aiming to obtain insights on different aspects of geospatial asset searching and purchasing: market activity, data assets, digital single market.

Market Activity. Most geospatial data consumers mostly purchase geospatial data assets only once or once a year, and a vast majority of geospatial data consumers use *open* geospatial data assets.

Data Assets. Consumers typically use all census, place names and socio-demographic types of georeferenced data assets. Most consumers use services similar to Google Maps, and many also use OGC, RESTFul and Geospatial Analytics services. The major challenges of consumers are data availability (77%), followed by the lack of information on the quality offered (62%), and the license/contract terms (52%). The surveys also uncovered that the greatest *challenges when purchasing* data assets are their completeness (61%), quality (60%), timeliness (44%), as well as general errors (41%), also illustrated in Fig. 1b.

Digital Single Market. More than 95% of the questioned data consumers are interested in participating in the marketplace. As part of the marketplace, the consumers expect to easily find and purchase assets (85%), to have access to transparent terms and restrictions before purchasing assets (74%), high quality data (65%), transparent costs (63%) and uniform formats (50%).

3.3 Summary

Surveying both data providers and consumers, we observed the indication of a significant market interest and demand for the portfolio of services offered or envisaged by the Topio marketplace.

We identified the need of a digital marketplace for geospatial data assets provision, as most data owners did not embark in offering their assets via a platform. As such, with Topio we plan to offer multiple channels for delivering, visualising and using the data assets in support for the providers who deliver their assets via their website, or even email and physical media.

The survey also indicated that the consumers are in line with the producers in terms of assets format (SHP is the preferred format by both parties) and the usage of services such as OGC, REST APIs. Still, most geospatial data asset consumers also use services similar to Google Maps, which is expected, given the popularity of Google Maps and the bundled functionalities it provides.

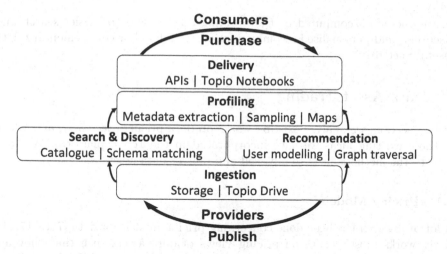

Fig. 2. Platform overview.

The major challenges indicated by the consumers perfectly frame and validate the issues addressed by Topio: make assets easier to publish and discover, and provide industry-focused and relevant metadata. Finally, these responses critically indicate that the actual quality and fit-for-use of a geospatial asset is largely an unknown entity before purchase, which deters both the use of the asset, as well as future purchases.

4   Platform Overview

The design of Topio marketplace is inspired from the insights gathered through surveys. Therefore, we focus on: (*i*) providing as much information about the assets as possible before acquisition; (*ii*) supporting multiple asset formats and delivering them via web services; and (*iii*) providing means to discover and integrate multiple assets with the aim to improve completeness, and quality. Through Topio design, we offer the absolute control of owners over their assets, and our flexible support for real-world value chain instances along the full lifecycle of geospatial data.

Figure 2 provides an overview of the components of Topio marketplace. First, the geospatial assets are ingested and stored in Topio Drive. A data asset is uploaded, versioned, curated, and stored in the underlying storage, and from there delivered to consumers directly transformed in their preferred format. The data asset lifecycle includes publishing, purchasing, delivery and also pricing based on the selected asset delivery option (Sect. 5).

We developed value-added services (VAS), including dataset discovery, recommender system, and profiler, to increase the benefits for the consumers. These benefits are twofold: (*i*) better understanding of the value of the assets based on the metadata computed by the profiling service, and (ii) easier search and discovery, and personalised recommendations of related or complementary data assets (Sect. 6).

5 Data Asset Trading

In this section, we analyze existing works on data pricing (Sect. 5.1), and which of these existing ideas we have incorporated in the Topio platform. We then turn to the methods used to buy, sell and deliver data assets (Sect. 5.2).

5.1 Pricing Models

A lot of research has been done concerning pricing models for data [7,10,17,21]. Early works mostly focus on pricing views of data assets such that they are arbitrage- and discount-free [17]. These pricing schemes are useful for ensuring that: (i) a buyer will not buy "cheaper" views of a dataset whose union costs less than the original dataset, and (ii) the use of these concepts in practice requires both training of the data providers but also a complete pricing market architecture to support such pricing schemes.

During our research for pricing schemes, we investigated the possibility of deriving the prices from selling either subsets of the datasets, or views of those datasets, but this came to be a very challenging task. When talking to data providers during our surveys (Sect. 3), the most common request was that the providers set a price for their dataset and a separate price for each of their derivatives (e.g., a subset of the businesses in France) set by the suppliers.

At this stage, Topio prices datasets in two main ways: (i) pay per dataset; and (ii) pay per API call on a value-added service. The former is the simplest form of pricing: a provider offers a dataset to consumers for a fixed price and can provide discounts on bundles of datasets. For the latter, as described in Sect. 6, when consumers read data from value-added service APIs, providers can set a price per API call. API calls are logged and the consumers are charged on a per-call basis. We also offer consumers the possibility to buy API-call credits e.g., buy 1M calls for a fixed price.

5.2 Data Asset Lifecycle

Asset Provision. The provider of an asset has full and highly-granular control over the asset and can define if, when, and how an asset will be available at any point in time of the asset's lifecycle. An asset (e.g., file, database, service) is provided in a stand-alone manner, as a file with small or ad-hoc transformations, or derived/integrated with other assets. An asset is published in the platform along with its license, price policy, price and contract terms. Publishing can be limited to metadata publishing alone or the metadata and the data asset itself.

Asset Acquisition. Once an asset is uploaded in Topio Drive, the asset is immediately available throughout the application and all the services. The consumers can browse the asset catalog and discover the desired assets based on the available metadata (Sect. 6.1). The consumer retains the right to access and use the assets within the Topio platform through notebooks or maps.

Asset Delivery. Topio delivers the assets and services in three main ways: (*i*) via Jupyter notebooks after establishing an appropriate contractual agreement with the interested party (the platform or another asset owner) governing how joint value is created and shared, (*ii*) a service in one of the available APIs, and frameworks or (*iii*) integrated/derived and provided as a file. Following, we outline the asset delivery approaches.

- *Topio Notebooks.* Topio enables the consumers to directly use all geospatial assets purchased and uploaded, and perform operations such as data cleaning and enrichment, geocoding and trend detection, and analyzing satellite imagery in an online notebook. The notebook is backed by resources provided by Topio, which are charged to the data consumer in a separate agreement. This way, data analysis and transformation can be done without the need to download the assets, enabling the use of high-value/size and complex assets with minimal effort. The integrated discovery service (Sect. 6.2) enables the consumer to discover relevant data for their data analysis workflows while working in the notebooks environment. This way, we can automatically recommend new data sources for enrichment and integration based on the data currently in use.
- *Topio Maps.* Topio Maps is a comprehensive framework for creating, using, sharing, and integrating interactive maps in web and mobile applications. The consumer can create custom maps using not only the data and services provided by the platform, but also proprietary data.
- *Physical Delivery.* Finally, the purchase and delivery of the asset is performed within or outside the platform, according to owner preferences and asset type. When the files are very large or other constraints become an issue (e.g., company policies), data assets can be physically shipped to consumers.

6 Value-Added Services

Our surveys indicate that both providers and consumers face challenges coming from the assets themselves, such as quality, geometry, schema and most important: completeness and accuracy. The value added services (VAS) provide a step forward towards facilitating asset completeness and accuracy, as they help discover new assets suitable for integration. Moreover, VAS help us to circumvent the deadlock where the consumer is unsure about the quality of the data, while the provider is not willing to reveal more information prior to payment.

As such, we have developed and integrated the following open-source value-added services: (*i*) data asset profiling (Sect. 6.1) to automatically extract various

Fig. 3. View of asset details and metadata before purchase.

kinds of information from the content of a given asset and enrich its description, (*ii*) data asset search and discovery (Sect. 6.2) which offers metadata-, faceted-, keyword-based search functionalities throughout `Topio`'s catalog, and helps the user find related assets, and (*iii*) data asset recommendation (Sect. 6.3) to recommend to the consumer new assets based on already purchased, used, or visualised assets.

6.1 Data Asset Profiling

According to the user surveys (Sect. 3), providing comprehensive and precise metadata to prospective buyers for a given asset before a purchase increase transparency and trust. These observations led us towards prioritizing and strengthening the generation of automated metadata as a differentiator and unique selling point for the `Topio` marketplace.

Data profiling[7] comprises a collection of operations and processes for extracting metadata from a given dataset [26]. Such metadata may involve schema information, statistics, samples, or other informative summaries over the data, thus offering extensive and objective indicators for assessing datasets. This com-

---

[7] https://github.com/OpertusMundi/profile.

Table 1. Metadata computed based on the asset type.

Type	Level	Metadata
Vector & Tabular	Dataset	Feature count
	Thematic attributes	Names, data types, cardinality, distribution, N-tiles, unique values, frequency, value pattern type, special data types, keywords per column numerical value patterns, numerical statistics, correlation among numerical attributes, equi-width histogram, date/time value distribution, geometry type distribution, attribute uniqueness, compliance to well-known schema
	Geometry	Native CRS, Spatial extent, convex/concave hull, heatmap, clusters, thumbnail generation
Raster	Dataset	Native CRS; Spatial extent
	Raster specific	Resolution; Width, height; COG
	Band related	Number of bands; Band statistics; Value distribution; Pixel (bit) depth; NoData Value(s)
Multi-dimensional	Dataset	Native CRS; Dimension count/info; Variable count/info
	Variable related	Spatial extent; Temporal range; Value distribution; NoData Value(s)

ponent can be internally invoked as part of the data publishing workflow, or on demand when searching and browsing for datasets, as illustrated in Fig. 3.

The geospatial datasets can be organized in various types, commonly vector (and tabular), raster, and multi-dimensional. Although some of the profiling metadata are common among various data types (e.g., native CRS and spatial extent for spatial data), in principle a different set of metadata is used for each data type. Some of the metadata characterize the dataset as a whole (e.g., feature count for vector and tabular assets), while other metadata apply only on a specific feature of the data type. A summary of the metadata computed based on the asset type is listed in Table 1.

To compute the data profiles and metadata, we created BigDataVoyant [23], which repurposes and extends various existing open source software, bundled together in a streamlined and scalable manner. Data profiling for each type of supported data type (i.e., vector, tabular, raster, multidimensional) is handled by a separate software component in the profiler, and specifically: (*i*) GeoVaex[8]

---

[8] https://github.com/OpertusMundi/geovaex.

(an extension of Vaex [5]) developed for out-of-memory processing of vector assets, (*ii*) GDAL/OGR for raster assets, and (*iii*) the netCDF Python module for multi-dimensional assets.

6.2 Data Asset Search and Discovery

Advanced Search. Topio offers rich search capabilities with a wide range of optional filtering criteria so that prospective data consumers can quickly identify assets of their interest. All search operations are powered by indexing all assets and their metadata in the backend and thus supporting various search conditions (textual, numerical, spatial, temporal, etc.). Some of the filtering conditions may come from a set of pre-defined choices (e.g., asset types, file formats), while others can be user-specified (e.g., price range), enabling potential consumers to narrow down their selection to assets that mostly match their preferences based on multiple filtering criteria. The platform uses tools such as Postgres full text indexing as well as Elasticsearch.

Data Asset Discovery. Dataset discovery is the process of navigating numerous datasets in order to find relevant ones and the relationships between them [16]. The output of a discovery process represents the initial step in a data management pipeline and the input for schema matching, mapping and the subsequent processes [16]. In Topio, the discovery service[9] allows end users to explore the collection of datasets by examining and understanding the relations between them and how they interconnect. This process enables the users to make informed purchasing decisions, as they get more knowledgeable and understand the different layers of relatedness between the assets.

The data asset discovery process is primarily used with tabular data, such as CSV, web tables, and spreadsheets [16]. For geospatial data assets, the typical discovery process adopts methods from the Semantic Web, primarily using RDF and ontologies [4,19], while data mining and knowledge discovery approaches put more emphasis on searching for co-location patterns given location points [13]. In the context of data market platforms, where different types of datasets can be published and transformed for purchasing, we employ the methodologies existing in structured tabular data for geospatial data. As such, we reduce system complexity by utilizing the metadata extracted using the profiler component of the platform, previously described in Sect. 6.1. Such metadata is used as a filtering step to reduce the number of datasets to process for discovery. We use open-source software to transform geodata into CSV, such as mapshaper [11]. The tool addresses the challenges posed by geodata formats (e.g., Shapefiles, GeoJSON), which are non-topological data formats (i.e., do not store topological relationships between adjacent polygons). As such, the transformed files are compatible with existing open-source discovery services [15], which rely on schema matching algorithms for capturing semantic or syntactic relationships between datasets [16].

---

[9] https://github.com/OpertusMundi/discovery-service

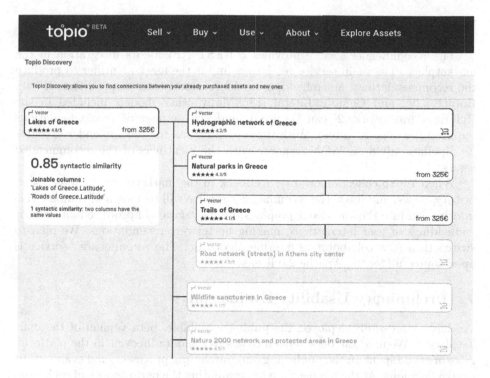

Fig. 4. View of the asset discovery and augmentation process.

Using the transformed assets, the discovery service is further used to discover assets which can be augmented. The approach leverages join paths traversal and ranking. We rank the join paths using a function integrated with feature importance measures, in order to reduce the set of joined tables returned to the user [15]. Then, using transitive joins, we determine the assets which are most appropriate for augmentation. Finally, we present all the assets used along the transitive join paths to improve the user experience through explanations. Figure 4 shows an example of the data asset discovery process used for augmentation.

6.3 Data Asset Recommendation

Topio provides contextualized asset recommendations to marketplace users, allowing the discovery of a wide range of related geospatial assets. Topio's recommender service combines several data sources from the marketplace into a consolidated knowledge graph following the DCAT[10] ontology. This knowledge graph serves as an expressive and powerful data structure that naturally models the user-item marketplace interactions. Then the recommender service applies knowledge graph embedding (KGE) models [9] to embed assets from the graph

---

[10] https://www.w3.org/TR/vocab-dcat-2/.

into a vector representation. Finally, the cosine function calculates the similarity among data assets in the graph.

The recommender service provides a REST API for its integration in the marketplace. The main service receives as input the asset identifier to produce the recommendations, an embedding model (currently, we support TransH [30], RotatE [29], and ComplExLiteral [18]. Many other models included in the PyKEEN framework [2] can be used), and the number of recommendations required (by default, three). With these parameters, the recommender executes its pipelines, giving a JSON response with the identifiers of the recommended assets.

When Topio collects more user feedback in the marketplace, such as search history, views, and buys, the recommender service will include and combine this information into the knowledge graph. More metadata will produce more robust embeddings of user interactions, making better recommendations. We plan to switch then to a collaborative filtering algorithm. The recommender service is open-source under the Apache 2.0 license[11].

7   Preliminary Usability Evaluation

We have successfully deployed the publicly available, beta version of the marketplace[12]. We used the beta version to assess the data lifecycle in the platform, measure time spent on the publishing and purchasing processes, and evaluate our design decisions. At the moment, we are evaluating the performance of each component (e.g., discovery service, recommender, profiler, etc.) using data gathered from the interactions of suppliers and consumers on our platform. However, this evaluation requires more users and specific experiments to be conducted. Until those experiments are completed, we have done preliminary investigation of how much time is required for publishing and purchasing assets. More specifically:

- Publishing an asset by an novice supplier (i.e., supplier with less than two assets published) takes on average three minutes from process start, to submission for review. We do not account for the time to upload an asset which is dependent on the size of the asset. Publishing an asset by an experienced supplier (i.e., supplier with more than five assets published) takes on average 25 s. Most suppliers opted to add optional metadata in the publishing wizard, which is a positive outcome as suppliers understand that the more metadata available, the easier for users to discover and purchase their assets.
- A supplier with an existing published asset spends, on average, five minutes to create an OGC service operationalized by topio.market. Most of this time is allocated to deciding the pricing of the created asset, rather than completing the wizard. This is an interesting insight as we did not observe it for data publishing; suppliers generally know well in advance the price they want to set. However, operationalizing their data represents a new market activity, and more consideration is needed to allocate the price point.

---

[11] https://github.com/OpertusMundi/recommender-system.
[12] https://beta.topio.market.

– The average time required for a prospective client to complete an asset purchase from visiting the cart, until asset delivery is 12 s. This is an expected duration as we based on the assumption that purchasing data assets does not differ from a standard e-shop.

8 Conclusion and Future Work

With Topio, we aim at laying the foundation for future open data marketplaces. The many components of the platform are openly available[13] and represent the starting point towards open web engineering and development. We have developed flexible and automated facilities for managing the entire lifecycle of geospatial asset trading, but these components can easily be extended to work beyond spatial data. By talking to data providers, we have come to the conclusion that commercial geodata products are updated and offered by data suppliers in regular intervals, which enables more research and development opportunities (e.g., (meta)data versioning, provenance, etc.). At the same time, providers find it very useful to use Topio to automatically offer and sell small regional data extracts/views (e.g. socio-demographics for three out of 11000 municipalities in Germany). Small regional views always require manual preparation, delivery and billing. For suppliers, there is always a lot of effort and little return, so Topio is of particular benefit to vendors in these cases. Consumers also benefit because the costs of the data extracts are reduced.

Future work for the market platform includes and is not limited to: (*i*) experimenting with different pricing algorithms and making them available for suppliers who are uncertain about pricing their assets, (*ii*) enhancing the user experience while working in Topio Notebooks by providing easy access to the data samples from the platform, (*iii*) giving the consumers the possibility to discover related assets and augmentation possibilities between existing assets from the marketplace and proprietary assets which they can upload on demand.

References

1. Agarwal, A., Dahleh, M., Sarkar, T.: A marketplace for data: an algorithmic solution. In: EC 2019, pp. 701–726 (2019)
2. Ali, M., et al.: PyKEEN 1.0: a Python library for training and evaluating knowledge graph embeddings. J. Mach. Learn. Res. **22**, 82:1–82:6 (2021)
3. Azcoitia, S.A., Laoutaris, N.: A survey of data marketplaces and their business models. SIGMOD Rec. **51**(3), 18–29 (2022)
4. Batcheller, J.K., Reitsma, F.: Implementing feature level semantics for spatial data discovery: supporting the reuse of legacy data using open source components. Comput. Environ. Urban Syst. **34**(4), 333–344 (2010)
5. Breddels, M.A., Veljanoski, J.: Vaex: big data exploration in the era of Gaia. Astron. Astrophys. **618**, A13 (2018)
6. Chapman, A., et al.: Dataset search: a survey. VLDB J. **29**(1), 251–272 (2020)

---

[13] https://github.com/OpertusMundi.

7. Chawla, S., Deep, S., Koutrisw, P., Teng, Y.: Revenue maximization for query pricing. Proc. VLDB Endow. **13**(1), 1–14 (2019)
8. Chen, L., Koutris, P., Kumar, A.: Towards model-based pricing for machine learning in a data marketplace. In: SIGMOD, pp. 1535–1552 (2019)
9. Chu, Y., Yao, J., Zhou, C., Yang, H.: Graph Neural Networks in Modern Recommender Systems. Springer, Singapore (2022)
10. Fernandez, R.C., Subramaniam, P., Franklin, M.J.: Data market platforms: trading data assets to solve data problems. Proc. VLDB Endow. **13**(12), 1933–1947 (2020)
11. Harrower, M., Bloch, M.: Mapshaper.org: a map generalization web service. IEEE Comput. Graph. Appl. **26**(4), 22–27 (2006)
12. Hayashi, T., Ohsawa, Y.: TEEDA: an interactive platform for matching data providers and users in the data marketplace. Information **11**(4), 218 (2020)
13. Huang, Y., Shekhar, S., Xiong, H.: Discovering colocation patterns from spatial data sets: a general approach. IEEE TKDE **16**(12), 1472–1485 (2004)
14. Ionescu, A., et al.: Topio marketplace: search and discovery of geospatial data. In: EDBT (2023)
15. Ionescu, A., Hai, R., Fragkoulis, M., Katsifodimos, A.: Join path-based data augmentation for decision trees. In: IEEE ICDEW, pp. 84–88. IEEE (2022)
16. Koutras, C., et al.: Valentine: evaluating matching techniques for dataset discovery. In: IEEE ICDE, pp. 468–479. IEEE (2021)
17. Koutris, P., Upadhyaya, P., Balazinska, M., Howe, B., Suciu, D.: Query-based data pricing. J. ACM (JACM) **62**(5), 1–44 (2015)
18. Kristiadi, A., Khan, M.A., Lukovnikov, D., Lehmann, J., Fischer, A.: Incorporating literals into knowledge graph embeddings. In: Ghidini, C., et al. (eds.) ISWC 2019. LNCS, vol. 11778, pp. 347–363. Springer, Cham (2019). https://doi.org/10.1007/978-3-030-30793-6_20
19. Lacasta, J., Nogueras-Iso, J., Béjar, R., Muro-Medrano, P.R., Zarazaga-Soria, F.J.: A web ontology service to facilitate interoperability within a spatial data infrastructure: applicability to discovery. Data Knowl. Eng. **63**(3), 947–971 (2007)
20. Li, Y., Yu, X., Koudas, N.: Data acquisition for improving machine learning models. Proc. VLDB Endow. **14**(10), 1832–1844 (2021)
21. Liang, F., Yu, W., An, D., Yang, Q., Fu, X., Zhao, W.: A survey on big data market: pricing, trading and protection. IEEE Access **6**, 15132–15154 (2018)
22. Miller, R.J., Nargesian, F., Zhu, E., Christodoulakis, C., Pu, K.Q., Andritsos, P.: Making open data transparent: data discovery on open data. IEEE Data Eng. Bull. **41**(2), 59–70 (2018)
23. Mitropoulos, P., Patroumpas, K., Skoutas, D., Vakkas, T., Athanasiou, S.: BigDataVoyant: automated profiling of large geospatial data. In: EDBT/ICDT Workshops (2021)
24. Mucha, T., Seppala, T.: Artificial intelligence platforms–a new research agenda for digital platform economy (2020)
25. Nargesian, F., Zhu, E., Miller, R.J., Pu, K.Q., Arocena, P.C.: Data lake management: challenges and opportunities. Proc. VLDB Endow. **12**(12), 1986–1989 (2019)
26. Naumann, F.: Data profiling revisited. ACM SIGMOD Rec. **42**(4), 40–49 (2014)
27. Niculescu, M.F., Wu, D., Xu, L.: Strategic intellectual property sharing: competition on an open technology platform under network effects. Inf. Syst. Res. **29**(2), 498–519 (2018)
28. de Reuver, M., Ofe, H., Agahari, W., Abbas, A.E., Zuiderwijk, A.: The openness of data platforms: a research agenda. In: Proceedings of the 1st International Workshop on Data Economy, pp. 34–41 (2022)

29. Sun, Z., Deng, Z., Nie, J., Tang, J.: Rotate: Knowledge graph embedding by relational rotation in complex space. In: 7th International Conference on Learning Representations, ICLR 2019, New Orleans, LA, USA, 6–9 May 2019 (2019)
30. Wang, Z., Zhang, J., Feng, J., Chen, Z.: Knowledge graph embedding by translating on hyperplanes. In: AAAI, pp. 1112–1119. AAAI Press (2014)

Demos and Posters

Creating Searchable Web Page Snapshots Using Semantic Technologies

Radek Burget[✉][iD] and Hamza Salem[iD]

Brno University of Technology, Faculty of Information Technology, Bozetechova 2, 61266 Brno, Czechia
burgetr@fit.vut.cz, xsalem00@stud.fit.vutbr.cz

Abstract. For many applications, it is necessary to create snapshots of web pages that accurately describe how the page appeared in a browser at a given point in time. Storing the original code (even if all referenced resources are included) and creating bitmap screenshots have many drawbacks when it comes to searching, viewing, and manipulating such snapshots. In this paper, we demonstrate a different approach that uses a remotely controlled web browser to render web pages. We capture the complete information about the rendered page and all of its content, transform it into an explicit RDF-based model representation, and store it in a repository. The stored page models can then be explored using interactive web-based tools, exported in various formats, linked to other data sources, and queried using SPARQL. We also include several application scenarios that demonstrate the benefits of the proposed approach.

Keywords: Web page snapshot · Page rendering · Web data extraction · RDF · SPARQL

1 Introduction

In many situations related to working with information published on the web, we need to create snapshots of web pages that capture the web page as it was rendered by the web browser at that particular moment as accurately as possible. The typical motivation for this is to document the source of information obtained from the web for different purposes, that include:

- Monitoring web content that changes over time (such as product prices, real estate, etc.)
- Creation of datasets for evaluation of various web content processing algorithms (such as data extraction, page segmentation, etc.) [1,3]
- Preparing training data for machine learning-based algorithms that analyze the visual presentation of the content [4], and more.

In many of these scenarios, the visual presentation of the content is as important as the content itself. In product monitoring, for example, we want to answer

I. Garrigós et al. (Eds.): ICWE 2023, LNCS 13893, pp. 355–358, 2023.
https://doi.org/10.1007/978-3-031-34444-2_26

questions retrospectively, such as: Was the product price visually marked as discounted? Was the information presented in the correct context? Also, many automated data extraction methods depend on the visual presentation of the content, and for their evaluation it is necessary to create the corresponding datasets [4,6,7]. In such scenarios, it is not sufficient to store the text content or the HTML code of the source page, as we lose the visual context.

Traditional approaches to archiving web pages typically rely on storing the HTML code of the web page along with other resources needed to render the page again. This is how the Internet Archive[1] works, for example. However, to reconstruct the visual appearance of the page from such a snapshot, we need to get a web browser to "replay" the archived content. This is a time-consuming task, and the result may not fully match the original appearance of the page because browsers evolve over time, they may run in different environments with different fonts available, and the pages may contain links to third-party dynamic content (such as advertisements) that cannot be efficiently stored [5]. The other option is to take a bitmap screenshot of the rendered page, which is easy to save and view later, but its content cannot be efficiently searched and/or annotated.

In this demo, we present a complementary approach that is based on capturing the complete information about a rendered page and each piece of its content from the web browser, transforming it into an explicit RDF model, and storing it in a central repository. We show, how the snapshots can be created, inspected via an interactive web interface, exported in a variety of formats ranging from XML and Turtle to plain bitmap screenshots, and possibly linked to other data such as structured data (JSON-LD) annotations.

Related Work. Traditional formats for archiving web pages include the standardized WARC[2] (ISO 28500), which stores the original HTML code along with additional resources such as style sheets, scripts, images, and other content referenced from HTML. The MHTML[3] file format and the HAR file format[4] are based on similar principles. Published datasets of web pages typically use one of these formats. For example, SWDE [3] or WEIR [1] consist of HTML files only, Kiesel et al. [5] use the WARC format, and Hotti et al. [4] use MHTML files. To annotate the captured pages with additional information, separate files in specific formats (such as text files or bitmap screenshots) must be used [1,3,6], or specific attributes can be added to the original HTML files [4]. In [2], the authors suggest building additional RDF-based semantic layers on top of such page archives to allow searching and linking of the stored documents and the data they contain.

The approach we present in this paper does not aim to replace the existing possibilities mentioned above. Unlike [2], we don't intend to semantically

---

[1] http://archive.org/.

[2] http://bibnum.bnf.fr/WARC/.

[3] https://www.rfc-editor.org/info/rfc2557.

[4] A W3C proposal that never became a standard but is supported by software tools such as Playwright.

describe the content of the pages, but rather their visual representation, which is missing in the archives. We provide an additional "searchable screenshot": A detailed representation of the rendered page, which is explicitly described using semantic technologies, can be browsed, linked to other data, and queried using the standard SPARQL language, allowing important information to be extracted from the collected set of pages. We also show how the content and presentation models can be combined to infer new knowledge from the web pages.

2 Creating an RDF Model of a Rendered Page

The rendering of an HTML document in modern browsers is driven by the CSS Visual Formatting Model[5]. In this model, each HTML element generates 0 to n boxes, which correspond to rectangular areas in the rendered page with the given position, size, and content. The visual properties of the content (such as colors and fonts) are defined by the computed style of the source element.

To obtain a model of the rendered page, we use the Puppeteer or Playwright library[6], which allows us to open the target page in a Chromium browser running in the background (headless mode) with configurable output media properties. After the page is rendered, we run our JavaScript code that extracts the generated boxes and their properties. This is not trivial, as the relevant APIs are partly experimental and not well documented, and many aspects of the browser behavior had to be discovered experimentally. Next, we organize the extracted boxes into a tree according to their visual nesting in the rendered page. The resulting box tree is similar to a DOM tree, but it describes the computed visual structure, which may differ from the structure of the code.

Finally, we describe the boxes and their relationships with RDF statements with the use of the vocabulary provided by our Box Model Ontology[7], which we published in [7]. We also describe the properties of the entire page, including an optional reference screenshot. The resulting model can be stored in an RDF repository and queried using SPARQL and/or serialized to a file.

The proposed architecture also allows the headless browser to be easily replaced by a client browser extension installed directly on the user's computer. This would allow to capture page snapshots interactively while preserving the user's current context. This is currently a work in progress.

3 Implementation and Applications

We implemented the described process using our FitLayout Web Page Analysis Framework[8]. It uses RDF4J as the RDF storage and also provides an interactive web GUI (Java backend with REST API and a Vue.js based frontend application) to inspect the created page snapshots and to submit SPARQL queries and browse the results.

---

[5] https://www.w3.org/TR/CSS22/visuren.html.
[6] We support both options with the same functionality.
[7] http://fitlayout.github.io/ontology/render.html.
[8] https://github.com/FitLayout/FitLayout.

```
SELECT ?label ?fsize ?area WHERE {
  ?area rdfs:label ?label . ?area b:fontSize ?fsize .
  ?area a:hasTag ?tag . ?tag map:isValueOf <http://schema.org/name>
} ORDER BY DESC(?fsize)
```

Fig. 1. SPARQL query to retrieve content elements that are linked to a given schema.org property, and the font sizes of those elements.

In addition to storing and later browsing a detailed model of a rendered page, the main applications considered include (i) creating links between structured data provided as JSON-LD or RDFa and its visual presentation on the page (see Fig. 1 for a sample query), (ii) discovering regular presentation patterns used in a page or set of pages, (iii) searching for specific content based on both textual and visual properties (e.g., position, font sizes, colors, text length, keyword occurrences, etc.), or even (iv) searching for content elements that have a visually represented relationship (e.g., all text strings preceded by a red label).

4   Conclusions

In this demo, we presented the use of semantic technologies to create an explicit model of a rendered page. The created model can be stored and linked to other data sources (such as JSON-LD content annotations based on schema.org or other vocabularies), and allows making SPARQL queries that involve the visual presentation, as we demonstrated in several applications.

Acknowledgements. This work was supported by project Smart information technology for a resilient society, FIT-S-23-8209, funded by Brno University of Technology.

References

1. Bronzi, M., Crescenzi, V., Merialdo, P., Papotti, P.: Extraction and integration of partially overlapping web sources. Proc. VLDB Endow. **6**(10), 805–816 (2013)
2. Fafalios, P., Holzmann, H., Kasturia, V., Nejdl, W.: Building and querying semantic layers for web archives. In: 2017 ACM/IEEE JCDL Conference, pp. 1–10 (2017)
3. Hao, Q., Cai, R., Pang, Y., Zhang, L.: From one tree to a forest: a unified solution for structured web data extraction, In: SIGIR 2011, NY, USA, pp. 775–784 (2011)
4. Hotti, A., Risuleo, R.S., Magureanu, S., Moradi, A., Lagergren, J.: Graph neural networks for nomination and representation learning of web elements (2021)
5. Kiesel, J., et al.: Reproducible web corpora: interactive archiving with automatic quality assessment. J. Data Inf. Qual. **10**(4), 1–25 (2018)
6. Kiesel, J., et al.: Web page segmentation revisited: evaluation framework and dataset. In: 29th ACM CKIM Conference, pp. 3047–3054. New York (2020)
7. Milička, M., Burget, R.: Information extraction from web sources based on multi-aspect content analysis. In: SemWebEval 2015 at ESWC 2015, pp. 81–92. No. 548 (2015)

Choose your Preferred Life Cycle and SofIA will do the Rest

María-José Escalona[1]([✉])[ID], Laura García-Borgoñon[2][ID],
Julián García-García[1][ID], Guillermo López-Nicolás[2][ID],
and Nora Parcus de Koch[1][ID]

[1] Universidad de Sevilla, Seville, Spain
{mjescalona,juliangg,norakoch}@us.es
[2] Instituto Tecnológico de Aragón, Zaragoza, Spain
{laurag,glopez}@itainnova.es
https://es3.us.es// , https://www.itainnova.es/es

Abstract. The importance of requirements engineering for software quality is well-understood in industry. It is also clear that requirements engineers need tools that do not prescribe only one type of development process. This paper presents an overview of SofIA, a CASE tool that provides maximum flexibility when modeling functionality, data or prototypes because it can use any given model to generate other models. SofIA is built on the experience acquired from having used the previous NDT-Suite in industrial projects for more than two decades. It achieves its objectives by supporting bidirectional transformations and guaranteeing traceability between all models. Initial evaluations performed in the academic environment have shown that students require less training and feel more comfortable when following their own modeling process.

Keywords: Requirements modeling · Mockups · Early testing · Model verification · Bidirectional traceability

1 Introduction

Quality software development is a complex issue that continues to pose many challenges. Development methodologies have evolved and have had to adapt to different life cycles, such as waterfall and iterative processes, and to different management models, including agile modes. SofIA (Software Methodology for Industrial Applications) is a proposal for models and artifacts that is accompanied by a CASE tool of the same name. In this work, we present an overview of the SofIA tool. SofIA is inspired by an earlier proposal called NDT (Navigational Development Techniques), and its corresponding tool, NDT-Suite [2]. NDT is a model-driven methodological environment that has been widely used in the industry over the last twenty years. Thanks to the lessons learned, SofIA

Supported by Nico Project (PID2019-105455GB-C31). Ministerio de Ciencia, Innovación y Universidades.

incorporates new research results that improve the NDT proposal and increase its applicability in industrial projects. The most notable features are: (1) SofIA proposes not just one specific life cycle but alternatives regarding on the models used as starting point. The artifacts of its metamodels are related by bidirectional traceability. (2) This bidirectional traceability allows the developers to start with the approach they find most comfortable. For example, some teams prefer to develop prototypes as the first element, while others prefer first to elaborate the functional requirements or to start with a conceptual model. SofIA supports all three of these approaches because they are all linked by transformations that allow a model to be generated from the others. (3) SofIA offers transformation-based model synchronization to guarantee consistency. This ensures that if either of two artifacts changes, the analyst can trace their relationship and check that the change does not produce any inconsistency between them. As mentioned, this work presents the tool that supports the SofIA methodology. Section 2 offers an overview of the tool and its architecture and explains how the three indicated improvements were implemented. Section 3 describes the first validations that were carried out. The article ends with some conclusions and ideas for future work in Sect. 4.

2   SofIA in a Nutshell

SofIA was designed using the four-level architecture [3], that has traditionally been used to establish relationship between models and metamodels (see Fig. 1): **M3 (metametamodel level).** Following the OMG MDA architecture, MOF was established as the meta-metamodeling language. **M2 (metamodel level).** Here, metamodels were defined describing M1 level models and the traceability between them. SofIA incorporates mainly aspects related to requirements (functional, UX/UI, interaction flow) and testing. **M1 (model level).** This level includes models that represent the reality of M0 level are included at this level. The following models were included in SofIA: class diagrams, use cases, scenarios, tests, prototypes, interaction flows. **M0 (real world level).** Real world data and information was incorporated. Two engines, denominated Driver and Quality, were developed. As can be seen, SofIA's main contribution was at the M2, M1 and M0 levels. At the M2 level, five metamodels representing the SofIA concepts and their relationships were defined: Conceptual, Functional Requirements, Prototype, Testing and Interaction Flow. A Traceability metamodel [1] was also included, establishing conceptual traceability connections between the different elements of the metamodels. The Traceability metamodel implements bidrectional formal transformations that help to keep the consistence between models. At the M1 level, models conforming to the previous metamodels used in the proposal were selected. Thus, for the Conceptual metamodel a UML class diagram was incorporated, while for the Functional Requirements metamodel a UML use case model and one or more scenario models were included. For the prototypes metamodel a mockups model was introduced and, the IFM metamodel incorporated an interaction flow model using the IFM Language. Finally, at the M0

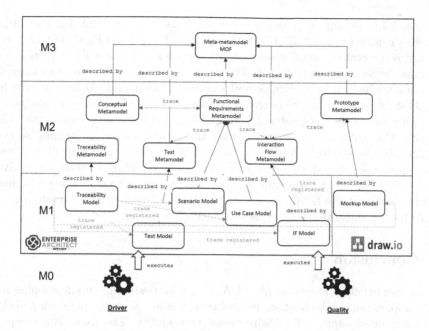

Fig. 1. SofIA's architecture

level, we included transformation (named Driver) and traceability (named Quality) engines to give SofIA three fundamental features: the engines perform transformations, establish and maintain bidirectional traceability between models as described in level M2, and ensure that models are well-formed, that is to say, they conform to the corresponding metamodels, including their constraints. In accordance with the definition of MDE solution proposed in [4], SofIA was built up by using the facilities provided by the Enterprise Architect (EA) and Draw.io tools to incorporate the necessary metamodels, models and transformations. EA offered the capability to extend base UML modeling elements through profiles to include our own metamodels and modeling tools (i.e., diagrams or toolboxes). It also provided an Add-In facility, which enabled us to extend default functionalities using our own code. Add-Ins are the best way to implement transformations and maintain bidirectional traceability. However, EA is not user friendly for the quick design of sketches as mockups, hence the inclusion in SofIA of Draw.io, an intuitive web tool, that makes it possible to develop their own toolboxes, add tags to convert elements into metaclasses, and import/export models into XML format to maintain consistency between prototypes and all other models.

3   Evaluation

SofIA is currently being evaluated in academic and industrial contexts, but some preliminary results from the academic environment can already be reported. In this regard, we have analyzed the number of meetings and training sessions requested by 29 computer engineering students using SOFIA for their Final Degree Projects (16 FDP; 55,17% ratio) and NDT-Suite (13 FDP; 44.83% ratio). Here, it is relevant to mention the evaluation context: (1) these FDPs were of similar complexity in terms of factors like use cases, data entities and mockups; (2) the students had just one a single SofIA training video; and (3) the students had 8 NDT-Suite audiovisual resources (manuals, YouTube videos, research papers, etc.) plus an example of a software project designed with the previous tool. Considering this scenario, we observed that the total number of training sessions required by the students was higher when the previous environment was used. More specifically, the students required 46 and 35 training sessions, respectively when using NDT-Suite and SofIA respectively. On average, these preliminary results show that the flexibility and automation offered by SofIA made it possible to reduce the training sessions by 23.91%.

4   Conclusions

This paper briefly presents SofIA, a CASE tool for designing and developing software applications, which offers flexibility regarding starting points for designs and automated support for bidirectional traceability. The focus is on requirements engineering and the building of mock-ups, use cases and data structure models. The SofIA architecture is based on the four levels M3 to MO of the OMG MDE definition and was created by extending the Enterprise Architect and Draw.io tools. So far, the tool has been validated by students working on their Final Degree Projects. In the future we will extend SofIA's metamodels to support modeling of additional requirements, such as security or accessibility. We also want to explore the possibility of adding heuristics, patterns, and even some machine learning protocols to help analysts define their requirements in a high quality. One future task will be to implementation additional alternatives regarding requirements models. We already started using SofIA in some transfer projects, but these are still in their initial phases, so it is still too early to present any results. We plan to use and evaluate SofIA in controlled software experiments in industrial projects in the near future.

References

1. Escalona, M.J., Koch, N., García-Borgoñón, L.: Lean requirements traceability automation enabled by model-driven engineering. PeerJ Comput. Sci. **8**, e817 (2022)
2. García García, J.A., Escalona, M.J., Domínguez, F.J., Salido, A.: NDT-Suite: a methodological tool solution in the model-driven engineering paradigm. J. Softw. Eng. Appl. **7**(4), 206–217 (2014)
3. González, C., Henderson, B.: Metamodelling for Software Engineering. Wiley, Hoboken (2008)
4. Molina, J.G., Rubio, F.O.G., Pelechano, V., Vallecillo, A., Vara, J.M., Vicente-Chicote, C.: Desarrollo de software dirigido por modelos: conceptos, métodos y herramientas. Alfaomega (2014)

SLA4OAI-Analyzer: Automated Validation of RESTful API Pricing Plans

Rafael Fresno-Aranda(✉)(iD), Pablo Fernández(iD), and Antonio Ruiz-Cortés(iD)

SCORE Lab, I3US Institute, Universidad de Sevilla, Seville, Spain
{rfresno,pablofm,aruiz}@us.es

Abstract. Nowadays, public web APIs are considered as business assets by many organizations. They provide data and functionality which other developers can integrate within their own services. These APIs are commercialized through pricings, which include a series of plans. Each plan contains features and limitations, coupled with a price. Developers who wish to use the API need to choose which plan better suits their needs. The formal description of pricings is not standardized, which hinders the ability to automate their analysis. The SLA4OAI specification aims to provide an extension for OpenAPI that allows pricings to be described. This specification paves the way for an ecosystem of tools that leverage the information of a pricing.

In this paper, we present SLA4OAI-Analyzer, a public API that automatically checks an SLA4OAI specification file for conflicts at different levels. We also provide an online Jupyter notebook to validate the API using different examples.

Keywords: Automation · Validity · REST · API · Pricing

1 Introduction

Nowadays, public web APIs are considered as business assets by many organizations. They provide data and functionality which other software developers can integrate within their own services. This has been boosted by the growing popularity of cloud-based and service-oriented architectures, which promote isolation and integration of different components through APIs. In this scenario, organizations commercialize their APIs through *pricings*, which include a series of *plans*. Each plan comprises a set of features and usage restrictions (limitations), coupled with a price that is usually a periodic subscription or pay-as-you-go.

This work has been partially supported by grants RTI2018-101204-B-C21, RTI2018-101204-B-C22, PID2021-126227NB-C21, PID2021-126227NB-C22, TED2021-131023B-C21, TED2021-131023B-C22, PDC2022-133521-I00 funded by MCIN/AEI/10.130 39/501100011033 and "ERDF a way of making Europe"; grants PYC20 RE 084 US, P18-FR-2895, US-1264651, US-1381595 funded by Junta de Andalucia/ERDF,UE; and FPU19/00666 funded by MCIN/AEI/10.13039/501100011033 and by "ESF Investing in your future".

I. Garrigós et al. (Eds.): ICWE 2023, LNCS 13893, pp. 363–366, 2023.
https://doi.org/10.1007/978-3-031-34444-2_28

Developers who wish to use the API need to choose between the different plans and subscribe to the one that better suits their needs.

Out of the different types of web APIs, RESTful APIs [8] are currently the most popular. They define each operation as an HTTP request that contains a URL, an HTTP method and a set of required or optional parameters. The RESTful paradigm integrates well within cloud-based architectures, in which different services communicate with each other through HTTP requests. There has been an ongoing effort to standardize the functional description of RESTful APIs. As of today, the de-facto standard is the OpenAPI Specification (OAS) [2], which has been adopted by many organizations to describe their APIs. This has fostered the creation of an ecosystem of tools that leverage the information in an OAS description for several purposes. Some examples include automated generation of mock servers or test cases [11].

Nonetheless, the non-functional description of an API (e.g. its pricing) is not part of OAS and its definition is up to the API provider [10]. This makes it harder to leverage the information included in a pricing, because each organization may describe it in a completely different way. Furthermore, it is difficult to check the validity and correctness of a pricing when its description is not standardized. In our previous work, we presented SLA4OAI[1] [6], a proposed extension of OAS that includes non-functional information and aims to overcome the aforementioned issues. It is a work-in-progress specification, written in JSON or YAML, that is under discussion by organizations and practitioners [7]. The formal description of an API pricing is useful, for example, to check for its correctness or automatically choose the best plans based on user needs [9].

In this demo, we present **SLA4OAI-Analyzer**, a RESTful API that automatically validates an SLA4OAI specification file and detects different types of conflicts. We also provide an online Jupyter notebook [5] to validate the API. The demo video is available at https://vimeo.com/803184037.

2   SLA4OAI-Analyzer

2.1   Validity of a Pricing

The **validity** of an SLA4OAI specification file, and thus the validity of a pricing, is defined as the absence of conflicts between the different elements of the pricing. A *pricing* consists of a series of *plans*, each of them having a series of *limitations*, and each limitation having a series of *limits*. A pricing is therefore valid when all of its elements are valid. For example, a pricing is not valid if a single limitation is not valid and has a conflict. An API provider would benefit from the automated validation of pricings, in order to ensure the coherence of its elements and, potentially, prevent users from exploiting the API.

Another element of an API worth mentioning is its **capacity**. The capacity of an API is the maximum workload that it can handle over a specific period of

---

[1] For historical reasons, we keep the name *SLA4OAI* even though the specification does not support Service Level Agreements, which are out of the scope of this paper.

time. It usually depends on the internal architecture and the deployment setup of the API. For example, a capacity of 1000 requests per second (RPS) means that the API can serve up to 1000 requests each second to its users.

In the following paragraphs, we present the validity criteria in a hierarchy. We start from fine-grained elements (limits and limitations) to coarse-grained ones (plans and pricing). Each criterion has multiple subcriteria, and all of them must be valid for the criterion to be valid.

VC1 - Valid limit A *limit* is valid if its threshold is a natural number (VC1.1).

VC2 - Valid limitation A *limitation* is valid if: all its *limits* are valid (VC2.1); there are no *limit consistency conflicts* between any pair of its *limits*, i.e. a limit over a longer period of time has a lower threshold than a limit over a shorter period (VC2.2); there are no *ambiguity conflicts* between any pair of its *limits*, i.e. multiple limits with different thresholds over the same period of time (VC2.3); and there is no *capacity conflict*, i.e. a limit is less restrictive than the *capacity* of the API (VC2.4).

VC3 - Valid plan A *plan* is valid if: all its *limitations* are valid (VC3.1); and there are no *limitation consistency conflicts* between any pair of its limitations, i.e. a limitation over a metric allows another limitation over a related metric (by a certain factor) to be exceeded (VC3.2).

VC4 - Valid pricing A *pricing* is valid if: all its *plans* are valid (VC4.1); and there are no *cost consistency conflicts* between any pair of its plans, i.e. a limitation in a plan with a lower cost is less restrictive than the equivalent limitation in a plan with a higher cost (VC4.2).

Listing 1.1 shows a simplified example of a pricing with a limit consistency conflict (VC2.2). Other examples can be found in our notebook [5].

```
1  Limitations:
2    Quota: 100 requests / 1 day
3    Quota: 10 requests / 1 week
```

Listing 1.1. Example of validity criterion VC2.2 (limit consistency conflict).

2.2   Pricing Validation API

The SLA4OAI-Analyzer API is available at [3]. Its code is publicly available at [4]. The API takes a URL that points to an SLA4OAI specification file as an input and checks for all conflicts that were presented in the previous subsection. The API returns a Boolean value that indicates whether the file is valid, and a detailed log showing the validity of each individual element of the pricing.

To validate the API, we provide an online Jupyter notebook that is available at [5]. Note that the notebook is shared with *execute* access, meaning that the cells can be executed but not modified. Nonetheless, they may be modified if the notebook is duplicated into your own Deepnote account. The notebook includes two examples for each validity subcriterion: one example has a conflict and the other does not. Because the full SLA4OAI specification files are complex and contain additional information that is not relevant for the detection of conflicts, each example includes a short pseudocode fragment, similar to listing 1.1, that shows the pricing elements that are actually relevant for this demo. The full SLA4OAI files are available at [1]. The examples in the notebook use these files. Alternatively, the API also accepts a full SLA4OAI file directly within the request body. There is a cell at the end of the notebook that contains an example.

3   Conclusions and Future Work

In this paper we presented SLA4OAI-Analyzer, a public API that automatically analyzes an SLA4OAI specification file and detects different types of conflicts at different levels of the specification. This tool is an example of how to leverage the information of a pricing when a formal description is available.

The current implementation of SLA4OAI-Analyzer has some limitations. It follows a strict syntax-guided approach, so small changes in the specification derive in important updates to the API. In the future, we aim to transform a pricing into a constraint satisfaction problem (CSP), which should allow for better maintainability and scalability of the API.

References

1. Full SLA4OAI Specification Files. https://github.com/isa-group/icwe23-demo-sla4oaianalyzer
2. OpenAPI Specification 3.1.0. https://spec.openapis.org/oas/v3.1.0
3. SLA4OAI-Analyzer API. https://sla4oai-analyzer-api.services.governify.io
4. SLA4OAI-Analyzer API Repository. https://github.com/isa-group/sla4oai-analyzer-api
5. SLA4OAI-Analyzer Deepnote Notebook. https://deepnote.com/workspace/rafael-fresno-ab85b312-0a6a-4a0d-8975-786d40a9e336/project/SLA4OAI-Conflicts-e39d1e11-8472-47c5-abd6-b4be10851a8d/notebook/Notebook%201-a14aeec4a0394c47bebbabbfe0c4dfce
6. SLA4OAI Research Specification. https://github.com/isa-group/SLA4OAI-ResearchSpecification
7. SLA4OAI Technical Committee. https://github.com/isa-group/SLA4OAI-TC
8. Fielding, R.T.: Architectural styles and the design of network-based software architectures. University of California, Irvine (2000)
9. Fresno-Aranda, R., Fernández, P., Durán, A., Ruiz-Cortés, A.: Semi-Automated Capacity Analysis of Limitation-Aware Microservices Architectures. In: Bañares, J.Á., Altmann, J., Agmon Ben-Yehuda, O., Djemame, K., Stankovski, V., Tuffin, B. (eds.) Economics of Grids, Clouds, Systems, and Services. GECON 2022. LNCS, vol. 13430, pp. 75–88. Springer, Cham (2022). https://doi.org/10.1007/978-3-031-29315-3_7
10. Gamez-Diaz, A., Fernandez, P., Ruiz-Cortes, A.: An analysis of RESTful APIs offerings in the industry. In: Maximilien, M., Vallecillo, A., Wang, J., Oriol, M. (eds.) ICSOC 2017. LNCS, vol. 10601, pp. 589–604. Springer, Cham (2017). https://doi.org/10.1007/978-3-319-69035-3_43
11. Martin-Lopez, A., Segura, S., Ruiz-Cortés, A.: RESTest: automated black-box testing of RESTful web APIs. In: Proceedings 30th ACM SIGSOFT International Symposium on Software Testing and Analysis (ISSTA), pp. 682–685 (2021)

Towards a Model-Driven Development of Environmental-Aware Web Augmenters Based on Open Data

Paula González-Martínez[1], César González-Mora[1]⬤, Irene Garrigós[1]⬤,
Jose-Norberto Mazón[1(✉)]⬤, and José M. Cecilia[2]⬤

[1] Department of Software and Computing Systems (DLSI), Universidad de Alicante,
Alicante, Spain
pgm136@gcloud.ua.es, {cgmora,igarrigos,jnmazon}@ua.es
[2] Department of Computing Engineering (DISCA), Universitat Politècnica de
València, València, Spain
jmcecilia@disca.upv.es

Abstract. In order to achieve the SDGs (Sustainable Development Goals), society must be able to consume open data to be aware of environmental situations. However, the existence of many related heterogeneous open data sets hampers citizens to use them to rise environmental awareness. In order to overcome this scenario, in this paper, we introduce a model-driven approach to automatically generate Web Augmenters that (i) homogeneously access environmental open data, and (ii) visualize this data while users are surfing the Web. In order to show the feasibility of our approach a case study is defined, based on generating a Web Augmenter that uses open data and Wikipedia related to "Mar Menor" coastal lagoon; a highly anthropized ecosystem located in South-East Spain.

Keywords: Web Augmentation · Open data · Environment ·
Sustainable Development Goals · Model-driven development

1 Introduction

Sustainable Development Goals (SDGs)[1] are an urgent call for action to reduce the inequality that includes strategies for improving health and education while tackling environmental issues, such as climate change and biodiversity preservation. Environmental public awareness, as well as citizen inclusiveness and engagement, are critical factors for SDGs success, rather than expert-driven big data analytics [3]. Interestingly, as proposed in [9], citizens could better participate in monitoring SDGs if novel techniques and tools that support data consumption were developed (i.e., data-collection techniques or analytic tools). However, there are no such tools specially fitted for citizens to raise public environmental awareness and involvement, as required for SDGs [10].

---

[1] https://sdgs.un.org/.

I. Garrigós et al. (Eds.): ICWE 2023, LNCS 13893, pp. 367–370, 2023.
https://doi.org/10.1007/978-3-031-34444-2_29

Developing biodiversity maps [7] is crucial for providing a better understanding of the environment. This kind of map has been proven as a useful mechanism for supporting practitioners and policy-makers in biodiversity monitoring to assess habitat degradation, invasive species, etc [8].

According to the challenges detected by Abadi et al. [1], two main issues should be considered when developing biodiversity maps for citizens [4]: (i) data that comes from several different sources (e.g., biological collections, field surveys or automated sensors, etc.) must be acquired and integrated before being ready for consumption; and (ii) data must be naturally consumed together with other data through continuous interaction with a well-known and widely used application such as a Web browser.

To overcome these problems and allow biodiversity maps to rise awareness of the environment among citizens, in this paper, we propose a model-driven approach to automatically generate Web Augmenters that (i) homogeneously access environmental open data, and (ii) visualize this data in biodiversity maps while users are surfing the Web. Finally, a case study is defined, based on generating a Web Augmenter that uses open data related to the "Mar Menor" coastal lagoon; a highly anthropized ecosystem located in South-East Spain.

2   Biodiversity Maps as Web Augmenters

In this section, we explain our model-driven approach for using Web augmenters as a mechanism to build and visualize biodiversity maps, while surfing the Web. Biodiversity data come from CSV files and our Web augmenter is specifically created for Wikipedia.

2.1   Data and Biodiversity Map Metamodel

Our model-driven approach starts from a specific model of the biodiversity data source that includes information about map to be generated and, eventually, shown as a Web augmenter. To do so, a new metamodel is developed to include concepts from biodiversity maps. This metamodel is inspired by the tabular data metamodel we developed in our previous work [6].

As shown in Fig. 1, metamodel consists of a map with identifier and scale (for zooming purposes), which will represent the habitat of a specific living being (with id, name, and minimum and maximum temperature as living conditions). Moreover, each map can have multiple layers represented by points. Data coming from sensors are related to a layer. There can be different kinds of sensors as subclasses; e.g., a temperature sensor, which indicates the specific point where the measurement is taken. Moreover, in the metamodel, the relation between the different objects is specified: a CSV file with its filename contains a set of rows, and a row with its position contains a set of cells with value and type.

Two datasets are used in our sample scenario to create the corresponding model based on the previously described metamodel: (i) environmental and water quality monitoring data coming from the "Mar Menor" lagoon in Southeast of

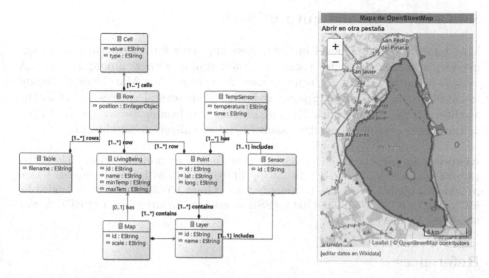

Fig. 1. Metamodel of biodiversity maps.   **Fig. 2.** Web augmenter.

Spain [2]. It includes, among others, measurements of "Mar Menor" temperature by using sensors in a buoy accessible as open data at https://zenodo.org/record/6798292; and (ii) data on the responses of some of the main coralligenous species living in the Mediterranean to thermal stress [5]. Data come from thermotolerance experiments with different temperature treatments (from 26 to 29 °C) with 10 species from different phyla (three anthozoans, six sponges, and one ascidian) and different structural roles. Corresponding open data is published at https://zenodo.org/record/5005552.

2.2   Augmenting the Web with Biodiversity Maps

From the previously-defined model containing data for biodiversity maps, a Web augmenter to be applied on the Wikipedia website is implemented. The resulting script in Tampermonkey is available online[2]. Specifically, infoboxes of Wikipedia entries for species of interest that appear in the model as "living being" are augmented with a biodiversity map. The biodiversity map contains data about the water temperature of the "Mar Menor" and species that survive under these conditions, just to rise awareness on the importance of environmental issues (such as temperature and climate change) among citizens. Wikipedia entry is augmented by using OpenStreetMap and LeafLet. The final result of a Wikipedia infobox augmented with a biodiversity map is shown in Fig. 2.

---

[2] https://greasyfork.org/es/scripts/460002-wikipedia-mapa-calor.

3   Conclusions and Future Work

This paper proposes a novel model-driven approach for considering Web augmenters as a mechanism for rising environmental awareness among citizens. A sample scenario is built by using sensor data from the "Mar Menor" lagoon (located in the South-East Spain) and data from several species living in the Mediterranean. Future work aims at creating environmental-aware Web augmenters that consider novel data sources and visualization capabilities.

Acknowledgements. This research has been funded by project projects TED2021-130890B funded by MCIN/AEI/10.13039/501100011033 and by the European Union NextGenerationEU/PRTR, and Ramon y Cajal Grant RYC2018-025580-I, funded by MCIN/AEI/10.13039/501100011033, "FSE invest in your future" and "ERDF A way of making Europe".

References

1. Abadi, D., et al.: The Seattle report on database research. ACM SIGMOD Rec. **48**(4), 44–53 (2020)
2. Blanco-Gómez, P., Jiménez-García, J.L., Cecilia, J.M.: Low-cost automated GPS, electrical conductivity and temperature sensing device (EC+ T track) and android platform for water quality monitoring campaigns. HardwareX **13**, e00381 (2023)
3. Del Río Castro, G., González Fernández, M.C., Uruburu Colsa, Á.: Unleashing the convergence amid digitalization and sustainability towards pursuing the sustainable development goals: a holistic review. J. Cleaner Prod. 280 (2021)
4. Gadelha Jr, L.M., et al.: A survey of biodiversity informatics: concepts, practices, and challenges. Wiley Interdisc. Rev. Data Min. Knowl. Discov. **11**(1), e1394 (2021)
5. Gómez-Gras, D., et al.: Response diversity in Mediterranean coralligenous assemblages facing climate change: insights from a multispecific thermotolerance experiment. Ecol. Evol. **9**(7), 4168–4180 (2019)
6. González-Mora, C., Garrigós, I., Zubcoff, J., Mazón, J.N.: Model-based generation of web application programming interfaces to access open data. J. Web Eng. 194–217 (2020)
7. Guralnick, R., Hill, A.: Biodiversity informatics: automated approaches for documenting global biodiversity patterns and processes. Bioinformatics **25**(4), 421–428 (2009)
8. Hoye, T.T., et al.: Biodiversity monitoring knowledge gaps and research & innovation priorities (2022)
9. Saner, R., Yiu, L., Nguyen, M.: Monitoring the SDGs: digital and social technologies to ensure citizen participation, inclusiveness and transparency. Dev. Policy Rev. **38**(4), 483–500 (2020)
10. Yamane, T., Kaneko, S.: Impact of raising awareness of sustainable development goals: a survey experiment eliciting stakeholder preferences for corporate behavior. J. Clean. Prod. **285**, 125291 (2021)

Enhancing Web Applications with Dynamic Code Migration Capabilities

Sebastian Heil[(✉)] , Jan-Ingo Haas , and Martin Gaedke

Technische Universität Chemnitz, Chemnitz, Germany
{sebastian.heil,jan.haas,martin.gaedke}@informatik.tu-chemnitz.de

Abstract. Dynamic migration of code between client and server of a web application allows to balance the needs of users for smooth and responsive user interactions with the interests of software providers to reduce costs and use resources efficiently. The ability to change the execution location of parts of the application logic at runtime means that depending on client capabilities, network speed and the current load of client and server, the code distribution can be optimized. In this demonstration, we showcase dynamic code migration for a sample e-commerce web application. The demonstrator is designed according to our novel DCM architecture and uses its infrastructure to automate compilation of code fragments and manage the migration at runtime, leveraging standardized Web technologies like WebAssembly and WebSockets. Demo participants will be able to interactively control the distribution of code fragments via a control user interface in the browser and interact with the e-commerce web application which was extended so that execution locations of application logic can be observed life. This demo provides a running prototypical implementation of the DCM architecture and aims at inspiring discussions about new possibilities for the Web platform from the widespread support of WebAssembly in all major browsers.

Keywords: Web Infrastructure · Software Architecture · Code Mobility · WebAssembly · WebSockets

1 Introduction

Code mobility in distributed systems has been a research interest for a long time since the concept was coined in the most influential paper of ICSE'97 [1]. For web applications, moving code execution between client and server allows to balance the needs of users for smooth and responsive user interactions with the interests of software providers to reduce costs and use resources efficiently. The ability to change the execution location of parts of the application logic at runtime means that depending on client capabilities, network speed, and the current load of client and server the code distribution can be optimized.

© The Author(s), under exclusive license to Springer Nature Switzerland AG 2023
I. Garrigós et al. (Eds.): ICWE 2023, LNCS 13893, pp. 371–375, 2023.
https://doi.org/10.1007/978-3-031-34444-2_30

The wide support of WebAssembly[1] provides the means for executing non-JavaScript application logic on the client side. Thus, a potentially uniform programming language on client and server establishes a new platform on top of which the vision of runtime code mobility becomes achievable for web applications, mitigating a main impediment of previous code mobility approaches [1].

Earlier Mobile Agents approaches in the web like HTML5 Agents [6] also make use of platform uniformity, based on JavaScript/NodeJS, however. Contemporary liquid computing approaches like Liquid.js [2] and Disclosure [4] make use of recent Web standards but are similarly specific to JavaScript. In contrast, WebAssembly opens the web environment's client side for arbitrary languages. We follow the idea of Mäkitalo et al. [5] to leverage WebAssembly modules as portable containers for code mobility, but unlike e.g. Blazor[2] at runtime.

This paper provides a brief overview of our novel software architecture for enabling the migration of application logic units between client and server side of a web application at runtime and outlines the interactive demonstration of an implementation of DCM in a Go-based e-commerce web application.

2   The DCM Architecture and Infrastructure in a Nutshell

This section summarizes the DCM architecture and supporting infrastructure for Web Engineers' adoption, shown in Fig. 1. A more detailed description of DCM, the related design challenges and design rationale can be found in [3].

Specification and Compilation of Code Fragments. DCM allows Web Engineers to designate parts of application logic, *Code Fragments*, for migration at runtime at the granularity of functions. A fragment is thus defined by its location in the codebase and migration-relevant metadata. Web Engineers specify fragments in a code fragment description (CFD). DCM infrastructure supports CFD creation by automatically extracting metadata such as source code, imports, function parameters/datatypes, through static analysis of the abstract syntax tree. To turn fragments into executable binary artifacts loadable at runtime, they are compiled as plugins for the server side and to WebAssembly modules for the client side. Before compiler invocation, DCM infrastructure modifies the codebase for dependency management and to enable redirection of control/data flow at runtime. The resulting artifacts and DCM runtime environment are then automatically deployed into the web application.

Dynamic Migration of Code Fragment Execution. At runtime, client and server `Code Distributor` handle execution of compiled code fragments. They keep track of available fragments and their state and handle fragment life cycle and dynamic migration when requested via the `API Controller`'s REST interface. Client-side fragments are executed as tasks via a pool of WebWorkers.

---

[1] https://www.w3.org/TR/wasm-core-1/.

[2] https://dotnet.microsoft.com/en-us/apps/aspnet/web-apps/blazor.

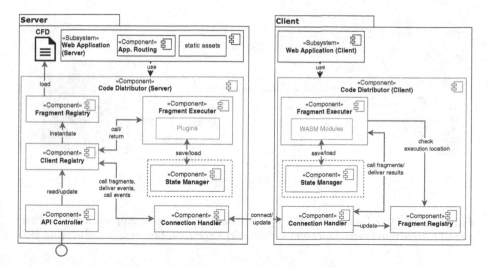

Fig. 1. Main Components and Interactions of the DCM Architecture. Supporting Infrastructure is in Blue, Automatically Generated Artifacts in Green. (Color figure online)

Client/Server communicate via WebSockets to synchronize incoming/outgoing data flows and events. To redirect control & data flow, `Fragment Executers` serve as proxies between the caller and the fragment code. Corresponding code modifications were automatically made before compilation. Control flow events are passed for fragment invocation/results. Data flow is forwarded and required transformations when entering/leaving the WebAssembly modules and serialization in the WebSocket connection are performed by the DCM infrastructure.

3   Demonstration

We built an interactive demonstrator[3] to showcase the DCM capabilities. As shown in Fig. 2, the scenario is a sample e-commerce application with basic article list, shopping cart, price/discount calculation functionalities. The application built according to the DCM architecture was extended with UI components to make the migration of fragments at runtime visible and controllable. Whenever application logic from a fragment is executed, an execution location indicator highlights its execution location – server or client. Demo participants can view the list of fragments and control their distribution via a dedicated fragment distribution control, allowing them to change the location of each fragment at runtime. By a second device or participants' own devices, we also demonstrate, that the fragment distribution can be chosen individually for each client, allowing for optimization according to individual load and hardware capabilities. An additional WASM Playground lets participants explore current corner-cases.

---

[3] source code available at: https://github.com/heseba/dcm-interactive-demo.

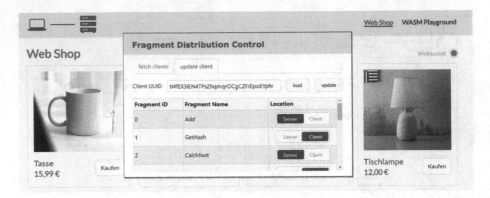

Fig. 2. Interactive Demonstrator: DCM-enabled E-Commerce Application with Fragment Distribution Control (center overlay) and Execution Location indicator (top left).

4 Conclusions and Future Work

DCM enables building web applications that can dynamically adapt execution of application logic at runtime for each client-server pair to better use available resources and balance users' and software providers' needs. This demo shows a working example using W3C-standardized web technologies and providing interactive code distribution controls. It aims at furthering the discussion about the Web platform in the light of new language-openness through WebAssembly.

Our future work targets the policy-based automation of fragment distribution decisions based on measurements of load and hardware capability detection. A second line of research focuses the combination of DCM with Web Components to enhance capabilities of building micro frontends for dynamic workflows.

Acknowledgements. The authors would like to thank Alexander Senger for his valuable contributions to the implementation of the DCM demonstrator.

References

1. Carzaniga, A., Picco, G.P., Vigna, G.: Is code still moving around? Looking back at a decade of code mobility. In: Proceedings of the ICSE 2007 Companion, pp. 9–20. IEEE (2007)
2. Gallidabino, A., Pautasso, C.: The liquid web worker API for horizontal offloading of stateless computations. J. Web Eng. **17**(6), 405–448 (2019)
3. Heil, S., Gaedke, M.: DCM: dynamic client-server code migration. In: Proceedings of the ICWE 2023. Springer, Cham (2023)
4. Kim, J.Y., Moon, S.M.: Disclosure: efficient instrumentation-based web app migration for liquid computing. In: Di Noia, T., Ko, I.Y., Schedl, M., Ardito, C. (eds.) ICWE 2022. Lecture Notes in Computer Science, vol. 13362, pp. 132–147. Springer, Cham (2022). https://doi.org/10.1007/978-3-031-09917-5_9

5. Mäkitalo, N., et al.: Web assembly modules as lightweight containers for liquid IoT applications. In: Brambilla, M., Chbeir, R., Frasincar, F., Manolescu, I. (eds.) ICWE 2021. LNCS, vol. 12706, pp. 328–336. Springer, Cham (2021). https://doi.org/10. 1007/978-3-030-74296-6_25
6. Voutilainen, J.P., Mattila, A.L., Systä, K., Mikkonen, T.: HTML5-based mobile agents for Web-of-Things. Informatica **40**(1), 43–51 (2016)

Macaroni: Crawling and Enriching Metadata from Public Model Zoos

Ziyu Li[(✉)], Henk Kant, Rihan Hai, Asterios Katsifodimos,
and Alessandro Bozzon

Delft University of Technology, Delft, The Netherlands
Z.Li-14@tudelft.nl

Abstract. Machine learning (ML) researchers and practitioners are building repositories of pre-trained models, called *model zoos*. These model zoos contain metadata that detail various properties of the ML models and datasets, which are useful for reporting, auditing, reproducibility, and interpretability. Unfortunately, the existing metadata representations come with limited expressivity and lack of standardization. Meanwhile, an interoperable method to store and query model zoo metadata is missing. These two gaps hinder model search, reuse, comparison, and composition. In this demo paper, we advocate for standardized ML model metadata representation, proposing *Macaroni*, a metadata search engine with toolkits that support practitioners to obtain and enrich that metadata.

Keywords: Machine Learning · Model Zoo · Metadata Representation

1 Introduction

Organizations are creating collections of pre-trained machine learning (ML) models, also known as *model zoos* or *model repositories*, as an incentive for sharing and reusing ML models. The most widely used model zoos include HuggingFace, Tensorflow Hub, and PyTorch Hub[1]. For a model zoo, metadata is essential. The metadata describes necessary information about an ML model in the model zoo, including its inference classes, architecture, training dataset, hyperparameter configurations, evaluation performance, etc. Metadata reporting is developed in the context of an ongoing effort to promote Trustworthy and Responsible AI[2].

In this work, we reveal that by querying and enriching metadata for model zoos, it facilitates MLOps and opens up new opportunities for abundant use cases. Practical use cases include but not limited to: i) model discovery and model selection for downstream tasks [2]; ii) (semi-)automatic model composition for complex analytic tasks [7]; iii) optimizing ML workloads on heterogeneous infrastructure [6]; iv) model reproducibility and documentation; v) and AutoML [5].

---

[1] https://huggingface.co/, https://pytorch.org/hub/, www.tensorflow.org/hub.

[2] https://partnershiponai.org/paper/responsible-publication-recommendations/.

© The Author(s), under exclusive license to Springer Nature Switzerland AG 2023
I. Garrigós et al. (Eds.): ICWE 2023, LNCS 13893, pp. 376–380, 2023.
https://doi.org/10.1007/978-3-031-34444-2_31

However, to fully explore the potential of model zoos for these use cases is non-trivial. A few challenges emerge due to the lack of structured and comprehensive metadata in existing solutions. First, aforementioned model zoos store various information about models, often in the form of model cards [4] with text fields primarily for human consumption. Model cards are not queryable, making it hard for automatic extension or management. Second, common ML model management tools/platforms, such as Amazon SageMaker, AzureML, MLflow, offer toolkits for practitioners to log metadata. However, logging the metadata is often optional, resulting in missing information and making it difficult for model discovery and model comparison. Moreover, existing model zoos often lack the support of fine-grained metadata. For instance, to select and fine-tune models for a specific task, e.g., sentiment analysis, an ML practitioner needs information regarding model definition, dataset statistics and the model's performance on the previous task. Such information is most times missing from model zoos such as HuggingFace. To summarize, a novel system that organizes the model zoo metadata in a *structured*, and *comprehensive* manner, is needed.

This demo paper represents an initial stride towards achieving our objective, wherein we introduce, *Macaroni*, a metadata search system for model zoos[3], along with a metadata model to represent ML models and related entities. Our system serves as a platform for querying and visualizing extensive metadata gathered from external model zoos or via offline automatic evaluations using easily-accessible APIs. Furthermore, Macaroni facilitates supplementing model cards and other Deep Learning benchmarks [1] by incorporating a wider range of evaluation metrics.

2 System Design

In this demo, we introduce the system architecture and the metadata model that represents different entities and relations. We also discuss the underlying technology components that obtain and enrich the metadata of model zoos. In particular, the main components include the metadata model, metadata crawler, and performance evaluation pipeline (on raw or perturbed datasets).

System Architecture. The system aims to query and enrich the metadata for model zoos. We present the system architecture in Fig. 1. The system includes a web-based interface as front-end and back-end with storage and computation. We collect metadata in two ways: crawling ML-related metadata from external model zoos; and enriching metadata, e.g., obtaining model performance by evaluating the model on raw or perturbed dataset. The metadata obtained is later stored in metadata storage supported by a metadata model. Macaroni allows users to i) interactively search/discover models, ii) compare multiple models on various objectives (e.g., accuracy, runtime, size), iii) and, specially, measure the robustness of models on perturbed dataset. These functionalities are novel compared to public model zoos and other metadata management tools, which can

---

[3] The prototype is available at metadatazoo.io.

be adopted seamlessly to support research studies such as explainable AI and AutoML.

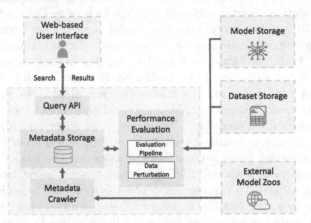

Fig. 1. The system architecture of Macaroni

Metadata Model. We present a conceptual view of our proposed metadata model [3], described using UML class diagrams. The metadata model is implemented with MangoDB (users can implement it in other database. The metadata model is comprised of four packages: i) `Configuration` package, which defines the ML models associated with architecture, hyperparameter settings, input and output. ii) `Dataset` packaged, includes both `Datasets` and their *Data Instances*. With the `Dataset` element, we represent the metadata of the datasets that is significant for data management and reporting, e.g., data source, data version. iii) `Execution` package describes the inference results (e.g., inference classes) of the model, possibly enriched with description from a knowledge graph. iv) `Evaluation` package, which presents the run-time metrics obtained in specified hardware settings. The instances of the `Evaluation` includes various types of evaluation metrics.

Metadata Crawler. The tool can automatically extract information from external model zoos, including HuggingFace and FiftyOne[4]. Metadata can be extracted from their APIs or information on the web pages and is recorded along with the source in the metadata storage. In particular, the model name, hyperparameters and task are obtained from the model cards from both model zoos through their APIs, and stored alongside the origin of the model. Information not available through their API (e.g., datasets and other tags) is parsed from the model's original readme files shown as the model cards. Other metadata could also be retrieved depending on the content provided by the external model zoos. Future work can investigate on extracting knowledge as metadata

---

[4] https://docs.voxel51.com/.

from the textual descriptions. Since more models will be added/updated , the crawling and extraction of the metadata shall be updated from time to time.

Model Evaluation Pipeline. The execution of models from different model zoos can be varied, differing by framework, algorithm, tasks, training dataset(s), and input format. To obtain the model performance and compare the evaluation results, we provide a unified evaluation pipeline, which facilitates evaluating models from different external model zoos on various datasets conveniently. Our pipeline is extensible, i.e., add support for new types of models or data after the initial pipeline deployment. We achieve extensibility in two ways. i) We apply a modular design, in which each evaluation module defines how to evaluate for a subset of models. ii) From each evaluation module, one or more evaluations are conducted, based on configuration of the module, such as which metrics to calculate or datasets to use.

Data Perturbation to Measure Model Capabilities. In addition to model performance on dedicated dataset, we also allow practitioners to investigate the model robustness on various types of data changes. Identifying the model performance on different data shifts is fundamental in understanding the model capabilities. We define a few types of perturbations on input dataset, e.g., converting to greyscale, flipping or mirroring the images, and observe the difference in performance. In such a way, we manage to identify how the model is generalized to data with different properties/changes. Future work can incorporate different perturbation methods, e.g., adversarial attacks, adding noise, on various modalities. We view the establishment of such a way to observe the model capabilities as the starting step, and further techniques and methods from explainable AI can enrich the description for model capabilities.

3 Conclusion and Future Work

We advocate for the need of structured, queryable, and comprehensive metadata for model zoos. We have proposed a platform for managing ML-related metadata including interactive web-based interface and related functionalities. To obtain the performance of models with various configurations, we also provide easily accessible APIs for model inference and evaluation. Our proposed platform can be used for building systems of AutoML, complex analytic tasks with model composition and explainable AI.

References

1. Coleman, C.: Dawnbench: an end-to-end deep learning benchmark and competition. Training **100**(101), 102 (2017)
2. Deshpande, A., et al.: A linearized framework and a new benchmark for model selection for fine-tuning. arXiv preprint arXiv:2102.00084 (2021)
3. Li, Z., Hai, R., et al.: Metadata representations for queryable ML model zoos. https://doi.org/10.48550/ARXIV.2207.09315, https://arxiv.org/abs/2207.09315

4. Mitchell, M., et al.: Model cards for model reporting. In: Proceedings of the Conference on Fairness, Accountability, and Transparency, pp. 220–229 (2019)
5. Vanschoren, J.: Meta-learning. In: Automated Machine Learning: Methods, Systems, Challenges, pp. 35–61 (2019)
6. Wu, Y., Lentz, M., Zhuo, D., Lu, Y.: Serving and optimizing machine learning workflows on heterogeneous infrastructures
7. Yang, Z., et al.: Optimizing machine learning inference queries with correlative proxy models. arXiv preprint arXiv:2201.00309 (2022)

WS3H: Webified Self-Sovereign Smart Home

Valentin Siegert(✉) ⓘ, Clemens Albrecht ⓘ, Mahda Noura ⓘ,
and Martin Gaedke ⓘ

Distributed and Self-organizing Systems, Chemnitz University of Technology,
Chemnitz, Germany
{valentin.siegert,mahda.noura,martin.gaedke}@informatik.tu-chemnitz.de,
clemens.albrecht@s2017.tu-chemnitz.de

Abstract. The Web of Things (WoT) concept proposes to integrate
the existing Web ecosystem with Things to provide an interoperable
infrastructure which goes beyond basic network connectivity. Existing
approaches unify the process to integrate the devices into the Web by
automatically generating Web APIs based on semantic device descriptions. However, they are either limited to specific protocols or do not
address transport security and authorization. In this paper, we demonstrate our approach on a Webified Self-Sovereign Smart Home that uses
self-sovereign identity to establish transport security and authorization
in a webified smart home. Our solution provides end user support with
easy deployment and addresses the local scope of a smart home due to
its self-sovereignty.

Keywords: Self-Sovereign Identity · Smart Home · Web of Things

1 Introduction and Related Work

Homes are becoming *smarter* by integrating Internet of Things (IoT) devices
to improve the user comfort through automation. Integrating IoT devices to the
Web – called the Web of Things (WoT) – provides an interoperable infrastructure
which simplifies their accessibility allowing to build IoT applications on top of
Web API's [5]. Although the WoT working group[1] advocates exposing physical
objects to the Web, they do not deal with the actual development of the Web
interface, which is a significant barrier to fast prototyping of WoT applications.
On the other hand, solutions like Matter[2] and WoTDL2API [5] propose an
abstraction layer to automate the process of integrating IoT devices into the
Web. Matter is an industry standard that builds on established technologies, all
of which use Internet Protocol version 6 (IPv6). WoTDL2API on the other hand
provides interoperable access to IoT devices by using a model-driven process to
generate automatically RESTful APIs from WoTDL instances.

---

[1] https://www.w3.org/WoT/wg/.
[2] https://buildwithmatter.com/.

I. Garrigós et al. (Eds.): ICWE 2023, LNCS 13893, pp. 381–385, 2023.
https://doi.org/10.1007/978-3-031-34444-2_32

Securing smart homes is in the end user's best interest, even though they may not think about security until after they purchase smart devices [3]. Unfortunately, the Mirai Botnet is only one example that insecure IoT devices can cause huge damage outside their owners interest [1]. Matter establishes unified APIs with a standardized security framework, but only supports devices of IPv6. Despite the motivation for a larger address range with IPv6, the rollout is not yet complete according to Google statistics[3]. WoTDL2API [5] is an application layer protocol that utilizes HTTP and can therefore also work with private IPv4 addresses. It is thus more suitable for Smart Homes, however it lacks support for transport security and authorization.

We therefore propose the **Webified Self-Sovereign Smart Home (WS3H)**; a secure, private and easy to use WoT solution for the Smart Home. It utilizes WoTDL2API [5] and Self-Sovereign Identity (SSI) for authentication and authorization based on the proposal for SSI in IoT [4]. Besides SSI, the two most prominent approaches for transport security and authorization are TLS [6] and Wireguard [2]. However, both impose a burden on end users because their initial adoption is difficult, which is easier in WS3H. TLS requires the establishment of a private CA or the use of a public CA, and in Wireguard the public key exchange of all smart home devices must be implemented by the end user. Our solution surpasses TLS and Wireguard by its ease of use for end users who do not want to deal with certificates or public and private keys.

The remainder of the paper presents WS3H and describes a demonstration on how a user can make use of WS3H within his home by connection a new device to WS3H.

2   Webified Self-Sovereign Smart Home (WS3H)

WS3H provides a secure and private solution. The application design of WS3H follows a hub-and-spoke topology and realizes SSI on behalf of standards provided by Hyperledger Aries[4]. The hub device provides the blockchain used by the SSI protocols. Furthermore, both the hub and the spoke devices provide an implementation of a Hyperledger Aries agent. The authentication and authorization of a new IoT device follows a three step procedure.

1. A spoke device starts a RFC 0160 Connection Protocol flow. It sends the hub its per-connection generated DID and public key, and the hub responds with its corresponding ones. From this point on, both peers can communicate over a DIDcomm-secured channel.
2. Then, the spoke device initiates RFC 0036 Issue Credential. After the hub receives the connection request, the only user interaction is to use notice and consent on whether to allow the spoke device to receive the credential. Using the device description provided by the spoke device, he can identify if it is the device he just connected to the network. Upon approval, the speaking device receives the credential, which it can now use to authenticate itself.

---

[3] https://www.google.com/intl/en/ipv6/statistics.html.
[4] https://github.com/hyperledger/aries-rfcs.

3. Using the Verifiable Credential (VC) it received in the previous step, the spoke device now starts the RFC 0037 Present Proof Protocol. It sends a verification request to the hub, which responds with a request for a matching credential. When the credential is verified, the hub confirms the confirmation and thus the spoke device is considered authenticated.

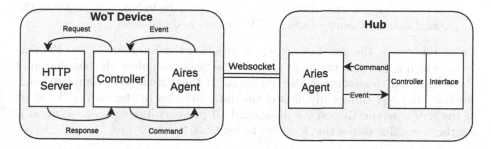

Fig. 1. WS3H Architecture

Figure 1 shows the architecture developed for WS3H. It shows the IoT device consisting of the WoTDL2API server, as well as the Aries Controller and Agent. The hub contains an agent and the Web server that performs the role of a controller and is responsible for presenting the Web UI.

3 Demonstration

The WS3H demo shows a typical smart home deployment scenario with two hosts. A Raspberry Pi connected to a light sensor, a motion sensor, and a volume sensor, and a laptop with a browser displaying the hub's UI. It demonstrates the use case of a dashboard that presents data about the user's home. The Raspberry Pi and the Laptop feature a full implementation of the hub-and-spoke concept with one spoke device. Both devices contain an implementation of an agent and a controller, and the Raspberry Pi contains the WoTDL2API server. To realize the concept, the following four components were used.

- The hub and the spoke device contain an Aries Cloudagent Python. This is a Python implementation of a full Hyperledger Aries Agent. It was chosen because it is currently the most complete implementation of such an agent. This agent provides the implementation of the protocols used to communicate between the two devices.
- To provide the blockchain implementation, the hub contains an implementation of the Hyperledger Indy blockchain using a VON Network Node Docker image. The Hyperledger Indy blockchain is currently the only supported option in Hyperledger Aries.

– The communication between the agent and the WoTDL2API server on the spoke device is handled using a custom Python application using Flask. It handles the packing and unpacking of the HTTP request and response, as well as performing the task of an agent controller.
– A custom Python application using Django implements the UI presented to the user. The UI implements the management of connected spoke devices as well as presenting the retrieved data to the user. This application also provides the agent controller implementation on the hub device as well as the packing and unpacking of the HTTP request and response.

Using this demo, the user can process connecting the Raspberry Pi to the network, which appears in the hub's UI. The user can then allow the connection of the device and the issuing of the credential. If these steps were completed successfully, the user can securly inspect the data provided by the sensors. A video[5] of the user's perspective on the dashboard UI presents how easy our solution is for the user after connecting a device to his Smart Home.

4   Conclusion

We demonstrated in this paper our Webified Self-Sovereign Smart Home (WS3H) approach, which secures Smart Homes' transport layer and establishes device authorization. It extends WoTDL2API [5] with a self-sovereign identity approach, targeting the use case of Smart Homes and its local scope. To establish secure channels within WS3H, the concept of self-sovereign identity for IoT devices [4] is implemented by using secure DIDcomm via VCs with the usage of Hyperledger Aries and Indy. The demonstration includes an example run of connecting a new device in a Smart Home and issuing credentials for it with ease for end users.

References

1. Antonakakis, M., April, T., Bailey, M., et al.: Understanding the mirai botnet. In: 26th USENIX Security Symposium (USENIX Security 17), pp. 1093–1110. USENIX Association, Vancouver, BC (2017). https://www.usenix.org/conference/usenixsecurity17/technical-sessions/presentation/antonakakis
2. Donenfeld, J.A.: Wireguard: next generation kernel network tunnel. In: NDSS, pp. 1–12 (2017). https://doi.org/10.14722/ndss.2017.23160
3. Emami-Naeini, P., Dixon, H., Agarwal, Y., et al.: Exploring how privacy and security factor into IoT device purchase behavior. In: Proceedings of the 2019 CHI Conference on Human Factors in Computing Systems, pp. 1–12. CHI 2019, Association for Computing Machinery, New York, NY, USA (2019). https://doi.org/10.1145/3290605.3300764
4. Fedrecheski, G., Rabaey, J.M., Costa, L.C.P., et al.: Self-sovereign identity for IoT environments: a perspective. In: 2020 Global Internet of Things Summit (GIoTS), pp. 1–6. IEEE, Dublin, Ireland (2020). https://doi.org/10.1109/GIOTS49054.2020.9119664

---

[5] https://youtu.be/-jrfGlrHfAc.

5. Noura, M., Heil, S., Gaedke, M.: Webifying heterogenous internet of things devices. In: Bakaev, M., Frasincar, F., Ko, I.-Y. (eds.) ICWE 2019. LNCS, vol. 11496, pp. 509–513. Springer, Cham (2019). https://doi.org/10.1007/978-3-030-19274-7_36
6. Rescorla, E.: The transport layer security (TLS) protocol version 1.3. Technical report (2018). https://www.rfc-editor.org/rfc/rfc8446

Ph.D Symposium

Quantum Web Services Orchestration and Management Using DevOps Techniques

Jaime Alvarado-Valiente[1]([⊠]) [iD], Javier Romero-Álvarez[1] [iD], Enrique Moguel[2] [iD], and José García-Alonso[1] [iD]

[1] University of Extremadura, Escuela Politécnica, Quercus Software Engineering Group, Av. de la Universidad, S/N, 10003, Cáceres, Spain
{jaimeav,jromero,jgaralo}@unex.es
[2] CénitS–COMPUTAEX (Extremadura Supercomputing, Technological Innovation and Research Center), Carretera Nacional 521, Km 41.8, 10071 Cáceres, Spain
enrique@unex.es

Abstract. Quantum computing is a new approach to computing based on quantum mechanics. It holds great promise for solving problems that classical computers cannot reach in a reasonable time, up to the point that it is already attracting the interest of the scientific and industrial communities. As quantum technology continues to advance and quantum computers become more prevalent, the need for hybrid systems that can integrate quantum software with classical information systems is becoming increasingly pressing. One of the most promising solutions for this integration is web engineering, which provides artifacts that are already well consolidated in classical computing and that can be integrated into quantum systems. Therefore, web engineering can provide a leap forward in the advancement of quantum computing. This thesis aims to design an orchestration method to coordinate and integrate quantum services into classic software systems and propose DevOps techniques for managing the life cycle of these systems.

Keywords: Quantum computing · Quantum web services · Quantum software · DevOps

1 Introduction and Motivation

Quantum computing is becoming a reality in the business world [1]. Several computer companies have already designed and built functional quantum computers, with dozens of programming languages and simulators created specifically for such machines. Currently, real quantum computers are now accessible through the cloud, which is motivating companies to create software and programs that can take advantage of quantum computing [2]. This is leading to the development of hybrid classical-quantum systems [3], where both classical and quantum software systems have to work together. It implies that traditional software must

I. Garrigós et al. (Eds.): ICWE 2023, LNCS 13893, pp. 389–394, 2023.
https://doi.org/10.1007/978-3-031-34444-2_33

cooperate and interact with new quantum software systems, and it seems that this situation will be enduring and is expected to continue.

Therefore, this could involve sharing data, exchanging information, or even running algorithms on both systems simultaneously to achieve the desired result. Current researchers aim to make these two kinds of software work together seamlessly without any conflicts or issues arising from their differences [3].

One of the solutions that allow integration in these hybrid systems is Service-Oriented Computing [4]. Conceptually, although a quantum service can be similar to a classic service, technically there are many differences. Quantum services require other resources than classical ones and cannot be reused as easily due to the accumulation of quantum resources [5]. Additionally, when integrating quantum services with traditional solutions, there are certain challenges that must be addressed to maintain the quality of the software engineering process. To achieve this, it is necessary to develop effective Quantum Software Engineering to provide the tools and methods needed to understand and use quantum computing [6]. Therefore, researchers in this field must design the necessary solutions so that programmers who need to use quantum services can do so by taking advantage of the benefits or lessons learned from classical software.

However, there are currently many areas that need to be analyzed and reviewed to provide methods and techniques that can be applied to quantum software development. This is reflected in the current lack of established standards and protocols, the difficulty to integrate and coordinate different quantum services, and the resulting increased complexity in the development of hybrid computing systems [6]. As a proven solution for the communication and integration of this kind of heterogeneous system, a way to carry out the development is through the use of web services. Therefore, it is necessary for software engineering tools for the orchestration and deployment of quantum elements to ensure interoperability and compatibility between different quantum services.

Furthermore, due to the complexity and asynchronous nature of quantum algorithms, as well as the unreliability of quantum computing hardware, efficient automation, and management of the quantum development life cycle becomes crucial. This is necessary to ensure scalability and consistent delivery of high-quality quantum applications, so a quantum DevOps process is necessary. In the context of quantum computing, a DevOps process would ensure that quantum web services are efficiently developed, tested, and deployed in a way that meets the needs of both developers and operations teams [7]. This would ultimately result in a more efficient and effective deployment of quantum web services.

As can be noticed, the current use of quantum services could compromise the integrity of the current software due to the complexity of quantum systems, the lack of standards, and the crucial interaction between classical and quantum software. This Ph.D. thesis aims to address these issues by proposing techniques and methodologies to this end, as will be seen in this paper.

2   Related Work

There are several areas of active research and development in the field of Quantum Software Engineering that attempt to solve the problems mentioned in the previous section. For example, I.D. Gheorghe-Pop et al. [8] perform an adaptation of the traditional DevOps process towards a quantum DevOps. The main contribution of this work is the introduction and motivation for a novel concept called Quantum DevOps, and the integration of quantum-based algorithms into development or testing stages. However, they only focus on how DevOps can be used to check the reliability of Noisy Intermediate-Scale Quantum (NISQ) and do not consider some aspects such as the integration of hybrid systems.

Other researchers are exploring approaches to combine quantum and classical computing hardware to create more powerful and efficient systems, such as J. Garcia-Alonso et al. [9] who propose a Quantum API Gateway that provides an optimization that allows developers to determine which quantum computer is best suited for each execution of a service at run-time. This can be a starting point for work to integrate this pattern with quantum orchestration by allowing user applications to communicate with a quantum computing back-end through a standardized and secure API.

Moreover, some researchers have also made significant contributions to simplify the development process of quantum services. F. Leymann et al. [10] focus on applying quantum computing to distributed systems and in their research they propose a knowledge-sharing platform for building applications on quantum computers.

Overall, the current approaches that attempt to solve quantum computing problems include the development of quantum programming languages, quantum compilers, and quantum software libraries, as well as the design and implementation of quantum software systems that allow developers to define quantum services at a high abstraction level. However, while these approaches focus on developing software and programming languages, as well as combining quantum and classical computing hardware, many challenges remain to be addressed in creating effective Quantum Software Engineering solutions, which are some of the aims of this work as explained in the following section.

3   Aims and Objectives

This Ph.D. thesis proposes the research and development of a methodology and an orchestration mechanism for the integration of quantum algorithms into classical web engineering solutions. The goal is to coordinate and control the execution of quantum services, to simplify the development process and increase the efficiency and reliability of these quantum services. To achieve this, some objectives have been established as the main scientific contributions of this thesis:

- How can existing orchestration techniques be adapted to support the needs of quantum software? New techniques or adaptations of existing **orchestration mechanisms** will be studied and proposed to adapt them to the needs arising from this quantum paradigm. So that the traditional software, used in web engineering, will be combined with quantum software to create hybrid systems to ensure service availability and performance. To this end, we propose the use of software engineering patterns that can be used to facilitate the development and orchestration of these hybrid systems, such as load balancers or the API Gateway pattern.

– How can we ensure the proper performance and maintenance of hybrid systems? **Life cycle management techniques** will be proposed to ensure that these hybrid systems run without problems. This is essential as there needs to be a mechanism for coordinating them with each other as well as with the classical components. It's not enough to have efficient ways of developing quantum web services to make them useful. These techniques are needed to ensure the proper operation and maintenance and help to preserve the integrity of quantum states to enable the development of new quantum applications.

– What is the possible approach to establish a software development and delivery process in quantum environments that enables efficient resource monitoring and management? **A quantum DevOps process** will be proposed, with the goal of ensuring that the service can cope with demand due to the complex and asynchronous nature of quantum algorithms. In addition, to enable monitoring while a quantum service has been deployed and is being invoked by users. Automation and optimization of the software development and delivery process in quantum web services environments are also targeted.

4   Research Methodology

To ensure the achievement of the different objectives and for being a research project in the field of Information Technology (IT), this research uses the Design-Science research methodology [11]. Design Science is a methodology oriented to research projects that attempts to give a more practical approach to the objectives of the research, such as the one addressed in this Ph.D. project. So, it is usually applied to projects in the field of Engineering and Computer Science, although it can be used in many other disciplines and fields.

Hevner et al. [11] focuses on applying this methodology to Information Systems research by defining guidelines to correctly plan the different activities. Following the guidelines proposed by this methodology, a research plan for this Ph.D. project is established and is shown in Fig. 1.

ACTIVITIES	2° semester	2023 1° semester	2° semester	2024 1° semester	2° semester	2025 1° semester
Finalize project description	■					
Literature review and analysis of current proposals	■	■				
Design of management and orchestration techniques			■	■		
Modeling of DevOps practices for quantum web services				■	■	
Development of hybrid classical-quantum tools					■	■
Evaluation and validation of the generated tools/models					■	■
Management activities and communication of project results		■	■	■	■	■
Research Communication. Writing and defense of the thesis						■

Fig. 1. Timeline for planned research work

Initial advances in this thesis research have included a proposed way of how quantum web services may be deployed and implemented for hybrid classical-quantum architectures [12] and a hybrid healthcare system that uses quantum simulations to help healthcare professionals make decisions about prescribing drugs for older adults [13]. As another key result, Fig. 2 shows a proposed life cycle architecture that reflects aspects of automation and efficiency, including elements such as integration, deployment, orchestration, and continuous testing for the development of quantum web services.

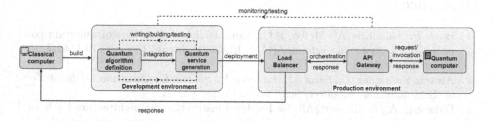

Fig. 2. Proposed system architecture

This architecture is mainly composed of a **development environment** which includes the whole process of defining quantum algorithms and the integration to carry out the generation of quantum services, and the iterative process that a quantum or classical developer performs when writing, compiling, and testing code. It is also composed of a **production environment** that, besides the invocation of quantum services, includes activities that are typically associated with a full DevOps cycle, such as monitoring or orchestration.

5 Conclusion

Quantum computing research focused on quantum software has grown in recent years. Currently, a need is emerging for research that focuses on service engineering for quantum software. Therefore, some works are appearing in Quantum Software Engineering that are moving towards applying the knowledge from classical software engineering to quantum software. For these reasons, it is necessary to make efforts for the integration and coexistence between quantum and classical computing, especially in the servitization line of quantum services.

Therein lies the main contribution of this thesis, providing a solution in the design of a method and a mechanism related to the integration and orchestration of quantum algorithms in classical web engineering solutions. Also, proposing a quantum DevOps process for such quantum systems can help with the efficient development and production of these systems. This will also allow quantum algorithms to be used in combination with existing web engineering solutions, allowing them to interact with each other and will ensure that they are efficiently managed and maintained throughout their life cycle.

Acknowledgments. This work is part of the Grant PID2021-124045408-C31 funded by MCIN/AEI /10.13039/50100011033 and by "ERDF A way of making Europe". It is also supported by the QSALUD project (EXP 00135977 / MIG-20201059); by the proyect 0786_CAP4ie_4_P (Interreg V-A España-Portugal 2021–2027); and by the Ministry of Economic Affairs and Digital Transformation of the Spanish Government through the Quantum ENIA project call - Quantum Spain project, and by the European Union through the Recovery, Transformation and Resilience Plan - NextGenerationEU within the framework of the Digital Spain 2025 Agenda.

References

1. Bova, F., Goldfarb, A., Melko, R.G.: Commercial applications of quantum computing. EPJ Quantum Technol. **8**(1), 1–13 (2021). https://doi.org/10.1140/epjqt/s40507-021-00091-1
2. Alvarez-Rodriguez, U., Sanz, M., Lamata, L., Solano, E.: Quantum artificial life in an IBM quantum computer. Sci. Rep. **8**(1), 1–9 (2018)
3. Dahlberg, A., et al.: NetQASM-a low-level instruction set architecture for hybrid quantum-classical programs in a quantum internet. Quantum Sci. Technol. **7**(3), 035023 (2022)
4. Moguel, E., Rojo, J., Valencia, D., Berrocal, J., Garcia-Alonso, J., Murillo, J.M.: Quantum service-oriented computing: current landscape and challenges. Softw. Qual. J. **30**(4), 983–1002 (2022)
5. Zhao, J.: Quantum software engineering: Landscapes and horizons. arXiv preprint arXiv:2007.07047 (2020)
6. Piattini, M., Peterssen, G., Pérez-Castillo, R.: Quantum computing: a new software engineering golden age. ACM SIGSOFT Softw. Eng. Notes **45**(3), 12–14 (2021)
7. Weder, B., Barzen, J., Leymann, F., Vietz, D.: Quantum software development lifecycle. In: Quantum Software Engineering, pp. 61–83. Springer, Cham (2022). https://doi.org/10.1007/978-3-031-05324-5_4
8. Gheorghe-Pop, I.D., Tcholtchev, N., Ritter, T., Hauswirth, M.: Quantum DevOps: towards reliable and applicable NISQ quantum computing. In: 2020 IEEE Globecom Workshops GC Wkshps, pp. 1–6. IEEE (2020)
9. Garcia-Alonso, J., Rojo, J., Valencia, D., Moguel, E., Berrocal, J., Murillo, J.M.: Quantum software as a service through a quantum API gateway. IEEE Internet Comput. **26**(1), 34–41 (2021)
10. Leymann, F., Barzen, J., Falkenthal, M.: Towards a platform for sharing quantum software. In: Proceedings of the 13th Advanced Summer School on Service Oriented Computing, pp. 70–74 (2019)
11. Hevner, A.R., March, S.T., Park, J., Ram, S.: Design science in information systems research. MIS Q. 75–105 (2004)
12. Alvarado-Valiente, J., Romero-Álvarez, J., Garcia-Alonso, J., Murillo, J.M.: A guide for quantum web services deployment. In: Di Noia, T., Ko, I.Y., Schedl, M., Ardito, C. (eds.) ICWE 2022. LNCS, vol. 13362, pp. 493–496. Springer, Cham (2022). https://doi.org/10.1007/978-3-031-09917-5_42
13. Romero-Álvarez, J., Alvarado-Valiente, J., Garcia-Alonso, J., Moguel, E., Murillo, J.M.: A graph-based healthcare system for quantum simulation of medication administration in the aging people. In: García-Alonso, J., Fonseca, C. (eds.) IWoG 2021. LNB, pp. 34–41. Springer, Cham (2022). https://doi.org/10.1007/978-3-030-97524-1_4

Using Emotions and Topics
to Understand Online Misinformation

Yuwei Chuai[(✉)], Arianna Rossi, and Gabriele Lenzini

SnT, University of Luxembourg, Luxembourg, Luxembourg
yuwei.chuai@uni.lu

Abstract. Misinformation has become one of the most pressing social issues in the twenty-first century. How the combinations of emotions and topics trigger the spread of misinformation, however, still remains to be revealed. This study comprehensively examines misinformation and its diffusion by correlating emotions and topics. First, we examine how specific emotions and topics are combined in misinformation. Second, we identify the effects of emotions and topics on the virality of misinformation. Finally, we further explore how to employ users' topic preferences and emotion reactions to detect and analyze echo chambers in misinformation cascades. The findings can help construct a detailed and consistent understanding on misinformation diffusion in terms of emotions and topics. Potential practical implications are also provided to prevent the spread of misinformation online.

Keywords: Misinformation · Social Networks · Emotions · Topics · Echo Chambers

1 Introduction

The prevalence of misinformation on social media strikes the stability of society, and contributes to various contentious events in politics, finance, and pandemics [5]. Combating online misinformation has become a major concern around the world [10]. Though massive related research emerged in recent years ranging from defining, characterizing, detecting, to intervening misinformation [5,8,16], the problem is still not well resolved. For example, because of the lack of counter-evidence, current detection methods are unrealistic to combat real-world misinformation [7]. Due to the pervasive nature of online misinformation, a major challenge has been to better understand its diffusion so as to design reliable interventions to mitigate it.

In this study, misinformation is defined as any piece of news that turns out to be false. Such a definition is generally accepted by current scholars [5,16]. Of note, before being identified, both true and false news items are all considered as rumors that contain uncertainty and get widely shared among the public [11].

G. Lenzini—Supported by FNR/FNRS 40008606. PhD supervisor.

I. Garrigós et al. (Eds.): ICWE 2023, LNCS 13893, pp. 395–400, 2023.
https://doi.org/10.1007/978-3-031-34444-2_34

Users tend not to question the credibility of information unless it violates their preconceptions or they are incentivized to do so [10]. The wide spread of rumors, both true and false, depends in part on specific content features, such as topics and emotions, and how users react to these content features [11]. Hence the driving factors of information diffusion and their use in misinformation need to be comprehensively explored to understand the nature of misinformation. For example, misinformation, which is often associated with social issues or events with high uncertainty and general attention, easily gets widely shared, polarizes public opinions, and even causes social panic [6,10,15]. Additionally, the writing style is of great importance to attract and convince other users to believe and share the information. For instance, misinformation peddlers link each other more frequently, adding to the spread of lies and conspiracies [14]. More importantly, the specific emotions, with which people react to the information, are regarded as a dominant driver of human behaviors, and play a unique role in enhancing online misinformation diffusion [2,3,11]. The effects (positive, negative, or neutral) of the same emotions on the spread of information, however, are inconsistent and even reversed in existing studies [11,15]. These studies all consider topic-specific variations, but the topic categories, such as politics and health, are too generalized to specify the variations. Given that the emotion distributions are different across different types of COVID-19 misinformation which are all belonging to a generalized health topic [1], examining the distributions of emotions under the control of topics at the event (issue) level provides a promising way to further understand the writing style of misinformation.

In addition to content analysis, misinformation diffusion networks and comments embedded in the networks give more details about the spreading patterns and user interactions. The overall assessment of diffusion networks has confirmed that false news spreads farther, faster, deeper, and more broadly than the real ones across all topic domains [15]. That is, misinformation is more viral than real information. Moreover, the emergence of echo chambers, in which users' opinions or beliefs are reinforced and go toward group polarization, has been identified in many studies [4]. However, echo chambers are much less widespread than is commonly assumed, and the real impact of echo chambers and their causal link with misinformation cascades are debated [4,13]. Users' opinions and emotional states towards specific topics are reinforced in echo chambers [4]. The combination of emotions and topics needs to be taken into account to better understand misinformation diffusion networks and echo chambers.

Taken together, despite many efforts in this regard, research on understanding the spread of misinformation is still in its infancy. Digging into the relationships between emotions and topics across content and context, this study aims to construct a detailed and consistent understanding on misinformation diffusion.

2   Research Objectives and Questions

This thesis takes fine-grained emotions and topics together into account in the analysis of the content and context of online (mis)information. First, we characterize the writing style of misinformation by identifying emotion words (anger, fear, etc.) and high-resolution topics (climate change, COVID-19 vaccine, etc.). Second, we analyze the network, namely whether the associations between emotions, topics, and veracity of information can predict the virality of online diffusion networks. Third, we analyze individual nodes (users), namely how to employ users' topic preferences and emotion reactions to detect echo chambers. To do so, the following questions are explored.

Research Question 1 (RQ1): Are there specific emotions particularly associated with certain topics in misinformation? We first compare the use of specific emotions in misinformation with that in real information under the control of topics to see whether the emotions are veracity-specific. Then, we explore how misinformation combines specific emotions and topics to make it distinct from real information.

Research Question 2 (RQ2): How do emotions and topics in the content associate with the virality of online misinformation? Many scholars only consider the retweet network to study the spread of misinformation [11,15]. Another type of diffusion networks, i.e., reply network, is also included in this study. We use cascade size and structural virality to measure the virality of online information.

Research Question 3 (RQ3): Can user's topic preferences and emotion reactions be used to detect echo chambers? Users' topic preferences can be estimated based on their prior posts, and emotion reactions also can be collected from their replies. Considering the two important context information from users, we try to design effective methods to detect echo chambers and identify the link between echo chambers and misinformation cascades.

By exploring the three questions, we will have a deep understanding about the effects of emotions, topics, and their interactions during the spread of misinformation. The findings can also provide insights into designing efficient interventions to combat misinformation ranging from content control to echo chamber mitigation.

3   Methodology

This study first collects data from fact-checking websites, social media platforms, and public datasets. Then, how we implement content and context analysis are introduced. Finally, the work we finished and future research plan are described.

3.1   Data Collection

To ensure the high quality of the datasets and mitigate sample selection bias, this study focuses on the most newsworthy and significant claims, both true and false, from authoritative fack-checking websites, such as PolitiFact.[1] We can

---

[1] https://www.politifact.com/.

scrutinize the content differences between true and false information based on the fact-checked claims collected.

This study further examines the online diffusion of misinformation by linking tweets on Twitter to fact-checked claims. Twitter is a unique platform that focuses on what is happening in the world, shares the freshest news, and captures the online trends of issues [6]. Twitter also provides developers with an easy-access API to retrieve data. Hence Twitter becomes an ideal workbench for researchers to study the spread of online information. Additionally, we also look for high-quality public datasets constructed for studying misinformation. Of note, the data collection process needs to be authorized by the data protection officer and the ethical review board to prevent privacy and ethical issues.

3.2   Content Analysis

Content analysis is based on the claims collected from fact-checking websites. First, this study considers six fine-grained cross-cultural basic emotions, namely, anger, disgust, joy, sadness, fear, and surprise. A popular multi-lingual emotion lexicon from the National Research Council of Canada (NRC) is employed to match emotion words in the content.[2] Additionally, we also use a state-of-the-art deep learning model as alternative method to detect emotions [9]. Second, for topic extraction, we transform each claim into a fixed-length vector using SentenceTransformers [12], which is a framework for state-of-the-art short-form text embeddings. The embeddings are fed into clustering algorithms, such as K-Means, to get topic clusters. Then we summarize topic categories according to the claims close to the cluster centers. Finally, controlling other content factors such as text length, we use regression models to examine the explainabilities of emotions, topics, and their interactions on the veracity (RQ1).

3.3   Context Analysis

Context analysis is based on the tweets collected from Twitter. First, we use keywords and SentenceTransformers to link claims to tweets according to their semantic similarities with a threshold. We then retrieve the online retweet and reply cascades of each tweet through the official Twitter API. Second, we explore structural properties including cascade size and structural virality. Finally, controlling covariables, we use regression models to explain how veracity, emotions, topics, and their interactions affect the structural properties (RQ2).

3.4   User Analysis

User analysis is mainly based on the users in the networks and their historical tweets. First, we use the topic distributions in users' historical tweets to estimate their topic preferences. We also calculate the similarities between users' prior tweets and the tweets they retweeted to analyze the changes in their interests.

---

[2] https://saifmohammad.com/WebPages/NRC-Emotion-Lexicon.htm.

Second, using the NRC emotion lexicon, we detect the emotion reactions of users in the replies, and identify the changes in emotion distributions compared to the original posts. Third, we detect echo chambers in the cascades based on users' topic preferences and emotion reactions. Finally, we use regression models to examine the link between echo chambers and misinformation cascades (RQ3).

4   Plan of Work and Time Schedule

Starting from October 2022, we are doing studies following the questions listed above. First, we did a literature review about the state of the art of misinformation analysis, detection, and intervention. Additionally, based on the literature review, a research proposal was completed. Second, 19,873 claims, including 5,407 true and 14,466 false ones, were already collected from PolitiFact. We also got the research API from Twitter. Third, how misinformation combines emotions and topics (RQ1) was in part answered. We found that misinformation has stronger politicization and partisan polarization than the real. The politicization entangled with out-group animosity contributes to the viral spread of misinformation. One paper "Stronger Politicization and Partisan Polarization as a Signature of Misinformation" is prepared for submission. Finally, Table 1 shows what the first author (PhD student) will do in the next three years.

Table 1. Time Schedule for Further Work

Time (Month)	Content	Expected Outcome
1–6	Keep studying RQ1	1 scientific article
6–18	Analyzing RQ2	2 scientific articles
18–30	Analyzing RQ3	2 scientific articles
30–36	Finishing the PhD thesis	Graduation

5   Potential Contributions

This study has some theoretical implications. First, this study can help better understand how emotions and topics are coordinated and make misinformation unique. Second, identifying the effects of fine grained emotions and topics on the diffusion of misinformation can explain the virality of misinformation and clarify previously inconsistent findings regarding emotions. Third, users' topic preferences and emotion reactions analysis can further reveal how users engage in echo chambers in misinformation.

In addition, this study also contributes some practical implications. First, understanding how misinformation employs emotions and topics can help design targeted nudging interventions via tagging tweets or browser extensions to shift users' attention towards accuracy and prevent the spread of misinformation at the very beginning. Second, more accurate detection methods can be developed according to the combinations of retweet networks, emotion networks, and topic preference networks. Third, based on the user analysis, echo chambers can be identified. The association between echo chambers and misinformation cascades also sheds light on mitigating group polarization in misinformation.

References

1. Charquero-Ballester, M., Walter, J.G., Nissen, I.A., Bechmann, A.: Different types of COVID-19 misinformation have different emotional valence on Twitter. Big Data Soc. **8**(2), 20539517211041280 (2021)
2. Chuai, Y., Chang, Y., Zhao, J.: What really drives the spread of COVID-19 Tweets: a revisit from perspective of content. In: 2022 IEEE 9th International Conference on Data Science and Advanced Analytics (DSAA), pp. 1–10. IEEE (2022)
3. Chuai, Y., Zhao, J.: Anger can make fake news viral online. Front. Phys. **10**, 970174 (2022)
4. Diaz-Diaz, F., San Miguel, M., Meloni, S.: Echo chambers and information transmission biases in homophilic and heterophilic networks. Sci. Rep. **12**(1), 9350 (2022)
5. Ecker, U.K., et al.: The psychological drivers of misinformation belief and its resistance to correction. Nat. Rev. Psychol. **1**(1), 13–29 (2022)
6. Falkenberg, M., et al.: Growing polarization around climate change on social media. Nat. Clim. Change **12**, 1114–1121 (2022)
7. Glockner, M., Hou, Y., Gurevych, I.: Missing counter-evidence renders NLP factchecking unrealistic for misinformation. arXiv (2022)
8. Gradoń, K.T., Hołyst, J.A., Moy, W.R., Sienkiewicz, J., Suchecki, K.: Countering misinformation: a multidisciplinary approach. Big Data Soc. **8**(1), 20539517211013850 (2021)
9. Hartmann, J.: Emotion english distilroberta-base. https://huggingface.co/j-hartmann/emotion-english-distilroberta-base/ (2022)
10. Lazer, D.M., et al.: The science of fake news. Science **359**(6380), 1094–1096 (2018)
11. Pröllochs, N., Bär, D., Feuerriegel, S.: Emotions in online rumor diffusion. EPJ Data Sci. **10**(1), 1–17 (2021). https://doi.org/10.1140/epjds/s13688-021-00307-5
12. Reimers, N., Gurevych, I.: Sentence-BERT: sentence embeddings using Siamese BERT-networks. In: Proceedings of the 2019 Conference on Empirical Methods in Natural Language Processing. Association for Computational Linguistics (2019)
13. Ross Arguedas, A., Robertson, C., Fletcher, R., Nielsen, R.: Echo chambers, filter bubbles, and polarisation: a literature review. Reuters Institute for the Study of Journalism (2022)
14. Sehgal, V., Peshin, A., Afroz, S., Farid, H.: Mutual hyperlinking among misinformation peddlers. arXiv (2021)
15. Vosoughi, S., Roy, D., Aral, S.: The spread of true and false news online. Science **359**, 1146–1151 (2018)
16. Wu, L., Morstatter, F., Carley, K.M., Liu, H.: Misinformation in social media: definition, manipulation, and detection. ACM SIGKDD Explor. Newsl. **21**(2), 80–90 (2019)

Learning-Based Quality of Experience Prediction for Selecting Web of Things Services in Public Spaces

KyeongDeok Baek[✉][iD] and In-Young Ko[iD]

School of Computing, Korea Advanced Institute of Science and Technology,
Daejeon, Republic of Korea
{kyeongdeok.baek,iko}@kaist.ac.kr

Abstract. In the age of the Web of Things (WoT), an increasing number of WoT devices will be deployed over public spaces and provide various services to users. Therefore, discovering and selecting public WoT services by predicting the expected Quality of Experience (QoE) become critical to satisfying users. However, because of the uncertain and dynamic nature of public WoT environments, accurately predicting and continuously maintaining the QoE of the services is challenging. We investigated the limitations of the traditional model-based QoE prediction in WoT environments and the potential of the learning-based approaches to deal with the challenges. In this work, we propose a distributed algorithm powered by learning-based QoE prediction for selecting public WoT services. Service agents predict the long-term QoE for the corresponding service based on attention mechanism and multi-agent reinforcement learning. Service agents learn the influence of hard-to-observe influencing factors in the environment, such as physical obstacles and interference from other services.

Keywords: Public WoT service selection · Learning-based QoE prediction · Attention-based multi-agent reinforcement learning

1 Introduction

Recently, an increasing number of Web of Things (WoT) devices provide various services to support people's daily lives. However, most WoT services are limited to private spaces with authorized users. Public WoT services have the potential to produce value on the fly for users based on users' needs in public spaces. As shown in Fig. 1, every user in the environment can freely request a service, such as news delivery and illumination, and the service agents will provide the requested services to the user.

In this situation, one of the challenges is to select the most appropriate service among the candidates that are functionally equivalent to the needs. The user

Ph.D Supervisor: Prof. In-Young Ko, School of Computing, KAIST.

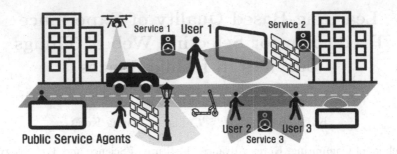

Fig. 1. A public WoT environment with various services

may select a service manually, but the user may have difficulties if excessively many candidate services are available or if the user cannot recognize or locate the corresponding WoT device in the space. Quality of Experience (QoE), which shows the users' satisfaction with the service, is the most critical criterion when selecting services. If the QoE of each candidate service is accurately predictable, the most promising service can be selected automatically.

Traditionally, model-based QoE prediction builds a prediction model that requires every influencing factor as input. However, in WoT environments, various environmental factors, such as physical obstacles and other services that may disturb the services, are hard to observe and require additional sensors. Furthermore, the prediction is short-sighted and only considers the current state of the service.

In this work, we propose a learning-based approach to predicting the long-term QoE of WoT services in public spaces for selection. Instead of building a generalized prediction model, we train specialized prediction models for each WoT service that learn the influences of hard-to-observe environmental factors. According to the QoE prediction results by the service agents, one of the service agents is selected to provide service to the user and may be replaced dynamically by an alternative agent if its QoE degrades. Based on the advantage of an attention mechanism and multi-agent reinforcement learning, service agents scalably collaborate to predict QoE and provide services continuously.

We state the research issues for the QoE prediction and selection of public WoT services in Sect. 2. We introduce our previous works for the research issues in Sect. 3. Finally, we propose a learning-based algorithm and research plans in Sect. 4.

2   Research Issues

The selection of Web services and the prediction of QoE have a long history of research [5,7]. Traditionally, service selection algorithms search for the best combination of Web services to form a composite service that optimizes objective metrics such as network latency, availability, and cost [5]. QoE prediction algorithms estimate subjective QoE from objective metrics to focus on users' perspectives. White-box prediction models predict QoE based on principles of psychophysics, while black-box prediction models predict QoE by learning the correlation between QoE and objective metrics from data [7].

2.1 Dynamic Selection and Replacement of Public WoT Services

In contrast to Web services, the complexity of selecting WoT services is not in the combinatorial explosion of composite services but in the high dynamicity of public environments. The QoE of WoT services may fluctuate because of the uncertain and dynamic nature of public environments. For instance, as shown in Fig. 1, Service 1 provides the content to User 1 appropriately at the moment but will degrade as the user moves far from the corresponding device. Therefore, continuously predicting the QoE of selected services and dynamically replacing the degraded service with alternatives is necessary to maintain QoE high.

2.2 QoE Prediction of Public WoT Services

One of the challenges to applying traditional QoE prediction algorithms to WoT service is that environmental factors, such as physical obstacles and interference from other services in the same space, are hard to observe and cannot be input into prediction models. For instance, as shown in Fig. 1, the sound from Service 2 would be blocked by a wall so that the user cannot perceive the content appropriately. The sound from Service 3 may disturb multiple users in front of the corresponding device. Traditional model-based QoE prediction approaches require (1) sophisticated modeling processes by domain experts for each type of service and (2) additional sensor devices to observe physical factors in the environment. Furthermore, to maintain the QoE of the selected service for a long time and reduce the number of replacements, the QoE prediction of WoT should be long-term.

3 Previous Works

3.1 Spatio-Cohesive and Dynamic Service Discovery

In our first work [1], we defined a new metric named spatio-cohesiveness that measures how the devices of the service composition are spatially close to each other. We assumed that a composition of WoT services with physical correlations on each other might be more effective when the corresponding devices are cohesive around the user. The algorithm discovers and selects appropriate services that satisfy the spatio-cohesiveness requirements representing how two devices or a device and the user should be close. However, extracting spatio-cohesiveness requirements is complicated, and high spatio-cohesiveness cannot guarantee a high perceived QoE of the user.

3.2   Learning-Based Service Selection and Handover

In our previous works [1–3], we extended service selection to dynamic handover that the services periodically hand over the user to alternative services when the quality of the services degrades. In contrast to relatively stable Web services, WoT services in public spaces are dynamic; therefore, their availability and effectiveness frequently fluctuate, and selected services should be monitored and replaced to provide the service continuously. We adopted reinforcement learning techniques [2,3] to train the agent that performs selections and makes handover decisions by predicting the expected long-term quality of each candidate. However, the quality prediction models of our proposed agents require every influencing factor as input, which requires additional sensor devices.

3.3   Effectiveness Model of Visual Services

In our recent work [3], we developed a new metric called visual service effectiveness that measures how effectively services can deliver content to the user visually through the corresponding display device. Based on the characteristics of light and the human vision system, we designed the visual service effectiveness model to examine whether the user can perceive the light from the display device. We evaluated the visual service effectiveness model in laboratory and Virtual Reality (VR) environments. However, the application domain of the visual service effectiveness model is limited to the services with display devices. In recent work [4], the authors developed a personalized and distributed quality prediction framework for WoT services. The framework efficiently deals with highly dynamic environments but not interference among services.

4   Research Plans

Our research question is: how can service agents predict long-term QoE without explicitly receiving hard-to-observe environmental factors? Currently, we are working on the learning-based QoE prediction algorithm for public WoT service selection based on attention mechanism and multi-agent reinforcement learning. Instead of building a global generalized prediction model that requires every influencing factor as input, we assign specialized prediction models for each service agent and let the service agents predict the long-term QoE of its service. As shown in Fig. 2, available service agents will receive requests from the user and return the long-term QoE prediction result so that the user can select the most promising service. After deployment, service agents provide service and collect feedback from the user. Based on the collected feedback, each service agent improves its QoE prediction model based on multi-agent reinforcement learning by implicitly learning the influence of hard-to-observe environmental factors such as physical obstacles and interference from other services. A service agent can summarize the environmental context based on an attention mechanism by receiving the status and calculating the importance of the other service agents.

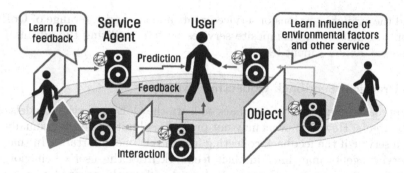

Fig. 2. Learning-based QoE prediction algorithm for public WoT service selection

4.1 Cold Start Problem

Our approach requires enough time and feedback data for learning until the QoE prediction models become accurate. However, the users may not be willing to report feedback, and positive feedback may be hardly obtainable with inaccurate QoE prediction results. Therefore, the amount of data in the field would be limited, and the training process of the service agents should require as fewer data as possible not to discomfort the users. We have plans to improve such data efficiency of the service agents to mitigate the cold-start problem of training data by adopting transfer learning [6] that utilizes the data of other service agents to accelerate the training of new agents.

4.2 Continual Adaptation of QoE Prediction Model

After a service agent learns the influence of environmental factors, the environment may change quickly or slowly, temporarily or permanently. For instance, the location of WoT devices may move, or a new obstacle may present. Such changes may critically decrease the accuracy of the QoE prediction model. Therefore, the service agents should continually adapt their QoE prediction models toward environmental changes. We plan to adopt domain-adaptation techniques [8] to let the service agents detect the statistical shift of data and adapt to maintain high accuracy of QoE prediction even though the environment changes frequently.

4.3 Collaboration of Service Agents

The service agents in the same environment may collaborate to provide more rich and complex services to users. Service handover is one of the collaborative actions the service agents can perform. In that sense, the service agents should communicate efficiently with each other to exchange their states and make collaborative and consistent decisions. For better practicality, we will design the collaboration of service agents that enables efficient communication and complex functions. Furthermore, the QoE prediction model of service agents also needs a further extension to deal with such collaboration. We have plans to extend the available actions of service agents and expand the range of QoE prediction to collaborative composite services by fully utilizing the advantages of multi-agent reinforcement learning.

4.4 Practical Feedback-Collecting System

Our approach requires users' feedback to learn the QoE prediction models of the service agents. However, users may not prefer to submit feedback manually after using a service if the feedback-collecting interface is uncomfortable. In that case, the service agents may infer implicit feedback from the user's behavior upon the service. For instance, the user will react differently according to whether the sound from the speaker device is perceptible. One of our plans is to develop a practical feedback-collecting system of WoT services that is easy to use and implicitly infer users' feedback to support the learning process of the agents.

Acknowledgements. This research was supported by the MSIT (Ministry of Science and ICT), Korea, under the ITRC (Information Technology Research Center) support program (IITP-2023-2020-0-01795) supervised by the IITP (Institute of Information & Communications Technology Planning & Evaluation).

References

1. Baek, K.-D., Ko, I.-Y.: Spatially cohesive service discovery and dynamic service handover for distributed IoT environments. In: Cabot, J., De Virgilio, R., Torlone, R. (eds.) ICWE 2017. LNCS, vol. 10360, pp. 60–78. Springer, Cham (2017). https://doi.org/10.1007/978-3-319-60131-1_4
2. Baek, K.D., Ko, I.-Y.: Spatio-cohesive service selection using machine learning in dynamic IoT environments. In: Mikkonen, T., Klamma, R., Hernández, J. (eds.) ICWE 2018. LNCS, vol. 10845, pp. 366–374. Springer, Cham (2018). https://doi.org/10.1007/978-3-319-91662-0_30
3. Baek, K., Ko, I.Y.: Dynamic and effect-driven output service selection for IoT environments using deep reinforcement learning. IEEE Internet of Things Journal (2022)
4. Li, X., Li, S., Li, Y., Zhou, Y., Chen, C., Zheng, Z.: A personalized federated tensor factorization framework for distributed IoT services QoS prediction from heterogeneous data. IEEE Internet Things J. 9(24), 25460–25473 (2022)
5. Moghaddam, M., Davis, J.G.: Service selection in web service composition: a comparative review of existing approaches. In: Bouguettaya, A., Sheng, Q., Daniel, F. (eds.) Web Services Foundations, pp. 321–346. Springer, New York (2014). https://doi.org/10.1007/978-1-4614-7518-7_13
6. Rajendran, J., Lakshminarayanan, A., Khapra, M.M., Prasanna, P., Ravindran, B.: Attend, adapt and transfer: attentive deep architecture for adaptive transfer from multiple sources in the same domain. In: International Conference on Learning Representations (2017)
7. Skorin-Kapov, L., Varela, M., Hoßfeld, T., Chen, K.T.: A survey of emerging concepts and challenges for QoE management of multimedia services. ACM Trans. Multimedia Comput. Commun. Appl. (TOMM) 14(2s), 1–29 (2018)
8. Steinparz, C.A., et al.: Reactive exploration to cope with non-stationarity in lifelong reinforcement learning. In: Conference on Lifelong Learning Agents, pp. 441–469. PMLR (2022)

Tutorials

A Practical Introduction for Developing and Operating Hybrid Quantum Applications

Martin Beisel[1], Felix Gemeinhardt[2(✉)], Marie Salm[1], and Benjamin Weder[1]

[1] Institute of Architecture of Application Systems, University of Stuttgart, Stuttgart, Germany
{Martin.Beisel,Marie.Salm,Benjamin.Weder}@iaas.uni-stuttgart.de
[2] Johannes Kepler University Linz, Linz, Austria
felix.gemeinhardt@jku.at

Abstract. With the increasing number of quantum computers available via the cloud, the research area of quantum software engineering is emerging. Its goal is the investigation of concepts and guidelines to develop and operate hybrid quantum applications, ensuring engineering principles such as modularity, reuse, and maintainability. In this tutorial, we provide an overview of state-of-the-art concepts and techniques in quantum computing, as well as quantum software engineering. It includes an introduction of selected essential quantum algorithms, limitations of current quantum computers, and a lifecycle for hybrid quantum applications. Furthermore, we show how the service-oriented development of hybrid quantum applications increases their modularity and reusability. Finally, we demonstrate the orchestration of the required classical and quantum programs using workflows and their automated deployment.

Keywords: Quantum Computing · Quantum Software Engineering · Hybrid Quantum Applications · SoC · Workflow Technology

1 Introduction

Quantum computers enable a computational advantage over classical computers by exploiting quantum mechanical phenomena, such as entanglement and superposition [4]. However, the capabilities of today's quantum computers are limited by high error rates and the number of provided qubits [5]. Multiple providers offer quantum computers with different characteristics, so choosing the most suitable one for the use case at hand can significantly improve performance [6]. Since many traditional tasks, such as data persistence, are not suitable for quantum computers, they serve as co-processors for specific problems [7]. Integrating and orchestrating the various classical and quantum programs comprising a hybrid quantum application is crucial [3]. Workflows are a proven approach to orchestrate hybrid quantum applications, as they enable the construction of scalable and robust applications [8]. To facilitate the development of quantum applications, it is good practice to modularize their functionalities in small

© The Author(s), under exclusive license to Springer Nature Switzerland AG 2023
I. Garrigós et al. (Eds.): ICWE 2023, LNCS 13893, pp. 409–412, 2023.
https://doi.org/10.1007/978-3-031-34444-2_36

packages [1]. Modularization enables, e.g., distributed deployment of the functionalities to benefit from heterogeneous cloud offerings depending on the user's requirements [2] and their reuse when composing new quantum applications [9].

2   Tutorial Overview

In the following, we provide the tutorial's structure, intended audience, and technical requirements, as well as the learning goals of the tutorial.

2.1   Intended Audience

Attendees of this tutorial do not require any previous knowledge of quantum computing or quantum software engineering. The tutorial aims to impart basic knowledge about designing, developing, deploying, and executing hybrid quantum applications. Therefore, it empowers attendees to use current quantum computers in different application areas and evaluate their suitability.

2.2   Tutorial Structure

The tutorial comprises six parts, including both lectures and practical activities:

- First, basic concepts and application areas of quantum computing are introduced. This comprises the presentation of a broad picture of the technology including its history, hardware, software, and limitations. Additionally, the basic working principles are outlined, and selected essential quantum algorithms for noisy and noise-free quantum computers will be explained.
- Second, a lifecycle for developing and operating hybrid quantum applications is introduced. It integrates the lifecycles of the different classical and quantum programs, as well as workflows, and shows their connection points.
- Third, the actual challenges of selecting existing quantum computers promising precise execution results based on given quantum programs are presented. Furthermore, a framework that tackles these challenges by enabling the automated selection of suitable quantum computers for quantum programs based on the requirements of the user is demonstrated.
- Next, a concept for modularizing quantum applications in a service-oriented manner is presented. To facilitate the integration of classical and quantum programs, a model-based orchestration approach using workflows is shown.
- Afterward, a practical session is planned in which attendees can model and execute a typical hybrid quantum application, solving the Maximum Cut problem with the Quantum Approximate Optimization Algorithm (QAOA), using workflows. The required services will be provided and attendants will focus on orchestrating them to build the quantum application.
- Finally, the automated deployment of hybrid quantum applications using TOSCA is presented in a lecture and practically shown in a demonstration.

2.3 Technical Requirements

For the practical part of the tutorial, a laptop with Docker and Docker Compose installed is required. Furthermore, to evaluate the modeled hybrid quantum application on state-of-the-art quantum computers, we utilize IBMQ and the SDK Qiskit. Thus, an IBMQ account is needed, which can be created free of charge. Alternatively, a local simulator can be used as described in the tutorial materials.

2.4 Learning Goals

Attendees will have obtained knowledge on:

- A holistic overview of quantum computing, promising application areas, and the basics of quantum software engineering.
- Hybrid quantum applications and their corresponding lifecycle.
- The importance of selecting a suitable quantum computer for a given quantum program and how to automate this process.
- Modular development of hybrid quantum applications, their orchestration using workflows, and automatic deployment using TOSCA.

2.5 Tutorial Material

The tutorial material consists of slides, videos, a detailed description of how to conduct the practical parts of the tutorial, as well as pointers to corresponding papers and tools. It is available at https://ust-quantil.github.io/icwe-tutorial/.

3 Biographies of Presenters

Below, a brief biography of the presenters can be found:

Martin Beisel is a research associate at the Institute of Architecture of Application Systems (IAAS) at the University of Stuttgart, Germany. He received his master's degree at the University of Stuttgart in Software Engineering in 2020. His research interests are in the field of quantum software engineering.

Felix Gemeinhardt joined the Christian Doppler Laboratory on Model-Integrated Smart Production (CDL-MINT) at the Johannes Kepler University Linz (JKU Linz) in 2020. He holds master's degrees in Physics and Business Management. His research interests are in applying Model-Driven Engineering and Automated Software Engineering techniques to Quantum Computing.

Marie Salm started working at the IAAS as a research associate and Ph.D. student in December 2019. She has a master's degree in Computer Science and works on the project PlanQK, a platform for quantum applications. Her research topic is the recommendation of quantum computers for quantum programs.

Benjamin Weder works as a research associate at the IAAS. He received his master's degree from the University of Stuttgart in Computer Science in 2018. He is the technical lead of the EniQmA project at the IAAS, developing techniques for holistic quantum software engineering and a corresponding toolchain.

Acknowledgment. Financial support by the Austrian Federal Ministry for Digital and Economic Affairs and the National Foundation for Research, Technology and Development and by the Austrian Science Fund (P 30525-N31) is gratefully acknowledged. Furthermore, this work was partially funded by the BMWK projects *PlanQK* (01MK20005N), *EniQmA* (01MQ22007B), and *SeQuenC* (01MQ22009B).

References

1. Beisel, M., Barzen, J., Garhofer, S., Leymann, F., Truger, F., Weder, B., Yussupov, V.: Quokka: a service ecosystem for workflow-based execution of variational quantum algorithms. In: Service-Oriented Computing - ICSOC 2022 Workshops. ICSOC 2022. Lecture Notes in Computer Science, vol. 13821, pp. 369–373. Springer, Cham (2023). https://doi.org/10.1007/978-3-031-26507-5_35
2. Binz, T., et al.: OpenTOSCA – a runtime for TOSCA-based cloud applications. In: Basu, S., Pautasso, C., Zhang, L., Fu, X. (eds.) ICSOC 2013. LNCS, vol. 8274, pp. 692–695. Springer, Heidelberg (2013). https://doi.org/10.1007/978-3-642-45005-1_62
3. Gemeinhardt, F., Garmendia, A., Wimmer, M.: Towards model-driven quantum software engineering. In: 2021 IEEE/ACM 2nd International Workshop on Quantum Software Engineering (Q-SE), pp. 13–15 (2021)
4. Nielsen, M.A., Chuang, I.: Quantum Computation and Quantum Information. AAPT (2010)
5. Preskill, J.: Quantum computing in the NISQ era and beyond. Quantum **2**, 79 (2018)
6. Salm, M., Barzen, J., Breitenbücher, U., Leymann, F., Weder, B., Wild, K.: The NISQ analyzer: automating the selection of quantum computers for quantum algorithms. In: Dustdar, S. (ed.) SummerSOC 2020. CCIS, vol. 1310, pp. 66–85. Springer, Cham (2020). https://doi.org/10.1007/978-3-030-64846-6_5
7. Weder, B., Barzen, J., Leymann, F., Vietz, D.: Quantum software development lifecycle. In: Serrano, M.A., Pèrez-Castillo, R., Piattini, M, pp. 61–83. Springer, Cham (2022). https://doi.org/10.1007/978-3-031-05324-5_4
8. Weder, B., Breitenbücher, U., Leymann, F., Wild, K.: integrating quantum computing into workflow modeling and execution. In: Proceedings of the 13th IEEE/ACM International Conference on Utility and Cloud Computing (UCC), pp. 279–291. IEEE Computer Society (2020)
9. Zhao, J.: Quantum Software Engineering: Landscapes and Horizons. arXiv preprint http://arxiv.org/abs/2007.07047arXiv:2007.07047 (2020)

Automated Web GUI Generation from High-Level Interaction Design with Discourse Models

Hermann Kaindl(✉) ⓘ

TU Wien, Vienna, Austria
kaindl@ict.tuwien.ac.at

Abstract. *Interaction design* is considered important for achieving usable Web user interfaces. *Communicative acts* as abstractions from speech acts can model basic building blocks ('atoms') of communication, like a question or an answer. When, e.g., a question and an answer are glued together as a so-called adjacency pair, a simple 'molecule' of a dialogue is modeled. Deliberately complex discourse structures can be modeled using relations from Rhetorical Structure Theory (RST). The content of a communicative act can refer to *ontologies* of the domain of discourse. Taking all this together, we created a new discourse metamodel that specifies what discourse models may look like. Such discourse models can specify an interaction design. Since manual creation of user interfaces is hard and expensive, automated generation may become more and more important. This tutorial also demonstrates how such an interaction design can be used for *automated Web GUI generation*. This is based on model-transformation rules according to the model-driven architecture. Based on AI optimization techniques, the graphical user interfaces (GUIs) are automatically tailored to a device such as a smartphone according to a given device specification. Since the usability of fully-automatically generated GUIs is still not satisfactory, unique *customization techniques* are employed as well. We also address *low-vision accessibility of Web-pages*, by combining automated design-time generation of Web-pages with *responsive design* for improving accessibility.

Keywords: Interaction design · Discourse models · Task models · Automated Web GUI generation · Customization · Low-vision accessibility of Web-pages

1 Intended Audience and Assumed Background

The target audience is interaction designers, Web designers, or project managers. Also educators can benefit from this tutorial.

The assumed attendee background is some familiarity with scenarios / use cases as well as interest in interaction design. There are no pre-requisites such as knowledge about Human-Computer Interaction in general.

© The Author(s), under exclusive license to Springer Nature Switzerland AG 2023
I. Garrigós et al. (Eds.): ICWE 2023, LNCS 13893, pp. 413–417, 2023.
https://doi.org/10.1007/978-3-031-34444-2_37

2 Tutorial Structure and List of Topics Covered

This tutorial is a combination of lectures, group discussions and exercises.

In order to provide a common basis for participants with different background, this tutorial starts with an overview of background material. An overview of discourse-based modeling follows, which is brief but sufficient for understanding the generation and customization of GUIs. This section concludes with an explanation of the duality of task- and discourse-based interaction design.

Based on that, this tutorial shows how GUIs can be generated automatically and, in this course tailored to different devices (as specified). This tutorial also shows how customization can be integrated into such a generation approach, both through custom rules and custom widgets.

Last but not least, this tutorial explains how low-vision accessibility can be improved through a combination with Responsive Design.

2.1 Summary of Topics Covered

- *Background*

  - Interaction design
  - Task-based modeling
  - Speech acts
  - Conversation Analysis
  - Model-driven transformation

- *Interaction Design based on Discourse Modeling*

  - Discourse example
  - Communicative Acts
  - Adjacency Pair
  - RST relations
  - Exercise: Understand given model
  - Duality of Task- and Discourse-based Design

- *GUI Generation*

  - Process of user-interface generation
  - Generation of Structural UI Model
  - Generation of Behavioral UI Model
  - Weaving of structural and behavioral models
  - Optimization for tailoring to device
  - Examples of generated user interfaces

- *Customization*

  - Custom rules
  - Custom widgets

- *Improving Low-vision Accessibility*

  - Combination with Responsive Design
  - Accessibility evaluation

- *Conclusion*

3 Learning Objectives and Outcomes

In this tutorial, participants learn about an open and fully implemented approach to GUI generation from models at the highest level of the Cameleon Reference Framework, i.e., the Tasks & Concepts Level. These models focus on the specification of (classes of) dialogues in contrast to tasks for modeling activities that can be performed by the user or the application (system). Participants will understand a duality of these approaches. Participants also get an overview of both generating and customizing GUIs.

References

1. Bogdan, C., et al.: Generating an abstract user interface from a discourse model inspired by human communication. In: Proceedings of the 41st Hawaii International Conference on System Sciences (HICSS 2008), Waikoloa, Big Island, Hawaii. IEEE (2008)
2. Bogdan, C., Kaindl, H., Falb, J., Popp, R.: Modeling of interaction design by end users through discourse modeling, In: Proceedings of the 2008 ACM International Conference on Intelligent User Interfaces (IUI 2008), Maspalomas, Gran Canaria, Spain. ACM Press (2008)
3. Falb, J., Kaindl, H., Horacek, H., Bogdan, C., Popp, R., Arnautovic, E.: A discourse model for interaction design based on theories of human communication. In: CHI'06 Extended Abstracts on Human Factors in Computing Systems, pp. 754–759, ACM Press (2006)
4. Falb, J., Kavaldjian, S., Popp, R., Raneburger, D., Arnautovic, E., Kaindl, H.: Fully automatic user interface generation from discourse models. In: Proceedings of the 2009 ACM International Conference on Intelligent User Interfaces (IUI 2009). ACM Press (2009). Tool demo paper
5. Falb, J., Popp, R., Röck, T., Jelinek, H., Arnautovic, E., Kaindl, H.: Using communicative acts in interface design specifications for automated synthesis of user interfaces. In: Proceedings of the 21st IEEE/ACM International Conference on Automated Software Engineering (ASE 2006), pp. 261–264 (2006)
6. Falb, J., Popp, R., Röck, T., Jelinek, H., Arnautovic, E., Kaindl, H.: UI prototyping for multiple devices through specifying interaction design. In: Baranauskas, C., Palanque, P., Abascal, J., Barbosa, S.D.J. (eds.) INTERACT 2007. LNCS, vol. 4662, pp. 136–149. Springer, Heidelberg (2007). https://doi.org/10.1007/978-3-540-74796-3_15
7. Kaindl, H., Popp, R., Raneburger, D.: Alternative interaction design patterns for automated GUI generation from discourse-based communication models. In: Proceedings of the 2014 IEEE International Conference on Systems, Man and Cybernetics (SMC 2014), San Diego, CA, USA. IEEE (2014)

8. Kavaldjian, S., Bogdan, C., Falb, J., Kaindl, H.: Transforming Discourse Models to Structural User Interface Models, Models in Software Engineering, MoDELS 2007 Workshops, LNCS 5002, pp. 77–88. Springer-Verlag, Berlin-Heidelberg (invited) (2008)
9. Kavaldjian, S., Falb, J., Kaindl, H.: Generating content presentation according to purpose. In: Proceedings of the 2009 IEEE International Conference on Systems, Man and Cybernetics (SMC 2009), San Antonio, TX, USA. IEEE (2009)
10. Popp, R., Falb, J., Raneburger, D., Kaindl, H.: A transformation engine for model-driven UI generation. In: Proceedings of the 4th ACM SIGCHI Symposium on Engineering Interactive Computing Systems (EICS 2012), Copenhagen, Denmark (2012)
11. Popp, R., Kaindl, H., Badalians Gholi Kandi, S., Raneburger, D., Paterno, F.: Duality of task- and discourse-based interaction design for GUI generation. In: Proceedings of the 2014 IEEE International Conference on Systems, Man, and Cybernetics (SMC 2014), pp. 3323–3328 (2014)
12. Popp, R., Kaindl, H., Raneburger, D.: Connecting interaction models and application logic for model-driven generation of web-based graphical user interfaces. In: Proceedings of the 20th Asia-Pacific Software Engineering Conference (APSEC 2013). ACM (2013)
13. Popp, R., Raneburger, D., and Kaindl, H.: Tool support for automated multi-device GUI generation from discourse-based communication models. In: Proceedings of the ACM SIGCHI Symposium on Engineering Interactive Computing Systems (EICS 2013) (2013)
14. Raneburger, D., Alonso-Ríos, D., Popp, R., Kaindl, H., Falb, J.: A user study with GUIs tailored for smartphones. In: Kotzé, P., Marsden, G., Lindgaard, G., Wesson, J., Winckler, M. (eds.) INTERACT 2013. LNCS, vol. 8118, pp. 505–512. Springer, Heidelberg (2013). https://doi.org/10.1007/978-3-642-40480-1_34
15. Raneburger, D., Kaindl, H., Popp, R.: Strategies for automated GUI tailoring for multiple devices. In: Proceedings of the 48st Annual Hawaii International Conference on System Sciences (HICSS-48) (2015)
16. Raneburger, D., Kaindl, H., Popp, R.: Model transformation rules for customization of multi-device graphical user interfaces. In: Proceedings of the 7th ACM SIGCHI Symposium on Engineering Interactive Computing Systems (EICS 2015), pp. 100–109 (2015)
17. Raneburger, D., Kaindl, H., Popp, R., Šajatovic, V., Armbruster, A.: A process for facilitating interaction design through automated GUI generation. In: Proceedings of the 29th ACM/SIGAPP Symposium on Applied Computing (SAC 2014) (2014)
18. Raneburger, D., Popp, R., Kaindl, H.: Model-driven transformation for optimizing PSMs: a case study of rule design for multi-device GUI generation. In Proceedings of the 8th International Joint Conference on Software Technologies (ICSOFT 2013). SciTePress (2013)
19. Raneburger, D., Popp, R., Kaindl, H.: A user study to evaluate the customization of automatically generated GUIs. In: Black, N.L., Neumann, W.P., Noy, I. (eds.) IEA 2021. LNNS, vol. 223, pp. 683–690. Springer, Cham (2022). https://doi.org/10.1007/978-3-030-74614-8_85
20. Raneburger, D., Popp, R., Kaindl, H., Armbruster, A., Šajatović, V.: An iterative and incremental process for interaction design through automated GUI generation. In: Kurosu, M. (ed.) HCI 2014. LNCS, vol. 8510, pp. 373–384. Springer, Cham (2014). https://doi.org/10.1007/978-3-319-07233-3_35
21. Raneburger, D., Popp, R., Kaindl, H., Falb, J.: Automated WIMP-UI behavior generation: parallelism and granularity of communication units. In: Proceedings of the 2011 IEEE International Conference on Systems, Man and Cybernetics (SMC 2011), pp. 2816–2821 (2011)
22. Raneburger, D., Popp, R., Kaindl, H., Falb, J., Ertl, D.: Automated generation of device-specific WIMP-UIs: weaving of structural and behavioral models. In: Proceedings of the 2011 SIGCHI Symposium on Engineering Interactive Computing Systems (EICS 2011) (2011)

Automated Web GUI Generation   417

23. Rathfux, T., Popp, R., Kaindl, H.,: Adding custom widgets to model-driven GUI generation. In: Proceedings of the 8th ACM SIGCHI Symposium on Engineering Interactive Computing Systems (EICS 2016), Brussels, Belgium (2016)
24. Rathfux, T., Thöner, J., Kaindl, H., Popp, R.: Combining design-time generation of web-pages with responsive design for improving low-vision accessibility. In: Proceedings of the ACM SIGCHI Symposium on Engineering Interactive Computing Systems (EICS 2018), Paris (2018)

Developing Distributed WoT Applications for the Cloud-to-thing Continuum

Sergio Laso[1]([✉])(iD) and Javier Berrocal[2](iD)

[1] Global Process and Product Improvement S.L.,
Calle Las Ocas 2, Cáceres 10004, Spain
slasom@unex.es
[2] Escuela Politécnica, Quercus Software Engineering Group,
University of Extremadura, Avda. de la Universidad s/n, Cáceres 10003, Spain
jberolm@unex.es

Abstract. The great popularity and acceptance of smart devices have encouraged the development of applications focused on the Internet of Things (IoT) and Web of Things (WoT) paradigms. These applications are normally based on cloud-centric architectures. However, the increasing amount of information exchanged and the need of IoT devices capable of adapting on real-time their behavior to the user context pose a challenge to these architectural assumptions. Recently, paradigms such as Fog, Edge, and Mist computing have been proposed along the Cloud-to-thing continuum to exploit the computational and storage capabilities of end devices (IoT devices, smartphones, etc.) in order to distribute some tasks on them, reducing the overhead both in the cloud and in the network, and increasing the response time. Currently, the implementation of these paradigms requires developers to be qualified and trained to create ad-hoc systems, as there is a lack of standards and tools to facilitate the development of these highly distributed applications. This tutorial delves into the deployment of WoT applications along the Cloud-to-thing continuum. It presents a framework based on existing standards to shorten the learning curve, the development time, and improve the software quality.

Keywords: Cloud-to-thing continuum · End devices · WoT applications · Internet of Things

1 Introduction

The capabilities of end devices have increased enormously. During the last few years, they have increased their storage and computing capabilities to sense more information from the environment and perform more complex tasks. This increase in device capabilities has favored the deployment of paradigms such as the Internet of Things (IoT) and the Web of Things (WoT) [2], where they are integrated into the network and use standard protocols for communication. This integration allows different devices to coordinate and expose services that can be

I. Garrigós et al. (Eds.): ICWE 2023, LNCS 13893, pp. 418–420, 2023.
https://doi.org/10.1007/978-3-031-34444-2_38

consumed by any application; thus making them more accessible to applications and humans [4].

The deployment and integration of the different modules of a WoT application is substantially determined by the architectural style applied. The most widespread architecture used by these applications and devices is the cloud-centric one, in which end devices act as simple clients that send the sensed information to the cloud and obtain from it the actions to be executed. However, the increase in the number of Internet-connected devices deployed every year [3], and the increase in their sensing capabilities may lead to network saturation due to the volume of information they have to publish and consume.

To try to solve these drawbacks, several research lines have proposed new architectural paradigms such as Fog Computing, Edge Computing, Mist Computing [7], etc. All these proposals fall within the Cloud-to-thing continuum umbrella [5], which are infrastructures that extend beyond centralized data centers, from the cloud to end devices. The goal of these paradigms is to distribute computing and storage services in different layers so that developers can exploit the capabilities of the nodes closer to the end-user (IoT devices, smartphones, fog/edge nodes, etc.), in order to reduce response time, network overhead, increase the privacy of managed data, and so on. In short, to facilitate the achievement of Quality of Service (QoS) attributes that allow the provision of acceptable quality for all users. However, it is necessary to bring the advances at the research level closer to the industry, so that we can reduce the effort required to develop of highly distributed WoT applications using the capabilities of the cloud-to-Thing continuum.

In this tutorial, we will explain the importance of the Cloud-to-thing continuum and the different proposals for WoT application development. We also present a framework that helps and facilitates the development of distributed WoT applications to be deployed along the Cloud-to-thing continuum, which allows for shortening the developers' learning curve and development time.

The rest of the paper is organized as follows. Section 2 presents the overview of the tutorial structure and Sect. 3 details the learning objectives and outcomes.

2   Overview of the Tutorial Structure

This tutorial has a duration of half-day (three hours) including both lectures and practical activities. It is divided into two parts:

- **Introduction:** The first part of the tutorial explains and details the importance of the Cloud-to-thing continuum and its benefits for WoT applications, the paradigms on which it is based, the different architectural styles on which it is composed, and all its possibilities for the deployment of distributed WoT applications.
- **Practical session:** The second part of the tutorial focuses on the development and deployment of distributed WoT applications. For this, it presents APIGEND [6] framework that allows developers to implement a WoT application composed of different services using the OpenAPI [1] standard. It can

be deployed in Cloud/Fog/Edge environments and on ends-device, such as smartphones or ESP32 microcontrollers.

3 Learning Objectives and Outcomes

At the end of the tutorial, attendees will get knowledge on:

- Distributed computing paradigms in the Cloud-to-Thing continuum.
- Generation of WoT application based on the OpenAPI standard.
- Development of WoT applications along the Cloud-to-Thing continuum.

Acknowledgment. This work has been partially funded by grant DIN2020-011586, funded by MCIN/ AEI/10.13039/501100011033 and by the European Union "Next GenerationEU /PRTR", by the Ministry of Science, Innovation, and Universities (projects TED2021-130913B-I00, PDC2022-133465-I00), by the Regional Ministry of Economy, Science and Digital Agenda of the Regional Government of Extremadura (GR21133) and the European Regional Development Fund.

References

1. The OpenAPI Specification Repository. Contribute to OAI/OpenAPI-Specification development by creating an account on GitHub. https://github.com/OAI/OpenAPI-Specification
2. Flores-Martin, D., Berrocal, J., García-Alonso, J., Murillo, J.M.: Towards dynamic and heterogeneous social IoT environments. Computing, 1–24 (2022)
3. Insights, T.: Number of internet of things (IoT) connected devices worldwide from 2019 to 2021, with forecasts from 2022 to 2030 (in billions). https://www.statista.com/statistics/1183457/iot-connected-devices-worldwide/
4. Laso, S., Berrocal, J., García-Alonso, J., Canal, C., Manuel Murillo, J.: Human microservices: a framework for turning humans into service providers. Softw. - Pract. Exp. (2021). https://doi.org/10.1002/spe.2976
5. Laso, S., et al.: Elastic data analytics for the cloud-to-things continuum. IEEE Internet Comput. **26**(6), 42–49 (2022). https://doi.org/10.1109/MIC.2021.3138153
6. Laso, S., Linaje, M., Garcia-Alonso, J., Murillo, J.M., Berrocal, J.: Artifact abstract: deployment of APIs on android mobile devices and microcontrollers. In: 2020 IEEE International Conference on Pervasive Computing and Communications (PerCom), pp. 1–2. IEEE (2020)
7. Yousefpour, A., et al.: All one needs to know about fog computing and related edge computing paradigms: a complete survey. J. Syst. Architect. **98**, 289–330 (2019)

Quantum Web Services: Development and Deployment

Javier Romero-Álvarez[1]([⊠])(iD), Jaime Alvarado-Valiente[1](iD), Enrique Moguel[2](iD), and Jose Garcia-Alonso[1](iD)

[1] University of Extremadura, Escuela Politécnica, Quercus Software Engineering Group, Av. de la Universidad, S/N, 10003 Cáceres, Spain
{jromero,jaimeav,jgaralo}@unex.es
[2] CénitS-COMPUTAEX (Extremadura Supercomputing, Technological Innovation and Research Center), Carretera Nacional 521, Km 41.8, 10071 Cáceres, Spain
enrique@unex.es

Abstract. Quantum computing has gained attention from the scientific community and industry, resulting in the development of increasingly powerful quantum computers and supporting technology. Major computer companies have created functional quantum computers, programming languages, and simulators that can be used by developers. This infrastructure is available through the cloud, similar to Infrastructure as a Service. However, utilizing these computers requires a deep understanding of quantum programming and hardware, which is different from traditional cloud computing. To enable a coexistence between quantum and classical computing, we believe that a transition period is necessary. One solution for coexistence is through web services. This tutorial will provide an overview of how quantum algorithms can be converted into web services, and how they can be deployed using the Amazon Braket platform for quantum computing and invoked through classical web service endpoints. Finally, we will propose a process for creating and deploying quantum services using an extension of OpenAPI and GitHub Actions. This extension allows developers to use the same methodology that they are used to for classical services.

Keywords: Quantum computing · Quantum web services · Quantum programming · OpenAPI

1 Introduction

Quantum computing has emerged as a powerful tool to solve problems that are intractable for classical computers. As this field advances, there is a growing need for developers to integrate quantum computing into their applications.

One promising approach to this challenge is the conversion of quantum algorithms into web services, which can be easily integrated into existing software applications [1]. By converting quantum algorithms into web services, it becomes possible to seamlessly integrate quantum computing capabilities into existing

I. Garrigós et al. (Eds.): ICWE 2023, LNCS 13893, pp. 421–423, 2023.
https://doi.org/10.1007/978-3-031-34444-2_39

software applications without requiring significant changes to the underlying code. This approach allows developers to take advantage of the strengths of both classical and quantum computing and can lead to more efficient and powerful computing solutions [2,3].

In this paper, we present a tutorial that provides an overview of how quantum algorithms can be converted into web services, and how they can be deployed using the Amazon Braket platform for quantum computing and invoked through classical web service endpoints.

This tutorial aims to provide a step-by-step guide to help developers understand the process of turning quantum algorithms into web services, deploying them in the cloud, and integrating them into existing applications.

We will also present a process for generating quantum services using OpenAPI, which allows developers to use a methodology they are familiar with for classic services [4] and automate the deployment of these quantum services with GitHub Action. Using OpenAPI, developers can easily define the inputs and outputs of their quantum services, making it easier for others to understand and use their code. In addition, automating the deployment of quantum services with GitHub Action makes the process of incorporating quantum computing into software development workflows faster.

This ICWE 2023 tutorial differs from the tutorial presented in 2022 [5] through its focus on the automation of the deployment of quantum services, and the inclusion of OpenAPI to define and generate quantum services.

2   Intended Audience

This tutorial is intended for people from academic and industrial backgrounds interested in quantum computing with a service-oriented approach. The attenders should possess a foundational understanding of quantum computing, that would include a basic knowledge of quantum software development, and familiarity with programming languages commonly used in quantum computing, such as Python, and open sources libraries like Amazon Braket.

Moreover, while understanding the underlying concepts does not require prior knowledge of web services, JSON files, and the use of GitHub Actions, these skills are necessary to follow the practical part of the tutorial.

Therefore, we recommend that tutorial participants attend the previous tutorial entitled *"A Practical Introduction for Developing and Operating Hybrid Quantum Applications"*, where fundamentals on quantum applications will be presented.

3   Overall Outline

This tutorial has a duration of half-day (three hours) including both lectures and practical activities. It will be divided into three parts:

1. **Introduction:** short lecture focused on quantum software servitization, and converting quantum algorithms into traditional web services, using Amazon Braket. Details of deployment and execution will be exemplified with Python libraries for classical web services and Postman for testing.
2. **Practical session:** attendees could deploy and use quantum web services. Shor's algorithm for factoring large numbers and a Travelling Salesman Problem solution will be used as examples of gate-based quantum computing. Attendees will use provided implementations of these algorithms, adapted to Amazon Braket, as traditional web services.
3. **Quantum OpenAPI:** presentation and demonstration of the tool with the proposed extension of the OpenAPI specification and GitHub Actions for the automatic definition and generation of quantum services, for their deployment and execution.

4 Learning Outcomes

By the end of the tutorial, attendees will have gained knowledge about the servitization of quantum algorithms, hybrid classical-quantum web services architectures automated generation of quantum web services for multiple providers using the OpenAPI specification and GitHub Actions, and the application of quantum web services in the real world using Amazon Braket.

Acknowledgement. This work is part of the Grant PID2021-124045OB-C31 funded by MCIN/AEI/ 10.13039/50100011033 and by "ERDF A way of making Europe". It is also supported by the QSALUD project (EXP 00135977 / MIG-20201059) in the lines of action of the Center for the Development of Industrial Technology (CDTI), and by the project 0786_CAP4ie_4_P (Interreg V-A España-Portugal 2021-2027).

References

1. Islam, M.M., Rahaman, M.: A review on progress and problems of quantum computing as a service (QcaaS) in the perspective of cloud computing. Global J. Comput. Sci. Technol. **15**(B4), 23–26 (2015)
2. Weder, B., Barzen, J., Leymann, F., Vietz, D.: Quantum software development lifecycle. In: Serrano, M.A., Perez-Castillo, R., Piattini, M. (eds.) Quantum Software Engineering, pp. 61–83. Springer, Cham (2022). https://doi.org/10.1007/978-3-031-05324-5_4
3. Garcia-Alonso, J.M., Rojo, J., Valencia, D., Moguel, E., Berrocal, J., Murillo, J.M.: Quantum software as a service through a quantum API gateway. IEEE Internet Comput. **26**(1), 34–41 (2021)
4. Laso, S., Berrocal, J., GarcíaAlonso, J., Canal, C., Manuel Murillo, J.: Human microservices: a framework for turning humans into service providers. Softw.: Pract. Exp. **51**(9), 1910–1935 (2021)
5. Alvarado-Valiente, J., Romero-Álvarez, J., Garcia-Alonso, J., Murillo, J.M.: A guide for quantum web services deployment. In: Di Noia, T., Ko, I.Y., Schedl, M., Ardito, C. (eds.) ICWE 2022. Lecture Notes in Computer Science, vol. 13362, pp. 493–496. Springer, Cham (2022). https://doi.org/10.1007/978-3-031-09917-5_42

Author Index

I. Garrigós et al. (Eds.): ICWE 2023, LNCS 13893, pp. 425–426, 2023.
https://doi.org/10.1007/978-3-031-34444-2